Hadoop: The Definitive Guide

Tom White
foreword by Doug Cutting

Beijing · Cambridge · Farnham · Köln · Sebastopol · Taipei · Tokyo

Hadoop: The Definitive Guide

by Tom White

Copyright © 2009 Tom White. All rights reserved.
Printed in the United States of America.

Published by O'Reilly Media, Inc., 1005 Gravenstein Highway North, Sebastopol, CA 95472.

O'Reilly books may be purchased for educational, business, or sales promotional use. Online editions are also available for most titles (*http://my.safaribooksonline.com*). For more information, contact our corporate/institutional sales department: (800) 998-9938 or *corporate@oreilly.com*.

Editor: Mike Loukides
Production Editor: Loranah Dimant
Proofreader: Nancy Kotary

Indexer: Ellen Troutman Zaig
Cover Designer: Karen Montgomery
Interior Designer: David Futato
Illustrator: Robert Romano

Printing History:

June 2009:   First Edition.

RepKover. This book uses RepKover™, a durable and flexible lay-flat binding.

ISBN: 978-0-596-52197-4

[M]   [9/09]

1251662666

For Eliane, Emilia, and Lottie

Table of Contents

Foreword

Hadoop got its start in Nutch. A few of us were attempting to build an open source web search engine and having trouble managing computations running on even a handful of computers. Once Google published its GFS and MapReduce papers, the route became clear. They'd devised systems to solve precisely the problems we were having with Nutch. So we started, two of us, half-time, to try to recreate these systems as a part of Nutch.

We managed to get Nutch limping along on 20 machines, but it soon became clear that to handle the Web's massive scale, we'd need to run it on thousands of machines and, moreover, that the job was bigger than two half-time developers could handle.

Around that time, Yahoo! got interested, and quickly put together a team that I joined. We split off the distributed computing part of Nutch, naming it Hadoop. With the help of Yahoo!, Hadoop soon grew into a technology that could truly scale to the Web.

In 2006, Tom White started contributing to Hadoop. I already knew Tom through an excellent article he'd written about Nutch, so I knew he could present complex ideas in clear prose. I soon learned that he could also develop software that was as pleasant to read as his prose.

From the beginning, Tom's contributions to Hadoop showed his concern for users and for the project. Unlike most open source contributors, Tom is not primarily interested in tweaking the system to better meet his own needs, but rather in making it easier for anyone to use.

Initially, Tom specialized in making Hadoop run well on Amazon's EC2 and S3 services. Then he moved on to tackle a wide variety of problems, including improving the MapReduce APIs, enhancing the website, and devising an object serialization framework. In all cases, Tom presented his ideas precisely. In short order, Tom earned the role of Hadoop committer and soon thereafter became a member of the Hadoop Project Management Committee.

Tom is now a respected senior member of the Hadoop developer community. Though he's an expert in many technical corners of the project, his specialty is making Hadoop easier to use and understand.

Given this, I was very pleased when I learned that Tom intended to write a book about Hadoop. Who could be better qualified? Now you have the opportunity to learn about Hadoop from a master—not only of the technology, but also of common sense and plain talk.

—Doug Cutting
Shed in the Yard, California

Preface

Martin Gardner, the mathematics and science writer, once said in an interview:

> Beyond calculus, I am lost. That was the secret of my column's success. It took me so long to understand what I was writing about that I knew how to write in a way most readers would understand.[*]

In many ways, this is how I feel about Hadoop. Its inner workings are complex, resting as they do on a mixture of distributed systems theory, practical engineering, and common sense. And to the uninitiated, Hadoop can appear alien.

But it doesn't need to be like this. Stripped to its core, the tools that Hadoop provides for building distributed systems—for data storage, data analysis, and coordination—are simple. If there's a common theme, it is about raising the level of abstraction—to create building blocks for programmers who just happen to have lots of data to store, or lots of data to analyze, or lots of machines to coordinate, and who don't have the time, the skill, or the inclination to become distributed systems experts to build the infrastructure to handle it.

With such a simple and generally applicable feature set, it seemed obvious to me when I started using it that Hadoop deserved to be widely used. However, at the time (in early 2006), setting up, configuring, and writing programs to use Hadoop was an art. Things have certainly improved since then: there is more documentation, there are more examples, and there are thriving mailing lists to go to when you have questions. And yet the biggest hurdle for newcomers is understanding what this technology is capable of, where it excels, and how to use it. That is why I wrote this book.

The Apache Hadoop community has come a long way. Over the course of three years, the Hadoop project has blossomed and spun off half a dozen subprojects. In this time, the software has made great leaps in performance, reliability, scalability, and manageability. To gain even wider adoption, however, I believe we need to make Hadoop even easier to use. This will involve writing more tools; integrating with more systems; and

---

[*] "The science of fun," Alex Bellos, *The Guardian*, May 31, 2008, *http://www.guardian.co.uk/science/2008/may/31/maths.science*.

writing new, improved APIs. I'm looking forward to being a part of this, and I hope this book will encourage and enable others to do so, too.

Administrative Notes

During discussion of a particular Java class in the text, I often omit its package name, to reduce clutter. If you need to know which package a class is in, you can easily look it up in Hadoop's Java API documentation for the relevant subproject, linked to from the Apache Hadoop home page at *http://hadoop.apache.org/*. Or if you're using an IDE, it can help using its auto-complete mechanism.

Similarly, although it deviates from usual style guidelines, program listings that import multiple classes from the same package may use the asterisk wildcard character to save space (for example: `import org.apache.hadoop.io.*`).

The sample programs in this book are available for download from the website that accompanies this book: *http://www.hadoopbook.com/*. You will also find instructions there for obtaining the datasets that are used in examples throughout the book, as well as further notes for running the programs in the book, and links to updates, additional resources, and my blog.

What's in This Book?

The rest of this book is organized as follows. Chapter 2 provides an introduction to MapReduce. Chapter 3 looks at Hadoop filesystems, and in particular HDFS, in depth. Chapter 4 covers the fundamentals of I/O in Hadoop: data integrity, compression, serialization, and file-based data structures.

The next four chapters cover MapReduce in depth. Chapter 5 goes through the practical steps needed to develop a MapReduce application. Chapter 6 looks at how MapReduce is implemented in Hadoop, from the point of view of a user. Chapter 7 is about the MapReduce programming model, and the various data formats that MapReduce can work with. Chapter 8 is on advanced MapReduce topics, including sorting and joining data.

Chapters 9 and 10 are for Hadoop administrators, and describe how to set up and maintain a Hadoop cluster running HDFS and MapReduce.

Chapters 11, 12, and 13 present Pig, HBase, and ZooKeeper, respectively.

Finally, Chapter 14 is a collection of case studies contributed by members of the Apache Hadoop community.

Conventions Used in This Book

The following typographical conventions are used in this book:

Italic

    Indicates new terms, URLs, email addresses, filenames, and file extensions.

`Constant width`

    Used for program listings, as well as within paragraphs to refer to program elements such as variable or function names, databases, data types, environment variables, statements, and keywords.

`Constant width bold`

    Shows commands or other text that should be typed literally by the user.

`Constant width italic`

    Shows text that should be replaced with user-supplied values or by values determined by context.

 This icon signifies a tip, suggestion, or general note.

 This icon indicates a warning or caution.

Using Code Examples

This book is here to help you get your job done. In general, you may use the code in this book in your programs and documentation. You do not need to contact us for permission unless you're reproducing a significant portion of the code. For example, writing a program that uses several chunks of code from this book does not require permission. Selling or distributing a CD-ROM of examples from O'Reilly books does require permission. Answering a question by citing this book and quoting example code does not require permission. Incorporating a significant amount of example code from this book into your product's documentation does require permission.

We appreciate, but do not require, attribution. An attribution usually includes the title, author, publisher, and ISBN. For example: "*Hadoop: The Definitive Guide*, by Tom White. Copyright 2009 Tom White, 978-0-596-52197-4."

If you feel your use of code examples falls outside fair use or the permission given above, feel free to contact us at *permissions@oreilly.com*.

Safari® Books Online

When you see a Safari® Books Online icon on the cover of your favorite technology book, that means the book is available online through the O'Reilly Network Safari Bookshelf.

Safari offers a solution that's better than e-books. It's a virtual library that lets you easily search thousands of top tech books, cut and paste code samples, download chapters, and find quick answers when you need the most accurate, current information. Try it for free at *http://my.safaribooksonline.com*.

How to Contact Us

Please address comments and questions concerning this book to the publisher:

O'Reilly Media, Inc.
1005 Gravenstein Highway North
Sebastopol, CA 95472
800-998-9938 (in the United States or Canada)
707-829-0515 (international or local)
707-829-0104 (fax)

We have a web page for this book, where we list errata, examples, and any additional information. You can access this page at:

http://www.oreilly.com/catalog/9780596521974

The author also has a site for this book at:

http://www.hadoopbook.com/

To comment or ask technical questions about this book, send email to:

bookquestions@oreilly.com

For more information about our books, conferences, Resource Centers, and the O'Reilly Network, see our website at:

http://www.oreilly.com

Acknowledgments

I have relied on many people, both directly and indirectly, in writing this book. I would like to thank the Hadoop community, from whom I have learned, and continue to learn, a great deal.

In particular, I would like to thank Michael Stack and Jonathan Gray for writing the chapter on HBase. Also thanks go to Adrian Woodhead, Marc de Palol, Joydeep Sen Sarma, Ashish Thusoo, Andrzej Białecki, Stu Hood, Chris K Wensel, and Owen

O'Malley for contributing case studies for Chapter 14. Matt Massie and Todd Lipcon wrote Appendix B, for which I am very grateful.

I would like to thank the following reviewers who contributed many helpful suggestions and improvements to my drafts: Raghu Angadi, Matt Biddulph, Christophe Bisciglia, Ryan Cox, Devaraj Das, Alex Dorman, Chris Douglas, Alan Gates, Lars George, Patrick Hunt, Aaron Kimball, Peter Krey, Hairong Kuang, Simon Maxen, Olga Natkovich, Benjamin Reed, Konstantin Shvachko, Allen Wittenauer, Matei Zaharia, and Philip Zeyliger. Ajay Anand kept the review process flowing smoothly. Philip ("flip") Kromer kindly helped me with the NCDC weather dataset featured in the examples in this book. Special thanks to Owen O'Malley and Arun C Murthy for explaining the intricacies of the MapReduce shuffle to me. Any errors that remain are, of course, to be laid at my door.

I am particularly grateful to Doug Cutting for his encouragement, support, and friendship, and for contributing the foreword.

Thanks also go to the many others with whom I have had conversations or email discussions over the course of writing the book.

Halfway through writing this book, I joined Cloudera, and I want to thank my colleagues for being incredibly supportive in allowing me the time to write, and to get it finished promptly.

I am grateful to my editor, Mike Loukides, and his colleagues at O'Reilly for their help in the preparation of this book. Mike has been there throughout to answer my questions, to read my first drafts, and to keep me on schedule.

Finally, the writing of this book has been a great deal of work, and I couldn't have done it without the constant support of my family. My wife, Eliane, not only kept the home going, but also stepped in to help review, edit, and chase case studies. My daughters, Emilia and Lottie, have been very understanding, and I'm looking forward to spending lots more time with all of them.

## CHAPTER 1

Meet Hadoop

> In pioneer days they used oxen for heavy pulling, and when one ox couldn't budge a log, they didn't try to grow a larger ox. We shouldn't be trying for bigger computers, but for more systems of computers.
>
> —Grace Hopper

Data!

We live in the data age. It's not easy to measure the total volume of data stored electronically, but an IDC estimate put the size of the "digital universe" at 0.18 zettabytes in 2006, and is forecasting a tenfold growth by 2011 to 1.8 zettabytes.[*] A zettabyte is 10^{21} bytes, or equivalently one thousand exabytes, one million petabytes, or one billion terabytes. That's roughly the same order of magnitude as one disk drive for every person in the world.

This flood of data is coming from many sources. Consider the following:[†]

- The New York Stock Exchange generates about one terabyte of new trade data per day.
- Facebook hosts approximately 10 billion photos, taking up one petabyte of storage.
- Ancestry.com, the genealogy site, stores around 2.5 petabytes of data.
- The Internet Archive stores around 2 petabytes of data, and is growing at a rate of 20 terabytes per month.
- The Large Hadron Collider near Geneva, Switzerland, will produce about 15 petabytes of data per year.

---

[*] From Gantz et al., "The Diverse and Exploding Digital Universe," March 2008 (*http://www.emc.com/collateral/analyst-reports/diverse-exploding-digital-universe.pdf*).

[†] *http://www.intelligententerprise.com/showArticle.jhtml?articleID=207800705*, *http://mashable.com/2008/10/15/facebook-10-billion-photos/*, *http://blog.familytreemagazine.com/insider/Inside+Ancestrycoms+TopSecret+Data+Center.aspx*, and *http://www.archive.org/about/faqs.php*, *http://www.interactions.org/cms/?pid=1027032*.

So there's a lot of data out there. But you are probably wondering how it affects you. Most of the data is locked up in the largest web properties (like search engines), or scientific or financial institutions, isn't it? Does the advent of "Big Data," as it is being called, affect smaller organizations or individuals?

I argue that it does. Take photos, for example. My wife's grandfather was an avid photographer, and took photographs throughout his adult life. His entire corpus of medium format, slide, and 35mm film, when scanned in at high-resolution, occupies around 10 gigabytes. Compare this to the digital photos that my family took last year, which take up about 5 gigabytes of space. My family is producing photographic data at 35 times the rate my wife's grandfather's did, and the rate is increasing every year as it becomes easier to take more and more photos.

More generally, the digital streams that individuals are producing are growing apace. Microsoft Research's MyLifeBits project (*http://research.microsoft.com/en-us/projects/ mylifebits/default.aspx*) gives a glimpse of archiving of personal information that may become commonplace in the near future. MyLifeBits was an experiment where an individual's interactions—phone calls, emails, documents—were captured electronically and stored for later access. The data gathered included a photo taken every minute, which resulted in an overall data volume of one gigabyte a month. When storage costs come down enough to make it feasible to store continuous audio and video, the data volume for a future MyLifeBits service will be many times that.

The trend is for every individual's data footprint to grow, but perhaps more importantly the amount of data generated by machines will be even greater than that generated by people. Machine logs, RFID readers, sensor networks, vehicle GPS traces, retail transactions—all of these contribute to the growing mountain of data.

The volume of data being made publicly available increases every year too. Organizations no longer have to merely manage their own data: success in the future will be dictated to a large extent by their ability to extract value from other organizations' data.

Initiatives such as Public Data Sets on Amazon Web Services (*http://aws.amazon.com/ publicdatasets/*), Infochimps.org (*http://infochimps.org/*), and theinfo.org (*http://theinfo .org/*) exist to foster the "information commons," where data can be freely (or in the case of AWS, for a modest price) shared for anyone to download and analyze. Mashups between different information sources make for unexpected and hitherto unimaginable applications.

Take, for example, the Astrometry.net (*http://astrometry.net/*) project, which watches the Astrometry group on Flickr for new photos of the night sky. It analyzes each image, and identifies which part of the sky it is from, and any interesting celestial bodies, such as stars or galaxies. Although it's still a new and experimental service, it shows the kind of things that are possible when data (in this case, tagged photographic images) is made available and used for something (image analysis) that was not anticipated by the creator.

It has been said that "More data usually beats better algorithms," which is to say that for some problems (such as recommending movies or music based on past preferences), however fiendish your algorithms are, they can often be beaten simply by having more data (and a less sophisticated algorithm).[‡]

The good news is that Big Data is here. The bad news is that we are struggling to store and analyze it.

Data Storage and Analysis

The problem is simple: while the storage capacities of hard drives have increased massively over the years, access speeds—the rate at which data can be read from drives—have not kept up. One typical drive from 1990 could store 1370 MB of data and had a transfer speed of 4.4 MB/s,[§] so you could read all the data from a full drive in around five minutes. Almost 20 years later one terabyte drives are the norm, but the transfer speed is around 100 MB/s, so it takes more than two and a half hours to read all the data off the disk.

This is a long time to read all data on a single drive—and writing is even slower. The obvious way to reduce the time is to read from multiple disks at once. Imagine if we had 100 drives, each holding one hundredth of the data. Working in parallel, we could read the data in under two minutes.

Only using one hundredth of a disk may seem wasteful. But we can store one hundred datasets, each of which is one terabyte, and provide shared access to them. We can imagine that the users of such a system would be happy to share access in return for shorter analysis times, and, statistically, that their analysis jobs would be likely to be spread over time, so they wouldn't interfere with each other too much.

There's more to being able to read and write data in parallel to or from multiple disks, though.

The first problem to solve is hardware failure: as soon as you start using many pieces of hardware, the chance that one will fail is fairly high. A common way of avoiding data loss is through replication: redundant copies of the data are kept by the system so that in the event of failure, there is another copy available. This is how RAID works, for instance, although Hadoop's filesystem, the Hadoop Distributed Filesystem (HDFS), takes a slightly different approach, as you shall see later.

The second problem is that most analysis tasks need to be able to combine the data in some way; data read from one disk may need to be combined with the data from any of the other 99 disks. Various distributed systems allow data to be combined from

---

[‡] The quote is from Anand Rajaraman writing about the Netflix Challenge (*http://anand.typepad.com/ datawocky/2008/03/more-data-usual.html*).

[§] These specifications are for the Seagate ST-41600n.

multiple sources, but doing this correctly is notoriously challenging. MapReduce provides a programming model that abstracts the problem from disk reads and writes, transforming it into a computation over sets of keys and values. We will look at the details of this model in later chapters, but the important point for the present discussion is that there are two parts to the computation, the map and the reduce, and it's the interface between the two where the "mixing" occurs. Like HDFS, MapReduce has reliability built-in.

This, in a nutshell, is what Hadoop provides: a reliable shared storage and analysis system. The storage is provided by HDFS, and analysis by MapReduce. There are other parts to Hadoop, but these capabilities are its kernel.

Comparison with Other Systems

The approach taken by MapReduce may seem like a brute-force approach. The premise is that the entire dataset—or at least a good portion of it—is processed for each query. But this is its power. MapReduce is a *batch* query processor, and the ability to run an ad hoc query against your whole dataset and get the results in a reasonable time is transformative. It changes the way you think about data, and unlocks data that was previously archived on tape or disk. It gives people the opportunity to innovate with data. Questions that took too long to get answered before can now be answered, which in turn leads to new questions and new insights.

For example, Mailtrust, Rackspace's mail division, used Hadoop for processing email logs. One ad hoc query they wrote was to find the geographic distribution of their users. In their words:

> This data was so useful that we've scheduled the MapReduce job to run monthly and we will be using this data to help us decide which Rackspace data centers to place new mail servers in as we grow.[||]

By bringing several hundred gigabytes of data together and having the tools to analyze it, the Rackspace engineers were able to gain an understanding of the data that they otherwise would never have had, and, furthermore, they were able to use what they had learned to improve the service for their customers. You can read more about how Rackspace uses Hadoop in Chapter 14.

RDBMS

Why can't we use databases with lots of disks to do large-scale batch analysis? Why is MapReduce needed?

The answer to these questions comes from another trend in disk drives: seek time is improving more slowly than transfer rate. Seeking is the process of moving the disk's

---

[||] *http://blog.racklabs.com/?p=66*

head to a particular place on the disk to read or write data. It characterizes the latency of a disk operation, whereas the transfer rate corresponds to a disk's bandwidth.

If the data access pattern is dominated by seeks, it will take longer to read or write large portions of the dataset than streaming through it, which operates at the transfer rate. On the other hand, for updating a small proportion of records in a database, a traditional B-Tree (the data structure used in relational databases, which is limited by the rate it can perform seeks) works well. For updating the majority of a database, a B-Tree is less efficient than MapReduce, which uses Sort/Merge to rebuild the database.

In many ways, MapReduce can be seen as a complement to an RDBMS. (The differences between the two systems are shown in Table 1-1.) MapReduce is a good fit for problems that need to analyze the whole dataset, in a batch fashion, particularly for ad hoc analysis. An RDBMS is good for point queries or updates, where the dataset has been indexed to deliver low-latency retrieval and update times of a relatively small amount of data. MapReduce suits applications where the data is written once, and read many times, whereas a relational database is good for datasets that are continually updated.

Table 1-1. RDBMS compared to MapReduce

	Traditional RDBMS	MapReduce
Data size	Gigabytes	Petabytes
Access	Interactive and batch	Batch
Updates	Read and write many times	Write once, read many times
Structure	Static schema	Dynamic schema
Integrity	High	Low
Scaling	Nonlinear	Linear

Another difference between MapReduce and an RDBMS is the amount of structure in the datasets that they operate on. *Structured data* is data that is organized into entities that have a defined format, such as XML documents or database tables that conform to a particular predefined schema. This is the realm of the RDBMS. *Semi-structured data*, on the other hand, is looser, and though there may be a schema, it is often ignored, so it may be used only as a guide to the structure of the data: for example, a spreadsheet, in which the structure is the grid of cells, although the cells themselves may hold any form of data. *Unstructured data* does not have any particular internal structure: for example, plain text or image data. MapReduce works well on unstructured or semi-structured data, since it is designed to interpret the data at processing time. In other words, the input keys and values for MapReduce are not an intrinsic property of the data, but they are chosen by the person analyzing the data.

Relational data is often *normalized* to retain its integrity, and remove redundancy. Normalization poses problems for MapReduce, since it makes reading a record a non-local operation, and one of the central assumptions that MapReduce makes is that it is possible to perform (high-speed) streaming reads and writes.

A web server log is a good example of a set of records that is *not* normalized (for example, the client hostnames are specified in full each time, even though the same client may appear many times), and this is one reason that logfiles of all kinds are particularly well-suited to analysis with MapReduce.

MapReduce is a linearly scalable programming model. The programmer writes two functions—a map function and a reduce function—each of which defines a mapping from one set of key-value pairs to another. These functions are oblivious to the size of the data or the cluster that they are operating on, so they can be used unchanged for a small dataset and for a massive one. More importantly, if you double the size of the input data, a job will run twice as slow. But if you also double the size of the cluster, a job will run as fast as the original one. This is not generally true of SQL queries.

Over time, however, the differences between relational databases and MapReduce systems are likely to blur. Both as relational databases start incorporating some of the ideas from MapReduce (such as Aster Data's and Greenplum's databases), and, from the other direction, as higher-level query languages built on MapReduce (such as Pig and Hive) make MapReduce systems more approachable to traditional database programmers.[#]

Grid Computing

The High Performance Computing (HPC) and Grid Computing communities have been doing large-scale data processing for years, using such APIs as Message Passing Interface (MPI). Broadly, the approach in HPC is to distribute the work across a cluster of machines, which access a shared filesystem, hosted by a SAN. This works well for predominantly compute-intensive jobs, but becomes a problem when nodes need to access larger data volumes (hundreds of gigabytes, the point at which MapReduce really starts to shine), since the network bandwidth is the bottleneck, and compute nodes become idle.

[#] In January 2007, David J. DeWitt and Michael Stonebraker caused a stir by publishing "MapReduce: A major step backwards" (*http://www.databasecolumn.com/2008/01/mapreduce-a-major-step-back.html*), in which they criticized MapReduce for being a poor substitute for relational databases. Many commentators argued that it was a false comparison (see, for example, Mark C. Chu-Carroll's "Databases are hammers; MapReduce is a screwdriver," *http://scienceblogs.com/goodmath/2008/01/databases_are_hammers_mapreduc.php*), and DeWitt and Stonebraker followed up with "MapReduce II" (*http://www.databasecolumn.com/2008/01/mapreduce-continued.html*), where they addressed the main topics brought up by others.

MapReduce tries to colocate the data with the compute node, so data access is fast since it is local.* This feature, known as *data locality*, is at the heart of MapReduce and is the reason for its good performance. Recognizing that network bandwidth is the most precious resource in a data center environment (it is easy to saturate network links by copying data around), MapReduce implementations go to great lengths to preserve it by explicitly modelling network topology. Notice that this arrangement does not preclude high-CPU analyses in MapReduce.

MPI gives great control to the programmer, but requires that he or she explicitly handle the mechanics of the data flow, exposed via low-level C routines and constructs, such as sockets, as well as the higher-level algorithm for the analysis. MapReduce operates only at the higher level: the programmer thinks in terms of functions of key and value pairs, and the data flow is implicit.

Coordinating the processes in a large-scale distributed computation is a challenge. The hardest aspect is gracefully handling partial failure—when you don't know if a remote process has failed or not—and still making progress with the overall computation. MapReduce spares the programmer from having to think about failure, since the implementation detects failed map or reduce tasks and reschedules replacements on machines that are healthy. MapReduce is able to do this since it is a *shared-nothing* architecture, meaning that tasks have no dependence on one other. (This is a slight oversimplification, since the output from mappers is fed to the reducers, but this is under the control of the MapReduce system; in this case, it needs to take more care rerunning a failed reducer than rerunning a failed map, since it has to make sure it can retrieve the necessary map outputs, and if not, regenerate them by running the relevant maps again.) So from the programmer's point of view, the order in which the tasks run doesn't matter. By contrast, MPI programs have to explicitly manage their own checkpointing and recovery, which gives more control to the programmer, but makes them more difficult to write.

MapReduce might sound like quite a restrictive programming model, and in a sense it is: you are limited to key and value types that are related in specified ways, and mappers and reducers run with very limited coordination between one another (the mappers pass keys and values to reducers). A natural question to ask is: can you do anything useful or nontrivial with it?

The answer is yes. MapReduce was invented by engineers at Google as a system for building production search indexes because they found themselves solving the same problem over and over again (and MapReduce was inspired by older ideas from the functional programming, distributed computing, and database communities), but it has since been used for many other applications in many other industries. It is pleasantly surprising to see the range of algorithms that can be expressed in MapReduce, from

---

* Jim Gray was an early advocate of putting the computation near the data. See "Distributed Computing Economics," March 2003, *http://research.microsoft.com/apps/pubs/default.aspx?id=70001*.

image analysis, to graph-based problems, to machine learning algorithms.[†] It can't solve every problem, of course, but it is a general data-processing tool.

You can see a sample of some of the applications that Hadoop has been used for in Chapter 14.

Volunteer Computing

When people first hear about Hadoop and MapReduce, they often ask, "How is it different from SETI@home?" SETI, the Search for Extra-Terrestrial Intelligence, runs a project called SETI@home (*http://setiathome.berkeley.edu/*) in which volunteers donate CPU time from their otherwise idle computers to analyze radio telescope data for signs of intelligent life outside earth. SETI@home is the most well-known of many *volunteer computing* projects; others include the Great Internet Mersenne Prime Search (to search for large prime numbers) and Folding@home (to understand protein folding, and how it relates to disease).

Volunteer computing projects work by breaking the problem they are trying to solve into chunks called *work units*, which are sent to computers around the world to be analyzed. For example, a SETI@home work unit is about 0.35 MB of radio telescope data, and takes hours or days to analyze on a typical home computer. When the analysis is completed, the results are sent back to the server, and the client gets another work unit. As a precaution to combat cheating, each work unit is sent to three different machines, and needs at least two results to agree to be accepted.

Although SETI@home may be superficially similar to MapReduce (breaking a problem into independent pieces to be worked on in parallel), there are some significant differences. The SETI@home problem is very CPU-intensive, which makes it suitable for running on hundreds of thousands of computers across the world,[‡] since the time to transfer the work unit is dwarfed by the time to run the computation on it. Volunteers are donating CPU cycles, not bandwidth.

MapReduce is designed to run jobs that last minutes or hours on trusted, dedicated hardware running in a single data center with very high aggregate bandwidth interconnects. By contrast, SETI@home runs a perpetual computation on untrusted machines on the Internet with highly variable connection speeds and no data locality.

[†] Apache Mahout (*http://lucene.apache.org/mahout/*) is a project to build machine learning libraries (such as classification and clustering algorithms) that run on Hadoop.

[‡] In January 2008, SETI@home was reported at *http://www.planetary.org/programs/projects/setiathome/setiathome_20080115.html* to be processing 300 gigabytes a day, using 320,000 computers (most of which are not dedicated to SETI@home; they are used for other things, too).

A Brief History of Hadoop

Hadoop was created by Doug Cutting, the creator of Apache Lucene, the widely used text search library. Hadoop has its origins in Apache Nutch, an open source web search engine, itself a part of the Lucene project.

The Origin of the Name "Hadoop"

The name Hadoop is not an acronym; it's a made-up name. The project's creator, Doug Cutting, explains how the name came about:

> The name my kid gave a stuffed yellow elephant. Short, relatively easy to spell and pronounce, meaningless, and not used elsewhere: those are my naming criteria. Kids are good at generating such. Googol is a kid's term.

Subprojects and "contrib" modules in Hadoop also tend to have names that are unrelated to their function, often with an elephant or other animal theme ("Pig," for example). Smaller components are given more descriptive (and therefore more mundane) names. This is a good principle, as it means you can generally work out what something does from its name. For example, the jobtracker[§] keeps track of MapReduce jobs.

Building a web search engine from scratch was an ambitious goal, for not only is the software required to crawl and index websites complex to write, but it is also a challenge to run without a dedicated operations team, since there are so many moving parts. It's expensive too: Mike Cafarella and Doug Cutting estimated a system supporting a 1-billion-page index would cost around half a million dollars in hardware, with a monthly running cost of $30,000.[‖] Nevertheless, they believed it was a worthy goal, as it would open up and ultimately democratize search engine algorithms.

Nutch was started in 2002, and a working crawler and search system quickly emerged. However, they realized that their architecture wouldn't scale to the billions of pages on the Web. Help was at hand with the publication of a paper in 2003 that described the architecture of Google's distributed filesystem, called GFS, which was being used in production at Google.[#] GFS, or something like it, would solve their storage needs for the very large files generated as a part of the web crawl and indexing process. In particular, GFS would free up time being spent on administrative tasks such as managing storage nodes. In 2004, they set about writing an open source implementation, the Nutch Distributed Filesystem (NDFS).

[§] In this book, we use the lowercase form, "jobtracker," to denote the entity when it's being referred to generally, and the CamelCase form `JobTracker` to denote the Java class that implements it.

[‖] Mike Cafarella and Doug Cutting, "Building Nutch: Open Source Search," *ACM Queue*, April 2004, *http://queue.acm.org/detail.cfm?id=988408*.

[#] Sanjay Ghemawat, Howard Gobioff, and Shun-Tak Leung, "The Google File System," October 2003, *http://labs.google.com/papers/gfs.html*.

In 2004, Google published the paper that introduced MapReduce to the world.[*] Early in 2005, the Nutch developers had a working MapReduce implementation in Nutch, and by the middle of that year all the major Nutch algorithms had been ported to run using MapReduce and NDFS.

NDFS and the MapReduce implementation in Nutch were applicable beyond the realm of search, and in February 2006 they moved out of Nutch to form an independent subproject of Lucene called Hadoop. At around the same time, Doug Cutting joined Yahoo!, which provided a dedicated team and the resources to turn Hadoop into a system that ran at web scale (see sidebar). This was demonstrated in February 2008 when Yahoo! announced that its production search index was being generated by a 10,000-core Hadoop cluster.[†]

In January 2008, Hadoop was made its own top-level project at Apache, confirming its success and its diverse, active community. By this timem Hadoop was being used by many other companies besides Yahoo!, such as Last.fm, Facebook, and the *New York Times* (some applications are covered in the case studies in Chapter 14 and on the Hadoop wiki (*http://wiki.apache.org/hadoop/PoweredBy*).

In one well-publicized feat, the *New York Times* used Amazon's EC2 compute cloud to crunch through four terabytes of scanned archives from the paper converting them to PDFs for the Web.[‡] The processing took less than 24 hours to run using 100 machines, and the project probably wouldn't have been embarked on without the combination of Amazon's pay-by-the-hour model (which allowed the NYT to access a large number of machines for a short period), and Hadoop's easy-to-use parallel programming model.

In April 2008, Hadoop broke a world record to become the fastest system to sort a terabyte of data. Running on a 910-node cluster, Hadoop sorted one terabyte in 209 seconds (just under 3½ minutes), beating the previous year's winner of 297 seconds (described in detail in "TeraByte Sort on Apache Hadoop" on page 461). In November of the same year, Google reported that its MapReduce implementation sorted one terabyte in 68 seconds.[§] As this book was going to press (May 2009), it was announced that a team at Yahoo! used Hadoop to sort one terabyte in 62 seconds.

[*] Jeffrey Dean and Sanjay Ghemawat, "MapReduce: Simplified Data Processing on Large Clusters ," December 2004, *http://labs.google.com/papers/mapreduce.html*.

[†] "Yahoo! Launches World's Largest Hadoop Production Application," 19 February 2008, *http://developer .yahoo.net/blogs/hadoop/2008/02/yahoo-worlds-largest-production-hadoop.html*.

[‡] Derek Gottfrid, "Self-service, Prorated Super Computing Fun!," 1 November 2007, *http://open.blogs.nytimes .com/2007/11/01/self-service-prorated-super-computing-fun/*.

[§] "Sorting 1PB with MapReduce," 21 November 2008, *http://googleblog.blogspot.com/2008/11/sorting-1pb -with-mapreduce.html*.

Hadoop at Yahoo!

Building Internet-scale search engines requires huge amounts of data and therefore large numbers of machines to process it. Yahoo! Search consists of four primary components: the *Crawler*, which downloads pages from web servers; the *WebMap*, which builds a graph of the known Web; the *Indexer*, which builds a reverse index to the best pages; and the *Runtime*, which answers users' queries. The WebMap is a graph that consists of roughly 1 trillion (10^{12}) edges each representing a web link and 100 billion (10^{11}) nodes each representing distinct URLs. Creating and analyzing such a large graph requires a large number of computers running for many days. In early 2005, the infrastructure for the WebMap, named *Dreadnaught*, needed to be redesigned to scale up to more nodes. Dreadnaught had successfully scaled from 20 to 600 nodes, but required a complete redesign to scale up further. Dreadnaught is similar to MapReduce in many ways, but provides more flexibility and less structure. In particular, each fragment in a Dreadnaught job can send output to each of the fragments in the next stage of the job, but the sort was all done in library code. In practice, most of the WebMap phases were pairs that corresponded to MapReduce. Therefore, the WebMap applications would not require extensive refactoring to fit into MapReduce.

Eric Baldeschwieler (Eric14) created a small team and we starting designing and prototyping a new framework written in C++ modeled after GFS and MapReduce to replace Dreadnaught. Although the immediate need was for a new framework for WebMap, it was clear that standardization of the batch platform across Yahoo! Search was critical and by making the framework general enough to support other users, we could better leverage investment in the new platform.

At the same time, we were watching Hadoop, which was part of Nutch, and its progress. In January 2006, Yahoo! hired Doug Cutting, and a month later we decided to abandon our prototype and adopt Hadoop. The advantage of Hadoop over our prototype and design was that it was already working with a real application (Nutch) on 20 nodes. That allowed us to bring up a research cluster two months later and start helping real customers use the new framework much sooner than we could have otherwise. Another advantage, of course, was that since Hadoop was already open source, it was easier (although far from easy!) to get permission from Yahoo!'s legal department to work in open source. So we set up a 200-node cluster for the researchers in early 2006 and put the WebMap conversion plans on hold while we supported and improved Hadoop for the research users.

Here's a quick timeline of how things have progressed:

- 2004—Initial versions of what is now Hadoop Distributed Filesystem and MapReduce implemented by Doug Cutting and Mike Cafarella.
- December 2005—Nutch ported to the new framework. Hadoop runs reliably on 20 nodes.
- January 2006—Doug Cutting joins Yahoo!.
- February 2006—Apache Hadoop project officially started to support the standalone development of MapReduce and HDFS.

- February 2006—Adoption of Hadoop by Yahoo! Grid team.
- April 2006—Sort benchmark (10 GB/node) run on 188 nodes in 47.9 hours.
- May 2006—Yahoo! set up a Hadoop research cluster—300 nodes.
- May 2006—Sort benchmark run on 500 nodes in 42 hours (better hardware than April benchmark).
- October 2006—Research cluster reaches 600 nodes.
- December 2006—Sort benchmark run on 20 nodes in 1.8 hours, 100 nodes in 3.3 hours, 500 nodes in 5.2 hours, 900 nodes in 7.8 hours.
- January 2007—Research cluster reaches 900 nodes.
- April 2007—Research clusters—2 clusters of 1000 nodes.
- April 2008—Won the 1 terabyte sort benchmark in 209 seconds on 900 nodes.
- October 2008—Loading 10 terabytes of data per a day on to research clusters.
- March 2009—17 clusters with a total of 24,000 nodes.
- April 2009—Won the minute sort by sorting 500 GB in 59 seconds (on 1400 nodes) and the 100 terabyte sort in 173 minutes (on 3400 nodes).

—Owen O'Malley

The Apache Hadoop Project

Today, Hadoop is a collection of related subprojects that fall under the umbrella of infrastructure for distributed computing. These projects are hosted by the Apache Software Foundation (*http://hadoop.apache.org/*), which provides support for a community of open source software projects. Although Hadoop is best known for MapReduce and its distributed filesystem (HDFS, renamed from NDFS), the other subprojects provide complementary services, or build on the core to add higher-level abstractions. The subprojects, and where they sit in the technology stack, are shown in Figure 1-1 and described briefly here:

Core
> A set of components and interfaces for distributed filesystems and general I/O (serialization, Java RPC, persistent data structures).

Avro
> A data serialization system for efficient, cross-language RPC, and persistent data storage. (At the time of this writing, Avro had been created only as a new subproject, and no other Hadoop subprojects were using it yet.)

MapReduce
> A distributed data processing model and execution environment that runs on large clusters of commodity machines.

HDFS
> A distributed filesystem that runs on large clusters of commodity machines.

Pig

A data flow language and execution environment for exploring very large datasets. Pig runs on HDFS and MapReduce clusters.

HBase

A distributed, column-oriented database. HBase uses HDFS for its underlying storage, and supports both batch-style computations using MapReduce and point queries (random reads).

ZooKeeper

A distributed, highly available coordination service. ZooKeeper provides primitives such as distributed locks that can be used for building distributed applications.

Hive

A distributed data warehouse. Hive manages data stored in HDFS and provides a query language based on SQL (and which is translated by the runtime engine to MapReduce jobs) for querying the data.

Chukwa

A distributed data collection and analysis system. Chukwa runs collectors that store data in HDFS, and it uses MapReduce to produce reports. (At the time of this writing, Chukwa had only recently graduated from a "contrib" module in Core to its own subproject.)

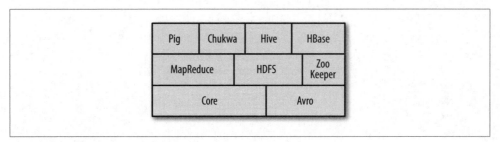

Figure 1-1. Hadoop subprojects

## CHAPTER 2

MapReduce

MapReduce is a programming model for data processing. The model is simple, yet not too simple to express useful programs in. Hadoop can run MapReduce programs written in various languages; in this chapter, we shall look at the same program expressed in Java, Ruby, Python, and C++. Most importantly, MapReduce programs are inherently parallel, thus putting very large-scale data analysis into the hands of anyone with enough machines at their disposal. MapReduce comes into its own for large datasets, so let's start by looking at one.

A Weather Dataset

For our example, we will write a program that mines weather data. Weather sensors collecting data every hour at many locations across the globe gather a large volume of log data, which is a good candidate for analysis with MapReduce, since it is semi-structured and record-oriented.

Data Format

The data we will use is from the National Climatic Data Center (NCDC, *http://www .ncdc.noaa.gov/*). The data is stored using a line-oriented ASCII format, in which each line is a record. The format supports a rich set of meteorological elements, many of which are optional or with variable data lengths. For simplicity, we shall focus on the basic elements, such as temperature, which are always present and are of fixed width.

Example 2-1 shows a sample line with some of the salient fields highlighted. The line has been split into multiple lines to show each field: in the real file, fields are packed into one line with no delimiters.

Example 2-1. Format of a National Climate Data Center record

```
0057
332130   # USAF weather station identifier
99999    # WBAN weather station identifier
19500101 # observation date
0300     # observation time
4
+51317   # latitude (degrees x 1000)
+028783  # longitude (degrees x 1000)
FM-12
+0171    # elevation (meters)
99999
V020
320      # wind direction (degrees)
1        # quality code
N
0072
1
00450    # sky ceiling height (meters)
1        # quality code
C
N
010000   # visibility distance (meters)
1        # quality code
N
9
-0128    # air temperature (degrees Celsius x 10)
1        # quality code
-0139    # dew point temperature (degrees Celsius x 10)
1        # quality code
10268    # atmospheric pressure (hectopascals x 10)
1        # quality code
```

Data files are organized by date and weather station. There is a directory for each year from 1901 to 2001, each containing a gzipped file for each weather station with its readings for that year. For example, here are the first entries for 1990:

```
% ls raw/1990 | head
010010-99999-1990.gz
010014-99999-1990.gz
010015-99999-1990.gz
010016-99999-1990.gz
010017-99999-1990.gz
010030-99999-1990.gz
010040-99999-1990.gz
010080-99999-1990.gz
010100-99999-1990.gz
010150-99999-1990.gz
```

Since there are tens of thousands of weather stations, the whole dataset is made up of a large number of relatively small files. It's generally easier and more efficient to process a smaller number of relatively large files, so the data was preprocessed so that each year's readings were concatenated into a single file. (The means by which this was carried out is described in Appendix C.)

Analyzing the Data with Unix Tools

What's the highest recorded global temperature for each year in the dataset? We will answer this first without using Hadoop, as this information will provide a performance baseline, as well as a useful means to check our results.

The classic tool for processing line-oriented data is *awk*. Example 2-2 is a small script to calculate the maximum temperature for each year.

Example 2-2. A program for finding the maximum recorded temperature by year from NCDC weather records

```
#!/usr/bin/env bash
for year in all/*
do
  echo -ne `basename $year .gz`"\t"
  gunzip -c $year | \
    awk '{ temp = substr($0, 88, 5) + 0;
           q = substr($0, 93, 1);
           if (temp !=9999 && q ~ /[01459]/ && temp > max) max = temp }
        END { print max }'
done
```

The script loops through the compressed year files, first printing the year, and then processing each file using *awk*. The *awk* script extracts two fields from the data: the air temperature and the quality code. The air temperature value is turned into an integer by adding 0. Next, a test is applied to see if the temperature is valid (the value 9999 signifies a missing value in the NCDC dataset), and if the quality code indicates that the reading is not suspect or erroneous. If the reading is OK, the value is compared with the maximum value seen so far, which is updated if a new maximum is found. The END block is executed after all the lines in the file have been processed, and prints the maximum value.

Here is the beginning of a run:

```
% ./max_temperature.sh
1901    317
1902    244
1903    289
1904    256
1905    283
...
```

The temperature values in the source file are scaled by a factor of 10, so this works out as a maximum temperature of 31.7°C for 1901 (there were very few readings at the beginning of the century, so this is plausible). The complete run for the century took 42 minutes in one run on a single EC2 High-CPU Extra Large Instance.

To speed up the processing, we need to run parts of the program in parallel. In theory, this is straightforward: we could process different years in different processes, using all the available hardware threads on a machine. There are a few problems with this, however.

First, dividing the work into equal-size pieces isn't always easy or obvious. In this case, the file size for different years varies widely, so some processes will finish much earlier than others. Even if they pick up further work, the whole run is dominated by the longest file. An alternative approach is to split the input into fixed-size chunks and assign each chunk to a process.

Second, combining the results from independent processes can need further processing. In this case, the result for each year is independent of other years and may be combined by concatenating all the results, and sorting by year. If using the fixed-size chunk approach, the combination is more delicate. For this example, data for a particular year will typically be split into several chunks, each processed independently. We'll end up with the maximum temperature for each chunk, so the final step is to look for the highest of these maximums, for each year.

Third, you are still limited by the processing capacity of a single machine. If the best time you can achieve is 20 minutes with the number of processors you have, then that's it. You can't make it go faster. Also, some datasets grow beyond the capacity of a single machine. When we start using multiple machines, a whole host of other factors come into play, mainly falling in the category of coordination and reliability. Who runs the overall job? How do we deal with failed processes?

So, though it's feasible to parallelize the processing, in practice it's messy. Using a framework like Hadoop to take care of these issues is a great help.

Analyzing the Data with Hadoop

To take advantage of the parallel processing that Hadoop provides, we need to express our query as a MapReduce job. After some local, small-scale testing, we will be able to run it on a cluster of machines.

Map and Reduce

MapReduce works by breaking the processing into two phases: the map phase and the reduce phase. Each phase has key-value pairs as input and output, the types of which may be chosen by the programmer. The programmer also specifies two functions: the map function and the reduce function.

The input to our map phase is the raw NCDC data. We choose a text input format that gives us each line in the dataset as a text value. The key is the offset of the beginning of the line from the beginning of the file, but as we have no need for this, we ignore it.

Our map function is simple. We pull out the year and the air temperature, since these are the only fields we are interested in. In this case, the map function is just a data preparation phase, setting up the data in such a way that the reducer function can do its work on it: finding the maximum temperature for each year. The map function is also a good place to drop bad records: here we filter out temperatures that are missing, suspect, or erroneous.

To visualize the way the map works, consider the following sample lines of input data (some unused columns have been dropped to fit the page, indicated by ellipses):

```
0067011990999991950051507004...9999999N9+00001+99999999999...
0043011990999991950051512004...9999999N9+00221+99999999999...
0043011990999991950051518004...9999999N9-00111+99999999999...
0043012650999991949032412004...0500001N9+01111+99999999999...
0043012650999991949032418004...0500001N9+00781+99999999999...
```

These lines are presented to the map function as the key-value pairs:

```
(0, 0067011990999991950051507004...9999999N9+00001+99999999999...)
(106, 0043011990999991950051512004...9999999N9+00221+99999999999...)
(212, 0043011990999991950051518004...9999999N9-00111+99999999999...)
(318, 0043012650999991949032412004...0500001N9+01111+99999999999...)
(424, 0043012650999991949032418004...0500001N9+00781+99999999999...)
```

The keys are the line offsets within the file, which we ignore in our map function. The map function merely extracts the year and the air temperature (indicated in bold text), and emits them as its output. (The temperature values have been interpreted as integers.)

```
(1950, 0)
(1950, 22)
(1950, -11)
(1949, 111)
(1949, 78)
```

The output from the map function is processed by the MapReduce framework before being sent to the reduce function. This processing sorts and groups the key-value pairs by key. So, continuing the example, our reduce function sees the following input:

```
(1949, [111, 78])
(1950, [0, 22, -11])
```

Each year appears with a list of all its air temperature readings. All the reduce function has to do now is iterate through the list and pick up the maximum reading:

```
(1949, 111)
(1950, 22)
```

This is the final output: the maximum global temperature recorded in each year.

The whole data flow is illustrated in Figure 2-1. At the bottom of the diagram is a Unix pipeline, which mimics the whole MapReduce flow, and which we will see again later in the chapter when we look at Hadoop Streaming.

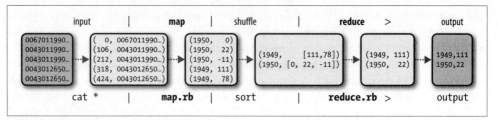

Figure 2-1. MapReduce logical data flow

Java MapReduce

Having run through how the MapReduce program works, the next step is to express it in code. We need three things: a map function, a reduce function, and some code to run the job. The map function is represented by an implementation of the Mapper interface, which declares a map() method. Example 2-3 shows the implementation of our map function.

Example 2-3. Mapper for maximum temperature example

```java
import java.io.IOException;

import org.apache.hadoop.io.IntWritable;
import org.apache.hadoop.io.LongWritable;
import org.apache.hadoop.io.Text;
import org.apache.hadoop.mapred.MapReduceBase;
import org.apache.hadoop.mapred.Mapper;
import org.apache.hadoop.mapred.OutputCollector;
import org.apache.hadoop.mapred.Reporter;

public class MaxTemperatureMapper extends MapReduceBase
  implements Mapper<LongWritable, Text, Text, IntWritable> {

  private static final int MISSING = 9999;

  public void map(LongWritable key, Text value,
      OutputCollector<Text, IntWritable> output, Reporter reporter)
      throws IOException {

    String line = value.toString();
    String year = line.substring(15, 19);
    int airTemperature;
    if (line.charAt(87) == '+') { // parseInt doesn't like leading plus signs
      airTemperature = Integer.parseInt(line.substring(88, 92));
    } else {
      airTemperature = Integer.parseInt(line.substring(87, 92));
    }
    String quality = line.substring(92, 93);
    if (airTemperature != MISSING && quality.matches("[01459]")) {
      output.collect(new Text(year), new IntWritable(airTemperature));
    }
  }
}
```

The Mapper interface is a generic type, with four formal type parameters that specify the input key, input value, output key, and output value types of the map function. For the present example, the input key is a long integer offset, the input value is a line of text, the output key is a year, and the output value is an air temperature (an integer). Rather than use built-in Java types, Hadoop provides its own set of basic types that are optimized for network serialization. These are found in the `org.apache.hadoop.io` package. Here we use `LongWritable`, which corresponds to a Java `Long`, `Text` (like Java `String`), and `IntWritable` (like Java `Integer`).

The `map()` method is passed a key and a value. We convert the `Text` value containing the line of input into a Java `String`, then use its `substring()` method to extract the columns we are interested in.

The `map()` method also provides an instance of `OutputCollector` to write the output to. In this case, we write the year as a `Text` object (since we are just using it as a key), and the temperature wrapped in an `IntWritable`. We write an output record only if the temperature is present and the quality code indicates the temperature reading is OK.

The reduce function is similarly defined using a `Reducer`, as illustrated in Example 2-4.

Example 2-4. Reducer for maximum temperature example

```java
import java.io.IOException;
import java.util.Iterator;

import org.apache.hadoop.io.IntWritable;
import org.apache.hadoop.io.Text;
import org.apache.hadoop.mapred.MapReduceBase;
import org.apache.hadoop.mapred.OutputCollector;
import org.apache.hadoop.mapred.Reducer;
import org.apache.hadoop.mapred.Reporter;

public class MaxTemperatureReducer extends MapReduceBase
  implements Reducer<Text, IntWritable, Text, IntWritable> {

  public void reduce(Text key, Iterator<IntWritable> values,
      OutputCollector<Text, IntWritable> output, Reporter reporter)
      throws IOException {

    int maxValue = Integer.MIN_VALUE;
    while (values.hasNext()) {
      maxValue = Math.max(maxValue, values.next().get());
    }
    output.collect(key, new IntWritable(maxValue));
  }
}
```

Again, four formal type parameters are used to specify the input and output types, this time for the reduce function. The input types of the reduce function must match the output type of the map function: `Text` and `IntWritable`. And in this case, the output types of the reduce function are `Text` and `IntWritable`, for a year and its maximum temperature, which we find by iterating through the temperatures and comparing each with a record of the highest found so far.

The third piece of code runs the MapReduce job (see Example 2-5).

Example 2-5. Application to find the maximum temperature in the weather dataset

```java
import java.io.IOException;

import org.apache.hadoop.fs.Path;
import org.apache.hadoop.io.IntWritable;
import org.apache.hadoop.io.Text;
import org.apache.hadoop.mapred.FileInputFormat;
import org.apache.hadoop.mapred.FileOutputFormat;
import org.apache.hadoop.mapred.JobClient;
import org.apache.hadoop.mapred.JobConf;

public class MaxTemperature {

  public static void main(String[] args) throws IOException {
    if (args.length != 2) {
      System.err.println("Usage: MaxTemperature <input path> <output path>");
      System.exit(-1);
    }

    JobConf conf = new JobConf(MaxTemperature.class);
    conf.setJobName("Max temperature");

    FileInputFormat.addInputPath(conf, new Path(args[0]));
    FileOutputFormat.setOutputPath(conf, new Path(args[1]));

    conf.setMapperClass(MaxTemperatureMapper.class);
    conf.setReducerClass(MaxTemperatureReducer.class);

    conf.setOutputKeyClass(Text.class);
    conf.setOutputValueClass(IntWritable.class);

    JobClient.runJob(conf);
  }
}
```

A JobConf object forms the specification of the job. It gives you control over how the job is run. When we run this job on a Hadoop cluster, we will package the code into a JAR file (which Hadoop will distribute round the cluster). Rather than explicitly specify the name of the JAR file, we can pass a class in the JobConf constructor, which Hadoop will use to locate the relevant JAR file by looking for the JAR file containing this class.

Having constructed a JobConf object, we specify the input and output paths. An input path is specified by calling the static addInputPath() method on FileInputFormat, and it can be a single file, a directory (in which case, the input forms all the files in that directory), or a file pattern. As the name suggests, addInputPath() can be called more than once to use input from multiple paths.

The output path (of which there is only one) is specified by the static setOutput Path() method on FileOutputFormat. It specifies a directory where the output files from the reducer functions are written. The directory shouldn't exist before running the job, as Hadoop will complain and not run the job. This precaution is to prevent data loss (it can be very annoying to accidentally overwrite the output of a long job with another).

Next, we specify the map and reduce types to use via the setMapperClass() and setReducerClass() methods.

The setOutputKeyClass() and setOutputValueClass() methods control the output types for the map and the reduce functions, which are often the same, as they are in our case. If they are different, then the map output types can be set using the methods setMapOutputKeyClass() and setMapOutputValueClass().

The input types are controlled via the input format, which we have not explicitly set since we are using the default TextInputFormat.

After setting the classes that define the map and reduce functions, we are ready to run the job. The static runJob() method on JobClient submits the job and waits for it to finish, writing information about its progress to the console.

A test run

After writing a MapReduce job, it's normal to try it out on a small dataset to flush out any immediate problems with the code. First install Hadoop in standalone mode— there are instructions for how to do this in Appendix A. This is the mode in which Hadoop runs using the local filesystem with a local job runner. Let's test it on the five-line sample discussed earlier (the output has been slightly reformatted to fit the page):

```
% export HADOOP_CLASSPATH=build/classes
% hadoop MaxTemperature input/ncdc/sample.txt output
09/04/07 12:34:35 INFO jvm.JvmMetrics: Initializing JVM Metrics with processName=Job
Tracker, sessionId=
09/04/07 12:34:35 WARN mapred.JobClient: Use GenericOptionsParser for parsing the
arguments. Applications should implement Tool for the same.
09/04/07 12:34:35 WARN mapred.JobClient: No job jar file set.  User classes may not
be found. See JobConf(Class) or JobConf#setJar(String).
09/04/07 12:34:35 INFO mapred.FileInputFormat: Total input paths to process : 1
09/04/07 12:34:35 INFO mapred.JobClient: Running job: job_local_0001
09/04/07 12:34:35 INFO mapred.FileInputFormat: Total input paths to process : 1
09/04/07 12:34:35 INFO mapred.MapTask: numReduceTasks: 1
09/04/07 12:34:35 INFO mapred.MapTask: io.sort.mb = 100
09/04/07 12:34:35 INFO mapred.MapTask: data buffer = 79691776/99614720
09/04/07 12:34:35 INFO mapred.MapTask: record buffer = 262144/327680
09/04/07 12:34:35 INFO mapred.MapTask: Starting flush of map output
09/04/07 12:34:36 INFO mapred.MapTask: Finished spill 0
09/04/07 12:34:36 INFO mapred.TaskRunner: Task:attempt_local_0001_m_000000_0 is
done. And is in the process of commiting
09/04/07 12:34:36 INFO mapred.LocalJobRunner: file:/Users/tom/workspace/htdg/input/n
cdc/sample.txt:0+529
09/04/07 12:34:36 INFO mapred.TaskRunner: Task 'attempt_local_0001_m_000000_0' done.
```

```
09/04/07 12:34:36 INFO mapred.LocalJobRunner:
09/04/07 12:34:36 INFO mapred.Merger: Merging 1 sorted segments
09/04/07 12:34:36 INFO mapred.Merger: Down to the last merge-pass, with 1 segments
left of total size: 57 bytes
09/04/07 12:34:36 INFO mapred.LocalJobRunner:
09/04/07 12:34:36 INFO mapred.TaskRunner: Task:attempt_local_0001_r_000000_0 is done
. And is in the process of commiting
09/04/07 12:34:36 INFO mapred.LocalJobRunner:
09/04/07 12:34:36 INFO mapred.TaskRunner: Task attempt_local_0001_r_000000_0 is
allowed to commit now
09/04/07 12:34:36 INFO mapred.FileOutputCommitter: Saved output of task
'attempt_local_0001_r_000000_0' to file:/Users/tom/workspace/htdg/output
09/04/07 12:34:36 INFO mapred.LocalJobRunner: reduce > reduce
09/04/07 12:34:36 INFO mapred.TaskRunner: Task 'attempt_local_0001_r_000000_0' done.
09/04/07 12:34:36 INFO mapred.JobClient:  map 100% reduce 100%
09/04/07 12:34:36 INFO mapred.JobClient: Job complete: job_local_0001
09/04/07 12:34:36 INFO mapred.JobClient: Counters: 13
09/04/07 12:34:36 INFO mapred.JobClient:    FileSystemCounters
09/04/07 12:34:36 INFO mapred.JobClient:      FILE_BYTES_READ=27571
09/04/07 12:34:36 INFO mapred.JobClient:      FILE_BYTES_WRITTEN=53907
09/04/07 12:34:36 INFO mapred.JobClient:    Map-Reduce Framework
09/04/07 12:34:36 INFO mapred.JobClient:      Reduce input groups=2
09/04/07 12:34:36 INFO mapred.JobClient:      Combine output records=0
09/04/07 12:34:36 INFO mapred.JobClient:      Map input records=5
09/04/07 12:34:36 INFO mapred.JobClient:      Reduce shuffle bytes=0
09/04/07 12:34:36 INFO mapred.JobClient:      Reduce output records=2
09/04/07 12:34:36 INFO mapred.JobClient:      Spilled Records=10
09/04/07 12:34:36 INFO mapred.JobClient:      Map output bytes=45
09/04/07 12:34:36 INFO mapred.JobClient:      Map input bytes=529
09/04/07 12:34:36 INFO mapred.JobClient:      Combine input records=0
09/04/07 12:34:36 INFO mapred.JobClient:      Map output records=5
09/04/07 12:34:36 INFO mapred.JobClient:      Reduce input records=5
```

When the hadoop command is invoked with a classname as the first argument, it launches a JVM to run the class. It is more convenient to use hadoop than straight java since the former adds the Hadoop libraries (and their dependencies) to the classpath, and picks up the Hadoop configuration too. To add the application classes to the classpath, we've defined an environment variable called HADOOP_CLASSPATH, which the hadoop script picks up.

When running in local (standalone) mode, the programs in this book all assume that you have set the HADOOP_CLASSPATH in this way. The commands should be run from the directory that the example code is installed in.

The output from running the job provides some useful information. (The warning about the job JAR file not being found is expected, since we are running in local mode without a JAR. We won't see this warning when we run on a cluster.) For example, we can see that the job was given an ID of job_local_0001, and it ran one map task and one reduce task (with the IDs attempt_local_0001_m_000000_0 and `attempt_local_0001_r_000000_0`). Knowing the job and task IDs can be very useful when debugging MapReduce jobs.

The last section of the output, entitled "Counters," shows the statistics that Hadoop generates for each job it runs. These are very useful for checking whether the amount of data processed is what you expected. For example, we can follow the number of records that went through the system: five map inputs produced five map outputs, then five reduce inputs in two groups produced two reduce outputs.

The output was written to the *output* directory, which contains one output file per reducer. The job had a single reducer, so we find a single file, named *part-00000*:

```
% cat output/part-00000
1949    111
1950    22
```

This result is the same as when we went through it by hand earlier. We interpret this as saying that the maximum temperature recorded in 1949 was 11.1°C, and in 1950 it was 2.2°C.

The new Java MapReduce API

Release 0.20.0 of Hadoop included a new Java MapReduce API, sometimes referred to as "Context Objects," designed to make the API easier to evolve in the future. The new API is type-incompatible with the old, however, so applications need to be rewritten to take advantage of it.[*]

There are several notable differences between the two APIs:

- The new API favors abstract classes over interfaces, since these are easier to evolve. For example, you can add a method (with a default implementation) to an abstract class without breaking old implementations of the class. In the new API, the `Mapper` and `Reducer` interfaces are now abstract classes.

- The new API is in the `org.apache.hadoop.mapreduce` package (and subpackages). The old API is found in `org.apache.hadoop.mapred`.

- The new API makes extensive use of context objects that allow the user code to communicate with the MapReduce system. The `MapContext`, for example, essentially unifies the role of the `JobConf`, the `OutputCollector`, and the `Reporter`.

- The new API supports both a "push" and a "pull" style of iteration. In both APIs, key-value record pairs are pushed to the mapper, but in addition, the new API allows a mapper to pull records from within the `map()` method. The same goes for the reducer. An example of how the "pull" style can be useful is processing records in batches, rather than one by one.

---

[*] At the time of this writing, not all of the MapReduce libraries in Hadoop have been ported to work with the new API. This book uses the old API for this reason. However, a copy of all of the examples in this book, rewritten to use the new API, will be made available on the book's website.

- Configuration has been unified. The old API has a special `JobConf` object for job configuration, which is an extension of Hadoop's vanilla `Configuration` object (used for configuring daemons; see "The Configuration API" on page 116). In the new API, this distinction is dropped, so job configuration is done through a `Configuration`.

- Job control is performed through the `Job` class, rather than `JobClient`, which no longer exists in the new API.

Example 2-6 shows the `MaxTemperature` application rewritten to use the new API. The differences are highlighted in bold.

Example 2-6. Application to find the maximum temperature in the weather dataset using the new context objects MapReduce API

```
public class NewMaxTemperature {

  static class NewMaxTemperatureMapper
    extends Mapper<LongWritable, Text, Text, IntWritable> {

    private static final int MISSING = 9999;

    public void map(LongWritable key, Text value, Context context)
        throws IOException, InterruptedException {

      String line = value.toString();
      String year = line.substring(15, 19);
      int airTemperature;
      if (line.charAt(87) == '+') { // parseInt doesn't like leading plus signs
        airTemperature = Integer.parseInt(line.substring(88, 92));
      } else {
        airTemperature = Integer.parseInt(line.substring(87, 92));
      }
      String quality = line.substring(92, 93);
      if (airTemperature != MISSING && quality.matches("[01459]")) {
        context.write(new Text(year), new IntWritable(airTemperature));
      }
    }
  }

  static class NewMaxTemperatureReducer
    extends Reducer<Text, IntWritable, Text, IntWritable> {

    public void reduce(Text key, Iterable<IntWritable> values,
        Context context)
        throws IOException, InterruptedException {

      int maxValue = Integer.MIN_VALUE;
      for (IntWritable value : values) {
        maxValue = Math.max(maxValue, value.get());
      }
      context.write(key, new IntWritable(maxValue));
    }
  }
```

```
public static void main(String[] args) throws Exception {
  if (args.length != 2) {
    System.err.println("Usage: NewMaxTemperature <input path> <output path>");
    System.exit(-1);
  }

  Job job = new Job();
  job.setJarByClass(NewMaxTemperature.class);

  FileInputFormat.addInputPath(job, new Path(args[0]));
  FileOutputFormat.setOutputPath(job, new Path(args[1]));

  job.setMapperClass(NewMaxTemperatureMapper.class);
  job.setReducerClass(NewMaxTemperatureReducer.class);

  job.setOutputKeyClass(Text.class);
  job.setOutputValueClass(IntWritable.class);

  System.exit(job.waitForCompletion(true) ? 0 : 1);
  }
}
```

Scaling Out

You've seen how MapReduce works for small inputs; now it's time to take a bird's-eye view of the system and look at the data flow for large inputs. For simplicity, the examples so far have used files on the local filesystem. However, to scale out, we need to store the data in a distributed filesystem, typically HDFS (which you'll learn about in the next chapter), to allow Hadoop to move the MapReduce computation to each machine hosting a part of the data. Let's see how this works.

Data Flow

First, some terminology. A MapReduce *job* is a unit of work that the client wants to be performed: it consists of the input data, the MapReduce program, and configuration information. Hadoop runs the job by dividing it into *tasks*, of which there are two types: *map tasks* and *reduce tasks*.

There are two types of nodes that control the job execution process: a *jobtracker* and a number of *tasktrackers*. The jobtracker coordinates all the jobs run on the system by scheduling tasks to run on tasktrackers. Tasktrackers run tasks and send progress reports to the jobtracker, which keeps a record of the overall progress of each job. If a tasks fails, the jobtracker can reschedule it on a different tasktracker.

Hadoop divides the input to a MapReduce job into fixed-size pieces called *input splits*, or just *splits*. Hadoop creates one map task for each split, which runs the user-defined map function for each *record* in the split.

Having many splits means the time taken to process each split is small compared to the time to process the whole input. So if we are processing the splits in parallel, the processing is better load-balanced if the splits are small, since a faster machine will be able to process proportionally more splits over the course of the job than a slower machine. Even if the machines are identical, failed processes or other jobs running concurrently make load balancing desirable, and the quality of the load balancing increases as the splits become more fine-grained.

On the other hand, if splits are too small, then the overhead of managing the splits and of map task creation begins to dominate the total job execution time. For most jobs, a good split size tends to be the size of a HDFS block, 64 MB by default, although this can be changed for the cluster (for all newly created files), or specified when each file is created.

Hadoop does its best to run the map task on a node where the input data resides in HDFS. This is called the *data locality optimization*. It should now be clear why the optimal split size is the same as the block size: it is the largest size of input that can be guaranteed to be stored on a single node. If the split spanned two blocks, it would be unlikely that any HDFS node stored both blocks, so some of the split would have to be transferred across the network to the node running the map task, which is clearly less efficient than running the whole map task using local data.

Map tasks write their output to local disk, not to HDFS. Why is this? Map output is intermediate output: it's processed by reduce tasks to produce the final output, and once the job is complete the map output can be thrown away. So storing it in HDFS, with replication, would be overkill. If the node running the map task fails before the map output has been consumed by the reduce task, then Hadoop will automatically rerun the map task on another node to recreate the map output.

Reduce tasks don't have the advantage of data locality—the input to a single reduce task is normally the output from all mappers. In the present example, we have a single reduce task that is fed by all of the map tasks. Therefore the sorted map outputs have to be transferred across the network to the node where the reduce task is running, where they are merged and then passed to the user-defined reduce function. The output of the reduce is normally stored in HDFS for reliability. As explained in Chapter 3, for each HDFS block of the reduce output, the first replica is stored on the local node, with other replicas being stored on off-rack nodes. Thus, writing the reduce output does consume network bandwidth, but only as much as a normal HDFS write pipeline consumes.

The whole data flow with a single reduce task is illustrated in Figure 2-2. The dotted boxes indicate nodes, the light arrows show data transfers on a node, and the heavy arrows show data transfers between nodes.

The number of reduce tasks is not governed by the size of the input, but is specified independently. In "The Default MapReduce Job" on page 178, you will see how to choose the number of reduce tasks for a given job.

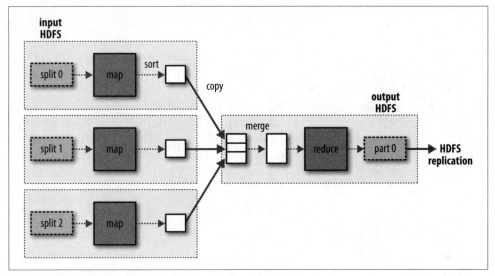

Figure 2-2. MapReduce data flow with a single reduce task

When there are multiple reducers, the map tasks *partition* their output, each creating one partition for each reduce task. There can be many keys (and their associated values) in each partition, but the records for every key are all in a single partition. The partitioning can be controlled by a user-defined partitioning function, but normally the default partitioner—which buckets keys using a hash function—works very well.

The data flow for the general case of multiple reduce tasks is illustrated in Figure 2-3. This diagram makes it clear why the data flow between map and reduce tasks is colloquially known as "the shuffle," as each reduce task is fed by many map tasks. The shuffle is more complicated than this diagram suggests, and tuning it can have a big impact on job execution time, as you will see in "Shuffle and Sort" on page 163.

Finally, it's also possible to have zero reduce tasks. This can be appropriate when you don't need the shuffle since the processing can be carried out entirely in parallel (a few examples are discussed in "NLineInputFormat" on page 198). In this case, the only off-node data transfer is when the map tasks write to HDFS (see Figure 2-4).

Combiner Functions

Many MapReduce jobs are limited by the bandwidth available on the cluster, so it pays to minimize the data transferred between map and reduce tasks. Hadoop allows the user to specify a *combiner function* to be run on the map output—the combiner function's output forms the input to the reduce function. Since the combiner function is an optimization, Hadoop does not provide a guarantee of how many times it will call it for a particular map output record, if at all. In other words, calling the combiner function zero, one, or many times should produce the same output from the reducer.

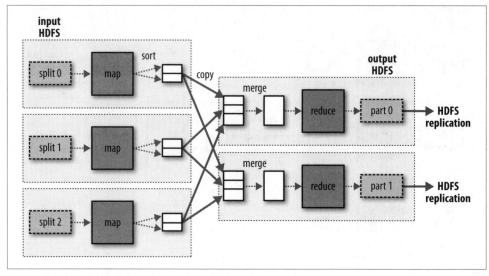

Figure 2-3. MapReduce data flow with multiple reduce tasks

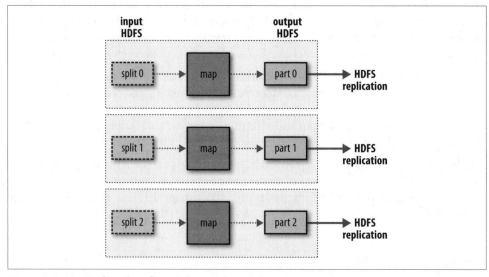

Figure 2-4. MapReduce data flow with no reduce tasks

The contract for the combiner function constrains the type of function that may be used. This is best illustrated with an example. Suppose that for the *maximum* temperature example, readings for the year 1950 were processed by two maps (because they were in different splits). Imagine the first map produced the output:

```
(1950, 0)
(1950, 20)
(1950, 10)
```

And the second produced:

```
(1950, 25)
(1950, 15)
```

The reduce function would be called with a list of all the values:

```
(1950, [0, 20, 10, 25, 15])
```

with output:

```
(1950, 25)
```

since 25 is the maximum value in the list. We could use a combiner function that, just like the reduce function, finds the maximum temperature for each map output. The reduce would then be called with:

```
(1950, [20, 25])
```

and the reduce would produce the same output as before. More succinctly, we may express the function calls on the temperature values in this case as follows:

```
max(0, 20, 10, 25, 15) = max(max(0, 20, 10), max(25, 15)) = max(20, 25) = 25
```

Not all functions possess this property.[†] For example, if we were calculating mean temperatures, then we couldn't use the mean as our combiner function, since:

```
mean(0, 20, 10, 25, 15) = 14
```

but:

```
mean(mean(0, 20, 10), mean(25, 15)) = mean(10, 20) = 15
```

The combiner function doesn't replace the reduce function. (How could it? The reduce function is still needed to process records with the same key from different maps.) But it can help cut down the amount of data shuffled between the maps and the reduces, and for this reason alone it is always worth considering whether you can use a combiner function in your MapReduce job.

Specifying a combiner function

Going back to the Java MapReduce program, the combiner function is defined using the Reducer interface, and for this application, it is the same implementation as the reducer function in MaxTemperatureReducer. The only change we need to make is to set the combiner class on the JobConf (see Example 2-7).

[†] Functions with this property are called *distributive* in the paper "Data Cube: A Relational Aggregation Operator Generalizing Group-By, Cross-Tab, and Sub-Totals," Gray et al. (1995).

Example 2-7. Application to find the maximum temperature, using a combiner function for efficiency

```java
public class MaxTemperatureWithCombiner {

  public static void main(String[] args) throws IOException {
    if (args.length != 2) {
      System.err.println("Usage: MaxTemperatureWithCombiner <input path> " +
          "<output path>");
      System.exit(-1);
    }

    JobConf conf = new JobConf(MaxTemperatureWithCombiner.class);
    conf.setJobName("Max temperature");

    FileInputFormat.addInputPath(conf, new Path(args[0]));
    FileOutputFormat.setOutputPath(conf, new Path(args[1]));

    conf.setMapperClass(MaxTemperatureMapper.class);
    conf.setCombinerClass(MaxTemperatureReducer.class);
    conf.setReducerClass(MaxTemperatureReducer.class);

    conf.setOutputKeyClass(Text.class);
    conf.setOutputValueClass(IntWritable.class);

    JobClient.runJob(conf);
  }
}
```

Running a Distributed MapReduce Job

The same program will run, without alteration, on a full dataset. This is the point of MapReduce: it scales to the size of your data and the size of your hardware. Here's one data point: on a 10-node EC2 cluster running High-CPU Extra Large Instances, the program took six minutes to run.[‡]

We'll go through the mechanics of running programs on a cluster in Chapter 5.

Hadoop Streaming

Hadoop provides an API to MapReduce that allows you to write your map and reduce functions in languages other than Java. *Hadoop Streaming* uses Unix standard streams as the interface between Hadoop and your program, so you can use any language that can read standard input and write to standard output to write your MapReduce program.

[‡] This is a factor of seven faster than the serial run on one machine using *awk*. The main reason it wasn't proportionately faster is because the input data wasn't evenly partitioned. For convenience, the input files were gzipped by year, resulting in large files for the later years in dataset, when the number of weather records was much higher.

Streaming is naturally suited for text processing (although as of version 0.21.0 it can handle binary streams, too), and when used in text mode, it has a line-oriented view of data. Map input data is passed over standard input to your map function, which processes it line by line and writes lines to standard output. A map output key-value pair is written as a single tab-delimited line. Input to the reduce function is in the same format—a tab-separated key-value pair—passed over standard input. The reduce function reads lines from standard input, which the framework guarantees are sorted by key, and writes its results to standard output.

Let's illustrate this by rewriting our MapReduce program for finding maximum temperatures by year in Streaming.

Ruby

The map function can be expressed in Ruby as shown in Example 2-8.

Example 2-8. Map function for maximum temperature in Ruby

```ruby
#!/usr/bin/env ruby

STDIN.each_line do |line|
  val = line
  year, temp, q = val[15,4], val[87,5], val[92,1]
  puts "#{year}\t#{temp}" if (temp != "+9999" && q =~ /[01459]/)
end
```

The program iterates over lines from standard input by executing a block for each line from STDIN (a global constant of type IO). The block pulls out the relevant fields from each input line, and, if the temperature is valid, writes the year and the temperature separated by a tab character \t to standard output (using puts).

> It's worth drawing out a design difference between Streaming and the Java MapReduce API. The Java API is geared toward processing your map function one record at a time. The framework calls the map() method on your Mapper for each record in the input, whereas with Streaming the map program can decide how to process the input—for example, it could easily read and process multiple lines at a time since it's in control of the reading. The user's Java map implementation is "pushed" records, but it's still possible to consider multiple lines at a time by accumulating previous lines in an instance variable in the Mapper.[§] In this case, you need to implement the close() method so that you know when the last record has been read, so you can finish processing the last group of lines.

[§] Alternatively, you could use "pull" style processing in the new MapReduce API—see "The new Java MapReduce API" on page 25.

Since the script just operates on standard input and output, it's trivial to test the script without using Hadoop, simply using Unix pipes:

```
% cat input/ncdc/sample.txt | src/main/ch02/ruby/max_temperature_map.rb
1950    +0000
1950    +0022
1950    -0011
1949    +0111
1949    +0078
```

The reduce function shown in Example 2-9 is a little more complex.

Example 2-9. Reduce function for maximum temperature in Ruby

```ruby
#!/usr/bin/env ruby

last_key, max_val = nil, 0
STDIN.each_line do |line|
  key, val = line.split("\t")
  if last_key && last_key != key
    puts "#{last_key}\t#{max_val}"
    last_key, max_val = key, val.to_i
  else
    last_key, max_val = key, [max_val, val.to_i].max
  end
end
puts "#{last_key}\t#{max_val}" if last_key
```

Again, the program iterates over lines from standard input, but this time we have to store some state as we process each key group. In this case, the keys are weather station identifiers, and we store the last key seen and the maximum temperature seen so far for that key. The MapReduce framework ensures that the keys are ordered, so we know that if a key is different from the previous one, we have moved into a new key group. In contrast to the Java API, where you are provided an iterator over each key group, in Streaming you have to find key group boundaries in your program.

For each line we pull out the key and value, then if we've just finished a group (`last_key && last_key != key`), we write the key and the maximum temperature for that group, separated by a tab character, before resetting the maximum temperature for the new key. If we haven't just finished a group, we just update the maximum temperature for the current key.

The last line of the program ensures that a line is written for the last key group in the input.

We can now simulate the whole MapReduce pipeline with a Unix pipeline (which is equivalent to the Unix pipeline shown in Figure 2-1):

```
% cat input/ncdc/sample.txt | src/main/ch02/ruby/max_temperature_map.rb | \
  sort | src/main/ch02/ruby/max_temperature_reduce.rb
1949    111
1950    22
```

The output is the same as the Java program, so the next step is to run it using Hadoop itself.

The `hadoop` command doesn't support a Streaming option; instead, you specify the Streaming JAR file along with the `jar` option. Options to the Streaming program specify the input and output paths, and the map and reduce scripts. This is what it looks like:

```
% hadoop jar $HADOOP_INSTALL/contrib/streaming/hadoop-*-streaming.jar \
  -input input/ncdc/sample.txt \
  -output output \
  -mapper src/main/ch02/ruby/max_temperature_map.rb \
  -reducer src/main/ch02/ruby/max_temperature_reduce.rb
```

When running on a large dataset on a cluster, we should set the combiner, using the `-combiner` option.

From release 0.21.0, the combiner can be any Streaming command. For earlier releases, the combiner had to be written in Java, so as a workaround it was common to do manual combining in the mapper, without having to resort to Java. In this case, we could change the mapper to be a pipeline:

```
% hadoop jar $HADOOP_INSTALL/contrib/streaming/hadoop-*-streaming.jar \
  -input input/ncdc/all \
  -output output \
  -mapper "ch02/ruby/max_temperature_map.rb | sort | ch02/ruby/max_temperature_reduce.rb" \
  -reducer src/main/ch02/ruby/max_temperature_reduce.rb \
  -file src/main/ch02/ruby/max_temperature_map.rb \
  -file src/main/ch02/ruby/max_temperature_reduce.rb
```

Note also the use of `-file`, which we use when running Streaming programs on the cluster to ship the scripts to the cluster.

Python

Streaming supports any programming language that can read from standard input, and write to standard output, so for readers more familiar with Python, here's the same example again.[||] The map script is in Example 2-10, and the reduce script is in Example 2-11.

Example 2-10. Map function for maximum temperature in Python

```python
#!/usr/bin/env python

import re
import sys

for line in sys.stdin:
  val = line.strip()
  (year, temp, q) = (val[15:19], val[87:92], val[92:93])
```

[||] As an alternative to Streaming, Python programmers should consider Dumbo (*http://www.last.fm/dumbo*), which makes the Streaming MapReduce interface more Pythonic, and easier to use.

```
  if (temp != "+9999" and re.match("[01459]", q)):
    print "%s\t%s" % (year, temp)
```

Example 2-11. Reduce function for maximum temperature in Python

```
#!/usr/bin/env python

import sys

(last_key, max_val) = (None, 0)
for line in sys.stdin:
  (key, val) = line.strip().split("\t")
  if last_key and last_key != key:
    print "%s\t%s" % (last_key, max_val)
    (last_key, max_val) = (key, int(val))
  else:
    (last_key, max_val) = (key, max(max_val, int(val)))

if last_key:
  print "%s\t%s" % (last_key, max_val)
```

We can test the programs and run the job in the same way we did in Ruby. For example, to run a test:

```
% cat input/ncdc/sample.txt | src/main/ch02/python/max_temperature_map.py | \
  sort | src/main/ch02/python/max_temperature_reduce.py
1949    111
1950    22
```

Hadoop Pipes

Hadoop Pipes is the name of the C++ interface to Hadoop MapReduce. Unlike Streaming, which uses standard input and output to communicate with the map and reduce code, Pipes uses sockets as the channel over which the tasktracker communicates with the process running the C++ map or reduce function. JNI is not used.

We'll rewrite the example running through the chapter in C++, and then we'll see how to run it using Pipes. Example 2-12 shows the source code for the map and reduce functions in C++.

Example 2-12. Maximum temperature in C++

```
#include <algorithm>
#include <limits>
#include <string>

#include "hadoop/Pipes.hh"
#include "hadoop/TemplateFactory.hh"
#include "hadoop/StringUtils.hh"

class MaxTemperatureMapper : public HadoopPipes::Mapper {
public:
  MaxTemperatureMapper(HadoopPipes::TaskContext& context) {
```

```
  }
  void map(HadoopPipes::MapContext& context) {
    std::string line = context.getInputValue();
    std::string year = line.substr(15, 4);
    std::string airTemperature = line.substr(87, 5);
    std::string q = line.substr(92, 1);
    if (airTemperature != "+9999" &&
        (q == "0" || q == "1" || q == "4" || q == "5" || q == "9")) {
      context.emit(year, airTemperature);
    }
  }
};

class MapTemperatureReducer : public HadoopPipes::Reducer {
public:
  MapTemperatureReducer(HadoopPipes::TaskContext& context) {
  }
  void reduce(HadoopPipes::ReduceContext& context) {
    int maxValue = INT_MIN;
    while (context.nextValue()) {
      maxValue = std::max(maxValue, HadoopUtils::toInt(context.getInputValue()));
    }
    context.emit(context.getInputKey(), HadoopUtils::toString(maxValue));
  }
};

int main(int argc, char *argv[]) {
  return HadoopPipes::runTask(HadoopPipes::TemplateFactory<MaxTemperatureMapper,
                              MapTemperatureReducer>());
}
```

The application links against the Hadoop C++ library, which is a thin wrapper for communicating with the tasktracker child process. The map and reduce functions are defined by extending the `Mapper` and `Reducer` classes defined in the `HadoopPipes` namespace and providing implementations of the `map()` and `reduce()` methods in each case. These methods take a context object (of type `MapContext` or `ReduceContext`), which provides the means for reading input and writing output, as well as accessing job configuration information via the `JobConf` class. The processing in this example is very similar to the Java equivalent.

Unlike the Java interface, keys and values in the C++ interface are byte buffers, represented as Standard Template Library (STL) strings. This makes the interface simpler, although it does put a slightly greater burden on the application developer, who has to convert to and from richer domain-level types. This is evident in `MapTemperatureReducer` where we have to convert the input value into an integer (using a convenience method in `HadoopUtils`) and then the maximum value back into a string before it's written out. In some cases, we can save on doing the conversion, such as in `MaxTemperatureMapper` where the `airTemperature` value is never converted to an integer since it is never processed as a number in the `map()` method.

The main() method is the application entry point. It calls HadoopPipes::runTask, which connects to the Java parent process and marshals data to and from the Mapper or Reducer. The runTask() method is passed a Factory so that it can create instances of the Mapper or Reducer. Which one it creates is controlled by the Java parent over the socket connection. There are overloaded template factory methods for setting a combiner, partitioner, record reader, or record writer.

Compiling and Running

Now we can compile and link our program using the Makefile in Example 2-13.

Example 2-13. Makefile for C++ MapReduce program

```
CC = g++
CPPFLAGS = -m32 -I$(HADOOP_INSTALL)/c++/$(PLATFORM)/include

max_temperature: max_temperature.cpp
    $(CC) $(CPPFLAGS) $< -Wall -L$(HADOOP_INSTALL)/c++/$(PLATFORM)/lib -lhadooppipes \
    -lhadooputils -lpthread -g -O2 -o $@
```

The Makefile expects a couple of environment variables to be set. Apart from HADOOP_INSTALL (which you should already have set if you followed the installation instructions in Appendix A), you need to define PLATFORM, which specifies the operating system, architecture, and data model (e.g., 32- or 64-bit). I ran it on a 32-bit Linux system with the following:

```
% export PLATFORM=Linux-i386-32
% make
```

On successful completion, you'll find the max_temperature executable in the current directory.

To run a Pipes job, we need to run Hadoop in *pseudo-distributed* mode (where all the daemons run on the local machine), for which there are setup instructions in Appendix A. Pipes doesn't run in standalone (local) mode, since it relies on Hadoop's distributed cache mechanism, which works only when HDFS is running.

With the Hadoop daemons now running, the first step is to copy the executable to HDFS so that it can be picked up by tasktrackers when they launch map and reduce tasks:

```
% hadoop fs -put max_temperature bin/max_temperature
```

The sample data also needs to be copied from the local filesystem into HDFS:

```
% hadoop fs -put input/ncdc/sample.txt sample.txt
```

Now we can run the job. For this, we use the Hadoop `pipes` command, passing the URI of the executable in HDFS using the `-program` argument:

```
% hadoop pipes \
  -D hadoop.pipes.java.recordreader=true \
  -D hadoop.pipes.java.recordwriter=true \
  -input sample.txt \
  -output output \
  -program bin/max_temperature
```

We specify two properties using the `-D` option: `hadoop.pipes.java.recordreader` and `hadoop.pipes.java.recordwriter`, setting both to `true` to say that we have not specified a C++ record reader or writer, but that we want to use the default Java ones (which are for text input and output). Pipes also allows you to set a Java mapper, reducer, combiner, or partitioner. In fact, you can have a mixture of Java or C++ classes within any one job.

The result is the same as the other versions of the same program that we ran.

## CHAPTER 3

The Hadoop Distributed Filesystem

When a dataset outgrows the storage capacity of a single physical machine, it becomes necessary to partition it across a number of separate machines. Filesystems that manage the storage across a network of machines are called *distributed filesystems*. Since they are network-based, all the complications of network programming kick in, thus making distributed filesystems more complex than regular disk filesystems. For example, one of the biggest challenges is making the filesystem tolerate node failure without suffering data loss.

Hadoop comes with a distributed filesystem called HDFS, which stands for *Hadoop Distributed Filesystem*. (You may sometimes see references to "DFS"—informally or in older documentation or configuration—which is the same thing.) HDFS is Hadoop's flagship filesystem and is the focus of this chapter, but Hadoop actually has a general-purpose filesystem abstraction, so we'll see along the way how Hadoop integrates with other storage systems (such as the local filesystem and Amazon S3).

The Design of HDFS

HDFS is a filesystem designed for storing very large files with streaming data access patterns, running on clusters on commodity hardware. Let's examine this statement in more detail:

Very large files
> "Very large" in this context means files that are hundreds of megabytes, gigabytes, or terabytes in size. There are Hadoop clusters running today that store petabytes of data.[*]

Streaming data access
> HDFS is built around the idea that the most efficient data processing pattern is a write-once, read-many-times pattern. A dataset is typically generated or copied

---

[*] "Scaling Hadoop to 4000 nodes at Yahoo!," *http://developer.yahoo.net/blogs/hadoop/2008/09/scaling_hadoop_to_4000_nodes_a.html*.

from source, then various analyses are performed on that dataset over time. Each analysis will involve a large proportion, if not all, of the dataset, so the time to read the whole dataset is more important than the latency in reading the first record.

Commodity hardware

Hadoop doesn't require expensive, highly reliable hardware to run on. It's designed to run on clusters of commodity hardware (commonly available hardware available from multiple vendors[†]) for which the chance of node failure across the cluster is high, at least for large clusters. HDFS is designed to carry on working without a noticeable interruption to the user in the face of such failure.

It is also worth examining the applications for which using HDFS does not work so well. While this may change in the future, these are areas where HDFS is not a good fit today:

Low-latency data access

Applications that require low-latency access to data, in the tens of milliseconds range, will not work well with HDFS. Remember HDFS is optimized for delivering a high throughput of data, and this may be at the expense of latency. HBase (Chapter 12) is currently a better choice for low-latency access.

Lots of small files

Since the namenode holds filesystem metadata in memory, the limit to the number of files in a filesystem is governed by the amount of memory on the namenode. As a rule of thumb, each file, directory, and block takes about 150 bytes. So, for example, if you had one million files, each taking one block, you would need at least 300 MB of memory. While storing millions of files is feasible, billions is beyond the capability of current hardware.

Multiple writers, arbitrary file modifications

Files in HDFS may be written to by a single writer. Writes are always made at the end of the file. There is no support for multiple writers, or for modifications at arbitrary offsets in the file. (These might be supported in the future, but they are likely to be relatively inefficient.)

HDFS Concepts

Blocks

A disk has a block size, which is the minimum amount of data that it can read or write. Filesystems for a single disk build on this by dealing with data in blocks, which are an integral multiple of the disk block size. Filesystem blocks are typically a few kilobytes in size, while disk blocks are normally 512 bytes. This is generally transparent to the

---

[†] See Chapter 9 for a typical machine specification.

filesystem user who is simply reading or writing a file—of whatever length. However, there are tools to do with filesystem maintenance, such as *df* and *fsck*, that operate on the filesystem block level.

HDFS too has the concept of a block, but it is a much larger unit—64 MB by default. Like in a filesystem for a single disk, files in HDFS are broken into block-sized chunks, which are stored as independent units. Unlike a filesystem for a single disk, a file in HDFS that is smaller than a single block does not occupy a full block's worth of underlying storage. When unqualified, the term "block" in this book refers to a block in HDFS.

Why Is a Block in HDFS So Large?

HDFS blocks are large compared to disk blocks, and the reason is to minimize the cost of seeks. By making a block large enough, the time to transfer the data from the disk can be made to be significantly larger than the time to seek to the start of the block. Thus the time to transfer a large file made of multiple blocks operates at the disk transfer rate.

A quick calculation shows that if the seek time is around 10ms, and the transfer rate is 100 MB/s, then to make the seek time 1% of the transfer time, we need to make the block size around 100 MB. The default is actually 64 MB, although many HDFS installations use 128 MB blocks. This figure will continue to be revised upward as transfer speeds grow with new generations of disk drives.

This argument shouldn't be taken too far, however. Map tasks in MapReduce normally operate on one block at a time, so if you have too few tasks (fewer than nodes in the cluster), your jobs will run slower than they could otherwise.

Having a block abstraction for a distributed filesystem brings several benefits. The first benefit is the most obvious: a file can be larger than any single disk in the network. There's nothing that requires the blocks from a file to be stored on the same disk, so they can take advantage of any of the disks in the cluster. In fact, it would be possible, if unusual, to store a single file on an HDFS cluster whose blocks filled all the disks in the cluster.

Second, making the unit of abstraction a block rather than a file simplifies the storage subsystem. Simplicity is something to strive for all in all systems, but is important for a distributed system in which the failure modes are so varied. The storage subsystem deals with blocks, simplifying storage management (since blocks are a fixed size, it is easy to calculate how many can be stored on a given disk), and eliminating metadata concerns (blocks are just a chunk of data to be stored—file metadata such as permissions information does not need to be stored with the blocks, so another system can handle metadata orthogonally).

Furthermore, blocks fit well with replication for providing fault tolerance and availability. To insure against corrupted blocks and disk and machine failure, each block is replicated to a small number of physically separate machines (typically three). If a block becomes unavailable, a copy can be read from another location in a way that is transparent to the client. A block that is no longer available due to corruption or machine failure can be replicated from their alternative locations to other live machines to bring the replication factor back to the normal level. (See "Data Integrity" on page 75 for more on guarding against corrupt data.) Similarly, some applications may choose to set a high replication factor for the blocks in a popular file to spread the read load on the cluster.

Like its disk filesystem cousin, HDFS's `fsck` command understands blocks. For example, running:

```
% hadoop fsck -files -blocks
```

will list the blocks that make up each file in the filesystem. (See also "Filesystem check (fsck)" on page 281.)

Namenodes and Datanodes

A HDFS cluster has two types of node operating in a master-worker pattern: a *namenode* (the master) and a number of *datanodes* (workers). The namenode manages the filesystem namespace. It maintains the filesystem tree and the metadata for all the files and directories in the tree. This information is stored persistently on the local disk in the form of two files: the namespace image and the edit log. The namenode also knows the datanodes on which all the blocks for a given file are located, however, it does not store block locations persistently, since this information is reconstructed from datanodes when the system starts.

A *client* accesses the filesystem on behalf of the user by communicating with the namenode and datanodes. The client presents a POSIX-like filesystem interface, so the user code does not need to know about the namenode and datanode to function.

Datanodes are the work horses of the filesystem. They store and retrieve blocks when they are told to (by clients or the namenode), and they report back to the namenode periodically with lists of blocks that they are storing.

Without the namenode, the filesystem cannot be used. In fact, if the machine running the namenode were obliterated, all the files on the filesystem would be lost since there would be no way of knowing how to reconstruct the files from the blocks on the datanodes. For this reason, it is important to make the namenode resilient to failure, and Hadoop provides two mechanisms for this.

The first way is to back up the files that make up the persistent state of the filesystem metadata. Hadoop can be configured so that the namenode writes its persistent state to multiple filesystems. These writes are synchronous and atomic. The usual configuration choice is to write to local disk as well as a remote NFS mount.

It is also possible to run a *secondary namenode*, which despite its name does not act as a namenode. Its main role is to periodically merge the namespace image with the edit log to prevent the edit log from becoming too large. The secondary namenode usually runs on a separate physical machine, since it requires plenty of CPU and as much memory as the namenode to perform the merge. It keeps a copy of the merged namespace image, which can be used in the event of the namenode failing. However, the state of the secondary namenode lags that of the primary, so in the event of total failure of the primary data, loss is almost guaranteed. The usual course of action in this case is to copy the namenode's metadata files that are on NFS to the secondary and run it as the new primary.

See "The filesystem image and edit log" on page 274 for more details.

The Command-Line Interface

We're going to have a look at HDFS by interacting with it from the command line. There are many other interfaces to HDFS, but the command line is one of the simplest, and to many developers the most familiar.

We are going to run HDFS on one machine, so first follow the instructions for setting up Hadoop in pseudo-distributed mode in Appendix A. Later you'll see how to run on a cluster of machines to give us scalability and fault tolerance.

There are two properties that we set in the pseudo-distributed configuration that deserve further explanation. The first is `fs.default.name`, set to *hdfs://localhost/*, which is used to set a default filesystem for Hadoop. Filesystems are specified by a URI, and here we have used a `hdfs` URI to configure Hadoop to use HDFS by default. The HDFS daemons will use this property to determine the host and port for the HDFS namenode. We'll be running it on `localhost`, on the default HDFS port, 8020. And HDFS clients will use this property to work out where the namenode is running so they can connect to it.

We set the second property, `dfs.replication`, to one so that HDFS doesn't replicate filesystem blocks by the usual default of three. When running with a single datanode, HDFS can't replicate blocks to three datanodes, so it would perpetually warn about blocks being under-replicated. This setting solves that problem.

Basic Filesystem Operations

The filesystem is ready to be used, and we can do all of the usual filesystem operations such as reading files, creating directories, moving files, deleting data, and listing directories. You can type `hadoop fs -help` to get detailed help on every command.

Start by copying a file from the local filesystem to HDFS:

```
% hadoop fs -copyFromLocal input/docs/quangle.txt hdfs://localhost/user/tom/quangle.txt
```

This command invokes Hadoop's filesystem shell command `fs`, which supports a number of subcommands—in this case, we are running `-copyFromLocal`. The local file *quangle.txt* is copied to the file */user/tom/quangle.txt* on the HDFS instance running on localhost. In fact, we could have omitted the scheme and host of the URI and picked up the default, `hdfs://localhost`, as specified in *core-site.xml*.

```
% hadoop fs -copyFromLocal input/docs/quangle.txt /user/tom/quangle.txt
```

We could also have used a relative path, and copied the file to our home directory in HDFS, which in this case is */user/tom*:

```
% hadoop fs -copyFromLocal input/docs/quangle.txt quangle.txt
```

Let's copy the file back to the local filesystem and check whether it's the same:

```
% hadoop fs -copyToLocal quangle.txt quangle.copy.txt
% md5 input/docs/quangle.txt quangle.copy.txt
MD5 (input/docs/quangle.txt) = a16f231da6b05e2ba7a339320e7dacd9
MD5 (quangle.copy.txt) = a16f231da6b05e2ba7a339320e7dacd9
```

The MD5 digests are the same, showing that the file survived its trip to HDFS and is back intact.

Finally, let's look at an HDFS file listing. We create a directory first just to see how it is displayed in the listing:

```
% hadoop fs -mkdir books
% hadoop fs -ls .
Found 2 items
drwxr-xr-x   - tom supergroup          0 2009-04-02 22:41 /user/tom/books
-rw-r--r--   1 tom supergroup        118 2009-04-02 22:29 /user/tom/quangle.txt
```

The information returned is very similar to the Unix command `ls -l`, with a few minor differences. The first column shows the file mode. The second column is the replication factor of the file (something a traditional Unix filesystems does not have). Remember we set the default replication factor in the site-wide configuration to be 1, which is why we see the same value here. The entry in this column is empty for directories since the concept of replication does not apply to them—directories are treated as metadata and stored by the namenode, not the datanodes. The third and fourth columns show the file owner and group. The fifth column is the size of the file in bytes, or zero for directories. The six and seventh columns are the last modified date and time. Finally, the eighth column is the absolute name of the file or directory.

File Permissions in HDFS

HDFS has a permissions model for files and directories that is much like POSIX.

There are three types of permission: the read permission (r), the write permission (w) and the execute permission (x). The read permission is required to read files or list the contents of a directory. The write permission is required to write a file, or for a directory, to create or delete files or directories in it. The execute permission is ignored for a file since you can't execute a file on HDFS (unlike POSIX), and for a directory it is required to access its children.

Each file and directory has an *owner*, a *group*, and a *mode*. The mode is made up of the permissions for the user who is the owner, the permissions for the users who are members of the group, and the permissions for users who are neither the owner nor members of the group.

A client's identity is determined by the username and groups of the process it is running in. Because clients are remote, this makes it possible to become an arbitrary user, simply by creating an account of that name on the remote system. Thus, permissions should be used only in a cooperative community of users, as a mechanism for sharing filesystem resources and for avoiding accidental data loss, and not for securing resources in a hostile environment. However, despite these drawbacks, it is worthwhile having permissions enabled (as it is by default; see the `dfs.permissions` property), to avoid accidental modification or deletion of substantial parts of the filesystem, either by users or by automated tools or programs.

When permissions checking is enabled, the owner permissions are checked if the client's username matches the owner, and the group permissions are checked if the client is a member of the group; otherwise, the other permissions are checked.

There is a concept of a super-user, which is the identity of the namenode process. Permissions checks are not performed for the super-user.

Hadoop Filesystems

Hadoop has an abstract notion of filesystem, of which HDFS is just one implementation. The Java abstract class `org.apache.hadoop.fs.FileSystem` represents a filesystem in Hadoop, and there are several concrete implementations, which are described in Table 3-1.

Table 3-1. Hadoop filesystems

Filesystem	URI scheme	Java implementation (all under org.apache.hadoop)	Description
Local	*file*	`fs.LocalFileSystem`	A filesystem for a locally connected disk with client-side checksums. Use `RawLocalFileSystem` for a local filesystem with no checksums. See "LocalFileSystem" on page 76.
HDFS	*hdfs*	`hdfs.DistributedFileSystem`	Hadoop's distributed filesystem. HDFS is designed to work efficiently in conjunction with Map-Reduce.
HFTP	*hftp*	`hdfs.HftpFileSystem`	A filesystem providing read-only access to HDFS over HTTP. (Despite its name, HFTP has no connection with FTP.) Often used with *distcp* ("Parallel Copying with distcp" on page 70) to copy data between HDFS clusters running different versions.
HSFTP	*hsftp*	`hdfs.HsftpFileSystem`	A filesystem providing read-only access to HDFS over HTTPS. (Again, this has no connection with FTP.)
HAR	*har*	`fs.HarFileSystem`	A filesystem layered on another filesystem for archiving files. Hadoop Archives are typically used for archiving files in HDFS to reduce the namenode's memory usage. See "Hadoop Archives" on page 71.
KFS (Cloud-Store)	*kfs*	`fs.kfs.KosmosFileSystem`	CloudStore (formerly Kosmos filesystem) is a distributed filesystem like HDFS or Google's GFS, written in C++. Find more information about it at *http://kosmosfs .sourceforge.net/*.
FTP	*ftp*	`fs.ftp.FTPFileSystem`	A filesystem backed by an FTP server.
S3 (native)	*s3n*	`fs.s3native.NativeS3FileSystem`	A filesystem backed by Amazon S3. See *http://wiki.apache.org/ha doop/AmazonS3*.
S3 (block-based)	*s3*	`fs.s3.S3FileSystem`	A filesystem backed by Amazon S3, which stores files in blocks (much like HDFS) to overcome S3's 5 GB file size limit.

Hadoop provides many interfaces to its filesystems, and it generally uses the URI scheme to pick the correct filesystem instance to communicate with. For example, the filesystem shell that we met in the previous section operates with all Hadoop filesystems. To list the files in the root directory of the local filesystem, type:

```
% hadoop fs -ls file:///
```

Although it is possible (and sometimes very convenient) to run MapReduce programs that access any of these filesystems, when you are processing large volumes of data, you should choose a distributed filesystem that has the data locality optimization, such as HDFS or KFS (see "Scaling Out" on page 27).

Interfaces

Hadoop is written in Java, and all Hadoop filesystem interactions are mediated through the Java API.[‡] The filesystem shell, for example, is a Java application that uses the Java `FileSystem` class to provide filesystem operations. The other filesystem interfaces are discussed briefly in this section. These interfaces are most commonly used with HDFS, since the other filesystems in Hadoop typically have existing tools to access the underlying filesystem (FTP clients for FTP, S3 tools for S3, etc.), but many of them will work with any Hadoop filesystem.

Thrift

By exposing its filesystem interface as a Java API, Hadoop makes it awkward for non-Java applications to access Hadoop filesystems. The Thrift API in the "thriftfs" contrib module remedies this deficiency by exposing Hadoop filesystems as an Apache Thrift service, making it easy for any language that has Thrift bindings to interact with a Hadoop filesystem, such as HDFS.

To use the Thrift API, run a Java server that exposes the Thrift service, and acts as a proxy to the Hadoop filesystem. Your application accesses the Thrift service, which is typically running on the same machine as your application.

The Thrift API comes with a number of pregenerated stubs for a variety of languages, including C++, Perl, PHP, Python, and Ruby. Thrift has support for versioning, so it's a good choice if you want to access different versions of a Hadoop filesystem from the same client code (you will need to run a proxy for each version of Hadoop to achieve this, however).

For installation and usage instructions, please refer to the documentation in the *src/contrib/thriftfs* directory of the Hadoop distribution.

[‡] The RPC interfaces in Hadoop are based on Hadoop's `Writable` interface, which is Java-centric. In the future, Hadoop will adopt another, cross-language, RPC serialization format, which will allow native HDFS clients to be written in languages other than Java.

C

Hadoop provides a C library called *libhdfs* that mirrors the Java `FileSystem` interface (it was written as a C library for accessing HDFS, but despite its name it can be used to access any Hadoop filesystem). It works using the *Java Native Interface* (JNI) to call a Java filesystem client.

The C API is very similar to the Java one, but it typically lags the Java one, so newer features may not be supported. You can find the generated documentation for the C API in the *libhdfs/docs/api* directory of the Hadoop distribution.

Hadoop comes with prebuilt *libhdfs* binaries for 32-bit Linux, but for other platforms, you will need to build them yourself using the instructions at *http://wiki.apache.org/hadoop/LibHDFS*.

FUSE

Filesystem in Userspace (FUSE) allows filesystems that are implemented in user space to be integrated as a Unix filesystem. Hadoop's Fuse-DFS contrib module allows any Hadoop filesystem (but typically HDFS) to be mounted as a standard filesystem. You can then use Unix utilities (such as `ls` and `cat`) to interact with the filesystem, as well as POSIX libraries to access the filesystem from any programming language.

Fuse-DFS is implemented in C using *libhdfs* as the interface to HDFS. Documentation for compiling and running Fuse-DFS is located in the *src/contrib/fuse-dfs* directory of the Hadoop distribution.

WebDAV

WebDAV is a set of extensions to HTTP to support editing and updating files. WebDAV shares can be mounted as filesystems on most operating systems, so by exposing HDFS (or other Hadoop filesystems) over WebDAV, it's possible to access HDFS as a standard filesystem.

At the time of this writing, WebDAV support in Hadoop (which is implemented by calling the Java API to Hadoop) is still under development, and can be tracked at *https://issues.apache.org/jira/browse/HADOOP-496*.

Other HDFS Interfaces

There are two interfaces that are specific to HDFS:

HTTP
> HDFS defines a read-only interface for retrieving directory listings and data over HTTP. Directory listings are served by the namenode's embedded web server (which runs on port 50070) in XML format, while file data is streamed from datanodes by their web servers (running on port 50075). This protocol is not tied to a specific HDFS version, making it possible to write clients that can use HTTP

to read data from HDFS clusters that run different versions of Hadoop. `HftpFileSystem` is a such a client: it is a Hadoop filesystem that talks to HDFS over HTTP (`HsftpFileSystem` is the HTTPS variant).

FTP

Although not complete at the time of this writing (*https://issues.apache.org/jira/browse/HADOOP-3199*), there is an FTP interface to HDFS, which permits the use of the FTP protocol to interact with HDFS. This interface is a convenient way to transfer data into and out of HDFS using existing FTP clients.

The FTP interface to HDFS is not to be confused with `FTPFileSystem`, which exposes any FTP server as a Hadoop filesystem.

The Java Interface

In this section, we dig into the Hadoop's `FileSystem` class: the API for interacting with one of Hadoop's filesystems.§ While we focus mainly on the HDFS implementation, `DistributedFileSystem`, in general you should strive to write your code against the `FileSystem` abstract class, to retain portability across filesystems. This is very useful when testing your program, for example, since you can rapidly run tests using data stored on the local filesystem.

Reading Data from a Hadoop URL

One of the simplest ways to read a file from a Hadoop filesystem is by using a `java.net.URL` object to open a stream to read the data from. The general idiom is:

```
InputStream in = null;
try {
  in = new URL("hdfs://host/path").openStream();
  // process in
} finally {
  IOUtils.closeStream(in);
}
```

There's a little bit more work required to make Java recognize Hadoop's `hdfs` URL scheme. This is achieved by calling the `setURLStreamHandlerFactory` method on `URL` with an instance of `FsUrlStreamHandlerFactory`. This method can only be called once per JVM, so it is typically executed in a static block. This limitation means that if some other part of your program—perhaps a third-party component outside your control—sets a `URLStreamHandlerFactory`, you won't be able to use this approach for reading data from Hadoop. The next section discusses an alternative.

---

§ There is a Java Specification Request (JSR 203, "NIO.2," *http://jcp.org/en/jsr/detail?id=203*) for an improved filesystem interface in Java, with the explicit goal of providing pluggable filesystem implementations. In the long term, it is possible that this new interface (which is slated to appear in Java 7) will replace Hadoop's `FileSystem` abstraction.

Example 3-1 shows a program for displaying files from Hadoop filesystems on standard output, like the Unix `cat` command.

Example 3-1. Displaying files from a Hadoop filesystem on standard output using a URLStreamHandler

```
public class URLCat {

  static {
    URL.setURLStreamHandlerFactory(new FsUrlStreamHandlerFactory());
  }

  public static void main(String[] args) throws Exception {
    InputStream in = null;
    try {
      in = new URL(args[0]).openStream();
      IOUtils.copyBytes(in, System.out, 4096, false);
    } finally {
      IOUtils.closeStream(in);
    }
  }
}
```

We make use of the handy `IOUtils` class that comes with Hadoop for closing the stream in the `finally` clause, and also for copying bytes between the input stream and the output stream (`System.out` in this case). The last two arguments to the `copyBytes` method are the buffer size used for copying, and whether to close the streams when the copy is complete. We close the input stream ourselves, and `System.out` doesn't need to be closed.

Here's a sample run:‖

```
% hadoop URLCat hdfs://localhost/user/tom/quangle.txt
On the top of the Crumpetty Tree
The Quangle Wangle sat,
But his face you could not see,
On account of his Beaver Hat.
```

Reading Data Using the FileSystem API

As the previous section explained, sometimes it is impossible to set a `URLStreamHandlerFactory` for your application. In this case, you will need to use the `FileSystem` API to open an input stream for a file.

A file in a Hadoop filesystem is represented by a Hadoop `Path` object (and not a `java.io.File` object, since its semantics are too closely tied to the local filesystem). You can think of a `Path` as a Hadoop filesystem URI, such as *hdfs://localhost/user/tom/quangle.txt*.

‖ The text is from *The Quangle Wangle's Hat* by Edward Lear.

`FileSystem` is a general filesystem API, so the first step is to retrieve an instance for the filesystem we want to use—HDFS in this case. There are two static factory methods for getting a `FileSystem` instance:

```
public static FileSystem get(Configuration conf) throws IOException
public static FileSystem get(URI uri, Configuration conf) throws IOException
```

A `Configuration` object encapsulates a client or server's configuration, which is set using configuration files read from the classpath, such as *conf/core-site.xml*. The first method returns the default filesystem (as specified in the file *conf/core-site.xml*, or the default local filesystem if not specified there). The second uses the given `URI`'s scheme and authority to determine the filesystem to use, falling back to the default filesystem if no scheme is specified in the given `URI`.

With a `FileSystem` instance in hand, we invoke an **open()** method to get the input stream for a file:

```
public FSDataInputStream open(Path f) throws IOException
public abstract FSDataInputStream open(Path f, int bufferSize) throws IOException
```

The first method uses a default buffer size of 4 K.

Putting this together, we can rewrite Example 3-1 as shown in Example 3-2.

Example 3-2. Displaying files from a Hadoop filesystem on standard output by using the FileSystem directly

```
public class FileSystemCat {

  public static void main(String[] args) throws Exception {
    String uri = args[0];
    Configuration conf = new Configuration();
    FileSystem fs = FileSystem.get(URI.create(uri), conf);
    InputStream in = null;
    try {
      in = fs.open(new Path(uri));
      IOUtils.copyBytes(in, System.out, 4096, false);
    } finally {
      IOUtils.closeStream(in);
    }
  }
}
```

The program runs as follows:

```
% hadoop FileSystemCat hdfs://localhost/user/tom/quangle.txt
On the top of the Crumpetty Tree
The Quangle Wangle sat,
But his face you could not see,
On account of his Beaver Hat.
```

FSDataInputStream

The open() method on FileSystem actually returns a FSDataInputStream rather than a standard java.io class. This class is a specialization of java.io.DataInputStream with support for random access, so you can read from any part of the stream.

```
package org.apache.hadoop.fs;

public class FSDataInputStream extends DataInputStream
    implements Seekable, PositionedReadable {
  // implementation elided
}
```

The Seekable interface permits seeking to a position in the file, and a query method for the current offset from the start of the file (getPos()):

```
public interface Seekable {
  void seek(long pos) throws IOException;
  long getPos() throws IOException;
  boolean seekToNewSource(long targetPos) throws IOException;
}
```

Calling seek() with a position that is greater than the length of the file will result in an IOException. Unlike the skip() method of java.io.InputStream which positions the stream at a point later than the current position, seek() can move to an arbitrary, absolute position in the file.

The seekToNewSource() method is not normally used by application writers. It attempts to find another copy of the data and seek to the offset targetPos in the new copy. This is used internally in HDFS to provide a reliable input stream of data to the client in the face of datanode failure.

Example 3-3 is a simple extension of Example 3-2 that writes a file to standard out twice: after writing it once, it seeks to the start of the file and streams through it once again.

Example 3-3. Displaying files from a Hadoop filesystem on standard output twice, by using seek

```
public class FileSystemDoubleCat {

  public static void main(String[] args) throws Exception {
    String uri = args[0];
    Configuration conf = new Configuration();
    FileSystem fs = FileSystem.get(URI.create(uri), conf);
    FSDataInputStream in = null;
    try {
      in = fs.open(new Path(uri));
      IOUtils.copyBytes(in, System.out, 4096, false);
      in.seek(0); // go back to the start of the file
      IOUtils.copyBytes(in, System.out, 4096, false);
    } finally {
      IOUtils.closeStream(in);
    }
}
```

```
    }
}
```

Here's the result of running it on a small file:

```
% hadoop FileSystemDoubleCat hdfs://localhost/user/tom/quangle.txt
On the top of the Crumpetty Tree
The Quangle Wangle sat,
But his face you could not see,
On account of his Beaver Hat.
On the top of the Crumpetty Tree
The Quangle Wangle sat,
But his face you could not see,
On account of his Beaver Hat.
```

FSDataInputStream also implements the PositionedReadable interface for reading parts of a file at a given offset:

```
public interface PositionedReadable {

  public int read(long position, byte[] buffer, int offset, int length)
    throws IOException;

  public void readFully(long position, byte[] buffer, int offset, int length)
    throws IOException;

  public void readFully(long position, byte[] buffer) throws IOException;
}
```

The read() method reads up to length bytes from the given position in the file into the buffer at the given offset in the buffer. The return value is the number of bytes actually read: callers should check this value as it may be less than length. The readFully() methods will read length bytes into the buffer (or buffer.length bytes for the version that just takes a byte array buffer), unless the end of the file is reached, in which case an EOFException is thrown.

All of these methods preserve the current offset in the file and are thread-safe, so they provide a convenient way to access another part of the file—metadata perhaps—while reading the main body of the file. In fact, they are just implemented using the Seekable interface using the following pattern:

```
long oldPos = getPos();
try {
  seek(position);
  // read data
} finally {
  seek(oldPos);
}
```

Finally, bear in mind that calling seek() is a relatively expensive operation, and should be used sparingly. You should structure your application access patterns to rely on streaming data, (by using MapReduce, for example) rather than performing a large number of seeks.

Writing Data

The `FileSystem` class has a number of methods for creating a file. The simplest is the method that takes a `Path` object for the file to be created and returns an output stream to write to:

```
public FSDataOutputStream create(Path f) throws IOException
```

There are overloaded versions of this method that allow you to specify whether to forcibly overwrite existing files, the replication factor of the file, the buffer size to use when writing the file, the block size for the file, and file permissions.

 The `create()` methods create any parent directories of the file to be written that don't already exist. Though convenient, this behavior may be unexpected. If you want the write to fail if the parent directory doesn't exist, then you should check for the existence of the parent directory first by calling the `exists()` method.

There's also an overloaded method for passing a callback interface, `Progressable`, so your application can be notified of the progress of the data being written to the datanodes:

```
package org.apache.hadoop.util;

public interface Progressable {
  public void progress();
}
```

As an alternative to creating a new file, you can append to an existing file using the `append()` method (there are also some other overloaded versions):

```
public FSDataOutputStream append(Path f) throws IOException
```

The append operation allows a single writer to modify an already written file by opening it and writing data from the final offset in the file. With this API, applications that produce unbounded files, such as logfiles, can write to an existing file after a restart, for example. The append operation is optional and not implemented by all Hadoop filesystems. For example, HDFS supports append, but S3 filesystems don't.

Example 3-4 shows how to copy a local file to a Hadoop filesystem. We illustrate progress by printing a period every time the `progress()` method is called by Hadoop, which is after each 64 K packet of data is written to the datanode pipeline. (Note that this particular behavior is not specified by the API, so it is subject to change in later versions of Hadoop. The API merely allows you to infer that "something is happening.")

Example 3-4. Copying a local file to a Hadoop filesystem, and shows progress

```
public class FileCopyWithProgress {
  public static void main(String[] args) throws Exception {
    String localSrc = args[0];
    String dst = args[1];
```

```
  InputStream in = new BufferedInputStream(new FileInputStream(localSrc));

  Configuration conf = new Configuration();
  FileSystem fs = FileSystem.get(URI.create(dst), conf);
  OutputStream out = fs.create(new Path(dst), new Progressable() {
    public void progress() {
      System.out.print(".");
    }
  });

  IOUtils.copyBytes(in, out, 4096, true);
  }
}
```

Typical usage:

```
% hadoop FileCopyWithProgress input/docs/1400-8.txt hdfs://localhost/user/tom/1400-8.txt
...............
```

Currently, none of the other Hadoop filesystems call **progress()** during writes. Progress is important in MapReduce applications, as you will see in later chapters.

FSDataOutputStream

The `create()` method on `FileSystem` returns a `FSDataOutputStream`, which, like `FSDataInputStream`, has a method for querying the current position in the file:

```
package org.apache.hadoop.fs;

public class FSDataOutputStream extends DataOutputStream implements Syncable {

  public long getPos() throws IOException {
    // implementation elided
  }

  // implementation elided

}
```

However, unlike `FSDataInputStream`, `FSDataOutputStream` does not permit seeking. This is because HDFS allows only sequential writes to an open file, or appends to an already written file. In other words, there is no support for writing to anywhere other than the end of the file, so there is no value in being able to seek while writing.

Directories

`FileSystem` provides a method to create a directory:

```
public boolean mkdirs(Path f) throws IOException
```

This method creates all of the necessary parent directories if they don't already exist, just like `java.io.File`'s `mkdirs()` method. It returns `true` if the directory (and all parent directories) was successfully created.

Often, you don't need to explicitly create a directory, since writing a file, by calling create(), will automatically create any parent directories.

Querying the Filesystem

File metadata: FileStatus

An important feature of any filesystem is the ability to navigate its directory structure and retrieve information about the files and directories that it stores. The FileStatus class encapsulates filesystem metadata for files and directories, including file length, block size, replication, modification time, ownership, and permission information.

The method getFileStatus() on FileSystem provides a way of getting a FileStatus object for a single file or directory. Example 3-5 shows an example of its use.

Example 3-5. Demonstrating file status information

```
public class ShowFileStatusTest {

  private MiniDFSCluster cluster; // use an in-process HDFS cluster for testing
  private FileSystem fs;

  @Before
  public void setUp() throws IOException {
    Configuration conf = new Configuration();
    if (System.getProperty("test.build.data") == null) {
      System.setProperty("test.build.data", "/tmp");
    }
    cluster = new MiniDFSCluster(conf, 1, true, null);
    fs = cluster.getFileSystem();
    OutputStream out = fs.create(new Path("/dir/file"));
    out.write("content".getBytes("UTF-8"));
    out.close();
  }

  @After
  public void tearDown() throws IOException {
    if (fs != null) { fs.close(); }
    if (cluster != null) { cluster.shutdown(); }
  }

  @Test(expected = FileNotFoundException.class)
  public void throwsFileNotFoundForNonExistentFile() throws IOException {
    fs.getFileStatus(new Path("no-such-file"));
  }

  @Test
  public void fileStatusForFile() throws IOException {
    Path file = new Path("/dir/file");
    FileStatus stat = fs.getFileStatus(file);
    assertThat(stat.getPath().toUri().getPath(), is("/dir/file"));
    assertThat(stat.isDir(), is(false));
    assertThat(stat.getLen(), is(7L));
```

```
  assertThat(stat.getModificationTime(),
      is(lessThanOrEqualTo(System.currentTimeMillis())));
  assertThat(stat.getReplication(), is((short) 1));
  assertThat(stat.getBlockSize(), is(64 * 1024 * 1024L));
  assertThat(stat.getOwner(), is("tom"));
  assertThat(stat.getGroup(), is("supergroup"));
  assertThat(stat.getPermission().toString(), is("rw-r--r--"));
}

@Test
public void fileStatusForDirectory() throws IOException {
  Path dir = new Path("/dir");
  FileStatus stat = fs.getFileStatus(dir);
  assertThat(stat.getPath().toUri().getPath(), is("/dir"));
  assertThat(stat.isDir(), is(true));
  assertThat(stat.getLen(), is(0L));
  assertThat(stat.getModificationTime(),
      is(lessThanOrEqualTo(System.currentTimeMillis())));
  assertThat(stat.getReplication(), is((short) 0));
  assertThat(stat.getBlockSize(), is(0L));
  assertThat(stat.getOwner(), is("tom"));
  assertThat(stat.getGroup(), is("supergroup"));
  assertThat(stat.getPermission().toString(), is("rwxr-xr-x"));
}

}
```

If no file or directory exists, a `FileNotFoundException` is thrown. However, if you are interested only in the existence of a file or directory, then the `exists()` method on FileSystem is more convenient:

```
public boolean exists(Path f) throws IOException
```

Listing files

Finding information on a single file or directory is useful, but you also often need to be able to list the contents of a directory. That's what FileSystem's `listStatus()` methods are for:

```
public FileStatus[] listStatus(Path f) throws IOException
public FileStatus[] listStatus(Path f, PathFilter filter) throws IOException
public FileStatus[] listStatus(Path[] files) throws IOException
public FileStatus[] listStatus(Path[] files, PathFilter filter) throws IOException
```

When the argument is a file, the simplest variant returns an array of FileStatus objects of length 1. When the argument is a directory it returns zero or more FileStatus objects representing the files and directories contained in the directory.

Overloaded variants allow a `PathFilter` to be supplied to restrict the files and directories to match—you will see an example in section "PathFilter" on page 61. Finally, if you specify an array of paths the result is a shortcut for calling the equivalent single-path `listStatus` method for each path in turn and accumulating the FileStatus object arrays in a single array. This can be useful for building up lists of input files to process from distinct parts of the filesystem tree. Example 3-6 is a simple demonstration of this idea. Note the use of `stat2Paths()` in `FileUtil` for turning an array of `FileStatus` objects to an array of `Path` objects.

Example 3-6. Showing the file statuses for a collection of paths in a Hadoop filesystem

```
public class ListStatus {

  public static void main(String[] args) throws Exception {
    String uri = args[0];
    Configuration conf = new Configuration();
    FileSystem fs = FileSystem.get(URI.create(uri), conf);

    Path[] paths = new Path[args.length];
    for (int i = 0; i < paths.length; i++) {
      paths[i] = new Path(args[i]);
    }

    FileStatus[] status = fs.listStatus(paths);
    Path[] listedPaths = FileUtil.stat2Paths(status);
    for (Path p : listedPaths) {
      System.out.println(p);
    }
  }
}
```

We can use this program to find the union of directory listings for a collection of paths:

```
% hadoop ListStatus hdfs://localhost/ hdfs://localhost/user/tom
hdfs://localhost/user
hdfs://localhost/user/tom/books
hdfs://localhost/user/tom/quangle.txt
```

File patterns

It is a common requirement to process sets of files in a single operation. For example, a MapReduce job for log processing might analyze a month worth of files, contained in a number of directories. Rather than having to enumerate each file and directory to specify the input, it is convenient to use wildcard characters to match multiple files with a single expression, an operation that is known as *globbing*. Hadoop provides two `FileSystem` methods for processing globs:

```
public FileStatus[] globStatus(Path pathPattern) throws IOException
public FileStatus[] globStatus(Path pathPattern, PathFilter filter) throws IOException
```

The `globStatus()` methods returns an array of `FileStatus` objects whose paths match the supplied pattern, sorted by path. An optional `PathFilter` can be specified to restrict the matches further.

Hadoop supports the same set of glob characters as Unix *bash* (see Table 3-2).

Table 3-2. Glob characters and their meanings

Glob	Name	Matches
*	asterisk	Matches zero or more characters
?	question mark	Matches a single character
[ab]	character class	Matches a single character in the set {a, b}
[^ab]	negated character class	Matches a single character that is not in the set {a, b}
[a-b]	character range	Matches a single character in the (closed) range [a, b], where a is lexicographically less than or equal to b
[^a-b]	negated character range	Matches a single character that is not in the (closed) range [a, b], where a is lexicographically less than or equal to b
{a,b}	alternation	Matches either expression a or b
\c	escaped character	Matches character c when it is a metacharacter

Imagine that logfiles are stored in a directory structure organized hierarchically by date. So, for example, logfiles for the last day of 2007 would go in a directory named */2007/12/31*. Suppose that the full file listing is:

- */2007/12/30*
- */2007/12/31*
- */2008/01/01*
- */2008/01/02*

Here are some file globs and their expansions:

Glob	Expansion
/*	/2007 /2008
/*/*	/2007/12 /2008/01
/*/12/*	/2007/12/30 /2007/12/31
/200?	/2007 /2008
/200[78]	/2007 /2008
/200[7-8]	/2007 /2008
/200[^01234569]	/2007 /2008
/*/*/{31,01}	/2007/12/31 /2008/01/01
/*/*/3{0,1}	/2007/12/30 /2007/12/31
/*/{12/31,01/01}	/2007/12/31 /2008/01/01

PathFilter

Glob patterns are not always powerful enough to describe a set of files you want to access. For example, it is not generally possible to exclude a particular file using a glob pattern. The listStatus() and globStatus() methods of FileSystem take an optional PathFilter, which allows programmatic control over matching:

```
package org.apache.hadoop.fs;

public interface PathFilter {
  boolean accept(Path path);
}
```

PathFilter is the equivalent of java.io.FileFilter for Path objects rather than File objects.

Example 3-7 shows a PathFilter for excluding paths that match a regular expression.

Example 3-7. A PathFilter for excluding paths that match a regular expression

```
public class RegexExcludePathFilter implements PathFilter {

  private final String regex;

  public RegexExcludePathFilter(String regex) {
    this.regex = regex;
  }

  public boolean accept(Path path) {
    return !path.toString().matches(regex);
  }
}
```

The filter passes only files that *don't* match the regular expression. We use the filter in conjunction with a glob that picks out an initial set of files to include: the filter is used to refine the results. For example:

```
fs.globStatus(new Path("/2007/*/*"), new RegexExcludeFilter("^.*/2007/12/31$"))
```

will expand to */2007/12/30*.

Filters can only act on a file's name, as represented by a Path. They can't use a file's properties, such as creation time, as the basis of the filter. Nevertheless, they can perform matching that neither glob patterns nor regular expressions can achieve. For example, if you store files in a directory structure that is laid out by date (like in the previous section), then you can write a PathFilter to pick out files that fall in a given date range.

Deleting Data

Use the delete() method on FileSystem to permanently remove files or directories:

```
public boolean delete(Path f, boolean recursive) throws IOException
```

If f is a file or an empty directory, then the value of recursive is ignored. A nonempty directory is only deleted, along with its contents, if recursive is true (otherwise an IOException is thrown).

Data Flow

Anatomy of a File Read

To get an idea of how data flows between the client interacting with HDFS, the namenode and the datanode, consider Figure 3-1, which shows the main sequence of events when reading a file.

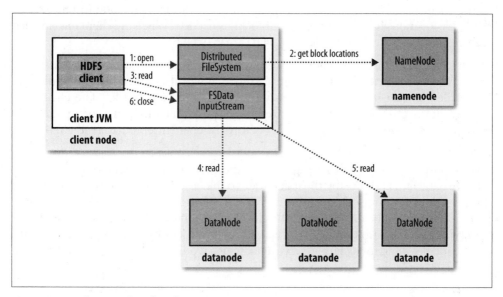

Figure 3-1. A client reading data from HDFS

The client opens the file it wishes to read by calling open() on the FileSystem object, which for HDFS is an instance of DistributedFileSystem (step 1 in Figure 3-1). DistributedFileSystem calls the namenode, using RPC, to determine the locations of the blocks for the first few blocks in the file (step 2). For each block, the namenode returns the addresses of the datanodes that have a copy of that block. Furthermore, the datanodes are sorted according to their proximity to the client (according to the topology of the cluster's network; see "Network Topology and Hadoop" on page 64). If the client is itself a datanode (in the case of a MapReduce task, for instance), then it will read from the local datanode.

The DistributedFileSystem returns a FSDataInputStream (an input stream that supports file seeks) to the client for it to read data from. FSDataInputStream in turn wraps a DFSInputStream, which manages the datanode and namenode I/O.

The client then calls `read()` on the stream (step 3). `DFSInputStream`, which has stored the datanode addresses for the first few blocks in the file, then connects to the first (closest) datanode for the first block in the file. Data is streamed from the datanode back to the client, which calls `read()` repeatedly on the stream (step 4). When the end of the block is reached, `DFSInputStream` will close the connection to the datanode, then find the best datanode for the next block (step 5). This happens transparently to the client, which from its point of view is just reading a continuous stream.

Blocks are read in order with the `DFSInputStream` opening new connections to datanodes as the client reads through the stream. It will also call the namenode to retrieve the datanode locations for the next batch of blocks as needed. When the client has finished reading, it calls `close()` on the `FSDataInputStream` (step 6).

During reading, if the client encounters an error while communicating with a datanode, then it will try the next closest one for that block. It will also remember datanodes that have failed so that it doesn't needlessly retry them for later blocks. The client also verifies checksums for the data transferred to it from the datanode. If a corrupted block is found, it is reported to the namenode, before the client attempts to read a replica of the block from another datanode.

One important aspect of this design is that the client contacts datanodes directly to retrieve data, and is guided by the namenode to the best datanode for each block. This design allows HDFS to scale to large number of concurrent clients, since the data traffic is spread across all the datanodes in the cluster. The namenode meanwhile merely has to service block location requests (which it stores in memory, making them very efficient), and does not, for example, serve data, which would quickly become a bottleneck as the number of clients grew.

Network Topology and Hadoop

What does it mean for two nodes in a local network to be "close" to each other? In the context of high-volume data processing, the limiting factor is the rate at which we can transfer data between nodes—bandwidth is a scarce commodity. The idea is to use the bandwidth between two nodes as a measure of distance.

Rather than measuring bandwidth between nodes, which can be difficult to do in practice (it requires a quiet cluster, and the number of pairs of nodes in a cluster grows as the square of the number of nodes), Hadoop takes a simple approach in which the network is represented as a tree and the distance between two nodes is the sum of their distances to their closest common ancestor. Levels in the tree are not predefined, but it is common to have levels that correspond to the data center, the rack, and the node that a process is running on. The idea is that the bandwidth available for each of the following scenarios becomes progressively less:

- Processes on the same node
- Different nodes on the same rack
- Nodes on different racks in the same data center
- Nodes in different data centers[#]

For example, imagine a node *n1* on rack *r1* in data center *d1*. This can be represented as */d1/r1/n1*. Using this notation, here are the distances for the four scenarios:

- *distance(/d1/r1/n1, /d1/r1/n1) = 0* (processes on the same node)
- *distance(/d1/r1/n1, /d1/r1/n2) = 2* (different nodes on the same rack)
- *distance(/d1/r1/n1, /d1/r2/n3) = 4* (nodes on different racks in the same data center)
- *distance(/d1/r1/n1, /d2/r3/n4) = 6* (nodes in different data centers)

This is illustrated schematically in Figure 3-2. (Mathematically inclined readers will notice that this is an example of a distance metric.)

Finally, it is important to realize that Hadoop cannot divine your network topology for you. It needs some help; we'll cover how to configure topology in "Network Topology" on page 247. By default though, it assumes that the network is flat—a single-level hierarchy—or in other words, that all nodes are on a single rack in a single data center. For small clusters, this may actually be the case, and no further configuration is required.

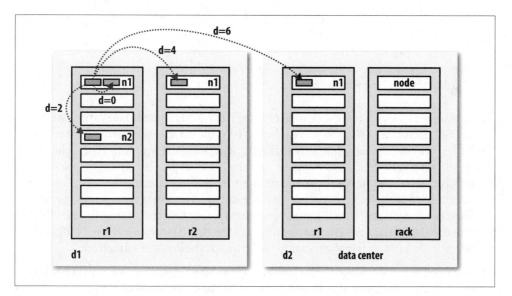

Figure 3-2. Network distance in Hadoop

[#] At the time of this writing, Hadoop is not suited for running across data centers.

Anatomy of a File Write

Next we'll look at how files are written to HDFS. Although quite detailed, it is instructive to understand the data flow since it clarifies HDFS's coherency model.

The case we're going to consider is the case of creating a new file, writing data to it, then closing the file. See Figure 3-3.

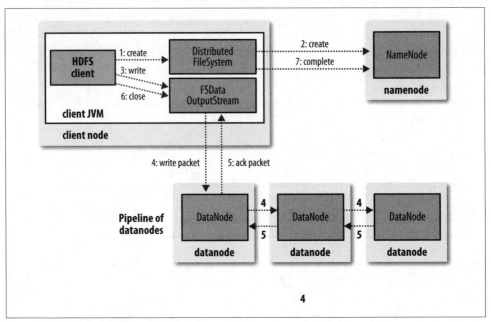

Figure 3-3. A client writing data to HDFS

The client creates the file by calling `create()` on `DistributedFileSystem` (step 1 in Figure 3-3). `DistributedFileSystem` makes an RPC call to the namenode to create a new file in the filesystem's namespace, with no blocks associated with it (step 2). The namenode performs various checks to make sure the file doesn't already exist, and that the client has the right permissions to create the file. If these checks pass, the namenode makes a record of the new file; otherwise, file creation fails and the client is thrown an `IOException`. The `DistributedFileSystem` returns a `FSDataOutputStream` for the client to start writing data to. Just as in the read case, `FSDataOutputStream` wraps a `DFSOutput Stream`, which handles communication with the datanodes and namenode.

As the client writes data (step 3), `DFSOutputStream` splits it into packets, which it writes to an internal queue, called the *data queue*. The data queue is consumed by the `Data Streamer`, whose responsibility it is to ask the namenode to allocate new blocks by picking a list of suitable datanodes to store the replicas. The list of datanodes forms a pipeline—we'll assume the replication level is 3, so there are three nodes in the pipeline. The `DataStreamer` streams the packets to the first datanode in the pipeline, which stores the packet and forwards it to the second datanode in the pipeline. Similarly, the second datanode stores the packet and forwards it to the third (and last) datanode in the pipeline (step 4).

`DFSOutputStream` also maintains an internal queue of packets that are waiting to be acknowledged by datanodes, called the *ack queue*. A packet is removed from the ack queue only when it has been acknowledged by all the datanodes in the pipeline (step 5).

If a datanode fails while data is being written to it, then the following actions are taken, which are transparent to the client writing the data. First the pipeline is closed, and any packets in the ack queue are added to the front of the data queue so that datanodes that are downstream from the failed node will not miss any packets. The current block on the good datanodes is given a new identity, which is communicated to the namenode, so that the partial block on the failed datanode will be deleted if the failed datanode recovers later on. The failed datanode is removed from the pipeline and the remainder of the block's data is written to the two good datanodes in the pipeline. The namenode notices that the block is under-replicated, and it arranges for a further replica to be created on another node. Subsequent blocks are then treated as normal.

It's possible, but unlikely, that multiple datanodes fail while a block is being written. As long as `dfs.replication.min` replicas (default one) are written the write will succeed, and the block will be asynchronously replicated across the cluster until its target replication factor is reached (`dfs.replication`, which defaults to three).

When the client has finished writing data it calls `close()` on the stream (step 6). This action flushes all the remaining packets to the datanode pipeline and waits for acknowledgments before contacting the namenode to signal that the file is complete (step 7). The namenode already knows which blocks the file is made up of (via `Data Streamer` asking for block allocations), so it only has to wait for blocks to be minimally replicated before returning successfully.

Replica Placement

How does the namenode choose which datanodes to store replicas on? There's a trade-off between reliability and write bandwidth and read bandwidth here. For example, placing all replicas on a single node incurs the lowest write bandwidth penalty since the replication pipeline runs on a single node, but this offers no real redundancy (if the node fails, the data for that block is lost). Also, the read bandwidth is high for off-rack reads. At the other extreme, placing replicas in different data centers may maximize redundancy, but at the cost of bandwidth. Even in the same data center (which is what all Hadoop clusters to date have run in), there are a variety of placement strategies. Indeed, Hadoop changed its placement strategy in release 0.17.0 to one that helps keep a fairly even distribution of blocks across the cluster. (See "balancer" on page 284 for details on keeping a cluster balanced.)

Hadoop's strategy is to place the first replica on the same node as the client (for clients running outside the cluster, a node is chosen at random, although the system tries not to pick nodes that are too full or too busy). The second replica is placed on a different rack from the first (*off-rack*), chosen at random. The third replica is placed on the same rack as the second, but on a different node chosen at random. Further replicas are placed on random nodes on the cluster, although the system tries to avoid placing too many replicas on the same rack.

Once the replica locations have been chosen, a pipeline is built, taking network topology into account. For a replication factor of 3, the pipeline might look like Figure 3-4.

Overall, this strategy gives a good balance between reliability (blocks are stored on two racks), write bandwidth (writes only have to traverse a single network switch), read performance (there's a choice of two racks to read from), and block distribution across the cluster (clients only write a single block on the local rack).

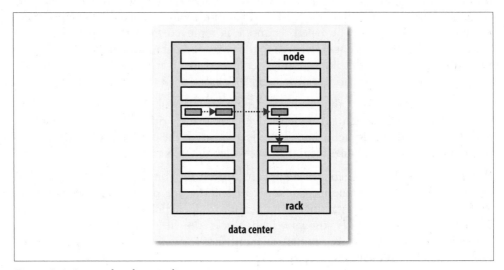

Figure 3-4. A typical replica pipeline

Coherency Model

A coherency model for a filesystem describes the data visibility of reads and writes for a file. HDFS trades off some POSIX requirements for performance, so some operations may behave differently than you expect them to.

After creating a file, it is visible in the filesystem namespace, as expected:

```
Path p = new Path("p");
fs.create(p);
assertThat(fs.exists(p), is(true));
```

However, any content written to the file is not guaranteed to be visible, even if the stream is flushed. So the file appears to have a length of zero:

```
Path p = new Path("p");
OutputStream out = fs.create(p);
```

```
out.write("content".getBytes("UTF-8"));
out.flush();
assertThat(fs.getFileStatus(p).getLen(), is(0L));
```

Once more than a block's worth of data has been written, the first block will be visible to new readers. This is true of subsequent blocks, too: it is always the current block being written that is not visible to other readers.

HDFS provides a method for forcing all buffers to be synchronized to the datanodes via the sync() method on FSDataOutputStream. After a successful return from sync(), HDFS guarantees that the data written up to that point in the file is persisted and visible to all new readers.[*] In the event of a crash (of the client or HDFS), the data will not be lost:

```
Path p = new Path("p");
FSDataOutputStream out = fs.create(p);
out.write("content".getBytes("UTF-8"));
out.flush();
out.sync();
assertThat(fs.getFileStatus(p).getLen(), is(((long) "content".length())));
```

This behavior is similar to the fsync system call in Unix that commits buffered data for a file descriptor. For example, using the Java API to write a local file, we are guaranteed to see the content after flushing the stream and synchronizing:

```
FileOutputStream out = new FileOutputStream(localFile);
out.write("content".getBytes("UTF-8"));
out.flush(); // flush to operating system
out.getFD().sync(); // sync to disk
assertThat(localFile.length(), is(((long) "content".length())));
```

Closing a file in HDFS performs an implicit sync(), too:

```
Path p = new Path("p");
OutputStream out = fs.create(p);
out.write("content".getBytes("UTF-8"));
out.close();
assertThat(fs.getFileStatus(p).getLen(), is(((long) "content".length())));
```

Consequences for application design

This coherency model has implications for the way you design applications. With no calls to sync(), you should be prepared to lose up to a block of data in the event of client or system failure. For many applications, this is unacceptable, so you should call sync() at suitable points, such as after writing a certain number of records or number of bytes. Though the sync() operation is designed to not unduly tax HDFS, it does have some overhead, so there is a trade-off between data robustness and throughput. What is an acceptable trade-off is application-dependent, and suitable values can be selected after measuring your application's performance with different sync() frequencies.

---

[*] At the time of this writing, the visibility guarantee is not honored. See *https://issues.apache.org/jira/browse/ HADOOP-4379*.

Parallel Copying with distcp

The HDFS access patterns that we have seen so far focus on single-threaded access. It's possible to act on a collection of files, by specifying file globs, for example, but for efficient, parallel processing of these files you would have to write a program yourself. Hadoop comes with a useful program called *distcp* for copying large amounts of data to and from Hadoop filesystems in parallel.

The canonical use case for *distcp* is for transferring data between two HDFS clusters. If the clusters are running identical versions of Hadoop, the *hdfs* scheme is appropriate:

```
% hadoop distcp hdfs://namenode1/foo hdfs://namenode2/bar
```

This will copy the */foo* directory (and its contents) from the first cluster to the */bar* directory on the second cluster, so the second cluster ends up with the directory structure */bar/foo*. If */bar* doesn't exist, it will be created first. You can specify multiple source paths, and all will be copied to the destination. Source paths must be absolute.

By default, *distcp* will skip files that already exist in the destination, but they can be overwritten by supplying the `-overwrite` option. You can also update only files that have changed using the `-update` option.

Using either (or both) of `-overwrite` or `-update` changes the how the source and destination paths are interpreted. This is best shown with an example. If we changed a file in the */foo* subtree on the first cluster from the previous example, then we could synchronize the change with the second cluster by running:

```
% hadoop distcp -update hdfs://namenode1/foo hdfs://namenode2/bar/foo
```

The extra trailing */foo* subdirectory is needed on the destination, as now the *contents* of the source directory are copied to the *contents* of the destination directory. (If you are familiar with *rsync*, you can think of the `-overwrite` or `-update` options as adding an implicit trailing slash to the source.)

If you are unsure of the effect of a *distcp* operation, it is a good idea to try it out on a small test directory tree first.

There are more options to control the behavior of *distcp*, including ones to preserve file attributes, ignore failures, and limit the number of files or total data copied. Run it with no options to see the usage instructions.

distcp is implemented as a MapReduce job where the work of copying is done by the maps that run in parallel across the cluster. There are no reducers. Each file is copied by a single map, and *distcp* tries to give each map approximately the same amount of data, by bucketing files into roughly equal allocations.

The number of maps is decided as follows. Since it's a good idea to get each map to copy a reasonable amount of data to minimize overheads in task setup, each map copies at least 256 MB (unless the total size of the input is less, in which case one map handles it all). For example, 1 GB of files will be given four map tasks. When the data size is very large, it becomes necessary to limit the number of maps in order to limit bandwidth and cluster utilization. By default, the maximum number of maps is 20 per (tasktracker) cluster node. For example, copying 1,000 GB of files to a 100-node cluster will allocate 2,000 maps (20 per node), so each will copy 512 MB on average. This can be reduced by specifying the -m argument to *distcp*. For example, -m 1000 would allocate 1,000 maps, each copying 1 GB on average.

If you try to use *distcp* between two HDFS clusters that are running different versions, the copy will fail if you use the *hdfs* protocol, since the RPC systems are incompatible. To remedy this, you can use the HTTP-based HFTP filesystem to read from the source. The job must run on the destination cluster so that the HDFS RPC versions are compatible. To repeat the previous example using HFTP:

```
% hadoop distcp hftp://namenode1:50070/foo hdfs://namenode2/bar
```

Note that you need to specify the namenode's web port in the source URI. This is determined by the dfs.http.address property, which defaults to 50070.

Keeping an HDFS Cluster Balanced

When copying data into HDFS, it's important to consider cluster balance. HDFS works best when the file blocks are evenly spread across the cluster, so you want to ensure that *distcp* doesn't disrupt this. Going back to the 1,000 GB example, by specifying -m 1 a single map would do the copy, which—apart from being slow and not using the cluster resources efficiently—would mean that the first replica of each block would reside on the node running the map (until the disk filled up). The second and third replicas would be spread across the cluster, but this one node would be unbalanced. By having more maps than nodes in the cluster, this problem is avoided—for this reason, it's best to start by running *distcp* with the default of 20 maps per node.

However, it's not always possible to prevent a cluster from becoming unbalanced. Perhaps you want to limit the number of maps so that some of the nodes can be used by other jobs. In this case, you can use the *balancer* tool (see "balancer" on page 284) to subsequently improve the block distribution across the cluster.

Hadoop Archives

HDFS stores small files inefficiently, since each file is stored in a block, and block metadata is held in memory by the namenode. Thus, a large number of small files can eat up a lot of memory on the namenode. (Note, however, that small files do not take up any more disk space than is required to store the raw contents of the file. For example, a 1 MB file stored with a block size of 128 MB uses 1 MB of disk space, not 128 MB.)

Hadoop Archives, or HAR files, are a file archiving facility that packs files into HDFS blocks more efficiently, thereby reducing namenode memory usage while still allowing transparent access to files. In particular, Hadoop Archives can be used as input to MapReduce.

Using Hadoop Archives

A Hadoop Archive is created from a collection of files using the *archive* tool. The tool runs a MapReduce job to process the input files in parallel, so to run it, you need a MapReduce cluster running to use it. Here are some files in HDFS that we would like to archive:

```
% hadoop fs -lsr /my/files
-rw-r--r--   1 tom supergroup          1 2009-04-09 19:13 /my/files/a
drwxr-xr-x   - tom supergroup          0 2009-04-09 19:13 /my/files/dir
-rw-r--r--   1 tom supergroup          1 2009-04-09 19:13 /my/files/dir/b
```

Now we can run the `archive` command:

```
% hadoop archive -archiveName files.har /my/files /my
```

The first option is the name of the archive, here *files.har*. HAR files always have a *.har* extension, which is mandatory for reasons you shall see later. Next comes the files to put in the archive. Here we are archiving only one source tree, the files in */my/ files* in HDFS, but the tool accepts multiple source trees. The final argument is the output directory for the HAR file. Let's see what the archive has created:

```
% hadoop fs -ls /my
Found 2 items
drwxr-xr-x   - tom supergroup          0 2009-04-09 19:13 /my/files
drwxr-xr-x   - tom supergroup          0 2009-04-09 19:13 /my/files.har
% hadoop fs -ls /my/files.har
Found 3 items
-rw-r--r--  10 tom supergroup        165 2009-04-09 19:13 /my/files.har/_index
-rw-r--r--  10 tom supergroup         23 2009-04-09 19:13 /my/files.har/_masterindex
-rw-r--r--   1 tom supergroup          2 2009-04-09 19:13 /my/files.har/part-0
```

The directory listing shows what a HAR file is made of: two index files and a collection of part files—just one in this example. The part files contain the contents of a number of the original files concatenated together, and the indexes make it possible to look up the part file that an archived file is contained in, and its offset and length. All these details are hidden from the application, however, which uses the *har* URI scheme to interact with HAR files, using a HAR filesystem that is layered on top of the underlying filesystem (HDFS in this case). The following command recursively lists the files in the archive:

```
% hadoop fs -lsr har:///my/files.har
drw-r--r--   - tom supergroup          0 2009-04-09 19:13 /my/files.har/my
drw-r--r--   - tom supergroup          0 2009-04-09 19:13 /my/files.har/my/files
```

```
-rw-r--r--   10 tom supergroup          1 2009-04-09 19:13 /my/files.har/my/files/a
drw-r--r--    - tom supergroup          0 2009-04-09 19:13 /my/files.har/my/files/dir
-rw-r--r--   10 tom supergroup          1 2009-04-09 19:13 /my/files.har/my/files/dir/b
```

This is quite straightforward if the filesystem that the HAR file is on is the default filesystem. On the other hand, if you want to refer to a HAR file on a different filesystem, then you need to use a different form of the path URI to normal. These two commands have the same effect, for example:

```
% hadoop fs -lsr har:///my/files.har/my/files/dir
% hadoop fs -lsr har://hdfs-localhost:8020/my/files.har/my/files/dir
```

Notice in the second form that the scheme is still *har* to signify a HAR filesystem, but the authority is *hdfs* to specify the underlying filesystem's scheme, followed by a dash and the HDFS host (localhost) and port (8020). We can now see why HAR files have to have a *.har* extension. The HAR filesystem translates the *har* URI into a URI for the underlying filesystem, by looking at the authority and path up to and including the component with the *.har* extension. In this case, it is *hdfs://localhost:8020/user/tom/files.har*. The remaining part of the path is the path of the file in the archive: */user/tom/files/dir*.

To delete a HAR file, you need to use the recursive form of delete, since to the underlying filesystem, the HAR file is a directory.

```
% hadoop fs -rmr /my/files.har
```

Limitations

There are a few limitations to be aware of with HAR files. Creating an archive creates a copy of the original files, so you need as much disk space as the files you are archiving to create the archive (although you can delete the originals once you have created the archive). There is currently no support for archive compression, although the files that go into the archive can be compressed (HAR files are like *tar* files in this respect).

Archives are immutable once they have been created. To add or remove files, you must recreate the archive. In practice, this is not a problem for files that don't change after being written, since they can be archived in batches on a regular basis, such as daily or weekly.

As noted earlier, HAR files can be used as input to MapReduce. However, there is no archive-aware `InputFormat` that can pack multiple files into a single MapReduce split, so processing lots of small files, even in a HAR file, can still be inefficient. "Small files and CombineFileInputFormat" on page 190 discusses another approach to this problem.

## CHAPTER 4

Hadoop I/O

Hadoop comes with a set of primitives for data I/O. Some of these are techniques that are more general than Hadoop, such as data integrity and compression, but deserve special consideration when dealing with multiterabyte datasets. Others are Hadoop tools or APIs that form the building blocks for developing distributed systems, such as serialization frameworks and on-disk data structures.

Data Integrity

Users of Hadoop rightly expect that no data will be lost or corrupted during storage or processing. However, since every I/O operation on the disk or network carries with it a small chance of introducing errors into the data that it is reading or writing, when the volumes of data flowing through the system are as large as the ones Hadoop is capable of handling, the chance of data corruption occurring is high.

The usual way of detecting corrupted data is by computing a *checksum* for the data when it first enters the system, and then whenever it is transmitted across a channel that is unreliable and hence capable of corrupting the data. The data is deemed to be corrupt if the newly generated checksum doesn't exactly match the original. This technique doesn't offer any way to fix the data—merely error detection. (And this is a reason for not using low-end hardware; in particular, be sure to use ECC memory.) Note that it is possible that it's the checksum that is corrupt, not the data, but this is very unlikely, since the checksum is much smaller than the data.

A commonly used error-detecting code is CRC-32 (cyclic redundancy check), which computes a 32-bit integer checksum for input of any size.

Data Integrity in HDFS

HDFS transparently checksums all data written to it and by default verifies checksums when reading data. A separate checksum is created for every `io.bytes.per.checksum` bytes of data. The default is 512 bytes, and since a CRC-32 checksum is 4 bytes long, the storage overhead is less than 1%.

Datanodes are responsible for verifying the data they receive before storing the data and its checksum. This applies to data that they receive from clients and from other datanodes during replication. A client writing data sends it to a pipeline of datanodes (as explained in Chapter 3), and the last datanode in the pipeline verifies the checksum. If it detects an error, the client receives a `ChecksumException`, a subclass of `IOException`.

When clients read data from datanodes, they verify checksums as well, comparing them with the ones stored at the datanode. Each datanode keeps a persistent log of checksum verifications, so it knows the last time each of its blocks was verified. When a client successfully verifies a block, it tells the datanode, which updates its log. Keeping statistics such as these is valuable in detecting bad disks.

Aside from block verification on client reads, each datanode runs a `DataBlockScanner` in a background thread that periodically verifies all the blocks stored on the datanode. This is to guard against corruption due to "bit rot" in the physical storage media. See "Datanode block scanner" on page 283 for details on how to access the scanner reports.

Since HDFS stores replicas of blocks, it can "heal" corrupted blocks by copying one of the good replicas to produce a new, uncorrupt replica. The way this works is that if a client detects an error when reading a block, it reports the bad block and the datanode it was trying to read from to the namenode before throwing a `ChecksumException`. The namenode marks the block replica as corrupt, so it doesn't direct clients to it, or try to copy this replica to another datanode. It then schedules a copy of the block to be replicated on another datanode, so its replication factor is back at the expected level. Once this has happened, the corrupt replica is deleted.

It is possible to disable verification of checksums by passing `false` to the `setVerify Checksum()` method on `FileSystem`, before using the `open()` method to read a file. The same effect is possible from the shell by using the `-ignoreCrc` option with the `-get` or the equivalent `-copyToLocal` command. This feature is useful if you have a corrupt file that you want to inspect so you can decide what to do with it. For example, you might want to see whether it can be salvaged before you delete it.

LocalFileSystem

The Hadoop `LocalFileSystem` performs client-side checksumming. This means that when you write a file called *filename*, the filesystem client transparently creates a hidden file, *.filename.crc*, in the same directory containing the checksums for each chunk of the file. Like HDFS, the chunk size is controlled by the `io.bytes.per.checksum` property, which defaults to 512 bytes. The chunk size is stored as metadata in the *.crc* file, so the file can be read back correctly even if the setting for the chunk size has changed. Checksums are verified when the file is read, and if an error is detected, `LocalFileSystem` throws a `ChecksumException`.

Checksums are fairly cheap to compute (in Java, they are implemented in native code), typically adding a few percent overhead to the time to read or write a file. For most applications, this is an acceptable price to pay for data integrity. It is, however, possible to disable checksums: the use case here is when the underlying filesystem support checksums natively. This is accomplished by using RawLocalFileSystem in place of LocalFileSystem. To do this globally in an application, it suffices to remap the implementation for *file* URIs by setting the property fs.file.impl to the value org.apache.hadoop.fs.RawLocalFileSystem. Alternatively, you can directly create a Raw LocalFileSystem instance, which may be useful if you want to disable checksum verification for only some reads; for example:

```
Configuration conf = ...
FileSystem fs = new RawLocalFileSystem();
fs.initialize(null, conf);
```

ChecksumFileSystem

LocalFileSystem uses ChecksumFileSystem to do its work, and this class makes it easy to add checksumming to other (nonchecksummed) filesystems, as ChecksumFileSystem is just a wrapper around FileSystem. The general idiom is as follows:

```
FileSystem rawFs = ...
FileSystem checksummedFs = new ChecksumFileSystem(rawFs);
```

The underlying filesystem is called the *raw* filesystem, and may be retrieved using the getRawFileSystem() method on ChecksumFileSystem. ChecksumFileSystem has a few more useful methods for working with checksums, such as getChecksumFile() for getting the path of a checksum file for any file. Check the documentation for the others.

If an error is detected by ChecksumFileSystem when reading a file, it will call its reportChecksumFailure() method. The default implementation does nothing, but LocalFileSystem moves the offending file and its checksum to a side directory on the same device called *bad_files*. Administrators should periodically check for these bad files and take action on them.

Compression

File compression brings two major benefits: it reduces the space needed to store files, and it speeds up data transfer across the network, or to or from disk. When dealing with large volumes of data, both of these savings can be significant, so it pays to carefully consider how to use compression in Hadoop.

There are many different compression formats, tools and algorithms, each with different characteristics. Table 4-1 lists some of the more common ones that can be used with Hadoop.[*]

Table 4-1. A summary of compression formats

Compression format	Tool	Algorithm	Filename extension	Multiple files	Splittable
DEFLATE[a]	N/A	DEFLATE	.deflate	No	No
gzip	gzip	DEFLATE	.gz	No	No
ZIP	zip	DEFLATE	.zip	Yes	Yes, at file boundaries
bzip2	bzip2	bzip2	.bz2	No	Yes
LZO	lzop	LZO	.lzo	No	No

[a] DEFLATE is a compression algorithm whose standard implementation is zlib. There is no commonly available command-line tool for producing files in DEFLATE format, as gzip is normally used. (Note that the gzip file format is DEFLATE with extra headers and a footer.) The *.deflate* filename extension is a Hadoop convention.

All compression algorithms exhibit a space/time trade-off: faster compression and decompression speeds usually come at the expense of smaller space savings. All of the tools listed in Table 4-1 give some control over this trade-off at compression time by offering nine different options: –1 means optimize for speed and -9 means optimize for space. For example, the following command creates a compressed file *file.gz* using the fastest compression method:

```
gzip -1 file
```

The different tools have very different compression characteristics. Both gzip and ZIP are general-purpose compressors, and sit in the middle of the space/time trade-off. Bzip2 compresses more effectively than gzip or ZIP, but is slower. Bzip2's decompression speed is faster than its compression speed, but it is still slower than the other formats. LZO, on the other hand, optimizes for speed: it is faster than gzip or ZIP (or any other compression or decompression tool[†]), but compresses slightly less effectively.

The "Splittable" column in Table 4-1 indicates whether the compression format supports splitting; that is, whether you can seek to any point in the stream and start reading from some point further on. Splittable compression formats are especially suitable for MapReduce; see "Compression and Input Splits" on page 83 for further discussion.

---

[*] At the time of this writing, Hadoop's ZIP integration is incomplete. See *https://issues.apache.org/jira/browse/HADOOP-1824*.

[†] Jeff Gilchrist's Archive Comparison Test at *http://compression.ca/act/act-summary.html* contains benchmarks for compression and decompression speed, and compression ratio for a wide range of tools.

Codecs

A *codec* is the implementation of a compression-decompression algorithm. In Hadoop, a codec is represented by an implementation of the `CompressionCodec` interface. So, for example, `GzipCodec` encapsulates the compression and decompression algorithm for gzip. Table 4-2 lists the codecs that are available for Hadoop.

Table 4-2. Hadoop compression codecs

Compression format	Hadoop CompressionCodec
DEFLATE	org.apache.hadoop.io.compress.DefaultCodec
gzip	org.apache.hadoop.io.compress.GzipCodec
bzip2	org.apache.hadoop.io.compress.BZip2Codec
LZO	com.hadoop.compression.lzo.LzopCodec

The LZO libraries are GPL-licensed and may not be included in Apache distributions, so for this reason the Hadoop codecs must be downloaded separately from *http://code .google.com/p/hadoop-gpl-compression/*. The `LzopCodec` is compatible with the `lzop` tool, which is essentially the LZO format with extra headers, and is the one you normally want. There is also a `LzoCodec` for the pure LZO format, which uses the *.lzo_deflate* filename extension (by analogy with DEFLATE, which is gzip without the headers).

Compressing and decompressing streams with CompressionCodec

`CompressionCodec` has two methods that allow you to easily compress or decompress data. To compress data being written to an output stream, use the `createOutput Stream(OutputStream out)` method to create a `CompressionOutputStream` to which you write your uncompressed data to have it written in compressed form to the underlying stream. Conversely, to decompress data being read from an input stream, call `createInputStream(InputStream in)` to obtain a `CompressionInputStream`, which allows you to read uncompressed data from the underlying stream.

`CompressionOutputStream` and `CompressionInputStream` are similar to `java.util.zip.DeflaterOutputStream` and `java.util.zip.DeflaterInputStream`, except that both of the former provide the ability to reset their underlying compressor or decompressor, which is important for applications that compress sections of the data stream as separate blocks, such as `SequenceFile`, described in "Sequence-File" on page 103.

Example 4-1 illustrates how to use the API to compress data read from standard input and write it to standard output.

Example 4-1. A program to compress data read from standard input and write it to standard output

```
public class StreamCompressor {

  public static void main(String[] args) throws Exception {
```

```
      String codecClassname = args[0];
      Class<?> codecClass = Class.forName(codecClassname);
      Configuration conf = new Configuration();
      CompressionCodec codec = (CompressionCodec)
        ReflectionUtils.newInstance(codecClass, conf);

      CompressionOutputStream out = codec.createOutputStream(System.out);
      IOUtils.copyBytes(System.in, out, 4096, false);
      out.finish();
    }
}
```

The application expects the fully qualified name of the CompressionCodec implementation as the first command-line argument. We use ReflectionUtils to construct a new instance of the codec, then obtain a compression wrapper around System.out. Then we call the utility method copyBytes() on IOUtils to copy the input to the output, which is compressed by the CompressionOutputStream. Finally, we call finish() on CompressionOutputStream, which tells the compressor to finish writing to the compressed stream, but doesn't close the stream. We can try it out with the following command line, which compresses the string "Text" using the StreamCompressor program with the GzipCodec, then decompresses it from standard input using *gunzip*:

```
% echo "Text" | hadoop StreamCompressor org.apache.hadoop.io.compress.GzipCodec \
  | gunzip -
Text
```

Inferring CompressionCodecs using CompressionCodecFactory

If you are reading a compressed file, you can normally infer the codec to use by looking at its filename extension. A file ending in *.gz* can be read with GzipCodec, and so on. The extension for each compression format is listed in Table 4-1.

CompressionCodecFactory provides a way of mapping a filename extension to a CompressionCodec using its getCodec() method, which takes a Path object for the file in question. Example 4-2 shows an application that uses this feature to decompress files.

Example 4-2. A program to decompress a compressed file using a codec inferred from the file's extension

```
public class FileDecompressor {

  public static void main(String[] args) throws Exception {
    String uri = args[0];
    Configuration conf = new Configuration();
    FileSystem fs = FileSystem.get(URI.create(uri), conf);

    Path inputPath = new Path(uri);
    CompressionCodecFactory factory = new CompressionCodecFactory(conf);
    CompressionCodec codec = factory.getCodec(inputPath);
    if (codec == null) {
      System.err.println("No codec found for " + uri);
      System.exit(1);
```

```
      }

      String outputUri =
        CompressionCodecFactory.removeSuffix(uri, codec.getDefaultExtension());

      InputStream in = null;
      OutputStream out = null;
      try {
        in = codec.createInputStream(fs.open(inputPath));
        out = fs.create(new Path(outputUri));
        IOUtils.copyBytes(in, out, conf);
      } finally {
        IOUtils.closeStream(in);
        IOUtils.closeStream(out);
      }
    }
  }
}
```

Once the codec has been found, it is used to strip off the file suffix to form the output filename (via the `removeSuffix()` static method of `CompressionCodecFactory`). In this way, a file named *file.gz* is decompressed to *file* by invoking the program as follows:

```
% hadoop FileDecompressor file.gz
```

`CompressionCodecFactory` finds codecs from a list defined by the `io.compression.codecs` configuration property. By default, this lists all the codecs provided by Hadoop (see Table 4-3), so you would need to alter it only if you have a custom codec that you wish to register (such as the externally hosted LZO codecs). Each codec knows its default filename extension, thus permitting `CompressionCodecFactory` to search through the registered codecs to find a match for a given extension (if any).

Table 4-3. Compression codec properties

Property name	Type	Default value	Description
io.compression.codecs	comma-separated Class names	org.apache.hadoop.io. compress.DefaultCodec, org.apache.hadoop.io. compress.GzipCodec, org.apache.hadoop.io. compress.Bzip2Codec	A list of the Compres sionCodec classes for compression/ decompression.

Native libraries

For performance, it is preferable to use a native library for compression and decompression. For example, in one test, using the native gzip libraries reduced decompression times by up to 50% and compression times by around 10% (compared to the built-in Java implementation). Table 4-4 shows the availability of Java and native implementations for each compression format. Not all formats have native implementations (bzip2, for example), whereas others are only available as a native implementation (LZO, for example).

Table 4-4. Compression library implementations

Compression format	Java implementation	Native implementation
DEFLATE	Yes	Yes
gzip	Yes	Yes
bzip2	Yes	No
LZO	No	Yes

Hadoop comes with prebuilt native compression libraries for 32- and 64-bit Linux, which you can find in the *lib/native* directory. For other platforms, you will need to compile the libraries yourself, following the instructions on the Hadoop wiki at *http:// wiki.apache.org/hadoop/NativeHadoop*.

The native libraries are picked up using the Java system property `java.library.path`. The *hadoop* script in the *bin* directory sets this property for you, but if you don't use this script, you will need to set the property in your application.

By default Hadoop looks for native libraries for the platform it is running on, and loads them automatically if they are found. This means you don't have to change any configuration settings to use the native libraries. In some circumstances, however, you may wish to disable use of native libraries, such as when you are debugging a compression-related problem. You can achieve this by setting the property `hadoop.native.lib` to `false`, which ensures that the built-in Java equivalents will be used (if they are available).

CodecPool. If you are using a native library and you are doing a lot of compression or decompression in your application, consider using `CodecPool`, which allows you to reuse compressors and decompressors, thereby amortizing the cost of creating these objects.

The code in Example 4-3 shows the API, although in this program, which only creates a single `Compressor`, there is really no need to use a pool.

Example 4-3. A program to compress data read from standard input and write it to standard output using a pooled compressor

```
public class PooledStreamCompressor {

  public static void main(String[] args) throws Exception {
    String codecClassname = args[0];
    Class<?> codecClass = Class.forName(codecClassname);
    Configuration conf = new Configuration();
    CompressionCodec codec = (CompressionCodec)
      ReflectionUtils.newInstance(codecClass, conf);
    Compressor compressor = null;
    try {
      compressor = CodecPool.getCompressor(codec);
      CompressionOutputStream out =
        codec.createOutputStream(System.out, compressor);
      IOUtils.copyBytes(System.in, out, 4096, false);
      out.finish();
```

```
    } finally {
      CodecPool.returnCompressor(compressor);
    }
  }
}
```

We retrieve a `Compressor` instance from the pool for a given `CompressionCodec`, which we use in the codec's overloaded `createOutputStream()` method. By using a `finally` block, we ensure that the compressor is returned to the pool even if there is an `IOException` while copying the bytes between the streams.

Compression and Input Splits

When considering how to compress data that will be processed by MapReduce, it is important to understand whether the compression format supports splitting. Consider an uncompressed file stored in HDFS whose size is 1 GB. With a HDFS block size of 64 MB, the file will be stored as 16 blocks, and a MapReduce job using this file as input will create 16 input splits, each processed independently as input to a separate map task.

Imagine now the file is a gzip-compressed file whose compressed size is 1 GB. As before, HDFS will store the file as 16 blocks. However, creating a split for each block won't work since it is impossible to start reading at an arbitrary point in the gzip stream, and therefore impossible for a map task to read its split independently of the others. The gzip format uses DEFLATE to store the compressed data, and DEFLATE stores data as a series of compressed blocks. The problem is that the start of each block is not distinguished in any way that would allow a reader positioned at an arbitrary point in the stream to advance to the beginning of the next block, thereby synchronizing itself with the stream. For this reason, gzip does not support splitting.

In this case, MapReduce will do the right thing, and not try to split the gzipped file, since it knows that the input is gzip-compressed (by looking at the filename extension) and that gzip does not support splitting. This will work, but at the expense of locality: a single map will process the 16 HDFS blocks, most of which will not be local to the map. Also, with fewer maps, the job is less granular, and so may take longer to run.

If the file in our hypothetical example were an LZO file, we would have the same problem since the underlying compression format does not provide a way for a reader to synchronize itself with the stream. A bzip2 file, however, does provide a synchronization marker between blocks (a 48-bit approximation of pi), so it does support splitting. (Table 4-1 lists whether each compression format supports splitting.)

For collections of files, the issues are slightly different. ZIP is an archive format, so it can combine multiple files into a single ZIP archive. Each file is compressed separately, and the locations of all the files in the archive are stored in a central directory at the end of the ZIP file. This property means that ZIP files support splitting at file boundaries, with each split containing one or more files from the ZIP archive. At the time of this writing, however, Hadoop does not support ZIP files as an input format.

Using Compression in MapReduce

As described in "Inferring CompressionCodecs using CompressionCodecFactory" on page 80, if your input files are compressed, they will be automatically decompressed as they are read by MapReduce, using the filename extension to determine the codec to use.

To compress the output of a MapReduce job, in the job configuration, set the `mapred.output.compress` property to `true`, and the `mapred.output.compression.codec` property to the classname of the compression codec you want to use, as shown in Example 4-4.

Example 4-4. Application to run the maximum temperature job producing compressed output

```java
public class MaxTemperatureWithCompression {

  public static void main(String[] args) throws IOException {
    if (args.length != 2) {
      System.err.println("Usage: MaxTemperatureWithCompression <input path> " +
          "<output path>");
      System.exit(-1);
    }

    JobConf conf = new JobConf(MaxTemperatureWithCompression.class);
```

```
conf.setJobName("Max temperature with output compression");

FileInputFormat.addInputPath(conf, new Path(args[0]));
FileOutputFormat.setOutputPath(conf, new Path(args[1]));

conf.setOutputKeyClass(Text.class);
conf.setOutputValueClass(IntWritable.class);

conf.setBoolean("mapred.output.compress", true);
conf.setClass("mapred.output.compression.codec", GzipCodec.class,
    CompressionCodec.class);

conf.setMapperClass(MaxTemperatureMapper.class);
conf.setCombinerClass(MaxTemperatureReducer.class);
conf.setReducerClass(MaxTemperatureReducer.class);

JobClient.runJob(conf);
  }
}
```

We run the program over compressed input (which doesn't have to use the same compression format as the output, although it does in this example) as follows:

```
% hadoop MaxTemperatureWithCompression input/ncdc/sample.txt.gz output
```

Each part of the final output is compressed; in this case, there is a single part:

```
% gunzip -c output/part-00000.gz
1949    111
1950    22
```

If you are emitting sequence files for your output, then you can set the `mapred.out put.compression.type` property to control the type of compression to use. The default is `RECORD`, which compresses individual records. Changing this to `BLOCK`, which compresses groups of records, is recommended since it compresses better (see "The SequenceFile Format" on page 109).

Compressing map output

Even if your MapReduce application reads and writes uncompressed data, it may benefit from compressing the intermediate output of the map phase. Since the map output is written to disk and transferred across the network to the reducer nodes, by using a fast compressor such as LZO, you can get performance gains simply because the volume of data to transfer is reduced. The configuration properties to enable compression for map outputs and to set the compression format are shown in Table 4-5.

Table 4-5. Map output compression properties

Property name	Type	Default value	Description
mapred.compress.map.output	boolean	false	Compress map outputs.
mapred.map.output.compression.codec	Class	org.apache.hadoop.io.compress.DefaultCodec	The compression codec to use for map outputs.

Here are the lines to add to enable gzip map output compression in your job:

```
conf.setCompressMapOutput(true);
conf.setMapOutputCompressorClass(GzipCodec.class);
```

Serialization

Serialization is the process of turning structured objects into a byte stream for transmission over a network or for writing to persistent storage. *Deserialization* is the process of turning a byte stream back into a series of structured objects.

Serialization appears in two quite distinct areas of distributed data processing: for interprocess communication and for persistent storage.

In Hadoop, interprocess communication between nodes in the system is implemented using *remote procedure calls* (RPCs). The RPC protocol uses serialization to render the message into a binary stream to be sent to the remote node, which then deserializes the binary stream into the original message. In general, it is desirable that an RPC serialization format is:

Compact
> A compact format makes the best use of network bandwidth, which is the most scarce resource in a data center.

Fast
> Interprocess communication forms the backbone for a distributed system, so it is essential that there is as little performance overhead as possible for the serialization and deserialization process.

Extensible
> Protocols change over time to meet new requirements, so it should be straightforward to evolve the protocol in a controlled manner for clients and servers. For example, it should be possible to add a new argument to a method call, and have the new servers accept messages in the old format (without the new argument) from old clients.

Interoperable
> For some systems, it is desirable to be able to support clients that are written in different languages to the server, so the format needs to be designed to make this possible.

On the face of it, the data format chosen for persistent storage would have different requirements from a serialization framework. After all, the lifespan of an RPC is less than a second, whereas persistent data may be read years after it was written. As it turns out, the four desirable properties of an RPC's serialization format are also crucial for a persistent storage format. We want the storage format to be compact (to make efficient use of storage space), fast (so the overhead in reading or writing terabytes of data is minimal), extensible (so we can transparently read data written in an older format), and interoperable (so we can read or write persistent data using different languages).

Hadoop uses its own serialization format, Writables, which is certainly compact and fast (but not so easy to extend, or use from languages other than Java). Since Writables are central to Hadoop (MapReduce programs use them for their key and value types), we look at them in some depth in the next section, before briefly turning to other well-known serialization frameworks, like Apache Thrift and Google Protocol Buffers.

The Writable Interface

The Writable interface defines two methods: one for writing its state to a DataOutput binary stream, and one for reading its state from a DataInput binary stream:

```
package org.apache.hadoop.io;

import java.io.DataOutput;
import java.io.DataInput;
import java.io.IOException;

public interface Writable {
  void write(DataOutput out) throws IOException;
  void readFields(DataInput in) throws IOException;
}
```

Let's look at a particular Writable to see what we can do with it. We will use IntWritable, a wrapper for a Java int. We can create one and set its value using the set() method:

```
IntWritable writable = new IntWritable();
writable.set(163);
```

Equivalently, we can use the constructor that takes the integer value:

```
IntWritable writable = new IntWritable(163);
```

To examine the serialized form of the IntWritable, we write a small helper method that wraps a java.io.ByteArrayOutputStream in a java.io.DataOutputStream (an implementation of java.io.DataOutput) to capture the bytes in the serialized stream:

```
public static byte[] serialize(Writable writable) throws IOException {
  ByteArrayOutputStream out = new ByteArrayOutputStream();
  DataOutputStream dataOut = new DataOutputStream(out);
  writable.write(dataOut);
  dataOut.close();
```

```
    return out.toByteArray();
}
```

An integer is written using four bytes (as we see using JUnit 4 assertions):

```
byte[] bytes = serialize(writable);
assertThat(bytes.length, is(4));
```

The bytes are written in big-endian order (so the most significant byte is written to the stream first, this is dictated by the `java.io.DataOutput` interface), and we can see their hexadecimal representation by using a method on Hadoop's `StringUtils`:

```
assertThat(StringUtils.byteToHexString(bytes), is("000000a3"));
```

Let's try deserialization. Again, we create a helper method to read a `Writable` object from a byte array:

```
public static byte[] deserialize(Writable writable, byte[] bytes)
    throws IOException {
  ByteArrayInputStream in = new ByteArrayInputStream(bytes);
  DataInputStream dataIn = new DataInputStream(in);
  writable.readFields(dataIn);
  dataIn.close();
  return bytes;
}
```

We construct a new, value-less, `IntWritable`, then call `deserialize()` to read from the output data that we just wrote. Then we check that its value, retrieved using the `get()` method, is the original value, 163:

```
IntWritable newWritable = new IntWritable();
deserialize(newWritable, bytes);
assertThat(newWritable.get(), is(163));
```

WritableComparable and comparators

`IntWritable` implements the `WritableComparable` interface, which is just a subinterface of the `Writable` and `java.lang.Comparable` interfaces:

```
package org.apache.hadoop.io;

public interface WritableComparable<T> extends Writable, Comparable<T> {
}
```

Comparison of types is crucial for MapReduce, where there is a sorting phase during which keys are compared with one another. One optimization that Hadoop provides is the `RawComparator` extension of Java's `Comparator`:

```
package org.apache.hadoop.io;

import java.util.Comparator;

public interface RawComparator<T> extends Comparator<T> {

  public int compare(byte[] b1, int s1, int l1, byte[] b2, int s2, int l2);
```

```
        }
```

This interface permits implementors to compare records read from a stream without deserializing them into objects, thereby avoiding any overhead of object creation. For example, the comparator for `IntWritable`s implements the raw `compare()` method by reading an integer from each of the byte arrays `b1` and `b2` and comparing them directly, from the given start positions (`s1` and `s2`) and lengths (`l1` and `l2`).

`WritableComparator` is a general-purpose implementation of `RawComparator` for `WritableComparable` classes. It provides two main functions. First, it provides a default implementation of the raw `compare()` method that deserializes the objects to be compared from the stream and invokes the object `compare()` method. Second, it acts as a factory for `RawComparator` instances (that `Writable` implementations have registered). For example, to obtain a comparator for `IntWritable`, we just use:

```
    RawComparator<IntWritable> comparator = WritableComparator.get(IntWritable.class);
```

The comparator can be used to compare two `IntWritable` objects:

```
    IntWritable w1 = new IntWritable(163);
    IntWritable w2 = new IntWritable(67);
    assertThat(comparator.compare(w1, w2), greaterThan(0));
```

or their serialized representations:

```
    byte[] b1 = serialize(w1);
    byte[] b2 = serialize(w2);
    assertThat(comparator.compare(b1, 0, b1.length, b2, 0, b2.length),
        greaterThan(0));
```

Writable Classes

Hadoop comes with a large selection of `Writable` classes in the `org.apache.hadoop.io` package. They form the class hierarchy shown in Figure 4-1.

Writable wrappers for Java primitives

There are `Writable` wrappers for all the Java primitive types (see Table 4-6) except `short` and `char` (both of which can be stored in an `IntWritable`). All have a `get()` and a `set()` method for retrieving and storing the wrapped value.

Table 4-6. Writable wrapper classes for Java primitives

Java primitive	Writable implementation	Serialized size (bytes)
boolean	BooleanWritable	1
byte	ByteWritable	1
int	IntWritable	4
	VIntWritable	1–5
float	FloatWritable	4

Java primitive	Writable implementation	Serialized size (bytes)
long	LongWritable	8
	VLongWritable	1–9
double	DoubleWritable	8

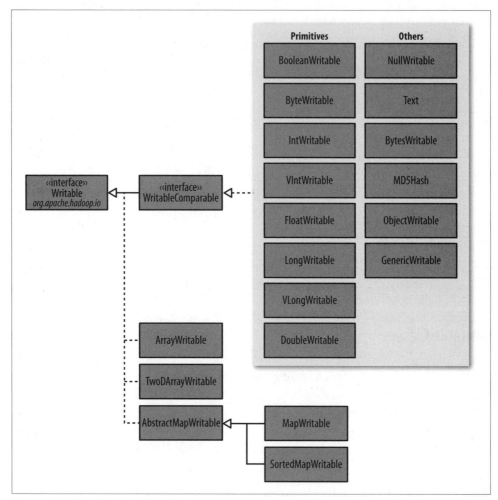

Figure 4-1. Writable class hierarchy

When it comes to encoding integers there is a choice between the fixed-length formats (IntWritable and LongWritable) and the variable-length formats (VIntWritable and VLongWritable). The variable-length formats use only a single byte to encode the value if it is small enough (between −112 and 127, inclusive); otherwise, they use the first byte to indicate whether the value is positive or negative, and how many bytes follow. For example, 163 requires two bytes:

```
byte[] data = serialize(new VIntWritable(163));
assertThat(StringUtils.byteToHexString(data), is("8fa3"));
```

How do you choose between a fixed-length and a variable-length encoding? Fixed-length encodings are good when the distribution of values is fairly uniform across the whole value space, such as a (well-designed) hash function. Most numeric variables tend to have nonuniform distributions, and on average the variable-length encoding will save space. Another advantage of variable-length encodings is that you can switch from VIntWritable to VLongWritable, since their encodings are actually the same. So by choosing a variable-length representation, you have room to grow without committing to an 8-byte long representation from the beginning.

Text

Text is a Writable for UTF-8 sequences. It can be thought of as the Writable equivalent of java.lang.String. Text is a replacement for the UTF8 class, which was deprecated because it didn't support strings whose encoding was over 32,767 bytes, and because it used Java's modified UTF-8.

The Text class uses an int (with a variable-length encoding) to store the number of bytes in the string encoding, so the maximum value is 2 GB. Furthermore, Text uses standard UTF-8, which makes it potentially easier to interoperate with other tools that understand UTF-8.

Indexing.   Because of its emphasis on using standard UTF-8, there are some differences between Text and the Java String class. Indexing for the Text class is in terms of position in the encoded byte sequence, not the Unicode character in the string, or the Java char code unit (as it is for String). For ASCII strings, these three concepts of index position coincide. Here is an example to demonstrate the use of the charAt() method:

```
Text t = new Text("hadoop");
assertThat(t.getLength(), is(6));
assertThat(t.getBytes().length, is(6));

assertThat(t.charAt(2), is((int) 'd'));
assertThat("Out of bounds", t.charAt(100), is(-1));
```

Notice that charAt() returns an int representing a Unicode code point, unlike the String variant that returns a char. Text also has a find() method, which is analogous to String's indexOf():

```
Text t = new Text("hadoop");
assertThat("Find a substring", t.find("do"), is(2));
assertThat("Finds first 'o'", t.find("o"), is(3));
assertThat("Finds 'o' from position 4 or later", t.find("o", 4), is(4));
assertThat("No match", t.find("pig"), is(-1));
```

Unicode. When we start using characters that are encoded with more than a single byte, the differences between `Text` and `String` become clear. Consider the Unicode characters shown in Table 4-7.[‡]

Table 4-7. Unicode characters

Unicode code point	U+0041	U+00DF	U+6771	U+10400
Name	LATIN CAPITAL LETTER A	LATIN SMALL LETTER SHARP S	N/A (a unified Han ideograph)	DESERET CAPITAL LETTER LONG I
UTF-8 code units	41	c3 9f	e6 9d b1	f0 90 90 80
Java representation	\u0041	\u00DF	\u6771	\uuD801\uDC00

All but the last character in the table, U+10400, can be expressed using a single Java `char`. U+10400 is a supplementary character and is represented by two Java `char`s, known as a surrogate pair. The tests in Example 4-5 show the differences between `String` and `Text` when processing a string of the four characters from Table 4-7.

Example 4-5. Tests showing the differences between the String and Text classes

```
public class StringTextComparisonTest {

  @Test
  public void string() throws UnsupportedEncodingException {

    String s = "\u0041\u00DF\u6771\uD801\uDC00";
    assertThat(s.length(), is(5));
    assertThat(s.getBytes("UTF-8").length, is(10));

    assertThat(s.indexOf("\u0041"), is(0));
    assertThat(s.indexOf("\u00DF"), is(1));
    assertThat(s.indexOf("\u6771"), is(2));
    assertThat(s.indexOf("\uD801\uDC00"), is(3));

    assertThat(s.charAt(0), is('\u0041'));
    assertThat(s.charAt(1), is('\u00DF'));
    assertThat(s.charAt(2), is('\u6771'));
    assertThat(s.charAt(3), is('\uD801'));
    assertThat(s.charAt(4), is('\uDC00'));

    assertThat(s.codePointAt(0), is(0x0041));
    assertThat(s.codePointAt(1), is(0x00DF));
    assertThat(s.codePointAt(2), is(0x6771));
    assertThat(s.codePointAt(3), is(0x10400));
  }

  @Test
  public void text() {
```

[‡] This example is based on one from the article Supplementary Characters in the Java Platform (*http://java.sun .com/developer/technicalArticles/Intl/Supplementary/*).

```
    Text t = new Text("\u0041\u00DF\u6771\uD801\uDC00");
    assertThat(t.getLength(), is(10));

    assertThat(t.find("\u0041"), is(0));
    assertThat(t.find("\u00DF"), is(1));
    assertThat(t.find("\u6771"), is(3));
    assertThat(t.find("\uD801\uDC00"), is(6));

    assertThat(t.charAt(0), is(0x0041));
    assertThat(t.charAt(1), is(0x00DF));
    assertThat(t.charAt(3), is(0x6771));
    assertThat(t.charAt(6), is(0x10400));
  }
}
```

The test confirms that the length of a String is the number of char code units it contains (5, one from each of the first three characters in the string, and a surrogate pair from the last), whereas the length of a Text object is the number of bytes in its UTF-8 encoding (10 = 1+2+3+4). Similarly, the indexOf() method in String returns an index in char code units, and find() for Text is a byte offset.

The charAt() method in String returns the char code unit for the given index, which in the case of a surrogate pair will not represent a whole Unicode character. The code PointAt() method, indexed by char code unit, is needed to retrieve a single Unicode character represented as an int. In fact, the charAt() method in Text is more like the codePointAt() method than its namesake in String. The only difference is that it is indexed by byte offset.

Iteration. Iterating over the Unicode characters in Text is complicated by the use of byte offsets for indexing, since you can't just increment the index. The idiom for iteration is a little obscure (see Example 4-6): turn the Text object into a java.nio.ByteBuffer, then repeatedly call the bytesToCodePoint() static method on Text with the buffer. This method extracts the next code point as an int and updates the position in the buffer. The end of the string is detected when bytesToCodePoint() returns −1.

Example 4-6. Iterating over the characters in a Text object

```
public class TextIterator {

  public static void main(String[] args) {
    Text t = new Text("\u0041\u00DF\u6771\uD801\uDC00");

    ByteBuffer buf = ByteBuffer.wrap(t.getBytes(), 0, t.getLength());
    int cp;
    while (buf.hasRemaining() && (cp = Text.bytesToCodePoint(buf)) != -1) {
      System.out.println(Integer.toHexString(cp));
    }
  }
}
```

Running the program prints the code points for the four characters in the string:

```
% hadoop TextIterator
41
df
6771
10400
```

Mutability. Another difference with `String` is that `Text` is mutable (like all `Writable` implementations in Hadoop, except `NullWritable`, which is a singleton). You can reuse a `Text` instance by calling one of the `set()` methods on it. For example:

```
Text t = new Text("hadoop");
t.set("pig");
assertThat(t.getLength(), is(3));
assertThat(t.getBytes().length, is(3));
```

 In some situations, the byte array returned by the `getBytes()` method may be longer than the length returned by `getLength()`:

```
Text t = new Text("hadoop");
t.set(new Text("pig"));
assertThat(t.getLength(), is(3));
assertThat("Byte length not shortened", t.getBytes().length, is(6));
```

This shows why it is imperative that you always call `getLength()` when calling `getBytes()`, so you know how much of the byte array is valid data.

Resorting to String. `Text` doesn't have as rich an API for manipulating strings as `java.lang.String`, so in many cases, you need to convert the `Text` object to a `String`. This is done in the usual way, using the `toString()` method.

```
assertThat(new Text("hadoop").toString(), is("hadoop"));
```

BytesWritable

`BytesWritable` is a wrapper for an array of binary data. Its serialized format is an integer field (4 bytes) that specifies the number of bytes to follow, followed by the bytes themselves. For example, the byte array of length two with values 3 and 5 is serialized as a 4-byte integer (`00000002`) followed by the two bytes from the array (`03` and `05`):

```
BytesWritable b = new BytesWritable(new byte[] { 3, 5 });
byte[] bytes = serialize(b);
assertThat(StringUtils.byteToHexString(bytes), is("000000020305"));
```

`BytesWritable` is mutable, and its value may be changed by calling its `set()` method. As with `Text`, the size of the byte array returned from the `getBytes()` method for `Byte sWritable`—the capacity—may not reflect the actual size of the data stored in the `BytesWritable`. You can determine the size of the `BytesWritable` by calling `get Length()`. To demonstrate:

```
b.setCapacity(11);
assertThat(b.getLength(), is(2));
assertThat(b.getBytes().length, is(11));
```

NullWritable

NullWritable is a special type of Writable, as it has a zero-length serialization. No bytes are written to, or read from, the stream. It is used as a placeholder; for example, in MapReduce, a key or a value can be declared as a NullWritable when you don't need to use that position—it effectively stores a constant empty value. NullWritable can also be useful as a key in SequenceFile when you want to store a list of values, as opposed to key-value pairs. It is an immutable singleton: the instance can be retrieved by calling NullWritable.get().

ObjectWritable and GenericWritable

ObjectWritable is a general-purpose wrapper for the following: Java primitives, String, enum, Writable, null, or arrays of any of these types. It is used in Hadoop RPC to marshal and unmarshal method arguments and return types.

ObjectWritable is useful when a field can be of more than one type: for example, if the values in a SequenceFile have multiple types, then you can declare the value type as an ObjectWritable and wrap each type in an ObjectWritable. Being a general-purpose mechanism, it's fairly wasteful of space since it writes the classname of the wrapped type every time it is serialized. In cases where the number of types is small and known ahead of time, this can be improved by having a static array of types, and using the index into the array as the serialized reference to the type. This is the approach that GenericWritable takes, and you have to subclass it to specify the types to support.

Writable collections

There are four Writable collection types in the org.apache.hadoop.io package: Array Writable, TwoDArrayWritable, MapWritable, and SortedMapWritable.

ArrayWritable and TwoDArrayWritable are Writable implementations for arrays and two-dimensional arrays (array of arrays) of Writable instances. All the elements of an ArrayWritable or a TwoDArrayWritable must be instances of the same class, which is specified at construction, as follows:

```
ArrayWritable writable = new ArrayWritable(Text.class);
```

In contexts where the Writable is defined by type, such as in SequenceFile keys or values, or as input to MapReduce in general, you need to subclass ArrayWritable (or TwoDArrayWritable, as appropriate) to set the type statically. For example:

```
public class TextArrayWritable extends ArrayWritable {
  public TextArrayWritable() {
    super(Text.class);
  }
}
```

ArrayWritable and TwoDArrayWritable both have get() and set() methods, as well as a toArray() method, which creates a shallow copy of the array (or 2D array).

MapWritable and SortedMapWritable are implementations of java.util.Map<Writable, Writable> and java.util.SortedMap<WritableComparable, Writable>, respectively. The type of each key and value field is a part of the serialization format for that field. The type is stored as a single byte that acts as an index into an array of types. The array is populated with the standard types in the org.apache.hadoop.io package, but custom Writable types are accommodated, too, by writing a header that encodes the type array for nonstandard types. As they are implemented, MapWritable and SortedMapWritable use positive **byte** values for custom types, so a maximum of 127 distinct nonstandard Writable classes can be used in any particular MapWritable or SortedMapWritable instance. Here's a demonstration of using a MapWritable with different types for keys and values:

```
MapWritable src = new MapWritable();
src.put(new IntWritable(1), new Text("cat"));
src.put(new VIntWritable(2), new LongWritable(163));

MapWritable dest = new MapWritable();
WritableUtils.cloneInto(dest, src);
assertThat((Text) dest.get(new IntWritable(1)), is(new Text("cat")));
assertThat((LongWritable) dest.get(new VIntWritable(2)), is(new LongWritable(163)));
```

Conspicuous by their absence are Writable collection implementations for sets and lists. A set can be emulated by using a MapWritable (or a SortedMapWritable for a sorted set), with NullWritable values. For lists of a single type of Writable, ArrayWritable is adequate, but to store different types of Writable in a single list, you can use GenericWritable to wrap the elements in an ArrayWritable. Alternatively, you could write a general ListWritable using the ideas from MapWritable.

Implementing a Custom Writable

Hadoop comes with a useful set of Writable implementations that serve most purposes; however, on occasion, you may need to write your own custom implementation. With a custom Writable, you have full control over the binary representation and the sort order. Because Writables are at the heart of the MapReduce data path, tuning the binary representation can have a significant effect on performance. The stock Writable implementations that come with Hadoop are well-tuned, but for more elaborate structures, it is often better to create a new Writable type, rather than compose the stock types.

To demonstrate how to create a custom Writable, we shall write an implementation that represents a pair of strings, called TextPair. The basic implementation is shown in Example 4-7.

Example 4-7. A Writable implementation that stores a pair of Text objects

```
import java.io.*;

import org.apache.hadoop.io.*;
```

```java
public class TextPair implements WritableComparable<TextPair> {

  private Text first;
  private Text second;

  public TextPair() {
    set(new Text(), new Text());
  }

  public TextPair(String first, String second) {
    set(new Text(first), new Text(second));
  }

  public TextPair(Text first, Text second) {
    set(first, second);
  }

  public void set(Text first, Text second) {
    this.first = first;
    this.second = second;
  }

  public Text getFirst() {
    return first;
  }

  public Text getSecond() {
    return second;
  }

  @Override
  public void write(DataOutput out) throws IOException {
    first.write(out);
    second.write(out);
  }

  @Override
  public void readFields(DataInput in) throws IOException {
    first.readFields(in);
    second.readFields(in);
  }

  @Override
  public int hashCode() {
    return first.hashCode() * 163 + second.hashCode();
  }

  @Override
  public boolean equals(Object o) {
    if (o instanceof TextPair) {
      TextPair tp = (TextPair) o;
      return first.equals(tp.first) && second.equals(tp.second);
    }
    return false;
  }
```

```
  @Override
  public String toString() {
    return first + "\t" + second;
  }

  @Override
  public int compareTo(TextPair tp) {
    int cmp = first.compareTo(tp.first);
    if (cmp != 0) {
      return cmp;
    }
    return second.compareTo(tp.second);
  }
}
```

The first part of the implementation is straightforward: there are two `Text` instance variables, `first` and `second`, and associated constructors, getters, and setters. All `Writable` implementations must have a default constructor so that the MapReduce framework can instantiate them, then populate their fields by calling `readFields()`. Writable instances are mutable and often reused, so you should take care to avoid allocating objects in the `write()` or `readFields()` methods.

`TextPair`'s `write()` method serializes each `Text` object in turn to the output stream, by delegating to the `Text` objects themselves. Similarly, `readFields()` deserializes the bytes from the input stream by delegating to each `Text` object. The `DataOutput` and `DataInput` interfaces have a rich set of methods for serializing and deserializing Java primitives, so, in general, you have complete control over the wire format of your `Writable` object.

Just as you would for any value object you write in Java, you should override the `hashCode()`, `equals()`, and `toString()` methods from `java.lang.Object`. The `hashCode()` method is used by the `HashPartitioner` (the default partitioner in MapReduce) to choose a reduce partition, so you should make sure that you write a good hash function that mixes well to ensure reduce partitions are of a similar size.

 If you ever plan to use your custom `Writable` with `TextOutputFormat`, then you must implement its `toString()` method. `TextOutputFormat` calls `toString()` on keys and values for their output representation. For `Text Pair`, we write the underlying `Text` objects as strings separated by a tab character.

`TextPair` is an implementation of `WritableComparable`, so it provides an implementation of the `compareTo()` method that imposes the ordering you would expect: it sorts by the first string followed by the second. Notice that `TextPair` differs from `TextArrayWrita ble` from the previous section (apart from the number of `Text` objects it can store), since `TextArrayWritable` is only a `Writable`, not a `WritableComparable`.

Implementing a RawComparator for speed

The code for TextPair in Example 4-7 will work as it stands; however, there is a further optimization we can make. As explained in "WritableComparable and comparators" on page 88, when TextPair is being used as a key in MapReduce, it will have to be deserialized into an object for the compareTo() method to be invoked. What if it were possible to compare two TextPair objects just by looking at their serialized representations?

It turns out that we can do this, since TextPair is the concatenation of two Text objects, and the binary representation of a Text object is a variable-length integer containing the number of bytes in the UTF-8 representation of the string, followed by the UTF-8 bytes themselves. The trick is to read the initial length, so we know how long the first Text object's byte representation is; then we can delegate to Text's RawComparator, and invoke it with the appropriate offsets for the first or second string. Example 4-8 gives the details (note that this code is nested in the TextPair class).

Example 4-8. A RawComparator for comparing TextPair byte representations

```
public static class Comparator extends WritableComparator {

  private static final Text.Comparator TEXT_COMPARATOR = new Text.Comparator();

  public Comparator() {
    super(TextPair.class);
  }

  @Override
  public int compare(byte[] b1, int s1, int l1,
                     byte[] b2, int s2, int l2) {

    try {
      int firstL1 = WritableUtils.decodeVIntSize(b1[s1]) + readVInt(b1, s1);
      int firstL2 = WritableUtils.decodeVIntSize(b2[s2]) + readVInt(b2, s2);
      int cmp = TEXT_COMPARATOR.compare(b1, s1, firstL1, b2, s2, firstL2);
      if (cmp != 0) {
        return cmp;
      }
      return TEXT_COMPARATOR.compare(b1, s1 + firstL1, l1 - firstL1,
                                     b2, s2 + firstL2, l2 - firstL2);
    } catch (IOException e) {
      throw new IllegalArgumentException(e);
    }
  }
}

static {
  WritableComparator.define(TextPair.class, new Comparator());
}
```

We actually subclass WritableComparator rather than implement RawComparator directly, since it provides some convenience methods and default implementations. The

subtle part of this code is calculating `firstL1` and `firstL2`, the lengths of the first
`Text` field in each byte stream. Each is made up of the length of the variable-length
integer (returned by `decodeVIntSize()` on `WritableUtils`), and the value it is encoding
(returned by `readVInt()`).

The static block registers the raw comparator so that whenever MapReduce sees the
`TextPair` class, it knows to use the raw comparator as its default comparator.

Custom comparators

As we can see with `TextPair`, writing raw comparators takes some care, since you have
to deal with details at the byte level. It is worth looking at some of the implementations
of `Writable` in the `org.apache.hadoop.io` package for further ideas, if you need to write
your own. The utility methods on `WritableUtils` are very handy too.

Custom comparators should also be written to be `RawComparator`s, if possible. These
are comparators that implement a different sort order to the natural sort order defined
by the default comparator. Example 4-9 shows a comparator for `TextPair`, called `First
Comparator`, that considers only the first string of the pair. Note that we override the
`compare()` method that takes objects so both `compare()` methods have the same
semantics.

We will make use of this comparator in Chapter 8, when we look at joins and secondary
sorting in MapReduce (see "Joins" on page 233).

Example 4-9. A custom RawComparator for comparing the first field of TextPair byte representations

```
public static class FirstComparator extends WritableComparator {

  private static final Text.Comparator TEXT_COMPARATOR = new Text.Comparator();

  public FirstComparator() {
    super(TextPair.class);
  }

  @Override
  public int compare(byte[] b1, int s1, int l1,
                     byte[] b2, int s2, int l2) {

    try {
      int firstL1 = WritableUtils.decodeVIntSize(b1[s1]) + readVInt(b1, s1);
      int firstL2 = WritableUtils.decodeVIntSize(b2[s2]) + readVInt(b2, s2);
      return TEXT_COMPARATOR.compare(b1, s1, firstL1, b2, s2, firstL2);
    } catch (IOException e) {
      throw new IllegalArgumentException(e);
    }
  }

  @Override
  public int compare(WritableComparable a, WritableComparable b) {
    if (a instanceof TextPair && b instanceof TextPair) {
      return ((TextPair) a).first.compareTo(((TextPair) b).first);
```

```
    }
    return super.compare(a, b);
  }
}
```

Serialization Frameworks

Although most MapReduce programs use `Writable` key and value types, this isn't mandated by the MapReduce API. In fact, any types can be used; the only requirement is that there be a mechanism that translates to and from a binary representation of each type.

To support this, Hadoop has an API for pluggable serialization frameworks. A serialization framework is represented by an implementation of `Serialization` (in the `org.apache.hadoop.io.serializer` package). `WritableSerialization`, for example, is the implementation of `Serialization` for `Writable` types.

A `Serialization` defines a mapping from types to `Serializer` instances (for turning an object into a byte stream) and `Deserializer` instances (for turning a byte stream into an object).

Set the `io.serializations` property to a comma-separated list of classnames to register `Serialization` implementations. Its default value is `org.apache.hadoop.io.serializer.WritableSerialization`, which means that only `Writable` objects can be serialized or deserialized out of the box.

Hadoop includes a class called `JavaSerialization` that uses Java Object Serialization. Although making it convenient to be able to use standard Java types in MapReduce programs, like `Integer` or `String`, Java Object Serialization is not as efficient as Writables, so it's not worth making this trade-off (see the sidebar).

Why Not Use Java Object Serialization?

Java comes with its own serialization mechanism, called Java Object Serialization (often referred to simply as "Java Serialization"), that is tightly integrated with the language, so it's natural to ask why this wasn't used in Hadoop. Here's what Doug Cutting said in response to that question:

> Why didn't I use Serialization when we first started Hadoop? Because it looked big and hairy and I thought we needed something lean and mean, where we had precise control over exactly how objects are written and read, since that is central to Hadoop. With Serialization you can get some control, but you have to fight for it.
>
> The logic for not using RMI was similar. Effective, high-performance inter-process communications are critical to Hadoop. I felt like we'd need to precisely control how things like connections, timeouts and buffers are handled, and RMI gives you little control over those.

The problem is that Java Serialization doesn't meet the criteria for a serialization format listed earlier: compact, fast, extensible, and interoperable.

Java Serialization is not compact: it writes the classname of each object being written to the stream—this is true of classes that implement `java.io.Serializable` or `java.io.Externalizable`. Subsequent instances of the same class write a reference handle to the first occurrence, which occupies only 5 bytes. However, reference handles don't work well with random access, since the referent class may occur at any point in the preceding stream—that is, there is state stored in the stream. Even worse, reference handles play havoc with sorting records in a serialized stream, since the first record of a particular class is distinguished and must be treated as a special case.

All these problems are avoided by not writing the classname to the stream at all, which is the approach that Writable takes. This makes the assumption that the client knows the expected type. The result is that the format is considerably more compact than Java Serialization, and random access and sorting work as expected since each record is independent of the others (so there is no stream state).

Java Serialization is a general-purpose mechanism for serializing graphs of objects, so it necessarily has some overhead for serialization and deserialization operations. What's more, the deserialization procedure creates a new instance for each object deserialized from the stream. Writable objects, on the other hand, can be (and often are) reused. For example, for a MapReduce job, which at its core serializes and deserializes billions of records of just a handful of different types, the savings gained by not having to allocate new objects are significant.

In terms of extensibility, Java Serialization has some support for evolving a type, but it is brittle and hard to use effectively (Writables have no support: the programmer has to manage them himself).

In principle, other languages could interpret the Java Serialization stream protocol (defined by the Java Object Serialization Specification), but in practice there are no widely used implementations in other languages, so it is a Java-only solution. The situation is the same for Writables.

Serialization IDL

There are a number of other serialization frameworks that approach the problem in a different way: rather than defining types through code, you define them in a language-neutral, declarative fashion, using an *interface description language* (IDL). The system can then generate types for different languages, which is good for interoperability. They also typically define versioning schemes that make type evolution straightforward.

Hadoop's own Record I/O (found in the `org.apache.hadoop.record` package) has an IDL that is compiled into Writable objects, which makes it convenient for generating types that are compatible with MapReduce. For whatever reason, however, Record I/O is not widely used.

Apache Thrift (*http://incubator.apache.org/thrift/*) and Google Protocol Buffers (*http://code.google.com/p/protobuf/*) are both popular serialization frameworks, and they are commonly used as a format for persistent binary data. There is limited support for these as MapReduce formats;[§] however, Thrift is used in parts of Hadoop to provide cross-language APIs, such as the "thriftfs" contrib module, where it is used to expose an API to Hadoop filesystems (see "Thrift" on page 49).

Finally, Avro is a new (at the time of this writing) Hadoop subproject that defines a serialization format. The goal is to migrate Hadoop's RPC mechanism to use Avro. Avro will also be suitable as a data format for large files.

File-Based Data Structures

For some applications, you need a specialized data structure to hold your data. For doing MapReduce-based processing, putting each blob of binary data into its own file doesn't scale, so Hadoop developed a number of higher-level containers for these situations.

SequenceFile

Imagine a logfile, where each log record is a new line of text. If you want to log binary types, plain text isn't a suitable format. Hadoop's `SequenceFile` class fits the bill in this situation, providing a persistent data structure for binary key-value pairs. To use it as a logfile format, you would choose a key, such as timestamp represented by a `LongWrit` `able`, and the value is a `Writable` that represents the quantity being logged.

`SequenceFile`s also work well as containers for smaller files. HDFS and MapReduce are optimized for large files, so packing files into a `SequenceFile` makes storing and processing the smaller files more efficient. ("Processing a whole file as a record" on page 192 contains a program to pack files into a `SequenceFile`.[‖])

Writing a SequenceFile

To create a `SequenceFile`, use one of its `createWriter()` static methods, which returns a `SequenceFile.Writer` instance. There are several overloaded versions, but they all require you to specify a stream to write to (either a `FSDataOutputStream` or a `FileSys` `tem` and `Path` pairing), a `Configuration` object, and the key and value types. Optional arguments include the compression type and codec, a `Progressable` callback to be informed of write progress, and a `Metadata` instance to be stored in the `SequenceFile` header.

The keys and values stored in a `SequenceFile` do not necessarily need to be `Writable`. Any types that can be serialized and deserialized by a `Serialization` may be used.

[§] You can find the latest status for a Thrift `Serialization` at *https://issues.apache.org/jira/browse/HADOOP* *-3787*, and a Protocol Buffers `Serialization` at *https://issues.apache.org/jira/browse/HADOOP-3788*.

[‖] In a similar vein, the blog post "A Million Little Files" by Stuart Sierra includes code for converting a *tar* file into a `SequenceFile` *http://stuartsierra.com/2008/04/24/a-million-little-files*.

Once you have a `SequenceFile.Writer`, you then write key-value pairs, using the `append()` method. Then when you've finished you call the `close()` method (Sequence File.Writer implements `java.io.Closeable`).

Example 4-10 shows a short program to write some key-value pairs to a Sequence File, using the API just described.

Example 4-10. Writing a SequenceFile

```
public class SequenceFileWriteDemo {

  private static final String[] DATA = {
    "One, two, buckle my shoe",
    "Three, four, shut the door",
    "Five, six, pick up sticks",
    "Seven, eight, lay them straight",
    "Nine, ten, a big fat hen"
  };

  public static void main(String[] args) throws IOException {
    String uri = args[0];
    Configuration conf = new Configuration();
    FileSystem fs = FileSystem.get(URI.create(uri), conf);
    Path path = new Path(uri);

    IntWritable key = new IntWritable();
    Text value = new Text();
    SequenceFile.Writer writer = null;
    try {
      writer = SequenceFile.createWriter(fs, conf, path,
          key.getClass(), value.getClass());

      for (int i = 0; i < 100; i++) {
        key.set(100 - i);
        value.set(DATA[i % DATA.length]);
        System.out.printf("[%s]\t%s\t%s\n", writer.getLength(), key, value);
        writer.append(key, value);
      }
    } finally {
      IOUtils.closeStream(writer);
    }
  }
}
```

The keys in the sequence file are integers counting down from 100 to 1, represented as `IntWritable` objects. The values are `Text` objects. Before each record is appended to the `SequenceFile.Writer`, we call the `getLength()` method to discover the current position in the file. (We will use this information about record boundaries in the next section when we read the file nonsequentially.) We write the position out to the console, along with the key and value pairs. The result of running it is shown here:

```
% hadoop SequenceFileWriteDemo numbers.seq
[128]   100     One, two, buckle my shoe
[173]   99      Three, four, shut the door
```

```
[220]    98    Five, six, pick up sticks
[264]    97    Seven, eight, lay them straight
[314]    96    Nine, ten, a big fat hen
[359]    95    One, two, buckle my shoe
[404]    94    Three, four, shut the door
[451]    93    Five, six, pick up sticks
[495]    92    Seven, eight, lay them straight
[545]    91    Nine, ten, a big fat hen
...
[1976]   60    One, two, buckle my shoe
[2021]   59    Three, four, shut the door
[2088]   58    Five, six, pick up sticks
[2132]   57    Seven, eight, lay them straight
[2182]   56    Nine, ten, a big fat hen
...
[4557]   5     One, two, buckle my shoe
[4602]   4     Three, four, shut the door
[4649]   3     Five, six, pick up sticks
[4693]   2     Seven, eight, lay them straight
[4743]   1     Nine, ten, a big fat hen
```

Reading a SequenceFile

Reading sequence files from beginning to end is a matter of creating an instance of `SequenceFile.Reader`, and iterating over records by repeatedly invoking one of the `next()` methods. Which one you use depends on the serialization framework you are using. If you are using `Writable` types, you can use the `next()` method that takes a key and a value argument, and reads the next key and value in the stream into these variables:

```
public boolean next(Writable key, Writable val)
```

The return value is `true` if a key-value pair was read and `false` if the end of the file has been reached.

For other, non-`Writable` serialization frameworks (such as Apache Thrift), you should use these two methods:

```
public Object next(Object key) throws IOException
public Object getCurrentValue(Object val) throws IOException
```

In this case, you need to make sure that the serialization you want to use has been set in the `io.serializations` property; see "Serialization Frameworks" on page 101.

If the `next()` method returns a non-null object, a key-value pair was read from the stream and the value can be retrieved using the `getCurrentValue()` method. Otherwise, if `next()` returns `null`, the end of the file has been reached.

The program in Example 4-11 demonstrates how to read a sequence file that has `Writable` keys and values. Note how the types are discovered from the `Sequence File.Reader` via calls to `getKeyClass()` and `getValueClass()`, then `ReflectionUtils` is used to create an instance for the key and an instance for the value. By using this technique, the program can be used with any sequence file that has `Writable` keys and values.

Example 4-11. Reading a SequenceFile

```java
public class SequenceFileReadDemo {

  public static void main(String[] args) throws IOException {
    String uri = args[0];
    Configuration conf = new Configuration();
    FileSystem fs = FileSystem.get(URI.create(uri), conf);
    Path path = new Path(uri);

    SequenceFile.Reader reader = null;
    try {
      reader = new SequenceFile.Reader(fs, path, conf);
      Writable key = (Writable)
        ReflectionUtils.newInstance(reader.getKeyClass(), conf);
      Writable value = (Writable)
        ReflectionUtils.newInstance(reader.getValueClass(), conf);
      long position = reader.getPosition();
      while (reader.next(key, value)) {
        String syncSeen = reader.syncSeen() ? "*" : "";
        System.out.printf("[%s%s]\t%s\t%s\n", position, syncSeen, key, value);
        position = reader.getPosition(); // beginning of next record
      }
    } finally {
      IOUtils.closeStream(reader);
    }
  }
}
```

Another feature of the program is that it displays the position of the *sync points* in the sequence file. A sync point is a point in the stream which can be used to resynchronize with a record boundary if the reader is "lost"—for example, after seeking to an arbitrary position in the stream. Sync points are recorded by `SequenceFile.Writer`, which inserts a special entry to mark the sync point every few records as a sequence file is being written. Such entries are small enough to incur only a modest storage overhead—less than 1%. Sync points always align with record boundaries.

Running the program in Example 4-11 shows the sync points in the sequence file as asterisks. The first one occurs at position 2021 (the second one occurs at position 4075, but is not shown in the output):

```
% hadoop SequenceFileReadDemo numbers.seq
[128]   100     One, two, buckle my shoe
[173]   99      Three, four, shut the door
[220]   98      Five, six, pick up sticks
[264]   97      Seven, eight, lay them straight
[314]   96      Nine, ten, a big fat hen
[359]   95      One, two, buckle my shoe
[404]   94      Three, four, shut the door
[451]   93      Five, six, pick up sticks
[495]   92      Seven, eight, lay them straight
[545]   91      Nine, ten, a big fat hen
[590]   90      One, two, buckle my shoe
...
```

```
[1976]    60      One, two, buckle my shoe
[2021*]   59      Three, four, shut the door
[2088]    58      Five, six, pick up sticks
[2132]    57      Seven, eight, lay them straight
[2182]    56      Nine, ten, a big fat hen
...
[4557]     5      One, two, buckle my shoe
[4602]     4      Three, four, shut the door
[4649]     3      Five, six, pick up sticks
[4693]     2      Seven, eight, lay them straight
[4743]     1      Nine, ten, a big fat hen
```

There are two ways to seek to a given position in a sequence file. The first is the seek() method, which positions the reader at the given point in the file. For example, seeking to a record boundary works as expected:

```
reader.seek(359);
assertThat(reader.next(key, value), is(true));
assertThat(((IntWritable) key).get(), is(95));
```

But if the position in the file is not at a record boundary, the reader fails when the next() method is called:

```
reader.seek(360);
reader.next(key, value); // fails with IOException
```

The second way to find a record boundary makes use of sync points. The sync(long position) method on SequenceFile.Reader positions the reader at the next sync point after position. (If there are no sync points in the file after this position, then the reader will be positioned at the end of the file.) Thus, we can call sync() with any position in the stream—a nonrecord boundary, for example—and the reader will be reestablish itself at the next sync point so reading can continue:

```
reader.sync(360);
assertThat(reader.getPosition(), is(2021L));
assertThat(reader.next(key, value), is(true));
assertThat(((IntWritable) key).get(), is(59));
```

> SequenceFile.Writer has a method called sync() for inserting a sync point at the current position in the stream. This is not to be confused with the identically named but otherwise unrelated sync() method defined by the Syncable interface for synchronizing buffers to the underlying device.

Sync points come into their own when using sequence files as input to MapReduce, since they permit the file to be split, so different portions of it can be processed independently by separate map tasks. See "SequenceFileInputFormat" on page 199.

Displaying a SequenceFile with the command-line interface

The hadoop fs command has a -text option to display sequence files in textual form. It looks at a file's magic number so that it can attempt to detect the type of the file and appropriately convert it to text. It can recognize gzipped files and sequence files; otherwise, it assumes the input is plain text.

For sequence files, this command is really useful only if the keys and values have a meaningful string representation (as defined by the `toString()` method). Also, if you have your own key or value classes, then you will need to make sure they are on Hadoop's classpath.

Running it on the sequence file we created in the previous section gives the following output:

```
% hadoop fs -text numbers.seq | head
100    One, two, buckle my shoe
99     Three, four, shut the door
98     Five, six, pick up sticks
97     Seven, eight, lay them straight
96     Nine, ten, a big fat hen
95     One, two, buckle my shoe
94     Three, four, shut the door
93     Five, six, pick up sticks
92     Seven, eight, lay them straight
91     Nine, ten, a big fat hen
```

Sorting and merging SequenceFiles

The most powerful way of sorting (and merging) one or more sequence files is to use MapReduce. MapReduce is inherently parallel and will let you specify the number of reducers to use, which determines the number of output partitions. For example, by specifying one reducer, you get a single output file. We can use the sort example that comes with Hadoop by specifying that the input and output are sequence files, and by setting the key and value types:

```
% hadoop jar $HADOOP_INSTALL/hadoop-*-examples.jar sort -r 1 \
  -inFormat org.apache.hadoop.mapred.SequenceFileInputFormat \
  -outFormat org.apache.hadoop.mapred.SequenceFileOutputFormat \
  -outKey org.apache.hadoop.io.IntWritable \
  -outValue org.apache.hadoop.io.Text \
  numbers.seq sorted
% hadoop fs -text sorted/part-00000 | head
1     Nine, ten, a big fat hen
2     Seven, eight, lay them straight
3     Five, six, pick up sticks
4     Three, four, shut the door
5     One, two, buckle my shoe
6     Nine, ten, a big fat hen
7     Seven, eight, lay them straight
8     Five, six, pick up sticks
9     Three, four, shut the door
10    One, two, buckle my shoe
```

Sorting is covered in more detail in "Sorting" on page 218.

As an alternative to using MapReduce for sort/merge, there is a `SequenceFile.Sorter` class that has a number of `sort()` and `merge()` methods. These functions predate Map-Reduce, and are lower-level functions than MapReduce (for example, to get parallelism, you need to partition your data manually), so in general MapReduce is the preferred approach to sort and merge sequence files.

The SequenceFile Format

A sequence file consists of a header followed by one or more records (see Figure 4-2). The first three bytes of a sequence file are the bytes `SEQ`, which acts a magic number, followed by a single byte representing the version number. The header contains other fields including the names of the key and value classes, compression details, user-defined metadata, and the sync marker.[#] Recall that the sync marker is used to allow a reader to synchronize to a record boundary from any position in the file. Each file has a randomly generated sync marker, whose value is stored in the header. Sync markers appear between records in the sequence file. They are designed to incur less than a 1% storage overhead, so they don't necessarily appear between every pair of records (such is the case for short records).

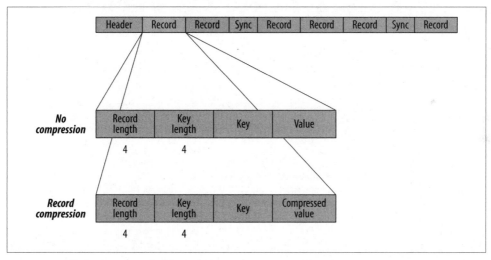

Figure 4-2. The internal structure of a sequence file with no compression and record compression

The internal format of the records depends on whether compression is enabled, and if it is, whether it is record compression or block compression.

[#] Full details of the format of these fields may be found in `SequenceFile`'s documentation (*http://hadoop.apache .org/core/docs/current/api/org/apache/hadoop/io/SequenceFile.html*) and source code.

If no compression is enabled (the default), then each record is made up of the record length (in bytes), the key length, the key and then the value. The length fields are written as four-byte integers adhering to the contract of the `writeInt()` method of `java.io.Data Output`. Keys and values are serialized using the `Serialization` defined for the class being written to the sequence file.

The format for record compression is almost identical to no compression, except the value bytes are compressed using the codec defined in the header. Note that keys are not compressed.

Block compression compresses multiple records at once; it is therefore more compact than and should generally be preferred over record compression because it has the opportunity to take advantage of similarities between records. (See Figure 4-3.) Records are added to a block until it reaches a minimum size in bytes, defined by the `io.seq file.compress.blocksize` property: the default is 1,000,000 bytes. A sync marker is written before the start of every block. The format of a block is a field indicating the number of records in the block, followed by four compressed fields: the key lengths, the keys, the value lengths, and the values.

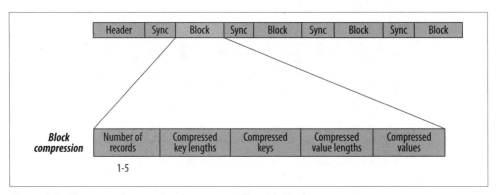

Figure 4-3. The internal structure of a sequence file with block compression

MapFile

A `MapFile` is a sorted `SequenceFile` with an index to permit lookups by key. `MapFile` can be thought of as a persistent form of `java.util.Map` (although it doesn't implement this interface), which is able to grow beyond the size of a `Map` that is kept in memory.

Writing a MapFile

Writing a `MapFile` is similar to writing a `SequenceFile`: you create an instance of `MapFile.Writer`, then call the `append()` method to add entries in order. (Attempting to add entries out of order will result in an `IOException`.) Keys must be instances of `WritableComparable`, and values must be `Writable`—contrast this to `SequenceFile`, which can use any serialization framework for its entries.

The program in Example 4-12 creates a `MapFile`, and writes some entries to it. It is very similar to the program in Example 4-10 for creating a `SequenceFile`.

Example 4-12. Writing a MapFile

```
public class MapFileWriteDemo {

  private static final String[] DATA = {
    "One, two, buckle my shoe",
    "Three, four, shut the door",
    "Five, six, pick up sticks",
    "Seven, eight, lay them straight",
    "Nine, ten, a big fat hen"
  };

  public static void main(String[] args) throws IOException {
    String uri = args[0];
    Configuration conf = new Configuration();
    FileSystem fs = FileSystem.get(URI.create(uri), conf);

    IntWritable key = new IntWritable();
    Text value = new Text();
    MapFile.Writer writer = null;
    try {
      writer = new MapFile.Writer(conf, fs, uri,
          key.getClass(), value.getClass());

      for (int i = 0; i < 1024; i++) {
        key.set(i + 1);
        value.set(DATA[i % DATA.length]);
        writer.append(key, value);
      }
    } finally {
      IOUtils.closeStream(writer);
    }
  }
}
```

Let's use this program to build a `MapFile`:

```
% hadoop MapFileWriteDemo numbers.map
```

If we look at the `MapFile`, we see it's actually a directory containing two files called *data* and *index*:

```
% ls -l numbers.map
total 104
-rw-r--r--   1 tom  tom  47898 Jul 29 22:06 data
-rw-r--r--   1 tom  tom    251 Jul 29 22:06 index
```

Both files are `SequenceFiles`. The *data* file contains all of the entries, in order:

```
% hadoop fs -text numbers.map/data | head
1       One, two, buckle my shoe
2       Three, four, shut the door
3       Five, six, pick up sticks
```

```
4        Seven, eight, lay them straight
5        Nine, ten, a big fat hen
6        One, two, buckle my shoe
7        Three, four, shut the door
8        Five, six, pick up sticks
9        Seven, eight, lay them straight
10       Nine, ten, a big fat hen
```

The *index* file contains a fraction of the keys, and contains a mapping from the key to that key's offset in the *data* file:

```
% hadoop fs -text numbers.map/index
1        128
129      6079
257      12054
385      18030
513      24002
641      29976
769      35947
897      41922
```

As we can see from the output, by default only every 128th key is included in the index, although you can change this value either by setting the `io.map.index.interval` property or by calling the `setIndexInterval()` method on the `MapFile.Writer` instance. A reason to increase the index interval would be to decrease the amount of memory that the `MapFile` needs to store the index. Conversely, you might decrease the interval to improve the time for random (since fewer records need to be skipped on average) at the expense of memory usage.

Since the index is only a partial index of keys, `MapFile` is not able to provide methods to enumerate, or even count, all the keys it contains. The only way to perform these operations is to read the whole file.

Reading a MapFile

Iterating through the entries in order in a `MapFile` is similar to the procedure for a `SequenceFile`: you create a `MapFile.Reader`, then call the `next()` method until it returns `false`, signifying that no entry was read because the end of the file was reached:

```
public boolean next(WritableComparable key, Writable val) throws IOException
```

A random access lookup can be performed by calling the `get()` method:

```
public Writable get(WritableComparable key, Writable val) throws IOException
```

The return value is used to determine if an entry was found in the `MapFile`; if it's `null`, then no value exists for the given key. If `key` was found, then the value for that key is read into `val`, as well as being returned from the method call.

It might be helpful to understand how this is implemented. Here is a snippet of code that retrieves an entry for the `MapFile` we created in the previous section:

```
Text value = new Text();
reader.get(new IntWritable(496), value);
assertThat(value.toString(), is("One, two, buckle my shoe"));
```

For this operation, the `MapFile.Reader` reads the *index* file into memory (this is cached so that subsequent random access calls will use the same in-memory index). The reader then performs a binary search on the in-memory index to find the key in the index that is less than or equal to the search key, 496. In this example, the index key found is 385, with value 18030, which is the offset in the *data* file. Next the reader seeks to this offset in the *data* file and reads entries until the key is greater than or equal to the search key, 496. In this case, a match is found and the value is read from the *data* file. Overall, a lookup takes a single disk seek and a scan through up to 128 entries on disk. For a random-access read, this is actually very efficient.

The `getClosest()` method is like `get()` except it returns the "closest" match to the specified key, rather than returning `null` on no match. More precisely, if the `MapFile` contains the specified key then that is the entry returned; otherwise, the key in the `MapFile` that is immediately after (or before, according to a `boolean` argument) the specified key is returned.

A very large `MapFile`'s index can take up a lot of memory. Rather than reindex to change the index interval, it is possible to load only a fraction of the index keys into memory when reading the `MapFile` by setting the `io.map.index.skip` property. This property is normally 0, which means no index keys are skipped; a value of 1 means skip one key for every key in the index (so every other key ends up in the index), 2 means skip two keys for every key in the index (so one third of the keys end up in the index), and so on. Larger skip values save memory but at the expense of lookup time, since more entries have to be scanned on disk, on average.

Converting a SequenceFile to a MapFile

One way of looking at a `MapFile` is as an indexed and sorted `SequenceFile`. So it's quite natural to want to be able to convert a `SequenceFile` into a `MapFile`. We covered how to sort a `SequenceFile` in "Sorting and merging SequenceFiles" on page 108, so here we look at how to create an index for a `SequenceFile`. The program in Example 4-13 hinges around the static utility method `fix()` on `MapFile`, which recreates the index for a `MapFile`.

Example 4-13. Recreating the index for a MapFile

```
public class MapFileFixer {

  public static void main(String[] args) throws Exception {
    String mapUri = args[0];

    Configuration conf = new Configuration();

    FileSystem fs = FileSystem.get(URI.create(mapUri), conf);
    Path map = new Path(mapUri);
```

```
    Path mapData = new Path(map, MapFile.DATA_FILE_NAME);

    // Get key and value types from data sequence file
    SequenceFile.Reader reader = new SequenceFile.Reader(fs, mapData, conf);
    Class keyClass = reader.getKeyClass();
    Class valueClass = reader.getValueClass();
    reader.close();

    // Create the map file index file
    long entries = MapFile.fix(fs, map, keyClass, valueClass, false, conf);
    System.out.printf("Created MapFile %s with %d entries\n", map, entries);
  }
}
```

The fix() method is usually used for recreating corrupted indexes, but since it creates a new index from scratch, it's exactly what we need here. The recipe is as follows:

1. Sort the sequence file *numbers.seq* into a new directory called *number.map* that will become the MapFile. (If the sequence file is already sorted, then you can skip this step. Instead, copy it to a file *number.map/data*, then go to step 3.)

    ```
    % hadoop jar $HADOOP_INSTALL/hadoop-*-examples.jar sort -r 1 \
      -inFormat org.apache.hadoop.mapred.SequenceFileInputFormat \
      -outFormat org.apache.hadoop.mapred.SequenceFileOutputFormat \
      -outKey org.apache.hadoop.io.IntWritable \
      -outValue org.apache.hadoop.io.Text \
      numbers.seq numbers.map
    ```

2. Rename the MapReduce output to be the *data* file:

    ```
    % hadoop fs -mv numbers.map/part-00000 numbers.map/data
    ```

3. Create the *index* file:

    ```
    % hadoop MapFileFixer numbers.map
    Created MapFile numbers.map with 100 entries
    ```

The MapFile *numbers.map* now exists and can be used.

## CHAPTER 5

Developing a MapReduce Application

In Chapter 2, we introduced the MapReduce model. In this chapter, we look at the practical aspects of developing a MapReduce application in Hadoop.

Writing a program in MapReduce has a certain flow to it. You start by writing your map and reduce functions, ideally with unit tests to make sure they do what you expect. Then you write a driver program to run a job, which can run from your IDE using a small subset of the data to check that it is working. If it fails, then you can use your IDE's debugger to find the source of the problem. With this information, you can expand your unit tests to cover this case, and improve your mapper or reducer as appropriate to handle such input correctly.

When the program runs as expected against the small dataset, you are ready to unleash it on a cluster. Running against the full dataset is likely to expose some more issues, which you can fix as before, by expanding your tests and mapper or reducer to handle the new cases. Debugging failing programs in the cluster is a challenge, but Hadoop provides some tools to help, such as an `IsolationRunner`, which allows you to run a task over the same input on which it failed, with a debugger attached, if necessary.

After the program is working, you may wish to do some tuning, first by running through some standard checks for making MapReduce programs faster and then by doing task profiling. Profiling distributed programs is not trivial, but Hadoop has hooks to aid the process.

Before we start writing a MapReduce program, we need to set up and configure the development environment. And to do that, we need to learn a bit about how Hadoop does configuration.

The Configuration API

Components in Hadoop are configured using Hadoop's own configuration API. An instance of the `Configuration` class (found in the `org.apache.hadoop.conf` package) represents a collection of configuration *properties* and their values. Each property is named by a `String`, and the type of a value may be one of several types, including Java primitives such as `boolean`, `int`, `long`, `float`, and other useful types such as `String`, `Class`, `java.io.File`, and collections of `String`s.

`Configuration`s read their properties from *resources*—XML files with a simple structure for defining name-value pairs. See Example 5-1.

Example 5-1. A simple configuration file, configuration-1.xml

```xml
<?xml version="1.0"?>
<configuration>
  <property>
    <name>color</name>
    <value>yellow</value>
    <description>Color</description>
  </property>

  <property>
    <name>size</name>
    <value>10</value>
    <description>Size</description>
  </property>

  <property>
    <name>weight</name>
    <value>heavy</value>
    <final>true</final>
    <description>Weight</description>
  </property>

  <property>
    <name>size-weight</name>
    <value>${size},${weight}</value>
    <description>Size and weight</description>
  </property>
</configuration>
```

Assuming this configuration file is in a file called *configuration-1.xml*, we can access its properties using a piece of code like this:

```
Configuration conf = new Configuration();
conf.addResource("configuration-1.xml");
assertThat(conf.get("color"), is("yellow"));
assertThat(conf.getInt("size", 0), is(10));
assertThat(conf.get("breadth", "wide"), is("wide"));
```

There are a couple of things to note: type information is not stored in the XML file; instead, properties can be interpreted as a given type when they are read. Also, the get() methods allow you to specify a default value, which is used if the property is not defined in the XML file, as in the case of breadth here.

Combining Resources

Things get interesting when more than one resource is used to define a configuration. This is used in Hadoop to separate out the default properties for the system, defined internally in a file called *core-default.xml*, from the site-specific overrides, in *core-site.xml*. The file in Example 5-2 defines the size and weight properties.

Example 5-2. A second configuration file, configuration-2.xml

```xml
<?xml version="1.0"?>
<configuration>
  <property>
    <name>size</name>
    <value>12</value>
  </property>

  <property>
    <name>weight</name>
    <value>light</value>
  </property>
</configuration>
```

Resources are added to a Configuration in order:

```
Configuration conf = new Configuration();
conf.addResource("configuration-1.xml");
conf.addResource("configuration-2.xml");
```

Properties defined in resources that are added later override the earlier definitions. So the size property takes its value from the second configuration file, *configuration-2.xml*:

```
assertThat(conf.getInt("size", 0), is(12));
```

However, properties that are marked as final cannot be overridden in later definitions. The weight property is final in the first configuration file, so the attempt to override it in the second fails and it takes the value from the first:

```
assertThat(conf.get("weight"), is("heavy"));
```

Attempting to override final properties usually indicates a configuration error, so this results in a warning message being logged to aid diagnosis. Administrators mark properties as final in the daemon's site files that they don't want users to change in their client-side configuration files, or job submission parameters.

Variable Expansion

Configuration properties can be defined in terms of other properties, or system properties. For example, the property size-weight in the first configuration file is defined as ${size},${weight}, and these properties are expanded using the values found in the configuration:

```
assertThat(conf.get("size-weight"), is("12,heavy"));
```

System properties take priority over properties defined in resource files:

```
System.setProperty("size", "14");
assertThat(conf.get("size-weight"), is("14,heavy"));
```

This feature is useful for overriding properties on the command line by using -D*property=value* JVM arguments.

Note that while configuration properties can be defined in terms of system properties, unless system properties are redefined using configuration properties, they are *not* accessible through the configuration API. Hence:

```
System.setProperty("length", "2");
assertThat(conf.get("length"), is((String) null));
```

Configuring the Development Environment

The first step is to download the version of Hadoop that you plan to use and unpack it on your development machine (this is described in Appendix A). Then, in your favorite IDE, create a new project and add all the JAR files from the top level of the unpacked distribution and from the *lib* directory to the classpath. You will then be able to compile Java Hadoop programs, and run them in local (standalone) mode within the IDE.

 For Eclipse users, there is a plug-in available for browsing HDFS and launching MapReduce programs. Instructions are available on the Hadoop wiki at *http://wiki.apache.org/hadoop/EclipsePlugIn*.

Managing Configuration

When developing Hadoop applications, it is common to switch between running the application locally and running it on a cluster. In fact, you may have several clusters you work with, or you may have a local "pseudo-distributed" cluster that you like to test on (a pseudo-distributed cluster is one whose daemons all run on the local machine; setting up this mode is covered in Appendix A, too).

One way to accommodate these variations is to have Hadoop configuration files containing the connection settings for each cluster you run against, and specify which one you are using when you run Hadoop applications or tools. As a matter of best practice, it's recommended to keep these files outside Hadoop's installation directory tree, as this makes it easy to switch between Hadoop versions without duplicating or losing settings.

For the purposes of this book, we assume the existence of a directory called *conf* that contains three configuration files: *hadoop-local.xml*, *hadoop-localhost.xml*, and *hadoop-cluster.xml* (these are available in the example code for this book). Note that there is nothing special about the names of these files—they are just convenient ways to package up some configuration settings. (Compare this to Table A-1 in Appendix A, which sets out the equivalent server-side configurations.)

The *hadoop-local.xml* file contains the default Hadoop configuration for the default filesystem and the jobtracker:

```xml
<?xml version="1.0"?>
<configuration>

  <property>
    <name>fs.default.name</name>
    <value>file:///</value>
  </property>

  <property>
    <name>mapred.job.tracker</name>
    <value>local</value>
  </property>

</configuration>
```

The settings in *hadoop-localhost.xml* point to a namenode and a jobtracker both running on localhost:

```xml
<?xml version="1.0"?>
<configuration>

  <property>
    <name>fs.default.name</name>
    <value>hdfs://localhost/</value>
  </property>

  <property>
    <name>mapred.job.tracker</name>
    <value>localhost:8021</value>
  </property>

</configuration>
```

Finally, *hadoop-cluster.xml* contains details of the cluster's namenode and jobtracker addresses. In practice, you would name the file after the name of the cluster, rather than "cluster" as we have here:

```xml
<?xml version="1.0"?>
<configuration>

  <property>
    <name>fs.default.name</name>
    <value>hdfs://namenode/</value>
  </property>
```

```
<property>
  <name>mapred.job.tracker</name>
  <value>jobtracker:8021</value>
</property>

</configuration>
```

You can add other configuration properties to these files as needed. For example, if you wanted to set your Hadoop username for a particular cluster, you could do it in the appropriate file.

Setting User Identity

The user identity that Hadoop uses for permissions in HDFS is determined by running the whoami command on the client system. Similarly, the group names are derived from the output of running groups.

If, however, your Hadoop user identity is different from the name of your user account on your client machine, then you can explicitly set your Hadoop username and group names by setting the hadoop.job.ugi property. The username and group names are specified as a comma-separated list of strings; e.g., preston,director,inventor would set the username to preston and the group names to director and inventor.

You can set the user identity that the HDFS web interface runs as by setting dfs.web.ugi using the same syntax. By default it is webuser,webgroup, which is not a super user, so system files are not accessible through the web interface.

Notice that there is no authentication with this system, a limitation that a future version of Hadoop will remedy.

With this setup, it is easy to use any configuration with the -conf command-line switch. For example, the following command shows a directory listing on the HDFS server running in pseudo-distributed mode on localhost:

```
% hadoop fs -conf conf/hadoop-localhost.xml -ls .
Found 2 items
drwxr-xr-x   - tom supergroup          0 2009-04-08 10:32 /user/tom/input
drwxr-xr-x   - tom supergroup          0 2009-04-08 13:09 /user/tom/output
```

If you omit the -conf option, then you pick up the Hadoop configuration in the *conf* subdirectory under $HADOOP_INSTALL. Depending on how you set this up, this may be for a standalone setup or a pseudo-distributed cluster.

Tools that come with Hadoop support the -conf option, but it's also straightforward to make your programs (such as programs that run MapReduce jobs) support it, too, using the Tool interface.

GenericOptionsParser, Tool, and ToolRunner

Hadoop comes with a few helper classes for making it easier to run jobs from the command line. GenericOptionsParser is a class that interprets common Hadoop command-line options and sets them on a Configuration object for your application to use as desired. You don't usually use GenericOptionsParser directly, as it's more convenient to implement the Tool interface and run your application with the ToolRunner, which uses GenericOptionsParser internally:

```
public interface Tool extends Configurable {
  int run(String [] args) throws Exception;
}
```

Example 5-3 shows a very simple implementation of Tool, for printing the keys and values of all the properties in the Tool's Configuration object.

Example 5-3. An example Tool implementation for printing the properties in a Configuration

```
public class ConfigurationPrinter extends Configured implements Tool {

  static {
    Configuration.addDefaultResource("hdfs-default.xml");
    Configuration.addDefaultResource("hdfs-site.xml");
    Configuration.addDefaultResource("mapred-default.xml");
    Configuration.addDefaultResource("mapred-site.xml");
  }

  @Override
  public int run(String[] args) throws Exception {
    Configuration conf = getConf();
    for (Entry<String, String> entry: conf) {
      System.out.printf("%s=%s\n", entry.getKey(), entry.getValue());
    }
    return 0;
  }

  public static void main(String[] args) throws Exception {
    int exitCode = ToolRunner.run(new ConfigurationPrinter(), args);
    System.exit(exitCode);
  }
}
```

We make ConfigurationPrinter a subclass of Configured, which is an implementation of the Configurable interface. All implementations of Tool need to implement Configurable (since Tool extends it), and subclassing Configured is often the easiest way to achieve this. The run() method obtains the Configuration using Configurable's getConf() method, and then iterates over it, printing each property to standard output.

The static block makes sure that the HDFS and MapReduce configurations are picked up in addition to the core ones (which Configuration knows about already).

ConfigurationPrinter's main() method does not invoke its own run() method directly. Instead, we call ToolRunner's static run() method, which takes care of creating a

Configuration object for the Tool, before calling its run() method. ToolRunner also uses a GenericOptionsParser to pick up any standard options specified on the command line, and set them on the Configuration instance. We can see the effect of picking up the properties specified in *conf/hadoop-localhost.xml* by running the following command:

```
% hadoop ConfigurationPrinter -conf conf/hadoop-localhost.xml \
  | grep mapred.job.tracker=
mapred.job.tracker=localhost:8021
```

Which Properties Can I Set?

ConfigurationPrinter is a useful tool for telling you what a property is set to in your environment.

You can also see the default settings for all the public properties in Hadoop by looking in the *docs* directory of your Hadoop installation for HTML files called *core-default.html*, *hdfs-default.html*, and *mapred-default.html*. Each property has a description which explains what it is for and what values it can be set to.

Be aware that some properties have no effect when set in the client configuration. For example, if in your job submission you set mapred.tasktracker.map.tasks.maximum with the expectation that it would change the number of task slots for the tasktrackers running your job then you would be disappointed, since this property only is only honored if set in the tasktracker's *mapred-site.html* file. In general, you can tell the component where a property should be set by its name, so the fact that mapred.task tracker.map.tasks.maximum starts with mapred.tasktracker gives you a clue that it can be set only for the tasktracker daemon. This is not a hard and fast rule, however, so in some cases you may need to resort to trial and error, or even reading the source.

We discuss many of Hadoop's most important configuration properties throughout this book. You can find a configuration property reference on the book's website at *http://www.hadoopbook.com*.

GenericOptionsParser also allows you to set individual properties. For example:

```
% hadoop ConfigurationPrinter -D color=yellow | grep color
color=yellow
```

The -D option is used to set the configuration property with key color to the value yellow. Options specified with -D take priority over properties from the configuration files. This is very useful: you can put defaults into configuration files, and then override them with the -D option as needed. A common example of this is setting the number of reducers for a MapReduce job via -D mapred.reduce.tasks=*n*. This will override the number of reducers set on the cluster, or if set in any client-side configuration files.

The other options that GenericOptionsParser and ToolRunner support are listed in Table 5-1. You can find more on Hadoop's configuration API in "The Configuration API" on page 116.

Do not confuse setting Hadoop properties using the -D *property=value* option to GenericOptionsParser (and ToolRunner) with setting JVM system properties using the -D*property=value* option to the java command. The syntax for JVM system properties does not allow any whitespace between the D and the property name, whereas GenericOptionsParser requires them to be separated by whitespace.

JVM system properties are retrieved from the java.lang.System class, whereas Hadoop properties are accessible only from a Configuration object. So, the following command will print nothing, since the System class is not used by ConfigurationPrinter:

```
% hadoop -Dcolor=yellow ConfigurationPrinter | grep color
```

If you want to be able to set configuration through system properties, then you need to mirror the system properties of interest in the configuration file. See "Variable Expansion" on page 117 for further discussion.

Table 5-1. GenericOptionsParser and ToolRunner options

Option	Description
-D *property=value*	Sets the given Hadoop configuration property to the given value. Overrides any default or site properties in the configuration, and any properties set via the -conf option.
-conf *filename* ...	Adds the given files to the list of resources in the configuration. This is a convenient way to set site properties, or to set a number of properties at once.
-fs *uri*	Sets the default filesystem to the given URI. Shortcut for -D fs.default.name=*uri*
-jt *host:port*	Sets the jobtracker to the given host and port. Shortcut for -D mapred.job.tracker=*host:port*
-files *file1,file2,...*	Copies the specified files from the local filesystem (or any filesystem if a scheme is specified) to the shared filesystem used by the jobtracker (usually HDFS) and makes them available to MapReduce programs in the task's working directory. (See "Distributed Cache" on page 239 for more on the distributed cache mechanism for copying files to tasktracker machines.)
-archives *archive1,archive2,...*	Copies the specified archives from the local filesystem (or any filesystem if a scheme is specified) to the shared filesystem used by the jobtracker (usually HDFS), unarchives them, and makes them available to MapReduce programs in the task's working directory.
-libjars *jar1,jar2,...*	Copies the specified JAR files from the local filesystem (or any filesystem if a scheme is specified) to the shared filesystem used by the jobtracker (usually HDFS), and adds them to the MapReduce task's classpath. This option is a useful way of shipping JAR files that a job is dependent on.

Writing a Unit Test

The map and reduce functions in MapReduce are easy to test in isolation, which is a consequence of their functional style. For known inputs, they produce known outputs.

However, since outputs are written to an `OutputCollector`, rather than simply being returned from the method call, the `OutputCollector` needs to be replaced with a mock so that its outputs can be verified. There are several Java mock object frameworks that can help build mocks; here we use Mockito, which is noted for its clean syntax, although any mock framework should work just as well.[*]

All of the tests described here can be run from within an IDE.

Mapper

The test for the mapper is shown in Example 5-4.

Example 5-4. Unit test for MaxTemperatureMapper

```
import static org.mockito.Matchers.anyObject;
import static org.mockito.Mockito.*;

import java.io.IOException;
import org.apache.hadoop.io.*;
import org.apache.hadoop.mapred.OutputCollector;
import org.junit.*;

public class MaxTemperatureMapperTest {

  @Test
  public void processesValidRecord() throws IOException {
    MaxTemperatureMapper mapper = new MaxTemperatureMapper();

    Text value = new Text("0043011990999991950051518004+68750+023550FM-12+0382" +
                                  // Year ^^^^
        "99999V0203201N00261220001CN9999999N9-00111+99999999999");
                                  // Temperature ^^^^^
    OutputCollector<Text, IntWritable> output = mock(OutputCollector.class);

    mapper.map(null, value, output, null);

    verify(output).collect(new Text("1950"), new IntWritable(-11));
  }
}
```

The test is very simple: it passes a weather record as input to the mapper, then checks the output is the year and temperature reading. The input key and `Reporter` are both ignored by the mapper, so we can pass in anything, including `null` as we do here. To create a mock `OutputCollector` we call Mockito's `mock()` method (a static import), passing the class of the type we want to mock. Then we invoke the mapper's `map()` method, which executes the code being tested. Finally, we verify that the mock object was called with the correct method and arguments, using Mockito's **verify()** method (again, statically imported). Here we verify that `OutputCollector`'s `collect()` method

---

[*] See also the MRUnit contrib module, which aims to make unit testing MapReduce programs easier.

was called with a `Text` object representing the year (1950) and an `IntWritable` representing the temperature (–1.1°C).

Proceeding in a test-driven fashion, we create a `Mapper` implementation that passes the test (see Example 5-5). Since we will be evolving the classes in this chapter, each is put in a different package indicating its version for ease of exposition. For example, `v1.MaxTemperatureMapper` is version 1 of `MaxTemperatureMapper`. In reality, of course, you would evolve classes without repackaging them.

Example 5-5. First version of a Mapper that passes MaxTemperatureMapperTest

```
public class MaxTemperatureMapper extends MapReduceBase
  implements Mapper<LongWritable, Text, Text, IntWritable> {

  public void map(LongWritable key, Text value,
      OutputCollector<Text, IntWritable> output, Reporter reporter)
      throws IOException {

    String line = value.toString();
    String year = line.substring(15, 19);
    int airTemperature = Integer.parseInt(line.substring(87, 92));
    output.collect(new Text(year), new IntWritable(airTemperature));
  }
}
```

This is a very simple implementation, which pulls the year and temperature fields from the line and emits them in the `OutputCollector`. Let's add a test for missing values, which in the raw data are represented by a temperature of +9999:

```
@Test
public void ignoresMissingTemperatureRecord() throws IOException {
  MaxTemperatureMapper mapper = new MaxTemperatureMapper();

  Text value = new Text("0043011990999991950051518004+68750+023550FM-12+0382" +
                                  // Year ^^^^
      "99999V0203201N00261220001CN9999999N9+99991+99999999999");
                                  // Temperature ^^^^^
  OutputCollector<Text, IntWritable> output = mock(OutputCollector.class);

  mapper.map(null, value, output, null);

  Text outputKey = anyObject();
  IntWritable outputValue = anyObject();
  verify(output, never()).collect(outputKey, outputValue);
}
```

Since records with missing temperatures should be filtered out, this test uses Mockito to verify that the collect method on the `OutputCollector` is *never* called for any `Text` key or `IntWritable` value.

The existing test fails with a `NumberFormatException`, as `parseInt()` cannot parse integers with a leading plus sign, so we fix up the implementation (version 2) to handle missing values:

```
public void map(LongWritable key, Text value,
    OutputCollector<Text, IntWritable> output, Reporter reporter)
    throws IOException {

  String line = value.toString();
  String year = line.substring(15, 19);
  String temp = line.substring(87, 92);
  if (!missing(temp)) {
      int airTemperature = Integer.parseInt(temp);
      output.collect(new Text(year), new IntWritable(airTemperature));
  }
}

private boolean missing(String temp) {
  return temp.equals("+9999");
}
```

With the test passing, we move on to writing the reducer.

Reducer

The reducer has to find the maximum value for a given key. Here's a simple test for this feature:

```
@Test
public void returnsMaximumIntegerInValues() throws IOException {
  MaxTemperatureReducer reducer = new MaxTemperatureReducer();

  Text key = new Text("1950");
  Iterator<IntWritable> values = Arrays.asList(
      new IntWritable(10), new IntWritable(5)).iterator();
  OutputCollector<Text, IntWritable> output = mock(OutputCollector.class);

  reducer.reduce(key, values, output, null);

  verify(output).collect(key, new IntWritable(10));
}
```

We construct an iterator over some IntWritable values and then verify that MaxTemperatureReducer picks the largest. The code in Example 5-6 is for an implementation of MaxTemperatureReducer that passes the test. Notice that we haven't tested the case of an empty values iterator, but arguably we don't need to, since MapReduce would never call the reducer in this case, as every key produced by a mapper has a value.

Example 5-6. Reducer for maximum temperature example

```
public class MaxTemperatureReducer extends MapReduceBase
  implements Reducer<Text, IntWritable, Text, IntWritable> {

  public void reduce(Text key, Iterator<IntWritable> values,
      OutputCollector<Text, IntWritable> output, Reporter reporter)
      throws IOException {

    int maxValue = Integer.MIN_VALUE;
```

```
    while (values.hasNext()) {
      maxValue = Math.max(maxValue, values.next().get());
    }
    output.collect(key, new IntWritable(maxValue));
  }
}
```

Running Locally on Test Data

Now that we've got the mapper and reducer working on controlled inputs, the next step is to write a job driver and run it on some test data on a development machine.

Running a Job in a Local Job Runner

Using the Tool interface introduced earlier in the chapter, it's easy to write a driver to run our MapReduce job for finding the maximum temperature by year (see MaxTemperatureDriver in Example 5-7).

Example 5-7. Application to find the maximum temperature

```
public class MaxTemperatureDriver extends Configured implements Tool {

  @Override
  public int run(String[] args) throws Exception {
    if (args.length != 2) {
      System.err.printf("Usage: %s [generic options] <input> <output>\n",
          getClass().getSimpleName());
      ToolRunner.printGenericCommandUsage(System.err);
      return -1;
    }

    JobConf conf = new JobConf(getConf(), getClass());
    conf.setJobName("Max temperature");

    FileInputFormat.addInputPath(conf, new Path(args[0]));
    FileOutputFormat.setOutputPath(conf, new Path(args[1]));

    conf.setOutputKeyClass(Text.class);
    conf.setOutputValueClass(IntWritable.class);

    conf.setMapperClass(MaxTemperatureMapper.class);
    conf.setCombinerClass(MaxTemperatureReducer.class);
    conf.setReducerClass(MaxTemperatureReducer.class);

    JobClient.runJob(conf);
    return 0;
  }

  public static void main(String[] args) throws Exception {
    int exitCode = ToolRunner.run(new MaxTemperatureDriver(), args);
    System.exit(exitCode);
```

```
    }
}
```

`MaxTemperatureDriver` implements the `Tool` interface, so we get the benefit of being able to set the options that `GenericOptionsParser` supports. The `run()` method constructs and configures a `JobConf` object, before launching a job described by the `JobConf`. Among the possible job configuration parameters, we set the input and output file paths, the mapper, reducer and combiner classes, and the output types (the input types are determined by the input format, which defaults to `TextInputFormat` and has `Long Writable` keys and `Text` values). It's also a good idea to set a name for the job so that you can pick it out in the job list during execution and after it has completed. By default, the name is the name of the JAR file, which is normally not particularly descriptive.

Now we can run this application against some local files. Hadoop comes with a local job runner, a cut-down version of the MapReduce execution engine for running Map-Reduce jobs in a single JVM. It's designed for testing, and is very convenient for use in an IDE, since you can run it in a debugger to step through the code in your mapper and reducer.

 The local job runner is only designed for simple testing of MapReduce programs, so inevitably it differs from the full MapReduce implementation. The biggest difference is that it can't run more than one reducer. (It can support the zero reducer case, too.) This is normally not a problem, as most applications can work with one reducer, although on a cluster you would choose a larger number to take advantage of parallelism. The thing to watch out for is that even if you set the number of reducers to a value over one, the local runner will silently ignore the setting and use a single reducer.

The local job runner also has no support for the `DistributedCache` feature (described in "Distributed Cache" on page 239).

Neither of these limitations is inherent in the local job runner, and future versions of Hadoop may relax these restrictions.

The local job runner is enabled by a configuration setting. Normally `mapred.job.tracker` is a `host:port` pair to specify the address of the jobtracker, but when it has the special value of `local`, the job is run in-process without accessing an external jobtracker.

From the command line, we can run the driver by typing:

```
% hadoop v2.MaxTemperatureDriver -conf conf/hadoop-local.xml \
  input/ncdc/micro max-temp
```

Equivalently, we could use the `-fs` and `-jt` options provided by `GenericOptionsParser`:

```
% hadoop v2.MaxTemperatureDriver -fs file:/// -jt local input/ncdc/micro max-temp
```

This command executes `MaxTemperatureDriver` using input from the local *input/ncdc/ micro* directory, producing output in the local *max-temp* directory. Note that although we've set `-fs` so we use the local filesystem (`file:///`), the local job runner will actually work fine against any filesystem, including HDFS (and it can be handy to do this if you have a few files that are on HDFS).

When we run the program it fails and prints the following exception:

```
java.lang.NumberFormatException: For input string: "+0000"
```

Fixing the mapper

This exception shows that the map method still can't parse positive temperatures. (If the stack trace hadn't given us enough information to diagnose the fault, we could run the test in a local debugger, since it runs in a single JVM.) Earlier, we made it handle the special case of missing temperature, +9999, but not the general case of any positive temperature. With more logic going into the mapper, it makes sense to factor out a parser class to encapsulate the parsing logic; see Example 5-8 (now on version 3).

Example 5-8. A class for parsing weather records in NCDC format

```java
public class NcdcRecordParser {

  private static final int MISSING_TEMPERATURE = 9999;

  private String year;
  private int airTemperature;
  private String quality;

  public void parse(String record) {
    year = record.substring(15, 19);
    String airTemperatureString;
    // Remove leading plus sign as parseInt doesn't like them
    if (record.charAt(87) == '+') {
      airTemperatureString = record.substring(88, 92);
    } else {
      airTemperatureString = record.substring(87, 92);
    }
    airTemperature = Integer.parseInt(airTemperatureString);
    quality = record.substring(92, 93);
  }

  public void parse(Text record) {
    parse(record.toString());
  }

  public boolean isValidTemperature() {
    return airTemperature != MISSING_TEMPERATURE && quality.matches("[01459]");
  }

  public String getYear() {
    return year;
  }
```

```
  public int getAirTemperature() {
    return airTemperature;
  }
}
```

The resulting mapper is much simpler (see Example 5-9). It just calls the parser's `parse()` method, which parses the fields of interest from a line of input, checks whether a valid temperature was found using the `isValidTemperature()` query method, and if it was retrieves the year and the temperature using the getter methods on the parser. Notice that we also check the quality status field as well as missing temperatures in `isValidTemperature()` to filter out poor temperature readings.

Another benefit of creating a parser class is that it makes it easy to write related mappers for similar jobs without duplicating code. It also gives us the opportunity to write unit tests directly against the parser, for more targeted testing.

Example 5-9. A Mapper that uses a utility class to parse records

```
public class MaxTemperatureMapper extends MapReduceBase
  implements Mapper<LongWritable, Text, Text, IntWritable> {

  private NcdcRecordParser parser = new NcdcRecordParser();

  public void map(LongWritable key, Text value,
      OutputCollector<Text, IntWritable> output, Reporter reporter)
      throws IOException {

    parser.parse(value);
    if (parser.isValidTemperature()) {
      output.collect(new Text(parser.getYear()),
          new IntWritable(parser.getAirTemperature()));
    }
  }
}
```

With these changes, the test passes.

Testing the Driver

Apart from the flexible configuration options offered by making your application implement `Tool`, you also make it more testable because it allows you to inject an arbitrary `Configuration`. You can take advantage of this to write a test that uses a local job runner to run a job against known input data, which checks that the output is as expected.

There are two approaches to doing this. The first is to use the local job runner and run the job against a test file on the local filesystem. The code in Example 5-10 gives an idea of how to do this.

Example 5-10. A test for MaxTemperatureDriver that uses a local, in-process job runner

```
@Test
public void test() throws Exception {
  JobConf conf = new JobConf();
  conf.set("fs.default.name", "file:///");
  conf.set("mapred.job.tracker", "local");

  Path input = new Path("input/ncdc/micro");
  Path output = new Path("output");

  FileSystem fs = FileSystem.getLocal(conf);
  fs.delete(output, true); // delete old output

  MaxTemperatureDriver driver = new MaxTemperatureDriver();
  driver.setConf(conf);

  int exitCode = driver.run(new String[] {
      input.toString(), output.toString() });
  assertThat(exitCode, is(0));

  checkOutput(conf, output);
}
```

The test explicitly sets `fs.default.name` and `mapred.job.tracker` so it uses the local filesystem and the local job runner. It then runs the `MaxTemperatureDriver` via its `Tool` interface against a small amount of known data. At the end of the test, the `checkOut put()` method is called to compare the actual output with the expected output, line by line.

The second way of testing the driver is to run it using a "mini-" cluster. Hadoop has a pair of testing classes, called `MiniDFSCluster` and `MiniMRCluster`, which provide a programmatic way of creating in-process clusters. Unlike the local job runner, these allow testing against the full HDFS and MapReduce machinery. Bear in mind too that task-trackers in a mini-cluster launch separate JVMs to run tasks in, which can make debugging more difficult.

Mini-clusters are used extensively in Hadoop's own automated test suite, but they can be used for testing user code too. Hadoop's `ClusterMapReduceTestCase` abstract class provides a useful base for writing such a test, handles the details of starting and stopping the in-process HDFS and MapReduce clusters in its `setUp()` and `tearDown()` methods, and generating a suitable `JobConf` object that is configured to work with them. Subclasses need populate only data in HDFS (perhaps by copying from a local file), run a MapReduce job, then confirm the output is as expected. Refer to the `MaxTemperature DriverMiniTest` class in the example code that comes with this book for the listing.

Tests like this serve as regression tests, and are a useful repository of input edge cases and their expected results. As you encounter more test cases, you can simply add them to the input file and update the file of expected output accordingly.

Running on a Cluster

Now that we are happy with the program running on a small test dataset, we are ready to try it on the full dataset on a Hadoop cluster. Chapter 9 covers how to set up a fully distributed cluster, although you can also work through this section on a pseudo-distributed cluster.

Packaging

We don't need to make any modifications to the program to run on a cluster rather than on a single machine, but we do need to package the program as a JAR file to send to the cluster. This is conveniently achieved using Ant, using a task such as this (you can find the complete build file in the example code):

```
<jar destfile="job.jar" basedir="${classes.dir}"/>
```

If you have a single job per JAR, then you can specify the main class to run in the JAR file's manifest. If the main class is not in the manifest, then it must be specified on the command line (as you will see shortly). Also, any dependent JAR files should be packaged in a *lib* subdirectory in the JAR file. (This is analogous to a Java *Web application archive*, or WAR file, except in that case the JAR files go in a *WEB-INF/lib* subdirectory in the WAR file.)

Launching a Job

To launch the job, we need to run the driver, specifying the cluster that we want to run the job on with the -conf option (we could equally have used the -fs and -jt options):

```
% hadoop jar job.jar v3.MaxTemperatureDriver -conf conf/hadoop-cluster.xml \
    input/ncdc/all max-temp
```

The runJob() method on JobClient launches the job and polls for progress, writing a line summarizing the map and reduce's progress whenever either changes. Here's the output (some lines have been removed for clarity):

```
09/04/11 08:15:52 INFO mapred.FileInputFormat: Total input paths to process : 101
09/04/11 08:15:53 INFO mapred.JobClient: Running job: job_200904110811_0002
09/04/11 08:15:54 INFO mapred.JobClient:  map 0% reduce 0%
09/04/11 08:16:06 INFO mapred.JobClient:  map 28% reduce 0%
09/04/11 08:16:07 INFO mapred.JobClient:  map 30% reduce 0%
...
09/04/11 08:21:36 INFO mapred.JobClient:  map 100% reduce 100%
09/04/11 08:21:38 INFO mapred.JobClient: Job complete: job_200904110811_0002
09/04/11 08:21:38 INFO mapred.JobClient: Counters: 19
09/04/11 08:21:38 INFO mapred.JobClient:   Job Counters
09/04/11 08:21:38 INFO mapred.JobClient:     Launched reduce tasks=32
09/04/11 08:21:38 INFO mapred.JobClient:     Rack-local map tasks=82
09/04/11 08:21:38 INFO mapred.JobClient:     Launched map tasks=127
09/04/11 08:21:38 INFO mapred.JobClient:     Data-local map tasks=45
09/04/11 08:21:38 INFO mapred.JobClient:   FileSystemCounters
```

```
09/04/11 08:21:38 INFO mapred.JobClient:     FILE_BYTES_READ=12667214
09/04/11 08:21:38 INFO mapred.JobClient:     HDFS_BYTES_READ=33485841275
09/04/11 08:21:38 INFO mapred.JobClient:     FILE_BYTES_WRITTEN=989397
09/04/11 08:21:38 INFO mapred.JobClient:     HDFS_BYTES_WRITTEN=904
09/04/11 08:21:38 INFO mapred.JobClient:   Map-Reduce Framework
09/04/11 08:21:38 INFO mapred.JobClient:     Reduce input groups=100
09/04/11 08:21:38 INFO mapred.JobClient:     Combine output records=4489
09/04/11 08:21:38 INFO mapred.JobClient:     Map input records=1209901509
09/04/11 08:21:38 INFO mapred.JobClient:     Reduce shuffle bytes=19140
09/04/11 08:21:38 INFO mapred.JobClient:     Reduce output records=100
09/04/11 08:21:38 INFO mapred.JobClient:     Spilled Records=9481
09/04/11 08:21:38 INFO mapred.JobClient:     Map output bytes=10282306995
09/04/11 08:21:38 INFO mapred.JobClient:     Map input bytes=274600205558
09/04/11 08:21:38 INFO mapred.JobClient:     Combine input records=1142482941
09/04/11 08:21:38 INFO mapred.JobClient:     Map output records=1142478555
09/04/11 08:21:38 INFO mapred.JobClient:     Reduce input records=103
```

The output includes more useful information. Before the job starts, its ID is printed: this is needed whenever you want to refer to the job, in logfiles for example, or when interrogating it via the hadoop job command. When the job is complete, its statistics (known as counters) are printed out. These are very useful for confirming that the job did what you expected. For example, for this job we can see that around 275 GB of input data was analyzed ("Map input bytes"), read from around 34 GB of compressed files on HDFS ("HDFS_BYTES_READ"). The input was broken into 101 gzipped files of reasonable size, so there was no problem with not being able to split them.

Job, Task, and Task Attempt IDs

The format of a job ID is composed of the time that the jobtracker (not the job) started, and an incrementing counter maintained by the jobtracker to uniquely identify the job to that instance of the jobtracker. So the job with this ID:

```
job_200904110811_0002
```

is the second (0002, job IDs are 1-based) job run by the jobtracker which started at 08:11 on April 11, 2009. The counter is formatted with leading zeros to make job IDs sort nicely—in directory listings, for example. However, when the counter reaches 10000 it is *not* reset, resulting in longer job IDs (which don't sort so well).

Tasks belong to a job, and their IDs are formed by replacing the job prefix of a job ID with a task prefix, and adding a suffix to identify the task within the job. For example,

```
task_200904110811_0002_m_000003
```

is the fourth (000003, task IDs are 0-based) map (m) task of the job with ID job_200904110811_0002. The task IDs are created for a job when it is initialized, so they do not necessarily dictate the order that the tasks will be executed in.

Tasks may be executed more than once, due to failure (see "Task Failure" on page 159) or speculative execution (see "Speculative Execution" on page 169), so to identify different instances of a task execution, task attempts are given unique IDs on the jobtracker. For example,

```
attempt_200904110811_0002_m_000003_0
```

is the first (0, attempt IDs are 0-based) attempt at running task task_200904110811_0002_m_000003. Task attempts are allocated during the job run as needed, so their ordering represents the order that they were created for tasktrackers to run.

The final count in the task attempt ID is incremented by one thousand if the job is restarted after the jobtracker is restarted and recovers its running jobs.

The MapReduce Web UI

Hadoop comes with a web UI for viewing information about your jobs. It is useful for following a job's progress while it is running, as well as finding job statistics and logs after the job has completed. You can find the UI at *http://jobtracker-host:50030/*.

The jobtracker page

A screenshot of the home page is shown in Figure 5-1. The first section of the page gives details of the Hadoop installation, such as the version number and when it was compiled, and the current state of the jobtracker (in this case, running), and when it was started.

Next is a summary of the cluster, which has measures of cluster capacity and utilization. This shows the number of maps and reduces currently running on the cluster, the total number of job submissions, the number of tasktracker nodes currently available, and the cluster's capacity: in terms of the number of map and reduce slots available across the cluster ("Map Task Capacity" and "Reduce Task Capacity"), and the number of available slots per node, on average. The number of tasktrackers that have been blacklisted by the jobtracker is listed as well (blacklisting is discussed in "Tasktracker Failure" on page 161).

Below the summary there is a section about the job scheduler that is running (here the default). You can click through to see job queues.

Further down we see sections for running, (successfully) completed, and failed jobs. Each of these sections has a table of jobs, with a row per job that shows the job's ID, owner, name (as set using JobConf's setJobName() method, which sets the mapred.job.name property) and progress information.

Finally, at the foot of the page, there are links to the jobtracker's logs, and the jobtracker's history: information on all the jobs that the jobtracker has run. The main display displays only 100 jobs (configurable via the mapred.jobtracker.completeuser jobs.maximum property), before consigning them to the history page. Note also that the job history is persistent, so you can find jobs here from previous runs of the jobtracker.

Figure 5-1. Screenshot of the jobtracker page

Job History

Job history refers to the events and configuration for a completed job. It is retained whether the job was successful or not. Job history is used to support job recovery after a jobtracker restart (see the `mapred.jobtracker.restart.recover` property), as well as providing interesting information for the user running a job.

Job history files are stored on the local filesystem of the jobtracker in a *history* subdirectory of the logs directory. It is possible to set the location to an arbitrary Hadoop filesystem via the `hadoop.job.history.location` property. The jobtracker's history files are kept for 30 days before being deleted by the system.

A second copy is also stored for the user, in the *_logs/history* subdirectory of the job's output directory. This location may be overridden by setting `hadoop.job.history.user.location`. By setting it to the special value none, no user job history is saved, although job history is still saved centrally. A user's job history files are never deleted by the system.

The history log includes job, task and attempt events, all of which are stored in a plain-text file. The history for a particular job may be viewed through the web UI, or via the command line, using `hadoop job -history` (which you point at the job's output directory).

The job page

Clicking on a job ID brings you to a page for the job, illustrated in Figure 5-2. At the top of the page is a summary of the job, with basic information such as job owner and name, and how long the job has been running for. The job file is the consolidated configuration file for the job, containing all the properties and their values that were in effect during the job run. If you are unsure of what a particular property was set to, you can click through to inspect the file.

While the job is running, you can monitor its progress on this page, which periodically updates itself. Below the summary is a table that shows the map progress and the reduce progress. "Num Tasks" shows the total number of map and reduce tasks for this job (a row for each). The other columns then show the state of these tasks: "Pending" (waiting to run), "Running," "Complete" (successfully run), "Killed" (tasks that have failed—this column would be more accurately labeled "Failed"). The final column shows the total number of failed and killed task attempts for all the map or reduce tasks for the job (task attempts may be marked as killed if they are a speculative execution duplicate, if the tasktracker they are running on dies, or if they are killed by a user). See "Task Failure" on page 159 for background on task failure.

Farther down the page, you can find completion graphs for each task that show their progress graphically. The reduce completion graph is divided into the three phases of the reduce task: copy (when the map outputs are being transferred to the reduce's tasktracker), sort (when the reduce inputs are being merged), and reduce (when the reduce function is being run to produce the final output). The phases are described in more detail in "Shuffle and Sort" on page 163.

In the middle of the page is a table of job counters. These are dynamically updated during the job run, and provide another useful window into the job's progress and general health. There is more information about what these counters mean in "Built-in Counters" on page 211.

Retrieving the Results

Once the job is finished, there are various ways to retrieve the results. Each reducer produces one output file, so there are 30 part files named *part-00000* to *part-00029* in the *max-temp* directory.

Hadoop job_200904110811_0002 on ip-10-250-110-47

User: root
Job Name: Max temperature
Job File: hdfs://ip-10-250-110-47.ec2.internal/mnt/hadoop/mapred/system/job_200904110811_0002/job.xml
Job Setup: Successful
Status: Running
Started at: Sat Apr 11 08:15:53 EDT 2009
Running for: 5mins, 38sec
Job Cleanup: Pending

Kind	% Complete	Num Tasks	Pending	Running	Complete	Killed	Failed/Killed Task Attempts
map	100.00%	101	0	0	101	0	0 / 26
reduce	70.74%	30	0	13	17	0	0 / 0

	Counter	Map	Reduce	Total
Job Counters	Launched reduce tasks	0	0	32
	Rack-local map tasks	0	0	82
	Launched map tasks	0	0	127
	Data-local map tasks	0	0	45
FileSystemCounters	FILE_BYTES_READ	12,665,901	564	12,666,465
	HDFS_BYTES_READ	33,485,841,275	0	33,485,841,275
	FILE_BYTES_WRITTEN	988,084	564	988,648
	HDFS_BYTES_WRITTEN	0	360	360
Map-Reduce Framework	Reduce input groups	0	40	40
	Combine output records	4,489	0	4,489
	Map input records	1,209,901,509	0	1,209,901,509
	Reduce shuffle bytes	0	18,397	18,397
	Reduce output records	0	40	40
	Spilled Records	9,378	42	9,420
	Map output bytes	10,282,306,995	0	10,282,306,995
	Map input bytes	274,600,205,558	0	274,600,205,558
	Map output records	1,142,478,555	0	1,142,478,555
	Combine input records	1,142,482,941	0	1,142,482,941
	Reduce input records	0	42	42

Map Completion Graph - close

Reduce Completion Graph - close

Go back to JobTracker

Hadoop, 2009.

Figure 5-2. Screenshot of the job page

A good way to think of these "part" files is as parts of the *max-temp* "file."

If the output is large (which it isn't in this case), then it is important to have multiple parts so that more than one reducer can work in parallel. Usually, if a file is in this partitioned form, it can still be used easily enough: as the input to another MapReduce job, for example. In some cases, you can exploit the structure of multiple partitions; to do a map-side join, for example, ("Map-Side Joins" on page 233) or a MapFile lookup ("An application: Partitioned MapFile lookups" on page 221).

This job produces a very small amount of output, so it is convenient to copy it from HDFS to our development machine. The `-getmerge` option to the `hadoop fs` command is useful here, as it gets all the files in the directory specified in the source pattern and merges them into a single file on the local filesystem:

```
% hadoop fs -getmerge max-temp max-temp-local
% sort max-temp-local | tail
1991    607
1992    605
1993    567
1994    568
1995    567
1996    561
1997    565
1998    568
1999    568
2000    558
```

We sorted the output, as the reduce output partitions are unordered (owing to the hash partition function). Doing a bit of postprocessing of data from MapReduce is very common, as is feeding it into analysis tools, such as R, a spreadsheet, or even a relational database.

Another way of retrieving the output if it is small is to use the `-cat` option to print the output files to the console:

```
% hadoop fs -cat max-temp/*
```

On closer inspection, we see that some of the results don't look plausible. For instance, the maximum temperature for 1951 (not shown here) is 590°C! How do we find out what's causing this? Is it corrupt input data or a bug in the program?

Debugging a Job

The time-honored way of debugging programs is via print statements, and this is certainly possible in Hadoop. However, there are complications to consider: with programs running on tens, hundreds, or thousands of nodes, how do we find and examine the output of the debug statements, which may be scattered across these nodes? For this particular case, where we are looking for (what we think is) an unusual case, we can use a debug statement to log to standard error, in conjunction with a message to update the task's status message to prompt us to look in the error log. The web UI makes this easy, as you will see.

We also create a custom counter, to count the total number of records with implausible temperatures in the whole dataset. This gives us valuable information about how to deal with the condition—if it turns out to be a common occurrence, then we might need to learn more about the condition and how to extract the temperature in these cases, rather than simply dropping the record. In fact, when trying to debug a job, you should always ask yourself if you can use a counter to get the information you need to find out what's happening. Even if you need to use logging or a status message, it may be useful to use a counter to gauge the extent of the problem. (There is more on counters in "Counters" on page 211.)

If the amount of log data you produce in the course of debugging is large, then you've got a couple of options. The first is to write the information to the map's output, rather than to standard error, for analysis and aggregation by the reduce. This approach usually necessitates structural changes to your program, so start with the other techniques first. Alternatively, you can write a program (in MapReduce of course) to analyze the logs produced by your job. There are tools to make this easier, such as Chukwa, a Hadoop subproject.

We add our debugging to the mapper (version 4), as opposed to the reducer, as we want to find out what the source data causing the anomalous output looks like:

```
public class MaxTemperatureMapper extends MapReduceBase
  implements Mapper<LongWritable, Text, Text, IntWritable> {

  enum Temperature {
    OVER_100
  }

  private NcdcRecordParser parser = new NcdcRecordParser();

  public void map(LongWritable key, Text value,
      OutputCollector<Text, IntWritable> output, Reporter reporter)
      throws IOException {

    parser.parse(value);
    if (parser.isValidTemperature()) {
      int airTemperature = parser.getAirTemperature();
      if (airTemperature > 1000) {
        System.err.println("Temperature over 100 degrees for input: " + value);
        reporter.setStatus("Detected possibly corrupt record: see logs.");
        reporter.incrCounter(Temperature.OVER_100, 1);
      }
      output.collect(new Text(parser.getYear()), new IntWritable(airTemperature));
    }
  }
}
```

If the temperature is over 100°C (represented by 1000, since temperatures are in tenths of a degree), we print a line to standard error with the suspect line, as well as updating the map's status message using the `setStatus()` method on `Reporter` directing us to look in the log. We also increment a counter, which in Java is represented by a field of an enum type. In this program, we have defined a single field `OVER_100` as a way to count the number of records with a temperature of over 100°C.

With this modification, we recompile the code, recreate the JAR file, then rerun the job, and while it's running go to the tasks page.

The tasks page

The job page has a number of links for look at the tasks in a job in more detail. For example, by clicking on the "map" link, you are brought to a page which lists information for all of the map tasks on one page. You can also see just the completed tasks. The screenshot in Figure 5-3 shows a portion of this page for the job run with our debugging statements. Each row in the table is a task, and it provides such information as the start and end times for each task, any errors reported back from the tasktracker, and a link to view the counters for an individual task.

Hadoop map task list for job_200904110811_0003 on ip-10-250-110-47

Completed Tasks

Task	Complete	Status	Start Time	Finish Time	Errors	Counters
task_200904110811_0003_m_000043	100.00%	hdfs://ip-10-250-110-47.ec2.internal/user/root/input/ncdc/all/1949.gz:0+220338475	11-Apr-2009 09:00:06	11-Apr-2009 09:01:25 (1mins, 18sec)		10
task_200904110811_0003_m_000044	100.00%	Detected possibly corrupt record: see logs.	11-Apr-2009 09:00:06	11-Apr-2009 09:01:28 (1mins, 21sec)		11
task_200904110811_0003_m_000045	100.00%	hdfs://ip-10-250-110-47.ec2.internal/user/root/input/ncdc/all/1970.gz:0+208374610	11-Apr-2009 09:00:06	11-Apr-2009 09:01:28 (1mins, 21sec)		10

Figure 5-3. Screenshot of the tasks page

Relevant to debugging is the Status column, which shows a task's latest status message. Before a task starts, it shows its status as "initializing," then once it starts reading records it shows the split information for the split it is reading as a filename with a byte offset and length. You can see the status we set for debugging for task `task_200811201130_0054_m_000000`, so let's click through to the logs page to find the associated debug message. (Notice too that there is an extra counter for this task, since our user counter has a nonzero count for this task.)

The task details page

From the tasks page, you can click on any task to get more information about it. The task details page, shown in Figure 5-4, shows each task attempt. In this case, there was one task attempt, which completed successfully. The table provides further useful data, such as the node the task attempt ran on, and links to task logfiles and counters.

Job job_200904110811_0003

All Task Attempts

Task Attempts	Machine	Status	Progress	Start Time	Finish Time	Errors	Task Logs	Counters	Actions
attempt_200904110811_0003_m_000044_0	/default-rack/ip-10-250-163-143.ec2.internal	SUCCEEDED	100.00%	11-Apr-2009 09:00:06	11-Apr-2009 09:01:25 (1mins, 19sec)		Last 4KB Last 8KB All	11	

Input Split Locations

/default-rack/10.250.202.127
/default-rack/10.250.123.223
/default-rack/10.250.115.79

Go back to the job
Go back to JobTracker

Hadoop, 2009.

Figure 5-4. Screenshot of the task details page

The "Actions" column contains links for killing a task attempt. By default, this is disabled, making the web UI a read-only interface. Set `webinterface.private.actions` to `true` to enable the actions links.

 By setting `webinterface.private.actions` to `true`, you also allow anyone with access to the HDFS web interface to delete files. The `dfs.web.ugi` property determines the user that the HDFS web UI runs as, thus controlling which files may be viewed and deleted.

For map tasks, there is also a section showing which nodes the input split was located on.

By following one of the links to the logfiles for the successful task attempt (you can see the last 4 KB or 8 KB of each logfile, or the entire file), we can find the suspect input record that we logged (the line is wrapped and truncated to fit on the page):

```
Temperature over 100 degrees for input:
0335999999433181957042302005+37950+139117SAO   +0004RJSN V02011359003150070356999994
33201957010100005+35317+139650SAO +000899999V02002359002650076249N004000599+0067...
```

This record seems to be in a different format to the others. For one thing, there are spaces in the line, which are not described in the specification.

When the job has finished, we can look at the value of the counter we defined to see how many records over 100°C there are in the whole dataset. Counters are accessible via the web UI, or the command line:

```
% hadoop job -counter job_200904110811_0003 'v4.MaxTemperatureMapper$Temperature' \
OVER_100
3
```

The -counter option takes the job ID, counter group name (which is the fully qualified classname here), and the counter name (the enum name). There are only three malformed records in the entire dataset of over a billion records. Throwing out bad records is standard for many big data problems, although we need to be careful in this case, since we are looking for an extreme value—the maximum temperature rather than an aggregate measure. Still, throwing away three records is probably not going to change the result.

Hadoop User Logs

Hadoop produces logs in various places, for various audiences. These are summarized in Table 5-2. Many of these files can be analyzed in aggregate using Chukwa, a Hadoop subproject.

As you have seen in this section, MapReduce task logs are accessible through the web UI, which is the most convenient way to view them. You can also find the logfiles on the local filesystem of the tasktracker that ran the task attempt, in a directory named by the task attempt. If task JVM reuse is enabled ("Task JVM Reuse" on page 170), then each logfile accumulates the logs for the entire JVM run, so multiple task attempts will be found in each logfile. The web UI hides this by showing only the portion that is relevant for the task attempt being viewed.

It is straightforward to write to these logfiles. Anything written to standard output, or standard error, is directed to the relevant logfile. (Of course, in Streaming, standard output is used for the map or reduce output, so it will not show up in the standard output log.)

In Java, you can write to the task's *syslog* file if you wish by using the Apache Commons Logging API. The actual logging is done by log4j in this case: the relevant log4j appender is called TLA (Task Log Appender) in the *log4j.properties* file in Hadoop's configuration directory.

There are some controls for managing retention and size of task logs. By default, logs are deleted after a minimum of 24 hours (set using the mapred.userlog.retain.hours property). You can also set a cap on the maximum size of each logfile using the mapred.userlog.limit.kb property, which is 0 by default, meaning there is no cap.

Table 5-2. Hadoop logs

Logs	Primary audience	Description	Further information
System daemon logs	Administrators	Each Hadoop daemon produces a logfile (using log4j) and another file that combines standard out and error. Written in the directory defined by the HADOOP_LOG_DIR environment variable.	"System log-files" on page 256.
HDFS audit logs	Administrators	A log of all HDFS requests, turned off by default. Written to the namenode's log, although this is configurable.	"Audit Log-ging" on page 280.
MapReduce job history logs	Users	A log of the events (such as task completion) that occur in the course of running a job. Saved centrally on the jobtracker, and in the job's output directory in a _logs/history subdirectory.	"Job His-tory" on page 135.
MapReduce task logs	Users	Each tasktracker child process produces a logfile using log4j (called *syslog*), a file for data sent to standard out (*stdout*), and a file for standard error (*stderr*). Written in the *userlogs* sub-directory of the directory defined by the HADOOP_LOG_DIR environment variable.	See next section.

Handling malformed data

Capturing input data that causes a problem is valuable, as we can use it in a test to check that the mapper does the right thing:

```
@Test
public void parsesMalformedTemperature() throws IOException {
  MaxTemperatureMapper mapper = new MaxTemperatureMapper();
  Text value = new Text("0335999999433181957042302005+37950+139117SAO  +0004" +
                              // Year ^^^^
      "RJSN V02011359003150070356999999433201957010100005+353");
                              // Temperature ^^^^^
  OutputCollector<Text, IntWritable> output = mock(OutputCollector.class);
  Reporter reporter = mock(Reporter.class);

  mapper.map(null, value, output, reporter);

  Text outputKey = anyObject();
  IntWritable outputValue = anyObject();
  verify(output, never()).collect(outputKey, outputValue);
  verify(reporter).incrCounter(MaxTemperatureMapper.Temperature.MALFORMED, 1);
}
```

The record that was causing the problem is of a different format to the other lines we've seen. Example 5-11 shows a modified program (version 5) using a parser that ignores each line with a temperature field that does not have a leading sign (plus or minus). We've also introduced a counter to measure the number of records that we are ignoring for this reason.

Example 5-11. Mapper for maximum temperature example

```java
public class MaxTemperatureMapper extends MapReduceBase
  implements Mapper<LongWritable, Text, Text, IntWritable> {

  enum Temperature {
    MALFORMED
  }

  private NcdcRecordParser parser = new NcdcRecordParser();

  public void map(LongWritable key, Text value,
      OutputCollector<Text, IntWritable> output, Reporter reporter)
      throws IOException {

    parser.parse(value);
    if (parser.isValidTemperature()) {
      int airTemperature = parser.getAirTemperature();
      output.collect(new Text(parser.getYear()), new IntWritable(airTemperature));
    } else if (parser.isMalformedTemperature()) {
      System.err.println("Ignoring possibly corrupt input: " + value);
      reporter.incrCounter(Temperature.MALFORMED, 1);
    }
  }
}
```

Using a Remote Debugger

When a task fails and there is not enough information logged to diagnose the error, you may want to resort to running a debugger for that task. This is hard to arrange when running the job on a cluster, as you don't know which node is going to process which part of the input, so you can't set up your debugger ahead of the failure. Instead, you run the job with a property set that instructs Hadoop to keep all the intermediate data generated during the job run. This data can then be used to rerun the failing task in isolation with a debugger attached. Note that the task is run in situ, on the same node that it failed on, which increases the chances of the error being reproducible.[†]

First, set the configuration property keep.failed.task.files to true, so that when tasks fail, the tasktracker keeps enough information to allow the task to be rerun over the same input data. Then run the job again and note which node the task fails on, and the task attempt ID (it begins with the string attempt_) using the web UI.

Next we need to run a special task runner called IsolationRunner with the retained files as input. Log into the node that the task failed on and look for the directory for that task attempt. It will be under one of the local MapReduce directories, as set by the mapred.local.dir property (covered in more detail in "Important Hadoop Daemon Properties" on page 258). If this property is a comma-separated list of directories (to

---

† This feature is currently broken in Hadoop 0.20.0. Track the fix under *https://issues.apache.org/jira/browse/HADOOP-4041*.

spread load across the physical disks on a machine), then you may need to look in all of the directories before you find the directory for that particular task attempt. The task attempt directory is in the following location:

```
mapred.local.dir/taskTracker/jobcache/job-ID/task-attempt-ID
```

This directory contains various files and directories, including *job.xml*, which contains all of the job configuration properties in effect during the task attempt, and which `IsolationRunner` uses to create a `JobConf` instance. For map tasks, this directory also contains a file containing a serialized representation of the input split, so the same input data can be fetched for the task. For reduce tasks, a copy of the map output, which forms the reduce input is stored in a directory named *output*.

There is also a directory called *work*, which is the working directory for the task attempt. We change into this directory to run the `IsolationRunner`. We need to set some options to allow the remote debugger to connect:‡

```
% export HADOOP_OPTS="-agentlib:jdwp=transport=dt_socket,server=y,suspend=y,\
address=8000"
```

The `suspend=y` option tells the JVM to wait until the debugger has attached before running code. The `IsolationRunner` is launched with the following command:

```
% hadoop org.apache.hadoop.mapred.IsolationRunner ../job.xml
```

Next, set breakpoints, attach your remote debugger (all the major Java IDEs support remote debugging—consult the documentation for instructions), and the task will be run under your control. You can rerun the task any number of times like this. With any luck, you'll be able to find and fix the error.

During the process, you can use other, standard, Java debugging techniques, such as `kill -QUIT` *pid* or `jstack` to get thread dumps.

More generally, it's worth knowing that this technique isn't only useful for failing tasks. You can keep the intermediate files for successful tasks too, which may be handy if you want to examine a task that isn't failing. In this case, set the property `keep.task.files.pattern` to a regular expression that matches the IDs of the tasks you want to keep.

Tuning a Job

After a job is working the question many developers ask is, "Can I make it run faster?"

There are a few Hadoop-specific "usual suspects" that are worth checking to see if they are responsible for a performance problem. You should run through the checklist in Table 5-3 before you start trying to profile or optimize at the task level.

---

‡ You can find details about debugging options on the Java Platform Debugger Architecture (*http://java.sun .com/javase/6/docs/technotes/guides/jpda/*) web page.

Table 5-3. Tuning checklist

Area	Best practice	Further information
Number of mappers	How long are you mappers running for? If they are only running for a few seconds on average, then you should see if there's a way to have fewer mappers and make them all run longer, a minute or so, as a rule of thumb. The extent to which this is possible depends on the input format you are using.	"Small files and CombineFileInputFormat" on page 190
Number of reducers	For maximum performance, the number of reducers should be slightly less than the number of reduce slots in the cluster. This allows the reducers to finish in one wave, and fully utilizes the cluster during the reduce phase.	"Choosing the Number of Reducers" on page 181
Combiners	Can your job take advantage of a combiner to reduce the amount of data in passing through the shuffle?	"Combiner Functions" on page 29
Intermediate compression	Job execution time can almost always benefit from enabling map output compression.	"Compressing map output" on page 85
Custom serialization	If you are using your own custom `Writable` objects, or custom comparators, then make sure you have implemented `RawComparator`.	"Implementing a RawComparator for speed" on page 99
Shuffle tweaks	The MapReduce shuffle exposes around a dozen tuning parameters for memory management, which may help you eke out the last bit of performance.	"Configuration Tuning" on page 166

Profiling Tasks

Like debugging, profiling a job running on a distributed system like MapReduce presents some challenges. Hadoop allows you to profile a fraction of the tasks in a job, and, as each task completes, pulls down the profile information to your machine for later analysis with standard profiling tools.

Of course, it's possible, and somewhat easier, to profile a job running in the local job runner. And provided you can run with enough input data to exercise the map and reduce tasks, this can be a valuable way of improving the performance of your mappers and reducers. There are a couple of caveats, however. The local job runner is a very different environment from a cluster, and the data flow patterns are very different. Optimizing the CPU performance of your code may be pointless if your MapReduce job is I/O-bound (as many jobs are). To be sure that any tuning is effective, you should compare the new execution time with the old running on a real cluster. Even this is easier said than done, since job execution times can vary due to resource contention with other jobs and the decisions the scheduler makes to do with task placement. To get a good idea of job execution time under these circumstances, perform a series of runs (with and without the change) and check whether any improvement is statistically significant.

It's unfortunately true that some problems (such as excessive memory use) can be reproduced only on the cluster, and in these cases the ability to profile in situ is indispensable.

The HPROF profiler

There are a number of configuration properties to control profiling, which are also exposed via convenience methods on `JobConf`. The following modification to `MaxTemperatureDriver` (version 6) will enable remote HPROF profiling. HPROF is a profiling tool that comes with the JDK that, although basic, can give valuable information about a program's CPU and heap usage.§

```
conf.setProfileEnabled(true);
conf.setProfileParams("-agentlib:hprof=cpu=samples,heap=sites,depth=6," +
        "force=n,thread=y,verbose=n,file=%s");
conf.setProfileTaskRange(true, "0-2");
```

The first line enables profiling, which by default is turned off. (This is equivalent to setting the configuration property `mapred.task.profile` to `true`).

Next we set the profile parameters, which are the extra command-line arguments to pass to the task's JVM. (When profiling is enabled, a new JVM is allocated for each task, even if JVM reuse is turned on; see "Task JVM Reuse" on page 170.) The default parameters specify the HPROF profiler; here we set an extra HPROF option, `depth=6`, to give more stack trace depth than the HPROF default. The `setProfileParams()` method on `JobConf` is equivalent to setting the `mapred.task.profile.params`.

Finally, we specify which tasks we want to profile. We normally only want profile information from a few tasks, so we use the `setProfileTaskRange()` method to specify the range of task IDs that we want profile information for. We've set it to `0-2` (which is actually the default), which means tasks with IDs 0, 1, and 2 are profiled. The first argument to the `setProfileTaskRange()` method dictates whether the range is for map or reduce tasks: `true` is for maps, `false` is for reduces. A set of ranges is permitted, using a notation that allows open ranges. For example, `0-1,4,6-` would specify all tasks except those with IDs 2, 3, and 5. The tasks to profile can also be controlled using the `mapred.task.profile.maps` property for map tasks, and `mapred.task.profile.reduces` for reduce tasks.

When we run a job with the modified driver, the profile output turns up at the end of the job in the directory we launched the job from. Since we are only profiling a few tasks, we can run the job on a subset of the dataset.

Here's a snippet of one of the mapper's profile files, which shows the CPU sampling information:

```
CPU SAMPLES BEGIN (total = 1002) Sat Apr 11 11:17:52 2009
rank   self  accum   count trace method
   1  3.49%  3.49%      35 307969 java.lang.Object.<init>
   2  3.39%  6.89%      34 307954 java.lang.Object.<init>
   3  3.19% 10.08%      32 307945 java.util.regex.Matcher.<init>
```

---

§ HPROF uses byte code insertion to profile your code, so you do not need to recompile your application with special options to use it. For more information on HPROF, see "HPROF: A Heap/CPU Profiling Tool in J2SE 5.0," by Kelly O'Hair at *http://java.sun.com/developer/technicalArticles/Programming/HPROF.html*.

```
    4  3.19% 13.27%     32 307963 java.lang.Object.<init>
    5  3.19% 16.47%     32 307973 java.lang.Object.<init>
```

Cross referencing the trace number 307973 gives us the stacktrace from the same file:

```
TRACE 307973: (thread=200001)
        java.lang.Object.<init>(Object.java:20)
        org.apache.hadoop.io.IntWritable.<init>(IntWritable.java:29)
        v5.MaxTemperatureMapper.map(MaxTemperatureMapper.java:30)
        v5.MaxTemperatureMapper.map(MaxTemperatureMapper.java:14)
        org.apache.hadoop.mapred.MapRunner.run(MapRunner.java:50)
        org.apache.hadoop.mapred.MapTask.runOldMapper(MapTask.java:356)
```

So it looks like the mapper is spending 3% of its time constructing `IntWritable` objects. This observation suggests that it might be worth reusing the `Writable` instances being output (version 7):

Example 5-12. Reusing the Text and IntWritable output objects

```
public class MaxTemperatureMapper extends MapReduceBase
  implements Mapper<LongWritable, Text, Text, IntWritable> {

  enum Temperature {
    MALFORMED
  }

  private NcdcRecordParser parser = new NcdcRecordParser();
  private Text year = new Text();
  private IntWritable temp = new IntWritable();

  public void map(LongWritable key, Text value,
      OutputCollector<Text, IntWritable> output, Reporter reporter)
      throws IOException {

    parser.parse(value);
    if (parser.isValidTemperature()) {
      year.set(parser.getYear());
      temp.set(parser.getAirTemperature());
      output.collect(year, temp);
    } else if (parser.isMalformedTemperature()) {
      System.err.println("Ignoring possibly corrupt input: " + value);
      reporter.incrCounter(Temperature.MALFORMED, 1);
    }
  }
}
```

However, we know if this is significant only if we can measure an improvement when running the job over the whole dataset. Running each variant five times on an otherwise quiet 11-node cluster showed no statistically significant difference in job execution time. Of course, this result holds only for this particular combination of code, data, and hardware, so you should perform similar benchmarks to see whether such a change is significant for your setup.

Other profilers

At the time of this writing, the mechanism for retrieving profile output is HPROF-specific. Until this is fixed, it should be possible to use Hadoop's profiling settings to trigger profiling using any profiler (see the documentation for the particular profiler), although it may be necessary to manually retrieve the profiler's output from tasktrackers for analysis.

If the profiler is not installed on all the tasktracker machines, consider using the Distributed Cache ("Distributed Cache" on page 239) for making the profiler binary available on the required machines.

MapReduce Workflows

So far in this chapter, you have seen the mechanics of writing a program using Map-Reduce. We haven't yet considered how to turn a data processing problem into the MapReduce model.

The data processing you have seen so far in this book is to solve a fairly simple problem (finding the maximum recorded temperature for given years). When the processing gets more complex, this complexity is generally manifested by having more MapReduce jobs, rather than having more complex map and reduce functions. In other words, as a rule of thumb, think about adding *more* jobs, rather than adding complexity *to* jobs.

For more complex problems, it is worth considering a higher-level language than Map-Reduce, such as Pig, Hive, or Cascading. One immediate benefit is that it frees you up from having to do the translation into MapReduce jobs, allowing you to concentrate on the analysis you are performing.

Decomposing a Problem into MapReduce Jobs

Let's look at an example of a more complex problem that we want to translate into a MapReduce workflow.

Imagine that we want to find the mean maximum recorded temperature for every day of the year and every weather station. In concrete terms, to calculate the mean maximum daily temperature recorded by station 029070-99999, say, on January 1, we take the mean of the maximum daily temperatures for this station for January 1, 1901; January 1, 1902; and so on up to January 1, 2000.

How can we compute this using MapReduce? The computation decomposes most naturally into two stages:

1. Compute the maximum daily temperature for every station-date pair.

   The MapReduce program in this case is a variant of the maximum temperature program, except that the keys in this case are a composite station-date pair, rather than just the year.

2. Compute the mean of the maximum daily temperatures for every station-day-month key.

   The mapper takes the output from the previous job (station-date, maximum temperature) records, and projects it into (station-day-month, maximum temperature) records by dropping the year component. The reduce function then takes the mean of the maximum temperatures, for each station-day-month key.

The output from first stage looks like this for the station we are interested in. (The *mean_max_daily_temp.sh* script in the examples provides an implementation in Hadoop Streaming.)

```
029070-99999    19010101    0
029070-99999    19020101    -94
...
```

The first two fields form the key, and the final column is the maximum temperature from all the readings for the given station and date. The second stage averages these daily maxima over years to yield:

```
029070-99999    0101    -68
```

which is interpreted as saying the mean maximum daily temperature on January 1 for station 029070-99999 over the century is –6.8°C.

It's possible to do this computation in one MapReduce stage, but it takes more work on the part of the programmer.‖

The arguments for having more (but simpler) MapReduce stages are that doing so leads to more composable and more maintainable mappers and reducers. The case studies in Chapter 14 cover a wide range of real-world problems that were solved using MapReduce, and in each case, the data processing task is implemented using two or more MapReduce jobs. The details in that chapter are invaluable for getting a better idea of how to decompose a processing problem into a MapReduce workflow.

It's possible to make map and reduce functions even more composable than we have done. A mapper commonly performs input format parsing, projection (selecting the relevant fields), and filtering (removing records that are not of interest). In the mappers you have seen so far, we have implemented all of these functions in a single mapper. However, there is a case for splitting these into distinct mappers and chaining them into a single mapper using the `ChainMapper` library class that comes with Hadoop. Combined with a `ChainReducer`, you can run a chain of mappers, followed by a reducer and another chain of mappers in a single MapReduce job.

‖ It's an interesting exercise to do this. Hint: use "Secondary Sort" on page 227.

Running Dependent Jobs

When there is more than one job in a MapReduce workflow, the question arises: how do you manage the jobs so they are executed in order? There are several approaches, and the main consideration is whether you have a linear chain of jobs, or a more complex directed acyclic graph (DAG) of jobs.

For a linear chain, the simplest approach is to run each job one after another, waiting until a job completes successfully before running the next.

```
JobClient.runJob(conf1);
JobClient.runJob(conf2);
```

If a job fails, the runJob() method will throw an IOException, so later jobs in the pipeline don't get executed. Depending on your application, you might want to catch the exception and clean up any intermediate data that was produced by any previous jobs.

For anything more complex than a linear chain, there are libraries that can help orchestrate your workflow (although they are suited to linear chains, or even one-off jobs, too). The simplest is in the org.apache.hadoop.mapred.jobcontrol package: the JobControl class. An instance of JobControl represents a graph of jobs to be run. You add the job configurations, then tell the JobControl instance the dependencies between jobs. You run the JobControl in a thread, and it runs the jobs in dependency order. You can poll for progress, and when the jobs have finished, you can query for all the jobs' statuses, and the associated errors for any failures. If a job fails, JobControl won't run its dependencies.

Unlike JobControl which runs on the client machine submitting the jobs, the *Hadoop Workflow Scheduler* (HWS)# runs as a server, and a client submits a workflow to the scheduler. When the workflow completes the scheduler can make an HTTP callback to the client to inform it of the jobs' statuses. HWS can run different types of jobs in the same workflow: a Pig job followed by a Java MapReduce job, for example.

At the time of this writing, the Hadoop Workflow Scheduler is still under development. See *https://issues .apache.org/jira/browse/HADOOP-5303*.

## CHAPTER 6

How MapReduce Works

In this chapter, we look at how MapReduce in Hadoop works in detail. This knowledge provides a good foundation for writing more advanced MapReduce programs, which we will cover in the following two chapters.

Anatomy of a MapReduce Job Run

You can run a MapReduce job with a single line of code: `JobClient.runJob(conf)`. It's very short, but it conceals a great deal of processing behind the scenes. This section uncovers the steps Hadoop takes to run a job.

The whole process is illustrated in Figure 6-1. At the highest level, there are four independent entities:

- The client, which submits the MapReduce job.
- The jobtracker, which coordinates the job run. The jobtracker is a Java application whose main class is `JobTracker`.
- The tasktrackers, which run the tasks that the job has been split into. Tasktrackers are Java applications whose main class is `TaskTracker`.
- The distributed filesystem (normally HDFS, covered in Chapter 3), which is used for sharing job files between the other entities.

Job Submission

The `runJob()` method on `JobClient` is a convenience method that creates a new `JobClient` instance and calls `submitJob()` on it (step 1 in Figure 6-1). Having submitted the job, `runJob()` polls the job's progress once a second, and reports the progress to the console if it has changed since the last report. When the job is complete, if it was successful, the job counters are displayed. Otherwise, the error that caused the job to fail is logged to the console.

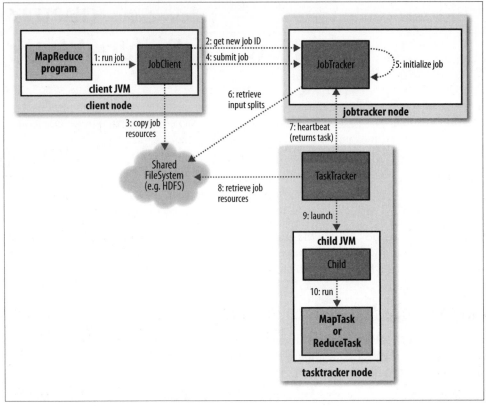

Figure 6-1. How Hadoop runs a MapReduce job

The job submission process implemented by JobClient's submitJob() method does the following:

- Asks the jobtracker for a new job ID (by calling getNewJobId() on JobTracker) (step 2).
- Checks the output specification of the job. For example, if the output directory has not been specified or it already exists, the job is not submitted and an error is thrown to the MapReduce program.
- Computes the input splits for the job. If the splits cannot be computed, because the input paths don't exist, for example, then the job is not submitted and an error is thrown to the MapReduce program.
- Copies the resources needed to run the job, including the job JAR file, the configuration file and the computed input splits, to the jobtracker's filesystem in a directory named after the job ID. The job JAR is copied with a high replication factor (controlled by the mapred.submit.replication property, which defaults to 10) so that there are lots of copies across the cluster for the tasktrackers to access when they run tasks for the job (step 3).

- Tells the jobtracker that the job is ready for execution (by calling `submitJob()` on `JobTracker`) (step 4).

Job Initialization

When the `JobTracker` receives a call to its `submitJob()` method, it puts it into an internal queue from where the job scheduler will pick it up and initialize it. Initialization involves creating an object to represent the job being run, which encapsulates its tasks, and bookkeeping information to keep track of the tasks' status and progress (step 5).

To create the list of tasks to run, the job scheduler first retrieves the input splits computed by the `JobClient` from the shared filesystem (step 6). It then creates one map task for each split. The number of reduce tasks to create is determined by the `mapred.reduce.tasks` property in the `JobConf`, which is set by the `setNumReduceTasks()` method, and the scheduler simply creates this number of reduce tasks to be run. Tasks are given IDs at this point.

Task Assignment

Tasktrackers run a simple loop that periodically sends heartbeat method calls to the jobtracker. Heartbeats tell the jobtracker that a tasktracker is alive, but they also double as a channel for messages. As a part of the heartbeat, a tasktracker will indicate whether it is ready to run a new task, and if it is, the jobtracker will allocate it a task, which it communicates to the tasktracker using the heartbeat return value (step 7).

Before it can choose a task for the tasktracker, the jobtracker must choose a job to select the task from. There are various scheduling algorithms as explained later in this chapter (see "Job Scheduling" on page 161), but the default one simply maintains a priority list of jobs. Having chosen a job, the jobtracker now chooses a task for the job.

Tasktrackers have a fixed number of slots for map tasks and for reduce tasks: for example, a tasktracker may be able to run two map tasks and two reduce tasks simultaneously. (The precise number depends on the number of cores and the amount of memory on the tasktracker; see "Memory" on page 254.) The default scheduler fills empty map task slots before reduce task slots, so if the tasktracker has at least one empty map task slot, the jobtracker will select a map task; otherwise, it will select a reduce task.

To choose a reduce task the jobtracker simply takes the next in its list of yet-to-be-run reduce tasks, since there are no data locality considerations. For a map task, however, it takes account of the tasktracker's network location and picks a task whose input split is as close as possible to the tasktracker. In the optimal case, the task is *data-local*, that is, running on the same node that the split resides on. Alternatively, the task may be *rack-local*: on the same rack, but not the same node, as the split. Some tasks are neither data-local nor rack-local and retrieve their data from a different rack from the one they are running on. You can tell the proportion of each type of task by looking at a job's counters (see "Built-in Counters" on page 211).

Task Execution

Now the tasktracker has been assigned a task, the next step is for it to run the task. First, it localizes the job JAR by copying it from the shared filesystem to the tasktracker's filesystem. It also copies any files needed from the distributed cache by the application to the local disk; see "Distributed Cache" on page 239 (step 8). Second, it creates a local working directory for the task, and un-jars the contents of the JAR into this directory. Third, it creates an instance of TaskRunner to run the task.

TaskRunner launches a new Java Virtual Machine (step 9) to run each task in (step 10), so that any bugs in the user-defined map and reduce functions don't affect the task-tracker (by causing it to crash or hang, for example). It is however possible to reuse the JVM between tasks; see "Task JVM Reuse" on page 170.

The child process communicates with its parent through the *umbilical* interface. This way it informs the parent of the task's progress every few seconds until the task is complete.

Streaming and Pipes

Both Streaming and Pipes run special map and reduce tasks for the purpose of launching the user-supplied executable and communicating with it (Figure 6-2).

In the case of Streaming, the Streaming task communicates with the process (which may be written in any language) using standard input and output streams. The Pipes task, on the other hand, listens on a socket and passes the C++ process a port number in its environment, so that on startup, the C++ process can establish a persistent socket connection back to the parent Java Pipes task.

In both cases, during execution of the task, the Java process passes input key-value pairs to the external process, which runs it through the user-defined map or reduce function and passes the output key-value pairs back to the Java process. From the tasktracker's point of view, it is as if the tasktracker child process ran the map or reduce code itself.

Progress and Status Updates

MapReduce jobs are long-running batch jobs, taking anything from minutes to hours to run. Because this is a significant length of time, it's important for the user to get feedback on how the job is progressing. A job and each of its tasks have a *status*, which includes such things as the state of the job or task (e.g., running, successfully completed, failed), the progress of maps and reduces, the values of the job's counters, and a status

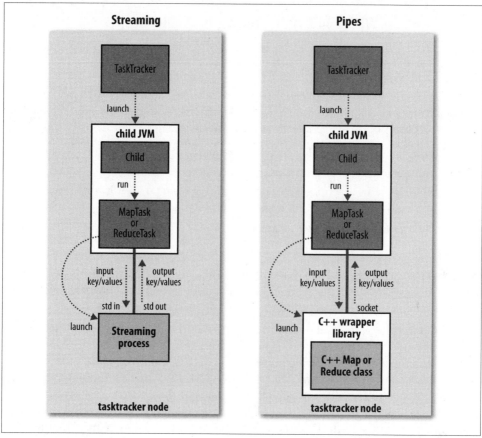

Figure 6-2. The relationship of the Streaming and Pipes executable to the tasktracker and its child

message or description (which may be set by user code). These statuses change over the course of the job, so how do they get communicated back to the client?

When a task is running, it keeps track of its *progress*, that is, the proportion of the task completed. For map tasks, this is the proportion of the input that has been processed. For reduce tasks, it's a little more complex, but the system can still estimate the proportion of the reduce input processed. It does this by dividing the total progress into three parts, corresponding to the three phases of the shuffle (see "Shuffle and Sort" on page 163). For example, if the task has run the reducer on half its input, then the task's progress is ⅚, since it has completed the copy and sort phases (⅓ each) and is half way through the reduce phase (⅙).

What Constitutes Progress in MapReduce?

Progress is not always measurable, but nevertheless it tells Hadoop that a task is doing something. For example, a task writing output records is making progress, even though it cannot be expressed as a percentage of the total number that will be written, since the latter figure may not be known, even by the task producing the output.

Progress reporting is important, as it means Hadoop will not fail a task that's making progress. All of the following operations constitute progress:

- Reading an input record (in a mapper or reducer)
- Writing an output record (in a mapper or reducer)
- Setting the status description on a reporter (using Reporter's setStatus() method)
- Incrementing a counter (using Reporter's incrCounter() method)
- Calling Reporter's progress() method

Tasks also have a set of counters that count various events as the task runs (we saw an example in "A test run" on page 23), either those built into the framework, such as the number of map output records written, or ones defined by users.

If a task reports progress, it sets a flag to indicate that the status change should be sent to the tasktracker. The flag is checked in a separate thread every three seconds, and if set it notifies the tasktracker of the current task status. Meanwhile, the tasktracker is sending heartbeats to the jobtracker every five seconds (this is a minimum, as the heartbeat interval is actually dependent on the size of the cluster: for larger clusters, the interval is longer), and the status of all the tasks being run by the tasktracker is sent in the call. Counters are sent less frequently than every five seconds, because they can be relatively high-bandwidth.

The jobtracker combines these updates to produce a global view of the status of all the jobs being run and their constituent tasks. Finally, as mentioned earlier, the JobClient receives the latest status by polling the jobtracker every second. Clients can also use JobClient's getJob() method to obtain a RunningJob instance, which contains all of the status information for the job.

The method calls are illustrated in Figure 6-3.

Job Completion

When the jobtracker receives a notification that the last task for a job is complete, it changes the status for the job to "successful." Then, when the JobClient polls for status, it learns that the job has completed successfully, so it prints a message to tell the user, and then returns from the runJob() method.

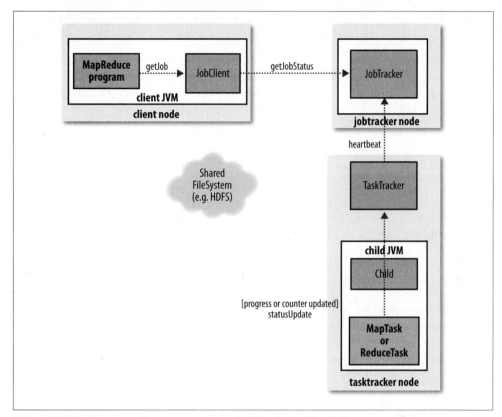

Figure 6-3. How status updates are propagated through the MapReduce system

The jobtracker also sends a HTTP job notification if it is configured to do so. This can be configured by clients wishing to receive callbacks, via the `job.end.notifica tion.url` property.

Last, the jobtracker cleans up its working state for the job, and instructs tasktrackers to do the same (so intermediate output is deleted, for example).

Failures

In the real world, user code is buggy, processes crash, and machines fail. One of the major benefits of using Hadoop is its ability to handle such failures and allow your job to complete.

Task Failure

Consider first the case of the child task failing. The most common way that this happens is when user code in the map or reduce task throws a runtime exception. If this happens, the child JVM reports the error back to its parent tasktracker, before it exits. The error ultimately makes it into the user logs. The tasktracker marks the task attempt as *failed*, freeing up a slot to run another task.

For Streaming tasks, if the Streaming process exits with a nonzero exit code, it is marked as failed. This behavior is governed by the `stream.non.zero.exit.is.failure` property (the default is `true`).

Another failure mode is the sudden exit of the child JVM—perhaps there is a JVM bug that causes the JVM to exit for a particular set of circumstances exposed by the Map-Reduce user code. In this case, the tasktracker notices that the process has exited, and marks the attempt as failed.

Hanging tasks are dealt with differently. The tasktracker notices that it hasn't received a progress update for a while, and proceeds to mark the task as failed. The child JVM process will be automatically killed after this period.[*] The timeout period after which tasks are considered failed is normally 10 minutes, and can be configured on a per-job basis (or a cluster basis) by setting the `mapred.task.timeout` property to a value in milliseconds.

Setting the timeout to a value of zero disables the timeout, so long-running tasks are never marked as failed. In this case, a hanging task will never free up its slot, and over time there may be cluster slowdown as a result. This approach should therefore be avoided, and making sure that a task is reporting progress periodically will suffice (see "What Constitutes Progress in MapReduce?" on page 158).

When the jobtracker is notified of a task attempt that has failed (by the tasktracker's heartbeat call) it will reschedule execution of the task. The jobtracker will try to avoid rescheduling the task on a tasktracker where it has previously failed. Furthermore, if a task fails more than four times, it will not be retried further. This value is configurable: the maximum number of attempts to run a task is controlled by the `mapred.map.max.attempts` property for map tasks, and `mapred.reduce.max.attempts` for reduce tasks. By default, if any task fails more than four times (or whatever the maximum number of attempts is configured to), the whole job fails.

For some applications it is undesirable to abort the job if a few tasks fail, as it may be possible to use the results of the job despite some failures. In this case, the maximum percentage of tasks that are allowed to fail without triggering job failure can be set for the job. Map tasks and reduce tasks are controlled independently, using the `mapred.max.map.failures.percent` and `mapred.max.reduce.failures.percent` properties.

---

[*] If a Streaming process hangs, the tasktracker does not try to kill it (although the JVM that launched it will be killed), so you should take precautions to monitor for this scenario, and kill orphaned processes by some other means.

A task attempt may also be *killed*, which is different from it failing. A task attempt may be killed because it is a speculative duplicate (for more, see "Speculative Execution" on page 169), or because the tasktracker it was running on failed, and the jobtracker marked all the task attempts running on it as killed. Killed task attempts do not count against the number of attempts to run the task (as set by `mapred.map.max.attempts` and `mapred.reduce.max.attempts`), since it wasn't the task's fault that an attempt was killed.

Users may also kill or fail task attempts using the web UI or the command line (type `hadoop job` to see the options). Jobs may also be killed by the same mechanisms.

Tasktracker Failure

Failure of a tasktracker is another failure mode. If a tasktracker fails by crashing, or running very slowly, it will stop sending heartbeats to the jobtracker (or send them very infrequently). The jobtracker will notice a tasktracker that has stopped sending heartbeats (if it hasn't received one for 10 minutes, configured via the `mapred.task tracker.expiry.interval` property, in milliseconds) and remove it from its pool of tasktrackers to schedule tasks on. The jobtracker arranges for map tasks that were run and completed successfully on that tasktracker to be rerun if they belong to incomplete jobs, since their intermediate output residing on the failed tasktracker's local filesystem may not be accessible to the reduce task. Any tasks in progress are also rescheduled.

A tasktracker can also be *blacklisted* by the jobtracker, even if the tasktracker has not failed. A tasktracker is blacklisted if the number of tasks that have failed on it is significantly higher than the average task failure rate on the cluster. Blacklisted tasktrackers can be restarted to remove them from the jobtracker's blacklist.

Jobtracker Failure

Failure of the jobtracker is the most serious failure mode. Currently, Hadoop has no mechanism for dealing with failure of the jobtracker—it is a single point of failure—so in this case the job fails. However, this failure mode has a low chance of occurring since the chance of a particular machine failing is low. It is possible that a future release of Hadoop will remove this limitation by running multiple jobtrackers, only one of which is the primary jobtracker at any time (using ZooKeeper as a coordination mechanism for the jobtrackers to decide who is the primary; see Chapter 13).

Job Scheduling

Early versions of Hadoop had a very simple approach to scheduling users' jobs: they ran in order of submission, using a FIFO scheduler. Typically each job would use the whole cluster, so jobs had to wait their turn. Although a shared cluster offers great potential for offering large resources to many users, the problem of sharing resources fairly between users requires a better scheduler. Production jobs need to complete in a timely manner, while allowing users who are making smaller ad hoc queries to get results back in a reasonable time.

Later on, the ability to set a job's priority was added, via the `mapred.job.priority` property or the `setJobPriority()` method on `JobClient` (both of which take one of the values `VERY_HIGH`, `HIGH`, `NORMAL`, `LOW`, `VERY_LOW`). When the job scheduler is choosing the next job to run, it selects one with the highest priority. However, with the FIFO scheduler, priorities do not support *preemption*, so a high-priority job can still be blocked by a long-running low priority job that started before the high-priority job was scheduled.

MapReduce in Hadoop now comes with a choice of schedulers. The default is the original FIFO queue-based scheduler, and there also a multi-user scheduler called the Fair Scheduler.

The Fair Scheduler

The Fair Scheduler aims to give every user a fair share of the cluster capacity over time. If a single job is running, it gets all of the cluster. As more jobs are submitted, free task slots are given to the jobs in such a way as to give each user a fair share of the cluster. A short job belonging to one user will complete in a reasonable time even while another user's long job is running, and the long job will still make progress.

Jobs are placed in pools, and by default, each user gets their own pool. A user who submits more jobs than a second user will not get any more cluster resources than the second, on average. It is also possible to define custom pools with guaranteed minimum capacities defined in terms of the number of map and reduce slots, and to set weightings for each pool.

The Fair Scheduler supports preemption, so if a pool has not received its fair share for a certain period of time, then the scheduler will kill tasks in pools running over capacity in order to give the slots to the pool running under capacity.

The Fair Scheduler is a "contrib" module. To enable it, place its JAR file on Hadoop's classpath, by copying it from Hadoop's *contrib/fairscheduler* directory to the *lib* directory. Then set the `mapred.jobtracker.taskScheduler` property to:

```
org.apache.hadoop.mapred.FairScheduler
```

The Fair Scheduler will work without further configuration, but to take full advantage of its features and how to configure it (including its web interface), refer to README in the *src/contrib/fairscheduler* directory of the distribution.

Shuffle and Sort

MapReduce makes the guarantee that the input to every reducer is sorted by key. The process by which the system performs the sort—and transfers the map outputs to the reducers as inputs—is known as the *shuffle*.[†] In this section, we look at how the shuffle works, as a basic understanding would be helpful, should you need to optimize a Map-Reduce program. The shuffle is an area of the codebase where refinements and improvements are continually being made, so the following description necessarily conceals many details (and may change over time). In many ways, the shuffle is the heart of MapReduce, and is where the "magic" happens.

The Map Side

When the map function starts producing output, it is not simply written to disk. The process is more involved, and takes advantage of buffering writes in memory and doing some presorting for efficiency reasons. Figure 6-4 shows what happens.

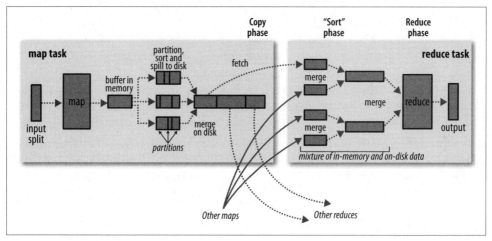

Figure 6-4. Shuffle and sort in MapReduce

Each map task has a circular memory buffer that it writes the output to. The buffer is 100 MB by default, a size which can be tuned by changing the `io.sort.mb` property. When the contents of the buffer reaches a certain threshold size (`io.sort.spill.per cent`, default `0.80`, or 80%) a background thread will start to *spill* the contents to disk. Map outputs will continue to be written to the buffer while the spill takes place, but if the buffer fills up during this time, the map will block until the spill is complete.

[†] The term *shuffle* is actually imprecise, since in some contexts it refers to only the part of the process where map outputs are fetched by reduce tasks. In this section, we take it to mean the whole process from the point where a map produces output to where a reduce consumes input.

Spills are written in round-robin fashion to the directories specified by the `mapred.local.dir` property, in a job-specific subdirectory.

Before it writes to disk, the thread first divides the data into partitions corresponding to the reducers that they will ultimately be sent to. Within each partition, the background thread performs an in-memory sort by key, and if there is a combiner function, it is run on the output of the sort.

Each time the memory buffer reaches the spill threshold, a new spill file is created, so after the map task has written its last output record there could be several spill files. Before the task is finished, the spill files are merged into a single partitioned and sorted output file. The configuration property `io.sort.factor` controls the maximum number of streams to merge at once; the default is 10.

If a combiner function has been specified, and the number of spills is at least three (the value of the `min.num.spills.for.combine` property), then the combiner is run before the output file is written. Recall that combiners may be run repeatedly over the input without affecting the final result. The point is that running combiners makes for a more compact map output, so there is less data to write to local disk and to transfer to the reducer.

It is often a good idea to compress the map output as it is written to disk, since doing so makes it faster to write to disk, saves disk space, and reduces the amount of data to transfer to the reducer. By default the output is not compressed, but it is easy to enable by setting `mapred.compress.map.output` to `true`. The compression library to use is specified by `mapred.map.output.compression.codec`; see "Compression" on page 77 for more on compression formats.

The output file's partitions are made available to the reducers over HTTP. The number of worker threads used to serve the file partitions is controlled by the `task tracker.http.threads` property—this setting is per tasktracker, not per map task slot. The default of 40 may need increasing for large clusters running large jobs.

The Reduce Side

Let's turn now to the reduce part of the process. The map output file is sitting on the local disk of the tasktracker that ran the map task (note that although map outputs always get written to the local disk of the map tasktracker, reduce outputs may not be), but now it is needed by the tasktracker that is about to run the reduce task for the partition. Furthermore, the reduce task needs the map output for its particular partition from several map tasks across the cluster. The map tasks may finish at different times, so the reduce task starts copying their outputs as soon as each completes. This is known as the *copy phase* of the reduce task. The reduce task has a small number of copier threads so that it can fetch map outputs in parallel. The default is five threads, but this number can be changed by setting the `mapred.reduce.parallel.copies` property.

How do reducers know which tasktrackers to fetch map output from?

As map tasks complete successfully, they notify their parent tasktracker of the status update, which in turn notifies the jobtracker. These notifications are transmitted over the heartbeat communication mechanism described earlier. Therefore, for a given job, the jobtracker knows the mapping between map outputs and tasktrackers. A thread in the reducer periodically asks the jobtracker for map output locations until it has retrieved them all.

Tasktrackers do not delete map outputs from disk as soon as the first reducer has retrieved them, as the reducer may fail. Instead, they wait until they are told to delete them by the jobtracker, which is after the job has completed.

The map outputs are copied to the reduce tasktracker's memory if they are small enough (the buffer's size is controlled by `mapred.job.shuffle.input.buffer.percent`, which specifies the proportion of the heap to use for this purpose); otherwise, they are copied to disk. When the in-memory buffer reaches a threshold size (controlled by `mapred.job.shuffle.merge.percent`), or reaches a threshold number of map outputs (`mapred.inmem.merge.threshold`), it is merged and spilled to disk.

As the copies accumulate on disk, a background thread merges them into larger, sorted files. This saves some time merging later on. Note that any map outputs that were compressed (by the map task) have to be decompressed in memory in order to perform a merge on them.

When all the map outputs have been copied, the reduce task moves into the *sort phase* (which should properly be called the *merge* phase, as the sorting was carried out on the map side), which merges the map outputs, maintaining their sort ordering. This is done in rounds. For example, if there were 50 map outputs, and the *merge factor* was 10 (the default, controlled by the `io.sort.factor` property, just like in the map's merge), then there would be 5 rounds. Each round would merge 10 files into one, so at the end there would be five intermediate files.

Rather than have a final round that merges these five files into a single sorted file, the merge saves a trip to disk by directly feeding the reduce function in what is the last phase: the *reduce phase*. This final merge can come from a mixture of in-memory and on-disk segments.

The number of files merged in each round is actually more subtle than this example suggests. The goal is to merge the minimum number of files to get to the merge factor for the final round. So if there were 40 files, the merge would not merge 10 files in each of the four rounds to get 4 files. Instead, the first round would merge only 4 files, and the subsequent three rounds would merge the full 10 files. The 4 merged files, and the 6 (as yet unmerged) files make a total of 10 files for the final round.

Note that this does not change the number of rounds, it's just an optimization to minimize the amount of data that is written to disk, since the final round always merges directly into the reduce.

During the reduce phase the reduce function is invoked for each key in the sorted output. The output of this phase is written directly to the output filesystem, typically HDFS. In the case of HDFS, since the tasktracker node is also running a datanode, the first block replica will be written to the local disk.

Configuration Tuning

We are now in a better position to understand how to tune the shuffle to improve MapReduce performance. The relevant settings, which can be used on a per-job basis (except where noted), are summarized in Tables 6-1 and 6-2, along with the defaults, which are good for general-purpose jobs.

The general principle is to give the shuffle as much memory as possible. However, there is a trade-off, in that you need to make sure that your map and reduce functions get enough memory to operate. This is why it is best to write your map and reduce functions to use as little memory as possible—certainly they should not use an unbounded amount of memory (by avoiding accumulating values in a map, for example).

The amount of memory given to the JVMs in which the map and reduce tasks run is set by the `mapred.child.java.opts` property. You should try to make this as large as possible for the amount of memory on you task nodes; the discussion in "Memory" on page 254 goes through the constraints to consider.

On the map side, the best performance can be obtained by avoiding multiple spills to disk; one is optimal. If you can estimate the size of your map outputs, then you can set the `io.sort.*` properties appropriately to minimize the number of spills. In particular, you should increase `io.sort.mb` if you can. There is a MapReduce counter ("Spilled records"; see "Counters" on page 211) that counts the total number of records that were spilled to disk over the course of a job, which can be useful for tuning. Note that the counter includes both map and reduce side spills.

On the reduce side, the best performance is obtained when the intermediate data can reside entirely in memory. By default, this does not happen, since for the general case all the memory is reserved for the reduce function. But if your reduce function has light memory requirements, then setting `mapred.inmem.merge.threshold` to 0 and `mapred.job.reduce.input.buffer.percent` to 1.0 (or a lower value; see Table 6-2) may bring a performance boost.

More generally, Hadoop's uses a buffer size of 4 KB by default, which is low, so you should increase this across the cluster (by setting `io.file.buffer.size`, see also "Other Hadoop Properties" on page 264).

In April 2008, Hadoop won the general-purpose terabyte sort benchmark (described in "TeraByte Sort on Apache Hadoop" on page 461), and one of the optimizations used was this one of keeping the intermediate data in memory on the reduce side.

Table 6-1. Map-side tuning properties

Property name	Type	Default value	Description
`io.sort.mb`	int	100	The size, in megabytes, of the memory buffer to use while sorting map output.
`io.sort.record.percent`	float	0.05	The proportion of `io.sort.mb` reserved for storing record boundaries of the map outputs. The remaining space is used for the map output records themselves.
`io.sort.spill.percent`	float	0.80	The threshold usage proportion for both the map output memory buffer and the record boundaries index to start the process of spilling to disk.
`io.sort.factor`	int	10	The maximum number of streams to merge at once when sorting files. This property is also used in the reduce. It's fairly common to increase this to 100.
`min.num.spills.for.combine`	int	3	The minimum number of spill files needed for the combiner to run (if a combiner is specified).
`mapred.compress.map.output`	boolean	false	Compress map outputs.
`mapred.map.output.compression.codec`	Class name	`org.apache.hadoop.io.compress.DefaultCodec`	The compression codec to use for map outputs.
`task tracker.http.threads`	int	40	The number of worker threads per tasktracker for serving the map outputs to reducers. This is a cluster-wide setting and cannot be set by individual jobs.

Table 6-2. Reduce-side tuning properties

Property name	Type	Default value	Description
`mapred.reduce.parallel.copies`	int	5	The number of threads used to copy map outputs to the reducer.
`mapred.reduce.copy.backoff`	int	300	The maximum amount of time, in seconds, to spend retrieving one map output for a reducer before declaring it as failed. The reducer may repeatedly reattempt a transfer within this time if it fails (using exponential backoff).
`io.sort.factor`	int	10	The maximum number of streams to merge at once when sorting files. This property is also used in the map.
`mapred.job.shuffle.input.buffer.percent`	float	0.70	The proportion of total heap size to be allocated to the map outputs buffer during the copy phase of the shuffle.
`mapred.job.shuffle.merge.percent`	float	0.66	The threshold usage proportion for the map outputs buffer (defined by `mapred.job.shuffle.input.buffer.percent`) for starting the process of merging the outputs and spilling to disk.
`mapred.inmem.merge.threshold`	int	1000	The threshold number of map outputs for starting the process of merging the outputs and spilling to disk. A value of 0 or less means there is no threshold, and the spill behavior is governed solely by `mapred.job.shuffle.merge.percent`.
`mapred.job.reduce.input.buffer.percent`	float	0.0	The proportion of total heap size to be used for retaining map outputs in memory during the reduce. For the reduce phase to begin, the size of map outputs in memory must be no more than this size. By default, all map outputs are merged to disk before the reduce begins, to give the reduces as much memory as possible. However, if your reducers require less memory, this value may be increased to minimize the number of trips to disk.

Task Execution

We saw how the MapReduce system executes tasks in the context of the overall job at the beginning of the chapter in "Anatomy of a MapReduce Job Run" on page 153. In this section, we'll look at some more controls that MapReduce users have over task execution.

Speculative Execution

The MapReduce model is to break jobs into tasks and run the tasks in parallel to make the overall job execution time smaller than it would otherwise be if the tasks ran sequentially. This makes job execution time sensitive to slow-running tasks, as it takes only one slow task to make the whole job take significantly longer than it would have done otherwise. When a job consists of hundreds or thousands of tasks, the possibility of a few straggling tasks is very real.

Tasks may be slow for various reasons, including hardware degradation, or software mis-configuration, but the causes may be hard to detect since the tasks still complete successfully, albeit after a longer time than expected. Hadoop doesn't try to diagnose and fix slow-running tasks; instead, it tries to detect when a task is running slower than expected and launches another, equivalent, task as a backup. This is termed *speculative execution* of tasks.

It's important to understand that speculative execution does not work by launching two duplicate tasks at about the same time so they can race each other. This would be wasteful of cluster resources. Rather, a speculative task is launched only after all the tasks for a job have been launched, and then only for tasks that have been running for some time (at least a minute), and have failed to make as much progress, on average, as the other tasks from the job. When a task completes successfully, any duplicate tasks that are running are killed since they are no longer needed. So if the original task completes before the speculative task then the speculative task is killed; on the other hand, if the speculative task finishes first, then the original is killed.

Speculative execution is an optimization, not a feature to make jobs run more reliably. If there are bugs that sometimes cause a task to hang or slow down, then relying on speculative execution to avoid these problems is unwise, and won't work reliably, since the same bugs are likely to affect the speculative task. You should fix the bug so that the task doesn't hang or slow down.

Speculative execution is turned on by default. It can be enabled or disabled independently for map tasks and reduce tasks, on a cluster-wide basis, or on a per-job basis. The relevant properties are shown in Table 6-3.

Table 6-3. Speculative execution properties

Property name	Type	Default value	Description
`mapred.map.tasks.speculative.execution`	boolean	true	Whether extra instances of map tasks may be launched if a task is making slow progress.
`mapred.reduce.tasks.speculative.execution`	boolean	true	Whether extra instances of reduce tasks may be launched if a task is making slow progress.

Why would you ever want to turn off speculative execution? The goal of speculative execution is reducing job execution time, but this comes at the cost of cluster efficiency. On a busy cluster speculative execution can reduce overall throughput, since redundant tasks are being executed in an attempt to bring down the execution time for a single job. For this reason, some cluster administrators prefer to turn it off on the cluster, and have users explicitly turn it on for individual jobs. This was especially relevant for older versions of Hadoop, when speculative execution could be overly aggressive in scheduling speculative tasks.

Task JVM Reuse

Hadoop runs tasks in their own Java Virtual Machine to isolate them from other running tasks. The overhead of starting a new JVM for each task can take around a second, which for jobs that run for a minute or so is insignificant. However, jobs that have a large number of very short-lived tasks (these are usually map tasks) or that have lengthy initialization, can see performance gains when the JVM is reused for subsequent tasks.

With task JVM reuse enabled, tasks do *not* run concurrently in a single JVM. The JVM runs tasks sequentially. Tasktrackers can however run more than one task at a time, but this is always done in separate JVMs. The properties for controlling the tasktrackers number of map task slots and reduce task slots are discussed in "Memory" on page 254.

The property for controlling task JVM reuse is `mapred.job.reuse.jvm.num.tasks`: it specifies the maximum number of tasks to run for a given job for each JVM launched, the default is 1 (see Table 6-4). Tasks from different jobs are always run in separate JVMs. If the property is set to −1, there is no limit to the number of tasks from the same job that may share a JVM. The method `setNumTasksToExecutePerJvm()` on `JobConf` can also be used to configure this property.

Table 6-4. Task JVM Reuse properties

Property name	Type	Default value	Description
`mapred.job.reuse.jvm.num.tasks`	int	1	The maximum number of tasks to run for a given job for each JVM on a tasktracker. A value of −1 indicates no limit: the same JVM may be used for all tasks for a job.

Tasks that are CPU-bound may also benefit from task JVM reuse by taking advantage of runtime optimizations applied by the HotSpot JVM. After running for a while, the HotSpot JVM builds up enough information to detect performance-critical sections in the code, and dynamically translates the Java byte codes of these hot spots into native machine code. This works well for long-running processes, but JVMs that run for seconds or a few minutes may not gain the full benefit of HotSpot. In these cases, it is worth enabling task JVM reuse.

Another place where a shared JVM is useful is for sharing state between the tasks of a job. By storing reference data in a static field, tasks get rapid access to the shared data.

Skipping Bad Records

Large datasets are messy. They often have corrupt records. They often have records that are in a different format. They often have missing fields. In an ideal world, your code would cope gracefully with all of these conditions. In practice, it is often expedient to ignore the offending records. Depending on the analysis being performed, if only a small percentage of records are affected, then skipping them may not significantly affect the result. However, if a task trips up when it encounters a bad record—by throwing a runtime exception—then the task fails. Failing tasks are retried (since the failure may be due to hardware failure or some other reason outside the task's control), but if a task fails four times, then the whole job is marked as failed (see "Task Failure" on page 159). If it is the data that is causing the task to throw an exception, rerunning the task won't help, since it will fail in exactly the same way each time.

> If you are using `TextInputFormat` ("TextInputFormat" on page 196), then you can set a maximum expected line length to safeguard against corrupted files. Corruption in a file can manifest itself as a very long line, which can cause out of memory errors and then task failure. By setting `mapred.linerecordreader.maxlength` to a value in bytes that fits in memory (and is comfortably greater than the length of lines in your input data), the record reader will skip the (long) corrupt lines without the task failing.

The best way to handle corrupt records is in your mapper or reducer code. You can detect the bad record and ignore it, or you can abort the job by throwing an exception. You can also count the total number of bad records in the job using counters to see how widespread the problem is.

In rare cases, though, you can't handle the problem because there is a bug in a third-party library that you can't work around in your mapper or reducer. In these cases, you can use Hadoop's optional *skipping mode* for automatically skipping bad records.

When skipping mode is enabled, tasks report the records being processed back to the tasktracker. When the task fails, the tasktracker retries the task, skipping the records that caused the failure. Because of the extra network traffic and bookkeeping to maintain the failed record ranges, skipping mode is turned on for a task only after it has failed twice.

Thus for a task consistently failing on a bad record, the tasktracker runs the following task attempts with these outcomes:

1. Task fails.
2. Task fails.
3. Skipping mode is enabled. Task fails but failed record is stored by the tasktracker.
4. Skipping mode is still enabled. Task succeeds by skipping the bad record that failed in the previous attempt.

Skipping mode is off by default; you enable it independently for map and reduce tasks using the `SkipBadRecords` class. It's important to note that skipping mode can detect only one bad record per task attempt, so this mechanism is appropriate only for detecting occasional bad records (a few per task, say). You may need to increase the maximum number of task attempts (via `mapred.map.max.attempts` and `mapred.reduce.max.attempts`) to give skipping mode enough attempts to detect and skip all the bad records in an input split.

Bad records that have been detected by Hadoop are saved as sequence files in the job's output directory under the *_logs/skip* subdirectory. These can be inspected for diagnostic purposes after the job has completed (using `hadoop fs -text`, for example).

The Task Execution Environment

Hadoop provides information to a map or reduce task about the environment in which it is running. For example, a map task can discover the name of the file it is processing (see "File information in the mapper" on page 192), and a map or reduce task can find out the attempt number of the task. The properties in Table 6-5 can be accessed from the job's configuration, obtained by providing an implementation of the `configure()` method for `Mapper` or `Reducer`, where the configuration is passed in as an argument.

Table 6-5. Task environment properties

Property name	Type	Description	Example
mapred.job.id	String	The job ID. (See "Job, Task, and Task Attempt IDs" on page 133 for a description of the format.)	job_200811201130_0004
mapred.tip.id	String	The task ID.	task_200811201130_0004_m_000003
mapred.task.id	String	The task attempt ID. (*Not* the task ID.)	attempt_200811201130_0004_m_000003_0
mapred.task.partition	int	The ID of the task within the job.	3
mapred.task.is.map	boolean	Whether this task is a map task.	true

Streaming environment variables

Hadoop sets job configuration parameters as environment variables for Streaming programs. However, it replaces nonalphanumeric characters with underscores to make sure they are valid names. The following Python expression illustrates how you can retrieve the value of the `mapred.job.id` property from within a Python Streaming script:

```
os.environ["mapred_job_id"]
```

You can also set environment variables for the Streaming processes launched by Map-Reduce by supplying the `-cmdenv` option to the Streaming launcher program (once for each variable you wish to set). For example, the following sets the `MAGIC_PARAMETER` environment variable:

```
-cmdenv MAGIC_PARAMETER=abracadabra
```

Task side-effect files

The usual way of writing output from map and reduce tasks is by using the `OutputCollector` to collect key-value pairs. Some applications need more flexibility than a single key-value pair model, so these applications write output files directly from the map or reduce task to a distributed filesystem, like HDFS. (There are other ways to produce multiple outputs, too, as described in "Multiple Outputs" on page 203.)

Care needs to be taken to ensure that multiple instances of the same task don't try to write to the same file. There are two problems to avoid: if a task failed and was retried, then the old partial output would still be present when the second task ran, and it would have to delete the old file first. Second, with speculative execution enabled, two instances of the same task could try to write to the same file simultaneously.

Hadoop solves this problem for the regular outputs from a task by writing outputs to a temporary directory that is specific to that task attempt. The directory is `${mapred.output.dir}/_temporary/${mapred.task.id}`. On successful completion of the task, the contents of the directory are copied to the job's output directory (`${mapred.output.dir}`). Thus if the task fails and is retried, the first attempt's partial output will just be cleaned up. A task and another speculative instance of the same task will get separate working directories, and only the first to finish will have the content of its working directory promoted to the output directory—the other will be discarded.

> The way that a task's output is committed on completion is implemented by an `OutputCommitter`, which is associated with the `OutputFormat`. The `OutputCommitter` for `FileOutputFormat` is a `FileOutputCommitter`, which implements the commit protocol described earlier. The `getOutputCommitter()` method on `OutputFormat` may be overridden to return a custom `OutputCommitter`, in case you want to implement the commit process in a different way.

Hadoop provides a mechanism for application writers to use this feature, too. A task may find its working directory by retrieving the value of the `mapred.work.output.dir` property from its configuration file. Alternatively, a MapReduce program using the Java API may call the `getWorkOutputPath()` static method on `FileOutputFormat` to get the `Path` object representing the working directory. The framework creates the working directory before executing the task, so you don't need to create it.

To take a simple example, imagine a program for converting image files from one format to another. One way to do this is to have a map-only job, where each map is given a set of images to convert (perhaps using `NLineInputFormat`; see "NLineInputFormat" on page 198). If a map task writes the converted images into its working directory, then they will be promoted to the output directory when the task successfully finishes.

## CHAPTER 7

MapReduce Types and Formats

MapReduce has a simple model of data processing: inputs and outputs for the map and reduce functions are key-value pairs. This chapter looks at the MapReduce model in detail, and, in particular, how data in various formats, from simple text to structured binary objects, can be used with this model.

MapReduce Types

The map and reduce functions in Hadoop MapReduce have the following general form:

```
map:    (K1, V1)         → list(K2, V2)
reduce: (K2, list(V2))   → list(K3, V3)
```

In general, the map input key and value types (K1 and V1) are different from the map output types (K2 and V2). However, the reduce input must have the same types as the map output, although the reduce output types may be different again (K3 and V3). The Java interfaces mirror this form:

```java
public interface Mapper<K1, V1, K2, V2> extends JobConfigurable, Closeable {

  void map(K1 key, V1 value, OutputCollector<K2, V2> output, Reporter reporter)
    throws IOException;
}

public interface Reducer<K2, V2, K3, V3> extends JobConfigurable, Closeable {

  void reduce(K2 key, Iterator<V2> values,
    OutputCollector<K3, V3> output, Reporter reporter) throws IOException;
}
```

Recall that the `OutputCollector` is purely for emitting key-value pairs (and is hence parameterized with their types), while the `Reporter` is for updating counters and status. (In the new MapReduce API in release 0.20.0 and later, these two functions are combined in a single context object.)

If a combine function is used then it is the same form as the reduce function (and is an implementation of `Reducer`), except its output types are the intermediate key and value types (K2 and V2), so they can feed the reduce function:

```
map: (K1, V1) → list(K2, V2)
combine: (K2, list(V2)) → list(K2, V2)
reduce: (K2, list(V2)) → list(K3, V3)
```

Often the combine and reduce functions are the same, in which case, K3 is the same as K2, and V3 is the same as V2.

The partition function operates on the intermediate key and value types (K2 and V2), and returns the partition index. In practice, the partition is determined solely by the key (the value is ignored):

```
partition: (K2, V2) → integer
```

Or in Java:

```
public interface Partitioner<K2, V2> extends JobConfigurable {

    int getPartition(K2 key, V2 value, int numPartitions);
}
```

So much for the theory, how does this help configure MapReduce jobs? Table 7-1 summarizes the configuration options. It is divided into the properties that determine the types, and those that have to be compatible with the configured types.

Table 7-1. *Configuration of MapReduce types*

Property	JobConf setter method	Input types		Intermediate types		Output types	
		K1	V1	K2	V2	K3	V3
Properties for configuring types:							
mapred.input.format.class	setInputFormat()	•	•				
mapred.mapoutput.key.class	setMapOutputKeyClass()			•			
mapred.mapoutput.value.class	setMapOutputValueClass()				•		
mapred.output.key.class	setOutputKeyClass()					•	
mapred.output.value.class	setOutputValueClass()						•
Properties that must be consistent with the types:							
mapred.mapper.class	setMapperClass()	•	•	•	•		
mapred.map.runner.class	setMapRunnerClass()	•	•	•	•		
mapred.combiner.class	setCombinerClass()			•	•		
mapred.partitioner.class	setPartitionerClass()			•	•		
mapred.output.key.comparator.class	setOutputKeyComparatorClass()			•			
mapred.output.value.groupfn.class	setOutputValueGroupingComparator()			•			
mapred.reducer.class	setReducerClass()			•	•	•	•
mapred.output.format.class	setOutputFormat()					•	•

Input types are set by the input format. So, for instance, a TextInputFormat generates keys of type LongWritable and values of type Text. The other types are set explicitly by calling the methods on the JobConf. If not set explicitly, the intermediate types default to the (final) output types, which default to LongWritable and Text. So if K2 and K3 are the same, you don't need to call setMapOutputKeyClass(), since it falls back to the type set by calling `setOutputKeyClass()`. Similarly, if V2 and V3 are the same, you only need to use `setOutputValueClass()`.

It may seem strange that these methods for setting the intermediate and final output types exist at all. After all, why can't the types be determined from a combination of the mapper and the reducer? The answer is that it's to do with a limitation in Java generics: type erasure means that the type information isn't always present at runtime, so Hadoop has to be given it explicitly. This also means that it's possible to configure a MapReduce job with incompatible types, because the configuration isn't checked at compile time. The settings that have to be compatible with the MapReduce types are listed in the lower part of Table 7-1. Type conflicts are detected at runtime during job execution, and for this reason, it is wise to run a test job using a small amount of data to flush out and fix any type incompatibilities.

The Default MapReduce Job

What happens when you run MapReduce without setting a mapper or a reducer? Let's try it by running this minimal MapReduce program:

```
public class MinimalMapReduce extends Configured implements Tool {

  @Override
  public int run(String[] args) throws Exception {
    if (args.length != 2) {
      System.err.printf("Usage: %s [generic options] <input> <output>\n",
          getClass().getSimpleName());
      ToolRunner.printGenericCommandUsage(System.err);
      return -1;
    }

    JobConf conf = new JobConf(getConf(), getClass());
    FileInputFormat.addInputPath(conf, new Path(args[0]));
    FileOutputFormat.setOutputPath(conf, new Path(args[1]));
    JobClient.runJob(conf);
    return 0;
  }

  public static void main(String[] args) throws Exception {
    int exitCode = ToolRunner.run(new MinimalMapReduce(), args);
    System.exit(exitCode);
  }
}
```

The only configuration that we set is an input path and an output path. We run it over a subset of our weather data with the following:

```
% hadoop MinimalMapReduce "input/ncdc/all/190{1,2}.gz" output
```

We do get some output: one file named *part-00000* in the output directory. Here's what the first few lines look like (truncated to fit the page):

0→0029029070999991901010106004+64333+023450FM-12+000599999V0202701N01591...
0→0035029070999991902010106004+64333+023450FM-12+000599999V0201401N01181...
135→0029029070999991901010113004+64333+023450FM-12+000599999V0202901N00821...
141→0035029070999991902010113004+64333+023450FM-12+000599999V0201401N01181...
270→0029029070999991901010120004+64333+023450FM-12+000599999V0209991C00001...
282→0035029070999991902010120004+64333+023450FM-12+000599999V0201401N01391...

Each line is an integer followed by a tab character, followed by the original weather data record. Admittedly, it's not a very useful program, but understanding how it produces its output does provide some insight into the defaults that Hadoop uses when running MapReduce jobs. Example 7-1 shows a program that has exactly the same effect as MinimalMapReduce, but explicitly sets the job settings to their defaults.

Example 7-1. A minimal MapReduce driver, with the defaults explicitly set

```java
public class MinimalMapReduceWithDefaults extends Configured implements Tool {

  @Override
  public int run(String[] args) throws IOException {
    JobConf conf = JobBuilder.parseInputAndOutput(this, getConf(), args);
    if (conf == null) {
      return -1;
    }

    conf.setInputFormat(TextInputFormat.class);

    conf.setNumMapTasks(1);
    conf.setMapperClass(IdentityMapper.class);
    conf.setMapRunnerClass(MapRunner.class);

    conf.setMapOutputKeyClass(LongWritable.class);
    conf.setMapOutputValueClass(Text.class);

    conf.setPartitionerClass(HashPartitioner.class);

    conf.setNumReduceTasks(1);
    conf.setReducerClass(IdentityReducer.class);

    conf.setOutputKeyClass(LongWritable.class);
    conf.setOutputValueClass(Text.class);

    conf.setOutputFormat(TextOutputFormat.class);

    JobClient.runJob(conf);
    return 0;
  }
  public static void main(String[] args) throws Exception {
    int exitCode = ToolRunner.run(new MinimalMapReduceWithDefaults(), args);
    System.exit(exitCode);
  }
}
```

We've simplified the first few lines of the run() method, by extracting the logic for printing usage and setting the input and output paths into a helper method. Almost all

MapReduce drivers take these two arguments (input and output), so reducing the boilerplate code here is a good thing. Here are the relevant methods in the `Job Builder` class for reference:

```
public static JobConf parseInputAndOutput(Tool tool, Configuration conf,
    String[] args) {

  if (args.length != 2) {
    printUsage(tool, "<input> <output>");
    return null;
  }
  JobConf jobConf = new JobConf(conf, tool.getClass());
  FileInputFormat.addInputPath(jobConf, new Path(args[0]));
  FileOutputFormat.setOutputPath(jobConf, new Path(args[1]));
  return jobConf;
}

public static void printUsage(Tool tool, String extraArgsUsage) {
  System.err.printf("Usage: %s [genericOptions] %s\n\n",
      tool.getClass().getSimpleName(), extraArgsUsage);
  GenericOptionsParser.printGenericCommandUsage(System.err);
}
```

Going back to `MinimalMapReduceWithDefaults` in Example 7-1, although there are many other default job settings, the ones highlighted are those most central to running a job. Let's go through them in turn.

The default input format is `TextInputFormat`, which produces keys of type `LongWritable` (the offset of the beginning of the line in the file) and values of type `Text` (the line of text). This explains where the integers in the final output come from: they are the line offsets.

Despite appearances, the `setNumMapTasks()` call does not necessarily set the number of map tasks to one, in fact. It is a hint, and the actual number of map tasks depends on the size of the input, and the file's block size (if the file is in HDFS). This is discussed further in "FileInputFormat input splits" on page 188.

The default mapper is `IdentityMapper`, which writes the input key and value unchanged to the output:

```
public class IdentityMapper<K, V>
    extends MapReduceBase implements Mapper<K, V, K, V> {

  public void map(K key, V val,
                  OutputCollector<K, V> output, Reporter reporter)
    throws IOException {
    output.collect(key, val);
  }
}
```

`IdentityMapper` is a generic type, which allows it to work with any key or value types, with the restriction that the map input and output keys are of the same type, and the map input and output values are of the same type. In this case, the map output key is `LongWritable` and the map output value is `Text`.

Map tasks are run by `MapRunner`, the default implementation of `MapRunnable` that calls the `Mapper`'s `map()` method sequentially with each record.

The default partitioner is `HashPartitioner`, which hashes a record's key to determine which partition the record belongs in. Each partition is processed by a reduce task, so the number of partitions is equal to the number of reduce tasks for the job:

```
public class HashPartitioner<K2, V2> implements Partitioner<K2, V2> {

  public void configure(JobConf job) {}

  public int getPartition(K2 key, V2 value,
                          int numPartitions) {
    return (key.hashCode() & Integer.MAX_VALUE) % numPartitions;
  }

}
```

The key's hash code is turned into a nonnegative integer by bitwise ANDing it with the largest integer value. It is then reduced modulo the number of partitions to find the index of the partition that the record belongs in.

By default, there is a single reducer, and therefore a single partition, so the action of the partitioner is irrelevant in this case since everything goes into one partition. However, it is important to understand the behavior of `HashPartitioner` when you have more than one reduce task. Assuming the key's hash function is a good one, the records will be evenly allocated across reduce tasks, with all records sharing the same key being processed by the same reduce task.

Choosing the Number of Reducers

The single reducer default is something of a gotcha for new users to Hadoop. Almost all real-world jobs should set this to a larger number; otherwise, the job will be very slow since all the intermediate data flows through a single reduce task. (Note that when running under the local job runner, only zero or one reducers are supported.)

The optimal number of reducers is related to the total number of available reducer slots in your cluster. The total number of slots is given by the product of the number of nodes in the cluster and the value of the `mapred.tasktracker.reduce.tasks.maximum` property (see "Environment Settings" on page 254).

One common setting is to have slightly fewer reducers than total slots, which gives one wave of reduce tasks (and tolerates a few failures, without extending job execution time). If your reduce tasks are very big, then it makes sense to have a larger number of reducers (resulting in two waves, for example) so that the tasks are more fine-grained, and failure doesn't affect job execution time significantly.

The default reducer is `IdentityReducer`, again a generic type, which simply writes all its input to its output:

```
public class IdentityReducer<K, V>
    extends MapReduceBase implements Reducer<K, V, K, V> {

  public void reduce(K key, Iterator<V> values,
                     OutputCollector<K, V> output, Reporter reporter)
    throws IOException {
    while (values.hasNext()) {
      output.collect(key, values.next());
    }
  }
}
```

For this job the output key is `LongWritable`, and the output value is `Text`. In fact, all the keys for this MapReduce program are `LongWritable`, and all the values are `Text`, since these are the input keys and values, and the map and reduce functions are both identity functions which by definition preserve type. Most MapReduce programs, however, don't use the same key or value types throughout, so you need to configure the job to declare the types you are using, as described in the previous section.

Records are sorted by the MapReduce system before being presented to the reducer. In this case the keys are sorted numerically, which has the effect of interleaving the lines from the input files into one combined output file.

The default output format is `TextOutputFormat`, which writes out records, one per line, by converting keys and values to strings and separating them with a tab character. This is why the output is tab-separated: it is a feature of `TextOutputFormat`.

The default Streaming job

In Streaming, the default job is similar, but not identical, to the Java equivalent. The minimal form is:

```
% hadoop jar $HADOOP_INSTALL/contrib/streaming/hadoop-*-streaming.jar \
  -input input/ncdc/sample.txt \
  -output output \
  -mapper /bin/cat
```

Notice that you have to supply a mapper: the default identity mapper will not work. The reason has to do with the default input format, `TextInputFormat`, which generates `LongWritable` keys and `Text` values. However, Streaming output keys and values (including the map keys and values) are always both of type `Text`.[*] The identity mapper cannot change `LongWritable` keys to `Text` keys, so it fails.

When we specify a non-Java mapper, and the input format is `TextInputFormat`, Streaming does something special. It doesn't pass the key to the mapper process, it just passes

---

[*] Except when used in binary mode, from version 0.21.0 onward, via the `-io rawbytes` or `-io typedbytes` options. Text mode (`-io text`) is the default.

the value. This is actually very useful, since the key is just the line offset in the file, and the value is the line, which is all most applications are interested in. The overall effect of this job is to perform a sort of the input.

With more of the defaults spelled out, the command looks like this:

```
% hadoop jar $HADOOP_INSTALL/contrib/streaming/hadoop-*-streaming.jar \
  -input input/ncdc/sample.txt \
  -output output \
  -inputformat org.apache.hadoop.mapred.TextInputFormat \
  -mapper /bin/cat \
  -partitioner org.apache.hadoop.mapred.lib.HashPartitioner \
  -numReduceTasks 1 \
  -reducer org.apache.hadoop.mapred.lib.IdentityReducer \
  -outputformat org.apache.hadoop.mapred.TextOutputFormat
```

The mapper and reducer arguments take a command or a Java class. A combiner may optionally be specified, using the -combiner argument.

Keys and values in Streaming

A Streaming application can control the separator that is used when a key-value pair is turned into a series of bytes and sent to the map or reduce process over standard input. The default is a tab character, but it is useful to be able to change it in the case that the keys or values themselves contain tab characters.

Similarly, when the map or reduce writes out key-value pairs, they may be separated by a configurable separator. Furthermore, the key from the output can be composed of more than the first field: it can be made up of the first n fields (defined by stream.num.map.output.key.fields or stream.num.reduce.output.key.fields), with the value being the remaining fields. For example, if the output from a Streaming process was a,b,c (and the separator is a comma), and n is two, then the key would be parsed as a,b and the value as c.

Separators may be configured independently for maps and reduces. The properties are listed in Table 7-2 and shown in a diagram of the data flow path in Figure 7-1.

These settings do not have any bearing on the input and output formats. For example, if stream.reduce.output.field.separator were set to be a colon, say, and the reduce stream process wrote the line a:b to standard out, then the Streaming reducer would know to extract the key as a and the value as b. With the standard TextOutputFormat, this record would be written to the output file with a tab separating a and b. You can change the separator that TextOutputFormat uses by setting mapred.textoutputformat.separator.

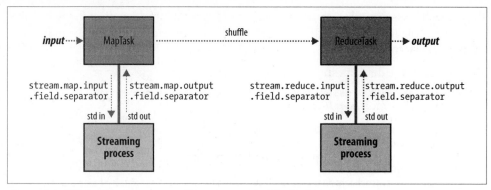

Figure 7-1. Where separators are used in a Streaming MapReduce job

Table 7-2. Streaming separator properties

Property name	Type	Default value	Description
stream.map.input.field.separator	String	\t	The separator to use when passing the input key and value strings to the stream map process as a stream of bytes.
stream.map.output.field.separator	String	\t	The separator to use when splitting the output from the stream map process into key and value strings for the map output.
stream.num.map.output.key.fields	int	1	The number of fields separated by stream.map.output.field.separator to treat as the map output key.
stream.reduce.input.field.separator	String	\t	The separator to use when passing the input key and value strings to the stream reduce process as a stream of bytes.
stream.reduce.output.field.separator	String	\t	The separator to use when splitting the output from the stream reduce process into key and value strings for the final reduce output.
stream.num.reduce.output.key.fields	int	1	The number of fields separated by stream.reduce.output.field.separator to treat as the reduce output key.

Input Formats

Hadoop can process many different types of data formats, from flat text files to databases. In this section, we explore the different formats available.

Input Splits and Records

As you saw in Chapter 2, an input split is a chunk of the input that is processed by a single map. Each map processes a single split. Each split is divided into records, and the map processes each record—a key-value pair—in turn. Splits and records are logical: there is nothing that requires them to be tied to files, for example, although in their most common incarnations, they are. In a database context, a split might correspond to a range of rows from a table, and a record to a row in that range (this is precisely what `DBInputFormat` does, an input format for reading data from a relational database).

Input splits are represented by the Java interface, `InputSplit` (which, like all of the classes mentioned in this section, is in the `org.apache.hadoop.mapred` package[†]):

```
public interface InputSplit extends Writable {

  long getLength() throws IOException;

  String[] getLocations() throws IOException;

}
```

An `InputSplit` has a length in bytes, and a set of storage locations, which are just hostname strings. Notice that a split doesn't contain the input data; it is just a reference to the data. The storage locations are used by the MapReduce system to place map tasks as close to the split's data as possible, and the size is used to order the splits so that the largest get processed first, in an attempt to minimize the job runtime (this is an instance of a greedy approximation algorithm).

As a MapReduce application writer, you don't need to deal with `InputSplit`s directly, as they are created by an `InputFormat`. An `InputFormat` is responsible for creating the input splits, and dividing them into records. Before we see some concrete examples of `InputFormat`, let's briefly examine how it is used in MapReduce. Here's the interface:

```
public interface InputFormat<K, V> {

  InputSplit[] getSplits(JobConf job, int numSplits) throws IOException;

  RecordReader<K, V> getRecordReader(InputSplit split,
                                     JobConf job,
                                     Reporter reporter) throws IOException;
}
```

The `JobClient` calls the `getSplits()` method, passing the desired number of map tasks as the `numSplits` argument. This number is treated as a hint, as `InputFormat` implementations are free to return a different number of splits to the number specified in `numSplits`. Having calculated the splits, the client sends them to the jobtracker, which uses their storage locations to schedule map tasks to process them on the tasktrackers.

[†] But see the new MapReduce classes in `org.apache.hadoop.mapreduce`, described in "The new Java MapReduce API" on page 25.

On a tasktracker, the map task passes the split to the `getRecordReader()` method on `InputFormat` to obtain a `RecordReader` for that split. A `RecordReader` is little more than an iterator over records, and the map task uses one to generate record key-value pairs, which it passes to the map function. A code snippet (based on the code in `MapRunner`) illustrates the idea:

```
K key = reader.createKey();
V value = reader.createValue();
while (reader.next(key, value)) {
  mapper.map(key, value, output, reporter);
}
```

Here the `RecordReader`'s `next()` method is called repeatedly to populate the key and value objects for the mapper. When the reader gets to the end of the stream, the `next()` method returns `false`, and the map task completes.

This code snippet makes it clear that the *same* key and value objects are used on each invocation of the `map()` method—only their contents are changed (by the reader's `next()` method). This can be a surprise to users, who might expect keys and values to be immutable. This causes problems when a reference to a key or value object is retained outside the `map()` method, as its value can change without warning. If you need to do this, make a copy of the object you want to hold on to. For example, for a `Text` object, you can use its copy constructor: `new Text(value)`.

The situation is similar with reducers. In this case the value objects in the reducer's iterator are reused, so you need to copy any that you need to retain between calls to the iterator (see Example 8-14).

Finally, note that `MapRunner` is only one way of running mappers. `MultithreadedMapRunner` is another implementation of the `MapRunnable` interface that runs mappers concurrently in a configurable number of threads (set by `mapred.map.multithreadedrunner.threads`). For most data processing tasks, it confers no advantage over `MapRunner`. However, for mappers that spend a long time processing each record, because they contact external servers, for example, it allows multiple mappers to run in one JVM with little contention. See "Fetcher: A multi-threaded MapRunner in action" on page 435 for an example of an application that uses `MultithreadedMapRunner`.

FileInputFormat

`FileInputFormat` is the base class for all implementations of `InputFormat` that use files as their data source (see Figure 7-2). It provides two things: a place to define which files are included as the input to a job, and an implementation for generating splits for the input files. The job of dividing splits into records is performed by subclasses.

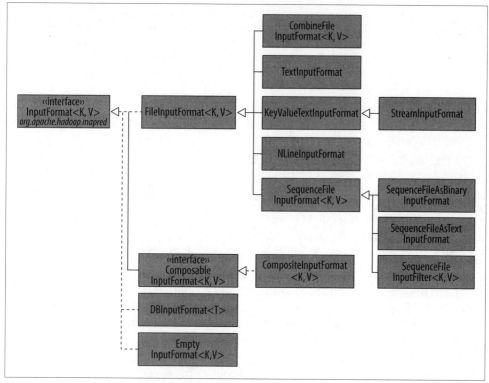

Figure 7-2. InputFormat class hierarchy

FileInputFormat input paths

The input to a job is specified as a collection of paths, which offers great flexibility in constraining the input to a job. FileInputFormat offers four static convenience methods for setting a JobConf's input paths:

```
public static void addInputPath(JobConf conf, Path path)
public static void addInputPaths(JobConf conf, String commaSeparatedPaths)
public static void setInputPaths(JobConf conf, Path... inputPaths)
public static void setInputPaths(JobConf conf, String commaSeparatedPaths)
```

The addInputPath() and addInputPaths() methods add a path or paths to the list of inputs. You can call these methods repeatedly to build the list of paths. The setInput Paths() methods set the entire list of paths in one go (replacing any paths set on the JobConf in previous calls).

A path may represent a file, a directory, or, by using a glob, a collection of files and directories. A path representing a directory includes all the files in the directory as input to the job. See "File patterns" on page 60 for more on using globs.

The contents of a directory specified as an input path are not processed recursively. In fact, the directory should only contain files: if the directory contains a subdirectory, it will be interpreted as a file, which will cause an error. The way to handle this case is to use a file glob or a filter to select only the files in the directory.

The add and set methods allow files to be specified by inclusion only. To exclude certain files from the input, you can set a filter using the `setInputPathFilter()` method on `FileInputFormat`:

```
public static void setInputPathFilter(JobConf conf,
                                      Class<? extends PathFilter> filter)
```

Filters are discussed in more detail in "PathFilter" on page 61.

Even if you don't set a filter, `FileInputFormat` uses a default filter that excludes hidden files (those whose names begin with a dot or an underscore). If you set a filter by calling `setInputPathFilter()`, it acts in addition to the default filter. In other words, only non-hidden files that are accepted by your filter get through.

Paths and filters can be set through configuration properties too (Table 7-3), which can be handy for Streaming and Pipes. Setting paths is done with the `-input` option for both Streaming and Pipes interfaces, so setting paths directly is not usually needed.

Table 7-3. Input path and filter properties

Property name	Type	Default value	Description
mapred.input.dir	comma-separated paths	none	The input files for a job. Paths that contain commas should have those commas escaped by a backslash character. For example, the glob {a,b} would be escaped as {a\,b}.
mapred.input.path Filter.class	PathFilter classname	none	The filter to apply to the input files for a job.

FileInputFormat input splits

Given a set of files, how does `FileInputFormat` turn them into splits? `FileInputFormat` splits only large files. Here "large" means larger than an HDFS block. The split size is normally the size of an HDFS block, which is appropriate for most applications; however, it is possible to control this value by setting various Hadoop properties, as shown in Table 7-4.

Table 7-4. Properties for controlling split size

Property name	Type	Default value	Description
`mapred.min.split.size`	`int`	1	The smallest valid size in bytes for a file split.
`mapred.max.split.size`[a]	`long`	`Long.MAX_VALUE`, that is 9223372036854775807	The largest valid size in bytes for a file split.
`dfs.block.size`	`long`	64 MB, that is 67108864	The size of a block in HDFS in bytes.

[a] This property is not present in the old MapReduce API (with the exception of `CombineFileInputFormat`). Instead, it is calculated indirectly as the size of the total input for the job, divided by the guide number of map tasks specified by `mapred.map.tasks` (or the `setNumMapTasks()` method on `JobConf`). Because `mapred.map.tasks` defaults to 1, this makes the maximum split size the size of the input.

The minimum split size is usually 1 byte, although some formats have a lower bound on the split size. (For example, sequence files insert sync entries every so often in the stream, so the minimum split size has to be large enough to ensure that every split has a sync point to allow the reader to resynchronize with a record boundary.)

Applications may impose a minimum split size: by setting this to a value larger than the block size, they can force splits to be larger than a block. There is no good reason for doing this when using HDFS, since doing so will increase the number of blocks that are not local to a map task.

The maximum split size defaults to the maximum value that can be represented by a Java `long` type. It has an effect only when it is less than the block size, forcing splits to be smaller than a block.

The split size is calculated by the formula (see the `computeSplitSize()` method in `FileInputFormat`):

```
max(minimumSize, min(maximumSize, blockSize))
```

by default:

```
minimumSize < blockSize < maximumSize
```

so the split size is `blockSize`. Various settings for these parameters and how they affect the final split size are illustrated in Table 7-5.

Table 7-5. Examples of how to control the split size

Minimum split size	Maximum split size	Block size	Split size	Comment
1 (default)	Long.MAX_VALUE (default)	64 MB (default)	64 MB	By default split size is the same as the default block size.
1 (default)	Long.MAX_VALUE (default)	128 MB	128 MB	The most natural way to increase the split size is to have larger blocks in HDFS, by setting dfs.block.size, or on a per-file basis at file construction time.
128 MB	Long.MAX_VALUE (default)	64 MB (default)	128 MB	Making the minimum split size greater than the block size increases the split size, but at the cost of locality.
1 (default)	32 MB	64 MB (default)	32 MB	Making the maximum split size less than the block size decreases the split size.

Small files and CombineFileInputFormat

Hadoop works better with a small number of large files than a large number of small files. One reason for this is that `FileInputFormat` generates splits in such a way that each split is all or part of a single file. If the file is very small ("small" means significantly smaller than an HDFS block) and there are a lot of them, then each map task will process very little input, and there will be a lot of them (one per file), each of which imposes extra bookkeeping overhead. Compare a 1 GB file broken into sixteen 64 MB blocks, and 10,000 or so 100 KB files. The 10,000 files use one map each, and the job time can be tens or hundreds of times slower than the equivalent one with a single input file and 16 map tasks.

The situation is alleviated somewhat by `CombineFileInputFormat`, which was designed to work well with small files. Where `FileInputFormat` creates a split per file, `CombineFileInputFormat` packs many files into each split so that each mapper has more to process. Crucially, `CombineFileInputFormat` takes node and rack locality into account when deciding which blocks to place in the same split, so it does not compromise the speed at which it can process the input in a typical MapReduce job.

Of course, if possible, it is still a good idea to avoid the many small files case since MapReduce works best when it can operate at the transfer rate of the disks in the cluster, and processing many small files increases the number of seeks that are needed to run a job. Also, storing large numbers of small files in HDFS is wasteful of the namenode's memory. One technique for avoiding the many small files case is to merge small files into larger files by using a SequenceFile: the keys can act as filenames (or a constant such as `NullWritable`, if not needed) and the values as file contents. See Example 7-4. But if you already have a large number of small files in HDFS, then `CombineFileInputFormat` is worth trying.

CombineFileInputFormat isn't just good for small files—it can bring benefits when processing large files too. Essentially, CombineFileInputFormat decouples the amount of data that a mapper consumes from the block size of the files in HDFS.

If your mappers can process each block in a matter of seconds, then you could use CombineFileInputFormat with the maximum split size set to a small multiple of the number of blocks (by setting the mapred.max.split.size property in bytes) so that each mapper processes more than one block. In return, the overall processing time falls, since proportionally fewer mappers run, which reduces the overhead in task bookkeeping and startup time associated with a large number of short-lived mappers.

Since CombineFileInputFormat is an abstract class without any concrete classes (unlike FileInputFormat), you need to do a bit more work to use it. (Hopefully, common implementations will be added to the library over time.) For example, to have the CombineFileInputFormat equivalent of TextInputFormat, you would create a concrete subclass of CombineFileInputFormat and implement the getRecordReader() method.

Preventing splitting

Some applications don't want files to be split so that a single mapper can process each input file in its entirety. For example, a simple way to check if all the records in a file are sorted is to go through the records in order, checking whether each record is not less than the preceding one. Implemented as a map task, this algorithm will work only if one map processes the whole file.[‡]

There are a couple of ways to ensure that an existing file is not split. The first (quick and dirty) way is to increase the minimum split size to be larger than the largest file in your system. Setting it to its maximum value, Long.MAX_VALUE, has this effect. The second is to subclass the concrete subclass of FileInputFormat that you want to use, to override the isSplitable() method[§] to return false. For example, here's a nonsplittable TextInputFormat:

```
import org.apache.hadoop.fs.*;
import org.apache.hadoop.mapred.TextInputFormat;

public class NonSplittableTextInputFormat extends TextInputFormat {
  @Override
  protected boolean isSplitable(FileSystem fs, Path file) {
    return false;
  }
}
```

[‡] This is how the mapper in SortValidator.RecordStatsChecker is implemented.

[§] In the method name isSplitable(), "splitable" has a single "t." It is usually spelled "splittable," which is the spelling I have used in this book.

File information in the mapper

A mapper processing a file input split can find information about the split by reading some special properties from its job configuration object, which may be obtained by implementing `configure()` in your `Mapper` implementation to get access to the `JobConf` object. Table 7-6 lists the properties available. These are in addition to the ones available to all mappers and reducers, listed in "The Task Execution Environment" on page 172.

Table 7-6. File split properties

Property name	Type	Description
map.input.file	String	The path of the input file being processed
map.input.start	long	The byte offset of the start of the split
map.input.length	long	The length of the split in bytes

In the next section, you shall see how to use this when we need to access the split's filename.

Processing a whole file as a record

A related requirement that sometimes crops up is for mappers to have access to the full contents of a file. Not splitting the file gets you part of the way there, but you also need to have a `RecordReader` that delivers the file contents as the value of the record. The listing for `WholeFileInputFormat` in Example 7-2 shows a way of doing this.

Example 7-2. An InputFormat for reading a whole file as a record

```
public class WholeFileInputFormat
    extends FileInputFormat<NullWritable, BytesWritable> {

  @Override
  protected boolean isSplitable(FileSystem fs, Path filename) {
    return false;
  }

  @Override
  public RecordReader<NullWritable, BytesWritable> getRecordReader(
      InputSplit split, JobConf job, Reporter reporter) throws IOException {

    return new WholeFileRecordReader((FileSplit) split, job);
  }
}
```

`WholeFileInputFormat` defines a format where the keys are not used, represented by `NullWritable`, and the values are the file contents, represented by `BytesWritable` instances. It defines two methods. First, the format is careful to specify that input files should never be split, by overriding `isSplitable()` to return `false`. Second, we implement getRecordReader() to return a custom implementation of RecordReader, which appears in Example 7-3.

Example 7-3. The RecordReader used by WholeFileInputFormat for reading a whole file as a record

```
class WholeFileRecordReader implements RecordReader<NullWritable, BytesWritable> {

  private FileSplit fileSplit;
  private Configuration conf;
  private boolean processed = false;

  public WholeFileRecordReader(FileSplit fileSplit, Configuration conf)
      throws IOException {
    this.fileSplit = fileSplit;
    this.conf = conf;
  }

  @Override
  public NullWritable createKey() {
    return NullWritable.get();
  }

  @Override
  public BytesWritable createValue() {
    return new BytesWritable();
  }

  @Override
  public long getPos() throws IOException {
    return processed ? fileSplit.getLength() : 0;
  }

  @Override
  public float getProgress() throws IOException {
    return processed ? 1.0f : 0.0f;
  }

  @Override
  public boolean next(NullWritable key, BytesWritable value) throws IOException {
    if (!processed) {
      byte[] contents = new byte[(int) fileSplit.getLength()];
      Path file = fileSplit.getPath();
      FileSystem fs = file.getFileSystem(conf);
      FSDataInputStream in = null;
      try {
        in = fs.open(file);
        IOUtils.readFully(in, contents, 0, contents.length);
        value.set(contents, 0, contents.length);
      } finally {
        IOUtils.closeStream(in);
      }
      processed = true;
      return true;
    }
    return false;
```

```
  }

  @Override
  public void close() throws IOException {
    // do nothing
  }
}
```

WholeFileRecordReader is responsible for taking a FileSplit and converting it into a single record, with a null key and a value containing the bytes of the file. Because there is only a single record, WholeFileRecordReader has either processed it or not, so it maintains a boolean called processed. If, when the next() method is called, the file has not been processed, then we open the file, create a byte array whose length is the length of the file, and use the Hadoop IOUtils class to slurp the file into the byte array. Then we set the array on the BytesWritable instance that was passed into the next() method, and return true to signal that a record has been read.

The other methods are straightforward bookkeeping methods for creating the correct key and value types, getting the position and progress of the reader, and a close() method, which is invoked by the MapReduce framework when the reader is done with.

To demonstrate how WholeFileInputFormat can be used, consider a MapReduce job for packaging small files into sequence files, where the key is the original filename, and the value is the content of the file. The listing is in Example 7-4.

Example 7-4. A MapReduce program for packaging a collection of small files as a single SequenceFile

```
public class SmallFilesToSequenceFileConverter extends Configured
  implements Tool {

  static class SequenceFileMapper extends MapReduceBase
      implements Mapper<NullWritable, BytesWritable, Text, BytesWritable> {

    private JobConf conf;

    @Override
    public void configure(JobConf conf) {
      this.conf = conf;
    }

    @Override
    public void map(NullWritable key, BytesWritable value,
        OutputCollector<Text, BytesWritable> output, Reporter reporter)
        throws IOException {

      String filename = conf.get("map.input.file");
      output.collect(new Text(filename), value);
    }

  }

  @Override
  public int run(String[] args) throws IOException {
```

```
    JobConf conf = JobBuilder.parseInputAndOutput(this, getConf(), args);
    if (conf == null) {
      return -1;
    }

    conf.setInputFormat(WholeFileInputFormat.class);
    conf.setOutputFormat(SequenceFileOutputFormat.class);

    conf.setOutputKeyClass(Text.class);
    conf.setOutputValueClass(BytesWritable.class);

    conf.setMapperClass(SequenceFileMapper.class);
    conf.setReducerClass(IdentityReducer.class);

    JobClient.runJob(conf);
    return 0;
  }

  public static void main(String[] args) throws Exception {
    int exitCode = ToolRunner.run(new SmallFilesToSequenceFileConverter(), args);
    System.exit(exitCode);
  }
}
```

Since the input format is a `WholeFileInputFormat`, the mapper has to find only the filename for the input file split. It does this by retrieving the `map.input.file` property from the `JobConf`, which is set to the split's filename by the MapReduce framework, but only for splits that are `FileSplit` instances (this includes most subclasses of `FileIn putFormat`). The reducer is the `IdentityReducer`, and the output format is a `SequenceFi leOutputFormat`.

Here's a run on a few small files. We've chosen to use two reducers, so we get two output sequence files:

```
% hadoop jar job.jar SmallFilesToSequenceFileConverter \
  -conf conf/hadoop-localhost.xml -D mapred.reduce.tasks=2 input/smallfiles output
```

Two part files are created, each of which is a sequence file, which we can inspect with the `-text` option to the filesystem shell:

```
% hadoop fs -conf conf/hadoop-localhost.xml -text output/part-00000
hdfs://localhost/user/tom/input/smallfiles/a   61 61 61 61 61 61 61 61 61 61
hdfs://localhost/user/tom/input/smallfiles/c   63 63 63 63 63 63 63 63 63 63
hdfs://localhost/user/tom/input/smallfiles/e
% hadoop fs -conf conf/hadoop-localhost.xml -text output/part-00001
hdfs://localhost/user/tom/input/smallfiles/b   62 62 62 62 62 62 62 62 62 62
hdfs://localhost/user/tom/input/smallfiles/d   64 64 64 64 64 64 64 64 64 64
hdfs://localhost/user/tom/input/smallfiles/f   66 66 66 66 66 66 66 66 66 66
```

The input files were named *a*, *b*, *c*, *d*, *e*, and *f*, and each contained 10 characters of the corresponding letter (so, for example, *a* contained 10 "a" characters), except *e*, which was empty. We can see this in the textual rendering of the sequence files, which prints the filename followed by the hex representation of the file.

There's at least one way we could improve this program. As mentioned earlier, having one mapper per file is inefficient, so subclassing `CombineFileInputFormat` instead of `FileInputFormat` is the better approach (there's code for this in the accompanying example code). Also, for a related technique of packing files into a Hadoop Archive, rather than a sequence file, see the section "Hadoop Archives" on page 71.

Text Input

Hadoop excels at processing unstructured text. In this section, we discuss the different `InputFormat`s that Hadoop provides to process text.

TextInputFormat

`TextInputFormat` is the default `InputFormat`. Each record is a line of input. The key, a `LongWritable`, is the byte offset within the file of the beginning of the line. The value is the contents of the line, excluding any line terminators (newline, carriage return), and is packaged as a `Text` object. So a file containing the following text:

```
On the top of the Crumpetty Tree
The Quangle Wangle sat,
But his face you could not see,
On account of his Beaver Hat.
```

is divided into one split of four records. The records are interpreted as the following key-value pairs:

```
(0, On the top of the Crumpetty Tree)
(33, The Quangle Wangle sat,)
(57, But his face you could not see,)
(89, On account of his Beaver Hat.)
```

Clearly, the keys are *not* line numbers. This would be impossible to implement in general, in that a file is broken into splits, at byte, not line, boundaries. Splits are processed independently. Line numbers are really a sequential notion: you have to keep a count of lines as you consume them, so knowing the line number within a split would be possible, but not within the file.

However, the offset within the file of each line is known by each split independently of the other splits, since each split knows the size of the preceding splits and just adds this on to the offsets within the split to produce a global file offset. The offset is usually sufficient for applications that need a unique identifier for each line. Combined with the file's name, it is unique within the filesystem. Of course, if all the lines are a fixed width, then calculating the line number is simply a matter of dividing the offset by the width.

The Relationship Between Input Splits and HDFS Blocks

The logical records that `FileInputFormat`s define do not usually fit neatly into HDFS blocks. For example, a `TextInputFormat`'s logical records are lines, which will cross HDFS boundaries more often than not. This has no bearing on the functioning of your program—lines are not missed or broken, for example—but it's worth knowing about, as it does mean that data-local maps (that is, maps that are running on the same host as their input data) will perform some remote reads. The slight overhead this causes is not normally significant.

Figure 7-3 shows an example. A single file is broken into lines, and the line boundaries do not correspond with the HDFS block boundaries. Splits honor logical record boundaries, in this case lines, so we see that the first split contains line 5, even though it spans the first and second block. The second split starts at line 6.

Figure 7-3. Logical records and HDFS blocks for TextInputFormat

KeyValueTextInputFormat

`TextInputFormat`'s keys, being simply the offset within the file, are not normally very useful. It is common for each line in a file to be a key-value pair, separated by a delimiter such as a tab character. For example, this is the output produced by `TextOutputFormat`, Hadoop's default `OutputFormat`. To interpret such files correctly, `KeyValueTextInputFormat` is appropriate.

You can specify the separator via the `key.value.separator.in.input.line` property. It is a tab character by default. Consider the following input file, where → represents a (horizontal) tab character:

```
line1→On the top of the Crumpetty Tree
line2→The Quangle Wangle sat,
line3→But his face you could not see,
line4→On account of his Beaver Hat.
```

Like in the `TextInputFormat` case, the input is in a single split comprising four records, although this time the keys are the Text sequences before the tab in each line:

```
(line1, On the top of the Crumpetty Tree)
(line2, The Quangle Wangle sat,)
(line3, But his face you could not see,)
(line4, On account of his Beaver Hat.)
```

NLineInputFormat

With `TextInputFormat` and `KeyValueTextInputFormat`, each mapper receives a variable number of lines of input. The number depends on the size of the split and the length of the lines. If you want your mappers to receive a fixed number of lines of input, then `NLineInputFormat` is the `InputFormat` to use. Like `TextInputFormat`, the keys are the byte offsets within the file and the values are the lines themselves.

N refers to the number of lines of input that each mapper receives. With N set to one (the default), each mapper receives exactly one line of input. The `mapred.line.input.format.linespermap` property controls the value of N. By way of example, consider these four lines again:

```
On the top of the Crumpetty Tree
The Quangle Wangle sat,
But his face you could not see,
On account of his Beaver Hat.
```

If, for example, N is two, then each split contains two lines. One mapper will receive the first two key-value pairs:

```
(0, On the top of the Crumpetty Tree)
(33, The Quangle Wangle sat,)
```

And another mapper will receive the second two key-value pairs:

```
(57, But his face you could not see,)
(89, On account of his Beaver Hat.)
```

The keys and values are the same as `TextInputFormat` produces. What is different is the way the splits are constructed.

Usually having a map task for a small number of lines of input is inefficient (due to the overhead in task setup), but there are applications that take a small amount of input data and run an extensive (that is, CPU-intensive) computation for it, then emit their output. Simulations are a good example. By creating an input file that specifies input parameters, one per line, you can perform a *parameter sweep*: run a set of simulations in parallel to find how a model varies as the parameter changes.

If you have long-running simulations, you may fall afoul of task time-outs. When a task doesn't report progress for more than 10 minutes, then the tasktracker assumes it has failed and aborts the process (see "Task Failure" on page 159).

The best way to guard against this is to report progress periodically, by writing a status message, or incrementing a counter, for example. See "What Constitutes Progress in MapReduce?" on page 158.

Another example is using Hadoop to bootstrap data loading from multiple data sources, such as databases. You create a "seed" input file which lists the data sources, one per line. Then each mapper is allocated a single data source, and it loads the data from that source into HDFS. The job doesn't need the reduce phase, so the number of re-ducers should be set to zero (by calling `setNumReduceTasks()` on `Job`). Furthermore, MapReduce jobs can be run to process the data loaded into HDFS. See Appendix C for an example.

XML

Most XML parsers operate on whole XML documents, so if a large XML document is made up of multiple input splits, then it is a challenge to parse these individually. Of course, you can process the entire XML document in one mapper (if it is not too large) using the technique in "Processing a whole file as a record" on page 192.

Large XML documents that are composed of a series of "records" (XML document fragments) can be broken into these records using simple string or regular-expression matching to find start and end tags of records. This alleviates the problem when the document is split by the framework, since the next start tag of a record is easy to find by simply scanning from the start of the split, just like `TextInputFormat` finds newline boundaries.

Hadoop comes with a class for this purpose called `StreamXmlRecordReader` (which is in the `org.apache.hadoop.streaming` package, although it can be used outside of Stream-ing). You can use it by setting your input format to `StreamInputFormat`, and setting the `stream.recordreader.class` property to `org.apache.hadoop.streaming.StreamXmlRecor dReader`. The reader is configured by setting job configuration properties to tell it the patterns for the start and end tags (see the class documentation for details).‖

To take an example, Wikipedia provides dumps of its content in XML form, which are appropriate for processing in parallel using MapReduce using this approach. The data is contained in one large XML wrapper document, which contains a series of elements, such as `page` elements that contain a page's content and associated metadata. Using `StreamXmlRecordReader`, the `page` elements can be interpreted as records for processing by a mapper.

Binary Input

Hadoop MapReduce is not just restricted to processing textual data—it has support for binary formats, too.

SequenceFileInputFormat

Hadoop's sequence file format stores sequences of binary key-value pairs. They are well suited as a format for MapReduce data since they are splittable (they have sync points so that readers can synchronize with record boundaries from an arbitrary point in the file, such as the start of a split), they support compression as a part of the format, and

---

‖ See *https://issues.apache.org/jira/browse/HADOOP-2439* for an improved XML input format.

they can store arbitrary types using a variety of serialization frameworks. (These topics are covered in "SequenceFile" on page 103.)

To use data from sequence files as the input to MapReduce, you use `SequenceFileIn` `putFormat`. The keys and values are determined by the sequence file, and you need to make sure that your map input types correspond. For example, if your sequence file has `IntWritable` keys and `Text` values, like the one created in Chapter 4, then the map signature would be `Mapper<IntWritable, Text, K, V>`, where K and V are the types of the map's output keys and values.

 Although its name doesn't give it away, `SequenceFileInputFormat` can read MapFiles as well as sequence files. If it finds a directory where it was expecting a sequence file, `SequenceFileInputFormat` assumes that it is reading a MapFile and uses its data file. This is why there is no `MapFileInputFormat` class.

SequenceFileAsTextInputFormat

`SequenceFileAsTextInputFormat` is a variant of `SequenceFileInputFormat` that converts the sequence file's keys and values to `Text` objects. The conversion is performed by calling `toString()` on the keys and values. This format makes sequence files suitable input for Streaming.

SequenceFileAsBinaryInputFormat

`SequenceFileAsBinaryInputFormat` is a variant of `SequenceFileInputFormat` that retrieves the sequence file's keys and values as opaque binary objects. They are encapsulated as `BytesWritable` objects, and the application is free to interpret the underlying byte array as it pleases. Combined with `SequenceFile.Reader`'s `appendRaw()` method, this provides a way to use any binary data types with MapReduce (packaged as a sequence file), although plugging into Hadoop's serialization mechanism is normally a cleaner alternative (see "Serialization Frameworks" on page 101).

Multiple Inputs

Although the input to a MapReduce job may consist of multiple input files (constructed by a combination of file globs, filters and plain paths), all of the input is interpreted by a single `InputFormat` and a single `Mapper`. What often happens, however, is that over time, the data format evolves, so you have to write your mapper to cope with all of your legacy formats. Or, you have data sources that provide the same type of data but in different formats. This arises in the case of performing joins of different datasets; see "Reduce-Side Joins" on page 235. For instance, one might be tab-separated plain text, the other a binary sequence file. Even if they are in the same format, they may have different representations, and therefore need to be parsed differently.

These cases are handled elegantly by using the `MultipleInputs` class, which allows you to specify the `InputFormat` and `Mapper` to use on a per-path basis. For example, if we had weather data from the U.K. Met Office[#] that we wanted to combine with the NCDC data for our maximum temperature analysis, then we might set up the input as follows:

```
MultipleInputs.addInputPath(conf, ncdcInputPath,
    TextInputFormat.class, MaxTemperatureMapper.class)
MultipleInputs.addInputPath(conf, metOfficeInputPath,
    TextInputFormat.class, MetOfficeMaxTemperatureMapper.class);
```

This code replaces the usual calls to `FileInputFormat.addInputPath()` and `conf.setMapperClass()`. Both Met Office and NCDC data is text-based, so we use `TextInputFormat` for each. But the line format of the two data sources is different, so we use two different mappers. The `MaxTemperatureMapper` reads NCDC input data and extracts the year and temperature fields. The `MetOfficeMaxTemperatureMapper` reads Met Office input data and extracts the year and temperature fields. The important thing is that the map outputs have the same types, since the reducers (which are all of the same type) see the aggregated map outputs and are not aware of the different mappers used to produce them.

The `MultipleInputs` class has an overloaded version of `addInputPath()` that doesn't take a mapper:

```
public static void addInputPath(JobConf conf, Path path,
                        Class<? extends InputFormat> inputFormatClass)
```

This is useful when you only have one mapper (set using the `JobConf`'s `setMapperClass()` method), but multiple input formats.

Database Input (and Output)

`DBInputFormat` is an input format for reading data from a relational database, using JDBC. Because it doesn't have any sharding capabilities, you need to be careful not to overwhelm the database you are reading from by running too many mappers. For this reason, it is best used for loading relatively small datasets, perhaps for joining with larger datasets from HDFS, using `MultipleInputs`. The corresponding output format is `DBOutputFormat`, which is useful for dumping job outputs (of modest size) into a database.[*]

[#] Met Office data is generally available only to the research and academic community. However, there is a small amount of monthly weather station data available at *http://www.metoffice.gov.uk/climate/uk/stationdata/*.

[*] Instructions for how to use these formats are provided in "Database Access with Hadoop," *http://www.cloudera.com/blog/2009/03/06/database-access-with-hadoop/*, by Aaron Kimball.

HBase's `TableInputFormat` is designed to allow a MapReduce program to operate on data stored in an HBase table. `TableOutputFormat` is for writing MapReduce outputs into an HBase table.

Output Formats

Hadoop has output data formats that correspond to the input formats covered in the previous section. The `OutputFormat` class hierarchy appears in Figure 7-4.

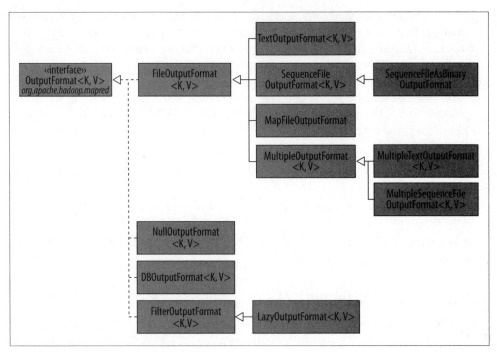

Figure 7-4. OutputFormat class hierarchy

Text Output

The default output format, `TextOutputFormat`, writes records as lines of text. Its keys and values may be of any type, since `TextOutputFormat` turns them to strings by calling `toString()` on them. Each key-value pair is separated by a tab character, although that may be changed using the `mapred.textoutputformat.separator` property. The counterpart to `TextOuputFormat` for reading in this case is `KeyValueTextInputFormat`, since it breaks lines into key-value pairs based on a configurable separator (see "KeyValue-TextInputFormat" on page 197).

You can suppress the key or the value (or both, making this output format equivalent to `NullOutputFormat`, which emits nothing) from the output using a `NullWritable` type.

This also causes no separator to be written, which makes the output suitable for reading in using TextInputFormat.

Binary Output

SequenceFileOutputFormat

As the name indicates, SequenceFileOutputFormat writes sequence files for its output. This is a good choice of output if it forms the input to a further MapReduce job, since it is compact, and is readily compressed. Compression is controlled via the static methods on SequenceFileOutputFormat, as described in "Using Compression in Map-Reduce" on page 84. For an example of how to use SequenceFileOutputFormat, see "Sorting" on page 218.

SequenceFileAsBinaryOutputFormat

SequenceFileAsBinaryOutputFormat is the counterpart to SequenceFileAsBinaryInput Format, and it writes keys and values in raw binary format into a SequenceFile container.

MapFileOutputFormat

MapFileOutputFormat writes MapFiles as output. The keys in a MapFile must be added in order, so you need to ensure that your reducers emit keys in sorted order.

> The reduce *input* keys are guaranteed to be sorted, but the output keys are under the control of the reduce function, and there is nothing in the general MapReduce contract that states that the reduce *output* keys have to be ordered in any way. The extra constraint of sorted reduce output keys is just needed for MapFileOutputFormat.

Multiple Outputs

FileOutputFormat and its subclasses generate a set of files in the output directory. There is one file per reducer and files are named by the partition number: *part-00000*, *part-00001*, etc. There is sometimes a need to have more control over the naming of the files, or to produce multiple files per reducer. MapReduce comes with two libraries to help you do this: MultipleOutputFormat and MultipleOutputs.

An example: Partitioning data

Consider the problem of partitioning the weather dataset by weather station. We would like to run a job whose output is a file per station, with each file containing all the records for that station.

One way of doing this is to have a reducer for each weather station. To arrange this, we need to do two things. First, write a partitioner that puts records from the same weather station into the same partition. Second, set the number of reducers on the job to be the number of weather stations. The partitioner would look like this:

```
public class StationPartitioner implements Partitioner<LongWritable, Text> {

  private NcdcRecordParser parser = new NcdcRecordParser();

  @Override
  public int getPartition(LongWritable key, Text value, int numPartitions) {
    parser.parse(value);
    return getPartition(parser.getStationId());
  }

  private int getPartition(String stationId) {
    ...
  }

  @Override
  public void configure(JobConf conf) { }
}
```

The getPartition(String) method, whose implementation is not shown, turns the station ID into a partition index. To do this, it needs a list of all the station IDs and then just returns the index of the station ID in the list.

There are two drawbacks to this approach. The first is that since the number of partitions needs to be known before the job is run, so does the number of weather stations. Although the NCDC provides metadata about its stations, there is no guarantee that the IDs encountered in the data match those in the metadata. A station that appears in the metadata but not in the data wastes a reducer slot. Worse, a station that appears in the data but not in the metadata doesn't get a reducer slot—it has to be thrown away. One way of mitigating this problem would be to write a job to extract the unique station IDs, but it's a shame that we need an extra job to do this.

The second drawback is more subtle. It is generally a bad idea to allow the number of partitions to be rigidly fixed by the application, since it can lead to small or uneven-sized partitions. Having many reducers doing a small amount of work isn't an efficient way of organizing a job: it's much better to get reducers to do more work and have fewer of them, as the overhead in running a task is then reduced. Uneven-sized partitions can be difficult to avoid too. Different weather stations will have gathered a widely varying amount of data: compare a station that opened one year ago to one that has been gathering data for one century. If a few reduce tasks take significantly longer than the others, they will dominate the job execution time and cause it to be longer than it needs to be.

There are two special cases when it does make sense to allow the application to set the number of partitions (or equivalently, the number of reducers):

Zero reducers
> This is a vacuous case: there are no partitions, as the application needs to run only map tasks.

One reducer
> It can be convenient to run small jobs to combine the output of previous jobs into a single file. This should only be attempted when the amount of data is small enough to be processed comfortably by one reducer.

It is much better to let the cluster drive the number of partitions for a job; the idea being that the more cluster reduce slots are available the faster the job can complete. This is why the default `HashPartitioner` works so well, as it works with any number of partitions and ensures each partition has a good mix of keys leading to more even-sized partitions.

If we go back to using `HashPartitioner`, each partition will contain multiple stations, so to create a file per station, we need to arrange for each reducer to write multiple files, which is where `MultipleOutputFormat` comes in.

MultipleOutputFormat

`MultipleOutputFormat` allows you to write data to multiple files whose names are derived from the output keys and values. `MultipleOutputFormat` is an abstract class with two concrete subclasses, `MultipleTextOutputFormat` and `MultipleSequenceFileOutput Format`, which are the multiple file equivalents of `TextOutputFormat` and `SequenceFi leOutputFormat`. `MultipleOutputFormat` provides a few protected methods that subclasses can override to control the output filename. In Example 7-5, we create a subclass of `MultipleTextOutputFormat` to override the `generateFileNameForKeyValue()` method to return the station ID, which we extracted from the record value.

Example 7-5. Partitioning whole dataset into files named by the station ID using MultipleOutputFormat

```
public class PartitionByStationUsingMultipleOutputFormat extends Configured
  implements Tool {

  static class StationMapper extends MapReduceBase
    implements Mapper<LongWritable, Text, Text, Text> {

    private NcdcRecordParser parser = new NcdcRecordParser();

    public void map(LongWritable key, Text value,
        OutputCollector<Text, Text> output, Reporter reporter)
        throws IOException {
```

```
      parser.parse(value);
      output.collect(new Text(parser.getStationId()), value);
    }
  }

  static class StationReducer extends MapReduceBase
    implements Reducer<Text, Text, NullWritable, Text> {

    @Override
    public void reduce(Text key, Iterator<Text> values,
        OutputCollector<NullWritable, Text> output, Reporter reporter)
        throws IOException {
      while (values.hasNext()) {
        output.collect(NullWritable.get(), values.next());
      }
    }
  }

  static class StationNameMultipleTextOutputFormat
    extends MultipleTextOutputFormat<NullWritable, Text> {

    private NcdcRecordParser parser = new NcdcRecordParser();

    protected String generateFileNameForKeyValue(NullWritable key, Text value,
        String name) {
      parser.parse(value);
      return parser.getStationId();
    }
  }

  @Override
  public int run(String[] args) throws IOException {
    JobConf conf = JobBuilder.parseInputAndOutput(this, getConf(), args);
    if (conf == null) {
      return -1;
    }

    conf.setMapperClass(StationMapper.class);
    conf.setMapOutputKeyClass(Text.class);
    conf.setReducerClass(StationReducer.class);
    conf.setOutputKeyClass(NullWritable.class);
    conf.setOutputFormat(StationNameMultipleTextOutputFormat.class);

    JobClient.runJob(conf);
    return 0;
  }

  public static void main(String[] args) throws Exception {
    int exitCode = ToolRunner.run(
        new PartitionByStationUsingMultipleOutputFormat(), args);
    System.exit(exitCode);
  }
}
```

`StationMapper` pulls the station ID from the record and uses it as the key. This causes records from the same station to go into the same partition. `StationReducer` replaces the key with a `NullWritable` so that when the final output is written using `StationName` `MultipleTextOutputFormat` (which like `TextOutputFormat` drops `NullWritable` keys), it consists solely of weather records (and not the station ID key).

The overall effect is to place all the records for one station in a file named by the station ID. Here is a few lines of output after running the program over a subset of the total dataset:

```
-rw-r--r--   3 root supergroup   2887145 2009-04-17 10:34 /output/010010-99999
-rw-r--r--   3 root supergroup   1395129 2009-04-17 10:33 /output/010050-99999
-rw-r--r--   3 root supergroup   2054455 2009-04-17 10:33 /output/010100-99999
-rw-r--r--   3 root supergroup   1422448 2009-04-17 10:34 /output/010280-99999
-rw-r--r--   3 root supergroup   1419378 2009-04-17 10:34 /output/010550-99999
-rw-r--r--   3 root supergroup   1384421 2009-04-17 10:33 /output/010980-99999
-rw-r--r--   3 root supergroup   1480077 2009-04-17 10:33 /output/011060-99999
-rw-r--r--   3 root supergroup   1400448 2009-04-17 10:33 /output/012030-99999
-rw-r--r--   3 root supergroup    307141 2009-04-17 10:34 /output/012350-99999
-rw-r--r--   3 root supergroup   1433994 2009-04-17 10:33 /output/012620-99999
```

The filename returned by `generateFileNameForKeyValue()` is actually a path that is interpreted relative to the output directory. It's possible to create subdirectories of arbitrary depth. For example, the following modification partitions the data by station and year so that each year's data is contained in a directory named by the station ID:

```java
protected String generateFileNameForKeyValue(NullWritable key, Text value,
    String name) {
  parser.parse(value);
  return parser.getStationId() + "/" + parser.getYear();
}
```

`MultipleOutputFormat` has more features that are not discussed here, such as the ability to copy the input directory structure and file naming for a map-only job. Please consult the Java documentation for details.

MultipleOutputs

There's a second library in Hadoop for generating multiple outputs, provided by the `MultipleOutputs` class. Unlike `MultipleOutputFormat`, `MultipleOutputs` can emit different types for each output. On the other hand, there is less control over the naming of outputs. The program in Example 7-6 shows how to use `MultipleOutputs` to partition the dataset by station.

Example 7-6. Partitioning whole dataset into files named by the station ID using MultipleOutputs

```java
public class PartitionByStationUsingMultipleOutputs extends Configured
  implements Tool {

  static class StationMapper extends MapReduceBase
    implements Mapper<LongWritable, Text, Text, Text> {
```

```
    private NcdcRecordParser parser = new NcdcRecordParser();

    public void map(LongWritable key, Text value,
        OutputCollector<Text, Text> output, Reporter reporter)
        throws IOException {

      parser.parse(value);
      output.collect(new Text(parser.getStationId()), value);
    }
  }

  static class MultipleOutputsReducer extends MapReduceBase
    implements Reducer<Text, Text, NullWritable, Text> {

    private MultipleOutputs multipleOutputs;

    @Override
    public void configure(JobConf conf) {
      multipleOutputs = new MultipleOutputs(conf);
    }

    public void reduce(Text key, Iterator<Text> values,
        OutputCollector<NullWritable, Text> output, Reporter reporter)
        throws IOException {

      OutputCollector collector = multipleOutputs.getCollector("station",
          key.toString().replace("-", ""), reporter);
      while (values.hasNext()) {
        collector.collect(NullWritable.get(), values.next());
      }
    }

    @Override
    public void close() throws IOException {
      multipleOutputs.close();
    }
  }

  @Override
  public int run(String[] args) throws IOException {
    JobConf conf = JobBuilder.parseInputAndOutput(this, getConf(), args);
    if (conf == null) {
      return -1;
    }

    conf.setMapperClass(StationMapper.class);
    conf.setMapOutputKeyClass(Text.class);
    conf.setReducerClass(MultipleOutputsReducer.class);
    conf.setOutputKeyClass(NullWritable.class);
    conf.setOutputFormat(NullOutputFormat.class); // suppress empty part file

    MultipleOutputs.addMultiNamedOutput(conf, "station", TextOutputFormat.class,
        NullWritable.class, Text.class);

    JobClient.runJob(conf);
```

```
      return 0;
    }
    public static void main(String[] args) throws Exception {
      int exitCode = ToolRunner.run(new PartitionByStationUsingMultipleOutputs(),
          args);
      System.exit(exitCode);
    }
}
```

The `MultipleOutputs` class is used to generate additional outputs to the usual output. Outputs are given names, and may be written to a single file (called *single named output*), or to multiple files (called *multi named output*). In this case, we want multiple files, one for each station, so we use a multi named output, which we initialize in the driver by calling the `addMultiNamedOutput()` method of `MultipleOutputs` to specify the name of the output (here `"station"`), the output format, and the output types. In addition, we set the regular output format to be `NullOutputFormat` in order to suppress the usual output.

In the reducer, where we generate the output, we construct an instance of `MultipleOut puts` in the `configure()` method, and assign it to an instance variable. We use the `MultipleOutputs` instance in the `reduce()` method to retrieve an `OutputCollector` for the multi named output. The `getCollector()` method takes the name of the output (`"station"` again) as well as a string identifying the part within the multi named output. Here we use the station identifier, with the "-" separator in the key removed, since only alphanumeric characters are allowed by `MultipleOutputs`.

The overall effect is to produce output files with the naming scheme `station_<station identifier>-r-<part_number>`. The `r` appears in the name because the output is produced by the reducer, and the part number is appended to be sure that there are no collisions resulting from different partitions (reducers) writing output for the same station. Since we partition by station, it cannot happen in this case (but it can in the general case).

In one run, the first few output files were named as follows (other columns from the directory listing have been dropped):

```
/output/station_01001099999-r-00027
/output/station_01005099999-r-00013
/output/station_01010099999-r-00015
/output/station_01028099999-r-00014
/output/station_01055099999-r-00000
/output/station_01098099999-r-00011
/output/station_01106099999-r-00025
/output/station_01203099999-r-00029
/output/station_01235099999-r-00018
/output/station_01262099999-r-00004
```

What's the Difference Between MultipleOutputFormat and MultipleOutputs?

It's unfortunate (although not necessarily unusual in an open source project) to have two libraries that do almost the same thing, since it is confusing for users. To help you choose which to use, here is a brief comparison.

Feature	MultipleOutputFormat	MultipleOutputs
Complete control over names of files and directories	Yes	No
Different key and value types for different outputs	No	Yes
Use from map and reduce in the same job	No	Yes
Multiple outputs per record	No	Yes
Use with any OutputFormat	No, need to subclass	Yes

So in summary, MultipleOutputs is more fully featured, but MultipleOutputFormat has more control over the output directory structure and file naming.

Lazy Output

FileOutputFormat subclasses will create output (*part-nnnnn*) files, even if they are empty. Some applications prefer that empty files not be created, which is where LazyOutput Format helps.[†] It is a wrapper output format that ensures that the output file is created only when the first record is emitted for a given partition. To use it, call its setOutput FormatClass() method with the JobConf and the underlying output format.

Streaming and Pipes support a -lazyOutput option to enable LazyOutputFormat.

Database Output

The output formats for writing to relational databases and to HBase are mentioned in "Database Input (and Output)" on page 201.

[†] LazyOutputFormat is available from release 0.21.0 of Hadoop.

## CHAPTER 8

MapReduce Features

This chapter looks at some of the more advanced features of MapReduce, including counters and sorting and joining datasets.

Counters

There are often things you would like to know about the data you are analyzing but which are peripheral to the analysis you are performing. For example, if you were counting invalid records, and discovered that the proportion of invalid records in the whole dataset was very high, you might be prompted to check why so many records were being marked as invalid—perhaps there is a bug in the part of the program that detects invalid records? Or if the data were of poor quality and genuinely did have very many invalid records, after discovering this, you might decide to increase the size of the dataset so that the number of good records was large enough for meaningful analysis.

Counters are a useful channel for gathering statistics about the job: for quality control, or for application level-statistics. They are also useful for problem diagnosis. If you are tempted to put a log message into your map or reduce task, then it is often better to see whether you can use a counter instead to record that a particular condition occurred. In addition to counter values being much easier to retrieve than log output for large distributed jobs, you get a record of the number of times that condition occurred, which is more work to obtain from a set of logfiles.

Built-in Counters

Hadoop maintains some built-in counters for every job (Table 8-1), which report various metrics for your job. For example, there are counters for the number of bytes and records processed, which allows you to confirm that the expected amount of input was consumed and the expected amount of output was produced.

Table 8-1. Built-in counters

Group	Counter	Description
Map-Reduce Framework	Map input records	The number of input records consumed by all the maps in the job. Incremented every time a record is read from a `RecordReader` and passed to the map's `map()` method by the framework.
	Map skipped records	The number of input records skipped by all the maps in the job. See "Skipping Bad Records" on page 171.
	Map input bytes	The number of bytes of uncompressed input consumed by all the maps in the job. Incremented every time a record is read from a `RecordReader` and passed to the map's `map()` method by the framework.
	Map output records	The number of map output records produced by all the maps in the job. Incremented every time the `collect()` method is called on a map's `OutputCollector`.
	Map output bytes	The number of bytes of uncompressed output produced by all the maps in the job. Incremented every time the `collect()` method is called on a map's `OutputCollector`.
	Combine input records	The number of input records consumed by all the combiners (if any) in the job. Incremented every time a value is read from the combiner's iterator over values. Note that this count is the number of values consumed by the combiner, not the number of distinct key groups (which would not be a useful metric, since there is not necessarily one group per key for a combiner; see "Combiner Functions" on page 29, and also "Shuffle and Sort" on page 163).
	Combine output records	The number of output records produced by all the combiners (if any) in the job. Incremented every time the `collect()` method is called on a combiner's `OutputCollector`.
	Reduce input groups	The number of distinct key groups consumed by all the reducers in the job. Incremented every time the reducer's `reduce()` method is called by the framework.
	Reduce input records	The number of input records consumed by all the reducers in the job. Incremented every time a value is read from the reducer's iterator over values. If reducers consume all of their inputs this count should be the same as the count for Map output records.
	Reduce output records	The number of reduce output records produced by all the maps in the job. Incremented every time the `collect()` method is called on a reducer's `OutputCollector`.
	Reduce skipped groups	The number of distinct key groups skipped by all the reducers in the job. See "Skipping Bad Records" on page 171.
	Reduce skipped ßrecords	The number of input records skipped by all the reducers in the job.
	Spilled records	The number of records spilled to disk in all map and reduce tasks in the job.
File Systems	*Filesystem* bytes read	The number of bytes read by each filesystem by map and reduce tasks. There is a counter for each filesystem: *Filesystem* may be Local, HDFS, S3, KFS, etc.
	Filesystem bytes written	The number of bytes written by each filesystem by map and reduce tasks.

Group	Counter	Description
Job Counters	Launched map tasks	The number of map tasks that were launched. Includes tasks that were started speculatively.
	Launched reduce tasks	The number of reduce tasks that were launched. Includes tasks that were started speculatively.
	Failed map tasks	The number of map tasks that failed. See "Task Failure" on page 159 for potential causes.
	Failed reduce tasks	The number of reduce tasks that failed.
	Data-local map tasks	The number of map tasks that ran on the same node as their input data.
	Rack-local map tasks	The number of map tasks that ran on a node in the same rack as their input data.
	Other local map tasks	The number of map tasks that ran on a node in a different rack to their input data. Inter-rack bandwidth is scarce, and Hadoop tries to place map tasks close to their input data, so this count should be low.

Counters are maintained by the task with which they are associated, and periodically sent to the tasktracker and then to the jobtracker, so they can be globally aggregated. (This is described in "Progress and Status Updates" on page 156.) The built-in Job Counters are actually maintained by the jobtracker, so they don't need to be sent across the network, unlike all other counters, including user-defined ones.

A task's counters are sent in full every time, rather than sending the counts since the last transmission, since this guards against errors due to lost messages. Furthermore, during a job run, counters may go down if a task fails. Counter values are definitive only once a job has successfully completed.

User-Defined Java Counters

MapReduce allows user code to define a set of counters, which are then incremented as desired in the mapper or reducer. Counters are defined by a Java enum, which serves to group related counters. A job may define an arbitrary number of enums, each with an arbitrary number of fields. The name of the enum is the group name, and the enum's fields are the counter names. Counters are global: the MapReduce framework aggregates them across all maps and reduces to produce a grand total at the end of the job.

We created some counters in Chapter 5 for counting malformed records in the weather dataset. The program in Example 8-1 extends that example to count the number of missing records and the distribution of temperature quality codes.

Example 8-1. Application to run the maximum temperature job, including counting missing and malformed fields and quality codes

```java
public class MaxTemperatureWithCounters extends Configured implements Tool {

  enum Temperature {
    MISSING,
    MALFORMED
  }

  static class MaxTemperatureMapperWithCounters extends MapReduceBase
    implements Mapper<LongWritable, Text, Text, IntWritable> {

    private NcdcRecordParser parser = new NcdcRecordParser();

    public void map(LongWritable key, Text value,
        OutputCollector<Text, IntWritable> output, Reporter reporter)
        throws IOException {

      parser.parse(value);
      if (parser.isValidTemperature()) {
        int airTemperature = parser.getAirTemperature();
        output.collect(new Text(parser.getYear()),
            new IntWritable(airTemperature));
      } else if (parser.isMalformedTemperature()) {
        System.err.println("Ignoring possibly corrupt input: " + value);
        reporter.incrCounter(Temperature.MALFORMED, 1);
      } else if (parser.isMissingTemperature()) {
        reporter.incrCounter(Temperature.MISSING, 1);
      }

      // dynamic counter
      reporter.incrCounter("TemperatureQuality", parser.getQuality(), 1);

    }
  }

  @Override
  public int run(String[] args) throws IOException {
    JobConf conf = JobBuilder.parseInputAndOutput(this, getConf(), args);
    if (conf == null) {
      return -1;
    }

    conf.setOutputKeyClass(Text.class);
    conf.setOutputValueClass(IntWritable.class);

    conf.setMapperClass(MaxTemperatureMapperWithCounters.class);
    conf.setCombinerClass(MaxTemperatureReducer.class);
    conf.setReducerClass(MaxTemperatureReducer.class);

    JobClient.runJob(conf);
    return 0;
  }
```

```
  public static void main(String[] args) throws Exception {
    int exitCode = ToolRunner.run(new MaxTemperatureWithCounters(), args);
    System.exit(exitCode);
  }
}
```

The best way to see what this program does is run it over the complete dataset:

```
% hadoop jar job.jar MaxTemperatureWithCounters input/ncdc/all output-counters
```

When the job has successfully completed, it prints out the counters at the end (this is done by JobClient's runJob() method). Here are the ones we are interested in:

```
09/04/20 06:33:36 INFO mapred.JobClient:     TemperatureQuality
09/04/20 06:33:36 INFO mapred.JobClient:       2=1246032
09/04/20 06:33:36 INFO mapred.JobClient:       1=973422173
09/04/20 06:33:36 INFO mapred.JobClient:       0=1
09/04/20 06:33:36 INFO mapred.JobClient:       6=40066
09/04/20 06:33:36 INFO mapred.JobClient:       5=158291879
09/04/20 06:33:36 INFO mapred.JobClient:       4=10764500
09/04/20 06:33:36 INFO mapred.JobClient:       9=66136858
09/04/20 06:33:36 INFO mapred.JobClient:     Air Temperature Records
09/04/20 06:33:36 INFO mapred.JobClient:       Malformed=3
09/04/20 06:33:36 INFO mapred.JobClient:       Missing=66136856
```

Dynamic counters

The code makes use of a dynamic counter—one that isn't defined by a Java enum. Since a Java enum's fields are defined at compile time, you can't create new counters on the fly using enums. Here we want to count the distribution of temperature quality codes, and though the format specification defines the values that it can take, it is more convenient to use a dynamic counter to emit the values that it actually takes. The method we use on the Reporter object takes a group and counter name using String names:

```
public void incrCounter(String group, String counter, long amount)
```

The two ways of creating and accessing counters—using enums and using Strings—are actually equivalent since Hadoop turns enums into Strings to send counters over RPC. Enums are slightly easier to work with, provide type safety, and are suitable for most jobs. For the odd occasion when you need to create counters dynamically, you can use the String interface.

Readable counter names

By default, a counter's name is the enum's fully qualified Java classname. These names are not very readable when they appear on the web UI, or in the console, so Hadoop provides a way to change the display names using resource bundles. We've done this here, so we see "Air Temperature Records" instead of "Temperature$MISSING." For dynamic counters, the group and counter names are used for the display names, so this is not normally an issue.

The recipe to provide readable names is as follows. Create a properties file named after the enum, using an underscore as a separator for nested classes. The properties file should be in the same directory as the top-level class containing the enum. The file is named *MaxTemperatureWithCounters_Temperature.properties* for the counters in Example 8-1.

The properties file should contain a single property named `CounterGroupName`, whose value is the display name for the whole group. Then each field in the enum should have a corresponding property defined for it, whose name is the name of the field suffixed with `.name`, and whose value is the display name for the counter. Here are the contents of *MaxTemperatureWithCounters_Temperature.properties*:

```
CounterGroupName=Air Temperature Records
MISSING.name=Missing
MALFORMED.name=Malformed
```

Hadoop uses the standard Java localization mechanisms to load the correct properties for the locale you are running in, so, for example, you can create a Chinese version of the properties in a file named *MaxTemperatureWithCounters_Tempera ture_zh_CN.properties* and they will be used when running in the `zh_CN` locale. Refer to the documentation for `java.util.PropertyResourceBundle` for more information.

Retrieving counters

In addition to being available via the web UI and the command line (using `hadoop job -counter`), you can retrieve counter values using the Java API. You can do this while the job is running, although it is more usual to get counters at the end of a job run, when they are stable. Example 8-2 shows a program that calculates the proportion of records that have missing temperature fields.

Example 8-2. Application to calculate the proportion of records with missing temperature fields

```java
import org.apache.hadoop.conf.Configured;
import org.apache.hadoop.mapred.*;
import org.apache.hadoop.util.*;

public class MissingTemperatureFields extends Configured implements Tool {

  @Override
  public int run(String[] args) throws Exception {
    if (args.length != 1) {
      JobBuilder.printUsage(this, "<job ID>");
      return -1;
    }
    JobClient jobClient = new JobClient(new JobConf(getConf()));
    String jobID = args[0];
    RunningJob job = jobClient.getJob(JobID.forName(jobID));
    if (job == null) {
      System.err.printf("No job with ID %s found.\n", jobID);
      return -1;
    }
```

```
  if (!job.isComplete()) {
    System.err.printf("Job %s is not complete.\n", jobID);
    return -1;
  }

  Counters counters = job.getCounters();
  long missing = counters.getCounter(
      MaxTemperatureWithCounters.Temperature.MISSING);

  long total = counters.findCounter("org.apache.hadoop.mapred.Task$Counter",
      "MAP_INPUT_RECORDS").getCounter();

  System.out.printf("Records with missing temperature fields: %.2f%%\n",
      100.0 * missing / total);
  return 0;
  }
  public static void main(String[] args) throws Exception {
    int exitCode = ToolRunner.run(new MissingTemperatureFields(), args);
    System.exit(exitCode);
  }
}
```

First we retrieve a `RunningJob` object from a `JobClient`, by calling the `getJob()` method with the job ID. We check whether there is actually a job with the given ID. There may not be, either because the ID was incorrectly specified or because the jobtracker no longer has a reference to the job (only the last 100 jobs are kept in memory, and all are cleared out if the jobtracker is restarted).

After confirming that the job has completed, we call the `RunningJob`'s `getCounters()` method, which returns a `Counters` object, encapsulating all the counters for a job. The `Counters` class provides various methods for finding the names and values of counters. We use the `getCounter()` method, which takes an enum to find the number of records that had a missing temperature field.

There are also `findCounter()` methods, all of which return a `Counter` object. We use this form to retrieve the built-in counter for map input records. To do this, we refer to the counter by its group name—the fully qualified Java classname for the enum—and counter name (both strings).[*]

Finally, we print the proportion of records that had a missing temperature field. Here's what we get for the whole weather dataset:

```
% hadoop jar job.jar MissingTemperatureFields job_200904200610_0003
Records with missing temperature fields: 5.47%
```

---

[*] The built-in counter's enums are not currently a part of the public API, so this is the only way to retrieve them. *https://issues.apache.org/jira/browse/HADOOP-4043* will remedy this deficiency.

User-Defined Streaming Counters

A Streaming MapReduce program can increment counters by sending a specially formatted line to the standard error stream, which is co-opted as a control channel in this case. The line must have the following format:

```
reporter:counter:group,counter,amount
```

This snippet in Python shows how to increment the "Missing" counter in the "Temperature" group by one:

```
sys.stderr.write("reporter:counter:Temperature,Missing,1\n")
```

In a similar way, a status message may be sent with a line formatted like this:

```
reporter:status:message
```

Sorting

The ability to sort data is at the heart of MapReduce. Even if your application isn't concerned with sorting per se, it may be able to use the sorting stage that MapReduce provides to organize its data. In this section, we will examine different ways of sorting datasets, and how you can control the sort order in MapReduce.

Preparation

We are going to sort the weather dataset by temperature. Storing temperatures as Text objects doesn't work for sorting purposes, since signed integers don't sort lexicographically.[†] Instead, we are going to store the data using sequence files whose IntWritable keys represent the temperature (and sort correctly), and whose Text values are the lines of data.

The MapReduce job in Example 8-3 is a map-only job that also filters the input to remove records that don't have a valid temperature reading. Each map creates a single block-compressed sequence file as output. It is invoked with the following command:

```
% hadoop jar job.jar SortDataPreprocessor input/ncdc/all input/ncdc/all-seq
```

Example 8-3. A MapReduce program for transforming the weather data into SequenceFile format

```
public class SortDataPreprocessor extends Configured implements Tool {

  static class CleanerMapper extends MapReduceBase
    implements Mapper<LongWritable, Text, IntWritable, Text> {

    private NcdcRecordParser parser = new NcdcRecordParser();
```

[†] One commonly used workaround for this problem—particularly in text-based Streaming applications—is to add an offset to eliminate all negative numbers, and left pad with zeros, so all numbers are the same number of characters. However, see "Streaming" on page 231 for another approach.

```java
    public void map(LongWritable key, Text value,
        OutputCollector<IntWritable, Text> output, Reporter reporter)
        throws IOException {

      parser.parse(value);
      if (parser.isValidTemperature()) {
        output.collect(new IntWritable(parser.getAirTemperature()), value);
      }
    }
  }

  @Override
  public int run(String[] args) throws IOException {
    JobConf conf = JobBuilder.parseInputAndOutput(this, getConf(), args);
    if (conf == null) {
      return -1;
    }

    conf.setMapperClass(CleanerMapper.class);
    conf.setOutputKeyClass(IntWritable.class);
    conf.setOutputValueClass(Text.class);
    conf.setNumReduceTasks(0);
    conf.setOutputFormat(SequenceFileOutputFormat.class);
    SequenceFileOutputFormat.setCompressOutput(conf, true);
    SequenceFileOutputFormat.setOutputCompressorClass(conf, GzipCodec.class);
    SequenceFileOutputFormat.setOutputCompressionType(conf,
        CompressionType.BLOCK);

    JobClient.runJob(conf);
    return 0;
  }
  public static void main(String[] args) throws Exception {
    int exitCode = ToolRunner.run(new SortDataPreprocessor(), args);
    System.exit(exitCode);
  }
}
```

Partial Sort

In "The Default MapReduce Job" on page 178, we saw that, by default, MapReduce
will sort input records by their keys. Example 8-4 is a variation for sorting sequence
files with IntWritable keys.

*Example 8-4. A MapReduce program for sorting a SequenceFile with IntWritable keys using the
default HashPartitioner*

```java
public class SortByTemperatureUsingHashPartitioner extends Configured
  implements Tool {

  @Override
  public int run(String[] args) throws IOException {
    JobConf conf = JobBuilder.parseInputAndOutput(this, getConf(), args);
    if (conf == null) {
      return -1;
```

```
    }

    conf.setInputFormat(SequenceFileInputFormat.class);
    conf.setOutputKeyClass(IntWritable.class);
    conf.setOutputFormat(SequenceFileOutputFormat.class);
    SequenceFileOutputFormat.setCompressOutput(conf, true);
    SequenceFileOutputFormat.setOutputCompressorClass(conf, GzipCodec.class);
    SequenceFileOutputFormat.setOutputCompressionType(conf,
        CompressionType.BLOCK);

    JobClient.runJob(conf);
    return 0;
  }

  public static void main(String[] args) throws Exception {
    int exitCode = ToolRunner.run(new SortByTemperatureUsingHashPartitioner(),
        args);
    System.exit(exitCode);
  }
}
```

Controlling Sort Order

The sort order for keys is controlled by a RawComparator, which is found as follows:

1. If the property mapred.output.key.comparator.class is set, an instance of that class is used. (The setOutputKeyComparatorClass() method on JobConf is a convenient way to set this property.)

2. Otherwise, keys must be a subclass of WritableComparable and the registered comparator for the key class is used.

3. If there is no registered comparator, then a RawComparator is used that deserializes the byte streams being compared into objects, and delegates to the WritableComparable's compareTo() method.

These rules reinforce why it's important to register optimized versions of RawComparators for your own custom Writable classes (which is covered in "Implementing a RawComparator for speed" on page 99), and also that it's straightforward to override the sort order by setting your own comparator (we do this in "Secondary Sort" on page 227).

Suppose we run this program using 30 reducers:[‡]

```
% hadoop jar job.jar SortByTemperatureUsingHashPartitioner \
  -D mapred.reduce.tasks=30 input/ncdc/all-seq output-hashsort
```

This command produces 30 output files, each of which is sorted. However, there is no easy way to combine the files (by concatenation, for example, in the case of plain-text

---

[‡] See "Sorting and merging SequenceFiles" on page 108 for how to do the same thing using the sort program example that comes with Hadoop.

files) to produce a globally sorted file. For many applications, this doesn't matter. For example, having a partially sorted set of files is fine if you want to do lookups.

An application: Partitioned MapFile lookups

To perform lookups by key, for instance, having multiple files works well. If we change the output format to be a `MapFileOutputFormat`, as shown in Example 8-5, then the output is 30 map files, which we can perform lookups against.

Example 8-5. A MapReduce program for sorting a SequenceFile and producing MapFiles as output

```
public class SortByTemperatureToMapFile extends Configured implements Tool {

  @Override
  public int run(String[] args) throws IOException {
    JobConf conf = JobBuilder.parseInputAndOutput(this, getConf(), args);
    if (conf == null) {
      return -1;
    }

    conf.setInputFormat(SequenceFileInputFormat.class);
    conf.setOutputKeyClass(IntWritable.class);
    conf.setOutputFormat(MapFileOutputFormat.class);
    SequenceFileOutputFormat.setCompressOutput(conf, true);
    SequenceFileOutputFormat.setOutputCompressorClass(conf, GzipCodec.class);
    SequenceFileOutputFormat.setOutputCompressionType(conf,
        CompressionType.BLOCK);

    JobClient.runJob(conf);
    return 0;
  }

  public static void main(String[] args) throws Exception {
    int exitCode = ToolRunner.run(new SortByTemperatureToMapFile(), args);
    System.exit(exitCode);
  }
}
```

`MapFileOutputFormat` provides a pair of convenience static methods for performing lookups against MapReduce output; their use is shown in Example 8-6.

Example 8-6. Retrieve the first entry with a given key from a collection of MapFiles

```
public class LookupRecordByTemperature extends Configured implements Tool {

  @Override
  public int run(String[] args) throws Exception {
    if (args.length != 2) {
      JobBuilder.printUsage(this, "<path> <key>");
      return -1;
    }
    Path path = new Path(args[0]);
    IntWritable key = new IntWritable(Integer.parseInt(args[1]));
    FileSystem fs = path.getFileSystem(getConf());
```

```
      Reader[] readers = MapFileOutputFormat.getReaders(fs, path, getConf());
      Partitioner<IntWritable, Text> partitioner =
        new HashPartitioner<IntWritable, Text>();
      Text val = new Text();
      Writable entry =
        MapFileOutputFormat.getEntry(readers, partitioner, key, val);
      if (entry == null) {
        System.err.println("Key not found: " + key);
        return -1;
      }
      NcdcRecordParser parser = new NcdcRecordParser();
      parser.parse(val.toString());
      System.out.printf("%s\t%s\n", parser.getStationId(), parser.getYear());
      return 0;
    }

    public static void main(String[] args) throws Exception {
      int exitCode = ToolRunner.run(new LookupRecordByTemperature(), args);
      System.exit(exitCode);
    }
  }
```

The getReaders() method opens a MapFile.Reader for each of the output files created
by the MapReduce job. The getEntry() method then uses the partitioner to choose the
reader for the key, and finds the value for that key by calling Reader's get() method. If
getEntry() returns null, it means no matching key was found. Otherwise, it returns
the value, which we translate into a station ID and year.

To see this in action, let's find the first entry for a temperature of –10°C (remember
that temperatures are stored as integers representing tenths of a degree, which is why
we ask for a temperature of -100):

```
% hadoop jar job.jar LookupRecordByTemperature output-hashmapsort -100
357460-99999    1956
```

We can also use the readers directly, in order to get all the records for a given key. The
array of readers that is returned is ordered by partition, so that the reader for a given
key may be found using the same partitioner that was used in the MapReduce job:

```
        Reader reader = readers[partitioner.getPartition(key, val, readers.length)];
```

Then once we have the reader, we get the first key using MapFile's get() method, then
repeatedly call next() to retrieve the next key and value, until the key changes. A program to do this is shown in Example 8-7.

Example 8-7. Retrieve all entries with a given key from a collection of MapFiles

```
public class LookupRecordsByTemperature extends Configured implements Tool {

  @Override
  public int run(String[] args) throws Exception {
    if (args.length != 2) {
      JobBuilder.printUsage(this, "<path> <key>");
```

```
    return -1;
  }
  Path path = new Path(args[0]);
  IntWritable key = new IntWritable(Integer.parseInt(args[1]));
  FileSystem fs = path.getFileSystem(getConf());

  Reader[] readers = MapFileOutputFormat.getReaders(fs, path, getConf());
  Partitioner<IntWritable, Text> partitioner =
    new HashPartitioner<IntWritable, Text>();
  Text val = new Text();

  Reader reader = readers[partitioner.getPartition(key, val, readers.length)];
  Writable entry = reader.get(key, val);
  if (entry == null) {
    System.err.println("Key not found: " + key);
    return -1;
  }
  NcdcRecordParser parser = new NcdcRecordParser();
  IntWritable nextKey = new IntWritable();
  do {
    parser.parse(val.toString());
    System.out.printf("%s\t%s\n", parser.getStationId(), parser.getYear());
  } while(reader.next(nextKey, val) && key.equals(nextKey));
  return 0;
}

public static void main(String[] args) throws Exception {
  int exitCode = ToolRunner.run(new LookupRecordsByTemperature(), args);
  System.exit(exitCode);
}
}
```

And here is a sample run to retrieve all readings of −10°C and count them:

```
% hadoop jar job.jar LookupRecordsByTemperature output-hashmapsort -100 \
  2> /dev/null | wc -l
1489272
```

Total Sort

How can you produce a globally sorted file using Hadoop? The naive answer is to use a single partition.[§] But this is incredibly inefficient for large files, since one machine has to process all of the output, so you are throwing away the benefits of the parallel architecture that MapReduce provides.

Instead it is possible to produce a set of sorted files that, if concatenated, would form a globally sorted file. The secret to doing this is to use a partitioner that respects the total order of the output. For example, if we had four partitions, we could put keys for temperatures less than −10°C in the first partition, those between −10°C and 0°C in the second, those between 0°C and 10°C in the third, and those over 10°C in the fourth.

[§] A better answer is to use Pig, which can sort with a single command. See "Sorting Data" on page 338.

Although this approach works, you have to choose your partition sizes carefully to ensure that they are fairly even so that job times aren't dominated by a single reducer. For the partitioning scheme just described, the relative sizes of the partitions are as follows:

Temperature range	< −10°C	[−10°C, 0°C)	[0°C, 10°C)	>= 10°C
Proportion of records	11%	13%	17%	59%

These partitions are not very even. To construct more even partitions, we need to have a better understanding of the temperature distribution for the whole dataset. It's fairly easy to write a MapReduce job to count the number of records that fall into a collection of temperature buckets. For example, Figure 8-1 shows the distribution for buckets of size 1°C, where each point on the plot corresponds to one bucket.

Figure 8-1. Temperature distribution for the weather dataset

While we could use this information to construct a very even set of partitions, the fact that we needed to run a job that used the entire dataset to construct them is not ideal. It's possible to get a fairly even set of partitions, by *sampling* the key space. The idea behind sampling is that you look at a small subset of the keys to approximate the key distribution, which is then used to construct partitions. Luckily, we don't have to write the code to do this ourselves, as Hadoop comes with a selection of samplers.

The InputSampler class defines a nested Sampler interface whose implementations return a sample of keys given an InputFormat and JobConf:

```
public interface Sampler<K,V> {
  K[] getSample(InputFormat<K,V> inf, JobConf job) throws IOException;
}
```

This interface is not usually called directly by clients. Instead, the writePartition File() static method on InputSampler is used, which creates a sequence file to store the keys that define the partitions:

```
public static <K,V> void writePartitionFile(JobConf job,
    Sampler<K,V> sampler) throws IOException
```

The sequence file is used by TotalOrderPartitioner to create partitions for the sort job. Example 8-8 puts it all together.

Example 8-8. A MapReduce program for sorting a SequenceFile with IntWritable keys using the TotalOrderPartitioner to globally sort the data

```
public class SortByTemperatureUsingTotalOrderPartitioner extends Configured
  implements Tool {

  @Override
  public int run(String[] args) throws Exception {
    JobConf conf = JobBuilder.parseInputAndOutput(this, getConf(), args);
    if (conf == null) {
      return -1;
    }

    conf.setInputFormat(SequenceFileInputFormat.class);
    conf.setOutputKeyClass(IntWritable.class);
    conf.setOutputFormat(SequenceFileOutputFormat.class);
    SequenceFileOutputFormat.setCompressOutput(conf, true);
    SequenceFileOutputFormat.setOutputCompressorClass(conf, GzipCodec.class);
    SequenceFileOutputFormat.setOutputCompressionType(conf,
        CompressionType.BLOCK);

    conf.setPartitionerClass(TotalOrderPartitioner.class);

    InputSampler.Sampler<IntWritable, Text> sampler =
      new InputSampler.RandomSampler<IntWritable, Text>(0.1, 10000, 10);

    Path input = FileInputFormat.getInputPaths(conf)[0];
    input = input.makeQualified(input.getFileSystem(conf));

    Path partitionFile = new Path(input, "_partitions");
    TotalOrderPartitioner.setPartitionFile(conf, partitionFile);
    InputSampler.writePartitionFile(conf, sampler);

    // Add to DistributedCache
    URI partitionUri = new URI(partitionFile.toString() + "#_partitions");
    DistributedCache.addCacheFile(partitionUri, conf);
    DistributedCache.createSymlink(conf);
```

```
    JobClient.runJob(conf);
    return 0;
  }

  public static void main(String[] args) throws Exception {
    int exitCode = ToolRunner.run(
        new SortByTemperatureUsingTotalOrderPartitioner(), args);
    System.exit(exitCode);
  }
}
```

We use a RandomSampler, which chooses keys with a uniform probability—here, 0.1. There are also parameters for the maximum number of samples to take, and the maximum number of splits to sample (here, 10,000 and 10, respectively; these settings are the defaults when InputSampler is run as an application), and the sampler stops when the first of these limits is met. Samplers run on the client, making it important to limit the number of splits that are downloaded, so the sampler runs quickly. In practice, the time taken to run the sampler is a small fraction of the overall job time.

The partition file that InputSampler writes is called _partitions_, which we have set to be in the input directory (it will not be picked up as an input file since it starts with an underscore). To share the partition file with the tasks running on the cluster, we add it to the distributed cache (see "Distributed Cache" on page 239).

On one run, the sampler chose −5.6°C, 13.9°C, and 22.0°C as partition boundaries (for four partitions), which translates into more even partition sizes that the earlier choice of partitions:

Temperature range	< −5.6°C	[−5.6°C, 13.9°C)	[13.9°C, 22.0°C)	>= 22.0°C
Proportion of records	29%	24%	23%	24%

Your input data determines the best sampler for you to use. For example, SplitSampler, which samples only the first _n_ records in a split, is not so good for sorted data[‖] because it doesn't select keys from throughout the split.

On the other hand, IntervalSampler chooses keys at regular intervals through the split, and makes a better choice for sorted data. RandomSampler is a good general-purpose sampler. If none of these suits your application (and remember that the point of sampling is to produce partitions that are _approximately_ equal in size), you can write your own implementation of the Sampler interface.

One of the nice properties of InputSampler and TotalOrderPartitioner is that you are free to choose the number of partitions. This choice is normally driven by the number of reducer slots in you cluster (choose a number slightly fewer than the total, to allow

---

[‖] In some applications, it's common for some of the input to already be sorted, or at least partially sorted. For example, the weather dataset is ordered by time, which may introduce certain biases, making the RandomSampler a safe choice.

for failures). However, `TotalOrderPartitioner` will work only if the partition boundaries are distinct: one problem with choosing a high number is that you may get collisions if you have a small key space.

Here's how we run it:

```
% hadoop jar job.jar SortByTemperatureUsingTotalOrderPartitioner \
  -D mapred.reduce.tasks=30 input/ncdc/all-seq output-totalsort
```

The program produces 30 output partitions, each of which is internally sorted; in addition, for these partitions, all the keys in partition *i* are less than the keys in partition *i* + 1.

Secondary Sort

The MapReduce framework sorts the records by key before they reach the reducers. For any particular key, however, the values are *not* sorted. The order that the values appear is not even stable from one run to the next, since they come from different map tasks, which may finish at different times from run to run. Generally speaking, most MapReduce programs are written so as not to depend on the order that the values appear to the reduce function. However, it is possible to impose an order on the values by sorting and grouping the keys in a particular way.

To illustrate the idea, consider the MapReduce program for calculating the maximum temperature for each year. If we arranged for the values (temperatures) to be sorted in descending order, we wouldn't have to iterate through them to find the maximum—we could take the first for each year and ignore the rest. (This approach isn't the most efficient way to solve this particular problem, but it illustrates how secondary sort works in general.)

To achieve this, we change our keys to be composite: a combination of year and temperature. We want the sort order for keys to be by year (ascending) and then by temperature (descending):

```
1900 35°C
1900 34°C
1900 34°C
...
1901 36°C
1901 35°C
```

If all we did was change the key, then this wouldn't help since now records for the same year would not (in general) go to the same reducer since they have different keys. For example, (1900, 35°C) and (1900, 34°C) could go to different reducers. By setting a partitioner to partition by the year part of the key, we can guarantee that records for the same year go to the same reducer. This still isn't enough to achieve our goal, however. A partitioner ensures only that one reducer receives all the records for a year; it doesn't change the fact that the reducer groups by key within the partition:

```
     Partition  Group
1900 35°C   |       |
1900 34°C   |       |
1900 34°C   |       |
   ...
1901 36°C   |       |
1901 35°C   |       |
```

The final piece of the puzzle is the setting to control the grouping. If we group values in the reducer by the year part of the key, then we will see all the records for the same year in one reduce group. And since they are sorted by temperature in descending order, the first is the maximum temperature:

```
     Partition  Group
1900 35°C   |       |
1900 34°C   |       |
1900 34°C   |       |
   ...
1901 36°C   |       |
1901 35°C   |       |
```

To summarize, there is a recipe here to get the effect of sorting by value:

- Make the key a composite of the natural key and the natural value.
- The key comparator should order by the composite key, that is, the natural key *and* natural value.
- The partitioner and grouping comparator for the composite key should consider only the natural key for partitioning and grouping.

Java code

Putting this all together results in the code in Example 8-9. This program uses the plain-text input again.

Example 8-9. Application to find the maximum temperature by sorting temperatures in the key

```java
public class MaxTemperatureUsingSecondarySort
  extends Configured implements Tool {

  static class MaxTemperatureMapper extends MapReduceBase
    implements Mapper<LongWritable, Text, IntPair, NullWritable> {

    private NcdcRecordParser parser = new NcdcRecordParser();

    public void map(LongWritable key, Text value,
        OutputCollector<IntPair, NullWritable> output, Reporter reporter)
        throws IOException {

      parser.parse(value);
      if (parser.isValidTemperature()) {
```

```
      output.collect(new IntPair(parser.getYearInt(),
          + parser.getAirTemperature()), NullWritable.get());
    }
  }
}

static class MaxTemperatureReducer extends MapReduceBase
  implements Reducer<IntPair, NullWritable, IntPair, NullWritable> {

  public void reduce(IntPair key, Iterator<NullWritable> values,
      OutputCollector<IntPair, NullWritable> output, Reporter reporter)
      throws IOException {

    output.collect(key, NullWritable.get());
  }
}

public static class FirstPartitioner
  implements Partitioner<IntPair, NullWritable> {

  @Override
  public void configure(JobConf job) {}

  @Override
  public int getPartition(IntPair key, NullWritable value, int numPartitions) {
    return Math.abs(key.getFirst() * 127) % numPartitions;
  }
}

public static class KeyComparator extends WritableComparator {
  protected KeyComparator() {
    super(IntPair.class, true);
  }
  @Override
  public int compare(WritableComparable w1, WritableComparable w2) {
    IntPair ip1 = (IntPair) w1;
    IntPair ip2 = (IntPair) w2;
    int cmp = IntPair.compare(ip1.getFirst(), ip2.getFirst());
    if (cmp != 0) {
      return cmp;
    }
    return -IntPair.compare(ip1.getSecond(), ip2.getSecond()); //reverse
  }
}

public static class GroupComparator extends WritableComparator {
  protected GroupComparator() {
    super(IntPair.class, true);
  }
  @Override
  public int compare(WritableComparable w1, WritableComparable w2) {
    IntPair ip1 = (IntPair) w1;
    IntPair ip2 = (IntPair) w2;
    return IntPair.compare(ip1.getFirst(), ip2.getFirst());
  }
```

```
  }

  @Override
  public int run(String[] args) throws IOException {
    JobConf conf = JobBuilder.parseInputAndOutput(this, getConf(), args);
    if (conf == null) {
      return -1;
    }

    conf.setMapperClass(MaxTemperatureMapper.class);
    conf.setPartitionerClass(FirstPartitioner.class);
    conf.setOutputKeyComparatorClass(KeyComparator.class);
    conf.setOutputValueGroupingComparator(GroupComparator.class);
    conf.setReducerClass(MaxTemperatureReducer.class);
    conf.setOutputKeyClass(IntPair.class);
    conf.setOutputValueClass(NullWritable.class);

    JobClient.runJob(conf);
    return 0;
  }

  public static void main(String[] args) throws Exception {
    int exitCode = ToolRunner.run(new MaxTemperatureUsingSecondarySort(), args);
    System.exit(exitCode);
  }
}
```

In the mapper, we create a key representing the year and temperature, using an `IntPair` `Writable` implementation. (`IntPair` is like the `TextPair` class we developed in "Implementing a Custom Writable" on page 96.) We don't need to carry any information in the value, since we can get the first (maximum) temperature in the reducer from the key, so we use a `NullWritable`. The reducer emits the first key, which due to the secondary sorting, is an `IntPair` for the year and its maximum temperature. `IntPair`'s `toString()` method creates a tab-separated string, so the output is a set of tab-separated year-temperature pairs.

 Many applications need to access all the sorted values, not just the first value as we have provided here. To do this, you need to populate the value fields since in the reducer you can retrieve only the first key. This necessitates some unavoidable duplication of information between key and value.

We set the partitioner to partition by the first field of the key (the year), using a custom partitioner. To sort keys by year (ascending) and temperature (descending), we use a custom key comparator that extracts the fields and performs the appropriate comparisons. Similarly, to group keys by year, we set a custom comparator, using `setOutput ValueGroupingComparator()`, to extract the first field of the key for comparison.[#]

Running this program gives the maximum temperatures for each year:

```
% hadoop jar job.jar MaxTemperatureUsingSecondarySort input/ncdc/all output-secondarysort
% hadoop fs -cat output-secondarysort/part-* | sort | head
1901    317
1902    244
1903    289
1904    256
1905    283
1906    294
1907    283
1908    289
1909    278
1910    294
```

Streaming

To do a secondary sort in Streaming, we can take advantage of a couple of library classes that Hadoop provides. Here's the driver that we can use to do a secondary sort:

```
hadoop jar $HADOOP_INSTALL/contrib/streaming/hadoop-*-streaming.jar \
  -D stream.num.map.output.key.fields=2 \
  -D mapred.text.key.partitioner.options=-k1,1 \
  -D mapred.output.key.comparator.class=\
org.apache.hadoop.mapred.lib.KeyFieldBasedComparator \
  -D mapred.text.key.comparator.options="-k1n -k2nr" \
  -input input/ncdc/all \
  -output output_secondarysort_streaming \
  -mapper src/main/ch08/python/secondary_sort_map.py \
  -partitioner org.apache.hadoop.mapred.lib.KeyFieldBasedPartitioner \
  -reducer src/main/ch08/python/secondary_sort_reduce.py \
  -file src/main/ch08/python/secondary_sort_map.py \
  -file src/main/ch08/python/secondary_sort_reduce.py
```

Our map function (Example 8-10) emits records with year and temperature fields. We want to treat the combination of both of these fields as the key, so we set `stream.num.map.output.key.fields` to 2. This means that values will be empty, just like in the Java case.

[#] For simplicity, these custom comparators as shown are not optimized; see "Implementing a RawComparator for speed" on page 99 for the steps we would need to take to make them faster.

Example 8-10. Map function for secondary sort in Python

```python
#!/usr/bin/env python

import re
import sys

for line in sys.stdin:
  val = line.strip()
  (year, temp, q) = (val[15:19], int(val[87:92]), val[92:93])
  if temp == 9999:
    sys.stderr.write("reporter:counter:Temperature,Missing,1\n")
  elif re.match("[01459]", q):
    print "%s\t%s" % (year, temp)
```

However, we don't want to partition by the entire key, so we use the `KeyFieldBased Partitioner` partitioner, which allows us to partition by a part of the key. The specification `mapred.text.key.partitioner.options` configures the partitioner. The value `-k1,1` instructs the partitioner to use only the first field of the key, where fields are assumed to be separated by a string defined by the `map.output.key.field.separator` property (a tab character by default).

Next, we want a comparator that sorts the year field in ascending order and the temperature field in descending order, so that the reduce function can simply return the first record in each group. Hadoop provides `KeyFieldBasedComparator`, which is ideal for this purpose. The comparison order is defined by a specification that is like the one used for GNU *sort*. It is set using the `mapred.text.key.comparator.options` property. The value `-k1n -k2nr` used in this example means "sort by the first field in numerical order, then by the second field in reverse numerical order." Like its partitioner cousin, `KeyFieldBasedPartitioner`, it uses the separator defined by the `map.out put.key.field.separator` to split a key into fields.

In the Java version, we had to set the grouping comparator; however, in Streaming groups are not demarcated in any way, so in the reduce function we have to detect the group boundaries ourselves by looking for when the year changes (Example 8-11).

Example 8-11. Reducer function for secondary sort in Python

```python
#!/usr/bin/env python

import sys

last_group = None
for line in sys.stdin:
  val = line.strip()
  (year, temp) = val.split("\t")
  group = year
  if last_group != group:
    print val
    last_group = group
```

When we run the streaming program, we get the same output as the Java version.

Finally, note that `KeyFieldBasedPartitioner` and `KeyFieldBasedComparator` are not confined to use in Streaming programs—they are applicable to Java MapReduce programs, too.

Joins

MapReduce can perform joins between large datasets, but writing the code to do joins from scratch is fairly involved. Rather than writing MapReduce programs, you might consider using a higher-level framework such as Pig, Hive, or Cascading, in which join operations are a core part of the implementation.

Let's briefly consider the problem we are trying to solve. We have two datasets; for example, the weather stations database, and the weather records—and we want to reconcile the two. For example, we want to see each station's history, with the station's metadata inlined in each output row. This is illustrated in Figure 8-2.

How we implement the join depends on how large the datasets are and how they are partitioned. If one dataset is large (the weather records) but the other one is small enough to be distributed to each node in the cluster (as the station metadata is), then the join can be effected by a MapReduce job that brings the records for each station together (a partial sort on station ID, for example). The mapper or reducer uses the smaller dataset to look up the station metadata for a station ID, so it can be written out with each record. See "Side Data Distribution" on page 238 for a discussion of this approach, where we focus on the mechanics of distributing the data to tasktrackers.

If both datasets are too large for either to be copied to each node in the cluster, then we can join them using MapReduce, using either a *map-side join* or a *reduce-side join*. One common example of this case is a user database, and a log of some user activity (such as access logs). For a popular service, it is not feasible to distribute the user database (or the logs) to all the MapReduce nodes.

Map-Side Joins

A map-side join works by performing the join before the data reaches the map function. For this to work, though, the inputs to each map must be partitioned and sorted in a particular way. Each input dataset must be divided into the same number of partitions, and it must be sorted by the same key (the join key) in each source. All the records for a particular key must reside in the same partition. This may sound like a strict requirement (and it is), but it actually fits the description of the output of a MapReduce job.

A map-side join can be used to join the outputs of several jobs that had the same number of reducers, the same keys, and output files that are not splittable (by being smaller than an HDFS block, or by virtue of being gzip compressed, for example). In the context of the weather example, if we ran a partial sort on the stations file by station ID, and another, identical sort on the records, again by station ID, and with the same number

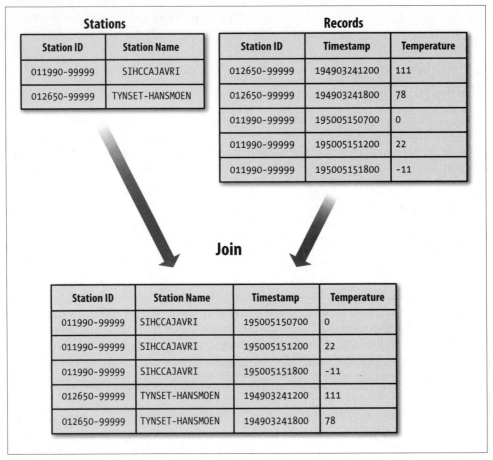

Figure 8-2. Inner join of two datasets

of reducers, then the two outputs would satisfy the conditions for running a map-side join.

Use a `CompositeInputFormat` from the `org.apache.hadoop.mapred.join` package to run a map-side join. The input sources and join type (inner or outer) for `CompositeInput Format` are configured through a join expression that is written according to a simple grammar. The package documentation has details and examples.

The `org.apache.hadoop.examples.Join` example is a general-purpose command-line program for running a map-side join, since it allows you to run a MapReduce job for any specified mapper and reducer, over multiple inputs that are joined with a given join operation.

Reduce-Side Joins

A reduce-side join is more general than a map-side join, in that the input datasets don't have to be structured in any particular way, but it is less efficient as both datasets have to go through the MapReduce shuffle. The basic idea is that the mapper tags each record with its source, and uses the join key as the map output key so that the records with the same key are brought together in the reducer. We use several ingredients to make this work in practice:

Multiple inputs

The input sources for the datasets have different formats, in general, so it is very convenient to use the `MultipleInputs` class (see "Multiple Inputs" on page 200) to separate the logic for parsing and tagging each source.

Secondary sort

As described, the reducer will see the records from both sources that have same key, but they are not guaranteed to be in any particular order. However, to perform the join, it is important to have the data from one source before another. For the weather data join, the station record must be the first of the values seen for each key, so the reducer can fill in the weather records with the station name and emit them straightaway. Of course, it would be possible to receive the records in any order if we buffered them in memory, but this should be avoided, since the number of records in any group may be very large and exceed the amount of memory available to the reducer.[*]

We saw in "Secondary Sort" on page 227 how to impose an order on the values for each key that the reducers see, so we use this technique here.

To tag each record, we use `TextPair` from Chapter 4 for the keys, to store the station ID, and the tag. The only requirement for the tag values is that they sort in such a way that the station records come before the weather records. This can be achieved by tagging station records as `0` and weather records as `1`. The mapper classes to do this are shown in Examples 8-12 and 8-13.

Example 8-12. Mapper for tagging station records for a reduce-side join

```
public class JoinStationMapper extends MapReduceBase
    implements Mapper<LongWritable, Text, TextPair, Text> {
  private NcdcStationMetadataParser parser = new NcdcStationMetadataParser();

  public void map(LongWritable key, Text value,
      OutputCollector<TextPair, Text> output, Reporter reporter)
      throws IOException {

    if (parser.parse(value)) {
      output.collect(new TextPair(parser.getStationId(), "0"),
```

---

[*] The `data_join` package in the *contrib* directory implements reduce-side joins by buffering records in memory, so it suffers from this limitation.

```
            new Text(parser.getStationName()));
    }
  }
}
```

Example 8-13. Mapper for tagging weather records for a reduce-side join

```
public class JoinRecordMapper extends MapReduceBase
    implements Mapper<LongWritable, Text, TextPair, Text> {
  private NcdcRecordParser parser = new NcdcRecordParser();

  public void map(LongWritable key, Text value,
      OutputCollector<TextPair, Text> output, Reporter reporter)
      throws IOException {

    parser.parse(value);
    output.collect(new TextPair(parser.getStationId(), "1"), value);
  }
}
```

The reducer knows that it will receive the station record first, so it extracts its name from the value and writes it out as a part of every output record (Example 8-14).

Example 8-14. Reducer for joining tagged station records with tagged weather records

```
public class JoinReducer extends MapReduceBase implements
    Reducer<TextPair, Text, Text, Text> {

  public void reduce(TextPair key, Iterator<Text> values,
      OutputCollector<Text, Text> output, Reporter reporter)
      throws IOException {

    Text stationName = new Text(values.next());
    while (values.hasNext()) {
      Text record = values.next();
      Text outValue = new Text(stationName.toString() + "\t" + record.toString());
      output.collect(key.getFirst(), outValue);
    }
  }
}
```

The code assumes that every station ID in the weather records has exactly one matching record in the station dataset. If this were not the case, we would need to generalize the code to put the tag into the value objects, by using another TextPair. The reduce() method would then be able to tell which entries were station names, and detect (and handle) missing or duplicate entries, before processing the weather records.

Because objects in the reducer's values iterator are re-used (for efficiency purposes), it is vital that the code makes a copy of the first Text object from the values iterator:

```
Text stationName = new Text(values.next());
```

If the copy is not made, then the stationName reference will refer to the value just read when it is turned into a string, which is a bug.

Tying the job together is the driver class, shown in Example 8-15. The essential point is that we partition and group on the first part of the key, the station ID, which we do with a custom Partitioner (KeyPartitioner), and a custom comparator, FirstCompara tor (from TextPair).

Example 8-15. Application to join weather records with station names

```
public class JoinRecordWithStationName extends Configured implements Tool {

  public static class KeyPartitioner implements Partitioner<TextPair, Text> {
    @Override
    public void configure(JobConf job) {}

    @Override
    public int getPartition(TextPair key, Text value, int numPartitions) {
      return (key.getFirst().hashCode() & Integer.MAX_VALUE) % numPartitions;
    }
  }

  @Override
  public int run(String[] args) throws Exception {
    if (args.length != 3) {
      JobBuilder.printUsage(this, "<ncdc input> <station input> <output>");
      return -1;
    }

    JobConf conf = new JobConf(getConf(), getClass());
    conf.setJobName("Join record with station name");

    Path ncdcInputPath = new Path(args[0]);
    Path stationInputPath = new Path(args[1]);
    Path outputPath = new Path(args[2]);

    MultipleInputs.addInputPath(conf, ncdcInputPath,
        TextInputFormat.class, JoinRecordMapper.class);
    MultipleInputs.addInputPath(conf, stationInputPath,
        TextInputFormat.class, JoinStationMapper.class);
    FileOutputFormat.setOutputPath(conf, outputPath);

    conf.setPartitionerClass(KeyPartitioner.class);
    conf.setOutputValueGroupingComparator(TextPair.FirstComparator.class);

    conf.setMapOutputKeyClass(TextPair.class);

    conf.setReducerClass(JoinReducer.class);
```

```
    conf.setOutputKeyClass(Text.class);

    JobClient.runJob(conf);
    return 0;
  }

  public static void main(String[] args) throws Exception {
    int exitCode = ToolRunner.run(new JoinRecordWithStationName(), args);
    System.exit(exitCode);
  }
}
```

Running the program on the sample data yields the following output:

```
011990-99999    SIHCCAJAVRI         0067011990999991950051507004+68750...
011990-99999    SIHCCAJAVRI         0043011990999991950051512004+68750...
011990-99999    SIHCCAJAVRI         0043011990999991950051518004+68750...
012650-99999    TYNSET-HANSMOEN     0043012650999991949032412004+62300...
012650-99999    TYNSET-HANSMOEN     0043012650999991949032418004+62300...
```

Side Data Distribution

Side data can be defined as extra read-only data needed by a job to process the main dataset. The challenge is to make side data available to all the map or reduce tasks (which are spread across the cluster) in a convenient and efficient fashion.

In addition to the distribution mechanisms described in this section, it is possible to cache side-data in memory in a static field, so that tasks of the same job that run in succession on the same tasktracker can share the data. "Task JVM Reuse" on page 170 describes how to enable this feature. If you take this approach, be aware of the amount of memory that you are using, as it might affect the memory needed by the shuffle (see "Shuffle and Sort" on page 163).

Using the Job Configuration

You can set arbitrary key-value pairs in the job configuration using the various setter methods on JobConf (inherited from Configuration). This is very useful if you need to pass a small piece of metadata to your tasks. To retrieve the values in the task, override the configure() method in the Mapper or Reducer and use a getter method on the JobConf object passed in.

Usually a primitive type is sufficient to encode your metadata, but for arbitrary objects you can either handle the serialization yourself (if you have an existing mechanism for turning objects to strings and back), or you can use Hadoop's Stringifier class. DefaultStringifier uses Hadoop's serialization framework to serialize objects (see "Serialization" on page 86).

You shouldn't use this mechanism for transferring more than a few kilobytes of data because it can put pressure on the memory usage in the Hadoop daemons, particularly in a system running hundreds of jobs. The job configuration is read by the jobtracker, the tasktracker, and the child JVM, and each time the configuration is read, all of its entries are read into memory, even if they are not used. User properties are not read on the jobtracker or the tasktracker, so they just waste time and memory.

Distributed Cache

Rather than serializing side data in the job configuration, it is preferable to distribute datasets using Hadoop's distributed cache mechanism. This provides a service for copying files and archives to the task nodes in time for the tasks to use them when they run. To save network bandwidth, files are normally copied to any particular node once per job.

Usage

For tools that use `GenericOptionsParser` (this includes many of the programs in this book—see "GenericOptionsParser, Tool, and ToolRunner" on page 121), you can specify the files to be distributed as a comma-separated list of URIs as the argument to the `-files` option. Files can be on the local filesystem, on HDFS, or on another Hadoop readable filesystem (such as S3). If no scheme is supplied, then the files are assumed to be local. (This is true even if the default filesystem is not the local filesystem.)

You can also copy archive files (JAR files, ZIP files, tar files, and gzipped tar files) to your tasks, using the `-archives` option; these are unarchived on the task node. The `-libjars` option will add JAR files to the classpath of the mapper and reducer tasks. This is useful if you haven't bundled library JAR files in your job JAR file.

> Streaming doesn't use the distributed cache for copying the streaming scripts across the cluster. You specify a file to be copied using the `-file` option (note the singular), which should be repeated for each file to be copied. Furthermore, files specified using the `-file` option must be file paths only, not URIs, so they must be accessible from the local filesystem of the client launching the Streaming job.
>
> Streaming also accepts the `-files` and `-archives` options for copying files into the distributed cache for use by your Streaming scripts.

Let's see how to use the distributed cache to share a metadata file for station names. The command we will run is:

```
% hadoop jar job.jar MaxTemperatureByStationNameUsingDistributedCacheFile \
  -files input/ncdc/metadata/stations-fixed-width.txt input/ncdc/all output
```

This command will copy the local file *stations-fixed-width.txt* (no scheme is supplied, so the path is automatically interpreted as a local file) to the task nodes, so we can use

it to look up station names. The listing for `MaxTemperatureByStationNameUsingDistri`
`butedCacheFile` appears in Example 8-16.

Example 8-16. Application to find the maximum temperature by station, showing station names from a lookup table passed as a distributed cache file

```java
public class MaxTemperatureByStationNameUsingDistributedCacheFile
  extends Configured implements Tool {

  static class StationTemperatureMapper extends MapReduceBase
    implements Mapper<LongWritable, Text, Text, IntWritable> {

    private NcdcRecordParser parser = new NcdcRecordParser();

    public void map(LongWritable key, Text value,
        OutputCollector<Text, IntWritable> output, Reporter reporter)
        throws IOException {

      parser.parse(value);
      if (parser.isValidTemperature()) {
        output.collect(new Text(parser.getStationId()),
            new IntWritable(parser.getAirTemperature()));
      }
    }
  }

  static class MaxTemperatureReducerWithStationLookup extends MapReduceBase
    implements Reducer<Text, IntWritable, Text, IntWritable> {

    private NcdcStationMetadata metadata;

    @Override
    public void configure(JobConf conf) {
      metadata = new NcdcStationMetadata();
      try {
        metadata.initialize(new File("stations-fixed-width.txt"));
      } catch (IOException e) {
        throw new RuntimeException(e);
      }
    }

    public void reduce(Text key, Iterator<IntWritable> values,
        OutputCollector<Text, IntWritable> output, Reporter reporter)
        throws IOException {

      String stationName = metadata.getStationName(key.toString());

      int maxValue = Integer.MIN_VALUE;
      while (values.hasNext()) {
        maxValue = Math.max(maxValue, values.next().get());
      }
      output.collect(new Text(stationName), new IntWritable(maxValue));
    }
  }
```

```
@Override
public int run(String[] args) throws IOException {
  JobConf conf = JobBuilder.parseInputAndOutput(this, getConf(), args);
  if (conf == null) {
    return -1;
  }

  conf.setOutputKeyClass(Text.class);
  conf.setOutputValueClass(IntWritable.class);

  conf.setMapperClass(StationTemperatureMapper.class);
  conf.setCombinerClass(MaxTemperatureReducer.class);
  conf.setReducerClass(MaxTemperatureReducerWithStationLookup.class);

  JobClient.runJob(conf);
  return 0;
}

public static void main(String[] args) throws Exception {
  int exitCode = ToolRunner.run(
      new MaxTemperatureByStationNameUsingDistributedCacheFile(), args);
  System.exit(exitCode);
}
}
```

The program finds the maximum temperature by weather station, so the mapper (StationTemperatureMapper) simply emits (station ID, temperature) pairs. For the combiner we reuse MaxTemperatureReducer (from Chapters 2 and 5) to pick the maximum temperature for any given group of map outputs on the map side. The reducer (MaxTemperatureReducerWithStationLookup) is different from the combiner, since in addition to finding the maximum temperature, it uses the cache file to look up the station name.

We use the reducer's configure() method to retrieve the cache file using its original name, relative to the working directory of the task.

 You can use the distributed cache for copying files that do not fit in memory. MapFiles are very useful in this regard, since they serve as an on-disk lookup format (see "MapFile" on page 110). Because MapFiles are a collection of files with a defined directory structure, you should put them into an archive format (JAR, ZIP, tar, or gzipped tar) and add them to the cache using the -archives option.

Here's a snippet of the output, showing some maximum temperatures for a few weather stations:

```
PEATS RIDGE WARATAH        372
STRATHALBYN RACECOU        410
SHEOAKS AWS                399
WANGARATTA AERO            409
```

```
MOOGARA          334
MACKAY AERO      331
```

How it works

When you launch a job, Hadoop copies the files specified by the `-files` and `-archives` options to the jobtracker's filesystem (normally HDFS). Then, before a task is run, the tasktracker copies the files from the jobtracker's filesystem to a local disk—the cache—so the task can access the files. From the task's point of view, the files are just there (and it doesn't care that they came from HDFS).

The tasktracker also maintains a reference count for the number of tasks using each file in the cache. After the task has run, the file's reference count is decreased by one, and when it reaches zero it is eligible for deletion. Files are deleted to make room for a new file when the cache exceeds a certain size—10 GB by default. The cache size may be changed by setting the configuration property `local.cache.size`, which is measured in bytes.

Although this design doesn't guarantee that subsequent tasks from the same job running on the same tasktracker will find the file in the cache, it is very likely that they will, since tasks from a job are usually scheduled to run at around the same time, so there isn't the opportunity for enough other jobs to run and cause the original task's file to be deleted from the cache.

Files are localized under the `${mapred.local.dir}/taskTracker/archive` directory on the tasktrackers. Applications don't have to know this, however, since the files are symbolically linked from the task's working directory.

The DistributedCache API

Most applications don't need to use the `DistributedCache` API because they can use the distributed cache indirectly via `GenericOptionsParser`. `GenericOptionsParser` makes it much more convenient to use the distributed cache: for example, it copies local files into HDFS and then the `JobClient` informs the `DistributedCache` of their locations in HDFS using the `addCacheFile()` and `addCacheArchive()` methods. The `JobClient` also gets `DistributedCache` to create symbolic links when the files are localized, by adding fragment identifiers to the files' URIs. For example, the file specified by the URI *hdfs://namenode/foo/bar#myfile* is symlinked as *myfile* in the task's working directory.

On the task node, it is most convenient to access the localized file directly; however, sometimes you may need to get a list of all the available cache files. `JobConf` has two methods for this purpose: `getLocalCacheFiles()` and `getLocalCacheArchives()`, which both return an array of `Path` objects pointing to local files.

MapReduce Library Classes

Hadoop comes with a library of mappers and reducers for commonly used functions. They are listed with brief descriptions in Table 8-2. For further information on how to use them, please consult their Java documentation.

Table 8-2. MapReduce library classes

Classes	Description
ChainMapper, ChainReducer	Run a chain of mappers in a single mapper, and a reducer followed by a chain of mappers in a single reducer. (Symbolically: M+RM*, where M is a mapper and R is a reducer.) This can substantially reduce the amount of disk I/O incurred compared to running multiple MapReduce jobs.
FieldSelectionMapReduce	A mapper and a reducer that can select fields (like the Unix cut command) from the input keys and values and emit them as output keys and values.
IntSumReducer, LongSumReducer	Reducers that sum integer values to produce a total for every key.
InverseMapper	A mapper that swaps keys and values.
TokenCounterMapper	A mapper that tokenizes the input value into words (using Java's StringTokenizer) and emits each word along with a count of one.
RegexMapper	A mapper that finds matches of a regular expression in the input value, and emits the matches along with a count of one.

## CHAPTER 9

Setting Up a Hadoop Cluster

This chapter explains how to set up Hadoop to run on a cluster of machines. Running HDFS and MapReduce on a single machine is great for learning about these systems, but to do useful work they need to run on multiple nodes.

There are a few options when it comes to getting a Hadoop cluster, from building your own to running on rented hardware, or using an offering that provides Hadoop as a service in the cloud. This chapter and the next give you enough information to set up and operate your own cluster, but even if you are using a Hadoop service in which a lot of the routine maintenance is done for you, these chapters still offer valuable information about how Hadoop works from an operations point of view.

Cluster Specification

Hadoop is designed to run on commodity hardware. That means that you are not tied to expensive, proprietary offerings from a single vendor; rather, you can choose standardized, commonly available hardware from any of a large range of vendors to build your cluster.

"Commodity" does not mean "low-end." Low-end machines often have cheap components, which have higher failure rates than more expensive (but still commodity-class) machines. When you are operating tens, hundreds, or thousands of machines, cheap components turn out to be a false economy, as the higher failure rate incurs a greater maintenance cost. On the other hand, large database class machines are not recommended either, since they don't score well on the price/performance curve. And even though you would need fewer of them to build a cluster of comparable performance to one built of mid-range commodity hardware, when one did fail it would have a bigger impact on the cluster, since a larger proportion of the cluster hardware would be unavailable.

Hardware specifications rapidly become obsolete, but for the sake of illustration, a typical choice of machine for running a Hadoop datanode and tasktracker in late 2008 would have the following specifications:

Processor
2 quad-core Intel Xeon 2.0GHz CPUs

Memory
8 GB ECC RAM[*]

Storage
41 TB SATA disks

Network
Gigabit Ethernet

While the hardware specification for your cluster will assuredly be different, Hadoop is designed to use multiple cores and disks, so it will be able to take full advantage of more powerful hardware.

Why Not Use RAID?

HDFS clusters do not benefit from using RAID (Redundant Array of Independent Disks) for datanode storage (although RAID is used for the namenode's disks, to protect against corruption of its metadata). The redundancy that RAID provides is not needed, since HDFS handles it by replication between nodes.

Furthermore, RAID striping (RAID 0) which is commonly used to increase performance, turns out to be *slower* than the JBOD (Just a Bunch Of Disks) configuration used by HDFS, which round-robins HDFS blocks between all disks. The reason for this is that RAID 0 read and write operations are limited by the speed of the slowest disk in the RAID array. In JBOD, disk operations are independent, so the average speed of operations is greater than that of the slowest disk. Disk performance often shows considerable variation in practice, even for disks of the same model. In some benchmarking carried out on a Yahoo! cluster (*http://markmail.org/message/xmzc45zi25htr7ry*), JBOD performed 10% faster than RAID 0 in one test (Gridmix), and 30% better in another (HDFS write throughput).

Finally, if a disk fails in a JBOD configuration, HDFS can continue to operate without the failed disk, whereas with RAID, failure of a single disk causes the whole array (and hence the node) to become unavailable.

The bulk of Hadoop is written in Java, and can therefore run on any platform with a JVM, although there are enough parts that harbor Unix assumptions (the control scripts, for example) to make it unwise to run on a non-Unix platform in production. In fact, Windows operating systems are not supported production platforms (although they can be used with Cygwin as a development platform; see Appendix A).

How large should your cluster be? There isn't an exact answer to this question, but the beauty of Hadoop is that you can start with a small cluster (say, 10 nodes) and grow it

---

[*] ECC memory is strongly recommended, as several Hadoop users have reported seeing many checksum errors when using non-ECC memory on Hadoop clusters.

as your storage and computational needs grow. In many ways, a better question is this: how fast does my cluster need to grow? You can get a good feel for this by considering storage capacity.

For example, if your data grows by 1 TB a week, and you have three-way HDFS replication, then you need an additional 3 TB of raw storage per week. Allow some room for intermediate files and logfiles (around 30%, say), and this works out at about one machine (2008 vintage) per week, on average. In practice, you wouldn't buy a new machine each week and add it to the cluster. The value of doing a back-of-the-envelope calculation like this is that it gives you a feel for how big your cluster should be: in this example, a cluster that holds two years of data needs 100 machines.

For a small cluster (on the order of 10 nodes), it is usually acceptable to run the namenode and the jobtracker on a single master machine (as long as at least one copy of the namenode's metadata is stored on a remote filesystem). As the cluster and the number of files stored in HDFS grow, the namenode needs more memory, so the namenode and jobtracker should be moved onto separate machines.

The secondary namenode can be run on the same machine as the namenode, but again for reasons of memory usage (the secondary has the same memory requirements as the primary), it is best to run it on a separate piece of hardware, especially for larger clusters. (This topic is discussed in more detail in "Master node scenarios" on page 254.) Machines running the namenodes should typically run on 64-bit hardware to avoid the 3 GB limit on Java heap size in 32-bit architectures.[†]

Network Topology

A common Hadoop cluster architecture consists of a two-level network topology, as illustrated in Figure 9-1. Typically there are 30 to 40 servers per rack, with a 1 GB switch for the rack (only three are shown in the diagram), and an uplink to a core switch or router (which is normally 1 GB or better). The salient point is that the aggregate bandwidth between nodes on the same rack is much greater than that between nodes on different racks.

Rack awareness

To get maximum performance out of Hadoop, it is important to configure Hadoop so that it knows the topology of your network. If your cluster runs on a single rack, then there is nothing more to do, since this is the default. However, for multirack clusters, you need to map nodes to racks. By doing this, Hadoop will prefer within-rack transfers (where there is more bandwidth available) to off-rack transfers when placing

---

[†] The traditional advice says other machines in the cluster (jobtracker, datanodes/tasktrackers) should be 32-bit to avoid the memory overhead of larger pointers. Sun's Java 6 update 14 features "compressed ordinary object pointers," which eliminates much of this overhead, so there's now no real downside to running on 64-bit hardware.

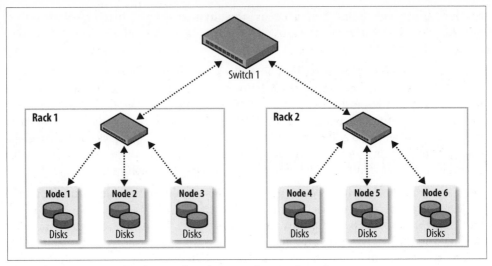

Figure 9-1. Typical two-level network architecture for a Hadoop cluster

MapReduce tasks on nodes. HDFS will be able to place replicas more intelligently to trade-off performance and resilience.

Network locations such as nodes and racks are represented in a tree, which reflects the network "distance" between locations. The namenode uses the network location when determining where to place block replicas (see "Network Topology and Hadoop" on page 64); the jobtracker uses network location to determine where the closest replica is as input for a map task that is scheduled to run on a tasktracker.

For the network in Figure 9-1, the rack topology is described by two network locations, say, */switch1/rack1* and */switch1/rack2*. Since there is only one top-level switch in this cluster, the locations can be simplified to */rack1* and */rack2*.

The Hadoop configuration must specify a map between node addresses and network locations. The map is described by a Java interface, DNSToSwitchMapping, whose signature is:

```
public interface DNSToSwitchMapping {
  public List<String> resolve(List<String> names);
}
```

The names parameter is a list of IP addresses, and the return value is a list of corresponding network location strings. The topology.node.switch.mapping.impl configuration property defines an implementation of the DNSToSwitchMapping interface that the namenode and the jobtracker use to resolve worker node network locations.

For the network in our example, we would map *node1*, *node2*, and *node3* to */rack1*, and *node4*, *node5*, and *node6* to */rack2*.

Most installations don't need to implement the interface themselves, however, since the default implementation is ScriptBasedMapping, which runs a user-defined script to determine the mapping. The script's location is controlled by the property `topology.script.file.name`. The script must accept a variable number of arguments that are the hostnames or IP addresses to be mapped, and it must emit the corresponding network locations to standard output, separated by whitespace. The example code includes a script for this purpose.

If no script location is specified, the default behavior is to map all nodes to a single network location, called *default-rack*.

Cluster Setup and Installation

Your hardware has arrived. The next steps are to get it racked up and install the software needed to run Hadoop.

There are various ways to install and configure Hadoop. This chapter describes how to do it from scratch using the Apache Hadoop distribution, and will give you the background to cover the things you need to think about when setting up Hadoop. Alternatively, if you would like to use RPMs or Debian packages for managing your Hadoop installation, then you might want to start with Cloudera's Distribution, described in Appendix B.

To ease the burden of installing and maintaining the same software on each node, it is normal to use an automated installation method like Red Hat Linux's Kickstart or Debian's Fully Automatic Installation. These tools allow you to automate the operating system installation by recording the answers to questions that are asked during the installation process (such as the disk partition layout), as well as which packages to install. Crucially, they also provide hooks to run scripts at the end of the process, which are invaluable for doing final system tweaks and customization that is not covered by the standard installer.

The following sections describe the customizations that are needed to run Hadoop. These should all be added to the installation script.

Installing Java

Java 6 or later is required to run Hadoop. The latest stable Sun JDK is the preferred option, although Java distributions from other vendors may work too. The following command confirms that Java was installed correctly:

```
% java -version
java version "1.6.0_12"
Java(TM) SE Runtime Environment (build 1.6.0_12-b04)
Java HotSpot(TM) 64-Bit Server VM (build 11.2-b01, mixed mode)
```

Creating a Hadoop User

It's good practice to create a dedicated Hadoop user account to separate the Hadoop installation from other services running on the same machine.

Some cluster administrators choose to make this user's home directory an NFS-mounted drive, to aid with SSH key distribution (see the following discussion). The NFS server is typically outside the Hadoop cluster. If you use NFS, it is worth considering autofs, which allows you to mount the NFS filesystem on demand, when the system accesses it. Autofs provides some protection against the NFS server failing, and also allows you to use replicated filesystems for failover. There are other NFS gotchas to watch out for, such as synchronizing UIDs and GIDs. For help setting up NFS on Linux, refer to the HOWTO at *http://nfs.sourceforge.net/nfs-howto/index.html*.

Installing Hadoop

Download Hadoop from the Apache Hadoop releases page (*http://hadoop.apache.org/core/releases.html*), and unpack the contents of the distribution in a sensible location, such as */usr/local* (*/opt* is another standard choice). Note that Hadoop is *not* installed in the hadoop user's home directory, as that may be an NFS-mounted directory.

```
% cd /usr/local
% sudo tar xzf hadoop-x.y.z.tar.gz
```

We also need to change the owner of the Hadoop files to be the hadoop user and group:

```
% sudo chown -R hadoop:hadoop hadoop-x.y.z
```

 Some administrators like to install HDFS and MapReduce in separate locations on the same system. At the time of this writing, only HDFS and MapReduce from the same Hadoop release are compatible with one another; however, in future releases, the compatibility requirements will be loosened. When this happens, having independent installations makes sense, as it gives more upgrade options (for more, see "Upgrades" on page 296). For example, it is convenient to be able to upgrade MapReduce—perhaps to patch a bug—while leaving HDFS running.

Note that separate installations of HDFS and MapReduce can still share configuration by using the --config option (when starting daemons) to refer to a common configuration directory. They can also log to the same directory, as the logfiles they produce are named in such a way as to avoid clashes.

Testing the Installation

Once you've created the installation file, you are ready to test it by installing it on the machines in your cluster. This will probably take a few iterations as you discover kinks in the install. When it's working, you can proceed to configure Hadoop and give it a test run. This process is documented in the following sections.

SSH Configuration

The Hadoop control scripts rely on SSH to perform cluster-wide operations. For example, there is a script for stopping and starting all the daemons in the cluster. Note that the control scripts are optional—cluster-wide operations can be performed by other mechanisms, too (such as a distributed shell).

To work seamlessly, SSH needs to be set up to allow password-less login for the hadoop user from machines in the cluster. The simplest way to achieve this is to generate a public/private key pair, and it will be shared across the cluster using NFS.

First, generate an RSA key pair by typing the following in the hadoop user account:

```
% ssh-keygen -t rsa -f ~/.ssh/id_rsa
```

Even though we want password-less logins, keys without passphrases are not considered good practice (it's OK to have an empty passphrase when running a local pseudo-distributed cluster, as described in Appendix A), so we specify a passphrase when prompted for one. We shall use *ssh-agent* to avoid the need to enter a password for each connection.

The private key is in the file specified by the -f option, *~/.ssh/id_rsa*, and the public key is stored in a file with the same name with *.pub* appended, *~/.ssh/id_rsa.pub*.

Next we need to make sure that the public key is in the *~/.ssh/authorized_keys* file on all the machines in the cluster that we want to connect to. If the hadoop user's home directory is an NFS filesystem, as described earlier, then the keys can be shared across the cluster by typing:

```
% cat ~/.ssh/id_rsa.pub >> ~/.ssh/authorized_keys
```

If the home directory is not shared using NFS, then the public keys will need to be shared by some other means.

Test that you can SSH from the master to a worker machine by making sure *ssh-agent* is running,[‡] and then run *ssh-add* to store your passphrase. You should be able to *ssh* to a worker without entering the passphrase again.

Hadoop Configuration

There are a handful of files for controlling the configuration of a Hadoop installation; the most important ones are listed in Table 9-1.

[‡] See its man page for instructions on how to start *ssh-agent*.

Table 9-1. Hadoop configuration files

Filename	Format	Description
hadoop-env.sh	Bash script	Environment variables that are used in the scripts to run Hadoop.
core-site.xml	Hadoop configuration XML	Configuration settings for Hadoop Core, such as I/O settings that are common to HDFS and MapReduce.
hdfs-site.xml	Hadoop configuration XML	Configuration settings for HDFS daemons: the namenode, the secondary namenode, and the datanodes.
mapred-site.xml	Hadoop configuration XML	Configuration settings for MapReduce daemons: the jobtracker, and the tasktrackers.
masters	Plain text	A list of machines (one per line) that each run a secondary namenode.
slaves	Plain text	A list of machines (one per line) that each run a datanode and a tasktracker.
hadoop-met rics.properties	Java Properties	Properties for controlling how metrics are published in Hadoop (see "Metrics" on page 286).
log4j.properties	Java Properties	Properties for system logfiles, the namenode audit log, and the task log for the tasktracker child process ("Hadoop User Logs" on page 142).

These files are all found in the *conf* directory of the Hadoop distribution. The configuration directory can be relocated to another part of the filesystem (outside the Hadoop installation, which makes upgrades marginally easier) as long as daemons are started with the `--config` option specifying the location of this directory on the local filesystem.

Configuration Management

Hadoop does not have a single, global location for configuration information. Instead, each Hadoop node in the cluster has its own set of configuration files, and it is up to administrators to ensure that they are kept in sync across the system. Hadoop provides a rudimentary facility for synchronizing configuration using *rsync* (see upcoming discussion), alternatively there are parallel shell tools that can help do this, like *dsh* or *pdsh*.

Hadoop is designed so that it is possible to have a single set of configuration files that are used for all master and worker machines. The great advantage of this is simplicity, both conceptually (since there is only one configuration to deal with) and operationally (as the Hadoop scripts are sufficient to manage a single configuration setup).

For some clusters, the one-size-fits-all configuration model breaks down. For example, if you expand the cluster with new machines that have a different hardware specification to the existing ones, then you need a different configuration for the new machines to take advantage of their extra resources.

In these cases, you need to have the concept of a *class* of machine, and maintain a separate configuration for each class. Hadoop doesn't provide tools to do this, but there are several excellent tools for doing precisely this type of configuration management, such as Puppet, cfengine, and bcfg2.

For a cluster of any size, it can be a challenge to keep all of the machines in sync: consider what happens if the machine is unavailable when you push out an update—who ensures it gets the update when it becomes available? This is a big problem and can lead to divergent installations, so even if you use the Hadoop control scripts for managing Hadoop, it may be a good idea to use configuration management tools for maintaining the cluster. These tools are also excellent for doing regular maintenance, such as patching security holes and updating system packages.

Control scripts

Hadoop comes with scripts for running commands, and starting and stopping daemons across the whole cluster. To use these scripts (which can be found in the *bin* directory), you need to tell Hadoop which machines are in the cluster. There are two files for this purpose, called *masters* and *slaves*, each of which contains a list of the machine hostnames or IP addresses, one per line. The *masters* file is actually a misleading name, in that it determines which machine or machines should run a secondary namenode. The *slaves* file lists the machines that the datanodes and tasktrackers should run on. Both *masters* and *slaves* files reside in the configuration directory, although the *slaves* file may be placed elsewhere (and given another name) by changing the HADOOP_SLAVES setting in *hadoop-env.sh*. Also, these files do not need to be distributed to worker nodes, since they are used only by the control scripts running on the namenode or jobtracker.

You don't need to specify which machine (or machines) the namenode and jobtracker runs on in the *masters* file, as this is determined by the machine the scripts are run on. (In fact, specifying these in the *masters* file would cause a secondary namenode to run there, which isn't always what you want.) For example, the *start-dfs.sh* script, which starts all the HDFS daemons in the cluster, runs the namenode on the machine the script is run on. In slightly more detail, it:

1. Starts a namenode on the local machine (the machine that the script is run on)
2. Starts a datanode on each machine listed in the *slaves* file
3. Starts a secondary namenode on each machine listed in the *masters* file

There is a similar script called *start-mapred.sh*, which starts all the MapReduce daemons in the cluster. More specifically, it:

1. Starts a jobtracker on the local machine
2. Starts a tasktracker on each machine listed in the *slaves* file

Note that *masters* is not used by the MapReduce control scripts.

Also provided are *stop-dfs.sh* and *stop-mapred.sh* scripts to stop the daemons started by the corresponding start script.

These scripts start and stop Hadoop daemons using the *hadoop-daemon.sh* script. If you use the aforementioned scripts, you shouldn't call *hadoop-daemon.sh* directly. But if you need to control Hadoop daemons from another system or from your own scripts, then the *hadoop-daemon.sh* script is a good integration point. Likewise, *hadoop-dae mons.sh* (with an "s") is handy for starting the same daemon on a set of hosts.

Master node scenarios

Depending on the size of the cluster, there are various configurations for running the master daemons: the namenode, secondary namenode, and jobtracker. On a small cluster (a few tens of nodes), it is convenient to put them on a single machine; however, as the cluster gets larger, there are good reasons to separate them.

The namenode has high memory requirements, as it holds file and block metadata for the entire namespace in memory. The secondary namenode, while idle most of the time, has a comparable memory footprint to the primary when it creates a checkpoint. (This is explained in detail in "The filesystem image and edit log" on page 274.) For filesystems with a large number of files, there may not be enough physical memory on one machine to run both the primary and secondary namenode.

The secondary namenode keeps a copy of the latest checkpoint of the filesystem metadata that it creates. Keeping this (stale) backup on a different node to the namenode allows recovery in the event of loss (or corruption) of all the namenode's metadata files. (This is discussed further in Chapter 10.)

On a busy cluster running lots of MapReduce jobs, the jobtracker uses considerable memory and CPU resources, so it should run on a dedicated node.

Whether the master daemons run on one or more nodes, the following instructions apply:

- Run the HDFS control scripts from the namenode machine. The masters file should contain the address of the secondary namenode.
- Run the MapReduce control scripts from the jobtracker machine.

When the namenode and jobtracker are on separate nodes, their *slaves* files need to be kept in sync, since each node in the cluster should run a datanode and a tasktracker.

Environment Settings

In this section, we consider how to set the variables in *hadoop-env.sh*.

Memory

By default, Hadoop allocates 1000 MB (1 GB) of memory to each daemon it runs. This is controlled by the HADOOP_HEAPSIZE setting in *hadoop-env.sh*. In addition, the task tracker launches separate child JVMs to run map and reduce tasks in, so we need to factor these into the total memory footprint of a worker machine.

The maximum number of map tasks that will be run on a tasktracker at one time is controlled by the mapred.tasktracker.map.tasks.maximum property, which defaults to two tasks. There is a corresponding property for reduce tasks, `mapred.task tracker.reduce.tasks.maximum`, which also defaults to two tasks. The memory given to each of these child JVMs can be changed by setting the `mapred.child.java.opts` property. The default setting is `-Xmx200m`, which gives each task 200 MB of memory. (Incidentally, you can provide extra JVM options here, too. For example, you might enable verbose GC logging to debug GC.) The default configuration therefore uses 2800 MB of memory for a worker machine (see Table 9-2).

Table 9-2. Worker node memory calculation

JVM	Default memory used (MB)	Memory used for 8 processors, 400 MB per child (MB)
Datanode	1000	1000
Tasktracker	1000	1000
Tasktracker child map task	2×200	7×400
Tasktracker child reduce task	2×200	7×400
Total	2800	7600

The number of tasks that can be run simultaneously on a tasktracker is governed by the number of processors available on the machine. Because MapReduce jobs are normally I/O-bound, it makes sense to have more tasks than processors to get better utilization. The amount of oversubscription depends on the CPU utilization of jobs you run, but a good rule of thumb is to have a factor of between one and two more tasks (counting both map and reduce tasks) than processors.

For example, if you had 8 processors and you wanted to run 2 processes on each processor, then you could set `mapred.tasktracker.map.tasks.maximum` and `mapred.task tracker.map.tasks.maximum` to both be 7 (not 8, since the datanode and the tasktracker each take one slot). If you also increased the memory available to each child task to 400 MB, then the total memory usage would be 7,600 MB (see Table 9-2).

Whether this Java memory allocation will fit into 8 GB of physical memory depends on the other processes that are running on the machine. If you are running Streaming or Pipes programs, this allocation will probably be inappropriate (and the memory allocated to the child should be dialled down), since it doesn't allow enough memory for users' (Streaming or Pipes) processes to run. The thing to avoid is processes being swapped out, as this it leads to severe performance degradation. The precise memory settings are necessarily very cluster-dependent, and can be optimized over time with experience gained from monitoring the memory usage across the cluster. Tools like Ganglia ("GangliaContext" on page 288) are good for gathering this information.

Hadoop also provides settings to control how much memory is used for MapReduce operations. These can be set on a per-job basis, and are covered in the section on "Shuffle and Sort" on page 163.

For the master node, each of the namenode, secondary namenode, and jobtracker daemons uses 1,000 MB by default, a total of 3,000 MB.

 A namenode can eat up memory, since a reference to every block of every file is maintained in memory. For example, 1,000 MB is enough for a few million files. You can increase the namenode's memory without changing the memory allocated to other Hadoop daemons by setting HADOOP_NAMENODE_OPTS in *hadoop-env.sh* to include a JVM option for setting the memory size. HADOOP_NAMENODE_OPTS allows you to pass extra options to the namenode's JVM. So, for example, if using a Sun JVM, -Xmx2000m would specify that 2000 MB of memory should be allocated to the namenode.

If you change the namenode's memory allocation, don't forget to do the same for the secondary namenode (using the HADOOP_SECONDARYNAME NODE_OPTS variable), since its memory requirements are comparable to the primary namenode's. You will probably also want to run the secondary namenode on a different machine, in this case.

There are corresponding environment variables for the other Hadoop daemons, so you can customize their memory allocations, if desired. See *hadoop-env.sh* for details.

Java

The location of the Java implementation to use is determined by the JAVA_HOME setting in *hadoop-env.sh*, or from the JAVA_HOME shell environment variable, if not set in *hadoop-env.sh*. It's a good idea to set the value in *hadoop-env.sh*, so that it is clearly defined in one place, and to ensure that the whole cluster is using the same version of Java.

System logfiles

System logfiles produced by Hadoop are stored in $HADOOP_INSTALL/logs by default. This can be changed using the HADOOP_LOG_DIR setting in *hadoop-env.sh*. It's a good idea to change this so that logfiles are kept out of the directory that Hadoop is installed in, since this keeps logfiles in one place even after the installation directory changes after an upgrade. A common choice is */var/log/hadoop*, set by including the following line in *hadoop-env.sh*:

```
export HADOOP_LOG_DIR=/var/log/hadoop
```

The log directory will be created if it doesn't already exist (if not, confirm that the Hadoop user has permission to create it). Each Hadoop daemon running on a machine produces two logfiles. The first is the log output written via log4j. This file, which ends in *.log*, should be the first port of call when diagnosing problems, since most application log messages are written here. The standard Hadoop log4j configuration uses a Daily Rolling File Appender to rotate logfiles. Old logfiles are never deleted, so you should arrange for them to be periodically deleted or archived, so as to not run out of disk space on the local node.

The second logfile is the combined standard output and standard error log. This logfile, which ends in *.out*, usually contains little or no output, since Hadoop uses log4j for logging. It is only rotated when the daemon is restarted, and only the last five logs are retained. Old logfiles are suffixed with a number between 1 and 5, with 5 being the oldest file.

Logfile names (of both types) are a combination of the name of the user running the daemon, the daemon name, and the machine hostname. For example, *hadoop-tom-datanode-sturges.local.log.2008-07-04* is the name of a logfile after it has been rotated. This naming structure makes it possible to archive logs from all machines in the cluster in a single directory, if needed, since the filenames are unique.

The username in the logfile name is actually the default for the `HADOOP_IDENT_STRING` setting in *hadoop-env.sh*. If you wish to give the Hadoop instance a different identity for the purposes of naming the logfiles, change `HADOOP_IDENT_STRING` to be the identifier you want.

SSH settings

The control scripts allow you to run commands on (remote) worker nodes from the master node using SSH. It can be useful to customize the SSH settings, for various reasons. For example, you may want to reduce the connection timeout (using the `ConnectTimeout` option) so the control scripts don't hang around waiting to see whether a dead node is going to respond. Obviously, this can be taken too far. If the timeout is too low, then busy nodes will be skipped, which is bad.

Another useful SSH setting is `StrictHostKeyChecking`, which can be set to `no` to automatically add new host keys to the known hosts files. The default, `ask`, is to prompt the user to confirm they have verified the key fingerprint, which is not a suitable setting in a large cluster environment.[§]

To pass extra options to SSH, define the `HADOOP_SSH_OPTS` environment variable in *hadoop-env.sh*. See the `ssh` and `ssh_config` manual pages for more SSH settings.

The Hadoop control scripts can distribute configuration files to all nodes of the cluster using rsync. This is not enabled by default, but by defining the `HADOOP_MASTER` setting in *hadoop-env.sh*, worker daemons will rsync the tree rooted at `HADOOP_MASTER` to the local node's `HADOOP_INSTALL` whenever the daemon starts up.

What if you have two masters—a namenode and a jobtracker on separate machines? You can pick one as the source, and the other can rsync from it, along with all the

---

[§] For more discussion on the security implications of SSH Host Keys, consult the article "SSH Host Key Protection" by Brian Hatch at *http://www.securityfocus.com/infocus/1806*.

workers. In fact, you could use any machine, even one outside the Hadoop cluster, to rsync from.

Because `HADOOP_MASTER` is unset by default, there is a bootstrapping problem: how do we make sure *hadoop-env.sh* with `HADOOP_MASTER` set is present on worker nodes? For small clusters, it is easy to write a small script to copy *hadoop-env.sh* from the master to all of the worker nodes. For larger clusters, tools like *dsh* can do the copies in parallel. Alternatively, a suitable *hadoop-env.sh* can be created as a part of the automated installation script (such as Kickstart).

When starting a large cluster with rsyncing enabled, the worker nodes can overwhelm the master node with rsync requests since the workers start at around the same time. To avoid this, set the `HADOOP_SLAVE_SLEEP` setting to a small number of seconds, such as `0.1`, for one-tenth of a second. When running commands on all nodes of the cluster, the master will sleep for this period between invoking the command on each worker machine in turn.

Important Hadoop Daemon Properties

Hadoop has a bewildering number of configuration properties. In this section, we address the ones that you need to define (or at least understand why the default is appropriate) for any real-world working cluster. These properties are set in the Hadoop site files: *core-site.xml*, *hdfs-site.xml*, and *mapred-site.xml*. Example 9-1 shows a typical example set of files. Notice that most are marked as final, in order to prevent them from being overridden by job configurations. You can learn more about how to write Hadoop's configuration files in "The Configuration API" on page 116.

Example 9-1. A typical set of site configuration files

```
<?xml version="1.0"?>
<!-- core-site.xml -->
<configuration>
  <property>
    <name>fs.default.name</name>
    <value>hdfs://namenode/</value>
    <final>true</final>
  </property>
</configuration>

<?xml version="1.0"?>
<!-- hdfs-site.xml -->
<configuration>
  <property>
    <name>dfs.name.dir</name>
    <value>/disk1/hdfs/name,/remote/hdfs/name</value>
    <final>true</final>
  </property>

  <property>
    <name>dfs.data.dir</name>
```

```
    <value>/disk1/hdfs/data,/disk2/hdfs/data</value>
    <final>true</final>
  </property>

  <property>
    <name>fs.checkpoint.dir</name>
    <value>/disk1/hdfs/namesecondary,/disk2/hdfs/namesecondary</value>
    <final>true</final>
  </property>
</configuration>

<?xml version="1.0"?>
<!-- mapred-site.xml -->
<configuration>
  <property>
    <name>mapred.job.tracker</name>
    <value>jobtracker:8021</value>
    <final>true</final>
  </property>

  <property>
    <name>mapred.local.dir</name>
    <value>/disk1/mapred/local,/disk2/mapred/local</value>
    <final>true</final>
  </property>

  <property>
    <name>mapred.system.dir</name>
    <value>/tmp/hadoop/mapred/system</value>
    <final>true</final>
  </property>

  <property>
    <name>mapred.tasktracker.map.tasks.maximum</name>
    <value>7</value>
    <final>true</final>
  </property>

  <property>
    <name>mapred.tasktracker.reduce.tasks.maximum</name>
    <value>7</value>
    <final>true</final>
  </property>

  <property>
    <name>mapred.child.java.opts</name>
    <value>-Xmx400m</value>
    <!-- Not marked as final so jobs can include JVM debugging options -->
  </property>
</configuration>
```

HDFS

To run HDFS, you need to designate one machine as a namenode. In this case, the property fs.default.name is a HDFS filesystem URI, whose host is the namenode's hostname or IP address, and port is the port that the namenode will listen on for RPCs. If no port is specified, the default of 8020 is used.

 The *masters* file that is used by the control scripts is not used by the HDFS (or MapReduce) daemons to determine hostnames. In fact, because the *masters* file is only used by the scripts, you can ignore it if you don't use them.

The `fs.default.name` property also doubles as specifying the default filesystem. The default filesystem is used to resolve relative paths, which are handy to use since they save typing (and avoid hardcoding knowledge of a particular namenode's address). For example, with the default filesystem defined in Example 9-1, the relative URI */a/b* is resolved to *hdfs://namenode/a/b*.

 If you are running HDFS, the fact that `fs.default.name` is used to specify both the HDFS namenode *and* the default filesystem means HDFS has to be the default filesystem in the server configuration. Bear in mind, however, that it is possible to specify a different filesystem as the default in the client configuration, for convenience.

For example, if you use both HDFS and S3 filesystems, then you have a choice of specifying either as the default in the client configuration, which allows you to refer to the default with a relative URI, and the other with an absolute URI.

There are a few other configuration properties you should set for HDFS: those that set the storage directories for the namenode and for datanodes. The property `dfs.name.dir` specifies a list of directories where the namenode stores persistent filesystem metadata (the edit log, and the filesystem image). A copy of each of the metadata files is stored in each directory for redundancy. It's common to configure `dfs.name.dir` so that the namenode metadata is written to one or two local disks, and a remote disk, such as a NFS-mounted directory. Such a setup guards against failure of a local disk, and failure of the entire namenode, since in both cases the files can be recovered and used to start a new namenode. (The secondary namenode takes only periodic checkpoints of the namenode, so it does not provide an up-to-date backup of the namenode.)

You should also set the `dfs.data.dir` property, which specifies a list of directories for a datanode to store its blocks. Unlike the namenode, which uses multiple directories for redundancy, a datanode round-robins writes between its storage directories, so for performance you should specify a storage directory for each local disk. Read performance also benefits from having multiple disks for storage, because blocks will be spread across them, and concurrent reads for distinct blocks will be correspondingly spread across disks.

For maximum performance, you should mount storage disks with the `noatime` option. This setting means that last accessed time information is not written on file reads, which gives significant performance gains.

Finally, you should configure where the secondary namenode stores its checkpoints of the filesystem. The `fs.checkpoint.dir` property specifies a list of directories where the checkpoints are kept. Like the storage directories for the namenode, which keep redundant copies of the namenode metadata, the checkpointed filesystem image is stored in each checkpoint directory for redundancy.

Table 9-3 summarizes the important configuration properties for HDFS.

Table 9-3. Important HDFS daemon properties

Property name	Type	Default value	Description
`fs.default.name`	URI	`file:///`	The default filesystem. The URI defines the hostname and port that the jobtracker's RPC server runs on. The default port is 8020. This property should be set in *core-site.xml*.
`dfs.name.dir`	comma-separated directory names	`${hadoop.tmp.dir}/dfs/name`	The list of directories where the namenode stores its persistent metadata. The namenode stores a copy of the metadata in each directory in the list.
`dfs.data.dir`	comma-separated directory names	`${hadoop.tmp.dir}/dfs/data`	A list of directories where the datanode stores blocks.
`fs.check point.dir`	comma-separated directory names	`${hadoop.tmp.dir}/dfs/namesecondary`	A list of directories where the secondary namenode stores checkpoints. It stores a copy of the checkpoint in each directory in the list.

Note that the storage directories for HDFS are under Hadoop's temporary directory by default (the `hadoop.tmp.dir` property, whose default is `/tmp/hadoop-${user.name}`). Therefore it is critical that these properties are set so that data is not lost by the system clearing out temporary directories.

MapReduce

To run MapReduce, you need to designate one machine as a jobtracker, which on small clusters may be the same machine as the namenode. To do this, set the `mapred.job.tracker` property to the hostname or IP address and port that the jobtracker will listen on. Note that this property is not a URI, but a host-port pair, separated by a colon. The port number 8021 is a common choice.

During a MapReduce job, intermediate data and working files are written to temporary local files. Since this data includes the potentially very large output of map tasks, you need to ensure that the `mapred.local.dir` property, which controls the location of local temporary storage, is configured to use disk partitions that are large enough. The `mapred.local.dir` property takes a comma-separated list of directory names, and you should use all available local disks to spread disk I/O. Typically, you will use the same disks and partitions (but different directories) for MapReduce temporary data as you use for datanode block storage, as governed by the `dfs.data.dir` property, discussed earlier.

MapReduce uses a distributed filesystem to share files (such as the job JAR file) with the tasktrackers that run the MapReduce tasks. The `mapred.system.dir` property is used to specify a directory where these files can be stored. This directory is resolved relative to the default filesystem (configured in `fs.default.name`), which is usually HDFS.

Finally, you should set the `mapred.tasktracker.map.tasks.maximum` and `mapred.task tracker.reduce.tasks.maximum` properties to reflect the number of available cores on the tasktracker machines and `mapred.child.java.opts` to reflect the amount of memory available for the tasktracker child JVMs. See the discussion in "Memory" on page 254.

Table 9-4 summarizes the important configuration properties for HDFS.

Table 9-4. Important MapReduce daemon properties

Property name	Type	Default value	Description
mapred.job.tracker	hostname and port	local	The hostname and port that the jobtracker's RPC server runs on. If set to the default value of local, then the jobtracker is run in-process on demand when you run a MapReduce job (you don't need to start the MapReduce daemons in this case).
mapred.local.dir	comma-separated directory names	${hadoop.tmp.dir} /mapred/local	A list of directories where the MapReduce stores intermediate data for jobs. The data is cleared out when the job ends.
mapred.system.dir	URI	${hadoop.tmp.dir} /mapred/system	The directory relative to fs.default.name where shared files are stored, during a job run.
mapred.task tracker.map.tasks. maximum	int	2	The number of map tasks that may be run on a tasktracker at any one time.

Property name	Type	Default value	Description
mapred.task tracker.reduce.tasks. maximum	int	2	The number of reduce tasks that may be run on a tasktracker at any one time.
mapred.child.java.opts	String	-Xmx200m	The JVM options used to launch the tasktracker child process that runs map and reduce tasks. This property can be set on a per-job basis, which can be useful for setting JVM properties for debugging, for example.

Hadoop Daemon Addresses and Ports

Hadoop daemons generally run both an RPC server (Table 9-5) for communication between daemons, and a HTTP server to provide web pages for human consumption (Table 9-6). Each server is configured by setting the network address and port number to listen on. By specifying the network address as 0.0.0.0, Hadoop will bind to all addresses on the machine. Alternatively, you can specify a single address to bind to. A port number of 0 instructs the server to start on a free port: this is generally discouraged, since it is incompatible with setting cluster-wide firewall policies.

Table 9-5. RPC server properties

Property name	Default value	Description
fs.default.name	file:///	When set to an HDFS URI, this property determines the namenode's RPC server address and port. The default port is 8020 if not specified.
dfs.datanode.ipc.address	0.0.0.0:50020	The datanode's RPC server address and port.
mapred.job.tracker	local	When set to a hostname and port, this property specifies the jobtracker's RPC server address and port. A commonly used port is 8021.
mapred.task.tracker.report.address	127.0.0.1:0	The tasktracker's RPC server address and port. This is used by the tasktracker's child JVM to communicate with the tasktracker. Using any free port is acceptable in this case, as the server only binds to the loopback address. You should change this setting only if the machine has no loopback address.

In addition to an RPC server, datanodes run a TCP/IP server for block transfers. The server address and port is set by the dfs.datanode.address property, and has a default value of 0.0.0.0:50010.

Table 9-6. HTTP server properties

Property name	Default value	Description
`mapred.job.tracker.http.address`	0.0.0.0:50030	The jobtracker's HTTP server address and port.
`mapred.task.tracker.http.address`	0.0.0.0:50060	The tasktracker's HTTP server address and port.
`dfs.http.address`	0.0.0.0:50070	The namenode's HTTP server address and port.
`dfs.datanode.http.address`	0.0.0.0:50075	The datanode's HTTP server address and port.
`dfs.secondary.http.address`	0.0.0.0:50090	The secondary namenode's HTTP server address and port.

There are also settings for controlling which network interfaces the datanodes and tasktrackers report as their IP addresses (for HTTP and RPC servers). The relevant properties are `dfs.datanode.dns.interface` and `mapred.tasktracker.dns.interface`, both of which are set to `default`, which will use the default network interface. You can set this explicitly to report the address of a particular interface; `eth0`, for example.

Other Hadoop Properties

This section discusses some other properties that you might consider setting.

Cluster membership

To aid the addition and removal of nodes in the future, you can specify a list of authorized machines that may join the cluster as datanodes or tasktrackers. The list is specified using the `dfs.hosts` (for datanodes) and `mapred.hosts` (for tasktrackers) properties, as well as the corresponding `dfs.hosts.exclude` and `mapred.hosts.exclude` files used for decommissioning. See "Commissioning and Decommissioning Nodes" on page 293 for further discussion.

Service-level authorization

You can define ACLs to control which users and groups have permission to connect to each Hadoop service. Services are defined at the protocol level, so there are ones for MapReduce job submission, namenode communication, and so on. By default, authorization is turned off (see the `hadoop.security.authorization` property) so all users may access all services. See the *hadoop-policy.xml* configuration file for more information.

Buffer size

Hadoop uses a buffer size of 4 KB (4096 bytes) for its I/O operations. This is a conservative setting, and with modern hardware and operating systems, you will likely see performance benefits by increasing it. 64 KB (65536 bytes) or 128 KB (131072 bytes) are common choices. Set this using the `io.file.buffer.size` property in *core-site.xml*.

HDFS block size

The HDFS block size is 64 MB by default, but many clusters use 128 MB (134,217,728 bytes) or even 256 MB (268,435,456 bytes) to give mappers more data to work on. Set this using the `dfs.block.size` property in *hdfs-site.xml*.

Reserved storage space

By default, datanodes will try to use all of the space available in their storage directories. If you want to reserve some space on the storage volumes for non-HDFS use, then you can set `dfs.datanode.du.reserved` to the amount, in bytes, of space to reserve.

Trash

Hadoop filesystems have a trash facility, in which deleted files are not actually deleted, but rather are moved to a trash folder, where they remain for a minimum period before being permanently deleted by the system. The minimum period in minutes that a file will remain in the trash is set using the `fs.trash.interval` configuration property in *core-site.xml*. By default the trash interval is zero, which disables trash.

Like in many operating systems, Hadoop's trash facility is a user-level feature, meaning that only files that are deleted using the filesystem shell are put in the trash. Files deleted programmatically are deleted immediately. It is possible to use the trash programmatically, however, by constructing a `Trash` instance, then calling its `moveToTrash()` method with the `Path` of the file intended for deletion. The method returns a value indicating success; a value of `false` means either that trash is not enabled or that the file is already in the trash.

When trash is enabled, each user has her own trash directory called *.Trash* in her home directory. File recovery is simple: you look for the file in a subdirectory of *.Trash* and move it out of the trash subtree.

HDFS will automatically delete files in trash folders, but other filesystems will not, so you have to arrange for this to be done periodically. You can *expunge* the trash, which will delete files that have been in the trash longer than their minimum period, using the filesystem shell:

```
% hadoop fs -expunge
```

The `Trash` class exposes an `expunge()` method that has the same effect.

Task memory limits

On a shared cluster, it shouldn't be possible for one user's errant MapReduce program to bring down nodes in the cluster. This can happen if the map or reduce task has a memory leak, for example, because the machine on which the tasktracker is running will run out of memory and may affect the other running processes. To prevent this situation, you can set `mapred.child.ulimit`, which sets a maximum limit on the virtual memory of the child process launched by the tasktracker. It is set in kilobytes, and should be comfortably larger than the memory of the JVM set by `mapred.child.java.opts`; otherwise, the child JVM might not start.

As an alternative, you can use *limits.conf* to set process limits at the operating system level.

Job scheduler

Particularly in a multiuser MapReduce setting, consider changing the default FIFO job scheduler to one of the more fully featured alternatives. See "Job Scheduling" on page 161.

Post Install

Once you have a Hadoop cluster up and running, you need to give users access to it. This involves creating a home directory for each user, and setting ownership permissions on it:

```
% hadoop fs -mkdir /user/username
% hadoop fs -chown username:username /user/username
```

This is a good time to set space limits on the directory. The following sets a 1 TB limit on the given user directory:

```
% hadoop dfsadmin -setSpaceQuota 1t /user/username
```

Benchmarking a Hadoop Cluster

Is the cluster set up correctly? The best way to answer this question is empirically: run some jobs and confirm that you get the expected results. Benchmarks make good tests, as you also get numbers that you can compare with other clusters as a sanity check on whether your new cluster is performing roughly as expected. And you can tune a cluster using benchmark results to squeeze the best performance out of it. This is often done with monitoring systems in place ("Monitoring" on page 285), so you can see how resources are being used across the cluster.

To get the best results, you should run benchmarks on a cluster that is not being used by others. In practice, this is just before it is put into service, and users start relying on it. Once users have periodically scheduled jobs on a cluster it is generally impossible to find a time when the cluster is not being used (unless you arrange downtime with users), so you should run benchmarks to your satisfaction before this happens.

Experience has shown that most hardware failures for new systems are hard drive failures. By running I/O intensive benchmarks—such as the ones described next—you can "burn in" the cluster before it goes live.

Hadoop Benchmarks

Hadoop comes with several benchmarks that you can run very easily with minimal setup cost. Benchmarks are packaged in the test JAR file, and you can get a list of them, with descriptions, by invoking the JAR file with no arguments:

```
% hadoop jar $HADOOP_INSTALL/hadoop-*-test.jar
```

Most of the benchmarks show usage instructions when invoked with no arguments. For example:

```
% hadoop jar $HADOOP_INSTALL/hadoop-*-test.jar TestDFSIO
TestFDSIO.0.0.4
Usage: TestFDSIO -read | -write | -clean [-nrFiles N] [-fileSize MB] [-resFile
resultFileName] [-bufferSize Bytes]
```

Benchmarking HDFS with TestDFSIO

`TestDFSIO` tests the I/O performance of HDFS. It does this by using a MapReduce job as a convenient way to read or write files in parallel. Each file is read or written in a separate map task, and the output of the map is used for collecting statistics relating to the file just processed. The statistics are accumulated in the reduce, to produce a summary.

The following command writes 10 files of 1,000 MB each:

```
% hadoop jar $HADOOP_INSTALL/hadoop-*-test.jar TestDFSIO -write -nrFiles 10
-fileSize 1000
```

At the end of the run, the results are written to the console and also recorded in a local file (which is appended to, so you can rerun the benchmark and not lose old results):

```
% cat TestDFSIO_results.log
----- TestDFSIO ----- : write
           Date & time: Sun Apr 12 07:14:09 EDT 2009
       Number of files: 10
Total MBytes processed: 10000
     Throughput mb/sec: 7.796340865378244
Average IO rate mb/sec: 7.8862199783325195
 IO rate std deviation: 0.9101254683525547
    Test exec time sec: 163.387
```

The files are written under the */benchmarks/TestDFSIO* directory by default (this can be changed by setting the `test.build.data` system property), in a directory called *io_data*.

To run a read benchmark, use the `-read` argument. Note that these files must already exist (having been written by TestDFSIO `-write`):

```
% hadoop jar $HADOOP_INSTALL/hadoop-*-test.jar TestDFSIO -read -nrFiles 10
-fileSize 1000
```

Here are the results for a real run:

```
----- TestDFSIO ----- : read
           Date & time: Sun Apr 12 07:24:28 EDT 2009
       Number of files: 10
 Total MBytes processed: 10000
    Throughput mb/sec: 80.25553361904304
 Average IO rate mb/sec: 98.6801528930664
  IO rate std deviation: 36.63507598174921
     Test exec time sec: 47.624
```

When you've finished benchmarking, you can delete all the generated files from HDFS using the -clean argument:

```
% hadoop jar $HADOOP_INSTALL/hadoop-*-test.jar TestDFSIO -clean
```

Benchmarking MapReduce with Sort

Hadoop comes with a MapReduce program that does a partial sort of its input. It is very useful for benchmarking the whole MapReduce system, as the full input dataset is transferred through the shuffle. The three steps are: generate some random data, perform the sort, then validate the results.

First we generate some random data using RandomWriter. It runs a MapReduce job with 10 maps per node, and each map generates (approximately) 10 GB of random binary data, with key and values of various sizes. You can change these values if you like by setting the properties test.randomwriter.maps_per_host and test.random write.bytes_per_map. There are also settings for the size ranges of the keys and values; see RandomWriter for details.

Here's how to invoke RandomWriter (found in the example JAR file, not the test one) to write its output to a directory called *random-data*:

```
% hadoop jar $HADOOP_INSTALL/hadoop-*-examples.jar randomwriter random-data
```

Next we can run the Sort program:

```
% hadoop jar $HADOOP_INSTALL/hadoop-*-examples.jar sort random-data sorted-data
```

The overall execution time of the sort is the metric we are interested in, but it's instructive to watch the job's progress via the web UI (*http://jobtracker-host:50030/*), where you can get a feel for how long each phase of the job takes. Adjusting the parameters mentioned in "Tuning a Job" on page 145 is a useful exercise, too.

As a final sanity check, we validate the data in *sorted-data* is, in fact, correctly sorted:

```
% hadoop jar $HADOOP_INSTALL/hadoop-*-test.jar testmapredsort -sortInput random-data \
    -sortOutput sorted-data
```

This command runs the SortValidator program, which performs a series of checks on the unsorted and sorted data to check whether the sort is accurate. It reports the outcome to the console at the end of its run:

```
SUCCESS! Validated the MapReduce framework's 'sort' successfully.
```

Other benchmarks

There are many more Hadoop benchmarks, but the following are widely used:

- MRBench (invoked with mrbench) runs a small job a number of times. It acts as a good counterpoint to sort, as it checks whether small job runs are responsive.
- NNBench (invoked with nnbench) is useful for load testing namenode hardware.
- *Gridmix* is a suite of benchmarks designed to model a realistic cluster workload, by mimicking a variety of data-access patterns seen in practice. See *src/benchmarks/gridmix2* in the distribution for further details.[||]

User Jobs

For tuning, it is best to include a few jobs that are representative of the jobs that your users run, so your cluster is tuned for these and not just for the standard benchmarks. If this is your first Hadoop cluster and you don't have any user jobs yet, then Gridmix is a good substitute.

When running your own jobs as benchmarks you should select a dataset for your user jobs that you use each time you run the benchmarks to allow comparisons between runs. When you set up a new cluster, or upgrade a cluster, you will be able to use the same dataset to compare the performance with previous runs.

Hadoop in the Cloud

Although many organizations choose to run Hadoop in-house, it is also popular to run Hadoop in the cloud on rented hardware or as a service. For instance, Cloudera offers tools for running Hadoop (see Appendix B) in a public or private cloud.

In this section, we look at running Hadoop on Amazon EC2, which is a great way to try out your own Hadoop cluster on a low-commitment, trial basis.

Hadoop on Amazon EC2

Amazon Elastic Compute Cloud (EC2) is a computing service that allows customers to rent computers (*instances*) on which they can run their own applications. A customer can launch and terminate instances on demand, paying by the hour for active instances.

Hadoop comes with a set of scripts that make is easy to run Hadoop on EC2. The scripts allow you to perform such operations as launching or terminating a cluster, or adding instances to an existing cluster.

Running Hadoop on EC2 is especially appropriate for certain workflows. For example, if you store data on Amazon S3, then you can run a cluster on EC2 and run MapReduce

---

[||] In a similar vein, *PigMix* is a set of benchmarks for Pig available from *http://wiki.apache.org/pig/PigMix*.

jobs that read the S3 data, and write output back to S3, before shutting down the cluster. If you're working with longer-lived clusters, you might copy S3 data onto HDFS running on EC2 for more efficient processing, as HDFS can take advantage of data locality, but S3 cannot (since S3 storage is not colocated with EC2 nodes).

EC2 Network Topology

The EC2 APIs offer no control over network topology to clients. At the time of this writing, it is not possible to give hints to direct placement of instances—to request that they are split between two racks, say. Nor is it possible to discover in which rack an instance is located after it has booted, which means that Hadoop considers the whole cluster to be situated in one rack ("Rack awareness" on page 247), even though in reality instances are likely to be spread across racks. Hadoop will still work, but not as efficiently as it might otherwise.

Setup

Before you can run Hadoop on EC2, you need to work through Amazon's Getting Started Guide (linked from the EC2 website *http://aws.amazon.com/ec2/*), which goes through setting up an account, installing the EC2 command-line tools, and launching an instance.

Next, get a copy of the Hadoop EC2 launch scripts. If you have already installed Apache Hadoop on your workstation (Appendix A), you will find them in the *src/contrib/ec2* subdirectory of the installation. If you haven't installed Hadoop, then do so now. (Note that the same scripts can be used to launch a cluster running Apache Hadoop, or Cloudera's Distribution for Hadoop, described in Appendix B.)

You need to configure the scripts to set your Amazon Web Service credentials, security key details, the version of Hadoop to run, and the EC2 instance type to use (the extra-large instances are most suitable for running Hadoop). Do this by editing the file *src/contrib/ec2/bin/hadoop-ec2-env.sh*: the comments in the file document how to set each variable.

Launching a cluster

We are now ready to launch a cluster. To launch a cluster named *test-hadoop-cluster* with one master node (running the namenode and jobtracker) and five worker nodes (running the datanodes and tasktackers), type:

```
% bin/hadoop-ec2 launch-cluster test-hadoop-cluster 5
```

This will create EC2 security groups for the cluster, if they don't already exist, and give the master and worker nodes unfettered access to one another. It will also enable SSH access from anywhere. Once the security groups have been set up, the master instance will be launched, then once it has started, the five worker instances will be launched. The reason that the worker nodes are launched separately is so that the master's hostname can be passed to the worker instances, and allow the datanodes and task-trackers to connect to the master when they start up.

Running a MapReduce job

Jobs need to be run from within EC2 (so EC2 hostnames resolve correctly), and to do this we need to transfer the job JAR file to the cluster. The scripts provide a convenient way to do this. The following command copies the JAR file to the master node:

```
% bin/hadoop-ec2 push test-hadoop-cluster /Users/tom/htdg-examples/job.jar
```

There is also a shortcut for logging into the cluster. This command logs into the master (using SSH), but it is also possible to specify the EC2 instance ID instead of the cluster name to log into any node in the cluster. (There is also a shortcut for the screen command that you may prefer.)

```
% bin/hadoop-ec2 login test-hadoop-cluster
```

The cluster's filesystem is empty, so before we run a job, we need to populate it with data. Doing a parallel copy from S3 (see "Hadoop Filesystems" on page 47 for more on the S3 filesystems in Hadoop) using Hadoop's *distcp* tool is an efficient way to transfer data into HDFS:

```
# hadoop distcp s3n://hadoopbook/ncdc/all input/ncdc/all
```

After the data has been copied, we can run a job in the usual way:

```
# hadoop jar job.jar MaxTemperatureWithCombiner input/ncdc/all output
```

Alternatively, we could have specified the input to be S3, which would have the same effect. When running multiple jobs over the same input data, it's best to copy the data to HDFS first to save bandwidth:

```
# hadoop jar job.jar MaxTemperatureWithCombiner s3n://hadoopbook/ncdc/all output
```

We can track the progress of the job using the jobtracker's web UI, found at *http://master_host:50030/*.

Terminating a cluster

To shut down the cluster, first log out from the EC2 node and issue the terminate-cluster command from your workstation:

```
# exit
% bin/hadoop-ec2 terminate-cluster test-hadoop-cluster
```

You will be asked to confirm that you want to terminate all the instances in the cluster.

## CHAPTER 10

Administering Hadoop

The previous chapter was devoted to setting up a Hadoop cluster. In this chapter, we look at the procedures to keep a cluster running smoothly.

HDFS

Persistent Data Structures

As an administrator, it is invaluable to have a basic understanding of how the components of HDFS—the namenode, the secondary namenode, and the datanodes—organize their persistent data on disk. Knowing which files are which can help you diagnose problems, or spot that something is awry.

Namenode directory structure

A newly formatted namenode creates the following directory structure:

```
${dfs.name.dir}/current/VERSION
                       /edits
                       /fsimage
                       /fstime
```

Recall from Chapter 9 that the dfs.name.dir property is a list of directories, with the same contents mirrored in each directory. This mechanism provides resilience, particularly if one of the directories is an NFS mount, as is recommended.

The *VERSION* file is a Java properties file that contains information about the version of HDFS that is running. Here are the contents of a typical file:

```
#Tue Mar 10 19:21:36 GMT 2009
namespaceID=134368441
cTime=0
storageType=NAME_NODE
layoutVersion=-18
```

The `layoutVersion` is a negative integer that defines the version of HDFS's persistent data structures. This version number has no relation to the release number of the Hadoop distribution. Whenever the layout changes the version number is decremented (for example, the version after –18 is –19). When this happens, HDFS needs to be upgraded, since a newer namenode (or datanode) will not operate if its storage layout is an older version. Upgrading HDFS is covered in "Upgrades" on page 296.

The `namespaceID` is a unique identifier for the filesystem, which is created when the filesystem is first formatted. The namenode uses it to identify new datanodes, since they will not know the `namespaceID` until they have registered with the namenode.

The `cTime` property marks the creation time of the namenode's storage. For newly formatted storage, the value is always zero, but it is updated to a timestamp whenever the filesystem is upgraded.

The `storageType` indicates that this storage directory contains data structures for a namenode.

The other files in the namenode's storage directory are *edits*, *fsimage*, and *fstime*. These are all binary files, which use Hadoop `Writable` objects as their serialization format (see "Serialization" on page 86). To understand what these files are for, we need to dig into the workings of the namenode a little more.

The filesystem image and edit log

When a filesystem client performs a write operation (such as creating or moving a file), it is first recorded in the edit log. The namenode also has an in-memory representation of the filesystem metadata, which it updates after the edit log has been modified. The in-memory metadata is used to serve read requests.

The edit log is flushed and synced after every write before a success code is returned to the client. For namenodes that write to multiple directories, the write must be flushed and synced to every copy before returning successfully. This ensures that no operation is lost due to machine failure.

The *fsimage* file is a persistent checkpoint of the filesystem metadata. However, it is *not* updated for every filesystem write operation, since writing out the *fsimage* file, which can grow to be gigabytes in size, would be very slow. This does not compromise resilience, however, because if the namenode fails, then the latest state of its metadata can be reconstructed by loading the *fsimage* from disk into memory, then applying each of the operations in the edit log. In fact, this is precisely what the namenode does when it starts up (see "Safe Mode" on page 278).

The *fsimage* file contains a serialized form of all the directory and file inodes in the filesystem. Each inode is an internal representation of a file or directory's metadata, and contains such information as the file's replication level, modification and access times, access permissions, block size, and the blocks a file is made up of. For directories, the modification time, permissions, and quota metadata is stored.

The *fsimage* file does *not* record the datanodes on which the blocks are stored. Instead the namenode keeps this mapping in memory, which it constructs by asking the datanodes for their block lists when they join the cluster, and periodically afterward to ensure the namenode's block mapping is up-to-date.

As described, the *edits* file would grow without bound. Though this state of affairs would have no impact on the system while the namenode is running, if the namenode were restarted, it would take a long time to apply each of the operations in its (very long) edit log. During this time the filesystem would be offline, which is generally undesirable.

The solution is to run the secondary namenode, whose purpose is to produce checkpoints of the primary's in-memory filesystem metadata.[*] The checkpointing process proceeds as follows (and is shown schematically in Figure 10-1):

1. The secondary asks the primary to roll its *edits* file, so new edits go to a new file.
2. The secondary retrieves *fsimage* and *edits* from the primary (using HTTP GET).
3. The secondary loads *fsimage* into memory, applies each operation from *edits*, then creates a new consolidated *fsimage* file.
4. The secondary sends the new *fsimage* back to the primary (using HTTP POST).
5. The primary replaces the old *fsimage* with the new one from the secondary, and the old *edits* file with the new one it started in step 1. It also updates the *fstime* file to record the time that the checkpoint was taken.

At the end of the process, the primary has an up-to-date *fsimage* file, and a shorter *edits* file (it is not necessarily empty, as it may have received some edits while the checkpoint was being taken). It is possible for an administrator to run this process manually while the namenode is in safe mode, using the `hadoop dfsadmin -saveNamespace` command.

---

[*] From Hadoop version 0.21.0 onward (which will be released after this book is due to be published), the secondary namenode will be replaced by a *checkpoint node*, which has the same functionality. At the same time, a new type of namenode, called a *backup node*, will be introduced whose purpose is to maintain an up-to-date copy of the namenode metadata, and will act as a replacement for storing a copy of the metadata on NFS.

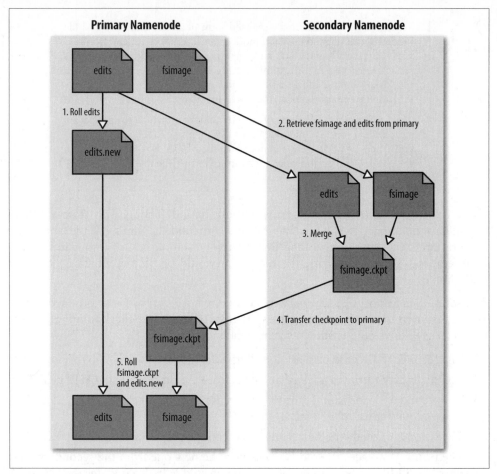

Figure 10-1. The checkpointing process

This procedure makes it clear why the secondary has similar memory requirements to the primary (since it loads the *fsimage* into memory), which is the reason that the secondary needs a dedicated machine on large clusters.

The schedule for checkpointing is controlled by two configuration parameters. The secondary namenode checkpoints every hour (`fs.checkpoint.period` in seconds) or sooner if the edit log has reached 64 MB (`fs.checkpoint.size` in bytes), which it checks every five minutes.

Secondary namenode directory structure

A useful side effect of the checkpointing process is that the secondary has a checkpoint at the end of the process, which can be found in a subdirectory called *previous.check point*. This can be used as a source for making (stale) backups of the namenode's metadata:

```
${fs.checkpoint.dir}/current/VERSION
                   /edits
                   /fsimage
                   /fstime
         /previous.checkpoint/VERSION
                             /edits
                             /fsimage
                             /fstime
```

The layout of this directory and of the secondary's *current* directory is identical to the namenode's. This is by design, since in the event of total namenode failure (when there are no recoverable backups, even from NFS), it allows recovery from a secondary namenode. This can be achieved either by copying the relevant storage directory to a new namenode, or, if the secondary is taking over as the new primary namenode, by using the -importCheckpoint option when starting the namenode daemon. The -importCheckpoint option will load the namenode metadata from the latest checkpoint in the directory defined by the fs.checkpoint.dir property, but only if there is no metadata in the dfs.name.dir directory, so there is no risk of overwriting precious metadata.

Datanode directory structure

Unlike namenodes, datanodes do not need to be explicitly formatted, since they create their storage directories automatically on startup. Here are the key files and directories:

```
${dfs.data.dir}/current/VERSION
                       /blk_<id_1>
                       /blk_<id_1>.meta
                       /blk_<id_2>
                       /blk_<id_2>.meta
                       /...
                       /blk_<id_64>
                       /blk_<id_64>.meta
                       /subdir0/
                       /subdir1/
                       /...
                       /subdir63/
```

A datanode's *VERSION* file is very similar to the namenode's:

```
#Tue Mar 10 21:32:31 GMT 2009
namespaceID=134368441
storageID=DS-547717739-172.16.85.1-50010-1236720751627
cTime=0
storageType=DATA_NODE
layoutVersion=-18
```

The namespaceID, cTime, and layoutVersion are all the same as the values in the namenode (in fact, the namespaceID is retrieved from the namenode when the datanode first connects). The storageID is unique to the datanode (it is the same across all storage directories), and is used by the namenode to uniquely identify the datanode. The storageType identifies this directory as a datanode storage directory.

The other files in the datanode's *current* storage directory are the files with the *blk_* prefix. There are two types: the HDFS blocks themselves (which just consist of the file's raw bytes) and the metadata for a block (with a *.meta* suffix). A block file just consists of the raw bytes of a portion of the file being stored; the metadata file is made up of a header with version and type information, followed by a series of checksums for sections of the block.

When the number of blocks in a directory grows to a certain size, the datanode creates a new subdirectory in which to place new blocks and their accompanying metadata. It creates a new subdirectory every time the number of blocks in a directory reaches 64 (set by the `dfs.datanode.numblocks` configuration property). The effect is to have a tree with high fan-out, so even for systems with a very large number of blocks, the directories will only be a few levels deep. By taking this measure, the datanode ensures that there is a manageable number of files per directory, which avoids the problems that most operating systems encounter when there are a large number of files (tens or hundreds of thousands) in a single directory.

If the configuration property `dfs.data.dir` specifies multiple directories (on different drives), blocks are written to each in a round-robin fashion. Note that blocks are *not* replicated on each drive on a single datanode: block replication is across distinct datanodes.

Safe Mode

When the namenode starts, the first thing it does is load its image file (*fsimage*) into memory and apply the edits from the edit log (*edits*). Once it has reconstructed a consistent in-memory image of the filesystem metadata, it creates a new *fsimage* file (effectively doing the checkpoint itself, without recourse to the secondary namenode) and an empty edit log. Only at this point does the namenode start listening for RPC and HTTP requests. However, the namenode is running in *safe mode*, which means that it offers only a read-only view of the filesystem to clients.

 Strictly speaking, in safe mode only filesystem operations that access the filesystem metadata (like producing a directory listing) are guaranteed to work. Reading a file will work only if the blocks are available on the current set of datanodes in the cluster; and file modifications (writes, deletes, or renames) will always fail.

Recall that the locations of blocks in the system are not persisted by the namenode—this information resides with the datanodes, in the form of a list of the blocks it is storing. During normal operation of the system, the namenode has a map of block locations stored in memory. Safe mode is needed to give the datanodes time to check in to the namenode with their block lists, so the namenode can be informed of enough block locations to run the filesystem effectively. If the namenode didn't wait for enough datanodes to check in, then it would start the process of replicating blocks to new datanodes, which would be unnecessary in most cases (since it only needed to wait for the extra datanodes to check in), and would put a great strain on the cluster's resources. Indeed, while in safe mode, the namenode does not issue any block replication or deletion instructions to datanodes.

Safe mode is exited when the *minimal replication condition* is reached, plus an extension time of 30 seconds. The minimal replication condition is when 99.9% of the blocks in the whole filesystem meet their minimum replication level (which defaults to one, and is set by `dfs.replication.min`).

When you are starting a newly formatted HDFS cluster, the namenode does not go into safe mode since there are no blocks in the system.

Table 10-1. Safe mode properties

Property name	Type	Default value	Description
dfs.replication.min	int	1	The minimum number of replicas that have to be written for a write to be successful.
dfs.safemode.threshold.pct	float	0.999	The proportion of blocks in the system that must meet the minimum replication level defined by `dfs.replication.min` before the namenode will exit safe mode. Setting this value to 0 or less forces the namenode not to start in safe mode. Setting this value to more than 1 means the namenode never exits safe mode.
dfs.safemode.extension	int	30000	The time, in milliseconds, to extend safe mode by after the minimum replication condition defined by `dfs.safemode.threshold.pct` has been satisfied. For small clusters (tens of nodes), it can be set to 0.

Entering and leaving safe mode

To see whether the namenode is in safe mode, you can use the `dfsadmin` command:

```
% hadoop dfsadmin -safemode get
Safe mode is ON
```

The front page of the HDFS web UI provides another indication of whether the namenode is in safe mode.

Sometimes you want to wait for the namenode to exit safe mode before carrying out a command, particularly in scripts. The `wait` option achieves this:

```
hadoop dfsadmin -safemode wait
# command to read or write a file
```

An administrator has the ability to make the namenode enter or leave safe mode at any time. It is sometimes necessary to do this when carrying out maintenance on the cluster, or after upgrading a cluster to confirm that data is still readable. To enter safe mode, use the following command:

```
% hadoop dfsadmin -safemode enter
Safe mode is ON
```

You can use this command when the namenode is still in safe mode while starting up to ensure that it never leaves safe mode. Another way of making sure that the namenode stays in safe mode indefinitely is to set the property `dfs.safemode.threshold.pct` to a value over one.

You can make the namenode leave safe mode by using:

```
% hadoop dfsadmin -safemode leave
Safe mode is OFF
```

Audit Logging

HDFS has the ability to log all filesystem access requests, a feature that some organizations require for auditing purposes. Audit logging is implemented using log4j logging at the `INFO` level, and in the default configuration it is disabled, as the log threshold is set to `WARN` in *log4j.properties*:

```
log4j.logger.org.apache.hadoop.fs.FSNamesystem.audit=WARN
```

You can enable audit logging by replacing `WARN` with `INFO`, and the result will be a log line written to the namenode's log for every HDFS event. Here's an example for a list status request on */user/tom*:

```
2009-03-13 07:11:22,982 INFO org.apache.hadoop.hdfs.server.namenode.FSNamesystem.audit:
  ugi=tom,staff,admin   ip=/127.0.0.1   cmd=listStatus   src=/user/tom   dst=null
  perm=null
```

It is a good idea to configure log4j so that the audit log is written to a separate file and isn't mixed up with the namenode's other log entries. An example of how to do this can be found on the Hadoop wiki at *http://wiki.apache.org/hadoop/HowToConfigure*.

Tools

dfsadmin

The *dfsadmin* tool is a multi-purpose tool for finding information about the state of HDFS, as well as performing administration operations on HDFS. It is invoked as `hadoop dfsadmin`. Commands that alter HDFS state typically require superuser privileges.

The available commands to *dfsadmin* are described in Table 10-2.

Table 10-2. dfsadmin commands

Command	Description
-help	Shows help for a given command, or all commands if no command is specified.
-report	Shows filesystem statistics (similar to that shown in the web UI) and information on connected datanodes.
-metasave	Dumps information to a file in Hadoop's log directory about blocks that are being replicated or deleted, and a list of connected datanodes.
-safemode	Changes or query the state of safe mode. See "Safe Mode" on page 278.
-saveNamespace	Saves the current in-memory filesystem image to a new *fsimage* file, and resets the *edits* file. This operation may be performed only in safe mode.
-refreshNodes	Updates the set of datanodes that are permitted to connect to the namenode. See "Commissioning and Decommissioning Nodes" on page 293.
-upgradeProgress	Gets information on the progress of a HDFS upgrade, or force an upgrade to proceed. See "Upgrades" on page 296.
-finalizeUpgrade	Removes the previous version of the datanodes' and namenode's storage directories. Used after an upgrade has been applied and the cluster is running successfully on the new version. See "Upgrades" on page 296.
-setQuota	Sets directory quotas. Directory quotas set a limit on the number of names (files or directories) in the directory tree. Directory quotas are useful for preventing users from creating large numbers of small files, a measure that helps preserve the namenode's memory (recall that accounting information for every file, directory, and block in the filesystem is stored in memory).
-clrQuota	Clears specified directory quotas.
-setSpaceQuota	Sets space quotas on directories. Space quotas set a limit on the size of files that may be stored in a directory tree. They are useful for giving users a limited amount of storage.
-clrSpaceQuota	Clears specified space quotas.
-refreshServiceAcl	Refreshes the namenode's service-level authorization policy file.

Filesystem check (fsck)

Hadoop provides an *fsck* utility for checking the health of files in HDFS. The tool looks for blocks that are missing from all datanodes, as well as under- or over-replicated blocks. Here is an example of checking the whole filesystem for a small cluster:

```
% hadoop fsck /
......................Status: HEALTHY
 Total size:    511799225 B
 Total dirs:    10
 Total files:   22
 Total blocks (validated):    22 (avg. block size 23263601 B)
 Minimally replicated blocks:    22 (100.0 %)
 Over-replicated blocks:    0 (0.0 %)
 Under-replicated blocks:    0 (0.0 %)
 Mis-replicated blocks:    0 (0.0 %)
 Default replication factor:    3
 Average block replication:    3.0
```

```
Corrupt blocks:        0
Missing replicas:        0 (0.0 %)
Number of data-nodes:        4
Number of racks:        1
```

```
The filesystem under path '/' is HEALTHY
```

fsck recursively walks the filesystem namespace, starting at the given path (here the filesystem root), and checks the files it finds. It prints a dot for every file it checks. To check a file, *fsck* retrieves the metadata for the file's blocks, and looks for problems or inconsistencies. Note that *fsck* retrieves all of its information from the namenode; it does not communicate with any datanodes to actually retrieve any block data.

Most of the output from *fsck* is self-explanatory, but here are some of the conditions it looks for:

Over-replicated blocks
> These are blocks that exceed their target replication for the file they belong to. Over-replication is not normally a problem, and HDFS will automatically delete excess replicas.

Under-replicated blocks
> These are blocks that do not meet their target replication for the file they belong to. HDFS will automatically create new replicas of under-replicated blocks until they meet the target replication. You can get information about the blocks being replicated (or waiting to be replicated) using `hadoop dfsadmin -metasave`.

Misreplicated blocks
> These are blocks that do not satisfy the block replica placement policy (see "Replica Placement" on page 67). For example, for a replication level of three in a multirack cluster, if all three replicas of a block are on the same rack, then the block is misreplicated since the replicas should be spread across at least two racks for resilience.

> A misreplicated block is not fixed automatically by HDFS (at the time of this writing). As a workaround, you can fix the problem manually by increasing the replication of the file the block belongs to (using `hadoop fs -setrep`), waiting until the block gets replicated, then decreasing the replication of the file back to its original value.

Corrupt blocks
> These are blocks whose replicas are all corrupt. Blocks with at least one noncorrupt replica are not reported as corrupt; the namenode will replicate the noncorrupt replica until the target replication is met.

Missing replicas
> These are blocks with no replicas anywhere in the cluster.

Corrupt or missing blocks are the biggest cause for concern, as it means data has been lost. By default, *fsck* leaves files with corrupt or missing blocks, but you can tell it to perform one of the following actions on them:

- *Move* the affected files to the */lost+found* directory in HDFS, using the -move option. Files are broken into chains of contiguous blocks to aid any salvaging efforts you may attempt.

- *Delete* the affected files, using the -delete option. Files cannot be recovered after being deleted.

Finding the blocks for a file. The *fsck* tool provides an easy way to find out which blocks are in any particular file. For example:

```
% hadoop fsck /user/tom/part-00007 -files -blocks -racks
/user/tom/part-00007 25582428 bytes, 1 block(s):  OK
0. blk_-3724870485760122836_1035 len=25582428 repl=3 [/default-rack/10.251.43.2:50010,
/default-rack/10.251.27.178:50010, /default-rack/10.251.123.163:50010]
```

This says that the file */user/tom/part-00007* is made up of one block, and shows the datanodes where the blocks are located. The *fsck* options used are as follows:

- The -files option shows the line with the filename, size, number of blocks, and its health (whether there are any missing blocks).

- The -blocks option shows information about each block in the file, one line per block.

- The -racks option displays the rack location and the datanode addresses for each block.

Running hadoop fsck without any arguments displays full usage instructions.

Datanode block scanner

Every datanode runs a block scanner, which periodically verifies all the blocks stored on the datanode. This allows bad blocks to be detected and fixed before they are read by clients. The DataBlockScanner maintains a list of blocks to verify, and scans them one by one for checksum errors. The scanner employs a throttling mechanism to preserve disk bandwidth on the datanode.

Blocks are periodically verified every three weeks to guard against disk errors over time (this is controlled by the dfs.datanode.scan.period.hours property, which defaults to 504 hours). Corrupt blocks are reported to the namenode to be fixed.

You can get a block verification report for a datanode by visiting the datanode's web interface at *http://datanode:50075/blockScannerReport*. Here's an example of a report, which should be self-explanatory:

```
Total Blocks                 :  21131
Verified in last hour        :     70
Verified in last day         :   1767
Verified in last week        :   7360
Verified in last four weeks  :  20057
Verified in SCAN_PERIOD      :  20057
Not yet verified             :   1074
Verified since restart       :  35912
```

```
Scans since restart             :    6541
Scan errors since restart       :       0
Transient scan errors           :       0
Current scan rate limit KBps    :    1024
Progress this period            :    109%
Time left in cur period         :  53.08%
```

By specifying the `listblocks` parameter, *http://datanode:50075/blockScannerReport? listblocks*, the report is preceded by a list of all the blocks on the datanode along with their latest verification status. Here is a snippet of the block list (lines are split to fit the page):

```
blk_6035596358209321442    : status : ok    type : none   scan time : 0
    not yet verified
blk_3065580480714947643    : status : ok    type : remote scan time : 1215755306400
    2008-07-11 05:48:26,400
blk_8729669677359108508    : status : ok    type : local  scan time : 1215755727345
    2008-07-11 05:55:27,345
```

The first column is the block ID, followed by some key-value pairs. The status can be one of `failed` or `ok` according to whether the last scan of the block detected a checksum error. The type of scan is `local` if it was performed by the background thread, `remote` if it was performed by a client or a remote datanode, or `none` if a scan of this block has yet to be made. The last piece of information is the scan time, which is displayed as the number of milliseconds since midnight 1 January 1970, and also as a more readable value.

balancer

Over time the distribution of blocks across datanodes can become unbalanced. An unbalanced cluster can affect locality for MapReduce, and it puts a greater strain on the highly utilized datanodes, so it's best avoided.

The *balancer* program is a Hadoop daemon that re-distributes blocks by moving them from over-utilized datanodes to under-utilized datanodes, while adhering to the block replica placement policy that makes data loss unlikely by placing block replicas on different racks (see "Replica Placement" on page 67). It moves blocks until the cluster is deemed to be balanced, which means that the utilization of every datanode (ratio of used space on the node to total capacity of the node) differs from the utilization of the cluster (ratio of used space on the cluster to total capacity of the cluster) by no more than a given threshold percentage. You can start the balancer with:

```
% start-balancer.sh
```

The `-threshold` argument specifies the threshold percentage that defines what it means for the cluster to be balanced. The flag is optional, in which case the threshold is 10%. At any one time, only one balancer may be running on the cluster.

The balancer runs until the cluster is balanced, it cannot move any more blocks, or it loses contact with the namenode. It produces a logfile in the standard log directory, where it writes a line for every iteration of redistribution that it carries out. Here is the output from a short run on a small cluster:

```
Time Stamp          Iteration#  Bytes Already Moved  Bytes Left To Move  Bytes Being Moved
Mar 18, 2009 5:23:42 PM  0                    0 KB            219.21 MB          150.29 MB
Mar 18, 2009 5:27:14 PM  1              195.24 MB             22.45 MB          150.29 MB
The cluster is balanced. Exiting...
Balancing took 6.072933333333333 minutes
```

The balancer is designed to run in the background without unduly taxing the cluster, or interfering with other clients using the cluster. It limits the bandwidth that it uses to copy a block from one node to another. The default is a modest 1 MB/s, but this can be changed by setting the `dfs.balance.bandwidthPerSec` property in *hdfs-site.xml*, specified in bytes.

Monitoring

Monitoring is an important part of system administration. In this section, we look at the monitoring facilities in Hadoop, and how they can hook into external monitoring systems.

The purpose of monitoring is to detect when the cluster is not providing the expected level of service. The master daemons are the most important to monitor: the namenodes (primary and secondary), and the jobtracker. Failure of datanodes and tasktrackers is to be expected, particularly on larger clusters, so you should provide extra capacity so that the cluster can tolerate having a small percentage of dead nodes at any time.

In addition to the facilities described next, some administrators run test jobs on a periodic basis as a test of the cluster's health.

There is lot of work going on to add more monitoring capabilities to Hadoop, which is not covered here. For example, Chukwa[†] is a data collection and monitoring system built on HDFS and MapReduce, and excels at mining log data for finding large-scale trends. Another example is the work to define a service lifecycle for Hadoop daemons, which includes adding a "ping" method to get a brief summary of a daemon's health.[‡]

Logging

All Hadoop daemons produce logfiles that can be very useful for finding out what is happening in the system. "System logfiles" on page 256 explains how to configure these files.

[†] *http://hadoop.apache.org/chukwa*

[‡] *https://issues.apache.org/jira/browse/HADOOP-3628*

Setting log levels

When debugging a problem, it is very convenient to be able to change the log level temporarily for a particular component in the system.

Hadoop daemons have a web page for changing the log level for any log4j log name, which can be found at */logLevel* in the daemon's web UI. By convention, log names in Hadoop correspond to the classname doing the logging, although there are exceptions to this rule, so you should consult the source code to find log names.

For example, to enable debug logging for the `JobTracker` class, we would visit the job-tracker's web UI at *http://jobtracker-host:50030/logLevel* and set the log name `org.apache.hadoop.mapred.JobTracker` to level `DEBUG`.

The same thing can be achieved from the command line as follows:

```
% hadoop daemonlog -setlevel jobtracker-host:50030 \
    org.apache.hadoop.mapred.JobTracker DEBUG
```

Log levels changed in this way are reset when the daemon restarts, which is usually what you want. However, to make a persistent change to a log level, simply change the *log4j.properties* file in the configuration directory. In this case, the line to add is:

```
log4j.logger.org.apache.hadoop.mapred.JobTracker=DEBUG
```

Getting stack traces

Hadoop daemons expose a web page (*/stacks* in the web UI) that produces a thread dump for all running threads in the daemon's JVM. For example, you can get a thread dump for a jobtracker from *http://jobtracker-host:50030/stacks*.

Metrics

The HDFS and MapReduce daemons collect information about events and measurements that are collectively known as *metrics*. For example, datanodes collect the following metrics (and many more): the number of bytes written, the number of blocks replicated, and the number of read requests from clients (both local and remote).

Metrics belong to a *context*, and Hadoop currently uses "dfs", "mapred", "rpc", and "jvm" contexts. Hadoop daemons usually collect metrics under several contexts. For example, datanodes collect metrics for the "dfs", "rpc", and "jvm" contexts.

How Do Metrics Differ from Counters?

The main difference is their scope: metrics are collected by Hadoop daemons, whereas counters (see "Counters" on page 211) are collected for MapReduce tasks, and aggregated for the whole job. They have different audiences, too: broadly speaking, metrics are for administrators, and counters are for MapReduce users.

The way they are collected and aggregated is also different. Counters are a MapReduce feature, and the MapReduce system ensures that counter values are propagated from

---

the tasktrackers where they are produced, back to the jobtracker, and finally back to the client running the MapReduce job. (Counters are propagated via RPC heartbeats; see "Progress and Status Updates" on page 156.) Both the tasktrackers and the jobtracker perform aggregation.

The collection mechanism for metrics is decoupled from the component that receives the updates, and there are various pluggable outputs, including local files, Ganglia, and JMX. The daemon collecting the metrics performs aggregation on them before they are sent to the output.

A context defines the unit of publication, you can choose to publish the "dfs" context, but not the "jvm" context, for instance. Metrics are configured in the *conf/hadoop-metrics.properties* file, and, by default, all contexts are configured so they do not publish their metrics. This is the contents of the default configuration file (minus the comments):

```
dfs.class=org.apache.hadoop.metrics.spi.NullContext
mapred.class=org.apache.hadoop.metrics.spi.NullContext
jvm.class=org.apache.hadoop.metrics.spi.NullContext
rpc.class=org.apache.hadoop.metrics.spi.NullContext
```

Each line in this file configures a different context, and specifies the class that handles the metrics for that context. The class must be an implementation of the `MetricsContext` interface; and, as the name suggests, the `NullContext` class neither publishes nor updates metrics.§

The other implementations of `MetricsContext` are covered in the following sections.

FileContext

`FileContext` writes metrics to a local file. It exposes two configuration properties: `fileName`, which specifies the absolute name of the file to write to, and `period`, for the time interval (in seconds) between file updates. Both properties are optional; if not set, the metrics will be written to standard output every five seconds.

Configuration properties apply to a context name, and are specified by appending the property name to the context name (separated by a dot). For example, to dump the "jvm" context to a file, we alter its configuration to be the following:

```
jvm.class=org.apache.hadoop.metrics.file.FileContext
jvm.fileName=/tmp/jvm_metrics.log
```

In the first line, we have changed the "jvm" context to use a `FileContext`, and in the second, we have set the "jvm" context's `fileName` property to be a temporary file. Here are two lines of output from the logfile, split over several lines to fit the page:

---

§ The term "context" is (perhaps unfortunately) overloaded here, since it can refer to either a collection of metrics (the "dfs" context, for example) or the class that publishes metrics (the `NullContext`, for example).

```
jvm.metrics: hostName=ip-10-250-59-159, processName=NameNode, sessionId=, gcCount=46, ↵
gcTimeMillis=394, logError=0, logFatal=0, logInfo=59, logWarn=1, ↵
memHeapCommittedM=4.9375, memHeapUsedM=2.5322647, memNonHeapCommittedM=18.25, ↵
memNonHeapUsedM=11.330269, threadsBlocked=0, threadsNew=0, threadsRunnable=6, ↵
threadsTerminated=0, threadsTimedWaiting=8, threadsWaiting=13
jvm.metrics: hostName=ip-10-250-59-159, processName=SecondaryNameNode, sessionId=, ↵
gcCount=36, gcTimeMillis=261, logError=0, logFatal=0, logInfo=18, logWarn=4, ↵
memHeapCommittedM=5.4414062, memHeapUsedM=4.46756, memNonHeapCommittedM=18.25, ↵
memNonHeapUsedM=10.624519, threadsBlocked=0, threadsNew=0, threadsRunnable=5, ↵
threadsTerminated=0, threadsTimedWaiting=4, threadsWaiting=2
```

FileContext can be useful on a local system for debugging purposes, but is unsuitable on a larger cluster since the output files are spread across the cluster, which makes analyzing them difficult.

GangliaContext

Ganglia (*http://ganglia.info/*) is an open source distributed monitoring system for very large clusters. It is designed to impose very low resource overheads on each node in the cluster. Ganglia itself collects metrics, such as CPU and memory usage; by using GangliaContext, you can inject Hadoop metrics into Ganglia.

GangliaContext has one required property, servers, which takes a space- and/or comma-separated list of Ganglia server host-port pairs. Further details on configuring this context can be found on the Hadoop wiki (*http://wiki.apache.org/hadoop/Ganglia Metrics*).

For a flavor of the kind of information you can get out of Ganglia, see Figure 10-2, which shows how the number of tasks in the jobtracker's queue varies over time.

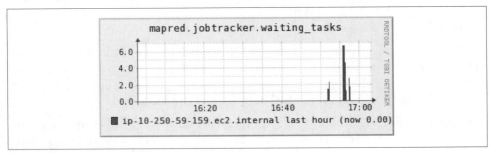

Figure 10-2. Ganglia plot of number of tasks in the jobtracker queue

NullContextWithUpdateThread

Both FileContext and a GangliaContext push metrics to an external system. However, some monitoring systems—notably JMX—need to pull metrics from Hadoop. Null ContextWithUpdateThread is designed for this. Like NullContext, it doesn't publish any metrics, but in addition it runs a timer that periodically updates the metrics stored in memory. This ensures that the metrics are up-to-date when they are fetched by another system.

All implementations of MetricsContext except NullContext perform this updating function (and they all expose a period property that defaults to five seconds), so you need to use NullContextWithUpdateThread only if you are not collecting metrics using another output. If you were using GangliaContext, for example, then it would ensure the metrics are updated, so you would be able to use JMX in addition with no further configuration of the metrics system. JMX is discussed in more detail shortly.

CompositeContext

CompositeContext allows you to output the same set of metrics to multiple contexts, such as a FileContext and a GangliaContext. The configuration is slightly tricky, and is best shown by an example:

```
jvm.class=org.apache.hadoop.metrics.spi.CompositeContext
jvm.arity=2
jvm.sub1.class=org.apache.hadoop.metrics.file.FileContext
jvm.fileName=/tmp/jvm_metrics.log
jvm.sub2.class=org.apache.hadoop.metrics.ganglia.GangliaContext
jvm.servers=ip-10-250-59-159.ec2.internal:8649
```

The arity property is used to specify the number of subcontexts; in this case, there are two. The property names for each subcontext are modified to have a part specifying the subcontext number, hence jvm.sub1.class and jvm.sub2.class.

Java Management Extensions

Java Management Extensions (JMX) is a standard Java API for monitoring and managing applications. Hadoop includes several managed beans (MBeans), which expose Hadoop metrics to JMX-aware applications. There are MBeans that expose the metrics in the "dfs" and "rpc" contexts, but none for the "mapred" context (at the time of this writing), or the "jvm" context (as the JVM itself exposes a richer set of JVM metrics). These MBeans are listed in Table 10-3.

Table 10-3. Hadoop MBeans

MBean Class	Daemons	Metrics
NameNodeActivityMBean	Namenode	Namenode activity metrics, such as the number of create file operations
FSNamesystemMBean	Namenode	Namenode status metrics, such as the number of connected datanodes
DataNodeActivityMBean	Datanode	Datanode activity metrics, such as number of bytes read
FSDatasetMBean	Datanode	Datanode storage metrics, such as capacity and free storage space

MBean Class	Daemons	Metrics
RpcActivityMBean	All daemons that use RPC: namenode, datanode, jobtracker, tasktracker	RPC statistics, such as average processing time

The JDK comes with a tool called JConsole for viewing MBeans in a running JVM. It's useful for browsing Hadoop metrics, as demonstrated in Figure 10-3.

Figure 10-3. JConsole view of a locally running namenode, showing metrics for the filesystem state

 Although you can see Hadoop metrics via JMX using the default metrics configuration, they will not be updated unless you change the MetricsContext implementation to something other than NullContext. For example, NullContextWithUpdateThread is appropriate if JMX is the only way you will be monitoring metrics.

Many third-party monitoring and alerting systems (such as Nagios or Hyperic) can query MBeans, making JMX the natural way to monitor your Hadoop cluster from an existing monitoring system. You will need to enable remote access to JMX, however, and choose a level of security that is appropriate for your cluster. The options here include password authentication, SSL connections, and SSL client-authentication. See the official Java documentation‖ for an in-depth guide on configuring these options.

‖ *http://java.sun.com/javase/6/docs/technotes/guides/management/agent.html*

All the options for enabling remote access to JMX involve setting Java system properties, which we do for Hadoop by editing the *conf/hadoop-env.sh* file. The following configuration settings show how to enable password-authenticated remote access to JMX on the namenode (with SSL disabled). The process is very similar for other Hadoop daemons:

```
export HADOOP_NAMENODE_OPTS="-Dcom.sun.management.jmxremote
-Dcom.sun.management.jmxremote.ssl=false
-Dcom.sun.management.jmxremote.password.file=$HADOOP_CONF_DIR/jmxremote.password
-Dcom.sun.management.jmxremote.port=8004 $HADOOP_NAMENODE_OPTS"
```

The *jmxremote.password* file lists the usernames and their passwords in plain text; the JMX documentation has further details on the format of this file.

With this configuration, we can use JConsole to browse MBeans on a remote namenode. Alternatively, we can use one of the many JMX tools to retrieve MBean attribute values. Here is an example of using the "jmxquery" command-line tool (and Nagios plug-in, available from *http://code.google.com/p/jmxquery/*) to retrieve the number of under-replicated blocks:

```
% ./check_jmx -U service:jmx:rmi:///jndi/rmi://namenode-host:8004/jmxrmi -O \
hadoop:service=NameNode,name=FSNamesystemState -A UnderReplicatedBlocks \
-w 100 -c 1000 -username monitorRole -password secret
JMX OK - UnderReplicatedBlocks is 0
```

This command establishes a JMX RMI connection to the host *namenode-host* on port 8004 and authenticates using the given username and password. It reads the attribute `UnderReplicatedBlocks` of the object named `hadoop:service=NameNode,name=FSNamesystemState` and prints out its value on the console.[#] The `-w` and `-c` options specify warning and critical levels for the value: the appropriate values of these are normally determined after operating a cluster for a while.

It's common to use Ganglia in conjunction with an alerting system like Nagios for monitoring a Hadoop cluster. Ganglia is good for efficiently collecting a large number of metrics and graphing them, whereas Nagios and similar systems are good at sending alerts when a critical threshold is reached in any of a smaller set of metrics.

[#] It's convenient to use JConsole to find the object names of the MBeans that you want to monitor. Note that MBeans for datanode metrics currently contain a random identifier, which makes it difficult to monitor them in anything but an ad hoc way. See *https://issues.apache.org/jira/browse/HADOOP-4482*.

Maintenance

Routine Administration Procedures

Metadata backups

If the namenode's persistent metadata is lost or damaged, the entire filesystem is rendered unusable, so it is critical that backups are made of these files. You should keep multiple copies of different ages (one hour, one day, one week, and one month, say) to protect against corruption, either in the copies themselves or in the live files running on the namenode.

A straightforward way to make backups is to write a script to periodically archive the secondary namenode's *previous.checkpoint* subdirectory (under the directory defined by the `fs.checkpoint.dir` property) to an offsite location. The script should additionally test the integrity of the copy. This can be done by starting a local namenode daemon, and verifying that it has successfully read the *fsimage* and *edits* files into memory (by scanning the namenode log for the appropriate success message, for example).[*]

Data backups

Although HDFS is designed to store data reliably, data loss can occur, just like in any storage system, and thus a backup strategy is essential. With the large data volumes that Hadoop can store, deciding what data to back up, and where to store it is a challenge. The key here is to prioritize your data. The highest priority is the data that cannot be regenerated, and which is critical to the business; though data that is straightforward to regenerate, or essentially disposable because it is of limited business value, is the lowest priority, and you may choose not to make backups of this category of data.

> Do not make the mistake of thinking that HDFS replication is a substitute for making backups. Bugs in HDFS can cause replicas to be lost. So can hardware failures. Although Hadoop is expressly designed so that hardware failure is very unlikely to result in data loss, the possibility can never be completely ruled out, particularly when combined with software bugs, or human error.
>
> When it comes to backups, think of HDFS in the same way as you would RAID. Although the data will survive the loss of an individual RAID disk, it may not if the RAID controller fails, or is buggy (perhaps overwriting some data), or the entire array is damaged.

---

[*] Hadoop 0.21.0 comes with an Offline Image Viewer, which can be used to check the integrity of the image files.

It's common to have a policy for user directories in HDFS. For example, they may have space quotas, and be backed up nightly. Whatever the policy, make sure your users know what it is, so they know what to expect.

The *distcp* tool is ideal for making backups to other HDFS clusters (preferably running on a different version of the software, to guard against loss due to bugs in HDFS) or other Hadoop filesystems (such as S3 or KFS), since it can copy files in parallel. Alternatively, you can employ an entirely different storage system for backups, using one of the ways to export data from HDFS described in "Hadoop Filesystems" on page 47.

Filesystem check (fsck)

It is advisable to run HDFS's *fsck* tool regularly (for example, daily) on the whole filesystem to proactively look for missing or corrupt blocks. See "Filesystem check (fsck)" on page 281.

Filesystem balancer

Run the balancer tool (see "balancer" on page 284) regularly to keep the filesystem datanodes evenly balanced.

Commissioning and Decommissioning Nodes

As an administrator of a Hadoop cluster, you will need to add or remove nodes from time to time. For example, to grow the storage available to a cluster, commission new nodes. Conversely, sometimes you may wish to shrink a cluster, and to do so, you decommission nodes. It can sometimes be necessary to decommission a node if it is misbehaving, perhaps because it is failing more often than it should or its performance is noticeably slow.

Nodes normally run both a datanode and a tasktracker, and both are typically commissioned or decommissioned in tandem.

Commissioning new nodes

Although commissioning a new node can be as simple as configuring the *hdfs-site.xml* file to point to the namenode and the *mapred-site.xml* file to point to the jobtracker and starting the datanode and jobtracker daemons, it is generally best to have a list of authorized nodes.

It is a potential security risk to allow any machine to connect to the namenode and act as a datanode, since the machine may gain access to data that it is not authorized to see. Furthermore, since such a machine is not a real datanode, it is not under your control, and may stop at any time, causing potential data loss. (Imagine what would happen if a number of such nodes were connected, and a block of data was present only on the "alien" nodes?) This scenario is a risk even inside a firewall, through misconfiguration, so datanodes (and tasktrackers) should be explicitly managed on all production clusters.

Datanodes that are permitted to connect to the namenode are specified in a file whose name is specified by the `dfs.hosts` property. The file resides on the namenode's local filesystem, and it contains a line for each datanode, specified by network address (as reported by the datanode—you can see what this is by looking at the namenode's web UI). If you need to specify multiple network addresses for a datanode, put them on one line, separated by whitespace.

Similarly, tasktrackers that may connect to the jobtracker are specified in a file whose name is specified by the `mapred.hosts` property. In most cases, there is one shared file, referred to as the *include file*, that both `dfs.hosts` and `mapred.hosts` refer to, since nodes in the cluster run both datanode and tasktracker daemons.

> The file (or files) specified by the `dfs.hosts` and `mapred.hosts` properties is different from the *slaves* file. The former is used by the namenode and jobtracker to determine which worker nodes may connect. The *slaves* file is used by the Hadoop control scripts to perform cluster-wide operations, such as cluster restarts. It is never used by the Hadoop daemons.

To add new nodes to the cluster:

1. Add the network addresses of the new nodes to the include file.
2. Update the namenode with the new set of permitted datanodes using this command:

   ```
   % hadoop dfsadmin -refreshNodes
   ```
3. Update the *slaves* file with the new nodes, so that they are included in future operations performed by the Hadoop control scripts.
4. Start the new datanodes.
5. Restart the MapReduce cluster.[†]
6. Check that the new datanodes and tasktrackers appear in the web UI.

HDFS will not move blocks from old datanodes to new datanodes to balance the cluster. To do this you should run the balancer described in "balancer" on page 284.

Decommissioning old nodes

Although HDFS is designed to tolerate datanode failures, this does not mean you can just terminate datanodes en masse with no ill effect. With a replication level of three,

---

[†] At the time of this writing, there is no command to refresh the set of permitted nodes in the jobtracker. Consider setting the `mapred.jobtracker.restart.recover` property to `true` to make the jobtracker recover running jobs after a restart.

for example, the chances are very high that you will lose data by simultaneously shutting down three datanodes if they are on different racks. The way to decommission datanodes is to inform the namenode of the nodes that you wish to take out of circulation, so that it can replicate the blocks to other datanodes before the datanodes are shut down.

With tasktrackers, Hadoop is more forgiving. If you shut down a tasktracker that is running tasks, the jobtracker will notice the failure and reschedule the tasks on other tasktrackers.

The decommissioning process is controlled by an *exclude file*, which for HDFS is set by the `dfs.hosts.exclude` property, and for MapReduce by the `mapred.hosts.exclude` property. It is often the case that these properties refer to the same file. The exclude file lists the nodes that are not permitted to connect to the cluster.

The rules for whether a tasktracker may connect to the jobtracker are simple: a tasktracker may connect only if it appears in the include file and does *not* appear in the exclude file. An unspecified or empty include file is taken to mean that all nodes are in the include file.

For HDFS, the rules are slightly different. If a datanode appears in both the include and the exclude file, then it may connect, but only to be decommissioned. Table 10-4 summarizes the different combinations for datanodes. As for tasktrackers, an unspecified or empty include file means all nodes are included.

Table 10-4. HDFS include and exclude file precedence

Node appears in include file	Node appears in exclude file	Interpretation
No	No	Node may not connect.
No	Yes	Node may not connect.
Yes	No	Node may connect.
Yes	Yes	Node may connect and will be decommissioned.

To remove nodes from the cluster:

1. Add the network addresses of the nodes to be decommissioned to the exclude file. Do not update the include file at this point.
2. Restart the MapReduce cluster to stop the tasktrackers on the nodes being decommissioned.
3. Update the namenode with the new set of permitted datanodes, with this command:

    ```
    % hadoop dfsadmin -refreshNodes
    ```
4. Go to the web UI and check whether the admin state has changed to "Decommission In Progress" for the datanodes being decommissioned. They will start copying their blocks to other datanodes in the cluster.

5. When all the datanodes report their state as "Decommissioned," then all the blocks have been replicated. Shut down the decommissioned nodes.

6. Remove the nodes from the include file, and run:

```
% hadoop dfsadmin -refreshNodes
```

7. Remove the nodes from the *slaves* file.

Upgrades

Upgrading an HDFS and MapReduce cluster requires careful planning. The most important consideration is the HDFS upgrade. If the layout version of the filesystem has changed, then the upgrade will automatically migrate the filesystem data and metadata to a format that is compatible with the new version. As with any procedure that involves data migration, there is a risk of data loss, so you should be sure that both your data and metadata is backed up (see "Routine Administration Procedures" on page 292).

Part of the planning process should include a trial run on a small test cluster with a copy of data that you can afford to lose. A trial run will allow you to familiarize yourself with the process, customize it to your particular cluster configuration and toolset, and iron out any snags before running the upgrade procedure on a production cluster. A test cluster also has the benefit of being available to test client upgrades on.

Version Compatibility

All pre-1.0 Hadoop components have very rigid version compatibility requirements. Only components from the same release are guaranteed to be compatible with each other, which means the whole system—from daemons to clients—has to be upgraded simultaneously, in lockstep. This necessitates a period of cluster downtime.

Version 1.0 of Hadoop promises to loosen these requirements so that, for example, older clients can talk to newer servers (within the same major release number). In later releases, rolling upgrades may be supported, which would allow cluster daemons to be upgraded in phases, so that the cluster would still be available to clients during the upgrade.

Upgrading a cluster when the filesystem layout has not changed is fairly straightforward: install the new versions of HDFS and MapReduce on the cluster (and on clients at the same time), shut down the old daemons, update configuration files, then start up the new daemons and switch clients to use the new libraries. This process is reversible, so rolling back an upgrade is also straightforward.

After every successful upgrade, you should perform a couple of final clean up steps:

• Remove the old installation and configuration files from the cluster.

• Fix any deprecation warnings in your code and configuration.

HDFS data and metadata upgrades

If you use the procedure just described to upgrade to a new version of HDFS and it expects a different layout version, then the namenode will refuse to run. A message like the following will appear in its log:

```
File system image contains an old layout version -16.
An upgrade to version -18 is required.
Please restart NameNode with -upgrade option.
```

The most reliable way of finding out whether you need to upgrade the filesystem is by performing a trial on a test cluster.

An upgrade of HDFS makes a copy of the previous version's metadata and data. Doing an upgrade does not double the storage requirements of the cluster, as the datanodes use hard links to keep two references (for the current and previous version) to the same block of data. This design makes it straightforward to roll back to the previous version of the filesystem, should you need to. You should understand that any changes made to the data on the upgraded system will be lost after the rollback completes.

You can keep only the previous version of the filesystem: you can't roll back several versions. Therefore, to carry out another upgrade to HDFS data and metadata, you will need to delete the previous version, a process called *finalizing the upgrade*. Once an upgrade is finalized, there is no procedure for rolling back to a previous version.

In general, you can skip releases when upgrading (for example, you can upgrade from release 0.18.3 to 0.20.0 without having to upgrade to a 0.19.x release first), but in some cases, you may have to go through intermediate releases. The release notes make it clear when this is required.

You should only attempt to upgrade a healthy filesystem. Before running the upgrade do a full *fsck* (see "Filesystem check (fsck)" on page 281). As an extra precaution, you can keep a copy of the *fsck* output that lists all the files and blocks in the system, so you can compare it with the output of running *fsck* after the upgrade.

It's also worth clearing out temporary files before doing the upgrade, both from the MapReduce system directory on HDFS and local temporary files.

With these preliminaries out of the way, here is the high-level procedure for upgrading a cluster when the filesystem layout needs to be migrated:

1. Make sure that any previous upgrade is finalized before proceeding with another upgrade.
2. Shut down MapReduce and kill any orphaned task processes on the tasktrackers.
3. Shut down HDFS and backup the namenode directories.
4. Install new versions of Hadoop HDFS and MapReduce on the cluster and on clients.
5. Start HDFS with the -upgrade option.

6. Wait until the upgrade is complete.

7. Perform some sanity checks on HDFS.

8. Start MapReduce.

9. Roll back or finalize the upgrade (optional).

While running the upgrade procedure, it is a good idea to remove the Hadoop scripts from your PATH environment variable. This forces you to be explicit about which version of the scripts you are running. It can be convenient to define two environment variables for the new installation directories; in the following instructions, we have defined OLD_HADOOP_INSTALL and NEW_HADOOP_INSTALL.

Start the upgrade. To perform the upgrade, run the following command (this is step 5 in the high-level upgrade procedure):

```
% $NEW_HADOOP_INSTALL/bin/start-dfs.sh -upgrade
```

This causes the namenode to upgrade its metadata, placing the previous version in a new directory called *previous*:

```
${dfs.name.dir}/current/VERSION
                /edits
                /fsimage
                /fstime
                    /previous/VERSION
                /edits
                /fsimage
                /fstime
```

Similarly, datanodes upgrade their storage directories, preserving the old copy in a directory called *previous*.

Wait until the upgrade is complete. The upgrade process is not instantaneous, but you can check the progress of an upgrade using *dfsadmin* (upgrade events also appear in the daemons' logfiles; step 6:

```
% $NEW_HADOOP_INSTALL/bin/hadoop dfsadmin -upgradeProgress status
Upgrade for version -18 has been completed.
Upgrade is not finalized.
```

Check the upgrade. This shows that the upgrade is complete. At this stage, you should run some sanity checks (step 7) on the filesystem (check files and blocks using *fsck*, basic file operations). You might choose to put HDFS into safe mode while you are running some of these checks (the ones that are read-only) to prevent others from making changes.

Roll back the upgrade (optional). If you find that the new version is not working correctly, you may choose to roll back to the previous version (step 9). This is only possible if you have not finalized the upgrade.

A rollback reverts the filesystem state to before the upgrade was performed, so any changes made in the meantime will be lost. In other words, it rolls back to the previous state of the filesystem, rather than downgrading the current state of the filesystem to a former version.

First, shut down the new daemons:

```
% $NEW_HADOOP_INSTALL/bin/stop-dfs.sh
```

Then start up the old version of HDFS with the -rollback option.

```
% $OLD_HADOOP_INSTALL/bin/start-dfs.sh -rollback
```

This command gets the namenode and datanodes to replace their current storage directories with their previous copies. The filesystem will be returned to its previous state.

Finalize the upgrade (optional). When you are happy with the new version of HDFS, you can finalize the upgrade (step 9) to remove the previous storage directories.

After an upgrade has been finalized, there is no way to roll back to the previous version.

This step is required before performing another upgrade:

```
% $NEW_HADOOP_INSTALL/bin/hadoop dfsadmin -finalizeUpgrade
% $NEW_HADOOP_INSTALL/bin/hadoop dfsadmin -upgradeProgress status
There are no upgrades in progress.
```

HDFS is now fully upgraded to the new version.

## CHAPTER 11

Pig

Pig raises the level of abstraction for processing large datasets. With MapReduce, there is a map function and there is a reduce function, and working out how to fit your data processing into this pattern, which often requires multiple MapReduce stages, can be a challenge. With Pig the data structures are much richer, typically being multivalued and nested; and the set of transformations you can apply to the data are much more powerful—they include joins, for example, which are not for the faint of heart in MapReduce.

Pig is made up of two pieces:

- The language used to express data flows, called *Pig Latin*.
- The execution environment to run Pig Latin programs. There are currently two environments: local execution in a single JVM and distributed execution on a Hadoop cluster.

A Pig Latin program is made up of a series of operations, or transformations, that are applied to the input data to produce output. Taken as a whole, the operations describe a data flow, which the Pig execution environment translates into an executable representation and then runs. Under the covers, Pig turns the transformations into a series of MapReduce jobs, but as a programmer you are mostly unaware of this, which allows you to focus on the data rather than the nature of the execution.

Pig is a scripting language for exploring large datasets. One criticism of MapReduce is that the development cycle is very long. Writing the mappers and reducers, compiling and packaging the code, submitting the job(s) and retrieving the results is a time-consuming business, and even with Streaming, which removes the compile and package step, the experience is still involved. Pig's sweet spot is its ability to process terabytes of data simply by issuing a half-dozen lines of Pig Latin from the console. Pig is very supportive of a programmer writing a query, since it provides several commands for introspecting the data structures in your program, as it is written. Even more useful, it can perform a sample run on a representative subset of your input data, so you can see whether there are errors in the processing before unleashing it on the full dataset.

Pig was designed to be extensible. Virtually all parts of the processing path are customizable: loading, storing, filtering, grouping, ordering, and joining can all be altered by user-defined functions (UDFs). These functions operate on Pig's nested data model, so they can integrate very deeply with Pig's operators. As another benefit, UDFs tend to be more reusable than the libraries developed for writing MapReduce programs.

Pig isn't suitable for all data processing tasks, however. Like MapReduce, it is designed for batch processing of data. If you want to perform a query that touches only a small amount of data in a large dataset, then Pig will not perform well, since it is set up to scan the whole dataset, or at least large portions of it.

Also, Pig doesn't perform as well as programs written in MapReduce. This is not surprising, as Pig is a general system that compiles queries into MapReduce jobs, so inevitably there will be some overhead in doing this. The good news, however, is that this overhead will come down as the Pig team optimizes the planner—all without you having to change your Pig queries.

Installing and Running Pig

Pig runs as a client-side application. Even if you want to run Pig on a Hadoop cluster, there is nothing extra to install on the cluster: Pig launches jobs and interacts with HDFS (or other Hadoop filesystems) from your workstation.

Installation is straightforward. Java 6 is a prerequisite (and on Windows, you will need Cygwin). Download a stable release from *http://hadoop.apache.org/pig/releases.html*, and unpack the tarball in a suitable place on your workstation:

```
% tar xzf pig-x.y.z.tar.gz
```

It's convenient to add Pig's binary directory to your command-line path. For example:

```
% export PIG_INSTALL=/home/tom/pig-x.y.z
% export PATH=$PATH:$PIG_INSTALL/bin
```

You also need to set the JAVA_HOME environment variable to point to a suitable Java installation.

Try typing pig -help to get usage instructions.

Execution Types

Pig has two execution types or modes: local mode and Hadoop mode.

Local mode

In local mode, Pig runs in a single JVM and accesses the local filesystem. This mode is suitable only for small datasets, and when trying out Pig. Local mode does not use Hadoop. In particular, it does not use Hadoop's local job runner; instead, Pig translates queries into a physical plan that it executes itself.

The execution type is set using the `-x` or `-exectype` option. To run in local mode, set the option to `local`:

```
% pig -x local
grunt>
```

This starts Grunt, the Pig interactive shell, which is discussed in more detail shortly.

Hadoop mode

In Hadoop mode, Pig translates queries into MapReduce jobs and runs them on a Hadoop cluster. The cluster may be a pseudo- or fully distributed cluster. Hadoop mode (with a fully distributed cluster) is what you use when you want to run Pig on large datasets.

To use Hadoop mode, you need to tell Pig which version of Hadoop you are using and where your cluster is running. Pig releases will work against only particular versions of Hadoop. For example, Pig 0.2.0 will run against only a Hadoop 0.17.x or 0.18.x release. The environment variable `PIG_HADOOP_VERSION` is used to tell Pig the version of Hadoop it is connecting to. For example, the following allows Pig to connect to any 0.18.x version of Hadoop:

```
% export PIG_HADOOP_VERSION=18
```

Next, you need to point Pig at the cluster's namenode and jobtracker. If you already have a Hadoop site file (or files) that define `fs.default.name` and `mapred.job.tracker`, you can simply add Hadoop's configuration directory to Pig's classpath:

```
% export PIG_CLASSPATH=$HADOOP_INSTALL/conf/
```

Alternatively, you can create a *pig.properties* file in Pig's *conf* directory (this directory may need creating, too), which sets these two properties. Here's an example for a pseudo-distributed setup:

```
fs.default.name=hdfs://localhost/
mapred.job.tracker=localhost:8021
```

Once you have configured Pig to connect to a Hadoop cluster, you can launch Pig, setting the `-x` option to `mapreduce`, or omitting it entirely, as Hadoop mode is the default:

```
% pig
2009-03-29 21:22:20,489 [main] INFO  org.apache.pig.backend.hadoop.executionengine.
HExecutionEngine - Connecting to hadoop file system at: hdfs://localhost/
2009-03-29 21:22:20,760 [main] INFO  org.apache.pig.backend.hadoop.executionengine.
HExecutionEngine - Connecting to map-reduce job tracker at: localhost:8021
grunt>
```

As you can see from the output, Pig reports the filesystem and jobtracker that it has connected to.

Running Pig Programs

There are three ways of executing Pig programs, all of which work in both local and Hadoop mode:

Script

> Pig can run a script file that contains Pig commands. For example, `pig script.pig` runs the commands in the local file *script.pig*. Alternatively, for very short scripts, you can use the `-e` option to run a script specified as a string on the command line.

Grunt

> Grunt is an interactive shell for running Pig commands. Grunt is started when no file is specified for Pig to run, and the `-e` option is not used. It is also possible to run Pig scripts from within Grunt using `run` and `exec`.

Embedded

> You can run Pig programs from Java, much like you can use JDBC to run SQL programs from Java. There are more details on the Pig wiki at *http://wiki.apache .org/pig/EmbeddedPig*.

Grunt

Grunt has line-editing facilities like those found in GNU Readline (used in the bash shell and many other command-line applications). For instance, the Ctrl-E key combination will move the cursor to the end of the line. Grunt remembers command history, too,[*] and you can recall lines in the history buffer using Ctrl-P or Ctrl-N (for previous and next), or, equivalently, the up or down cursor keys.

Another handy feature is Grunt's completion mechanism, which will try to complete Pig Latin keywords and functions when you press the Tab key. For example, consider the following incomplete line:

```
grunt> a = foreach b ge
```

If you press the Tab key at this point, ge will expand to `generate`, a Pig Latin keyword:

```
grunt> a = foreach b generate
```

You can customize the completion tokens by creating a file named *autocomplete*, and placing it on Pig's classpath (such as in the *conf* directory in Pig's install directory), or in the directory you invoked Grunt from. The file should have one token per line, and tokens must not contain any whitespace. Matching is case-sensitive. It can be very handy to add commonly used file paths (especially because Pig does not perform filename completion), or the names of any user-defined functions you have created.

---

[*] History is stored in a file called *.pig_history* in your home directory.

You can get a list of commands using the `help` command. When you've finished your Grunt session, you can exit with the `quit` command.

Pig Latin Editors

PigPen is an Eclipse plug-in that provides an environment for developing Pig programs. It includes a Pig script text editor, an example generator (equivalent to the ILLUS-TRATE command), and a button for running the script on a Hadoop cluster. There is also an operator graph window, which shows a script in graph form, for visualizing the data flow. For full installation and usage instructions, please refer to the Pig wiki at *http://wiki.apache.org/pig/PigPen*.

There are also Pig Latin syntax highlighters for other editors, including Vim and Text-Mate. Details are available on the Pig wiki.

An Example

Let's look at a simple example by writing the program to calculate the maximum recorded temperature by year for the weather dataset in Pig Latin (just like we did using MapReduce in Chapter 2). The complete program is only a few lines long:

```
-- max_temp.pig: Finds the maximum temperature by year
records = LOAD 'input/ncdc/micro-tab/sample.txt'
  AS (year:chararray, temperature:int, quality:int);
filtered_records = FILTER records BY temperature != 9999 AND
  (quality == 0 OR quality == 1 OR quality == 4 OR quality == 5 OR quality == 9);
grouped_records = GROUP filtered_records BY year;
max_temp = FOREACH grouped_records GENERATE group,
  MAX(filtered_records.temperature);
DUMP max_temp;
```

To explore what's going on, we'll use Pig's Grunt interpreter, which allows us to enter lines and interact with the program to understand what it's doing. Start up Grunt in local mode, then enter the first line of the Pig script:

```
grunt> records = LOAD 'input/ncdc/micro-tab/sample.txt'
>>    AS (year:chararray, temperature:int, quality:int);
```

For simplicity, the program assumes that the input is tab-delimited text, with each line having just year, temperature, and quality fields. (Pig actually has more flexibility than this with regard to the input formats it accepts, as you'll see later.) This line describes the input data we want to process. The `year:chararray` notation describes the field's name and type; a `chararray` is like a Java string, and an `int` is like a Java `int`. The LOAD operator takes a URI argument; here we are just using a local file, but we could refer to an HDFS URI. The AS clause (which is optional) gives the fields names to make it convenient to refer to them in subsequent statements.

The result of the LOAD operator, indeed any operator in Pig Latin, is a *relation*, which is just a set of tuples. A *tuple* is just like a row of data in a database table, with multiple fields in a particular order. In this example, the LOAD function produces a set of (year, temperature, quality) tuples that are present in the input file. We write a relation with one tuple per line, where tuples are represented as comma-separated items in parentheses:

```
(1950,0,1)
(1950,22,1)
(1950,-11,1)
(1949,111,1)
```

Relations are given names, or *aliases*, so they can be referred to. This relation is given the records alias. We can examine the contents of an alias using the DUMP operator:

```
grunt> DUMP records;
(1950,0,1)
(1950,22,1)
(1950,-11,1)
(1949,111,1)
(1949,78,1)
```

We can also see the structure of a relation—the relation's *schema*—using the DESCRIBE operator on the relation's alias:

```
grunt> DESCRIBE records;
records: {year: chararray,temperature: int,quality: int}
```

This tells us that records has three fields, with aliases year, temperature, and quality, which are the names we gave them in the AS clause. The fields have the types given to them in the AS clause, too. We shall examine types in Pig in more detail later.

The second statement removes records that have a missing temperature (indicated by a value of 9999), or an unsatisfactory quality reading. For this small dataset, no records are filtered out:

```
grunt> filtered_records = FILTER records BY temperature != 9999 AND
>>   (quality == 0 OR quality == 1 OR quality == 4 OR quality == 5 OR quality == 9);
grunt> DUMP filtered_records;
(1950,0,1)
(1950,22,1)
(1950,-11,1)
(1949,111,1)
(1949,78,1)
```

The third statement uses the GROUP function to group the records relation by the year field. Let's use DUMP to see what it produces:

```
grunt> grouped_records = GROUP filtered_records BY year;
grunt> DUMP grouped_records;
(1949,{(1949,111,1),(1949,78,1)})
(1950,{(1950,0,1),(1950,22,1),(1950,-11,1)})
```

We now have two rows, or tuples, one for each year in the input data. The first field in each tuple is the field being grouped by (the year), and the second field is a bag of tuples for that year. A *bag* is just an unordered collection of tuples, which in Pig Latin is represented using curly braces.

By grouping the data in this way, we have created a row per year, so now all that remains is to find the maximum temperature for the tuples in each bag. Before we do this, let's understand the structure of the grouped_records relation:

```
grunt> DESCRIBE grouped_records;
grouped_records: {group: chararray,filtered_records: {year: chararray,
temperature: int,quality: int}}
```

This tells us that the grouping field is given the alias group by Pig, and the second field is the same structure as the filtered_records relation that was being grouped. With this information, we can try the fourth transformation:

```
grunt> max_temp = FOREACH grouped_records GENERATE group,
>>    MAX(filtered_records.temperature);
```

FOREACH processes every row to generate a derived set of rows, using a GENERATE clause to define the fields in each derived row. In this example, the first field is group, which is just the year. The second field is a little more complex. The filtered_records.temperature reference is to the temperature field of the fil tered_records bag in the grouped_records relation. MAX is a built-in function for calculating the maximum value of fields in a bag. In this case, it calculates the maximum temperature for the fields in each filtered_records bag. Let's check the result:

```
grunt> DUMP max_temp;
(1949,111)
(1950,22)
```

So we've successfully calculated the maximum temperature for each year.

Generating Examples

In this example, we've used a small sample dataset with just a handful of rows to make it easier to follow the data flow and aid debugging. Creating a cut-down dataset is an art, as ideally it should be rich enough to cover all the cases to exercise your queries (the *completeness* property), yet be small enough to reason about by the programmer (the *conciseness* property). Using a random sample doesn't work well in general, since join and filter operations tend to remove all random data, leaving an empty result, which is not illustrative of the general flow.

With the ILLUSTRATE operator, Pig provides a tool for generating a reasonably complete and concise dataset. Although it can't generate examples for all queries (it doesn't support LIMIT, SPLIT, or nested FOREACH statements, for example), it can generate useful examples for many queries. ILLUSTRATE works only if the relation has a schema.

Here is the output from running ILLUSTRATE (slightly reformatted to fit the page):

```
grunt> ILLUSTRATE max_temp;
```

records	year: bytearray	temperature: bytearray	quality: bytearray
	1949	9999	1
	1949	111	1
	1949	78	1

records	year: chararray	temperature: int	quality: int
	1949	9999	1
	1949	111	1
	1949	78	1

filtered_records	year: chararray	temperature: int	quality: int
	1949	111	1
	1949	78	1

grouped_records	group: chararray	filtered_records: bag({year: chararray, temperature: int,quality: int})
	1949	{(1949, 111, 1), (1949, 78, 1)}

max_temp	group: chararray	int
	1949	111

Notice that Pig used some of the original data (this is important to keep the generated dataset realistic), as well as creating some new data. It noticed the special value 9999 in the query and created a tuple containing this value to exercise the FILTER statement.

In summary, the output of the ILLUSTRATE is easy to follow and can help you understand what your query is doing.

Comparison with Databases

Having seen Pig in action, it might seem that Pig Latin is similar to SQL. The presence of such operators as GROUP BY and DESCRIBE reinforces this impression. However, there are several differences between the two languages, and between Pig and RDBMSs in general.

The most significant difference is that Pig Latin is a data flow programming language, whereas SQL is a declarative programming language. In other words, a Pig Latin program is a step-by-step set of operations on an input relation, in which each step is a single transformation. By contrast, SQL statements are a set of constraints that taken together define the output. In many ways, programming in Pig Latin is like working at the level of an RDBMS query planner, which figures out how to turn a declarative statement into a system of steps.

RDBMSs store data in tables, with tightly predefined schemas. Pig is more relaxed about the data that it processes: you can define a schema at runtime, but it's optional. Essentially, it will operate on any source of tuples (although the source should support being read in parallel, by being in multiple files, for example), where a UDF is used to read the tuples from their raw representation.[†] The most common representation is a text file with tab-separated fields, and Pig provides a built-in load function for this format. Unlike with a traditional database, there is no data import process to load the data into the RDBMS. The data is loaded from the filesystem (usually HDFS) as the first step in the processing.

Pig's support for complex, nested data structures differentiates it from SQL, which operates on flatter data structures. Also, Pig's ability to use UDFs and streaming operators that are tightly integrated with the language and Pig's nested data structures makes Pig Latin more customizable than most SQL dialects.

There are several features to support online, low-latency queries that RDBMSs have that are absent in Pig, such as transactions and indexes. As mentioned earlier, Pig does not support random reads or queries in the order of tens of milliseconds. Nor does it support random writes, to update small portions of data; all writes are bulk, streaming writes, just like MapReduce.

Hive is a subproject of Hadoop that sits between Pig and conventional RDBMSs. Like Pig, Hive is designed to use HDFS for storage, but otherwise there are some significant differences. Its query language, Hive QL, is based on SQL, and anyone who is familiar with SQL would have little trouble writing queries in Hive QL. Like RDBMSs, Hive mandates that all data be stored in tables, with a schema under its management; however, it can associate a schema with preexisting data in HDFS, so the load step is optional. Hive does not support low-latency queries, a characteristic it shares with Pig. Hive is discussed further in "Hadoop and Hive at Facebook" on page 414.

Pig Latin

This section gives an informal description of the syntax and semantics of the Pig Latin programming language.[‡] It is not meant to offer a complete reference to the

---

[†] Or as the Pig Philosophy (*http://hadoop.apache.org/pig/philosophy.html*) has it, "Pigs eat anything."

[‡] Not to be confused with Pig Latin the language game. English words are translated into Pig Latin by moving the initial consonant sound to the end of the word and adding an "ay" sound. For example, "pig" becomes "ig-pay," and "Hadoop" becomes "Adoop-hay."

language,§ but there should be enough here for you to get a good understanding of Pig Latin's constructs.

Structure

A Pig Latin program consists of a collection of statements. A statement can be thought of as an operation, or a command.‖ For example, a GROUP operation is a type of statement:

```
grouped_records = GROUP records BY year;
```

The command to list the files in a Hadoop filesystem is another example of a statement:

```
ls /
```

Statements are usually terminated with a semicolon, as in the example of the GROUP statement. In fact, this is an example of a statement that must be terminated with a semicolon: it is a syntax error to omit it. The ls command, on the other hand, does not have to be terminated with a semicolon. As a general guideline, statements or commands for interactive use in Grunt do not need the terminating semicolon. This group includes the interactive Hadoop commands, as well as the diagnostic operators like DESCRIBE. It's never an error to add a terminating semicolon, so if in doubt, it's simplest to add one.

Statements that have to be terminated with a semicolon can be split across multiple lines for readability:

```
records = LOAD 'input/ncdc/micro-tab/sample.txt'
  AS (year:chararray, temperature:int, quality:int);
```

Pig Latin has two forms of comments. Double hyphens are single-line comments. Everything from the first hyphen to the end of the line is ignored by the Pig Latin interpreter:

```
-- My program
DUMP A; -- What's in A?
```

C-style comments are more flexible since they delimit the beginning and end of the comment block with /* and */ markers. They can span lines or be embedded in a single line:

```
/*
 * Description of my program spanning
 * multiple lines.
 */
A = LOAD 'input/pig/join/A';
B = LOAD 'input/pig/join/B';
```

§ Pig Latin does not have a formal language definition as such, but there is a comprehensive guide to the language that can be found linked to from the Pig wiki at *http://wiki.apache.org/pig/*.

‖ You sometimes these terms being used interchangeably in documentation on Pig Latin. For example, "GROUP command, " "GROUP operation," "GROUP statement."

```
C = JOIN A BY $0, /* ignored */ B BY $1;
DUMP C;
```

Pig Latin has a list of keywords that have a special meaning in the language and cannot be used as identifiers. These include the operators (LOAD, ILLUSTRATE), commands (cat, ls), expressions (matches, FLATTEN), and functions (DIFF, MAX)—all of which are covered in the following sections.

Pig Latin has mixed rules on case sensitivity. Operators and commands are not case-sensitive (to make interactive use more forgiving); however, aliases and function names are case-sensitive.

Statements

As a Pig Latin program is executed, each statement is parsed in turn. If there are syntax errors, or other (semantic) problems such as undefined aliases, the interpreter will halt and display an error message. The interpreter builds a *logical plan* for every relational operation, which forms the core of a Pig Latin program. The logical plan for the statement is added to the logical plan for the program so far, then the interpreter moves on to the next statement.

It's important to note that no data processing takes place while the logical plan of the program is being constructed. For example, consider again the Pig Latin program from the first example:

```
-- max_temp.pig: Finds the maximum temperature by year
records = LOAD 'input/ncdc/micro-tab/sample.txt'
  AS (year:chararray, temperature:int, quality:int);
filtered_records = FILTER records BY temperature != 9999 AND
  (quality == 0 OR quality == 1 OR quality == 4 OR quality == 5 OR quality == 9);
grouped_records = GROUP filtered_records BY year;
max_temp = FOREACH grouped_records GENERATE group,
  MAX(filtered_records.temperature);
DUMP max_temp;
```

When the Pig Latin interpreter sees the first line containing the LOAD statement, it confirms that it is syntactically and semantically correct, and adds it to the logical plan, but it does *not* load the data from the file (or even check whether the file exists). Indeed, where would it load it? Into memory? Even if it did fit into memory, what would it do with the data? Perhaps not all the input data is needed (since later statements filter it, for example), so it would be pointless to load it. The point is that it makes no sense to start any processing until the whole flow is defined. Similarly, Pig validates the GROUP and FOREACH ... GENERATE statements, and adds them to the logical plan without executing them. The trigger for Pig to start processing is the DUMP statement (a STORE statement also triggers processing). At that point, the logical plan is compiled into a physical plan and executed.

The type of physical plan that Pig prepares depends on the execution environment. For local execution, Pig will create a physical plan that runs in a single local JVM, whereas for execution on Hadoop, Pig compiles the logical plan into a series of MapReduce jobs.

 You can see the logical and physical plans created by Pig using the EXPLAIN command on a relation (EXPLAIN max_temp; for example). In MapReduce mode, EXPLAIN will also show the MapReduce plan, which shows how the physical operators are grouped into MapReduce jobs. This is a good way to find out how many MapReduce jobs Pig will run for your query.

The relational operators that can be a part of a logical plan in Pig are summarized in Table 11-1. We shall go through each operator in more detail in "Data Processing Operators" on page 331.

Table 11-1. Pig Latin relational operators

Category	Operator	Description
Loading and storing	LOAD	Loads data from the filesystem or other storage into a relation
	STORE	Saves a relation to the filesystem or other storage
	DUMP	Prints a relation to the console
Filtering	FILTER	Removes unwanted rows from a relation
	DISTINCT	Removes duplicate rows from a relation
	FOREACH ... GENERATE	Adds or removes fields from a relation
	STREAM	Transforms a relation using an external program
Grouping and joining	JOIN	Joins two or more relations
	COGROUP	Groups the data in two or more relations
	GROUP	Groups the data in a single relation
	CROSS	Creates the cross product of two or more relations
Sorting	ORDER	Sorts a relation by one or more fields
	LIMIT	Limits the size of a relation to a maximum number of tuples
Combining and splitting	UNION	Combines two or more relations into one
	SPLIT	Splits a relation into two or more relations

There are other types of statement that are not added to the logical plan. For example, the diagnostic operators, DESCRIBE, EXPLAIN, and ILLUSTRATE are provided to allow the user to interact with the logical plan, for debugging purposes (see Table 11-2). DUMP is a sort of diagnostic operator too, since it is used only to allow interactive debugging of small result sets, or in combination with LIMIT to retrieve a few rows from a larger relation. The STORE statement should be used when the size of the output is more than a few lines, as it writes to a file, rather than to the console.

Table 11-2. Pig Latin diagnostic operators

Operator	Description
DESCRIBE	Prints a relation's schema
EXPLAIN	Prints the logical and physical plans
ILLUSTRATE	Shows a sample execution of the logical plan, using a generated subset of the input

Pig Latin provides two statements, REGISTER and DEFINE, to make it possible to incorporate user-defined functions into Pig scripts (see Table 11-3).

Table 11-3. Pig Latin UDF statements

Statement	Description
REGISTER	Registers a JAR file with the Pig runtime
DEFINE	Creates an alias for a UDF, streaming script, or a command specification

Since they do not process relations, commands are not added to the logical plan; instead, they are executed immediately. Pig provides commands to interact with Hadoop filesystems (which are very handy for moving data around before or after processing with Pig) and MapReduce, as well as a few utility commands (described in Table 11-4).

Table 11-4. Pig Latin commands

Category	Command	Description
Hadoop Filesystem	cat	Prints the contents of one or more files
	cd	Changes the current directory
	copyFromLocal	Copies a local file or directory to a Hadoop filesystem
	copyToLocal	Copies a file or directory on a Hadoop filesystem to the local filesystem
	cp	Copies a file or directory to another directory
	ls	Lists files
	mkdir	Creates a new directory
	mv	Moves a file or directory to another directory
	pwd	Prints the path of the current working directory
	rm	Deletes a file or directory
	rmf	Forcibly deletes a file or directory (does not fail if the file or directory does not exist)
Hadoop MapReduce	kill	Kills a MapReduce job
Utility	help	Shows the available commands and options
	quit	Exits the interpreter
	set	Sets Pig options

The filesystem commands can operate on files or directories in any Hadoop filesystem, and they are very similar to the `hadoop fs` commands (which is not surprising, as both are simple wrappers around the Hadoop `FileSystem` interface). Precisely which Hadoop filesystem is used is determined by the `fs.default.name` property in the site file for Hadoop Core. See "The Command-Line Interface" on page 45 for more details on how to configure this file.

These commands are mostly self-explanatory, except `set`, which is used to set options that control Pig's behavior. The `debug` option is used to turn debug logging on or off from within a script (you can also control the log level when launching Pig, using the `-d` or `-debug` option).

```
grunt> set debug on
```

Another useful option is the `job.name` option, which gives a Pig job a meaningful name, making it easier to pick out your Pig MapReduce jobs when running on a shared Hadoop cluster. If Pig is running a script (rather than being an interactive query from Grunt), its job name defaults to a value based on the script name.

Expressions

An expression is something that is evaluated to yield a value. Expressions can be used in Pig as a part of a statement containing a relational operator. Pig has a rich variety of expressions, many of which will be familiar from other programming languages. They are listed in Table 11-5, with brief descriptions and examples. We shall examples of many of these expressions throughout the chapter.

Table 11-5. Pig Latin expressions

Category	Expressions	Description	Examples
Constant	Literal	Constant value (see also literals in Table 11-6)	`1.0, 'a'`
Field (by position)	$n	Field in position n (zero-based)	`$0`
Field (by name)	f	Field named f	`year`
Projection	$c.\$n, c.f$	Field in container c (relation, bag, or tuple) by position, by name	`records.$0, records.year`
Map lookup	$m\#k$	Value associated with key k in map m	`items#'Coat'`
Cast	$(t)\ f$	Cast of field f to type t	`(int) year`
Arithmetic	$x + y, x - y$	Addition, subtraction	`$1 + $2, $1 - $2`
	$x * y, x / y$	Multiplication, division	`$1 * $2, $1 / $2`
	$x\ \%\ y$	Modulo, the remainder of x divided by y	`$1 % $2`
	$+x, -x$	Unary positive, negation	`+1, -1`
Conditional	$x\ ?\ y : z$	Bincond/ternary, y if x evaluates to true, z otherwise	`quality == 0 ? 0 : 1`

Category	Expressions	Description	Examples
Comparison	x == y, x != y	Equals, not equals	quality == 0, tempera ture != 9999
	x > y, x < y	Greater than, less than	quality > 0, quality < 10
	x >= y, x <= y	Greater than or equal to, less than or equal to	quality >= 1, quality <= 9
	x matches y	Pattern matching with regular expression	quality matches '[01459]'
	x is null	Is null	temperature is null
	x is not null	Is not null	temperature is not null
Boolean	x or y	Logical or	q == 0 or q == 1
	x and y	Logical and	q == 0 and r == 0
	not x	Logical negation	not q matches '[01459]'
Functional	fn(f1,f2,…)	Invocation of function fn on fields f1, f2, etc.	isGood(quality)
Flatten	FLATTEN(f)	Removal of nesting from bags and tuples	FLATTEN(group)

Types

So far you have seen some of the simple types in Pig, such as int and chararray. Here we will discuss Pig's built-in types in more detail.

Pig has four numeric types: int, long, float, and double, which are identical to their Java counterparts. There is also a bytearray type, like Java's byte array type for representing a blob of binary data; and chararray, which, like java.lang.String, represents textual data in UTF-16 format, although it can be loaded or stored in UTF-8 format. Pig does not have types corresponding to Java's boolean,[#] byte, short, or char primitive types. These are all easily represented using Pig's int type, or chararray for char.

The numeric, textual, and binary types are simple atomic types. Pig Latin also has three complex types for representing nested structures: tuple, bag, and map. All of Pig Latin's types are listed in Table 11-6.

[#] Although there is no boolean type for data, Pig has the concept of an expression evaluating to true or false, for testing conditions (such as in a FILTER statement). However, Pig does not allow a boolean expression to be stored in a field.

Table 11-6. Pig Latin types

Category	Type	Description	Literal example
Numeric	int	32-bit signed integer	1
	long	64-bit signed integer	1L
	float	32-bit floating-point number	1.0F
	double	64-bit floating-point number	1.0
Text	chararray	Character array in UTF-16 format	'a'
Binary	bytearray	Byte array	Not supported
Complex	tuple	Sequence of fields of any type	(1,'pomegranate')
	bag	An unordered collection of tuples, possibly with duplicates	{(1,'pomegranate'),(2)}
	map	A set of key-value pairs. Keys must be atoms, values may be any type	[1#'pomegranate']

The complex types are usually loaded from files or constructed using relational operators. Be aware, however, that the literal form in Table 11-6 is used when a constant value is created from within a Pig Latin program. The raw form in a file is usually different when using the standard `PigStorage` loader. For example, the representation in a file of the bag in Table 11-6 would be `{(1,pomegranate),(2)}` (note the lack of quotes), and with a suitable schema, this would be loaded as a relation with a single field and row, whose value was the bag.

Maps are always loaded from files, since there is no relational operator in Pig that produces a map. It's possible to write a UDF to generate maps, if desired.

Although relations and bags are conceptually the same (an unordered collection of tuples), in practice Pig treats them slightly differently. A relation is a top-level construct, whereas a bag has to be contained in a relation. Normally you don't have to worry about this, but there are a few restrictions that can trip up the uninitiated. For example, it's not possible to create a relation from a bag literal. So the following statement fails:

```
A = {(1,2),(3,4)}; -- Error
```

The simplest workaround in this case is to load the data from a file using the LOAD statement.

As another example, you can't treat a relation like a bag and project a field into a new relation ($0 refers to the first field of A, using the positional notation):

```
B = A.$0;
```

Instead, you have to use a relational operator to turn the relation A into relation B:

```
B = FOREACH A GENERATE $0;
```

It's possible that a future version of Pig Latin will remove these inconsistencies and treat relations and bags in the same way.

Schemas

A relation in Pig may have an associated schema, which gives the fields in the relation names and types. We've seen how an AS clause in a LOAD statement is used to attach a schema to a relation:

```
grunt> records = LOAD 'input/ncdc/micro-tab/sample.txt'
>>    AS (year:int, temperature:int, quality:int);
grunt> DESCRIBE records;
records: {year: int,temperature: int,quality: int}
```

This time we've declared the year to be an integer, rather than of type chararray, even though the file it is being loaded from is the same. An integer may be more appropriate if we needed to manipulate the year arithmetically (to turn it into a timestamp, for example), whereas the chararray representation might be more appropriate when it's being used as a simple identifier. Pig's flexibility in the degree to which schemas are declared contrasts with schemas in traditional SQL databases, which are declared before the data is loaded into to the system. Pig is designed for analyzing plain input files with no associated type information, so it is quite natural to choose types for fields later than you would with an RDBMS.

It's possible to omit type declarations completely, too:

```
grunt> records = LOAD 'input/ncdc/micro-tab/sample.txt'
>>    AS (year, temperature, quality);
grunt> DESCRIBE records;
records: {year: bytearray,temperature: bytearray,quality: bytearray}
```

In this case, we have specified only the names of the fields in the schema, year, temperature, and quality. The types default to bytearray, the most general type, representing a binary string.

You don't need to specify types for every field; you can leave some to default to bytearray, as we have done for year in this declaration:

```
grunt> records = LOAD 'input/ncdc/micro-tab/sample.txt'
>>    AS (year, temperature:int, quality:int);
grunt> DESCRIBE records;
records: {year: bytearray,temperature: int,quality: int}
```

However, if you specify a schema in this way, you do need to specify every field. Also there's no way to specify the type of a field without specifying the name. On the other hand, the schema is entirely optional, and can be omitted by not specifying an AS clause:

```
grunt> records = LOAD 'input/ncdc/micro-tab/sample.txt';
grunt> DESCRIBE records;
Schema for records unknown.
```

Fields in a relation with no schema can be referenced only using positional notation: $0 refers to the first field in a relation, $1 to the second, and so on. Their types default to bytearray:

```
grunt> projected_records = FOREACH records GENERATE $0, $1, $2;
grunt> DUMP projected_records;
(1950,0,1)
(1950,22,1)
(1950,-11,1)
(1949,111,1)
(1949,78,1)
grunt> DESCRIBE projected_records;
projected_records: {bytearray,bytearray,bytearray}
```

Although it can be convenient not to have to assign types to fields (particularly in the first stages of writing a query), doing so can improve the clarity and efficiency of Pig Latin programs, and is generally recommended.

 Declaring a schema as a part of the query is flexible, but doesn't lend itself to schema reuse. A set of Pig queries over the same input data will often have the same schema repeated in each query. If the query processes a large number of fields, this repetition can become hard to maintain, since Pig (unlike Hive) doesn't have a way to associate a schema with data outside of a query. One way to solve this problem is to write your own load function, which encapsulates the schema. This is described in more detail in "A Load UDF" on page 327.

Validation and nulls

A SQL database will enforce the constraints in a table's schema at load time: for example, trying to load a string into a column that is declared to be a numeric type will fail. In Pig, if the value cannot be cast to the type declared in the schema, then it will substitute a null value. Let's see how this works if we have the following input for the weather data, which has an "e" character in place of an integer:

```
1950    0    1
1950    22   1
1950    e    1
1949    111  1
1949    78   1
```

Pig handles the corrupt line by producing a null for the offending value, which is displayed as the absence of a value when dumped to screen (and also when saved using STORE):

```
grunt> records = LOAD 'input/ncdc/micro-tab/sample_corrupt.txt'
>>    AS (year:chararray, temperature:int, quality:int);
grunt> DUMP records;
(1950,0,1)
(1950,22,1)
(1950,,1)
(1949,111,1)
(1949,78,1)
```

Pig produces a warning for the invalid field (not shown here), but does not halt its processing. For large datasets, it is very common to have corrupt, invalid, or merely unexpected data, and it is generally infeasible to incrementally fix every unparsable record. Instead, we can pull out all of the invalid records in one go, so we can take action on them, perhaps by fixing our program (because they indicate we have made a mistake), or by filtering them out (because the data is genuinely unusable).

```
grunt> corrupt_records = FILTER records BY temperature is null;
grunt> DUMP corrupt_records;
(1950,,1)
```

Note the use of the is null operator, which is analogous to SQL. In practice, we would include more information from the original record such as an identifier and the value that could not be parsed, to help our analysis of the bad data.

We can find the number of corrupt records using the following idiom for counting the number of rows in a relation:

```
grunt> grouped = GROUP corrupt_records ALL;
grunt> all_grouped = FOREACH grouped GENERATE group, COUNT(corrupt_records);
grunt> DUMP all_grouped;
(all,1L)
```

Another useful technique is to use the SPLIT operator to partition the data into "good" and "bad" relations, which can then be analyzed separately:

```
grunt> SPLIT records INTO good_records IF temperature is not null,
>>    bad_records IF temperature is null;
grunt> DUMP good_records;
(1950,0,1)
(1950,22,1)
(1949,111,1)
(1949,78,1)
grunt> DUMP bad_records;
(1950,,1)
```

Going back to the case in which temperature's type was left undeclared, the corrupt data cannot be easily detected, since it doesn't surface as a null:

```
grunt> records = LOAD 'input/ncdc/micro-tab/sample_corrupt.txt'
>>    AS (year:chararray, temperature, quality:int);
grunt> DUMP records;
(1950,0,1)
(1950,22,1)
(1950,e,1)
(1949,111,1)
(1949,78,1)
grunt> filtered_records = FILTER records BY temperature != 9999 AND
>>    (quality == 0 OR quality == 1 OR quality == 4 OR quality == 5 OR quality == 9);
grunt> grouped_records = GROUP filtered_records BY year;
grunt> max_temp = FOREACH grouped_records GENERATE group,
>>    MAX(filtered_records.temperature);
grunt> DUMP max_temp;
(1949,111.0)
(1950,22.0)
```

What happens in this case is that the `temperature` field is interpreted as a `bytearray`, so the corrupt field is not detected when the input is loaded. When passed to the `MAX` function the `temperature` field is cast to a `double`, since `MAX` works only with numeric types. The corrupt field can not be represented as a `double`, so it becomes a `null`, which `MAX` silently ignores. The best approach is generally to declare types for your data on loading, and look for missing or corrupt values in the relations themselves before you do your main processing.

Sometimes corrupt data shows up as smaller tuples since fields are simply missing. You can filter these out by using the SIZE function as follows:

```
grunt> A = LOAD 'input/pig/corrupt/missing_fields';
grunt> DUMP A;
(2,Tie)
(4,Coat)
(3)
(1,Scarf)
grunt> B = FILTER A BY SIZE(*) > 1;
grunt> DUMP B;
(2,Tie)
(4,Coat)
(1,Scarf)
```

Schema merging

In Pig, you don't declare the schema for every new relation in the data flow. In most cases, Pig can figure out the resulting schema for the output of a relational operation by considering the schema of the input relation.

How are schemas propagated to new relations? Some relational operators don't change the schema, so the relation produced by the LIMIT operator (which restricts a relation to a maximum number of tuples), for example, has the same schema as the relation it operates on. For other operators, the situation is more complicated. UNION, for example, combines two or more relations into one, and tries to merge the input relations schemas. If the schemas are incompatible, due to different types or number of fields, then the schema of the result of the UNION is unknown.

You can find out the schema for any relation in the data flow using the DESCRIBE operator. If you want to redefine the schema for a relation, you can use the FORE-ACH ... GENERATE operator with AS clauses to define the schema for some or all of the fields of the input relation.

See "User-Defined Functions" on page 322 for further discussion of schemas.

Functions

Functions in Pig come in five types:

Eval function

A function that takes one or more expressions and returns another expression. An example of a built-in eval function is MAX, which returns the maximum value of the entries in a bag. Some eval functions are *aggregate functions*, which means they operate on a bag of data to produce a scalar value; MAX is an example of an aggregate function. Furthermore, many aggregate functions are *algebraic*, which means that the result of the function may be calculated incrementally. In MapReduce terms, algebraic functions make use of the combiner, and are much more efficient to calculate (see "Combiner Functions" on page 29). MAX is an algebraic function, whereas a function to calculate the median of a collection of values is an example of a function that is not algebraic.

Filter function

A special type of eval function that returns a logical boolean result. As the name suggests, filter functions are used in the FILTER operator to remove unwanted rows. They can also be used in other relational operators that take boolean conditions, and in general expressions using boolean or conditional expressions. An example of a built-in filter function is IsEmpty, which tests whether a bag or a map contains any items.

Comparison function

A function that can impose an ordering on a pair of tuples. You can specify the comparison function to use in an ORDER clause to control the sort order.

Load function

A function that specifies how to load data into a relation from external storage.

Store function

A function that specifies how to save the contents of a relation to external storage. Often load and store functions are implemented by the same type. For example, PigStorage, which loads data from delimited text files, can store data in the same format.

Pig has a small collection of built-in functions, which are listed in Table 11-7.

Table 11-7. Pig built-in functions

Category	Function	Description
Eval	AVG	Calculates the average (mean) value of entries in a bag.
	CONCAT	Concatenates two byte arrays or two character arrays together.
	COUNT	Calculates the number of entries in a bag.
	DIFF	Calculates the set difference of two bags. If the two arguments are not bags, then returns a bag containing both if they are equal; otherwise, returns an empty bag.
	MAX	Calculates the maximum value of entries in a bag.
	MIN	Calculates the minimum value of entries in a bag.

Category	Function	Description
	SIZE	Calculates the size of a type. The size of numeric types is always one, for character arrays it is the number of characters, for byte arrays the number of bytes, and for containers (tuple, bag, map) it is the number of entries.
	SUM	Calculates the sum of the values of entries in a bag.
	TOKENIZE	Tokenizes a character array into a bag of its constituent words.
Filter	IsEmpty	Tests if a bag or map is empty.
Load/Store	PigStorage	Loads or stores relations using a field-delimited text format. Each line is broken into fields using a configurable field delimiter (defaults to a tab character) to be stored in the tuple's fields. It is the default storage when none is specified.
	BinStorage	Loads or stores relations from or to binary files. An internal Pig format is used that uses Hadoop Writable objects.
	BinaryStorage	Loads or stores relations containing only single-field tuples with a value of type byte array from or to binary files. The bytes of the bytearray values are stored verbatim. Used with Pig streaming.
	TextLoader	Loads relations from a plain-text format. Each line corresponds to a tuple whose single field is the line of text.
	PigDump	Stores relations by writing the toString() representation of tuples, one per line. Useful for debugging.

If the function you need is not available, you can write your own. Before you do that, however, have a look in the *Piggy Bank*, a repository of Pig functions shared by the Pig community. There are details on the Pig wiki at *http://wiki.apache.org/pig/PiggyBank* on how to browse and obtain the Piggy Bank functions. If the Piggy Bank doesn't have what you need, you can write your own function (and if it is sufficiently general, you might consider contributing it to the Piggy Bank so that others can benefit from it, too). These are known as *user-defined functions*, or UDFs.

User-Defined Functions

Pig's designers realized that the ability to plug-in custom code is crucial for all but the most trivial data processing jobs. For this reason, they made it easy to define and use user-defined functions.

A Filter UDF

Let's demonstrate by writing a filter function for filtering out weather records that do not have a temperature quality reading of satisfactory (or better). The idea is to change this line:

```
filtered_records = FILTER records BY temperature != 9999 AND
  (quality == 0 OR quality == 1 OR quality == 4 OR quality == 5 OR quality == 9);
```

to:

```
filtered_records = FILTER records BY temperature != 9999 AND isGood(quality);
```

This achieves two things: it makes the Pig script more concise, and it encapsulates the logic in one place so that it can be easily reused in other scripts. If we were just writing an ad hoc query, then we probably wouldn't bother to write a UDF. It's when you start doing the same kind of processing over and over again that you see opportunities for reusable UDFs.

UDFs are written in Java, and filter functions are all subclasses of `FilterFunc`, which itself is a subclass of `EvalFunc`. We'll look at `EvalFunc` in more detail later, but for the moment just note that, in essence, `EvalFunc` looks like the following class:

```java
public abstract class EvalFunc<T> {
  public abstract T exec(Tuple input) throws IOException;
}
```

`EvalFunc`'s only abstract method, `exec()`, takes a tuple and returns a single value, the (parameterized) type `T`. The fields in the input tuple consist of the expressions passed to the function; in this case, a single integer. For `FilterFunc`, `T` is `Boolean`, so the method should return `true` only for those tuples that should not be filtered out.

For the quality filter, we write a class, `IsGoodQuality`, that extends `FilterFunc` and implements the `exec()` method. See Example 11-1. The `Tuple` class is essentially a list of objects with associated types. Here we are concerned only with the first field (since the function only has a single argument), which we extract by index using the `get()` method on `Tuple`. The field is an integer, so if it's not `null`, we cast it and check whether the value is one that signifies the temperature was a good reading, returning the appropriate value, `true` or `false`.

Example 11-1. A FilterFunc UDF to remove records with unsatisfactory temperature quality readings

```java
package com.hadoopbook.pig;

import java.io.IOException;
import java.util.ArrayList;
import java.util.List;

import org.apache.pig.FilterFunc;

import org.apache.pig.backend.executionengine.ExecException;
import org.apache.pig.data.DataType;
import org.apache.pig.data.Tuple;
import org.apache.pig.impl.logicalLayer.FrontendException;

public class IsGoodQuality extends FilterFunc {

  @Override
  public Boolean exec(Tuple tuple) throws IOException {
    if (tuple == null || tuple.size() == 0) {
      return false;
    }
```

```
    try {
      Object object = tuple.get(0);
      if (object == null) {
        return false;
      }
      int i = (Integer) object;
      return i == 0 || i == 1 || i == 4 || i == 5 || i == 9;
    } catch (ExecException e) {
      throw new IOException(e);
    }
  }

}
```

To use the new function, we first compile it, and package it in a JAR file (in the example code that accompanies this book, we can do this by typing ant pig). Then we tell Pig about the JAR file with the REGISTER operator, which is given the local path to the filename (and is *not* enclosed in quotes):

```
grunt> REGISTER pig.jar;
```

Finally, we can invoke the function:

```
grunt> filtered_records = FILTER records BY temperature != 9999 AND
>>     com.hadoopbook.pig.IsGoodQuality(quality);
```

Pig resolves function calls by treating the function's name as a Java classname and attempting to load a class of that name. (This, incidentally, is why function names are case-sensitive: because Java classnames are.) When searching for classes, Pig uses a classloader that includes the JAR files that have been registered. When running in distributed mode, Pig will ensure that your JAR files get shipped to the cluster.

For the UDF in this example, Pig looks for a class with the name com.hadoop book.pig.IsGoodQuality, which it finds in the JAR file we registered.

Resolution of built-in functions proceeds in the same way, except for one difference: Pig has a set of built-in package names that it searches, so the function call does not have to be a fully qualified name. For example, the function MAX is actually implemented by a class MAX in the package org.apache.pig.builtin. This is one of the packages that Pig looks in, so we can write MAX rather than org.apache.pig.builtin.MAX in our Pig programs.

We can't register our package with Pig, but we can shorten the function name by defining an alias, using the DEFINE operator:

```
grunt> DEFINE isGood com.hadoopbook.pig.IsGoodQuality();
grunt> filtered_records = FILTER records BY temperature != 9999 AND isGood(quality);
```

Defining an alias is a good idea if you want to use the function several times in the same script. It's also necessary if you want to pass arguments to the constructor of the UDF's implementation class.

Leveraging types

The filter works when the quality field is declared to be of type int, but if the type information is absent, then the UDF fails! This happens because the field is the default type, bytearray, represented by the DataByteArray class. Because DataByteArray is not an Integer, the cast fails.

The obvious way to fix this is to convert the field to an integer in the exec() method. However, there is a better way, which is to tell Pig the types of the fields that the function expects. The getArgToFuncMapping() method on EvalFunc is provided for precisely this reason. We can override it to tell Pig that the first field should be an integer:

```
@Override
public List<FuncSpec> getArgToFuncMapping() throws FrontendException {
  List<FuncSpec> funcSpecs = new ArrayList<FuncSpec>();
  funcSpecs.add(new FuncSpec(this.getClass().getName(),
      new Schema(new Schema.FieldSchema(null, DataType.INTEGER))));

  return funcSpecs;
}
```

This method returns a FuncSpec object corresponding to each of the fields of the tuple that are passed to the exec() method. Here there is a single field, and we construct an anonymous FieldSchema (the name is passed as null, since Pig ignores the name when doing type conversion). The type is specified using the INTEGER constant on Pig's Data Type class.

With the amended function, Pig will attempt to convert the argument passed to the function to an integer. If the field cannot be converted, then a null is passed for the field. The exec() method always returns false if the field is null. For this application this behavior is appropriate, as we want to filter out records whose quality field is unintelligible.

Here's the final program using the new function:

```
-- max_temp_filter_udf.pig
REGISTER pig.jar;
DEFINE isGood com.hadoopbook.pig.IsGoodQuality();
records = LOAD 'input/ncdc/micro-tab/sample.txt'
  AS (year:chararray, temperature:int, quality:int);
filtered_records = FILTER records BY temperature != 9999 AND isGood(quality);
grouped_records = GROUP filtered_records BY year;
max_temp = FOREACH grouped_records GENERATE group,
  MAX(filtered_records.temperature);
DUMP max_temp;
```

An Eval UDF

Writing an eval function is a small step up from writing a filter function. Consider a UDF (see Example 11-2) for trimming leading and trailing whitespace from chararray values, just like the trim() method on java.lang.String. We will use this UDF later in the chapter.

Example 11-2. An EvalFunc UDF to trim leading and trailing whitespace from chararray values

```
public class Trim extends EvalFunc<String> {

  @Override
  public String exec(Tuple input) throws IOException {
    if (input == null || input.size() == 0) {
      return null;
    }
    try {
      Object object = input.get(0);
      if (object == null) {
        return null;
      }
      return ((String) object).trim();
    } catch (ExecException e) {
      throw new IOException(e);
    }
  }

  @Override
  public List<FuncSpec> getArgToFuncMapping() throws FrontendException {
    List<FuncSpec> funcList = new ArrayList<FuncSpec>();
    funcList.add(new FuncSpec(this.getClass().getName(), new Schema(
        new Schema.FieldSchema(null, DataType.CHARARRAY))));

    return funcList;
  }
}
```

The exec() and getArgToFuncMapping() methods are straightforward; like the ones in the IsGoodQuality UDF.

When you write an eval function, you need to consider what the output's schema looks like. In the following statement, the schema of B is determined by the function udf:

```
B = FOREACH A GENERATE udf($0);
```

If udf creates tuples with scalar fields, then Pig can determine B's schema through reflection. For complex types such as bags, tuples, or maps, Pig needs more help, and you should implement the outputSchema() method to give Pig the information about the output schema.

The Trim UDF returns a string, which Pig translates as a chararray, as can be seen from the following session:

```
grunt> DUMP A;
( pomegranate)
(banana   )
(apple)
(  lychee )
grunt> DESCRIBE A;
```

```
A: {fruit: chararray}
grunt> B = FOREACH A GENERATE com.hadoopbook.pig.Trim(fruit);
grunt> DUMP B;
(pomegranate)
(banana)
(apple)
(lychee)
grunt> DESCRIBE B;
B: {chararray}
```

A has `chararray` fields that have leading and trailing spaces. We create B from A by applying the `Trim` function to the first field in A (named `fruit`). B's fields are correctly inferred to be of type `chararray`.

A Load UDF

We'll demonstrate a custom load function that can read plain-text column ranges as fields, very much like the Unix `cut` command. It is used as follows:

```
grunt> records = LOAD 'input/ncdc/micro/sample.txt'
>>    USING com.hadoopbook.pig.CutLoadFunc('16-19,88-92,93-93')
>>    AS (year:int, temperature:int, quality:int);
grunt> DUMP records;
(1950,0,1)
(1950,22,1)
(1950,-11,1)
(1949,111,1)
(1949,78,1)
```

The string passed to `CutLoadFunc` is the column specification; each comma-separated range defines a field, which is assigned a name and type in the AS clause. Let's examine the implementation of `CutLoadFunc`, shown in Example 11-3.

Example 11-3. A LoadFunc UDF to load tuple fields as column ranges

```java
public class CutLoadFunc extends Utf8StorageConverter implements LoadFunc {

  private static final Log LOG = LogFactory.getLog(CutLoadFunc.class);

  private static final Charset UTF8 = Charset.forName("UTF-8");
  private static final byte RECORD_DELIMITER = (byte) '\n';

  private TupleFactory tupleFactory = TupleFactory.getInstance();
  private BufferedPositionedInputStream in;
  private long end = Long.MAX_VALUE;
  private List<Range> ranges;

  public CutLoadFunc(String cutPattern) {
    ranges = Range.parse(cutPattern);
  }

  @Override
  public void bindTo(String fileName, BufferedPositionedInputStream in,
      long offset, long end) throws IOException {
```

```
      this.in = in;
      this.end = end;

      // Throw away the first (partial) record - it will be picked up by another
      // instance
      if (offset != 0) {
        getNext();
      }
    }
  }

  @Override
  public Tuple getNext() throws IOException {
    if (in == null || in.getPosition() > end) {
      return null;
    }

    String line;
    while ((line = in.readLine(UTF8, RECORD_DELIMITER)) != null) {
      Tuple tuple = tupleFactory.newTuple(ranges.size());
      for (int i = 0; i < ranges.size(); i++) {
        try {
          Range range = ranges.get(i);
          if (range.getEnd() > line.length()) {
            LOG.warn(String.format(
                "Range end (%s) is longer than line length (%s)",
                range.getEnd(), line.length()));
            continue;
          }
          tuple.set(i, new DataByteArray(range.getSubstring(line)));
        } catch (ExecException e) {
          throw new IOException(e);
        }
      }
      return tuple;
    }
    return null;
  }

  @Override
  public void fieldsToRead(Schema schema) {
    // Can't use this information to optimize, so ignore it
  }

  @Override
  public Schema determineSchema(String fileName, ExecType execType,
      DataStorage storage) throws IOException {
    // Cannot determine schema in general
    return null;
  }
}
```

When Pig is using the Hadoop execution engine, data loading takes place in the mapper, so it is important that the input can be split into portions that are independently handled by each mapper (see "Input Splits and Records" on page 185 for background).

In Pig, load functions are asked to load a portion of the input, specified as a byte range. The start and end offsets are typically not on record boundaries (since they correspond to HDFS blocks), so on initialization, in the `bindTo()` method, the load function needs to find the start of the next record boundary. The Pig runtime then calls `getNext()` repeatedly, and the load function reads tuples from the stream until it gets past the byte range it was asked to load. At this point, it returns `null` to signal that there are no more tuples to be read.

`CutLoadFunc` is constructed with a string that specifies the column ranges to use for each field. The logic for parsing this string and creating a list of internal `Range` objects that encapsulates these ranges is contained in the `Range` class, and is not shown here (it is available in the example code that accompanies this book).

In `CutLoadFunc`'s `bindTo()` method, we find the next record boundary. If we are at the beginning of the stream, we know the stream is positioned at the first record boundary. Otherwise, we call `getNext()` to discard the first partial line, since it will be handled in full by another instance of `CutLoadFunc`—the one whose byte range immediately proceeds the current one. In some cases, the start offset may fall on a line boundary, but it is not possible to detect this case, so we always have to discard the first line. This is not a problem, since we always read lines until the position of the input stream is strictly past the end offset. In others words, if the end offset is on a line boundary, then we will read one further line. In this way we can be sure that no lines are omitted by the load function. (The situation is analogous to the one described and illustrated in "TextInputFormat" on page 196.)

The role of the `getNext()` implementation is to turn lines of the input file into `Tuple` objects. It does this by means of a `TupleFactory`, a Pig class for creating `Tuple` instances. The `newTuple()` method creates a new tuple with the required number of fields, which is just the number of `Range` classes, and the fields are populated using substrings of the line, which are determined by the `Range` objects.

We need to think about what to do if the line is shorter than the range asked for. One option is to throw an exception, and stop further processing. This is appropriate if your application cannot tolerate incomplete or corrupt records. In many cases, it is better to return a tuple with `null` fields and let the Pig script handle the incomplete data as it sees fit. This is the approach we take here, by exiting the for loop if the range end is past the end of the line, we leave the current field, and any subsequent fields in the tuple, with their default value of `null`.

Using a schema

Let's now consider the type of the fields being loaded. If the user has specified a schema, then the fields need converting to the relevant types. However, this is performed lazily by Pig, and so the loader should always construct tuples of type `bytearray`, using the `DataByteArray` type. The loader function still has the opportunity to do the conversion, however, since it must implement a collection of conversion methods for this purpose:

```
public interface LoadFunc {

    // Cast methods
    public Integer bytesToInteger(byte[] b) throws IOException;
    public Long bytesToLong(byte[] b) throws IOException;
    public Float bytesToFloat(byte[] b) throws IOException;
    public Double bytesToDouble(byte[] b) throws IOException;
    public String bytesToCharArray(byte[] b) throws IOException;
    public Map<Object, Object> bytesToMap(byte[] b) throws IOException;
    public Tuple bytesToTuple(byte[] b) throws IOException;
    public DataBag bytesToBag(byte[] b) throws IOException;

    // Other methods omitted
}
```

CutLoadFunc doesn't implement these methods itself, since it extends Pig's Utf8Stora
geConverter, which provides standard conversions between UTF-8 encoded data and
Pig data types.

In some cases, the load function itself can determine the schema. For example, if we
were loading self-describing data like XML or JSON, we could create a schema for Pig
by looking at the data. Alternatively, the load function may determine the schema in
another way, such as an external file, or being passed information in its constructor.
To support such cases, the load function can provide an implementation of determine
Schema() that returns a schema. Note, however, that if a user supplies a schema in the
AS clause of LOAD, then it takes precedence over the schema returned by the load
function's determineSchema() method.

For CutLoadFunc, we return null in determineSchema(), so there is a schema only if the
user supplies one.

Finally, LoadFunc has a fieldsToRead() method that lets the loader function find out
which columns the query is asking for. This is can be a useful optimization for column-
oriented storage, so the loader only loads the columns that are needed by the query.
There is no obvious way for CutLoadFunc to load only a subset of columns, since it reads
the whole line for each tuple, so we ignore this information.

Advanced loading with Slicer

For more control over the data loading process, your load function can implement the
Slicer interface, in addition to LoadFunc. A Slicer implementation is free to use the
location information passed to LOAD in any way it chooses: it doesn't have to be a
Hadoop path, but could be interpreted as a database reference, or in some other way.
Furthermore, it is up to the Slicer to split the input dataset into Slice objects, where
each Slice is processed by a single MapReduce mapper. A custom Slicer can therefore
split the input in a different way to Pig's standard slicing behavior, which is to break
files into HDFS block-sized slices. For example, a Slicer for processing large image or
video files might create one file per slice.

You can learn more about writing a `Slicer` on the Pig wiki at *http://wiki.apache.org/pig/ UDFManual*.

Data Processing Operators

Loading and Storing Data

Throughout this chapter we have seen how to load data from external storage for processing in Pig. Storing results is straightforward, too. Here's an example of using Pig-Storage to store tuples as plain-text values separated by a colon character:

```
grunt> STORE A INTO 'out' USING PigStorage(':');
grunt> cat out
Joe:cherry:2
Ali:apple:3
Joe:banana:2
Eve:apple:7
```

Other built-in storage functions are described in Table 11-7.

Filtering Data

Once you have some data loaded into a relation, the next step is often to filter it to remove the data that you are not interested in. By filtering early in the processing pipeline, you minimize the amount of data flowing through the system, which can improve efficiency.

FOREACH .. GENERATE

We have already seen how to remove rows from a relation using the FILTER operator with simple expressions and a UDF. The FOREACH .. GENERATE operator is used to act on every row in a relation. It can be used to remove fields, or to generate new ones. In this example, we do both:

```
grunt> DUMP A;
(Joe,cherry,2)
(Ali,apple,3)
(Joe,banana,2)
(Eve,apple,7)
grunt> B = FOREACH A GENERATE $0, $2+1, 'Constant';
grunt> DUMP B;
(Joe,3,Constant)
(Ali,4,Constant)
(Joe,3,Constant)
(Eve,8,Constant)
```

Here we have created a new relation B with three fields. Its first field is a projection of the first field ($0) of A. B's second field is the third field of A ($1) with one added to it.

B's third field is a constant field (every row in B has the same third field) with the chararray value Constant.

The FOREACH .. GENERATE operator has a nested form for to support more complex processing. In the following example, we compute various statistics for the weather dataset:

```
-- year_stats.pig
REGISTER pig.jar;
DEFINE isGood com.hadoopbook.pig.IsGoodQuality();
records = LOAD 'input/ncdc/all/19{1,2,3,4,5}0*'
  USING com.hadoopbook.pig.CutLoadFunc('5-10,11-15,16-19,88-92,93-93')
  AS (usaf:chararray, wban:chararray, year:int, temperature:int, quality:int);

grouped_records = GROUP records BY year PARALLEL 30;

year_stats = FOREACH grouped_records {
  uniq_stations = DISTINCT records.usaf;
  good_records = FILTER records BY isGood(quality);
  GENERATE FLATTEN(group), COUNT(uniq_stations) AS station_count,
    COUNT(good_records) AS good_record_count, COUNT(records) AS record_count;
}

DUMP year_stats;
```

Using the cut UDF we developed earlier, we load various fields from the input dataset into the records relation. Next we group records by year. Notice the PARALLEL keyword for setting the number of reducers to use; this is vital when running on a cluster. Then we process each group using a nested FOREACH .. GENERATE operator. The first nested statement creates a relation for the distinct USAF identifiers for stations using the DISTINCT operator. The second nested statement creates a relation for the records with "good" readings using the FILTER operator, and a UDF. The final nested statement is a GENERATE statement (a nested FOREACH .. GENERATE must always have a GENERATE statement as the last nested statement) that generates the summary fields of interest using the grouped records, as well as the relations created in the nested block.

Running it on a few years of data, we get the following:

```
(1920,8L,8595L,8595L)
(1950,1988L,8635452L,8641353L)
(1930,121L,89245L,89262L)
(1910,7L,7650L,7650L)
(1940,732L,1052333L,1052976L)
```

The fields are year, number of unique stations, total number of good readings, and total number of readings. We can see how the number of weather stations and readings grew over time.

STREAM

The STREAM operator allows you to transform data in a relation using an external program or script. It is named by analogy with Hadoop Streaming, which provides a similar capability for MapReduce (see "Hadoop Streaming" on page 32).

STREAM can use built-in commands with arguments. Here is an example that uses the Unix cut command to extract the second field of each tuple in A. Note that the command and its arguments are enclosed in backticks:

```
grunt> C = STREAM A THROUGH `cut -f 2`;
grunt> DUMP C;
(cherry)
(apple)
(banana)
(apple)
```

The STREAM operator uses PigStorage to serialize and deserialize relations to and from the program's standard input and output streams. Tuples in A are converted to tab-delimited lines that are passed to the script. The output of the script is read one line at a time and split on tabs to create new tuples for the output relation C. You can provide a custom serializer and deserializer using the DEFINE command.

Pig streaming is most powerful when you write custom processing scripts. The following Python script filters out bad weather records:

```python
#!/usr/bin/env python

import re
import string
import sys

for line in sys.stdin:
  (year, temp, q) = string.strip().split(line)
  if (temp != "9999" and re.match("[01459]", q)):
    print "%s\t%s" % (year, temp)
```

To use the script, you need to ship it to the cluster. This is achieved via a DEFINE clause, which also creates an alias for the STREAM command. The STREAM statement can then refer to the alias, as the following Pig script shows:

```
-- max_temp_filter_stream.pig
DEFINE is_good_quality `is_good_quality.py`
  SHIP ('src/main/ch11/python/is_good_quality.py');
records = LOAD 'input/ncdc/micro-tab/sample.txt'
  AS (year:chararray, temperature:int, quality:int);
filtered_records = STREAM records THROUGH is_good_quality
  AS (year:chararray, temperature:int);
grouped_records = GROUP filtered_records BY year;
max_temp = FOREACH grouped_records GENERATE group,
  MAX(filtered_records.temperature);
DUMP max_temp;
```

Grouping and Joining Data

Joining datasets in MapReduce takes some work on the part of the programmer (see "Joins" on page 233), whereas Pig has very good built-in support for join operations, making it much more approachable. Since the large datasets that are suitable for analysis by Pig (and MapReduce in general), are not normalized, joins are used more infrequently in Pig than they are in SQL.

JOIN

Let's look at an example of an inner join. Consider the relations A and B:

```
grunt> DUMP A;
(2,Tie)
(4,Coat)
(3,Hat)
(1,Scarf)
grunt> DUMP B;
(Joe,2)
(Hank,4)
(Ali,0)
(Eve,3)
(Hank,2)
```

We can join the two relations on the numerical (identity) field in each:

```
grunt> C = JOIN A BY $0, B BY $1;
grunt> DUMP C;
(2,Tie,Joe,2)
(2,Tie,Hank,2)
(3,Hat,Eve,3)
(4,Coat,Hank,4)
```

This is a classic inner join, where each match between the two relations corresponds to a row in the result. (It's actually an equijoin since the join predicate is equality.) The result's fields are made up of all the fields of all the input relations.

You should use the general join operator if all the relations being joined are too large to fit in memory. If one of the relations is small enough to fit in memory, there is a special type of join called a *fragment replicate join*, which is implemented by distributing the small input to all the mappers, and performing a map-side join using an in-memory lookup table against the (fragmented) larger relation. There is a special syntax for telling Pig to use a fragment replicate join:

```
grunt> C = JOIN A BY $0, B BY $1 USING "replicated";
```

The first relation must be the large one, followed by one or more small ones.

COGROUP

JOIN always gives a flat structure: a set of tuples. The COGROUP statement is similar to JOIN, but creates a nested set of output tuples. This can be useful if you want to exploit the structure in subsequent statements:

```
grunt> D = COGROUP A BY $0, B BY $1;
grunt> DUMP D;
(0,{},{(Ali,0)})
(1,{(1,Scarf)},{})
(2,{(2,Tie)},{(Joe,2),(Hank,2)})
(3,{(3,Hat)},{(Eve,3)})
(4,{(4,Coat)},{(Hank,4)})
```

COGROUP generates a tuple for each unique grouping key. The first field of each tuple is the key, and the remaining fields are bags of tuples from the relations with a matching key. The first bag contains the matching tuples from relation A with the same key. Similarly, the second bag contains the matching tuples from relation B with the same key.

If for a particular key a relation has no matching key, then the bag for that relation is empty. For example, since no one has bought a scarf (with ID 1), the second bag in the tuple for that row is empty. This is an example of an outer join, which is the default type for COGROUP. It can be made explicit using the OUTER keyword; making this COGROUP statement the same as the previous one:

```
D = COGROUP A BY $0 OUTER, B BY $1 OUTER;
```

You can suppress rows with empty bags by using the INNER keyword, which gives the COGROUP inner join semantics. The INNER keyword is applied per relation, so the following only suppresses rows when relation A has no match (dropping the unknown product 0 here):

```
grunt> E = COGROUP A BY $0 INNER, B BY $1;
grunt> DUMP E;
(1,{(1,Scarf)},{})
(2,{(2,Tie)},{(Joe,2),(Hank,2)})
(3,{(3,Hat)},{(Eve,3)})
(4,{(4,Coat)},{(Hank,4)})
```

We can flatten this structure to discover who bought each of the items in relation A:

```
grunt> F = FOREACH E GENERATE FLATTEN(A), B.$0;
grunt> DUMP F;
(1,Scarf,{})
(2,Tie,{(Joe),(Hank)})
(3,Hat,{(Eve)})
(4,Coat,{(Hank)})
```

Using a combination of COGROUP, INNER, and FLATTEN (which removes nesting) it's possible to simulate a JOIN:

```
grunt> G = COGROUP A BY $0 INNER, B BY $1 INNER;
grunt> H = FOREACH G GENERATE FLATTEN($1), FLATTEN($2);
```

```
grunt> DUMP H;
(2,Tie,Joe,2)
(2,Tie,Hank,2)
(3,Hat,Eve,3)
(4,Coat,Hank,4)
```

This gives the same result as JOIN A BY $0, B BY $1.

If the join key is composed of several fields, you can specify them all in the BY clauses of the JOIN or COGROUP statement. Make sure that the number of fields in each BY clause is the same.

Here's another example of a join in Pig, in a script for calculating the maximum temperature of for every station over a time period controlled by the input:

```
-- max_temp_station_name.pig
REGISTER pig.jar;
DEFINE isGood com.hadoopbook.pig.IsGoodQuality();

stations = LOAD 'input/ncdc/metadata/stations-fixed-width.txt'
  USING com.hadoopbook.pig.CutLoadFunc('1-6,8-12,14-42')
  AS (usaf:chararray, wban:chararray, name:chararray);

trimmed_stations = FOREACH stations GENERATE usaf, wban,
  com.hadoopbook.pig.Trim(name);

records = LOAD 'input/ncdc/all/191*'
  USING com.hadoopbook.pig.CutLoadFunc('5-10,11-15,88-92,93-93')
  AS (usaf:chararray, wban:chararray, temperature:int, quality:int);

filtered_records = FILTER records BY temperature != 9999 AND isGood(quality);
grouped_records = GROUP filtered_records BY (usaf, wban) PARALLEL 30;
max_temp = FOREACH grouped_records GENERATE FLATTEN(group),
  MAX(filtered_records.temperature);
max_temp_named = JOIN max_temp BY (usaf, wban), trimmed_stations BY (usaf, wban)
  PARALLEL 30;
max_temp_result = FOREACH max_temp_named GENERATE $0, $1, $5, $2;

STORE max_temp_result INTO 'max_temp_by_station';
```

We use the cut UDF we developed earlier to load one relation holding the station IDs (USAF and WBAN identifiers) and names, and one relation holding all the weather records, keyed by station ID. We group the filtered weather records by station ID and aggregate by maximum temperature, before joining with the stations. Finally, we project out the fields we want in the final result: USAF, WBAN, station name, maximum temperature.

Here are a few results for the 1910s:

```
228020      99999      SORTAVALA       322
029110      99999      VAASA AIRPORT   300
040650      99999      GRIMSEY         378
```

This query could be made more efficient by using a fragment replicate join, as the station metadata is small.

CROSS

Pig Latin includes the cross product operator (also known as the cartesian product), which joins every tuple in a relation with every tuple in a second relation (and with every tuple in further relations if supplied). The size of the output is the product of the size of the inputs, potentially making the output very large:

```
grunt> I = CROSS A, B;
grunt> DUMP I;
(2,Tie,Joe,2)
(2,Tie,Hank,4)
(2,Tie,Ali,0)
(2,Tie,Eve,3)
(2,Tie,Hank,2)
(4,Coat,Joe,2)
(4,Coat,Hank,4)
(4,Coat,Ali,0)
(4,Coat,Eve,3)
(4,Coat,Hank,2)
(3,Hat,Joe,2)
(3,Hat,Hank,4)
(3,Hat,Ali,0)
(3,Hat,Eve,3)
(3,Hat,Hank,2)
(1,Scarf,Joe,2)
(1,Scarf,Hank,4)
(1,Scarf,Ali,0)
(1,Scarf,Eve,3)
(1,Scarf,Hank,2)
```

When dealing with large datasets, you should try to avoid operations that generate intermediate representations that are quadratic (or worse) in size. Computing the cross product of the whole input dataset is rarely needed, if ever.

For example, at first blush one might expect that calculating pairwise document similarity in a corpus of documents would require every document pair to be generated before calculating their similarity. However, if one starts with the insight that most document pairs have a similarity score of zero (that is, they are unrelated), then we can find a way to a better algorithm.

In this case, the key idea is to focus on the entities that we are using to calculate similarity (terms in a document, for example), and make them the center of the algorithm. In practice, we also remove terms that don't help discriminate between documents (stopwords) and this reduces the problem space still further. Using this technique to analyze a set of roughly one million (10^6) documents generates in the order of one billion (10^9) intermediate pairs,[*] rather than the one trillion (10^{12}) produced by the naive approach (generating the cross product of the input), or the approach with no stopword removal.

---

[*] "Pairwise Document Similarity in Large Collections with MapReduce," Elsayed, Lin, and Oard (2008, College Park, MD: University of Maryland).

GROUP

Although COGROUP groups the data in two or more relations, the GROUP statement groups the data in a single relation. GROUP supports grouping by more than equality of keys: you can use an expression or user-defined function as the group key. For example, consider the following relation A:

```
grunt> DUMP A;
(Joe,cherry)
(Ali,apple)
(Joe,banana)
(Eve,apple)
```

Let's group by the number of characters in the second field:

```
grunt> B = GROUP A BY SIZE($1);
grunt> DUMP B;
(5L,{(Ali,apple),(Eve,apple)})
(6L,{(Joe,cherry),(Joe,banana)})
```

GROUP creates a relation whose first field is the grouping field, which is given the alias group. The second field is a bag containing the grouped fields with the same schema as the original relation (in this case, A).

There are also two special grouping operations: ALL and ANY. ALL groups all the tuples in a relation in a single group, as if the GROUP function was a constant:

```
grunt> C = GROUP A ALL;
grunt> DUMP C;
(all,{(Joe,cherry),(Ali,apple),(Joe,banana),(Eve,apple)})
```

Note that there is no BY in this form of the GROUP statement. The ALL grouping is commonly used to count the number of tuples in a relation, as shown in "Validation and nulls" on page 318.

The ANY keyword is used to group the tuples in a relation randomly, which can be useful for sampling.

Sorting Data

Relations are unordered in Pig. Consider a relation A:

```
grunt> DUMP A;
(2,3)
(1,2)
(2,4)
```

There is no guarantee which order the rows will be processed in. In particular, when retrieving the contents of A using DUMP or STORE, the rows may be written in any order. If you want to impose an order on the output you can use the ORDER operator to sort a relation by one or more fields. The default sort order compares fields of the same type using the natural ordering, and different types are given an arbitrary, but deterministic, ordering (a tuple is always "less than" a bag, for example). A different ordering may be imposed with a USING clause that specifies a UDF that extends Pig's `ComparisonFunc` class.

The following example sorts A by the first field in ascending order, and by the second field in descending order:

```
grunt> B = ORDER A BY $0, $1 DESC;
grunt> DUMP B;
(1,2)
(2,4)
(2,3)
```

Any further processing on a sorted relation does not guarantee to retain its order. For example:

```
grunt> C = FOREACH B GENERATE *;
```

Even though relation C has the same contents as relation B, its tuples may be emitted in any order by a DUMP or a STORE. It is for this reason that it is usual to perform the ORDER operation just before retrieving the output.

The LIMIT statement is useful for limiting the number of results, as a quick and dirty way to get a sample of a relation; prototyping (the ILLUSTRATE command should be preferred for generating more representative samples of the data). It can be used immediately after the ORDER statement to retrieve the first n tuples. Usually LIMIT will select any n tuples from a relation, but when used immediately after an ORDER statement, the order is retained (in an exception to the rule that processing a relation does not retain its order).

```
grunt> D = LIMIT B 2;
grunt> DUMP D;
(1,2)
(2,4)
```

If the limit is greater than the number of tuples in the relation, all tuples are returned (so LIMIT has no effect).

Using LIMIT can improve the performance of a query because Pig tries to apply the limit as early as possible in the processing pipeline, to minimize the amount of data that needs to be processed. For this reason, you should always use LIMIT if you are not interested in the entire output.

Combining and Splitting Data

Sometimes you have several relations that you would like to combine into one. For this, the UNION statement is used. For example:

```
grunt> DUMP A;
(2,3)
(1,2)
(2,4)
grunt> DUMP B;
```

```
(z,x,8)
(w,y,1)
grunt> C = UNION A, B;
grunt> DUMP C;
(2,3)
(z,x,8)
(1,2)
(w,y,1)
(2,4)
```

C is the union of relations A and B, and since relations are unordered, the order of the tuples in C is undefined. Also, it's possible to form the union of two relations with different schemas or with different numbers of fields, as we have done here. Pig attempts to merge the schemas from the relations that UNION is operating on. In this case, they are incompatible, so C has no schema:

```
grunt> DESCRIBE A;
A: {f0: int,f1: int}
grunt> DESCRIBE B;
B: {f0: chararray,f1: chararray,f2: int}
grunt> DESCRIBE C;
Schema for C unknown.
```

If the output relation has no schema, your script needs to be able to handle tuples that vary in the number of fields and/or types.

The SPLIT operator is the opposite of UNION; it partitions a relation into two or more relations. See "Validation and nulls" on page 318 for an example of how to use it.

Pig in Practice

There are some practical techniques that are worth knowing about when you are developing and running Pig programs. This section covers some of them.

Parallelism

When running in Hadoop mode, you need to tell Pig how many reducers you want for each job. You do this using a PARALLEL clause for operators that run in the reduce phase, which includes all the grouping and joining operators (GROUP, COGROUP, JOIN, CROSS), as well as DISTINCT and ORDER. By default the number of reducers is one (just like for MapReduce), so it is important to set the degree of parallelism when running on a large dataset. The following line sets the number of reducers to 30 for the GROUP:

```
grouped_records = GROUP records BY year PARALLEL 30;
```

A good setting for the number of reduce tasks is slightly fewer than the number of reduce slots in the cluster. See "Choosing the Number of Reducers" on page 181 for further discussion.

The number of map tasks is set by the size of the input (with one map per HDFS block), and is not affected by the PARALLEL clause.

Parameter Substitution

If you have a Pig script that you run on a regular basis, then it's quite common to want to be able to run the same script with different parameters. For example, a script that runs daily may use the date to determine which input files it runs over. Pig supports *parameter substitution*, where parameters in the script are substituted with values supplied at runtime. Parameters are denoted by identifiers prefixed with a $ character; for example $input and $output, used in the following script to specify the input and output paths:

```
-- max_temp_param.pig
records = LOAD '$input' AS (year:chararray, temperature:int, quality:int);
filtered_records = FILTER records BY temperature != 9999 AND
  (quality == 0 OR quality == 1 OR quality == 4 OR quality == 5 OR quality == 9);
grouped_records = GROUP filtered_records BY year;
max_temp = FOREACH grouped_records GENERATE group,
  MAX(filtered_records.temperature);
STORE max_temp into '$output';
```

Parameters can be specified when launching Pig, using the -param option, one for each parameter:

```
% pig \
        -param input=/user/tom/input/ncdc/micro-tab/sample.txt \
        -param output=/tmp/out \
        src/main/ch11/pig/max_temp_param.pig
```

You can also put parameters in a file, and pass them to Pig using the -param_file option. For example, we can achieve the same result as the previous command by placing the parameter definitions in a file:

```
# Input file
input=/user/tom/input/ncdc/micro-tab/sample.txt
# Output file
output=/tmp/out
```

The *pig* invocation then becomes:

```
% pig \
        -param_file src/main/ch11/pig/max_temp_param.param \
        src/main/ch11/pig/max_temp_param.pig
```

You can specify multiple parameter files using -param_file repeatedly. You can also use a combination of -param and -param_file options, and if any parameter is defined in both a parameter file and on the command line, the last value on the command line takes precedence.

Dynamic parameters

For parameters that are supplied using the -param option, it is easy to make the value dynamic by running a command or script. Many Unix shells support command substitution for a command enclosed in backticks, and we can use this to make the output directory date-based:

```
% pig \
        -param input=/user/tom/input/ncdc/micro-tab/sample.txt \
        -param output=/tmp/`date "+%Y-%m-%d"`/out \
        src/main/ch11/pig/max_temp_param.pig
```

Pig also supports backticks in parameter files, by executing the enclosed command in a shell and using the shell output as the substituted value. If the command or scripts exits with a nonzero exit status, then the error message is reported and execution halts. Backtick support in parameter files is a useful feature; it means that parameters can be defined in the same way if they are defined in a file or on the command line.

Parameter substitution processing

Parameter substitution occurs as a preprocessing step before the script is run. You can see the substitutions that the preprocessor made by executing Pig with the -dryrun option. In dry run mode, Pig performs parameter substitution and generates a copy of the original script with substituted values, but does not execute the script. You can inspect the generated script and check that the substitutions look sane (because they are dynamically generated, for example) before running it in normal mode.

At the time of this writing, Grunt does not support parameter substitution.

## CHAPTER 12

HBase

Jonathan Gray and Michael Stack

HBasics

HBase is a distributed column-oriented database built on top of HDFS. HBase is the Hadoop application to use when you require real-time read/write random-access to very large datasets.

Although there are countless strategies and implementations for database storage and retrieval, most solutions—especially those of the relational variety—are not built with very large scale and distribution in mind. Many vendors offer replication and partitioning solutions to grow the database beyond the confines of a single node but these add-ons are generally an afterthought and are complicated to install and maintain. They also come at some severe compromise to the RDBMS feature set. Joins, complex queries, triggers, views, and foreign-key constraints become prohibitively expensive to run on a scaled RDBMS or do not work at all.

HBase comes at the scaling problem from the opposite direction. It is built from the ground-up to scale linearly just by adding nodes. HBase is not relational and does not support SQL, but given the proper problem space it is able to do what an RDBMS cannot: ably host very large, sparsely populated tables on clusters made from commodity hardware.

The canonical HBase use case is the *webtable*, a table of crawled web pages and their attributes (such as language and MIME type) keyed by the web page URL. The webtable is large with row counts that run into the billions. Batch analytic and parsing MapReduce jobs are continuously run against the webtable deriving statistics and adding new columns of MIME type and parsed text content for later indexing by a search engine. Concurrently, the table is randomly accessed by crawlers running at various rates updating random rows while random web pages are served in real time as users click on a website's cached-page feature.

Backdrop

The HBase project was started toward the end of 2006 by Chad Walters and Jim Kellerman of Powerset. It was modeled after Google's "Bigtable: A Distributed Storage System for Structured Data" by Chang et al. (*http://labs.google.com/papers/bigtable .html*), which had just been published. In February 2007, Mike Cafarella made a code drop of a mostly working system that Jim Kellerman then carried forward.

The first HBase release was bundled as part of Hadoop 0.15.0. At the start of 2008, HBase became a Hadoop subproject at *http://hadoop.apache.org/hbase* (or *http://hbase .org*). HBase has been in production use at Powerset since late 2007. Other production users of HBase include WorldLingo, Streamy.com, OpenPlaces, and groups at Yahoo! and Adobe.

Concepts

In this section, we provide a quick overview of core HBase concepts. At a minimum, a passing familiarity will ease the digestion of all that follows.[*]

Whirlwind Tour of the Data Model

Applications store data into labeled tables. Tables are made of rows and columns. Table cells—the intersection of row and column coordinates—are versioned. By default, their version is a timestamp auto-assigned by HBase at the time of cell insertion. A cell's content is an uninterpreted array of bytes.

Table row keys are also byte arrays, so theoretically anything can serve as a row key from strings to binary representations of longs or even serialized data structures. Table rows are sorted by row key, the table's primary key. By default, the sort is byte-ordered. All table accesses are via the table primary key.[†]

Row columns are grouped into *column families*. All column family members have a common prefix, so, for example, the columns *temperature:air* and *temperature:dew_point* are both members of the *temperature* column family, whereas *station:identifier* belongs to the *station* family.[‡] The column family prefix must be composed of *printable* characters. The qualifying tail can be made of any arbitrary bytes.

---

[*] For more detail than is provided here, see the HBase Architecture page *http://wiki.apache.org/hadoop/Hbase/ HbaseArchitecture* on the HBase wiki.

[†] Though there are facilities in HBase to support secondary indices, these are ancillary rather than core and are likely to be moved to their own project.

[‡] In HBase, by convention, the colon character (:) delimits the column family from the column family *qualifier*. It is hardcoded.

A table's column families must be specified up front as part of the table schema definition, but new column family members can be added on demand. For example, a new column *station:address* can be offered by a client as part of an update, and its value persisted, as long as the column family *station* is already in existence on the targeted table.

Physically, all column family members are stored together on the filesystem. So, though earlier we described HBase as a column-oriented store, it would be more accurate if it were described as a column-*family*-oriented store. Because tunings and storage specifications are done at the column family level, it is advised that all column family members have the same general access pattern and size characteristics.

In synopsis, HBase tables are like those in an RDBMS, only cells are versioned, rows are sorted, and columns can be added on the fly by the client as long as the column family they belong to preexists.

Regions

Tables are automatically partitioned horizontally by HBase into *regions*. Each region comprises a subset of a table's rows. A region is defined by its first row, inclusive, and last row, exclusive, plus a randomly generated region identifier. Initially a table comprises a single region but as the size of the region grows, after it crosses a configurable size threshold, it splits at a row boundary into two new regions of approximately equal size. Until this first split happens, all loading will be against the single server hosting the original region. As the table grows, the number of its regions grows. Regions are the units that get distributed over an HBase cluster. In this way, a table that is too big for any one server can be carried by a cluster of servers with each node hosting a subset of the table's total regions. This is also the means by which the loading on a table gets distributed. At any one time, the online set of sorted regions comprises the table's total content.

Locking

Row updates are atomic, no matter how many row columns constitute the row-level transaction. This keeps the locking model simple.

Implementation

Just as HDFS and MapReduce are built of clients, slaves and a coordinating master—*namenode* and *datanodes* in HDFS and *jobtracker* and *tasktrackers* in MapReduce—so is HBase characterized with an HBase *master* node orchestrating a cluster of one or more *regionserver* slaves (see Figure 12-1). The HBase master is responsible for bootstrapping a virgin install, for assigning regions to registered regionservers, and for recovering regionserver failures. The master node is lightly loaded. The regionservers carry zero or more regions and field client read/write requests. They also manage region splits informing the HBase master about the new daughter regions for it to manage the offlining of parent region and assignment of the replacement daughters. HBase depends on ZooKeeper (Chapter 13) and by default it manages a ZooKeeper instance as the authority on cluster state.[§]

Regionserver slave nodes are listed in the HBase *conf/regionservers* file as you would list datanodes and tasktrackers in the Hadoop *conf/slaves* file. Start and stop scripts are like those in Hadoop using the same SSH-based running of remote commands mechanism. Cluster site-specific configuration is made in the HBase *conf/hbase-site.xml* and *conf/hbase-env.sh* files, which have the same format as that of their equivalents up in the Hadoop parent project (see Chapter 9).

 Where there is commonality to be found, HBase directly uses or subclasses the parent Hadoop implementation, whether a service or type. When this is not possible, HBase will follow the Hadoop model where it can. For example, HBase uses the Hadoop Configuration system so configuration files have the same format. What this means for you, the user, is that you can leverage any Hadoop familiarity in your exploration of HBase. HBase deviates from this rule only when adding its specializations.

HBase persists data via the Hadoop filesystem API. Since there are multiple implementations of the filesystem interface—one for the local filesystem, one for the KFS filesystem, Amazon's S3, and HDFS (the Hadoop Distributed Filesystem)—HBase can persist to any of these implementations. Most experience though has been had using HDFS, though by default, unless told otherwise, HBase writes the local filesystem. The local filesystem is fine for experimenting with your initial HBase install, but thereafter, usually the first configuration made in an HBase cluster involves pointing HBase at the HDFS cluster to use.

HBase in operation

HBase, internally, keeps special catalog tables named *-ROOT-* and *.META.* within which it maintains the current list, state, recent history, and location of all regions afloat on the cluster. The *-ROOT-* table holds the list of *.META.* table regions. The *.META.* table holds the list of all user-space regions. Entries in these tables are keyed using the region's start row. Row keys, as noted previously, are sorted so finding the region that hosts a particular row is a matter of a lookup to find the first entry whose key is greater than or equal to that of the requested row key. As regions transition—are split, disabled/enabled, deleted, redeployed by the region load balancer, or redeployed due to a regionserver crash—the catalog tables are updated so the state of all regions on the cluster is kept current.

[§] HBase can be configured to use an existing ZooKeeper cluster instead.

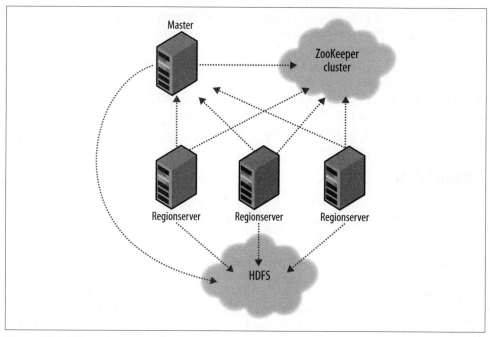

Figure 12-1. HBase cluster members

Fresh clients connect to the ZooKeeper cluster first to learn the location of -ROOT-. Clients consult -ROOT- to elicit the location of the .META. region whose scope covers that of the requested row. The client then does a lookup against the found .META. region to figure the hosting user-space region and its location. Thereafter the client interacts directly with the hosting regionserver.

To save on having to make three round-trips per row operation, clients cache all they learn traversing -ROOT- and .META. caching locations as well as user-space region start and stop rows so they can figure hosting regions themselves without having to go back to the .META. table. Clients continue to use the cached entry as they work until there is a fault. When this happens—the region has moved—the client consults the .META. again to learn the new location. If, in turn, the consulted .META. region has moved, then -ROOT- is reconsulted.

Writes arriving at a regionserver are first appended to a commit log and then are added to an in-memory cache. When this cache fills, its content is flushed to the filesystem.

The commit log is hosted on HDFS, so it remains available through a regionserver crash. When the master notices that a regionserver is no longer reachable, it splits the dead regionserver's commit log by region. On reassignment, regions that were on the dead regionserver, before they open for business, pick up their just-split file of not yet persisted edits and replay them to bring themselves up-to-date with the state they had just before the failure.

Reading, the region's memcache is consulted first. If sufficient versions are found to satisfy the query, we return. Otherwise, flush files are consulted in order, from newest to oldest until sufficient versions are found or until we run out of flush files to consult. A background process compacts flush files once their number has broached a threshold, rewriting many files as one, because the fewer files a read consults, the more performant it will be. On compaction, versions beyond the configured maximum, deletes and expired cells are cleaned out. A separate process running in the regionserver monitors flush file sizes splitting the region when they grow in excess of the configured maximum.

Installation

Download a stable release from the HBase Release page (*http://hadoop.apache.org/hbase/releases.html*) and unpack it somewhere on your filesystem. For example:

```
% tar xzf hbase-x.y.z.tar.gz
```

As with Hadoop, you first need to tell HBase where Java is located on your system. If you have the JAVA_HOME environment variable set to point to a suitable Java installation, then that will be used, and you don't have to configure anything further. Otherwise, you can set the Java installation that HBase uses by editing HBase's *conf/hbase-env.sh*, and specifying the JAVA_HOME variable (see Appendix A for some examples) to point to version 1.6.0 of Java.

HBase, just like Hadoop, requires Java 6.

For convenience, add the HBase binary directory to your command-line path. For example:

```
% export HBASE_INSTALL=/home/hbase/hbase-x.y.z
% export PATH=$PATH:$HBASE_INSTALL/bin
```

To get the list of HBase options, type:

```
% hbase
Usage: hbase <command>
where <command> is one of:
  shell            run the HBase shell
  master           run an HBase HMaster node
  regionserver     run an HBase HRegionServer node
  rest             run an HBase REST server
  thrift           run an HBase Thrift server
  zookeeper        run a Zookeeper server
  migrate          upgrade an hbase.rootdir
 or
  CLASSNAME        run the class named CLASSNAME
Most commands print help when invoked w/o parameters.
```

Test Drive

To start a temporary instance of HBase that uses the */tmp* directory on the local filesystem for persistence, type

```
% start-hbase.sh
```

This will launch two daemons: a standalone HBase instance that persists to the local filesystem—by default, HBase will write to */tmp/hbase-${USERID}*—and a single instance of ZooKeeper to host cluster state.‖

To administer your HBase instance, launch the HBase shell by typing:

```
% hbase shell
HBase Shell; enter 'help<RETURN>' for list of supported commands.
Version: 0.19.1, r751874, Thu Mar 12 22:54:22 PDT 2009
hbase(main):001:0>
```

This will bring up a JRuby IRB interpreter that has had some HBase-specific commands added to it. Type help and then RETURN to see the list of shell commands that are available. The list is long. Each listed command includes an example of how its used. Commands use Ruby formatting, specifying lists and dictionaries. See the end of the help screen for a quick tutorial.

Now let us create a simple table, add some data, and then clean up.

To create a table, you must name your table and define its schema. A table's schema comprises table attributes and the list of table column families. Column families themselves have attributes that you in turn set at schema definition time. Examples of column family attributes include whether the family content should be compressed on the filesystem and how many versions of a cell to keep. Schemas can be later edited by offlining the table using the shell `disable` command, making the necessary alterations using `alter`, then putting the table back on line with `enable`.

To create a table named *test* with a single column family name *data* using defaults for table and column family attributes, enter:

```
hbase(main):007:0> create 'test', 'data'
0 row(s) in 4.3066 seconds
```

 If the previous command does not complete successfully, and the shell displays an error and a stack trace, your install was not successful. Check the master logs under the HBase *logs* directory for a clue as to where things went awry.

See the `help` output for examples adding table and column family attributes when specifying a schema.

‖ In standalone mode, HBase master and regionserver are both run in the same JVM.

To prove the new table was created successfully, run the `list` command. This will output all tables in the user space:

```
hbase(main):019:0> list
test
1 row(s) in 0.1485 seconds
```

To insert data into three different rows and columns in the *data* column family, and then list the table content, do the following:

```
hbase(main):021:0> put 'test', 'row1', 'data:1', 'value1'
0 row(s) in 0.0454 seconds
hbase(main):022:0> put 'test', 'row2', 'data:2', 'value2'
0 row(s) in 0.0035 seconds
hbase(main):023:0> put 'test', 'row3', 'data:3', 'value3'
0 row(s) in 0.0090 seconds
hbase(main):024:0> scan 'test'
ROW                     COLUMN+CELL
 row1                   column=data:1, timestamp=1240148026198, value=value1
 row2                   column=data:2, timestamp=1240148040035, value=value2
 row3                   column=data:3, timestamp=1240148047497, value=value3
3 row(s) in 0.0825 seconds
```

Notice how we added three new columns without changing the schema.#

To remove the table, you must first disable it before dropping it:

```
hbase(main):025:0> disable 'test'
09/04/19 06:40:13 INFO client.HBaseAdmin: Disabled test
0 row(s) in 6.0426 seconds
hbase(main):026:0> drop 'test'
09/04/19 06:40:17 INFO client.HBaseAdmin: Deleted test
0 row(s) in 0.0210 seconds
hbase(main):027:0> list
0 row(s) in 2.0645 seconds
```

Shut down your HBase instance by running:

```
% stop-hbase.sh
```

To learn how to set up a distributed HBase and point it at a running HDFS, see the Getting Started (*http://hadoop.apache.org/hbase/docs/current/api/overview-summary .html#overview_description*) section of the HBase documentation.

Clients

There are a number of client options for interacting with an HBase cluster.

To quickly load one million 1 k rows, run `PerformanceEvaluation` as shown here. This will launch a single client running the PerformanceEvaluation *sequentialWriter* script. It will create a table named *TestTable* with a single column family and then populate it. For more on the `PerformanceEvaluation` scripts, see the HBase wiki page on the subject (*http://wiki.apache.org/hadoop/Hbase/PerformanceEvaluation*).

```
% hbase org.apache.hadoop.hbase.PerformanceEvaluation sequentialWrite 1
```

Java

HBase, like Hadoop, is written in Java. Later in this chapter, in "Example" on page 354, there is sample code for uploading data to an HBase table and for reading and updating the uploaded data in HBase tables. In the case of the examples, where we are interacting with preexisting tables, we use the HBase `HTable` class as the gateway for fetching and updating HBase table instances. Administering your cluster (adding, enabling or dropping tables), you would use a different class, `HBaseAdmin`. Both of these classes are in the `org.apache.hadoop.hbase.client` package.

MapReduce

HBase classes and utilities in the `org.apache.hadoop.hbase.mapred` package facilitate using HBase as a source and/or sink in MapReduce jobs. The `TableInputFormat` class makes splits on region boundaries so maps are handed a single region to work on. The `TableOutputFormat` will write the result of reduce into HBase. The `RowCounter` class in Example 12-1 can be found in the HBase `mapred` package. It runs a map task to count rows using `TableInputFormat`.

Example 12-1. A MapReduce application to count the number of rows in an HBase table

```
public class RowCounter extends Configured implements Tool {
  // Name of this 'program'
  static final String NAME = "rowcounter";

  static class RowCounterMapper
  implements TableMap<ImmutableBytesWritable, RowResult> {
    private static enum Counters {ROWS}

    public void map(ImmutableBytesWritable row, RowResult value,
        OutputCollector<ImmutableBytesWritable, RowResult> output,
        Reporter reporter)
    throws IOException {
      boolean content = false;
      for (Map.Entry<byte [], Cell> e: value.entrySet()) {
        Cell cell = e.getValue();
        if (cell != null && cell.getValue().length > 0) {
          content = true;
          break;
        }
      }
      if (!content) {
        // Don't count rows that are all empty values.
        return;
      }
      // Give out same value every time.  We're only interested in the row/key
      reporter.incrCounter(Counters.ROWS, 1);
    }

    public void configure(JobConf jc) {
      // Nothing to do.
    }
```

```
  public void close() throws IOException {
    // Nothing to do.
  }
}

public JobConf createSubmittableJob(String[] args) throws IOException {
  JobConf c = new JobConf(getConf(), getClass());
  c.setJobName(NAME);
  // Columns are space delimited
  StringBuilder sb = new StringBuilder();
  final int columnoffset = 2;
  for (int i = columnoffset; i < args.length; i++) {
    if (i > columnoffset) {
      sb.append(" ");
    }
    sb.append(args[i]);
  }
  // Second argument is the table name.
  TableMapReduceUtil.initTableMapJob(args[1], sb.toString(),
    RowCounterMapper.class, ImmutableBytesWritable.class, RowResult.class, c);
  c.setNumReduceTasks(0);
  // First arg is the output directory.
  FileOutputFormat.setOutputPath(c, new Path(args[0]));
  return c;
}

static int printUsage() {
  System.out.println(NAME +
    " <outputdir> <tablename> <column1> [<column2>...]");
  return -1;
}

public int run(final String[] args) throws Exception {
  // Make sure there are at least 3 parameters
  if (args.length < 3) {
    System.err.println("ERROR: Wrong number of parameters: " + args.length);
    return printUsage();
  }
  JobClient.runJob(createSubmittableJob(args));
  return 0;
}

public static void main(String[] args) throws Exception {
  HBaseConfiguration c = new HBaseConfiguration();
  int errCode = ToolRunner.run(c, new RowCounter(), args);
  System.exit(errCode);
}
}
```

This class implements Tool, which is discussed in "GenericOptionsParser, Tool, and ToolRunner" on page 121, and the HBase TableMap interface, a specialization of org.apache.hadoop.mapred.Mapper that sets the map inputs types passed by TableInput Format. The createSubmittableJob() method parses arguments added to the configuration that were passed on the command line figuring the table and columns we are to run `RowCounter` against. It also invokes the `TableMapReduceUtil.initTableMapJob()` utility method, which among other things such as setting the map class to use, sets the input format to `TableInputFormat`. The map is simple. It checks all columns. If all are empty, it doesn't count the row. Otherwise, it increments `Counters.ROWS` by one.

REST and Thrift

HBase ships with REST and thrift interfaces. These are useful when the interacting application is written in a language other than Java. In both cases, a Java server hosts an instance of the HBase client brokering application REST and thrift requests in and out of the HBase cluster. This extra work proxying requests and responses means these interfaces are slower than using the Java client directly.

REST

To put up the REST, start it using the following command:

```
% hbase-daemon.sh start rest
```

This will start a server instance, by default on port 60050, background it, and catch any emissions by the server into a logfile under the HBase *logs* directory.

Clients can ask for the response to be formatted as JSON or as XML, depending on how the client *HTTP Accept* header is set. See the REST wiki page (*http://wiki.apache .org/hadoop/Hbase/HbaseRest*) for documentation and examples of making REST client requests.

To stop the REST server, type:

```
% hbase-daemon.sh stop rest
```

Thrift

Similarly, start a thrift service by putting up a server to field thrift clients by running the following:

```
% hbase-daemon.sh start thrift
```

This will start the server instance, by default on port 9090, background it, and catch any emissions by the server into a logfile under the HBase *logs* directory. The HBase thrift documentation[*] notes the thrift version used generating classes. The HBase thrift IDL can be found at *src/java/org/apache/hadoop/hbase/thrift/Hbase.thrift* in the HBase source code.

To stop the thrift server, type:

```
% hbase-daemon.sh stop thrift
```

---

[*] *http://hadoop.apache.org/hbase/docs/current/api/org/apache/hadoop/hbase/thrift/package-summary.html*

Example

Although HDFS and MapReduce are powerful tools for processing batch operations over large datasets, they do not provide ways to read or write individual records efficiently. In this example, we'll explore HBase as the tool to fill this gap.

The existing weather dataset described in previous chapters contains observations for tens of thousands of stations over 100 years and this data is growing without bound. In this example, we will build a simple web interface that allows a user to navigate the different stations and page through their historical temperature observations in time order. For the sake of this example, let us allow that the dataset is massive, that the observations run to the billions, and that the rate at which temperature updates arrive is significant—say hundreds to thousands of updates a second from around the world across the whole range of weather stations. Also let us allow that it is a requirement that the web application must display the most up-to-date observation within a second or so of receipt.

The first size requirement should preclude our use of a simple RDBMS instance and make HBase a candidate store. The second latency requirement rules out plain HDFS. A MapReduce job could build initial indices that allowed random-access over all of the observation data but keeping up this index as the updates arrived is not what HDFS and MapReduce are good at.

Schemas

In our example, there will be two tables:

Stations
> This table holds station data. Let the row key be the `stationid`. Let this table have a column family *info* that acts as a key/val dictionary for station information. Let the keys be name, location, and description. This table is static and the *info* family, in this case, closely mirrors a typical RDBMS table design.

Observations
> This table holds temperature observations. Let the row key be a composite key of `stationid` + reverse order timestamp. Give this table a column family `data` that will contain one column `airtemp` with the observed temperature as the column value.

Our choice of schema is derived from how we want to most efficiently read from HBase. Rows and columns are stored in increasing lexicographical order. Though there are facilities for secondary indexing and regular expression matching, they come at a performance penalty.[†] It is vital that you understand how you want to most efficiently query your data in order to most effectively store and access it.

[†] The bundled HBase secondary index mechanism make use of TransactionalHBase, which is powerful but not performant. If you need good performance, it is recommended, for now, that you manage your own secondary index tables or make use of an external index implementation like Lucene.

For the stations table, the choice of stationid as key is obvious because we will always access information for a particular station by its id. The observations table, however, uses a composite key that adds the observation timestamp at the end. This will group all observations for a particular station together, and by using a reverse order timestamp (Long.MAX_VALUE - epoch) and storing it as binary, observations for each station will be ordered with most recent observation first.

In the shell, you would define your tables as follows:

```
hbase(main):036:0> create 'stations', {NAME => 'info', VERSIONS => 1}
0 row(s) in 0.1304 seconds
hbase(main):037:0> create 'observations', {NAME => 'data', VERSIONS => 1}
0 row(s) in 0.1332 seconds
```

In both cases, we are interested only in the latest version of a table cell, so set VERSIONS to 1.

Loading Data

There are a relatively small number of stations, so their static data is easily inserted using any of the available interfaces.

However, let's assume that there are billions of individual observations to be loaded. This kind of import is normally an extremely complex and long-running database operation, but MapReduce and HBase's distribution model allow us to make full use of the cluster. Copy the raw input data onto HDFS and then run a MapReduce job that can read the input and write to HBase, eventually reading from and writing to all nodes. At the beginning, as the import runs, your table will have only one region, so writes will go to only one server. As the import progresses and tables split, regions will be distributed across the cluster along with your writes.

Example 12-2 shows an example MapReduce job that imports observations to HBase from the same input file used in the previous chapters' examples.

Example 12-2. A MapReduce application to import temperature data from HDFS into an HBase table

```
public class HBaseTemperatureImporter extends Configured implements Tool {

  // Inner-class for map
  static class HBaseTemperatureMapper<K, V> extends MapReduceBase implements
      Mapper<LongWritable, Text, K, V> {
    private NcdcRecordParser parser = new NcdcRecordParser();
    private HTable table;

    public void map(LongWritable key, Text value,
        OutputCollector<K, V> output, Reporter reporter)
      throws IOException {
      parser.parse(value.toString());
      if (parser.isValidTemperature()) {
        byte[] rowKey = RowKeyConverter.makeObservationRowKey(parser.getStationId(),
          parser.getObservationDate().getTime());
```

Example | 355

```
        BatchUpdate bu = new BatchUpdate(rowKey);
        bu.put("data:airtemp", Bytes.toBytes(parser.getAirTemperature()));
        table.commit(bu);
      }
    }

    public void configure(JobConf jc) {
      super.configure(jc);
      // Create the HBase table client once up-front and keep it around
      // rather than create on each map invocation.
      try {
        this.table = new HTable(new HBaseConfiguration(jc), "observations");
      } catch (IOException e) {
        throw new RuntimeException("Failed HTable construction", e);
      }
    }
  }

  public int run(String[] args) throws IOException {
    if (args.length != 1) {
      System.err.println("Usage: HBaseTemperatureImporter <input>");
      return -1;
    }
    JobConf jc = new JobConf(getConf(), getClass());
    FileInputFormat.addInputPath(jc, new Path(args[0]));
    jc.setMapperClass(HBaseTemperatureMapper.class);
    jc.setNumReduceTasks(0);
    jc.setOutputFormat(NullOutputFormat.class);
    JobClient.runJob(jc);
    return 0;
  }

  public static void main(String[] args) throws Exception {
    int exitCode = ToolRunner.run(new HBaseConfiguration(),
        new HBaseTemperatureImporter(), args);
    System.exit(exitCode);
  }
}
```

HBaseTemperatureImporter has an inner class named HBaseTemperatureMapper that is like the MaxTemperatureMapper class from Chapter 5. The outer class implements Tool and does the setup to launch the HBaseTemperatureMapper inner class. HBaseTemperatureMapper takes the same input as MaxTemperatureMapper and does the same parse—using the NcdcRecordParser introduced in Chapter 5—to check for valid temperatures, but rather than add valid temperatures to the output collector as MaxTemperatureMapper does, instead it adds valid temperatures to the observations HBase table into the *data:airtemp* column. In the configure() method, we create an HTable instance once against the observations table and use it afterward in map invocations talking to HBase.

The row key used is created in the makeObservationRowKey() method on RowKey Converter from the station ID and observation time:

```
public class RowKeyConverter {

  private static final int STATION_ID_LENGTH = 12;

  /**
   * @return A row key whose format is: <station_id> <reverse_order_epoch>
   */
  public static byte[] makeObservationRowKey(String stationId,
      long observationTime) {
    byte[] row = new byte[STATION_ID_LENGTH + Bytes.SIZEOF_LONG];
    Bytes.putBytes(row, 0, Bytes.toBytes(stationId), 0, STATION_ID_LENGTH);
    long reverseOrderEpoch = Long.MAX_VALUE - observationTime;
    Bytes.putLong(row, STATION_ID_LENGTH, reverseOrderEpoch);
    return row;
  }

}
```

The conversion takes advantage of the fact that the station ID is a fixed-length string. The `Bytes` class used in `makeObservationRowKey()` is from the HBase utility package. It includes methods for converting between byte arrays and common Java and Hadoop types. In `makeObservationRowKey()`, the `Bytes.putLong()` method is used to fill the key byte array. The `Bytes.SIZEOF_LONG` constant is used for sizing and positioning in the row key array.

We can run the program with the following:

```
% hbase HBaseTemperatureImporter input/ncdc/all
```

Optimization notes

- Watch for the phenomenon where the import walks in lock-step through the table with all clients in concert pounding one of the table's regions (and thus, a single node), then moving on to the next, and so on, rather than evenly distributing the load over all regions. This is usually brought on by some interaction between sorted input and how the splitter works. Randomizing the ordering of your row keys prior to insertion may help. In our example, given the distribution of **stationid** values and how `TextInputFormat` makes splits, the upload should be sufficiently distributed.[‡]

- Only obtain one `HTable` instance per task. There is a cost instantiating an `HTable`, so if you do this for each insert, you may have a negative impact on performance. Hence our setup of `HTable` in the `configure()` step.

[‡] If a table is new, it will have only one region and initially all updates will be to this single region until it splits. This will happen even if row keys are randomly distributed. This startup phenomenon means uploads run slow at first until there are sufficient regions distributed so all cluster members are able to participate in the upload. Do not confuse this phenomenon with that of the one described earlier.

Example | 357

- By default, each `HTable.commit(BatchUpdate)` actually performs the insert without any buffering. You can disable HTable auto-flush feature using `HTable.setAuto Flush(false)` and then set the size of configurable write buffer. When the inserts committed fill the write buffer, it is then flushed. Remember though, you must call a manual `HTable.flushCommits()` at the end of each task to ensure that nothing is left unflushed in the buffer. You could do this in an override of the mapper's `close()` method.

- HBase includes `TableInputFormat` and `TableOutputFormat` to help with MapReduce jobs that source and sink HBase (see Example 12-1). One way to write the previous example would have been to use `MaxTemperatureMapper` from Chapter 5 as is but add a reducer task that takes the output of the `MaxTemperatureMapper` and feeds it to HBase via `TableOutputFormat`.

Web Queries

To implement the web application, we will use the HBase Java API directly. Here it becomes clear how important your choice of schema and storage format is.

The simplest query will be to get the static station information. This type of query is simple in a traditional database, but HBase gives you additional control and flexibility. Using the `info` family as a key/value dictionary (column names as keys, column values as values), the code would look like this:

```
public Map<String, String> getStationInfo(HTable table, String stationId)
    throws IOException {
  byte[][] columns = { Bytes.toBytes("info:") };
  RowResult res = table.getRow(Bytes.toBytes(stationId), columns);
  if (res == null) {
    return null;
  }
  Map<String, String> resultMap = new HashMap<String, String>();
  resultMap.put("name", getValue(res, "info:name"));
  resultMap.put("location", getValue(res, "info:location"));
  resultMap.put("description", getValue(res, "info:description"));
  return resultMap;
}

private static String getValue(RowResult res, String key) {
  Cell c = res.get(key.getBytes());
  if (c == null) {
    return "";
  }
  return Bytes.toString(c.getValue());
}
```

In this example, getStationInfo() takes an HTable instance and a station ID. To get the station info, we use HTable.getRow(). Use this method when fetching more than one column from a row. Passing a column family name info: rather than explicit column names will return all columns on that family.§ The getRow() results are returned in RowResult, an implementation of SortedMap with the row key as a data member. It is keyed by the column name as a byte array. Values are Cell data structures that hold a timestamp and the cell content in a byte array. The getStationInfo() method converts the RowResult Map into a more friendly Map of String keys and values.

We can already see how there is a need for utility functions when using HBase. There are an increasing number of abstractions being built atop HBase to deal with this low-level interaction, but it's important to understand how this works and how storage choices make a difference.

One of the strengths of HBase over a relational database is that you don't have to prespecify the columns. So, in the future, if each station now has at least these three attributes but there are hundreds of optional ones, we can just insert them without modifying the schema. Your applications reading and writing code would of course need to be changed. The example code might change in this case to looping through RowResult.entrySet() rather than explicitly grabbing each value from the RowResult.

We will make use of HBase scanners for retrieval of observations in our web application.

Here we are after a Map<ObservationTime, ObservedTemp> result. We will use a NavigableMap<Long, Integer> because it is sorted and has a descendingMap() method, so we can access observations in both ascending or descending order. The code is in Example 12-3.

Example 12-3. Methods for retrieving a range of rows of weather station observations from an HBase table

```
public NavigableMap<Long, Integer> getStationObservations(HTable table,
    String stationId, long maxStamp, int maxCount) throws IOException {
  byte[][] columns = { Bytes.toBytes("data:airtemp") };
  byte[] startRow = RowKeyConverter.makeObservationRowKey(stationId, maxStamp);
  RowResult res = null;
  NavigableMap<Long, Integer> resultMap = new TreeMap<Long, Integer>();
  byte[] airtempColumn = Bytes.toBytes("data:airtemp");
  Scanner s = table.getScanner(columns, startRow);
  int count = 0;
  try {
    while ((res = s.next()) != null && count++ < maxCount) {
      byte[] row = res.getRow();
      byte[] value = res.get(airtempColumn).getValue();
      Long stamp = Long.MAX_VALUE -
        Bytes.toLong(row, row.length - Bytes.SIZEOF_LONG, Bytes.SIZEOF_LONG);
```

---

§ A column name without a qualifier designates a column family. The colon is required. If you pass info only for column family name, rather than info:, HBase will complain the column name is incorrectly formatted.

Example | 359

```
      Integer temp = Bytes.toInt(value);
      resultMap.put(stamp, temp);
    }
  } finally {
    s.close();
  }
  return resultMap;
}

/**
 * Return the last ten observations.
 */
public NavigableMap<Long, Integer> getStationObservations(HTable table,
    String stationId) throws IOException {
  return getStationObservations(table, stationId, Long.MAX_VALUE, 10);
}
```

The getStationObservations() method takes a station ID and a range defined by max
Stamp and a maximum number of rows (maxCount). Note that the NavigableMap that is
returned is actually now in descending time order. If you want to read through it in
ascending order, you would make use of NavigableMap.descendingMap().

The advantage of storing things as Long.MAX_VALUE - stamp may not be clear in the
previous example. It has more use when you want to get the newest observations for a
given offset and limit, which is often the case in web applications. If the observations
were stored with the actual stamps, we would be able to get only the oldest observations
for a given offset and limit efficiently. Getting the newest would mean getting all of
them, and then grabbing them off the end. One of the prime reasons for moving from
RDBMS to HBase is to allow for these types of "early-out" scenarios.

Scanners

HBase scanners are like cursors in a traditional database or Java iterators, except—
unlike the latter—they have to be closed after use. Scanners return rows in order. Users
obtain a scanner on an HBase table by calling HTable.getScanner(). A number of overloaded variants allow the user to pass a row at which to start the scanner, a row at which
to stop the scanner on, which columns in a row to return in the row result, and op-
tionally, a filter to run on the server side.[||] The Scanner interface absent Javadoc is as
follows:

```
public interface Scanner extends Closeable, Iterable<RowResult> {
  public RowResult next() throws IOException;
  public RowResult [] next(int nbRows) throws IOException;
  public void close();
}
```

[||] To learn more about the server-side filtering mechanism in HBase, see *http://hadoop.apache.org/hbase/
docs/current/api/org/apache/hadoop/hbase/filter/package-summary.html*.

You can ask for the next row's results or a number of rows. Each invocation of next() involves a trip back to the regionserver, so grabbing a bunch of rows at once can make for significant performance savings.[#]

HBase Versus RDBMS

HBase and other column-oriented databases are often compared to more traditional and popular relational databases or RDBMSs. Although they differ dramatically in their implementations and in what they set out to accomplish, the fact that they are potential solutions to the same problems means that despite their enormous differences, the comparison is a fair one to make.

As described previously, HBase is a distributed, column-oriented data storage system. It picks up where Hadoop left off by providing random reads and writes on top of HDFS. It has been designed from the ground up with a focus on scale in every direction: tall in numbers of rows (billions), wide in numbers of columns (millions), and to be horizontally partitioned and replicated across thousands of commodity nodes automatically. The table schemas mirror the physical storage, creating a system for efficient data structure serialization, storage, and retrieval. The burden is on the application developer to make use of this storage and retrieval in the right way.

Strictly speaking, an RDBMS is a database that follows Codd's 12 Rules (*http://en.wikipedia.org/wiki/Codd%27s_12_rules*). Typical RDBMSs are fixed-schema, row-oriented databases with ACID properties and a sophisticated SQL query engine. The emphasis is on strong consistency, referential integrity, abstraction from the physical layer, and complex queries through the SQL language. You can easily create secondary indexes, perform complex inner and outer joins, count, sum, sort, group, and page your data across a number of tables, rows, and columns.

For a majority of small- to medium-volume applications, there is no substitute for the ease of use, flexibility, maturity, and powerful feature set of available open source RDBMS solutions like MySQL and PostgreSQL. However, if you need to scale up in terms of dataset size, read/write concurrency, or both, you'll soon find that the conveniences of an RDBMS come at an enormous performance penalty and make distribution inherently difficult. The scaling of an RDBMS usually involves breaking Codd's rules, loosening ACID restrictions, forgetting conventional DBA wisdom, and on the way losing most of the desirable properties that made relational databases so convenient in the first place.

[#] The hbase.client.scanner.caching configuration option is set to 1 by default. Scanners will, under the covers, fetch this many results at a time, bringing them client side, and returning to the server to fetch the next batch only after the current batch has been exhausted. Higher caching values will enable faster scanning but will eat up more memory in the client.

Successful Service

Here is a synopsis of how the typical RDBMS scaling story runs. The following list presumes a successful growing service:

Initial public launch
> Move from local workstation to shared, remote hosted MySQL instance with a well-defined schema.

Service becomes more popular; too many reads hitting the database
> Add memcached to cache common queries. Reads are now no longer strictly ACID; cached data must expire.

Service continues to grow in popularity; too many writes hitting the database
> Scale MySQL vertically by buying a beefed up server with 16 cores, 128 GB of RAM, and banks of 15 k RPM hard drives. Costly.

New features increases query complexity; now we have too many joins
> Denormalize your data to reduce joins. (That's not what they taught me in DBA school!)

Rising popularity swamps the server; things are too slow
> Stop doing any server-side computations.

Some queries are still too slow
> Periodically prematerialize the most complex queries, try to stop joining in most cases.

Reads are OK, but writes are getting slower and slower
> Drop secondary indexes and triggers (no indexes?).

At this point, there are no clear solutions for how to solve your scaling problems. In any case, you'll need to begin to scale horizontally. You can attempt to build some type of partitioning on your largest tables, or look into some of the commercial solutions that provide multiple master capabilities.

Countless applications, businesses, and websites have successfully achieved scalable, fault-tolerant, and distributed data systems built on top of RDBMSs and are likely using many of the previous strategies. But what you end up with is something that is no longer a true RDBMS, sacrificing features and conveniences for compromises and complexities. Any form of slave replication or external caching introduces weak consistency into your now denormalized data. The inefficiency of joins and secondary indexes means almost all queries become primary key lookups. A multiwriter setup likely means no real joins at all and distributed transactions are a nightmare. There's now an incredibly complex network topology to manage with an entirely separate cluster for caching. Even with this system and the compromises made, you will still worry about your primary master crashing and the daunting possibility of having 10 times the data and 10 times the load in a few months.

HBase

Enter HBase, which has the following characteristics:

No real indexes
> Rows are stored sequentially, as are the columns within each row. Therefore, no issues with index bloat, and insert performance is independent of table size.

Automatic partitioning
> As your tables grow, they will automatically be split into regions and distributed across all available nodes.

Scale linearly and automatically with new nodes
> Add a node, point it to the existing cluster, and run the regionserver. Regions will automatically rebalance and load will spread evenly.

Commodity hardware
> Clusters are built on $1,000–$5,000 nodes rather than $50,000 nodes. RDBMS are hungry I/O, which is the most costly type of hardware.

Fault tolerance
> Lots of nodes means each is relatively insignificant. No need to worry about individual node downtime.

Batch processing
> MapReduce integration allows fully parallel, distributed jobs against your data with locality awareness.

If you stay up at night worrying about your database (uptime, scale, or speed), then you should seriously consider making a jump from the RDBMS world to HBase. Utilize a solution that was intended to scale rather than a solution based on stripping down and throwing money at what used to work. With HBase, the software is free, the hardware is cheap, the distribution is intrinsic, and there are no black boxes to step on your toes.

Use Case: HBase at streamy.com

Streamy.com is a real-time news aggregator and social sharing platform. With a broad feature set, we started out with a complex implementation on top of PostgreSQL. It's a terrific product with a great community and a beautiful codebase. We tried every trick in the book to keep things fast as we scaled, going so far as to modify the code directly to suit our needs. Originally taking advantage of all RDBMS goodies, we found that eventually, one by one, we had to let them all go. Along the way, our entire team became the DBA.

We did manage to solve many of the issues that we ran into, but there were two that eventually led to the decision to find another solution from outside the world of RDBMS.

Streamy crawls thousands of RSS feeds and aggregates hundreds of millions of items from them. In addition to having to store these items, one of our more complex queries reads a time-ordered list of all items from a set of sources. At the high end, this can run to several thousand sources and all of their items all in a single query.

Very large items tables

At first, this was a single items table, but the high number of secondary indexes made inserts and updates very slow. We started to divide items up into several one-to-one link tables to store other information, separating static fields from dynamic ones, grouping fields based on how they were queried, and denormalizing everything along the way. Even with these changes, single updates required rewriting the entire record, so tracking statistics on items was difficult to scale. The rewriting of records and having to update indexes along the way are intrinsic properties of the RDBMS we were using. They could not be decoupled. We partitioned our tables, which was not too difficult because of the natural partition of time, but the complexity got out of hand fast. We needed another solution!

Very large sort merges

Performing sorted merges of time-ordered lists is common in many Web 2.0 applications. An example SQL query might look like this:

```
SELECT id, stamp, type FROM streams
  WHERE type IN ('type1','type2','type3','type4',...,'typeN')
  ORDER BY stamp DESC LIMIT 10 OFFSET 0;
```

Assuming id is a primary key on streams, and that stamp and type have secondary indexes, an RDBMS query planner treats this query as follows:

```
MERGE (
  SELECT id, stamp, type FROM streams
    WHERE type = 'type1' ORDER BY stamp DESC,
  ...,
  SELECT id, stamp, type FROM streams
    WHERE type = 'typeN' ORDER BY stamp DESC
) ORDER BY stamp DESC LIMIT 10 OFFSET 0;
```

The problem here is that we are after only the top 10 IDs, but the query planner actually materializes an entire merge and then limits at the end. A simple heapsort across each of the types would allow you to "early out" once you have the top 10. In our case, each type could have tens of thousands of IDs in it, so materializing the entire list and sorting it was extremely slow and unnecessary. We actually went so far as to write a custom PL/Python script that performed a heapsort using a series of queries like the following:

```
SELECT id, stamp, type FROM streams
  WHERE type = 'typeN'
  ORDER BY stamp DESC LIMIT 1 OFFSET 0;
```

If we ended up taking from typeN (it was the next most recent in the heap), we would run another query:

```
SELECT id, stamp, type FROM streams
  WHERE type = 'typeN'
  ORDER BY stamp DESC LIMIT 1 OFFSET 1;
```

In nearly all cases, this outperformed the native SQL implementation and the query planner's strategy. In the worst cases for SQL, we were more than an order of magnitude faster using the Python procedure. We found ourselves continually trying to outsmart the query planner.

Again, at this point, we really needed another solution.

Life with HBase

Our RDBMS-based system was always capable of correctly implementing our requirements; the issue was scaling. When you start to focus on scale and performance rather than correctness, you end up short-cutting and optimizing for your domain-specific use cases everywhere possible. Once you start implementing your own solutions to your data problems, the overhead and complexity of an RDBMS gets in your way. The abstraction from the storage layer and ACID requirements are an enormous barrier and luxury that you cannot always afford when building for scale. HBase is a distributed, column-oriented, sorted map store and not much else. The only major part that is abstracted from the user is the distribution, and that's exactly what we don't want to deal with. Business logic, on the other hand, is very specialized and optimized. With HBase not trying to solve all of our problems, we've been able to solve them better ourselves and rely on HBase for scaling our storage, not our logic. It was an extremely liberating experience to be able to focus on our applications and logic rather than the scaling of the data itself.

We currently have tables with hundreds of millions of rows and tens of thousands of columns; the thought of storing billions of rows and millions of columns is exciting, not scary.

Praxis

In this section, we discuss some of the common issues users run into running an HBase instance that moves beyond basic examples.

Versions

First, ensure you are running compatible versions of Hadoop and HBase. Compatible versions have their major and minor version numbers in common. Although an HBase 0.18.0 cannot talk to an Hadoop 0.19.0 version cluster—they disagree in their minor numbers—an HBase 0.19.2 can run on a Hadoop 0.19.1 HDFS. Incompatible versions will throw an exception complaining about the version mismatch, if you are lucky. If they cannot talk to each sufficiently to pass versions, you may see your HBase cluster hang indefinitely, soon after startup. The mismatch exception or HBase hang can also happen on upgrade if older versions of either HBase or Hadoop can still be found on the CLASSPATH because of imperfect cleanup of the old software.

Love and Hate: HBase and HDFS

HBase's use of HDFS is very different from how its used by MapReduce. In MapReduce, generally, HDFS files are opened, their content streamed through a map task and then closed. In HBase, data files are opened on cluster startup and kept open so that we avoid paying the file open costs on each access. Because of this, HBase tends to see issues not normally encountered by MapReduce clients:

Running out of file descriptors

Because we keep files open, on a loaded cluster, it doesn't take long before we run into system- and Hadoop-imposed limits. For instance, say we have a cluster that has three nodes each running an instance of a datanode and a regionserver and we're running an upload into a table that is currently at 100 regions and 10 column families. Allow that each column family has on average two flush files. Doing the math, we can have $100 \times 10 \times 2$, or 2,000, files open at any one time. Add to this total miscellaneous other descriptors consumed by outstanding scanners, Java libraries. Each open file consumes at least one descriptor over on the remote datanode. The default limit on the number of file descriptors per process is 1024. When we exceed the filesystem *ulimit*, we'll see the complaint about *Too many open files* in logs but often you'll first see indeterminate behavior in HBase. The fix requires increasing the file descriptor *ulimit* count.[*] You can verify that the HBase process is running with sufficient file descriptors by looking at the first few lines of a regionservers log. It emits vitals on such as the JVM being used and environment settings such as the file descriptor *ulimit*.

Running out of datanode threads

Similarly, the Hadoop datanode has an upper bound of 256 on the number of threads it can run at any one time. Given the same table statistics quoted in the preceding bullet, it's easy to see how we can exceed this upper bound relatively early, given that in the datanode as of this writing each open connection to a file block consumes a thread.[†] If you look in the datanode log, you'll see a complaint like *xceiverCount 258 exceeds the limit of concurrent xcievers 256* but again, you'll likely see HBase act erratically before you encounter this log entry. Increase the `dfs.datanode.max.xcievers` (note that the property name is misspelled) count in HDFS and restart your cluster.[‡]

---

[*] See the HBase FAQ (*http://wiki.apache.org/hadoop/Hbase/FAQ*) for how to up the *ulimit* on your cluster.

[†] See HADOOP-3856 Asynchronous IO Handling in Hadoop and HDFS (*https://issues.apache.org/jira/browse/HADOOP-3856*).

[‡] See the HBase troubleshooting guide (*http://wiki.apache.org/hadoop/Hbase/Troubleshooting*) for more detail on this issue.

Bad blocks

The DFSClient hosted in your long-running regionserver will tend to mark file blocks as bad if, on an access, the server is currently heavily loaded. Since blocks by default are replicated three times, the regionserver DFSClient will move on to the next replica. But if this replica is accessed during a time of heavy loading, we now have two of the three blocks marked as bad. If the third block is found to be bad, we start see complaint *No live nodes contain current block* in regionserver logs. During startup, there is lots of churn and contention as regions are opened and deployed. During this time, the *No live nodes contain current block* can come on quickly. At an extreme, set `dfs.datanode.socket.write.timeout` to zero. Note that this configuration needs to be set in a location that can be seen by the HBase DFSClient; set it in the *hbase-site.xml* or by symlinking the *hadoop-site.xml* (or *hdfs-site.xml* in recent versions) into your HBase *conf* directory.[§]

UI

HBase runs a web server on the master to present a view on the state of your running cluster. By default, it listens on port 60010. The master UI displays a list of basic attributes such as software versions, cluster load, request rates, lists of cluster tables and participating regionservers. Click on a regionserver in the master UI and you are taken to the web server running on the individual regionserver. It lists the regions this server is carrying and basic metrics such as resources consumed and request rates.

Metrics

Hadoop has a metrics system that can be used emitting vitals over a period to a *context* (this is covered in "Metrics" on page 286). Enabling Hadoop metrics, and in particular tying them to Ganglia, helps the development of view on what is happening on your cluster currently and in the recent past. HBase also adds metrics of its own—request rates, counts of vitals, resources used—that can be caught by a Hadoop context. See the file *hadoop-metrics.properties* under the HBase *conf* directory.[||]

Schema Design

HBase tables are like those in an RDBMS, except that cells are versioned, rows are sorted, and columns can be added on the fly by the client as long as the column family they belong to preexists. The following factors should be considered when designing schemas for HBase. The other property to keep in mind when designing schemas is that a defining attribute of column(-family)-oriented stores (*http://en.wikipedia.org/*

[§] Again, see the HBase troubleshooting guide (*http://wiki.apache.org/hadoop/Hbase/Troubleshooting*) for more detail on this issue.

[||] Yes, this file named for Hadoop, though it's for setting up HBase metrics.

wiki/Column-oriented_DBMS), like HBase, is that it can host wide and sparsely populated tables at no incurred cost.#

Joins

There is no native database join facility in HBase, but wide tables can make it so that there is no need for database joins pulling from secondary or tertiary tables. A wide row can sometimes be made to hold all data that pertains to a particular primary key.

Row keys

Take time designing your row key. In the weather data example in this chapter, the compound row key has a station prefix that served to group temperatures by station. The reversed timestamp suffix made it so temperatures could be scanned ordered from most recent to oldest. A smart compound key can be used clustering data in ways amenable to how it will be accessed.

Designing compound keys, you may have to zero-pad number components so row keys sort properly. Otherwise, you will run into the issue where 10 sorts before 2 when only byte-order is considered (02 sorts before 10).

If your keys are integers, use a binary representation rather than persist the string version of a number—it consumes less space.

"Column-Stores for Wide and Sparse Data" (*http://db.csail.mit.edu/projects/cstore/abadicidr07.pdf*) by Daniel J. Abadi.

ZooKeeper

So far in this book, we have been studying large-scale data processing. This chapter is different: it is about building general distributed applications using Hadoop's distributed coordination service, called ZooKeeper.

Writing distributed applications is hard. It's hard primarily because of partial failure. When a message is sent across the network between two nodes and the network fails, the sender does not know whether the receiver got the message. It may have gotten through before the network failed, or it may not have. Or perhaps the receiver's process died. The only way that the sender can find out what happened is to reconnect to the receiver and ask it. This is partial failure: when we don't even know if an operation failed.

ZooKeeper can't make partial failures go away, since they are intrinsic to distributed systems. It certainly does not hide partial failures, either.[*] But what ZooKeeper does do is give you a set of tools to build distributed applications that can safely handle partial failures.

ZooKeeper also has the following characteristics:

ZooKeeper is simple
> ZooKeeper is, at its core, a stripped-down filesystem that exposes a few simple operations, and some extra abstractions such as ordering and notifications.

ZooKeeper is expressive
> The ZooKeeper primitives are a rich set of building blocks that can be used to build a large class of coordination data structures and protocols. Examples include: distributed queues, distributed locks, and leader election among a group of peers.

---

[*] This is the message of J. Waldo et al., "A Note on Distributed Computing," (1994), *http://research.sun.com/techrep/1994/smli_tr-94-29.pdf*. That is, distributed programming is fundamentally different from local programming, and the differences cannot simply be papered over.

ZooKeeper is highly available

ZooKeeper runs on a collection of machines and is designed to be highly available, so applications can depend on it. ZooKeeper can help you avoid introducing single points of failure into your system, so you can build a reliable application.

ZooKeeper facilitates loosely coupled interactions

ZooKeeper interactions support participants that do not need to know about one another. For example, ZooKeeper can be used as a rendezvous mechanism so that processes that otherwise don't know of each other's existence (or network details) can discover each other and interact. Coordinating parties may not even be contemporaneous, since one process may leave a message in ZooKeeper that is read by another after the first has shut down.

ZooKeeper is a library

ZooKeeper provides an open source, shared repository of implementations and recipes of common coordination patterns. Individual programmers are spared the burden of writing common protocols themselves (which are often difficult to get right). Over time the community can add to, and improve, the libraries, which is to everyone's benefit.

ZooKeeper is highly performant, too. At Yahoo!, where it was created, ZooKeeper's throughput has been benchmarked at approximately 10,000 operations per second for write-dominant workloads. For workloads where reads dominate, which is the norm, the throughput is several times higher.

Installing and Running ZooKeeper

When trying out ZooKeeper for the first time, it's simplest to run it in standalone mode with a single ZooKeeper server. You can do this on a development machine, for example. ZooKeeper requires Java 6 to run, so make sure you have it installed first. If you are running ZooKeeper on Windows (Windows is supported only as a development platform, not as a production platform), you need to install Cygwin, too.

Download a stable release of ZooKeeper from the Apache ZooKeeper releases page at *http://hadoop.apache.org/zookeeper/releases.html*, and unpack the tarball in a suitable location:

```
% tar xzf zookeeper-x.y.z.tar.gz
```

ZooKeeper provides a few binaries to run and interact with the service, and it's convenient to put the directory containing the binaries on your command-line path:

```
% export ZOOKEEPER_INSTALL=/home/tom/zookeeper-x.y.z
% export PATH=$PATH:$ZOOKEEPER_INSTALL/bin
```

Before running the ZooKeeper service, we need to set up a configuration file. The configuration file is conventionally called *zoo.cfg* and placed in the *conf* subdirectory (although you can also place it in */etc/zookeeper*, or in the directory defined by the `ZOOCFGDIR` environment variable, if set). Here's an example:

```
tickTime=2000
dataDir=/Users/tom/zookeeper
clientPort=2181
```

This is a standard Java properties file, and the three properties defined in this example are the minimum required for running ZooKeeper in standalone mode. Briefly, `tickTime` is the basic time unit in ZooKeeper (specified in milliseconds), `dataDir` is the local filesystem location where ZooKeeper stores persistent data, and `clientPort` is the port the ZooKeeper listens on for client connections (2181 is a common choice). You should change `dataDir` to an appropriate setting for your system.

With a suitable configuration defined, we are now ready to start a local ZooKeeper server:

```
% zkServer.sh start
```

To check whether ZooKeeper is running, send the `ruok` command ("Are you OK?") to the client port using `nc` (`telnet` works, too):

```
% echo ruok | nc localhost 2181
imok
```

That's ZooKeeper saying "I'm OK." There are other commands, known as the "four-letter words," for interacting with ZooKeeper. Most are queries: `dump` lists sessions and ephemeral znodes, `envi` lists server properties, `reqs` lists outstanding requests, and `stat` lists service statistics and connected clients. However, you can also update Zoo-Keeper's state: `srst` resets the service statistics, and `kill` shuts down ZooKeeper if issued from the host running the ZooKeeper server.

For more extensive ZooKeeper monitoring, have a look at its JMX support, which is covered in the ZooKeeper documentation (linked from *http://hadoop.apache.org/zoo keeper/*).

An Example

Imagine a group of servers that provide some service to clients. We want clients to be able to locate one of the servers, so they can use the service. One of the challenges is maintaining the list of servers in the group.

The membership list clearly cannot be stored on a single node in the network, as the failure of that node would mean the failure of the whole system (we would like the list to be highly available). Suppose for a moment that we had a robust way of storing the list. We would still have the problem of how to remove a server from the list if it failed. Some process needs to be responsible for removing failed servers, but note that it can't be the servers themselves, since they are no longer running!

What we are describing is not a passive distributed data structure, but an active one, and one that can change the state of an entry when some external event occurs. Zoo-Keeper provides this service, so let's see how to build this group membership application (as it is known) with it.

Group Membership in ZooKeeper

One way of understanding ZooKeeper is to think of it as providing a high-availability filesystem. It doesn't have files and directories, but a unified concept of a node, called a *znode*, which acts both as a container of data (like a file) and a container of other znodes (like a directory). Znodes form a hierarchical namespace, and a natural way to build a membership list is to create a parent znode with the name of the group, and child znodes with the name of the group members (servers). This is shown in Figure 13-1.

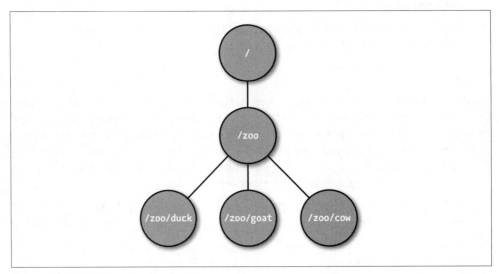

Figure 13-1. ZooKeeper znodes

In this example, we won't store data in any of the znodes, but in a real application, you could imagine storing data about the members in their znodes, such as hostname.

Creating the Group

Let's introduce ZooKeeper's Java API by writing a program to create a znode for the group, */zoo* in this example. See Example 13-1.

Example 13-1. A program to create a znode representing a group in ZooKeeper

```
public class CreateGroup implements Watcher {
```

```java
private static final int SESSION_TIMEOUT = 5000;

private ZooKeeper zk;
private CountDownLatch connectedSignal = new CountDownLatch(1);

public void connect(String hosts) throws IOException, InterruptedException {
  zk = new ZooKeeper(hosts, SESSION_TIMEOUT, this);
  connectedSignal.await();
}

@Override
public void process(WatchedEvent event) { // Watcher interface
  if (event.getState() == KeeperState.SyncConnected) {
    connectedSignal.countDown();
  }
}

public void create(String groupName) throws KeeperException,
    InterruptedException {
  String path = "/" + groupName;
  String createdPath = zk.create(path, null/*data*/, Ids.OPEN_ACL_UNSAFE,
      CreateMode.PERSISTENT);
  System.out.println("Created " + createdPath);
}

public void close() throws InterruptedException {
  zk.close();
}

public static void main(String[] args) throws Exception {
  CreateGroup createGroup = new CreateGroup();
  createGroup.connect(args[0]);
  createGroup.create(args[1]);
  createGroup.close();
}
}
```

When the main() method is run, it creates a CreateGroup instance and then calls its connect() method. This method instantiates a new ZooKeeper object, the main class of the client API and the one that maintains the connection between the client and the ZooKeeper service. The constructor takes three arguments: the first is the host address (and optional port, which defaults to 2181) of the ZooKeeper service;[†] the second is the session timeout in milliseconds (which we set to 5 seconds), explained in more detail later; and the third is an instance of a Watcher object. The Watcher object receives callbacks from ZooKeeper to inform it of various events. In this case, CreateGroup is a Watcher, so we pass this to the ZooKeeper constructor.

When a ZooKeeper instance is created, it starts a thread to connect to the ZooKeeper service. The call to the constructor returns immediately, so it is important to wait for

---

[†] For a replicated ZooKeeper service, this parameter is the comma-separated list of servers (host and optional port) in the ensemble.

the connection to be established before using the ZooKeeper object. We make use of Java's CountDownLatch class (in the java.util.concurrent package) to block until the ZooKeeper instance is ready. This is where the Watcher comes in. The Watcher interface has a single method:

```
public void process(WatchedEvent event);
```

When the client has connected to ZooKeeper, the Watcher receives a call to its process() method with an event indicating that it has connected. On receiving a connection event (represented by the Watcher.Event.KeeperState enum, with value SyncConnected), we decrement the counter in the CountDownLatch, using its count Down() method. The latch was created with a count of one, representing the number of events that need to occur before it releases all waiting threads. After calling count Down() once, the counter reaches zero and the await() method returns.

The connect() method has now returned, and the next method to be invoked on the CreateGroup is the create() method. In this method, we create a new ZooKeeper znode using the create() method on the ZooKeeper instance. The arguments it takes are the path (represented by a string), the contents of the znode (a byte array, null here), an access control list (or ACL for short, which here is a completely open ACL, allowing any client to read or write the znode), and the nature of the znode to be created.

Znodes may be ephemeral or persistent. An ephemeral znode will be deleted by the ZooKeeper service when the client that created it disconnects, either by explicitly disconnecting or if the client terminates for whatever reason. A persistent znode, on the other hand, is not deleted when the client disconnects. We want the znode representing a group to live longer than the lifetime of the program that creates it, so we create a persistent znode.

The return value of the create() method is the path that was created by ZooKeeper. We use it to print a message that the path was successfully created. We will see how the path returned by create() may differ from the one passed in to the method when we look at sequential znodes.

To see the program in action, we need to have ZooKeeper running on the local machine, and then we can type:

```
% export CLASSPATH=build/classes:$ZOOKEEPER_INSTALL/*:$ZOOKEEPER_INSTALL/lib/*:\
$ZOOKEEPER_INSTALL/conf
% java CreateGroup localhost zoo
Created /zoo
```

Joining a Group

The next part of the application is a program to register a member in a group. Each member will run as a program and join a group. When the program exits, it should be removed from the group, which we can do by creating an ephemeral znode that represents it in the ZooKeeper namespace.

The JoinGroup program implements this idea, and its listing is in Example 13-2. The logic for creating and connecting to a ZooKeeper instance has been refactored into a base class, ConnectionWatcher, and appears in Example 13-3.

Example 13-2. A program that joins a group

```
public class JoinGroup extends ConnectionWatcher {

  public void join(String groupName, String memberName) throws KeeperException,
      InterruptedException {
    String path = "/" + groupName + "/" + memberName;
    String createdPath = zk.create(path, null/*data*/, Ids.OPEN_ACL_UNSAFE,
      CreateMode.EPHEMERAL);
    System.out.println("Created " + createdPath);
  }

  public static void main(String[] args) throws Exception {
    JoinGroup joinGroup = new JoinGroup();
    joinGroup.connect(args[0]);
    joinGroup.join(args[1], args[2]);

    // stay alive until process is killed or thread is interrupted
    Thread.sleep(Long.MAX_VALUE);
  }
}
```

Example 13-3. A helper class that waits for the connection to ZooKeeper to be established

```
public class ConnectionWatcher implements Watcher {

  private static final int SESSION_TIMEOUT = 5000;

  protected ZooKeeper zk;
  private CountDownLatch connectedSignal = new CountDownLatch(1);

  public void connect(String hosts) throws IOException, InterruptedException {
    zk = new ZooKeeper(hosts, SESSION_TIMEOUT, this);
    connectedSignal.await();
  }

  @Override
  public void process(WatchedEvent event) {
    if (event.getState() == KeeperState.SyncConnected) {
      connectedSignal.countDown();
    }
  }

  public void close() throws InterruptedException {
    zk.close();
  }
}
```

The code for JoinGroup is very similar to CreateGroup. It creates an ephemeral znode as a child of the group znode in its join() method, then simulates doing work of some kind by sleeping until the process is forcibly terminated. Later, you will see that upon termination, the ephemeral znode is removed by ZooKeeper.

Listing Members in a Group

Now we need a program to find the members in a group (see Example 13-4).

Example 13-4. A program to list the members in a group

```java
public class ListGroup extends ConnectionWatcher {

  public void list(String groupName) throws KeeperException,
      InterruptedException {
    String path = "/" + groupName;

    try {
      List<String> children = zk.getChildren(path, false);
      if (children.isEmpty()) {
        System.out.printf("No members in group %s\n", groupName);
        System.exit(1);
      }
      for (String child : children) {
        System.out.println(child);
      }
    } catch (KeeperException.NoNodeException e) {
      System.out.printf("Group %s does not exist\n", groupName);
      System.exit(1);
    }
  }

  public static void main(String[] args) throws Exception {
    ListGroup listGroup = new ListGroup();
    listGroup.connect(args[0]);
    listGroup.list(args[1]);
    listGroup.close();
  }
}
```

In the list() method, we call getChildren() with a znode path and a watch flag to retrieve a list of child paths for the znode, which we print out. Placing a watch on a znode causes the registered Watcher to be triggered if the znode changes state. Although we're not using it here, watching a znode's children would permit a program to get notifications of members joining or leaving the group, or of the group being deleted.

We catch KeeperException.NoNodeException, which is thrown in the case when the group's znode does not exist.

Let's see ListGroup in action. As expected, the zoo group is empty, since we haven't added any members yet:

```
% java ListGroup localhost zoo
No members in group zoo
```

We can use `JoinGroup` to add some members. We launch them as background processes, since they don't terminate on their own (due to the sleep statement):

```
% java JoinGroup localhost zoo duck &
% java JoinGroup localhost zoo cow &
% java JoinGroup localhost zoo goat &
% goat_pid=$!
```

The last line saves the process ID of the Java process running the program that adds goat as a member. We need to remember the ID so that we can kill the process in a moment, after checking the members:

```
% java ListGroup localhost zoo
goat
duck
cow
```

To remove a member, we kill its process:

```
% kill $goat_pid
```

And a few seconds later, it has disappeared from the group because the process's Zoo-Keeper session has terminated (the timeout was set to 5 seconds) and its associated ephemeral node has been removed:

```
% java ListGroup localhost zoo
duck
cow
```

Let's stand back and see what we've built here. We have a way of building up a list of a group of nodes that are participating in a distributed system. The nodes may have no knowledge of each other. A service that wants to use the nodes in the list to perform some work, for example, can discover the nodes without them being aware of the service's existence.

Finally, note that group membership is not a substitution for handling network errors when communicating with a node. Even if a node is a group member, communications with it may fail, and such failures must be handled in the usual manner.

ZooKeeper command-line tools

ZooKeeper comes with a command-line tool for interacting with the ZooKeeper namespace. We can use it to list the znodes under the */zoo* znode as follows:

```
% zkCli.sh localhost ls /zoo
Processing ls
WatchedEvent: Server state change. New state: SyncConnected
[duck, cow]
```

You can run the command without arguments to display usage instructions.

Deleting a Group

To round off the example, let's see how to delete a group. The ZooKeeper class provides a delete() method that takes a path and a version number. ZooKeeper will delete a znode only if the version number specified is the same as the version number of the znode it is trying to delete, an optimistic locking mechanism that allows clients to detect conflicts over znode modification. You can bypass the version check, however, by using a version number of -1 to delete the znode regardless of its version number.

There is no recursive delete operation in ZooKeeper, so you have to delete child znodes before parents. This is what we do in the DeleteGroup class, which will remove a group and all its members (Example 13-5).

Example 13-5. A program to delete a group and its members

```java
public class DeleteGroup extends ConnectionWatcher {

  public void delete(String groupName) throws KeeperException,
      InterruptedException {
    String path = "/" + groupName;

    try {
      List<String> children = zk.getChildren(path, false);
      for (String child : children) {
        zk.delete(path + "/" + child, -1);
      }
      zk.delete(path, -1);
    } catch (KeeperException.NoNodeException e) {
      System.out.printf("Group %s does not exist\n", groupName);
      System.exit(1);
    }
  }

  public static void main(String[] args) throws Exception {
    DeleteGroup deleteGroup = new DeleteGroup();
    deleteGroup.connect(args[0]);
    deleteGroup.delete(args[1]);
    deleteGroup.close();
  }
}
```

Finally, we can delete the zoo group that we created earlier:

```
% java DeleteGroup localhost zoo
% java ListGroup localhost zoo
Group zoo does not exist
```

The ZooKeeper Service

ZooKeeper is a highly available, high-performance coordination service. In this section, we look at the nature of the service it provides: its model, operations, and implementation.

Data Model

ZooKeeper maintains a hierarchical tree of nodes called znodes. A znode stores data and has an associated ACL. ZooKeeper is designed for coordination (which typically uses small data files), not high-volume data storage, so there is a limit of 1 MB on the amount of data that may be stored in any znode.

Data access is atomic. A client reading the data stored at a znode will never receive only some of the data; the data will be delivered in its entirety (or the read will fail). Similarly, a write will replace all the data associated with a znode. ZooKeeper guarantees that the write will either succeed or fail; there is no such thing as a partial write, where only some of the data written by the client is stored. ZooKeeper does not support an append operation. These characteristics contrast with HDFS, which is designed for high-volume data storage, with streaming data access, and provides an append operation.

Znodes are referenced by paths, which in ZooKeeper are represented as slash-delimited Unicode character strings, like filesystem paths in Unix. Paths must be absolute, so they must begin with a slash character. Furthermore, they are canonical, which means that each path has a single representation, and so paths do not undergo resolution. For example, in Unix, a file with the path */a/b* can equivalently be referred to by the path */a/./b*, since "." refers to the current directory at the point it is encountered in the path. In ZooKeeper "." does not have this special meaning, and is actually illegal as a path component (as is ".." for the parent of the current directory).

Path components are composed of Unicode characters, with a few restrictions (these are spelled out in the ZooKeeper reference documentation). The string "zookeeper" is a reserved word, and may not be used as a path component. In particular, ZooKeeper uses the */zookeeper* subtree to store management information, such as information on quotas.

Note that paths are not URIs, and they are represented in the Java API by a `java.lang.String`, rather than the Hadoop `Path` class (or by the `java.net.URI` class, for that matter).

Znodes have some properties that are very useful for building distributed applications, which we discuss in the following sections.

Ephemeral znodes

Znodes can be one of two types: ephemeral or persistent. A znode's type is set at creation time and may not be changed later. An ephemeral znode is deleted by ZooKeeper when the creating client's session ends. By contrast, a persistent znode is not tied to the client's session, and is deleted only when explicitly deleted by a client (not necessarily the one that created it). An ephemeral znode may not have children, not even ephemeral ones.

Even though ephemeral nodes are tied to a client session, they are visible to all clients (subject to their ACL policy, of course).

Ephemeral znodes are ideal for building applications that needs to know when certain distributed resources are available. The example earlier in this chapter uses ephemeral znodes to implement a group membership service, so any process can discover the members of the group at any particular time.

Sequence numbers

A *sequential* znode is given a sequence number by ZooKeeper as a part of its name. If a znode is created with the sequential flag set, then the value of a monotonically increasing counter (maintained by the parent znode) is appended to its name.

If a client asks to create a sequential znode with the name */a/b-*, for example, then the znode created may actually have the name */a/b-3*.[‡] If, later on, another sequential znode with the name */a/b-* is created, then it will be given a unique name with a larger value of the counter—for example, */a/b-5*. In the Java API, the actual path given to sequential znodes is communicated back to the client as the return value of the `create()` call.

Sequence numbers can be used to impose a global ordering on events in a distributed system, and may be used by the client to infer the ordering. In "A Lock Service" on page 398, you will learn how to use sequential znodes to build a shared lock.

Watches

Watches allow clients to get notifications when a znode changes in some way. Watches are set by operations on the ZooKeeper service, and are triggered by other operations on the service. For example, a client might call the `exists` operation on a znode, placing a watch on it at the same time. If the znode doesn't exist, then the `exists` operation will return false. If, some time later, the znode is created by a second client, then the watch is triggered, notifying the first client of the znode's creation. You will see precisely which operations trigger others in the next section.

Watchers are triggered only once.[§] To receive multiple notifications, a client needs to reregister the watch. If the client in the previous example wishes to receive further notifications for the znode's existence (to be notified when it is deleted, for example), it needs to call the `exists` operation again to set a new watch.

There is an example in "A Configuration Service" on page 391 demonstrating how to use watches to update configuration across a cluster.

Operations

There are nine basic operations in ZooKeeper, listed in Table 13-1.

[‡] It is conventional (but not required) to have a trailing dash on path names for sequential nodes, to make their sequence numbers easy to read and parse (by the application).

[§] Except for callbacks for connection events, which do not need re-registration.

Table 13-1. Operations in the ZooKeeper service

Operation	Description
create	Creates a znode (the parent znode must already exist)
delete	Deletes a znode (the znode may not have any children)
exists	Tests whether a znode exists and retrieves its metadata
getACL, setACL	Gets/sets the ACL for a znode
getChildren	Gets a list of the children of a znode
getData, setData	Gets/sets the data associated with a znode
sync	Synchronizes a client's view of a znode with ZooKeeper

Update operations in ZooKeeper are conditional. A `delete` or `setData` operation has to specify the version number of the znode that is being updated (which is found from a previous `exists` call). If the version number does not match, the update will fail. Updates are a nonblocking operation, so a client that loses an update (because another process updated the znode in the meantime) can decide whether to try again or take some other action, and it can do so without blocking the progress of any other process.

Although ZooKeeper can be viewed as a filesystem, there are some filesystem primitives that it does away with in the name of simplicity. Because files are small and are written and read in their entirety, there is no need to provide open, close, or seek operations.

> The `sync` operation is not like `fsync()` in POSIX filesystems. As mentioned earlier, writes in ZooKeeper are atomic, and a successful write operation is guaranteed to have been written to persistent storage on a majority of ZooKeeper servers. However, it is permissible for reads to lag the latest state of ZooKeeper service, and the `sync` operation exists to allow a client to bring itself up-to-date. This topic is covered in more detail in the section on "Consistency" on page 386.

APIs

There are two core language bindings for ZooKeeper clients, one for Java and one for C; there are also `contrib` bindings for Perl, Python, and REST clients. For each binding, there is a choice between performing operations synchronously or asynchronously. We've already seen the synchronous Java API. Here's the signature for the `exists` operation, which returns a `Stat` object encapsulating the znode's metadata, or `null` if the znode doesn't exist:

```
public Stat exists(String path, Watcher watcher) throws KeeperException,
    InterruptedException
```

The asynchronous equivalent, which is also found in the `ZooKeeper` class, looks like this:

```
public void exists(String path, Watcher watcher, StatCallback cb, Object ctx)
```

In the Java API, all the asynchronous methods have **void** return types, since the result of the operation is conveyed via a callback. The caller passes a callback implementation, whose method is invoked when a response is received from ZooKeeper. In this case, the callback is the `StatCallback` interface, which has the following method:

```
public void processResult(int rc, String path, Object ctx, Stat stat);
```

The `rc` argument is the return code, corresponding to the codes defined by `KeeperEx ception`. A nonzero code represents an exception, in which case the `stat` parameter will be null. The `path` and `ctx` arguments correspond to the equivalent arguments passed by the client to the `exists()` method, and can be used to identify the request for which this callback is a response. The `ctx` parameter can be an arbitrary object that may be used by the client when the path does not give enough context to disambiguate the request. If not needed, it may be set to `null`.

There are actually two C shared libraries. The single-threaded library, `zookeeper_st`, supports only the asynchronous API and is intended for platforms where the `pthread` library is not available or stable. Most developers will use the multithreaded library, `zookeeper_mt`, as it supports both the synchronous and asynchronous APIs. For details on how to build and use the C API, please refer to the *README* file in the *src/c* directory of the ZooKeeper distribution.

Should I Use the Synchronous or Asynchronous API?

Both APIs offer the same functionality, so the one you use is largely a matter of style. The asynchronous API is appropriate if you have an event-driven programming model, for example.

The asynchronous API allows you to pipeline requests, which in some scenarios can offer better throughput. Imagine that you want to read a large batch of znodes and process them independently. Using the synchronous API, each read would block until it returned, whereas with the asynchronous API, you can fire off all the asynchronous reads very quickly and process the responses in a separate thread as they come back.

Watch triggers

The read operations `exists`, `getChildren`, and `getData` may have watches set on them, and the watches are triggered by write operations: `create`, `delete`, and `setData`. ACL operations do not participate in watches. When a watch is triggered, a watch event is generated, and the watch event's type depends both on the watch and the operation that triggered it:

- A watch set on an `exists` operation will be triggered when the znode being watched is created, deleted, or has its data updated.

- A watch set on a `getData` operation will be triggered when the znode being watched is deleted or has its data updated. No trigger can occur on creation, since the znode must already exist for the `getData` operation to succeed.

- A watch set on a `getChildren` operation will be triggered when a child of the znode being watched is created or deleted, or when the znode itself is deleted. You can tell whether the znode or its child was deleted by looking at the watch event type: `NodeDeleted` shows the znode was deleted, and `NodeChildrenChanged` indicates that it was a child that was deleted.

The combinations are summarized in Table 13-2.

Table 13-2. Watch creation operations and their corresponding triggers

	Watch trigger				
Watch creation	create		delete		setData
	znode	child	znode	child	
exists	NodeCreated		NodeDeleted		NodeData Changed
getData			NodeDeleted		NodeData Changed
getChildren		NodeChildren Changed	NodeDeleted	NodeChildren Changed	

A watch event includes the path of the znode that was involved in the event, so for `NodeCreated` and `NodeDeleted` events, you can tell which node was created or deleted simply by inspecting the path. To discover which children have changed after a `NodeChildrenChanged` event, you need to call `getChildren` again to retrieve the new list of children. Similarly, to discover the new data for a `NodeDataChanged` event, you need to call `getData`. In both of these cases, the state of the znodes may have changed between receiving the watch event and performing the read operation, so you should bear this in mind when writing applications.

ACLs

A znode is created with a list of ACLs, which determines who can perform certain operations on it.

ACLs depend on authentication, the process by which the client identifies itself to ZooKeeper. There are a few authentication schemes that ZooKeeper provides:

digest
> The client is identified by a username and password.

host
> The client is identified by his hostname.

ip
The client is identified by his IP address.

Clients may authenticate themselves after establishing a ZooKeeper session. Authentication is optional, although a znode's ACL may require an authenticated client, in which case the client must authenticate itself to access the znode. Here is an example of using the *digest* scheme to authenticate with a username and password:

```
zk.addAuthInfo("digest", "tom:secret".getBytes());
```

An ACL is the combination of an authentication scheme, an identity for that scheme, and a set of permissions. For example, if we wanted to give clients in the domain *example.com* read access to a znode, we would set an ACL on the znode with the host scheme, an ID of example.com, and READ permission. In Java, we would create the ACL object as follows:

```
new ACL(Perms.READ, new Id("host", "example.com"));
```

The full set of permissions are listed in Table 13-3. Note that the exists operation is not governed by an ACL permission, so any client may call exists to find the Stat for a znode or to discover that a znode does not in fact exist.

Table 13-3. ACL permissions

ACL permission	Permitted operations
CREATE	create (a child znode)
READ	getChildren
	getData
WRITE	setData
DELETE	delete (a child znode)
ADMIN	setACL

There are a number of predefined ACLs defined in the ZooDefs.Ids class, including OPEN_ACL_UNSAFE, which gives all permissions (except ADMIN permission) to everyone.

In addition, ZooKeeper has a pluggable authentication mechanism, which makes it possible to integrate third-party authentication systems if needed.

Implementation

The ZooKeeper service can run in two modes. In *standalone mode*, there is a single ZooKeeper server, which is useful for testing due to its simplicity (it can even be embedded in unit tests), but provides no guarantees of high-availability or resilience. In production, ZooKeeper runs in *replicated mode*, on a cluster of machines called an *ensemble*. ZooKeeper achieves high-availability through replication, and can provide a service as long as a majority of the machines in the ensemble are up. For example, in a five-node ensemble, any two machines can fail and the service will still work because a majority of three remain. Note that a six-node ensemble can also tolerate only two machines failing, since with three failures the remaining three do not constitute a majority of the six. For this reason, it is usual to have an odd number of machines in an ensemble.

Conceptually, ZooKeeper is very simple: all it has to do is ensure that every modification to the tree of znodes is replicated to a majority of the ensemble. If a minority of the machines fail, then a minimum of one machine will survive with the latest state. The other remaining replicas will eventually catch up with this state.

The implementation of this simple idea, however, is nontrivial. ZooKeeper uses a protocol called Zab that runs in two phases, which may be repeated indefinitely:

Phase 1: Leader election
> The machines in an ensemble go through a process of electing a distinguished member, called the *leader*. The other machines are termed *followers*. This phase is finished once a majority (or *quorum*) of followers have synchronized their state with the leader.

Phase 2: Atomic broadcast
> All write requests are forwarded to the leader, which broadcasts the update to the followers. When a majority have persisted the change, the leader commits the update, and the client gets a response saying the update succeeded. The protocol for achieving consensus is designed to be atomic, so a change either succeeds or fails. It resembles two-phase commit.

Does ZooKeeper Use Paxos?

No. ZooKeeper's Zab protocol is not the same as the well-known Paxos algorithm (Leslie Lamport, "Paxos Made Simple," *ACM SIGACT News [Distributed Computing Column] 32*, 4 [Whole Number 121, December 2001] 51–58.). Zab is similar, but it differs in several aspects of its operation, such as relying on TCP for its message ordering guarantees.

Zab is described in "A simple totally ordered broadcast protocol" by Benjamin Reed and Flavio Junqueira (Proceedings of the Second Workshop on Large-Scale Distributed Systems and Middleware [LADIS'08] 2008, IBM TJ Watson Research Center, Yorktown Heights, NY, USA. To appear in ACM International Conference Proceedings Series, ACM Press, 2009. ISBN: 978-1-60558-296-2).

Google's Chubby Lock Service (Mike Burrows, "The Chubby Lock Service for Loosely-Coupled Distributed Systems," November 2006, *http://labs.google.com/papers/chubby .html*), which shares similar goals with ZooKeeper, is based on Paxos.

If the leader fails, the remaining machines hold another leader election and continue as before with the new leader. If the old leader later recovers, it then starts as a follower. Leader election is very fast, around 200 ms according to one published result,[||] so performance does not noticeably degrade during an election.

All machines in the ensemble write updates to disk before updating their in-memory copy of the znode tree. Read requests may be serviced from any machine, and since they involve only a lookup from memory, they are very fast.

Consistency

Understanding the basis of ZooKeeper's implementation helps in understanding the consistency guarantees that the service makes. The terms "leader" and "follower" for the machines in an ensemble are apt, for they make the point that a follower may lag the leader by a number of updates. This is a consequence of the fact that only a majority and not all of the ensemble needs to have persisted a change before it is committed. A good mental model for ZooKeeper is of clients connected to ZooKeeper servers that are following the leader. A client may actually be connected to the leader, but it has no control over this, and cannot even know if this is the case.[#] See Figure 13-2.

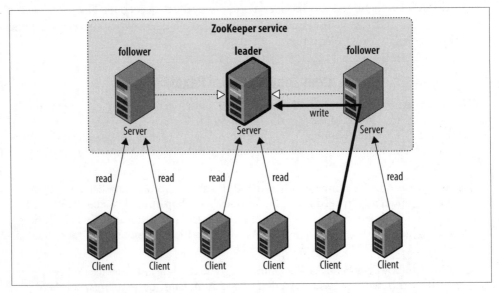

Figure 13-2. Reads are satisfied by followers, while writes are committed by the leader

---

[||] Reported by Yahoo! at *http://hadoop.apache.org/zookeeper/docs/current/zookeeperOver.html*.

[#] It is possible to configure ZooKeeper so that the leader does not accept client connections. In this case, its only job is to coordinate updates. Do this by setting the `leaderServes` property to no. This is recommended for ensembles of more than three servers.

Every update made to the znode tree is given a globally unique identifier, called a *zxid* (which stands for "ZooKeeper transaction ID"). Updates are ordered, so if *zxid* z_1 is less than z_2, then z_1 happened before z_2, according to ZooKeeper, which is the single authority on ordering in the distributed system.

The following guarantees for data consistency flow from ZooKeeper's design:

Sequential consistency
> Updates from any particular client are applied in the order that they are sent. This means that if a client updates the znode z to the value a, and in a later operation, it updates z to the value b, then no client will ever see z with value a after it has seen it with value b (if no other updates are made to z).

Atomicity
> Updates either succeed or fail. This means that if an update fails, no client will ever see it.

Single system image
> A client will see the same view of the system regardless of the server it connects to. This means that if a client connects to a new server during the same session, it will not see an older state of the system than the one it saw with the previous server. When a server fails and a client tries to connect to another in the ensemble, a server that is behind the one that failed will not accept connections from the client until it has caught up with the failed server.

Durability
> Once an update has succeeded, it will persist and will not be undone. This means updates will survive server failures.

Timeliness
> The lag in any client's view of the system is bounded, so it will not be out of date by more than some multiple of tens of seconds. This means that rather than allow a client to see data that is very stale, a server will shut down, forcing the client to switch to a more up-to-date server.

For performance reasons, reads are satisfied from a ZooKeeper's server's memory and do not participate in the global ordering of writes. This property can lead to the appearance of inconsistent ZooKeeper states from clients that communicate through a mechanism outside ZooKeeper.

For example, client A updates znode z from a to a', A tells B to read z, B reads the value of z as a, not a'. This is perfectly compatible with the guarantees that ZooKeeper makes (this condition that it does *not* promise is called "Simultaneously Consistent Cross-Client Views"). To prevent this condition from happening, B should call sync on z, before reading z's value. The sync operation forces the ZooKeeper server that B is connected to to "catch up" with the leader, so that when B reads z's value it will be the one that A set (or a later value).

Slightly confusingly, the sync operation is only available as an *asynchronous* call. The reason for this is that you don't need to wait for it to return, since ZooKeeper guarantees that any subsequent operation will happen after the sync completes on the server, even if the operation is issued before the sync completes.

Sessions

A ZooKeeper client is configured with the list of servers in the ensemble. On startup, it tries to connect to one of the servers in the list. If the connection fails, it tries another server in the list, and so on, until it either successfully connects to one of them, or fails if all ZooKeeper servers are unavailable.

Once a connection has been made with a ZooKeeper server, the server creates a new session for the client. A session has a timeout period that is decided on by the application that creates it. If the server hasn't received a request within the timeout period, it may expire the session. Once a session has expired, it may not be reopened, and any ephemeral nodes associated with the session will be lost. Although session expiry is a comparatively rare event, since sessions are long-lived, it is important for applications to handle it (which you will see how in "The Resilient ZooKeeper Application" on page 394).

Sessions are kept alive by the client sending ping requests (also known as heartbeats) whenever the session is idle for longer than a certain period. (Pings are automatically sent by the ZooKeeper client library, so your code doesn't need to worry about maintaining the session.) The period is chosen to be low enough to detect server failure (manifested by a read timeout) and reconnect to another server within the session timeout period.

Failover to another ZooKeeper server is handled automatically by the ZooKeeper client, and, crucially, sessions (and associated ephemeral znodes) are still valid after another server takes over from the failed one.

During failover, the application will receive notifications of disconnections and connections to the service. Watch notifications will not be delivered while the client is disconnected, but they will be delivered when the client successfully reconnects. Also, if the application tries to perform an operation while the client is reconnecting to another server, the operation will fail. This underlines the importance of handling connection loss exceptions in real-world ZooKeeper applications (described in "The Resilient ZooKeeper Application" on page 394).

Time

There are several time parameters in ZooKeeper. The *tick time* is the fundamental period of time in ZooKeeper and is used by servers in the ensemble to define the schedule on which their interactions run. Other settings are defined in terms of tick time, or are at least constrained by it. The session timeout, for example, may not be less than 2 ticks or more than 20. If you attempt to set a session timeout outside this range, it will be modified to fall within the range.

A common tick time setting is 2 seconds (2,000 milliseconds). This translates to an allowable session timeout of between 4 and 40 seconds. There are a few considerations in selecting a session timeout.

A low session timeout leads to faster detection of machine failure. In the group membership example, the session timeout is the time it takes for a failed machine to be removed from the group. Beware of setting the session timeout too low, however, since a busy network can cause packets to be delayed and may cause inadvertent session expiry. In such an event, a machine would appear to "flap": leaving and then rejoining the group repeatedly in a short space of time.

Applications that create more complex ephemeral state should favor longer session timeouts, as the cost of reconstruction is higher. In some cases, it is possible to design the application so it can restart within the session timeout period, and avoid session expiry. (This might be desirable to perform maintenance or upgrades.) Every session is given a unique identity and password by the server, and if these are passed to ZooKeeper while a connection is being made, it is possible to recover a session (as long as it hasn't expired). An application can therefore arrange a graceful shutdown, whereby it stores the session identity and password to stable storage before restarting the process, retrieving the stored session identity and password, and recovering the session.

You should view this feature as an optimization, which can help avoid expire sessions. It does not remove the need to handle session expiry, which can still occur if a machine fails unexpectedly, or even if an application is shut down gracefully but does not restart before its session expires—for whatever reason.

As a general rule, the larger the ZooKeeper ensemble, the larger the session timeout should be. Connection timeouts, read timeouts, and ping periods are all defined internally as a function of the number of servers in the ensemble, so as the ensemble grows, these periods decrease. Consider increasing the timeout if you experience frequent connection loss. You can monitor ZooKeeper metrics—such as request latency statistics—using JMX.

States

The ZooKeeper object transitions through different states in its lifecycle (see Figure 13-3). You can query its state at any time by using the getState() method:

```
public States getState()
```

States is an enum representing the different states that a ZooKeeper object may be in. (Despite the enum's name, an instance of ZooKeeper may only be in one state at a time.) A newly constructed ZooKeeper instance is in the CONNECTING state, while it tries to

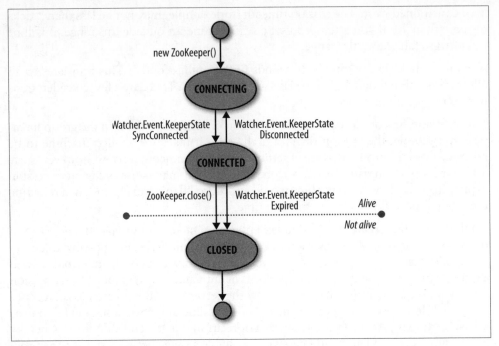

Figure 13-3. *ZooKeeper state transitions*

establish a connection with the ZooKeeper service. Once a connection is established, it goes into the CONNECTED state.

A client using the ZooKeeper object can receive notifications of the state transitions by registering a Watcher object. On entering the CONNECTED state, the watcher receives a WatchedEvent whose KeeperState value is SyncConnected.

 A ZooKeeper Watcher object serves double duty: it can be used to be notified of changes in the ZooKeeper state (as described in this section), and it can be used to be notified of changes in znodes (described in "Watch triggers" on page 382). The (default) watcher passed in to the ZooKeeper object constructor is used for state changes, but znode changes may either use a dedicated instance of Watcher (by passing one in to the appropriate read operation), or they may share the default one if using the form of the read operation that takes a boolean flag to specify whether to use a watcher.

The ZooKeeper instance may disconnect and reconnect to the ZooKeeper service, moving between the CONNECTED and CONNECTING states. If it disconnects, the watcher receives a Disconnected event. Note that these state transitions are initiated by the ZooKeeper instance itself, and it will automatically try to reconnect if the connection is lost.

The ZooKeeper instance may transition to a third state, CLOSED, if either the close() method is called or the session times out as indicated by a KeeperState of type Expired. Once in the CLOSED state, the ZooKeeper object is no longer considered to be alive (this can be tested using the isAlive() method on States), and cannot be reused. To reconnect to the ZooKeeper service, the client must construct a new ZooKeeper instance.

Building Applications with ZooKeeper

Having covered ZooKeeper in some depth, let's turn back to writing some useful applications with it.

A Configuration Service

One of the most basic services that a distributed application needs is a configuration service so that common pieces of configuration information can be shared by machines in a cluster. At the simplest level, ZooKeeper can act as a highly available store for configuration, allowing application participants to retrieve or update configuration files. Using ZooKeeper watches, it is possible to create an active configuration service, where interested clients are notified of changes in configuration.

Let's write such a service. We make a couple of assumptions that simplify the implementation (they could be removed with a little more work). First, the only configuration values we need to store are strings, and keys are just znode paths, so we use a znode to store each key-value pair. Second, there is a single client that performs updates at any one time. Among other things, this model fits with the idea of a master (such as the namenode in HDFS) that wishes to update information that its workers need to follow.

We wrap the code up in a class called ActiveKeyValueStore:

```
public class ActiveKeyValueStore extends ConnectionWatcher {

  private static final Charset CHARSET = Charset.forName("UTF-8");

  public void write(String path, String value) throws InterruptedException,
      KeeperException {
    Stat stat = zk.exists(path, false);
    if (stat == null) {
      zk.create(path, value.getBytes(CHARSET), Ids.OPEN_ACL_UNSAFE,
          CreateMode.PERSISTENT);
    } else {
      zk.setData(path, value.getBytes(CHARSET), -1);
    }
  }
}
```

The contract of the write() method is that a key with the given value is written to ZooKeeper. It hides the difference between creating a new znode and updating an existing znode with a new value, by testing first for the znode using the exists operation and then performing the appropriate operation. The other detail worth mentioning is the need to convert the string value to a byte array, for which we just use the `getBytes()` method with a UTF-8 encoding.

To illustrate the use of the `ActiveKeyValueStore`, consider a `ConfigUpdater` class that updates a configuration property with a value. The listing appears in Example 13-6.

Example 13-6. An application that updates a property in ZooKeeper at random times

```java
public class ConfigUpdater {

  public static final String PATH = "/config";

  private ActiveKeyValueStore store;
  private Random random = new Random();

  public ConfigUpdater(String hosts) throws IOException, InterruptedException {
    store = new ActiveKeyValueStore();
    store.connect(hosts);
  }

  public void run() throws InterruptedException, KeeperException {
    while (true) {
      String value = random.nextInt(100) + "";
      store.write(PATH, value);
      System.out.printf("Set %s to %s\n", PATH, value);
      TimeUnit.SECONDS.sleep(random.nextInt(10));
    }
  }

  public static void main(String[] args) throws Exception {
    ConfigUpdater configUpdater = new ConfigUpdater(args[0]);
    configUpdater.run();
  }
}
```

The program is simple. A `ConfigUpdater` has an `ActiveKeyValueStore` that connects to ZooKeeper in `ConfigUpdater`'s constructor. The `run()` method loops forever, updating the */config* znode at random times with random values.

Next, let's look at how to read the */config* configuration property. First we add a read method to `ActiveKeyValueStore`:

```java
public String read(String path, Watcher watcher) throws InterruptedException,
    KeeperException {
  byte[] data = zk.getData(path, watcher, null/*stat*/);
  return new String(data, CHARSET);
}
```

The `getData()` method of ZooKeeper takes the path, a `Watcher`, and a `Stat` object. The `Stat` object is filled in with values by `getData()`, and is used to pass information back to the caller. In this way, the caller can get both the data and the metadata for a znode, although in this case, we pass a null `Stat` because we are not interested in the metadata.

As a consumer of the service, ConfigWatcher (see Example 13-7) creates an ActiveKey ValueStore, and after starting, calls the store's read() method (in its displayConfig() method) passing a reference to itself as the watcher. It displays the initial value of the configuration that it reads.

Example 13-7. An application that watches for updates of a property in ZooKeeper and prints them to the console

```java
public class ConfigWatcher implements Watcher {

  private ActiveKeyValueStore store;

  public ConfigWatcher(String hosts) throws IOException, InterruptedException {
    store = new ActiveKeyValueStore();
    store.connect(hosts);
  }

  public void displayConfig() throws InterruptedException, KeeperException {
    String value = store.read(ConfigUpdater.PATH, this);
    System.out.printf("Read %s as %s\n", ConfigUpdater.PATH, value);
  }

  @Override
  public void process(WatchedEvent event) {
    if (event.getType() == EventType.NodeDataChanged) {
      try {
        displayConfig();
      } catch (InterruptedException e) {
        System.err.println("Interrupted. Exiting.");
        Thread.currentThread().interrupt();
      } catch (KeeperException e) {
        System.err.printf("KeeperException: %s. Exiting.\n", e);
      }
    }
  }

  public static void main(String[] args) throws Exception {
    ConfigWatcher configWatcher = new ConfigWatcher(args[0]);
    configWatcher.displayConfig();

    // stay alive until process is killed or thread is interrupted
    Thread.sleep(Long.MAX_VALUE);
  }
}
```

When the ConfigUpdater updates the znode, ZooKeeper causes the watcher to fire with an event type of EventType.NodeDataChanged. ConfigWatcher acts on this event in its process() method by reading and displaying the latest version of the config.

Because watches are one-time signals, we tell ZooKeeper of the new watch each time we call read() on ActiveKeyValueStore—this ensures we see future updates. Furthermore, we are not guaranteed to receive every update, since between the receipt of the watch event and the next read, the znode may have been updated, possibly many times, and as the client has no watch registered during that period, it is not notified. For the configuration service, this is not a problem because clients care only about the latest value of a property, as it takes precedence over previous values, but in general you should be aware of this potential limitation.

Let's see the code in action. Launch the ConfigUpdater in one terminal window:

```
% java ConfigUpdater localhost
Set /config to 79
Set /config to 14
Set /config to 78
```

Then launch the ConfigWatcher in another window immediately afterward:

```
% java ConfigWatcher localhost
Read /config as 79
Read /config as 14
Read /config as 78
```

The Resilient ZooKeeper Application

The first of the Fallacies of Distributed Computing[*] states that "The network is reliable." As they stand, the programs so far have been assuming a reliable network, so when they run on a real network, they can fail in several ways. Let's examine possible failure modes, and what we can do to correct them so that our programs are resilient in the face of failure.

Every ZooKeeper operation in the Java API declares two types of exception in its throws clause: InterruptedException and KeeperException.

InterruptedException

An InterruptedException is thrown if the operation is interrupted. There is a standard Java mechanism for canceling blocking methods, which is to call interrupt() on the thread from which the blocking method was called. A successful cancelation will result in an InterruptedException. ZooKeeper adheres to this standard, so you can cancel a ZooKeeper operation in this way. Classes or libraries that use ZooKeeper should usually propagate the InterruptedException so that their clients can cancel their operations.[†]

An InterruptedException does not indicate a failure, but rather that the operation has been canceled, so in the configuration application, it is appropriate to propagate the exception, causing the application to terminate.

---

[*] See *http://en.wikipedia.org/wiki/Fallacies_of_Distributed_Computing*.

[†] For more detail, see the excellent article "Dealing with InterruptedException" (*http://www.ibm.com/developerworks/java/library/j-jtp05236.html*) by Brian Goetz.

KeeperException

A `KeeperException` is thrown if the ZooKeeper server signals an error, or if there is a communication problem with the server. There are various subclasses of `KeeperException` for different error cases. For example, `KeeperException.NoNodeException` is a subclass of `KeeperException` that is thrown if you try to perform an operation on a znode that doesn't exist.

Every subclass of `KeeperException` has a corresponding code with information about the type of error. For example, for `KeeperException.NoNodeException` the code is `KeeperException.Code.NONODE` (an enum value).

There are two ways then to handle `KeeperException`: either catch `KeeperException` and test its code to determine what remedying action to take, or catch the equivalent `KeeperException` subclasses and perform the appropriate action in each catch block.

`KeeperException`s fall into three broad categories.

State exceptions. A state exception occurs when the operation fails because it cannot be applied to the znode tree. State exceptions usually happen because another process is mutating a znode at the same time. For example, a `setData` operation with a version number will fail with a `KeeperException.BadVersionException` if the znode is updated by another process first, since the version number does not match. The programmer is usually aware that this kind of conflict is possible, and will code to deal with it.

Some state exceptions indicate an error in the program, such as `KeeperException.NoChildrenForEphemeralsException`, which is thrown when trying to create a child znode of an ephemeral znode.

Recoverable exceptions. Recoverable exceptions are those from which the application can recover within the same ZooKeeper session. A recoverable exception is manifested by `KeeperException.ConnectionLossException`, which means that the connection to Zoo-Keeper has been lost. ZooKeeper will try to reconnect, and in most cases the reconnection will succeed and ensure that the session is intact.

However, ZooKeeper cannot tell whether the operation that failed with `KeeperException.ConnectionLossException` was applied. This is an example of partial failure (which we introduced at the beginning of the chapter). The onus is therefore on the programmer to deal with the uncertainty, and the action that should be taken depends on the application.

At this point, it is useful to make a distinction between *idempotent* and *nonidempotent* operations. An idempotent operation is one that may be applied one or more times with the same result, such as a read request or an unconditional `setData`. These can simply be retried.

A nonidempotent operation cannot be indiscriminately retried, as the effect of applying it multiple times is not the same as applying it once. The program needs a way of detecting whether its update was applied by encoding information in the znode's path name or its data. We shall discuss how to deal with failed nonidempotent operations in "Recoverable exceptions" on page 399, when we look at the implementation of a lock service.

Unrecoverable exceptions. In some cases, the ZooKeeper session becomes invalid—perhaps because of a timeout or because the session was closed (both get a KeeperEx ception.SessionExpiredException), or perhaps because authentication failed (Keeper Exception.AuthFailedException). In any case, all ephemeral nodes associated with the session will be lost, so the application needs to rebuild its state before reconnecting to ZooKeeper.

A reliable configuration service

Going back to the write() method in ActiveKeyValueStore, recall that it is composed of an exists operation followed by either a create or a setData:

```java
public void write(String path, String value) throws InterruptedException,
    KeeperException {
  Stat stat = zk.exists(path, false);
  if (stat == null) {
    zk.create(path, value.getBytes(CHARSET), Ids.OPEN_ACL_UNSAFE,
        CreateMode.PERSISTENT);
  } else {
    zk.setData(path, value.getBytes(CHARSET), -1);
  }
}
```

Taken as a whole, the write() method is idempotent, so we can afford to unconditionally retry it. Here's a modified version of the write() method that retries in a loop. It is set to try a maximum number of retries (MAX_RETRIES) and sleeps for RETRY_PERIOD_SECONDS between each attempt:

```java
public void write(String path, String value) throws InterruptedException,
    KeeperException {
  int retries = 0;
  while (true) {
    try {
      Stat stat = zk.exists(path, false);
      if (stat == null) {
        zk.create(path, value.getBytes(CHARSET), Ids.OPEN_ACL_UNSAFE,
            CreateMode.PERSISTENT);
      } else {
        zk.setData(path, value.getBytes(CHARSET), stat.getVersion());
      }
    } catch (KeeperException.SessionExpiredException e) {
      throw e;
    } catch (KeeperException e) {
      if (retries++ == MAX_RETRIES) {
        throw e;
      }
      // sleep then retry
      TimeUnit.SECONDS.sleep(RETRY_PERIOD_SECONDS);
```

```
        }
      }
    }
```

The code is careful not to retry `KeeperException.SessionExpiredException`, since when a session expires, the `ZooKeeper` object enters the `CLOSED` state, from which it can never reconnect (refer to Figure 13-3). We simply rethrow the exception[‡] and let the caller create a new `ZooKeeper` instance, so that the whole `write()` method can be retried. A simple way to create a new instance is to create a new `ConfigUpdater` (which we've actually renamed `ResilientConfigUpdater`) to recover from an expired session:

```java
public static void main(String[] args) throws Exception {
  while (true) {
    try {
      ResilientConfigUpdater configUpdater =
        new ResilientConfigUpdater(args[0]);
      configUpdater.run();
    } catch (KeeperException.SessionExpiredException e) {
      // start a new session
    } catch (KeeperException e) {
      // already retried, so exit
      e.printStackTrace();
      break;
    }
  }
}
```

An alternative way of dealing with session expiry would be to look for a `KeeperState` of type `Expired` in the watcher (that would be the `ConnectionWatcher` in the example here), and create a new connection when this is detected. This way, we would just keep retrying in the `write()` method, even if we got a `KeeperException.SessionExpiredException`, since the connection should eventually be re-established. Regardless of the precise mechanics of how we recover from an expired session, the important point is that it is a different kind of failure from connection loss and needs to be handled differently.

> There's actually another failure mode that we've ignored here. When the `ZooKeeper` object is created, it tries to connect to a ZooKeeper server. If the connection fails or times out, then it tries another server in the ensemble. If, after trying all of the servers in the ensemble, it can't connect, then it throws an `IOException`. The likelihood of all ZooKeeper servers being unavailable is low; nevertheless, some applications may choose to retry the operation in a loop until ZooKeeper is available.

This is just one strategy for retry handling—there are many others, such as using exponential backoff where the period between retries is multiplied by a constant each

---

[‡] Another way of writing the code would be to have a single catch block, just for `KeeperException`, and a test to see whether its code has the value `KeeperException.Code.SESSIONEXPIRED`. Which method you use is a matter of style, since they both behave in the same way.

time. The `org.apache.hadoop.io.retry` package in Hadoop Core is a set of utilities for adding retry logic into your code in a reusable way, and may be helpful for building ZooKeeper applications.

A Lock Service

A distributed lock is a mechanism for providing mutual exclusion between a collection of processes. At any one time, only a single process may hold the lock. Distributed locks can be used for leader election in a large distributed system, where the leader is the process that holds the lock at any point in time.

> Do not confuse ZooKeeper's own leader election with a general leader election service, which can be built using ZooKeeper primitives. Zoo-Keeper's own leader election is not exposed publicly, unlike the type of general leader election service we are describing here, which is designed to be used by distributed systems that need to agree upon a master process.

To implement a distributed lock using ZooKeeper, we use sequential znodes to impose an order on the processes vying for the lock. The idea is simple: first designate a lock znode, typically describing the entity being locked on, say */leader*; then clients that want to acquire the lock create sequential ephemeral znodes as children of the lock znode. At any point in time, the client with the lowest sequence number holds the lock. For example, if two clients create znodes at around the same time, */leader/lock-1* and */leader/lock-2*, then the client that created */leader/lock-1* holds the lock, since its znode has the lowest sequence number. The ZooKeeper service is the arbiter of order, since it assigns the sequence numbers.

The lock may be released simply by deleting the znode */leader/lock-1*; alternatively, if the client process dies, it will be deleted by virtue of it being an ephemeral znode. The client that created */leader/lock-2* will then hold the lock, since it has the next lowest sequence number. It will be notified that it has the lock by creating a watch that fires when znodes go away.

The pseudocode for lock acquisition is as follows:

1. Create an ephemeral sequential znode named *lock-* under the lock znode and re-member its actual path name (the return value of the **create** operation).
2. Get the children of the lock znode and set a watch.
3. If the path name of the znode created in 1 has the lowest number of the children returned in 2, then the lock has been acquired. Exit.
4. Wait for the notification from the watch set in 2 and go to step 2.

The herd effect

Although this algorithm is correct, there are some problems with it. The first problem is that this implementation suffers from the *herd effect*. Consider hundreds or thousands of clients, all trying to acquire the lock. Each client places a watch on the lock znode for changes in its set of children. Every time the lock is released, or another process starts the lock acquisition process, the watch fires and every client receives a notification. The "herd effect" refers to a large number of clients being notified of the same event, when only a small number of them can actually proceed. In this case, only one client will successfully acquire the lock, and the process of maintaining and sending watch events to all clients causes traffic spikes, which put pressure on the ZooKeeper servers.

To avoid the herd effect, we need to refine the condition for notification. The key observation for implementing locks is that a client needs to be notified only when the child znode with the *previous* sequence number goes away, not when any child znode is deleted (or created). In our example, if clients have created the znodes */leader/lock-1*, */leader/lock-2*, and */leader/lock-3*, then the client holding */leader/lock-3* only needs to be notified when */leader/lock-2* disappears. It does not need to be notified when */leader/lock-1* disappears, or when a new znode */leader/lock-4* is added.

Recoverable exceptions

Another problem with the lock algorithm as it stands is that it doesn't handle the case when the create operation fails due to connection loss. Recall that in this case we do not know if the operation succeeded or failed. Creating a sequential znode is a nonidempotent operation, so we can't simply retry, since if the first create had succeeded, we would have an orphaned znode that would never be deleted (until the client session ended, at least). Deadlock would be the unfortunate result.

The problem is that after reconnecting, the client can't tell whether it created any of the child znodes. By embedding an identifier in the znode name, if it suffers a connection loss, it can check to see whether any of the children of the lock node have its identifier in their name. If a child contains its identifier, it knows that the create operation succeeded, and it shouldn't create another child znode. If no child has the identifier in its name, then the client can safely create a new sequential child znode.

The client's session identifier is a long integer that is unique for the ZooKeeper service and therefore ideal for the purpose of identifying a client across connection loss events. The session identifier can be obtained by calling the `getSessionId()` method on the `ZooKeeper` Java class.

The ephemeral sequential znode should be created with a name of the form *lock-<sessionId>-*, so that when the sequence number is appended by ZooKeeper, the name becomes *lock-<sessionId>-<sequenceNumber>*. The sequence numbers are unique to the parent, not to the name of the child, so this technique allows the child znodes to identify their creators as well as impose an order of creation.

Unrecoverable exceptions

If a client's ZooKeeper session expires, the ephemeral znode created by the client will be deleted, effectively relinquishing the lock, or at least forfeiting the client's turn to acquire the lock. The application using the lock should realize that it no longer holds the lock, clean up its state, then start again, by creating a new lock object, and trying to acquire it. Notice that it is the application that controls this process, not the lock implementation, since it cannot second-guess how the application needs to clean up its state.

Implementation

Implementing a distributed lock correctly is a delicate matter, since accounting for all of the failure modes is nontrivial. ZooKeeper comes with a production-quality lock implementation in Java called `WriteLock` (from ZooKeeper 3.2.0 onward) that is very easy for clients to use.

More Distributed Data Structures and Protocols

There are many distributed data structures and protocols that can be built with Zoo-Keeper, such as barriers, queues, and two-phase commit. One interesting thing to note is that these are synchronous protocols, even though we use asynchronous ZooKeeper primitives (such as notifications) to build them.

The ZooKeeper website (*http://hadoop.apache.org/zookeeper/*) describes several such data structures and protocols in pseudocode. At the time of this writing, standard implementations were not available as a part of ZooKeeper, but over time it is expected that they will be added to the codebase.

BookKeeper

BookKeeper is a highly available and reliable logging service. It can be used to provide write-ahead logging, which is a common technique for ensuring data integrity in storage systems. In a system using write-ahead logging, every write operation is written to the transaction log before it is applied. Using this procedure, we don't have to write the data to permanent storage after every write operation because in the event of a system failure, the latest state may be recovered by replaying the transaction log for any writes that had not been applied.

BookKeeper clients create logs called *ledgers*, and each record appended to a ledger is called a *ledger entry*, which is simply a byte array. Ledgers are managed by *bookies*, which are servers that replicate the ledger data. Note that ledger data is not stored in ZooKeeper, only metadata is.

Traditionally, the challenge has been to make systems that use write-ahead logging robust in the face of failure of the node writing the transaction log. This is usually done by replicating the transaction log in some manner. Hadoop's HDFS namenode, for instance, writes its edit log to multiple disks, one of which is typically an NFS mounted disk. However, in the event of failure of the primary, failover is still manual. By providing logging as a highly available service, BookKeeper promises to make failover transparent, since it can tolerate the loss of bookie servers.

BookKeeper is provided in the *contrib* directory of the ZooKeeper distribution, where you can find more information on how to use it.

ZooKeeper in Production

In production, you should run ZooKeeper in replicated mode. Here we will cover some of the considerations for running an ensemble of ZooKeeper servers. However, this section is not exhaustive, so you should consult the ZooKeeper Administrator's Guide (*http://hadoop.apache.org/zookeeper/docs/current/*) for detailed up-to-date instructions, including supported platforms, recommended hardware, maintenance procedures, and configuration properties.

Resilience and Performance

ZooKeeper machines should be located to minimize the impact of machine and network failure. In practice, this means that servers should be spread across racks, power supplies, and switches, so that the failure of any one of these does not cause the ensemble to lose a majority of its servers. ZooKeeper replies on having low-latency connections between all of the servers in the ensemble, so for that reason an ensemble should be confined to a single data center.

ZooKeeper is a highly available system, and it is critical that it can perform its functions in a timely manner. Therefore, ZooKeeper should run on machines that are dedicated to ZooKeeper alone. Having other applications contend for resources can cause ZooKeeper's performance to degrade significantly.

Configure ZooKeeper to keep its transaction log on a different disk drive from its snapshots. By default, both go in the directory specified by the `dataDir` property, but by specifying a location for `dataLogDir`, the transaction log will be written there. By having its own dedicated device (not just a partition) a ZooKeeper server can maximize the rate at which it writes log entries to disk, which is does sequentially, without seeking. Since all writes go through the leader, write throughput does not scale by adding servers, so it is crucial that writes are as fast as possible.

If the process swaps to disk, performance will suffer adversely. This can be avoided by setting the Java heap size to less than the amount of physical memory available on the machine. The ZooKeeper scripts will source a file called *java.env* from its configuration directory, and this can be used to set the `JVMFLAGS` environment variable to set the heap size (and any other desired JVM arguments).

Configuration

Each server in the ensemble of ZooKeeper servers has a numeric identifier that is unique within the ensemble, and must fall between 1 and 255. The server number is specified in plain text in a file named *myid* in the directory specified by the dataDir property.

Setting each server number is only half of the job. We also need to give all the servers all the identities and network locations of the others in the ensemble. The ZooKeeper configuration file must include a line for each server, of the form:

    server.n=hostname:port:port

The value of *n* is replaced by the server number. There are two port settings: the first is the port that followers use to connect to the leader, and the second is used for leader election. Here is a sample configuration for a three-machine replicated ZooKeeper ensemble:

```
tickTime=2000
dataDir=/disk1/zookeeper
dataLogDir=/disk2/zookeeper
clientPort=2181
initLimit=5
syncLimit=2
server.1=zookeeper1:2888:3888
server.2=zookeeper2:2888:3888
server.3=zookeeper3:2888:3888
```

Servers listen on three ports: 2181 for client connections; 2888 for follower connections, if they are the leader; and 3888 for other server connections during the leader election phase. When a ZooKeeper server starts up, it reads the *myid* file to determine which server it is, then reads the configuration file to determine the ports it should listen on, as well as the network addresses of the other servers in the ensemble.

Clients connecting to this ZooKeeper ensemble should use zookeeper1:2181,zookeeper2:2181,zookeeper3:2181 as the host string in the constructor for the ZooKeeper object.

In replicated mode, there are two extra mandatory properties: initLimit and syncLimit, both measured in multiples of tickTime.

initLimit is the amount of time to allow for followers to connect to and sync with the leader. If a majority of followers fail to sync within this period, then the leader renounces its leadership status and another leader election takes place. If this happens often (and you can discover if this is the case because it is logged), it is a sign that the setting is too low.

syncLimit is the amount of time to allow a follower to sync with the leader. If a follower fails to sync within this period, it will restart itself. Clients that were attached to this follower will connect to another one.

These are the minimum settings needed to get up and running with a cluster of Zoo-Keeper servers. There are, however, more configuration options, particularly for tuning performance, documented in the ZooKeeper Administrator's Guide.

Case Studies

Hadoop Usage at Last.fm

Last.fm: The Social Music Revolution

Founded in 2002, Last.fm is an Internet radio and music community website that offers many services to its users, such as free music streams and downloads, music and event recommendations, personalized charts, and much more. There are about 25 million people who use Last.fm every month, generating huge amounts of data that need to be processed. One example of this is users transmitting information indicating which songs they are listening to (this is known as "scrobbling"). This data is processed and stored by Last.fm, so the user can access it directly (in the form of charts), and it is also used to make decisions about users' musical tastes and compatibility, and artist and track similarity.

Hadoop at Last.fm

As Last.fm's service developed and the number of users grew from thousands to millions, storing, processing and managing all the incoming data became increasingly challenging. Fortunately, Hadoop was quickly becoming stable enough and was enthusiastically adopted as it became clear how many problems it solved. It was first used at Last.fm in early 2006 and was put into production a few months later. There were several reasons for adopting Hadoop at Last.fm:

- The distributed filesystem provided redundant backups for the data stored on it (e.g., web logs, user listening data) at no extra cost.
- Scalability was simplified through the ability to add cheap, commodity hardware when required.
- The cost was right (free) at a time when Last.fm had limited financial resources.
- The open source code and active community meant that Last.fm could freely modify Hadoop to add custom features and patches.

- Hadoop provided a flexible framework for running distributed computing algorithms with a relatively easy learning curve.

Hadoop has now become a crucial part of Last.fm's infrastructure, currently consisting of two Hadoop clusters spanning over 50 machines, 300 cores, and 100 TB of disk space. Hundreds of daily jobs are run on the clusters performing operations, such as logfile analysis, evaluation of A/B tests, ad hoc processing, and charts generation. This case study will focus on the process of generating charts, as this was the first usage of Hadoop at Last.fm and illustrates the power and flexibility that Hadoop provides over other approaches when working with very large datasets.

Generating Charts with Hadoop

Last.fm uses user-generated track listening data to produce many different types of charts, such as weekly charts for tracks, per country and per user. A number of Hadoop programs are used to process the listening data and generate these charts, and these run on a daily, weekly, or monthly basis. Figure 14-1 shows an example of how this data is displayed on the site; in this case, the weekly top tracks.

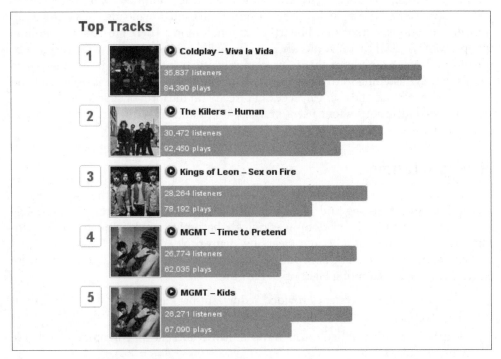

Figure 14-1. Last.fm top tracks chart

Listening data typically arrives at Last.fm from one of two sources:

- A user plays a track of her own (e.g., listening to an MP3 file on a PC or other device), and this information is sent to Last.fm using either the official Last.fm client application or one of many hundreds of third-party applications.

- A user tunes into one of Last.fm's Internet radio stations and streams a song to her computer. The Last.fm player or website can be used to access these streams and extra functionality is made available to the user, allowing her to love, skip, or ban each track that she listens to.

When processing the received data, we distinguish between a track listen submitted by a user (the first source above, referred to as a *scrobble* from here on) and a track listened to on the Last.fm radio (the second source, mentioned earlier, referred to as a *radio listen* from here on). This distinction is very important in order to prevent a feedback loop in the Last.fm recommendation system, which is based only on scrobbles. One of the most fundamental Hadoop jobs at Last.fm takes the incoming listening data and summarizes it into a format that can be used for display purposes on the Last.fm website as well as input to other Hadoop programs. This is achieved by the Track Statistics program, which is the example described in the following sections.

The Track Statistics Program

When track listening data is submitted to Last.fm, it undergoes a validation and conversion phase, the end result of which is a number of space-delimited text files containing the user ID, the track ID, the number of times the track was scrobbled, the number of times the track was listened to on the radio, and the number of times it was skipped. Table 14-1 contains sample listening data, which is used in the following examples as input to the Track Statistics program (the real data is gigabytes in size and includes many more fields that have been omitted here for simplicity's sake).

Table 14-1. Listening data

UserId	TrackId	Scrobble	Radio	Skip
111115	222	0	1	0
111113	225	1	0	0
111117	223	0	1	1
111115	225	1	0	0

These text files are the initial input provided to the Track Statistics program, which consists of two jobs that calculate various values from this data and a third job that merges the results (see Figure 14-2).

The Unique Listeners job calculates the total number of unique listeners for a track by counting the first listen by a user and ignoring all other listens by the same user. The Sum job accumulates the total listens, scrobbles, radio listens, and skips for each track by counting these values for all listens by all users. Although the input format of these

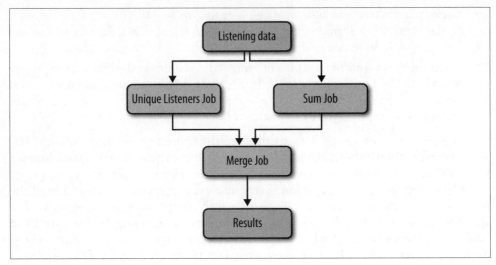

Figure 14-2. TrackStats jobs

two jobs is identical, two separate jobs are needed, as the Unique Listeners job is responsible for emitting values per track per user, and the Sum job emits values per track. The final "Merge" job is responsible for merging the intermediate output of the two other jobs into the final result. The end results of running the program are the following values per track:

- Number of unique listeners
- Number of times the track was scrobbled
- Number of times the track was listened to on the radio
- Number of times the track was listened to in total
- Number of times the track was skipped on the radio

Each job and its MapReduce phases are described in more detail next. Please note that the provided code snippets have been simplified due to space constraints; for download details for the full code listings, refer to the preface.

Calculating the number of unique listeners

The Unique Listeners job calculates, per track, the number of unique listeners.

UniqueListenerMapper. The `UniqueListenersMapper` processes the space-delimited raw listening data and emits the user ID associated with each track ID:

```
public void map(LongWritable position, Text rawLine, OutputCollector<IntWritable,
    IntWritable> output, Reporter reporter) throws IOException {

  String[] parts = (rawLine.toString()).split(" ");

  int scrobbles = Integer.parseInt(parts[TrackStatisticsProgram.COL_SCROBBLES]);
```

```
int radioListens = Integer.parseInt(parts[TrackStatisticsProgram.COL_RADIO]);
// if track somehow is marked with zero plays - ignore
if (scrobbles <= 0 && radioListens <= 0) {
  return;
}
// if we get to here then user has listened to track,
// so output user id against track id
IntWritable trackId = new IntWritable(
  Integer.parseInt(parts[TrackStatisticsProgram.COL_TRACKID]));
IntWritable userId = new IntWritable(
  Integer.parseInt(parts[TrackStatisticsProgram.COL_USERID]));
output.collect(trackId, userId);
}
```

UniqueListenersReducer. The UniqueListenersReducers receives a list of user IDs per track ID, and puts these IDs into a **Set** to remove any duplicates. The size of this set is then emitted (i.e., the number of unique listeners) for each track ID. Storing all the reduce values in a **Set** runs the risk of running out of memory if there are many values for a certain key. This hasn't happened in practice, but to overcome this, an extra MapReduce step could be introduced to remove all the duplicate values or a secondary sort could be used. (For more details, see "Secondary Sort" on page 227.)

```
public void reduce(IntWritable trackId, Iterator<IntWritable> values,
    OutputCollector<IntWritable, IntWritable> output, Reporter reporter)
    throws IOException {

  Set<Integer> userIds = new HashSet<Integer>();
  // add all userIds to the set, duplicates automatically removed (set contract)
  while (values.hasNext()) {
    IntWritable userId = values.next();
    userIds.add(Integer.valueOf(userId.get()));
  }
  // output trackId -> number of unique listeners per track
  output.collect(trackId, new IntWritable(userIds.size()));
}
```

Table 14-2 shows the sample input data for the job. The map output appears in Table 14-3 and the reduce output in Table 14-4.

Table 14-2. Job input

Line of file	UserId	TrackId	Scrobbled	Radio play	Skip
LongWritable	IntWritable	IntWritableBoolean		Boolean	Boolean
0	11115	222	0	1	0
1	11113	225	1	0	0
2	11117	223	0	1	1
3	11115	225	1	0	0

Table 14-3. Mapper output

TrackId	UserId
IntWritable	IntWritable
222	11115
225	11113
223	11117
225	11115

Table 14-4. Reducer output

TrackId	#listeners
IntWritable	IntWritable
222	1
225	2
223	1

Summing the track totals

The Sum job is relatively simple; it just adds up the values we are interested in for each track.

SumMapper. The input data is again the raw text files, but in this case, it is handled quite differently. The desired end result is a number of totals (unique listener count, play count, scrobble count, radio listen count, skip count) associated with each track. To simplify things, we use an intermediate TrackStats object generated using Hadoop Record I/O, which implements WritableComparable (so it can be used as output) to hold these values. The mapper creates a TrackStats object and sets the values on it for each line in the file, except for the unique listener count, which is left empty (it will be filled in by the final merge job):

```
public void map(LongWritable position, Text rawLine,
    OutputCollector<IntWritable, TrackStats> output, Reporter reporter)
    throws IOException {

  String[] parts = (rawLine.toString()).split(" ");
  int trackId = Integer.parseInt(parts[TrackStatisticsProgram.COL_TRACKID]);
  int scrobbles = Integer.parseInt(parts[TrackStatisticsProgram.COL_SCROBBLES]);
  int radio = Integer.parseInt(parts[TrackStatisticsProgram.COL_RADIO]);
  int skip = Integer.parseInt(parts[TrackStatisticsProgram.COL_SKIP]);
  // set number of listeners to 0 (this is calculated later)
  // and other values as provided in text file
  TrackStats trackstat = new TrackStats(0, scrobbles + radio, scrobbles, radio, skip);
  output.collect(new IntWritable(trackId), trackstat);
}
```

SumReducer. In this case, the reducer performs a very similar function to the mapper—it sums the statistics per track and returns an overall total:

```
public void reduce(IntWritable trackId, Iterator<TrackStats> values,
    OutputCollector<IntWritable, TrackStats> output, Reporter reporter)
    throws IOException {

  TrackStats sum = new TrackStats(); // holds the totals for this track
  while (values.hasNext()) {
    TrackStats trackStats = (TrackStats) values.next();
    sum.setListeners(sum.getListeners() + trackStats.getListeners());
    sum.setPlays(sum.getPlays() + trackStats.getPlays());
    sum.setSkips(sum.getSkips() + trackStats.getSkips());
    sum.setScrobbles(sum.getScrobbles() + trackStats.getScrobbles());
    sum.setRadioPlays(sum.getRadioPlays() + trackStats.getRadioPlays());
  }
  output.collect(trackId, sum);
}
```

Table 14-5 shows the input data for the job (the same as for the Unique Listeners job). The map output appears in Table 14-6 and the reduce output in Table 14-7.

Table 14-5. Job input

Line	UserId	TrackId	Scrobbled	Radio play	Skip
LongWritable	IntWritable	IntWritable	Boolean	Boolean	Boolean
0	11115	222	0	1	0
1	11113	225	1	0	0
2	11117	223	0	1	1
3	11115	225	1	0	0

Table 14-6. Map output

TrackId	#listeners	#plays	#scrobbles	#radio plays	#skips
IntWritable	IntWritable	IntWritable	IntWritable	IntWritable	IntWritable
222	0	1	0	1	0
225	0	1	1	0	0
223	0	1	0	1	1
225	0	1	1	0	0

Table 14-7. Reduce output

TrackId	#listeners	#plays	#scrobbles	#radio plays	#skips
IntWritable	IntWritable	IntWritable	IntWritable	IntWritable	IntWritable
222	0	1	0	1	0
225	0	2	2	0	0
223	0	1	0	1	1

Merging the results

The final job needs to merge the output from the two previous jobs: the number of unique listeners per track and the statistics per track. In order to be able to merge these different inputs, two different mappers (one for each type of input) are used. The two intermediate jobs are configured to write their results to different paths, and the `MultipleInputs` class is used to specify which mapper will process which files. The following code shows how the `JobConf` for the job is set up to do this:

```
MultipleInputs.addInputPath(conf, sumInputDir,
    SequenceFileInputFormat.class, IdentityMapper.class);

MultipleInputs.addInputPath(conf, listenersInputDir,
    SequenceFileInputFormat.class, MergeListenersMapper.class);
```

It is possible to use a single mapper to handle different inputs, but the example solution is more convenient and elegant.

MergeListenersMapper. This mapper is used to process the `UniqueListenerJob`'s output of unique listeners per track. It creates a `TrackStats` object in a similar manner to the `SumMapper`, but this time, it fills in only the unique listener count per track and leaves the other values empty:

```
public void map(IntWritable trackId, IntWritable uniqueListenerCount,
    OutputCollector<IntWritable, TrackStats> output, Reporter reporter)
    throws IOException {
  TrackStats trackStats = new TrackStats();
  trackStats.setListeners(uniqueListenerCount.get());
  output.collect(trackId, trackStats);
}
```

Table 14-8 shows some input for the mapper; the corresponding output is shown in Table 14-9.

Table 14-8. MergeListenersMapper input

TrackId	#listeners
IntWritable	IntWritable
222	1
225	2
223	1

Table 14-9. MergeListenersMapper output

TrackId	#listeners	#plays	#scrobbles	#radio	#skips
222	1	0	0	0	0
225	2	0	0	0	0
223	2	0	0	0	0

IdentityMapper. The IdentityMapper is configured to process the SumJob's output of TrackStats objects and, as no additional processing is required, it directly emits the input data (see Table 14-10).

Table 14-10. IdentityMapper input and output

TrackId	#listeners	#plays	#scrobbles	#radio	#skips
IntWritable	IntWritable	IntWritable	IntWritable	IntWritable	IntWritable
222	0	1	0	1	0
225	0	2	2	0	0
223	0	1	0	1	1

SumReducer. The two mappers above emit values of the same type: a TrackStats object per track, with different values filled in. The final reduce phase can reuse the SumReducer described earlier to create a TrackStats object per track, sum up all the values, and emit it (see Table 14-11).

Table 14-11. Final SumReducer output

TrackId	#listeners	#plays	#scrobbles	#radio	#skips
IntWritable	IntWritable	IntWritable	IntWritable	IntWritable	IntWritable
222	1	1	0	1	0
225	2	2	2	0	0
223	1	1	0	1	1

The final output files are then accumulated and copied to a server where a web service makes the data available to the Last.fm website for display. An example of this is shown in Figure 14-3, where the total number of listeners and plays are displayed for a track.

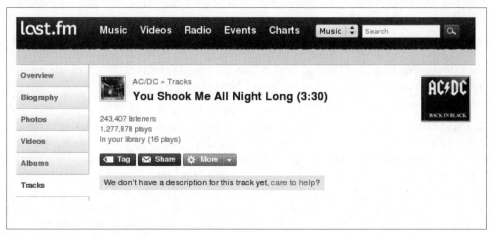

Figure 14-3. TrackStats result

Summary

Hadoop has become an essential part of Last.fm's infrastructure and is used to generate and process a wide variety of datasets ranging from web logs to user listening data. The example covered here has been simplified considerably in order to get the key concepts across; in real-world usage the input data has a more complicated structure and the code that processes it is more complex. Hadoop itself, while mature enough for production use, is still in active development and new features and improvements are added by the Hadoop community every week. We at Last.fm are happy to be part of this community as a contributor of code and ideas, and as end users of a great piece of open source technology.

—Adrian Woodhead and Marc de Palol

Hadoop and Hive at Facebook

Introduction

Hadoop can be used to form core backend batch and near real-time computing infrastructures. It can also be used to store and archive massive datasets. In this case study, we will explore backend data architectures and the role Hadoop can play in them. We will describe hypothetical Hadoop configurations, potential uses of Hive—an open source data warehousing and SQL infrastructure built on top of Hadoop—and the different kinds of business and product applications that have been built using this infrastructure.

Hadoop at Facebook

History

The amount of log and dimension data in Facebook that needs to be processed and stored has exploded as the usage of the site has increased. A key requirement for any data processing platform for this environment is the ability to be able to scale rapidly in tandem. Further, engineering resources being limited, the system should be very reliable and easy to use and maintain.

Initially, data warehousing at Facebook was performed entirely on an Oracle instance. After we started hitting scalability and performance problems, we investigated whether there were open source technologies that could be used in our environment. As part of this investigation, we deployed a relatively small Hadoop instance and started publishing some of our core datasets into this instance. Hadoop was attractive because Yahoo! was using it internally for its batch processing needs and also because we were familiar with the simplicity and scalability of the MapReduce model as popularized by Google.

Our initial prototype was very successful: the engineers loved the ability to process massive amounts of data in reasonable timeframes, an ability that we just did not have before. They also loved being able to use their favorite programming language for processing (using Hadoop streaming). Having our core datasets published in one centralized data store was also very convenient. At around the same time, we started developing Hive. This made it even easier for users to process data in the Hadoop cluster by being able to express common computations in the form of SQL, a language with which most engineers and analysts are familiar.

As a result, the cluster size and usage grew leaps and bounds, and today Facebook is running the second largest Hadoop cluster in the world. As of this writing, we hold more than 2 PB of data in Hadoop and load more than 10 TB of data into it every day. Our Hadoop instance has 2,400 cores and about 9 TB of memory and runs at 100% utilization at many points during the day. We are able to scale out this cluster rapidly in response to our growth, and we have been able to take advantage of open source by modifying Hadoop where required to suit our needs. We have contributed back to open source, both in the form of contributions to some core components of Hadoop as well as by open-sourcing Hive, which is now a Hadoop subproject.

Use cases

There are at least four interrelated but distinct classes of uses for Hadoop at Facebook:

- Producing daily and hourly summaries over large amounts of data. These summaries are used for a number of different purposes within the company:
  - Reports based on these summaries are used by engineering and nonengineering functional teams to drive product decisions. These summaries include reports on growth of the users, page views, and average time spent on the site by the users.
  - Providing performance numbers about advertisement campaigns that are run on Facebook.
  - Backend processing for site features such as people you may like and applications you may like.
- Running ad hoc jobs over historical data. These analyses help answer questions from our product groups and executive team.
- As a de facto long-term archival store for our log datasets.
- To look up log events by specific attributes (where logs are indexed by such attributes), which is used to maintain the integrity of the site and protect users against spambots.

Data architecture

Figure 14-4 shows the basic components of our architecture and the data flow within these components.

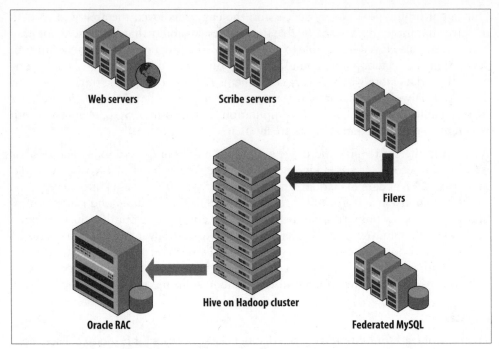

Figure 14-4. Data warehousing architecture at Facebook

As shown in Figure 14-4, the following components are used in processing data:

Scribe

Log data is generated by web servers as well as internal services such as the Search backend. We use Scribe, an open source log collection service developed in Facebook that deposits hundreds of log datasets with daily volume in tens of terabytes into a handful of NFS servers.

HDFS

A large fraction of this log data is copied into one central HDFS instance. Dimension data is also scraped from our internal MySQL databases and copied over into HDFS daily.

Hive/Hadoop

We use Hive, a Hadoop subproject developed in Facebook, to build a data warehouse over all the data collected in HDFS. Files in HDFS, including log data from Scribe and dimension data from the MySQL tier, are made available as tables with logical partitions. A SQL-like query language provided by Hive is used in conjunction with MapReduce to create/publish a variety of summaries and reports, as well as to perform historical analysis over these tables.

Tools

Browser-based interfaces built on top of Hive allow users to compose and launch Hive queries (which in turn launch MapReduce jobs) using just a few mouse clicks.

Traditional RDBMS

> We use Oracle and MySQL databases to publish these summaries. The volume of data here is relatively small, but the query rate is high and needs real-time response.

DataBee

> An in-house ETL workflow software that is used to provide a common framework for reliable batch processing across all data processing jobs.

Data from the NFS tier storing Scribe data is continuously replicated to the HDFS cluster by copier jobs. The NFS devices are mounted on the Hadoop tier and the copier processes run as map-only jobs on the Hadoop cluster. This makes it easy to scale the copier processes and also makes them fault-resilient. Currently we copy over 6 TB per day from Scribe to HDFS in this manner. We also download up to 4 TB of dimension data from our MySQL tier to HDFS every day. These are also conveniently arranged on the Hadoop cluster, as map-only jobs that copy data out of MySQL boxes.

Hadoop configuration

The central philosophy behind our Hadoop deployment is consolidation. We use a single HDFS instance, and a vast majority of processing is done in a single MapReduce cluster (running a single jobtracker). The reasons for this are fairly straightforward:

- We can minimize the administrative overheads by operating a single cluster.
- Data does not need to be duplicated. All data is available in a single place for all the use cases described previously.
- By using the same compute cluster across all departments, we get tremendous efficiencies.
- Our users work in a collaborative environment, so requirements in terms of quality of service are not onerous (yet).

We also have a single shared Hive metastore (using a MySQL database) that holds metadata about all the Hive tables stored in HDFS.

Hypothetical Use Case Studies

In this section, we will describe some typical problems that are common for large websites, which are difficult to solve through traditional warehousing technologies, simply because the costs and scales involved are prohibitively high. Hadoop and Hive can provide a more scalable and more cost-effective solution in such situations.

Advertiser insights and performance

One of the most common uses of Hadoop is to produce summaries from large volumes of data. It is very typical of large ad networks such as Facebook ad network, Google AdSense, and many others to provide advertisers with standard aggregated statistics about their ads that help the advertisers to tune their campaigns effectively. Computing advertisement performance numbers on large datasets is a very data-intensive operation, and the scalability and cost advantages of Hadoop and Hive can really help in computing these numbers in a reasonable time frame and at a reasonable cost.

Many ad networks provide standardized CPC- and CPM-based ad-units to the advertisers. The CPC ads are cost-per-click ads: the advertiser pays the ad network amounts that are dependent on the number of clicks that the particular ad gets from the users visiting the site. The CPM ads, on the other hand, bill the advertisers amounts that are proportional to the number of users that see the ad on the site. Apart from these standardized ad units, in the last few years ads that have more dynamic content that is tailored to each individual user have also become common in the online advertisement industry. Yahoo! does this through SmartAds, whereas Facebook provides its advertisers with Social Ads. The latter allows the advertisers to embed information from a user's network of friends; for example, a Nike ad may refer to a friend of the user who recently fanned Nike and shared that information with his friends on Facebook. In addition, Facebook also provides Engagement Ad units to the advertisers, wherein the users can more effectively interact with the ad, be it by commenting on it or by playing embedded videos. In general, there is a wide variety of ads that are provided to the advertisers by the online ad networks, and this variety also adds yet another dimension to the various kinds of performance numbers that the advertisers are interested in getting about their campaigns.

At the most basic level, advertisers are interested in knowing the total and the number of unique users that have seen the ad or have clicked on it. For more dynamic ads, they may even be interested in getting the breakdown of these aggregated numbers by the kind of dynamic information shown in the ad unit or the kind of engagement action undertaken by the users on the ad. For example, a particular advertisement may have been shown 100,000 times to 30,000 unique users. Similarly a video embedded inside an Engagement Ad may have been watched by 100,000 unique users. In addition, these performance numbers are typically reported for each ad, campaign, and account. An account may have multiple campaigns with each campaign running multiple ads on the network. Finally, these numbers are typically reported for different time durations by the ad networks. Typical durations are daily, rolling week, month to date, rolling month, and sometimes even for the entire lifetime of the campaign. Moreover, advertisers also look at the geographic breakdown of these numbers among other ways of slicing and dicing this data, such as what percentage of the total viewers or clickers of a particular ad are in the Asia Pacific region.

As is evident, there are four predominant dimension hierarchies: the account, campaign, and ad dimension; the time period; the type of interaction; and the user dimension. The last of these is used to report unique numbers, whereas the other three are the reporting dimensions. The user dimension is also used to create aggregated geographic profiles for the viewers and clickers of ads. All this information in totality allows the advertisers to tune their campaigns to improve their effectiveness on any given ad network. Aside from the multidimensional nature of this set of pipelines, the volumes of data processed and the rate at which this data is growing on a daily basis make this difficult to scale without a technology like Hadoop for large ad networks. As of this writing, for example, the ad log volume that is processed for ad performance numbers at Facebook is approximately 1 TB per day of (uncompressed) logs. This volume has seen a 30-fold increase since January 2008, when the volumes were in the range of 30 GB per day. Hadoop's ability to scale with hardware has been a major factor behind the ability of these pipelines to keep up with this data growth with minor tweaking of job configurations. Typically, these configuration changes involve increasing the number of reducers for the Hadoop jobs that are processing the intensive portions of these pipelines. The largest of these stages currently run with 400 reducers (an increase of eight times from the 50 reducers that were being used in January 2008).

Ad hoc analysis and product feedback

Apart from regular reports, another primary use case for a data warehousing solution is to be able to support ad hoc analysis and product feedback solutions. Any typical website, for example, makes product changes, and it is typical for product managers or engineers to understand the impact of a new feature, based on user engagement as well as on the click-through rate on that feature. The product team may even wish to do a deeper analysis on what is the impact of the change based on various regions and countries, such as whether this change increases the click-through rate of the users in U.S. or whether it reduces the engagement of users in India. A lot of this type of analysis could be done with Hadoop by using Hive and regular SQL. The measurement of click-through rate can be easily expressed as a join of the impressions and clicks for the particular link related to the feature. This information can be joined with geographic information to compute the effect of product changes on different regions. Subsequently one can compute average click-through rate for different geographic regions by performing aggregations over them. All of these are easily expressible in Hive using a couple of SQL queries (that would in turn generate multiple Hadoop jobs). If only an estimate were required, the same queries can be run for a sample set of the users using sampling functionality natively supported by Hive. Some of this analysis needs the use of custom map and reduce scripts in conjunction with the Hive SQL and that is also easy to plug into a Hive query.

A good example of a more complex analysis is estimating the peak number of users logging into the site per minute for the entire past year. This would involve sampling page view logs (because the total page view data for a popular website is huge), grouping it by time and then finding the number of new users at different time points via a custom reduce script. This is a good example where both SQL and MapReduce are required for solving the end user problem and something that is possible to achieve easily with Hive.

Data analysis

Hive and Hadoop can be easily used for training and scoring for data analysis applications. These data analysis applications can span multiple domains such as popular websites, bioinformatics companies, and oil exploration companies. A typical example of such an application in the online ad network industry would be the prediction of what features of an ad makes it more likely to be noticed by the user. The training phase typically would involve identifying the response metric and the predictive features. In this case, a good metric to measure the effectiveness of an ad could be its click-through rate. Some interesting features of the ad could be the industry vertical that it belongs to, the content of the ad, the placement of the ad on the page, and so on. Hive is easily useful for assembling training data and then feeding the same into a data analysis engine (typically R or user programs written in MapReduce). In this particular case, different ad performance numbers and features can be structured as tables in Hive. One can easily sample this data (sampling is required as R can only handle limited data volume) and perform the appropriate aggregations and joins using Hive queries to assemble a response table that contains the most important ad features that determine the effectiveness of an advertisement. However, since sampling loses information, some of the more important data analysis applications use parallel implementations of popular data analysis kernels using MapReduce framework.

Once the model has been trained, it may be deployed for scoring on a daily basis. The bulk of the data analysis tasks do not perform daily scoring though. Many of them are ad hoc in nature and require one-time analysis that can be used as input into product design process.

Hive

Overview

When we started using Hadoop, we very quickly became impressed by its scalability and availability. However, we were worried about widespread adoption, primarily because of the complexity involved in writing MapReduce programs in Java (as well as the cost of training users to write them). We were aware that a lot of engineers and analysts in the company understood SQL as a tool to query and analyze data and that a lot of them were proficient in a number of scripting languages like PHP and Python. As a result, it was imperative for us to develop software that could bridge this gap between the languages that the users were proficient in and the languages required to program Hadoop.

It was also evident that a lot of our datasets were structured and could be easily partitioned. The natural consequence of these requirements was a system that could model data as tables and partitions and that could also provide a SQL-like language for query and analysis. Also essential was the ability to plug in customized MapReduce programs written in the programming language of the user's choice into the query. This system was called Hive. Hive is a data warehouse infrastructure built on top of Hadoop and serves as the predominant tool that is used to query the data stored in Hadoop at Facebook. In the following sections, we describe this system in more detail.

Data organization

Data is organized consistently across all datasets and is stored compressed, partitioned, and sorted:

Compression
> Almost all datasets are stored as sequence files using gzip codec. Older datasets are recompressed to use the bzip codec that gives substantially more compression than gzip. Bzip is slower than gzip, but older data is accessed much less frequently and this performance hit is well worth the savings in terms of disk space.

Partitioning
> Most datasets are partitioned by date. Individual partitions are loaded into Hive, which loads each partition into a separate HDFS directory. In most cases, this partitioning is based simply on datestamps associated with scribe logfiles. However, in some cases, we scan data and collate them based on timestamp available inside a log entry. Going forward, we are also going to be partitioning data on multiple attributes (for example, country and date).

Sorting
> Each partition within a table is often sorted (and hash-partitioned) by unique ID (if one is present). This has a few key advantages:

* It is easy to run sampled queries on such datasets.
* We can build indexes on sorted data.
* Aggregates and joins involving unique IDs can be done very efficiently on such datasets.

Loading data into this long-term format is done by daily MapReduce jobs (and is distinct from the near real-time data import processes).

Query language

The Hive Query language is very SQL-like. It has traditional SQL constructs like joins, group bys, where, select, from clauses and from clause subqueries. It tries to convert SQL commands into a set of MapReduce jobs. Apart from the normal SQL clauses, it has a bunch of other extensions, like the ability to specify custom mapper and reducer scripts in the query itself, the ability to insert into multiple tables, partitions, HDFS or local files while doing a single scan of the data and the ability to run the query on data samples rather than the full dataset (this ability is fairly useful while testing queries). The Hive metastore stores the metadata for a table and provides this metadata to the Hive compiler for converting SQL commands to MapReduce jobs. Through partition pruning, map-side aggregations, and other features, the compiler tries to create plans that can optimize the runtime for the query.

Data pipelines using Hive

Additionally, the ability provided by Hive in terms of expressing data pipelines in SQL can and has provided the much needed flexibility in putting these pipelines together in an easy and expedient manner. This is especially useful for organizations and products that are still evolving and growing. Many of the operations needed in processing data pipelines are the well-understood SQL operations like join, group by, and distinct aggregations. With Hive's ability to convert SQL into a series of Hadoop MapReduce jobs, it becomes fairly easy to create and maintain these pipelines. We illustrate these facets of Hive in this section by using an example of a hypothetical ad network and showing how some typical aggregated reports needed by the advertisers can be computed using Hive. As an example, assuming that an online ad network stores information on ads in a table named `dim_ads` and stores all the impressions served to that ad in a table named `impression_logs` in Hive, with the latter table being partitioned by date, the daily impression numbers (both unique and total by campaign, that are routinely given by ad networks to the advertisers) for 2008-12-01 are expressible as the following SQL in Hive:

```
SELECT a.campaign_id, count(1), count(DISTINCT b.user_id)
FROM dim_ads a JOIN impression_logs b ON(b.ad_id = a.ad_id)
WHERE b.dateid = '2008-12-01'
GROUP BY a.campaign_id;
```

This would also be the typical SQL statement that one could use in other RDBMSs such as Oracle, DB2, and so on.

In order to compute the daily impression numbers by ad and account from the same joined data as earlier, Hive provides the ability to do multiple group bys simultaneously as shown in the following query (SQL-like but not strictly SQL):

```
FROM(
  SELECT a.ad_id, a.campaign_id, a.account_id, b.user_id
  FROM dim_ads a JOIN impression_logs b ON (b.ad_id = a.ad_id)
  WHERE b.dateid = '2008-12-01') x
INSERT OVERWRITE DIRECTORY 'results_gby_adid'
  SELECT x.ad_id, count(1), count(DISTINCT x.user_id) GROUP BY x.ad_id
INSERT OVERWRITE DIRECTORY 'results_gby_campaignid'
  SELECT x.campaign_id, count(1), count(DISTINCT x.user_id) GROUP BY x.campaign_id
INSERT OVERWRITE DIRECTORY 'results_gby_accountid'
  SELECT x.account_id, count(1), count(DISTINCT x.user_id) GROUP BY x.account_id;
```

In one of the optimizations that is being added to Hive, the query can be converted into a sequence of Hadoop MapReduce jobs that are able to scale with data skew. Essentially, the join is converted into one MapReduce job and the three group bys are converted into four MapReduce jobs with the first one generating a partial aggregate on `unique_id`. This is especially useful because the distribution of `impression_logs` over `unique_id` is much more uniform as compared to `ad_id` (typically in an ad network, a few ads dominate in that they are shown more uniformly to the users). As a result, computing the partial aggregation by `unique_id` allows the pipeline to distribute the work more uniformly to the reducers. The same template can be used to compute performance numbers for different time periods by simply changing the date predicate in the query.

Computing the lifetime numbers can be more tricky though, as using the strategy described previously, one would have to scan all the partitions of the `impression_logs` table. Therefore, in order to compute the lifetime numbers, a more viable strategy is to store the lifetime counts on a per `ad_id`, `unique_id` grouping every day in a partition of an intermediate table. The data in this table combined with the next days `impression_logs` can be used to incrementally generate the lifetime ad performance numbers. As an example, in order to get the impression numbers for 2008-12-01, the intermediate table partition for 2008-11-30 is used. The Hive queries that can be used to achieve this are as follows:

```
INSERT OVERWRITE lifetime_partial_imps PARTITION(dateid='2008-12-01')
SELECT x.ad_id, x.user_id, sum(x.cnt)
FROM (
  SELECT a.ad_id, a.user_id, a.cnt
  FROM lifetime_partial_imps a
  WHERE a.dateid = '2008-11-30'
  UNION ALL
  SELECT b.ad_id, b.user_id, 1 as cnt
  FROM impression_log b
  WHERE b.dateid = '2008-12-01'
) x
GROUP BY x.ad_id, x.user_id;
```

This query computes the partial sums for 2008-12-01, which can be used for computing the 2008-12-01 numbers as well as the 2008-12-02 numbers (not shown here). The SQL is converted to a single Hadoop MapReduce job that essentially computes the group by on the combined stream of inputs. This SQL can be followed by the following Hive query, which computes the actual numbers for different groupings (similar to the one in the daily pipelines):

```
FROM(
  SELECT a.ad_id, a.campaign_id, a.account_id, b.user_id, b.cnt
    FROM dim_ads a JOIN lifetime_partial_imps b ON (b.ad_id = a.ad_id)
    WHERE b.dateid = '2008-12-01') x
INSERT OVERWRITE DIRECTORY 'results_gby_adid'
  SELECT x.ad_id, sum(x.cnt), count(DISTINCT x.user_id) GROUP BY x.ad_id
INSERT OVERWRITE DIRECTORY 'results_gby_campaignid'
  SELECT x.campaign_id, sum(x.cnt), count(DISTINCT x.user_id) GROUP BY x.campaign_id
INSERT OVERWRITE DIRECTORY 'results_gby_accountid'
  SELECT x.account_id, sum(x.cnt), count(DISTINCT x.user_id) GROUP BY x.account_id;
```

Hive and Hadoop are batch processing systems that cannot serve the computed data with the same latency as a usual RDBMS such as Oracle or MySQL. Therefore, on many occasions, it is still useful to load the summaries generated through Hive and Hadoop to a more traditional RDBMS for serving this data to users through different BI tools or even though a web portal.

Problems and Future Work

Fair sharing

Hadoop clusters typically run a mix of production daily jobs that need to finish computation within a reasonable time frame as well as ad hoc jobs that may be of different priorities and sizes. In typical installations, these jobs tend to run overnight, when interference from ad hoc jobs run by users is minimal. However, overlap between large ad hoc and production jobs is often unavoidable and, without adequate safeguards, can impact the latency of production jobs. ETL processing also contains several near real-time jobs that must be performed at hourly intervals (these include processes to copy Scribe data from NFS servers as well as hourly summaries computed over some datasets). It also means that a single rogue job can bring down the entire cluster and put production processes at risk.

The fair-sharing Hadoop jobscheduler, developed at Facebook and contributed back to Hadoop, provides a solution to many of these issues. It reserves guaranteed compute resources for specific pools of jobs while at the same time letting idle resources be used by everyone. It also prevents large jobs from hogging cluster resources by allocating compute resources in a fair manner across these pools. Memory can become one of the most contended resources in the cluster. We have made some changes to Hadoop so that if the JobTracker is low on memory, Hadoop job submissions are throttled. This can allow the user processes to run with reasonable per-process memory limits, and it is possible to put in place some monitoring scripts in order to prevent MapReduce jobs from impacting HDFS daemons (due primarily to high memory consumption) running on the same node. Log directories are stored in separate disk partitions and cleaned regularly, and we think it can also be useful to put MapReduce intermediate storage in separate disk partitions as well.

Space management

Capacity management continues to be a big challenge—utilization is increasing at a fast rate with growth of data. Many growing companies with growing datasets have the same pain. In many situations, much of this data is temporary in nature. In such cases, one can use retention settings in Hive and also recompress older data in bzip format to save on space. Although configurations are largely symmetrical from a disk storage point of view, adding a separate tier of high-storage-density machines to hold older data may prove beneficial. This will make it cheaper to store archival data in Hadoop. However, access to such data should be transparent. We are currently working on a data archival layer to make this possible and to unify all the aspects of dealing with older data.

Scribe-HDFS integration

Currently, Scribe writes to a handful of NFS filers from where data is picked up and delivered to HDFS by custom copier jobs as described earlier. We are working on making Scribe write directly to another HDFS instance. This will make it very easy to scale and administer Scribe. Due to the high uptime requirements for Scribe, its target HDFS instance is likely to be different from the production HDFS instance (so that it is isolated from any load/downtime issues due to user jobs).

Improvements to Hive

Hive is still under active development. A number of key features are being worked on such as order by and having clause support, more aggregate functions, more built in functions, datetime, data type, and so on. At the same time, a number of performance optimizations are being worked on, such as predicate pushdown and common subexpression elimination. On the integration side, JDBC and ODBC drivers are being developed in order to integrate with OLAP and BI tools. With all these optimizations, we hope that we can unlock the power of MapReduce and Hadoop and bring it closer to nonengineering communities as well within Facebook. For more information on this project, please visit *http://hadoop.apache.org/hive/*.

—Joydeep Sen Sarma and Ashish Thusoo

Nutch Search Engine

Background

Nutch is a framework for building scalable Internet crawlers and search engines. It's an Apache Software Foundation project, and a subproject of Lucene, and it's available under the Apache 2.0 license.

We won't go deeply into the anatomy of a web crawler as such—the purpose of this case study is to show how Hadoop can be used to implement various complex processing tasks typical for a search engine. Interested readers can find plenty of Nutch-specific information on the official site of the project (*http://lucene.apache.org/nutch*). Suffice to say that in order to create and maintain a search engine, one needs the following subsystems:

Database of pages
> This database keeps track of all pages known to the crawler and their status, such as the last time it visited the page, its fetching status, refresh interval, content checksum, etc. In Nutch terminology, this database is called *CrawlDb*.

List of pages to fetch
> As crawlers periodically refresh their view of the Web, they download new pages (previously unseen) or refresh pages that they think already expired. Nutch calls such a list of candidate pages prepared for fetching a *fetchlist*.

Raw page data
> Page content is downloaded from remote sites, and stored locally in the original uninterpreted format, as a byte array. This data is called the *page content* in Nutch.

Parsed page data
> Page content is then parsed using a suitable parser—Nutch provides parsers for documents in many popular formats, such as HTML, PDF, Open Office and Microsoft Office, RSS, and others.

Link graph database
> This database is necessary to compute link-based page ranking scores, such as PageRank. For each URL known to Nutch, it contains a list of other URLs pointing to it, and their associated anchor text (from HTML `<a href="..">anchor text</a>` elements). This database is called *LinkDb*.

Full-text search index
> This is a classical inverted index, built from the collected page metadata and from the extracted plain-text content. It is implemented using the excellent Lucene library (*http://lucene.apache.org/java*).

We briefly mentioned before that Hadoop began its life as a component in Nutch, intended to improve its scalability and to address clear performance bottlenecks caused by a centralized data processing model. Nutch was also the first public proof-of-concept application ported to the framework that would later become Hadoop, and the effort required to port Nutch algorithms and data structures to Hadoop proved to be surprisingly small. This probably encouraged the following development of Hadoop as a separate subproject with the aim of providing a reusable framework for applications other than Nutch.

Currently nearly all Nutch tools process data by running one or more MapReduce jobs.

Data Structures

There are several major data structures maintained in Nutch, and they all make use of Hadoop I/O classes and formats. Depending on the purpose of the data, and the way it's accessed once it's created, the data is kept either using Hadoop map files or sequence files.

Since the data is produced and processed by MapReduce jobs, which in turn run several map and reduce tasks, its on-disk layout corresponds to the common Hadoop output formats, that is, `MapFileOutputFormat` and `SequenceFileOutputFormat`. So to be precise, we should say that data is kept in several partial map files or sequence files, with as many parts as there were reduce tasks in the job that created the data. For simplicity, we omit this distinction in the following sections.

CrawlDb

CrawlDb stores the current status of each URL, as a map file of `<url, CrawlDatum>`, where keys use `Text` and values use a Nutch-specific `CrawlDatum` class (which implements the `Writable` interface).

In order to provide a quick random access to the records (sometimes useful for diagnostic reasons, when users want to examine individual records in CrawlDb), this data is stored in map files and not in sequence files.

CrawlDb is initially created using the Injector tool, which simply converts a plain-text representation of the initial list of URLs (called the seed list) to a map file in the format described earlier. Subsequently it is updated with the information from the fetched and parsed pages—more on that shortly.

LinkDb

This database stores the incoming link information for every URL known to Nutch. It is a map file of `<url, Inlinks>`, where Inlinks is a list of URL and anchor text data. It's worth noting that this information is not immediately available during page collection, but the reverse information is available, namely that of outgoing links from a page. The process of inverting this relationship is implemented as a MapReduce job, described shortly.

Segments

Segments in Nutch parlance correspond to fetching and parsing a batch of URLs. Figure 14-5 presents how segments are created and processed.

A segment (which is really a directory in a filesystem) contains the following parts (which are simply subdirectories containing `MapFileOutputFormat` or `SequenceFileOut putFormat` data):

content
> Contains the raw data of downloaded pages, as a map file of `<url, Content>`. Nutch uses a map file here, because it needs fast random access in order to present a cached view of a page.

crawl_generate
> Contains the list of URLs to be fetched, together with their current status retrieved from CrawlDb, as a sequence file of `<url, CrawlDatum>`. This data uses sequence file, first because it's processed sequentially, and second because we couldn't satisfy the map file invariants of sorted keys. We need to spread URLs that belong to the same host as far apart as possible to minimize the load per target host, and this means that records are sorted more or less randomly.

crawl_fetch

Contains status reports from the fetching, that is, whether it was successful, what was the response code, etc. This is stored in a map file of `<url, CrawlDatum>`.

crawl_parse

The list of outlinks for each successfully fetched and parsed page is stored here so that Nutch can expand its crawling frontier by learning new URLs.

parse_data

Metadata collected during parsing; among others, the list of outgoing links (outlinks) for a page. This information is crucial later on to build an inverted graph (of incoming links—inlinks).

parse_text

Plain-text version of the page, suitable for indexing in Lucene. These are stored as a map file of `<url, ParseText>` so that Nutch can access them quickly when building summaries (snippets) to display the list of search results.

New segments are created from CrawlDb when the Generator tool is run (1 in Figure 14-5), and initially contain just a list of URLs to fetch (the *crawl_generate* subdirectory). As this list is processed in several steps, the segment collects output data from the processing tools in a set of subdirectories.

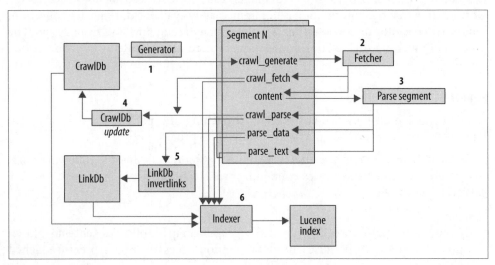

Figure 14-5. Segments

For example, the *content* part is populated by a tool called Fetcher, which downloads raw data from URLs on the fetchlist (2). This tool also saves the status information in *crawl_fetch* so that this data can be used later on for updating the status of the page in CrawlDb.

The remaining parts of the segment are populated by the Parse segment tool (3), which reads the content section, selects appropriate content parser based on the declared (or detected) MIME type, and saves the results of parsing in three parts: *crawl_parse*, *parse_data*, and *parse_text*. This data is then used to update the CrawlDb with new information (4) and to create the LinkDb (5).

Segments are kept around until all pages present in them are expired. Nutch applies a configurable maximum time limit, after which a page is forcibly selected for refetching; this helps the operator phase out all segments older than this limit (because he can be sure that by that time all pages in this segment would have been refetched).

Segment data is used to create Lucene indexes ([6]—primarily the *parse_text* and *parse_data* parts), but it also provides a data storage mechanism for quick retrieval of plain text and raw content data. The former is needed so that Nutch can generate snippets (fragments of document text best matching a query); the latter provides the ability to present a "cached view" of the page. In both cases, this data is accessed directly from map files in response to requests for snippet generation or for cached content. In practice, even for large collections the performance of accessing data directly from map files is quite sufficient.

Selected Examples of Hadoop Data Processing in Nutch

The following sections present relevant details of some Nutch tools to illustrate how the MapReduce paradigm is applied to a concrete data processing task in Nutch.

Link inversion

HTML pages collected during crawling contain HTML links, which may point either to the same page (internal links) or to other pages. HTML links are directed from source page to target page. See Figure 14-6.

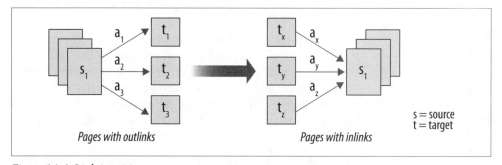

Figure 14-6. Link inversion

However, most algorithms for calculating a page's importance (or quality) need the opposite information, that is, what pages contain outlinks that point to the current page. This information is not readily available when crawling. Also, the indexing process benefits from taking into account the anchor text on inlinks so that this text may semantically enrich the text of the current page.

As mentioned earlier, Nutch collects the outlink information and then uses this data to build a LinkDb, which contains this reversed link data in the form of inlinks and anchor text.

This section presents a rough outline of the implementation of the LinkDb tool—many details have been omitted (such as URL normalization and filtering) in order to present a clear picture of the process. What's left gives a classical example of why the MapReduce paradigm fits so well with the key data transformation processes required to run a search engine. Large search engines need to deal with massive web graph data (many pages with a lot of outlinks/inlinks), and the parallelism and fault tolerance offered by Hadoop make this possible. Additionally, it's easy to express the link inversion using the map-sort-reduce primitives, as illustrated next.

The snippet below presents the job initialization of the LinkDb tool:

```
JobConf job = new JobConf(configuration);
FileInputFormat.addInputPath(job, new Path(segmentPath, "parse_data"));
job.setInputFormat(SequenceFileInputFormat.class);
job.setMapperClass(LinkDb.class);
job.setReducerClass(LinkDb.class);
job.setOutputKeyClass(Text.class);
job.setOutputValueClass(Inlinks.class);
job.setOutputFormat(MapFileOutputFormat.class);
FileOutputFormat.setOutputPath(job, newLinkDbPath);
```

As we can see, the source data for this job is the list of fetched URLs (keys) and the corresponding ParseData records that contain among others the outlink information for each page, as an array of outlinks. An outlink contains both the target URL and the anchor text.

The output from the job is again a list of URLs (keys), but the values are instances of inlinks, which is simply a specialized Set of inlinks that contain target URLs and anchor text.

Perhaps surprisingly, URLs are typically stored and processed as plain text and not as java.net.URL or java.net.URI instances. There are several reasons for this: URLs extracted from downloaded content usually need normalization (e.g., converting hostnames to lowercase, resolving relative paths), are often broken or invalid, or refer to unsupported protocols. Many normalization and filtering operations are better expressed as text patterns that span several parts of a URL. Also, for the purpose of link analysis, we may still want to process and count invalid URLs.

Let's take a closer look now at the map() and reduce() implementations—in this case, they are simple enough to be implemented in the body of the same class:

```
public void map(Text fromUrl, ParseData parseData,
    OutputCollector<Text, Inlinks> output, Reporter reporter) {
  ...
  Outlink[] outlinks = parseData.getOutlinks();
  Inlinks inlinks = new Inlinks();
  for (Outlink out : outlinks) {
```

```
        inlinks.clear(); // instance reuse to avoid excessive GC
        String toUrl = out.getToUrl();
        String anchor = out.getAnchor();
        inlinks.add(new Inlink(fromUrl, anchor));
        output.collect(new Text(toUrl), inlinks);
    }
}
```

You can see from this listing that for each `Outlink` our `map()` implementation produces a pair of `<toUrl, Inlinks>`, where `Inlinks` contains just a single `Inlink` containing `fromUrl` and the anchor text. The direction of the link has been inverted.

Subsequently, these one-element-long `Inlinks` are aggregated in the `reduce()` method:

```
public void reduce(Text toUrl, Iterator<Inlinks> values,
    OutputCollector<Text, Inlinks> output, Reporter reporter) {
  Inlinks result = new Inlinks();
  while (values.hasNext()) {
    result.add(values.next());
  }
  output.collect(toUrl, result);
}
```

From this code, it's obvious that we have got exactly what we wanted—that is, a list of all `fromUrls` that point to our `toUrl`, together with their anchor text. The inversion process has been accomplished.

This data is then saved using the `MapFileOutputFormat` and becomes the new version of LinkDb.

Generation of fetchlists

Let's take a look now at a more complicated use case. Fetchlists are produced from the CrawlDb (which is a map file of `<url, crawlDatum>`, with the `crawlDatum` containing a status of this URL), and they contain URLs ready to be fetched, which are then processed by the Nutch Fetcher tool. Fetcher is itself a MapReduce application (described shortly). This means that the input data (partitioned in N parts) will be processed by N map tasks—the Fetcher tool enforces that `SequenceFileInputFormat` should not further split the data in more parts than there are already input partitions. We mentioned earlier briefly that fetchlists need to be generated in a special way so that the data in each part of the fetchlist (and consequently processed in each map task) meets certain requirements:

1. All URLs from the same host need to end up in the same partition. This is required so that Nutch can easily implement in-JVM host-level blocking to avoid overwhelming target hosts.
2. URLs from the same host should be as far apart as possible (i.e., well mixed with URLs from other hosts) in order to minimize the host-level blocking.

3. There should be no more than x URLs from any single host so that large sites with many URLs don't dominate smaller sites (and URLs from smaller sites still have a chance to be scheduled for fetching).

4. URLs with high scores should be preferred over URLs with low scores.

5. There should be at most y URLs in total in the fetchlist.

6. The number of output partitions should match the optimum number of fetching map tasks.

In this case, two MapReduce jobs are needed to satisfy all these requirements, as illustrated in Figure 14-7. Again, in the following listings, we are going to skip some details of these steps for the sake of brevity.

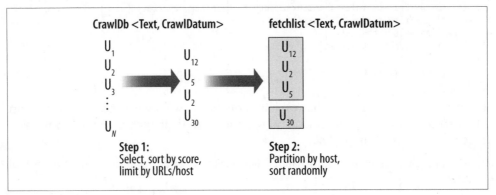

Figure 14-7. Generation of fetchlists

Step 1: Select, sort by score, limit by URL count per host. In this step, Nutch runs a MapReduce job to select URLs that are considered eligible for fetching, and to sort them by their score (a floating-point value assigned to each URL, e.g., a PageRank score). The input data comes from CrawlDb, which is a map file of `<url, datum>`. The output from this job is a sequence file with `<score, <url, datum>>`, sorted in descending order by score.

First, let's look at the job setup:

```
FileInputFormat.addInputPath(job, crawlDbPath);
job.setInputFormat(SequenceFileInputFormat.class);
job.setMapperClass(Selector.class);
job.setPartitionerClass(Selector.class);
job.setReducerClass(Selector.class);
FileOutputFormat.setOutputPath(job, tempDir);
job.setOutputFormat(SequenceFileOutputFormat.class);
job.setOutputKeyClass(FloatWritable.class);
job.setOutputKeyComparatorClass(DecreasingFloatComparator.class);
job.setOutputValueClass(SelectorEntry.class);
```

The `Selector` class implements three functions: mapper, reducer, and partitioner. The last function is especially interesting: `Selector` uses a custom `Partitioner` to assign URLs from the same host to the same reduce task so that we can satisfy criteria 3–5 from the previous list. If we didn't override the default partitioner, URLs from the same host would end up in different partitions of the output, and we wouldn't be able to track and limit the total counts, because MapReduce tasks don't communicate between themselves. As it is now, all URLs that belong to the same host will end up being processed by the same reduce task, which means we can control how many URLs per host are selected.

It's easy to implement a custom partitioner so that data that needs to be processed in the same task ends up in the same partition. Let's take a look first at how the `Selector` class implements the `Partitioner` interface (which consists of a single method):

```
/** Partition by host. */
public int getPartition(FloatWritable key, Writable value, int numReduceTasks) {
  return hostPartitioner.getPartition(((SelectorEntry)value).url, key, numReduceTasks);
}
```

The method returns an integer number from 0 to `numReduceTasks` - 1. It simply replaces the key with the original URL from `SelectorEntry` to pass the URL (instead of score) to an instance of `PartitionUrlByHost`, where the partition number is calculated:

```
/** Hash by hostname. */
public int getPartition(Text key, Writable value, int numReduceTasks) {
  String urlString = key.toString();
  URL url = null;
  try {
    url = new URL(urlString);
  } catch (MalformedURLException e) {
    LOG.warn("Malformed URL: '" + urlString + "'");
  }
  int hashCode = (url == null ? urlString : url.getHost()).hashCode();
  // make hosts wind up in different partitions on different runs
  hashCode ^= seed;

  return (hashCode & Integer.MAX_VALUE) % numReduceTasks;
}
```

As you can see from the code snippet, the partition number is a function of only the host part of the URL, which means that all URLs that belong to the same host will end up in the same partition.

The output from this job is sorted in decreasing order by score. Since there are many records in CrawlDb with the same score, we couldn't use `MapFileOutputFormat` because we would violate the map file's invariant of strict key ordering.

Observant readers will notice that as we had to use something other than the original keys, but we still want to preserve the original key-value pairs, we use here a `Selector Entry` class to pass the original key-value pairs to the next step of processing.

`Selector.reduce()` keeps track of the total number of URLs and the maximum number of URLs per host, and simply discards excessive records. Please note that the enforcement of the total count limit is necessarily approximate. We calculate the limit for the current task as the total limit divided by the number of reduce tasks. But we don't know for sure from within the task that it is going to get an equal share of URLs; indeed, in most cases, it doesn't because of the uneven distribution of URLs among hosts. However, for Nutch this approximation is sufficient.

Step 2: Invert, partition by host, sort randomly. In the previous step, we ended up with a sequence file of `<score, selectorEntry>`. Now we have to produce a sequence file of `<url, datum>` and satisfy criteria 1, 2, and 6 just described. The input data for this step is the output data produced in step 1.

The following is a snippet showing the setup of this job:

```
FileInputFormat.addInputPath(job, tempDir);
job.setInputFormat(SequenceFileInputFormat.class);
job.setMapperClass(SelectorInverseMapper.class);
job.setMapOutputKeyClass(Text.class);
job.setMapOutputValueClass(SelectorEntry.class);
job.setPartitionerClass(PartitionUrlByHost.class);
job.setReducerClass(PartitionReducer.class);
job.setNumReduceTasks(numParts);
FileOutputFormat.setOutputPath(job, output);
job.setOutputFormat(SequenceFileOutputFormat.class);
job.setOutputKeyClass(Text.class);
job.setOutputValueClass(CrawlDatum.class);
job.setOutputKeyComparatorClass(HashComparator.class);
```

The `SelectorInverseMapper` class simply discards the current key (the score value), extracts the original URL and uses it as a key, and uses the `SelectorEntry` as the value. Careful readers may wonder why we don't go one step further, extracting also the original `CrawlDatum` and using it as the value—more on this shortly.

The final output from this job is a sequence file of `<Text, CrawlDatum>`, but our output from the map phase uses `<Text, SelectorEntry>`. We have to specify that we use different key/value classes for the map output, using the `setMapOutputKeyClass()` and `setMapOutputValueClass()` setters—otherwise, Hadoop assumes that we use the same classes as declared for the reduce output (this conflict usually would cause a job to fail).

The output from the map phase is partitioned using `PartitionUrlByHost` class so that it again assigns URLs from the same host to the same partition. This satisfies requirement 1.

Once the data is shuffled from map to reduce tasks, it's sorted by Hadoop according to the output key comparator, in this case the `HashComparator`. This class uses a simple hashing scheme to mix URLs in a way that is least likely to put URLs from the same host close to each other.

In order to meet requirement 6, we set the number of reduce tasks to the desired number of `Fetcher` map tasks (the `numParts` mentioned earlier), keeping in mind that each reduce partition will be used later on to create a single `Fetcher` map task.

`PartitionReducer` class is responsible for the final step, that is, to convert `<url, selectorEntry>` to `<url, crawlDatum>`. A surprising side effect of using `HashCompara tor` is that several URLs may be hashed to the same hash value, and Hadoop will call `reduce()` method passing only the first such key—all other keys considered equal will be discarded. Now it becomes clear why we had to preserve all URLs in `SelectorEn try` records, because now we can extract them from the iterated values. Here is the implementation of this method:

```
public void reduce(Text key, Iterator<SelectorEntry> values,
    OutputCollector<Text, CrawlDatum> output, Reporter reporter) throws IOException {
  // when using HashComparator, we get only one input key in case of hash collisions
  // so use only URLs extracted from values
  while (values.hasNext()) {
    SelectorEntry entry = values.next();
    output.collect(entry.url, entry.datum);
  }
}
```

Finally, the output from reduce tasks is stored as a `SequenceFileOutputFormat` in a Nutch segment directory, in a *crawl_generate* subdirectory. This output satisfies all criteria from 1 to 6.

Fetcher: A multi-threaded MapRunner in action

The Fetcher application in Nutch is responsible for downloading the page content from remote sites. As such, it is important that the process uses every opportunity for parallelism, in order to minimize the time it takes to crawl a fetchlist.

There is already one level of parallelism present in Fetcher—multiple parts of the input fetchlists are assigned to multiple map tasks. However, in practice this is not sufficient: sequential download of URLs, from different hosts (see the earlier section on `HashCom parator`), would be a tremendous waste of time. For this reason the Fetcher map tasks process this data using multiple worker threads.

Hadoop uses the `MapRunner` class to implement the sequential processing of input data records. The `Fetcher` class implements its own `MapRunner` that uses multiple threads to process input records in parallel.

Let's begin with the setup of the job:

```
job.setSpeculativeExecution(false);
FileInputFormat.addInputPath(job, "segment/crawl_generate");
job.setInputFormat(InputFormat.class);
job.setMapRunnerClass(Fetcher.class);
FileOutputFormat.setOutputPath(job, segment);
job.setOutputFormat(FetcherOutputFormat.class);
job.setOutputKeyClass(Text.class);
job.setOutputValueClass(NutchWritable.class);
```

First, we turn off speculative execution. We can't run several map tasks downloading content from the same hosts because it would violate the host-level load limits (such as the number of concurrent requests and the number of requests per second).

Next, we use a custom `InputFormat` implementation that prevents Hadoop from splitting partitions of input data into smaller chunks (splits), thus creating more map tasks than there are input partitions. This again ensures that we control host-level access limits.

Output data is stored using a custom `OutputFormat` implementation, which creates several output map files and sequence files created using data contained in `NutchWrita ble` values. The `NutchWritable` class is a subclass of `GenericWritable`, able to pass instances of several different `Writable` classes declared in advance.

The Fetcher class implements the `MapRunner` interface, and we set this class as the job's `MapRunner` implementation. The relevant parts of the code are listed here:

```
public void run(RecordReader<Text, CrawlDatum> input,
    OutputCollector<Text, NutchWritable> output,
            Reporter reporter) throws IOException {
  int threadCount = getConf().getInt("fetcher.threads.fetch", 10);
  feeder = new QueueFeeder(input, fetchQueues, threadCount * 50);
  feeder.start();

  for (int i = 0; i < threadCount; i++) {        // spawn threads
    new FetcherThread(getConf()).start();
  }
  do {                                           // wait for threads to exit
    try {
      Thread.sleep(1000);
    } catch (InterruptedException e) {}
    reportStatus(reporter);
  } while (activeThreads.get() > 0);
}
```

`Fetcher` reads many input records in advance, using the `QueueFeeder` thread that puts input records into a set of per-host queues. Then several `FetcherThread` instances are started, which consume items from per-host queues, while `QueueFeeder` keeps reading input data to keep the queues filled. Each `FetcherThread` consumes items from any nonempty queue.

In the meantime, the main thread of the map task spins around waiting for all threads to finish their job. Periodically it reports the status to the framework to ensure that Hadoop doesn't consider this task to be dead and kill it. Once all items are processed, the loop is finished and the control is returned to Hadoop, which considers this map task to be completed.

Indexer: Using custom OutputFormat

This is an example of a MapReduce application that doesn't produce sequence file or map file output—instead, the output from this application is a Lucene index. Again, as MapReduce applications may consist of several reduce tasks, the output from this application may consist of several partial Lucene indexes.

Nutch Indexer tool uses information from CrawlDb, LinkDb, and Nutch segments (fetch status, parsing status, page metadata, and plain-text data), so the job setup section involves adding several input paths:

```
FileInputFormat.addInputPath(job, crawlDbPath);
FileInputFormat.addInputPath(job, linkDbPath);
// add segment data
FileInputFormat.addInputPath(job, "segment/crawl_fetch");
FileInputFormat.addInputPath(job, "segment/crawl_parse");
FileInputFormat.addInputPath(job, "segment/parse_data");
FileInputFormat.addInputPath(job, "segment/parse_text");
job.setInputFormat(SequenceFileInputFormat.class);
job.setMapperClass(Indexer.class);
job.setReducerClass(Indexer.class);
FileOutputFormat.setOutputPath(job, indexDir);
job.setOutputFormat(OutputFormat.class);
job.setOutputKeyClass(Text.class);
job.setOutputValueClass(LuceneDocumentWrapper.class);
```

All corresponding records for a URL dispersed among these input locations need to be combined to create Lucene documents to be added to the index.

The Mapper implementation in Indexer simply wraps input data, whatever its source and implementation class, in a NutchWritable, so that the reduce phase may receive data from different sources, using different classes, and still be able to consistently declare a single output value class (as NutchWritable) from both map and reduce steps.

The Reducer implementation iterates over all values that fall under the same key (URL), unwraps the data (fetch CrawlDatum, CrawlDb CrawlDatum, LinkDb Inlinks, Parse Data and ParseText) and, using this information, builds a Lucene document, which is then wrapped in a Writable LuceneDocumentWrapper and collected. In addition to all textual content (coming either from the plain-text data or from metadata), this document also contains a PageRank-like score information (obtained from CrawlDb data). Nutch uses this score to set the boost value of Lucene document.

The OutputFormat implementation is the most interesting part of this tool:

```
public static class OutputFormat extends
    FileOutputFormat<WritableComparable, LuceneDocumentWrapper> {

  public RecordWriter<WritableComparable, LuceneDocumentWrapper>
      getRecordWriter(final FileSystem fs, JobConf job,
                      String name, final Progressable progress) throws IOException {
    final Path out = new Path(FileOutputFormat.getOutputPath(job), name);
    final IndexWriter writer = new IndexWriter(out.toString(),
                      new NutchDocumentAnalyzer(job), true);

    return new RecordWriter<WritableComparable, LuceneDocumentWrapper>() {
      boolean closed;
      public void write(WritableComparable key, LuceneDocumentWrapper value)
```

```
        throws IOException {                          // unwrap & index doc
    Document doc = value.get();
    writer.addDocument(doc);
    progress.progress();
}

public void close(final Reporter reporter) throws IOException {
    // spawn a thread to give progress heartbeats
    Thread prog = new Thread() {
        public void run() {
            while (!closed) {
                try {
                    reporter.setStatus("closing");
                    Thread.sleep(1000);
                } catch (InterruptedException e) { continue; }
                catch (Throwable e) { return; }
            }
        }
    };

    try {
        prog.start();
        // optimize & close index
        writer.optimize();
        writer.close();
    } finally {
        closed = true;
    }
}
    };
}
```

When an instance of `RecordWriter` is requested, the `OutputFormat` creates a new Lucene index by opening an `IndexWriter`. Then, for each new output record collected in the reduce method, it unwraps the Lucene document from `LuceneDocumentWrapper` value and adds it to the index.

When a reduce task is finished, Hadoop will try to close the `RecordWriter`. In this case, the process of closing may take a long time, because we would like to optimize the index before closing. During this time, Hadoop may conclude that the task is hung, since there are no progress updates, and it may attempt to kill it. For this reason, we first start a background thread to give reassuring progress updates, and then proceed to perform the index optimization. Once the optimization is completed, we stop the progress updater thread. The output index is now created, optimized, and is closed, and ready for use in a searcher application.

Summary

This short overview of Nutch necessarily omits many details, such as error handling, logging, URL filtering and normalization, dealing with redirects or other forms of "aliased" pages (such as mirrors), removing duplicate content, calculating PageRank scoring, etc. You can find this and much more information on the official page of the project and on the wiki (*http://wiki.apache.org/nutch*).

Today, Nutch is used by many organizations and individual users. Still, operating a search engine requires nontrivial investment in hardware, integration, and customization, and the maintenance of the index, so in most cases Nutch is used to build commercial vertical- or field-specific search engines.

Nutch is under active development, and the project follows closely new releases of Hadoop. As such, it will continue to be a practical example of a real-life application that uses Hadoop at its core, with excellent results.

—Andrzej Białecki

Log Processing at Rackspace

Rackspace Hosting has always provided managed systems for enterprises, and in that vein, Mailtrust became Rackspace's mail division in the Fall 2007. Rackspace currently hosts email for over 1 million users and thousands of companies on hundreds of servers.

Requirements/The Problem

Transferring the mail generated by Rackspace customers through the system generates a considerable "paper" trail, in the form of around 150 GB per day of logs in various formats. It is extremely helpful to aggregate that data for growth planning purposes and to understand how customers use our applications, and the records are also a boon for troubleshooting problems in the system.

If an email fails to be delivered, or a customer is unable to log in, it is vital that our customer support team is able to find enough information about the problem to begin the debugging process. To make it possible to find that information quickly, we cannot leave the logs on the machines that generated them or in their original format. Instead, we use Hadoop to do a considerable amount of processing, with the end result being Lucene indexes that customer support can query.

Logs

Two of our highest volume log formats are produced by the Postfix mail transfer agent and Microsoft Exchange Server. All mail that travels through our systems touches Postfix at some point, and the majority of messages travel through multiple Postfix servers. The Exchange environment is independent by necessity, but one class of Postfix machines acts as an added layer of protection, and uses SMTP to transfer messages between mailboxes hosted in each environment.

The messages travel through many machines, but each server only knows enough about the destination of the mail to transfer it to the next responsible server. Thus, in order to build the complete history of a message, our log processing system needs to have a global view of the system. This is where Hadoop helps us immensely: as our system grows, so does the volume of logs. For our log processing logic to stay viable, we had to ensure that it would scale, and MapReduce was the perfect framework for that growth.

Brief History

Earlier versions of our log processing system were based on MySQL, but as we gained more and more logging machines, we reached the limits of what a single MySQL server could process. The database schema was already reasonably denormalized, which would have made it less difficult to shard, but MySQL's partitioning support was still very weak at that point in time. Rather than implementing our own sharding and processing solution around MySQL, we chose to use Hadoop.

Choosing Hadoop

As soon as you shard the data in a RDBMS system, you lose a lot of the advantages of SQL for performing analysis of your dataset. Hadoop gives us the ability to easily process all of our data in parallel using the same algorithms we would for smaller datasets.

Collection and Storage

Log collection

The servers generating the logs we process are distributed across multiple data centers, but we currently have a single Hadoop cluster, located in one of those data centers (see Figure 14-8). In order to aggregate the logs and place them into the cluster, we use the Unix syslog replacement syslog-ng and some simple scripts to control the creation of files in Hadoop.

Within a data center, syslog-ng is used to transfer logs from a *source* machine to a load-balanced set of *collector* machines. On the collectors, each type of log is aggregated into a single stream, and lightly compressed with gzip (step A in Figure 14-8). From remote collectors, logs can be transferred through an SSH tunnel cross-data center to collectors that are local to the Hadoop cluster (step B).

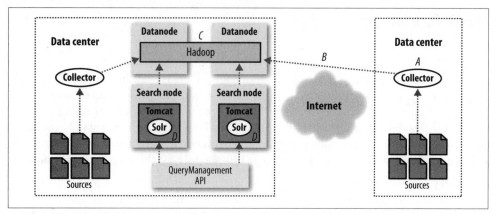

Figure 14-8. Hadoop data flow at Rackspace

Once the compressed log stream reaches a local collector, it can be written to Hadoop (step C). We currently use a simple Python script that buffers input data to disk, and periodically pushes the data into the Hadoop cluster using the Hadoop command-line interface. The script copies the log buffers to input folders in Hadoop when they reach a multiple of the Hadoop block size, or when enough time has passed.

This method of securely aggregating logs from different data centers was developed before SOCKS support was added to Hadoop via the `hadoop.rpc.socket.fac` `tory.class.default` parameter and `SocksSocketFactory` class. By using SOCKS support and the HDFS API directly from remote collectors, we could eliminate one disk write and a lot of complexity from the system. We plan to implement a replacement using these features in future development sprints.

Once the raw logs have been placed in Hadoop, they are ready for processing by our MapReduce jobs.

Log storage

Our Hadoop cluster currently contains 15 datanodes with commodity CPUs and three 500 GB disks each. We use a default replication factor of three for files that need to survive for our archive period of six months, and two for anything else.

The Hadoop namenode uses hardware identical to the datanodes. To provide reasonably high availability, we use two secondary namenodes, and a virtual IP that can easily be pointed at any of the three machines with snapshots of the HDFS. This means that in a failover situation, there is potential for us to lose up to 30 minutes of data, depending on the ages of the snapshots on the secondary namenodes. This is acceptable for our log processing application, but other Hadoop applications may require lossless failover by using shared storage for the namenode's image.

MapReduce for Logs

Processing

In distributed systems, the sad truth of unique identifiers is that they are rarely actually unique. All email messages have a (supposedly) unique identifier called a *message-id* that is generated by the host where they originated, but a bad client could easily send out duplicates. In addition, since the designers of Postfix could not trust the message-id to uniquely identify the message, they were forced to come up with a separate ID called a *queue-id*, which is guaranteed to be unique only for the lifetime of the message on a local machine.

Although the message-id tends to be the definitive identifier for a message, in Postfix logs, it is necessary to use queue-ids to find the message-id. Looking at the second line in Example 14-1 (which is formatted to better fit the page), you will see the hex string 1DBD21B48AE, which is the queue-id of the message that the log line refers to. Because information about a message (including its message-id) is output as separate lines when it is collected (potentially hours apart), it is necessary for our parsing code to keep state about messages.

Example 14-1. Postfix log lines

```
Nov 12 17:36:54 gate8.gate.sat.mlsrvr.com postfix/smtpd[2552]: connect from hostname
Nov 12 17:36:54 relay2.relay.sat.mlsrvr.com postfix/qmgr[9489]: 1DBD21B48AE:
from=<mapreduce@rackspace.com>, size=5950, nrcpt=1 (queue active)
Nov 12 17:36:54 relay2.relay.sat.mlsrvr.com postfix/smtpd[28085]: disconnect from
hostname
Nov 12 17:36:54 gate5.gate.sat.mlsrvr.com postfix/smtpd[22593]: too many errors
after DATA from hostname
Nov 12 17:36:54 gate5.gate.sat.mlsrvr.com postfix/smtpd[22593]: disconnect from
hostname
Nov 12 17:36:54 gate10.gate.sat.mlsrvr.com postfix/smtpd[10311]: connect from
hostname
Nov 12 17:36:54 relay2.relay.sat.mlsrvr.com postfix/smtp[28107]: D42001B48B5:
to=<mapreduce@rackspace.com>, relay=hostname[ip], delay=0.32, delays=0.28/0/0/0.04,
dsn=2.0.0, status=sent (250 2.0.0 Ok: queued as 1DBD21B48AE)
Nov 12 17:36:54 gate20.gate.sat.mlsrvr.com postfix/smtpd[27168]: disconnect from
hostname
Nov 12 17:36:54 gate5.gate.sat.mlsrvr.com postfix/qmgr[1209]: 645965A0224: removed
Nov 12 17:36:54 gate2.gate.sat.mlsrvr.com postfix/smtp[15928]: 732196384ED: to=<m
apreduce@rackspace.com>, relay=hostname[ip], conn_use=2, delay=0.69, delays=0.04/
0.44/0.04/0.17, dsn=2.0.0, status=sent (250 2.0.0 Ok: queued as 02E1544C005)
Nov 12 17:36:54 gate2.gate.sat.mlsrvr.com postfix/qmgr[13764]: 732196384ED: removed
Nov 12 17:36:54 gate1.gate.sat.mlsrvr.com postfix/smtpd[26394]: NOQUEUE: reject: RCP
T from hostname 554 5.7.1 <mapreduce@rackspace.com>: Client host rejected: The
sender's mail server is blocked; from=<mapreduce@rackspace.com> to=<mapred
uce@rackspace.com> proto=ESMTP helo=<mapreduce@rackspace.com>
```

From a MapReduce perspective, each line of the log is a single key-value pair. In phase 1, we need to map all lines with a single queue-id key together, and then reduce them to determine if the log message values indicate that the queue-id is complete.

Similarly, once we have a completed queue-id for a message, we need to group by the message-id in phase 2. We Map each completed queue-id with its message-id as key, and a list of its log lines as the value. In Reduce, we determine whether all of the queue-ids for the message-id indicate that the message left our system.

Together, the two phases of the mail log MapReduce job and their `InputFormat` and `OutputFormat` form a type of *staged event-driven architecture* (SEDA). In SEDA, an application is broken up into multiple "stages," that are separated by queues. In a Hadoop context, a queue could be either an input folder in HDFS that a MapReduce job consumes from, or the implicit queue that MapReduce forms between the Map and Reduce steps.

In Figure 14-9, the arrows between stages represent the queues, with a dashed arrow being the implicit MapReduce queue. Each stage can send a key-value pair (SEDA calls them events or messages) to another stage via these queues.

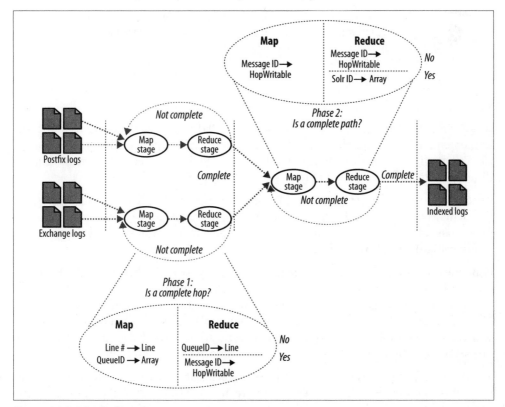

Figure 14-9. MapReduce chain

Phase 1: Map. During the first phase of our Mail log processing job, the inputs to the Map stage are either a line number key and log message value or a queue-id key to an array of log-message values. The first type of input is generated when we process a raw logfile from the queue of input files, and the second type is an intermediate format that represents the state of a queue-id we have already attempted to process, but which was requeued because it was incomplete.

In order to accomplish this dual input, we implemented a Hadoop `InputFormat` that delegates the work to an underlying `SequenceFileRecordReader` or `LineRecordReader`, depending on the file extension of the input `FileSplit`. The two input formats come from different input folders (queues) in HDFS.

Phase 1: Reduce. During this phase, the Reduce stage determines whether the queue-id has enough lines to be considered completed. If the queue-id is completed, we output the message-id as key, and a `HopWritable` object as value. Otherwise, the queue-id is set as the key, and the array of log lines is requeued to be Mapped with the next set of raw logs. This will continue until we complete the queue-id, or until it times out.

 The `HopWritable` object is a POJO that implements Hadoop's `Writable` interface. It completely describes a message from the viewpoint of a single server, including the sending address and IP, attempts to deliver the message to other servers, and typical message header information.

This split output is accomplished with an `OutputFormat` implementation that is somewhat symmetrical with our dual `InputFormat`. Our `MultiSequenceFileOutputFormat` was implemented before the Hadoop API added a `MultipleSequenceFileOutputFormat` in r0.17.0, but fulfills the same type of goal: we needed our Reduce output pairs to go to different files depending on characteristics of their keys.

Phase 2: Map. In the next stage of the Mail log processing job, the input is a message-id key, with a `HopWritable` value from the previous phase. This stage does not contain any logic: instead, it simply combines the inputs from the first phase using the standard `SequenceFileInputFormat` and `IdentityMapper`.

Phase 2: Reduce. In the final Reduce stage, we want to see whether all of the `HopWritables` we have collected for the message-id represent a complete message path through our system. A message path is essentially a directed graph (which is typically acyclic, but it may contain loops if servers are misconfigured). In this graph, a vertex is a server, which can be labeled with multiple queue-ids, and attempts to deliver the message from one server to another are edges. For this processing, we use the JGraphT graph library.

For output, we again use the `MultiSequenceFileOutputFormat`. If the Reducer decides that all of the queue-ids for a message-id create a complete message path, then the message is serialized and queued for the `SolrOutputFormat`. Otherwise, the `HopWritables` for the message are queued for phase 2: Map stage to be reprocessed with the next batch of queue-ids.

The `SolrOutputFormat` contains an embedded Apache Solr instance—in the fashion that was originally recommended by the Solr wiki (*http://wiki.apache.org/solr/Embedded Solr*)—to generate an index on local disk. Closing the `OutputFormat` then involves compressing the disk index to the final destination for the output file. This approach has a few advantages over using Solr's HTTP interface or using Lucene directly:

- We can enforce a Solr schema (*http://wiki.apache.org/solr/SchemaXml*)
- Map and Reduce remain idempotent
- Indexing load is removed from the Search nodes

We currently use the default `HashPartitioner` class to decide which Reduce task will receive particular keys, which means that the keys are semirandomly distributed. In a future iteration of the system, we'd like to implement a new `Partitioner` to split by sending address instead (our most common search term). Once the indexes are split by sender, we can use the hash of the address to determine where to merge or query for an index, and our search API will only need to communicate with the relevant nodes.

Merging for near-term search

After a set of MapReduce phases have completed, a different set of machines are notified of the new indexes, and can pull them for merging. These Search nodes are running Apache Tomcat and Solr instances to host completed indexes, along with a service to pull and merge the indexes to local disk (step D in Figure 14-8).

Each compressed file from `SolrOutputFormat` is a complete Lucene index, and Lucene provides the `IndexWriter.addIndexes()` methods for quickly merging multiple indexes. Our `MergeAgent` service decompresses each new index into a Lucene `RAMDirectory` or `FSDirectory` (depending on size), merges them to local disk, and sends a `<commit/>` request to the Solr instance hosting the index to make the changed index visible to queries.

Sharding.   The Query/Management API is a thin layer of PHP code that handles sharding the output indexes across all of the Search nodes. We use a simple implementation of consistent hashing to decide which Search nodes are responsible for each index file. Currently, indexes are sharded by their creation time, and then by their hashed filename, but we plan to replace the filename hash with a sending address hash at some point in the future (see phase 2: Reduce).

Because HDFS already handles replication of the Lucene indexes, there is no need to keep multiple copies available in Solr. Instead, in a failover situation, the Search node is completely removed, and other nodes become responsible for merging the indexes.

Search results.   With this system, we've achieved a 15-minute turnaround time from log generation to availability of a search result for our Customer Support team.

Our search API supports the full Lucene query syntax, so we commonly see complex queries like:

```
sender:"mapreduce@rackspace.com" -recipient:"hadoop@rackspace.com"
  recipient:"@rackspace.com" short-status:deferred timestamp:[1228140900 TO 2145916799]
```

Each result returned by a query is a complete serialized message path, which indicates whether individual servers and recipients received the message. We currently display the path as a 2D graph (Figure 14-10) that the user can interact with to expand points of interest, but there is a lot of room for improvement in the visualization of this data.

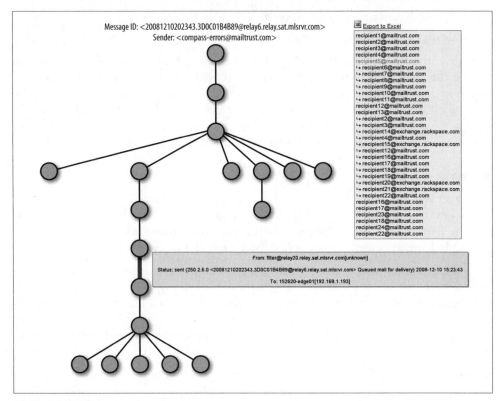

Figure 14-10. Data tree

Archiving for analysis

In addition to providing short-term search for Customer Support, we are also interested in performing analysis of our log data.

Every night, we run a series of MapReduce jobs with the day's indexes as input. We implemented a `SolrInputFormat` that can pull and decompress an index, and emit each document as a key-value pair. With this `InputFormat`, we can iterate over all message paths for a day, and answer almost any question about our mail system, including:

- Per domain data (viruses, spam, connections, recipients)
- Most effective spam rules

- Load generated by specific users
- Reasons for message bounces
- Geographical sources of connections
- Average latency between specific machines

Since we have months of compressed indexes archived in Hadoop, we are also able to retrospectively answer questions that our nightly log summaries leave out. For instance, we recently wanted to determine the top sending IP addresses per month, which we accomplished with a simple one-off MapReduce job.

—Stu Hood

Cascading

Cascading is an open source Java library and application programming interface (API) that provides an abstraction layer for MapReduce. It allows developers to build complex, mission-critical data processing applications that run on Hadoop clusters.

The Cascading project began in the summer of 2007. Its first public release, version 0.1, launched in January 2008. Version 1.0 was released in January 2009. Binaries, source code, and add-on modules can be downloaded from the project website, *http://www.cascading.org/*.

"Map" and "Reduce" operations offer powerful primitives. However, they tend to be at the wrong level of granularity for creating sophisticated, highly composable code that can be shared among different developers. Moreover, many developers find it difficult to "think" in terms of MapReduce when faced with real-world problems.

To address the first issue, Cascading substitutes the "keys" and "values" used in MapReduce with simple field names and a data tuple model, where a tuple is simply a list of values. For the second issue, Cascading departs from Map and Reduce operations directly by introducing higher-level abstractions as alternatives: Functions, Filters, Aggregators, and Buffers.

Other alternatives began to emerge at about the same time as the project's initial public release, but Cascading was designed to complement them. Consider that most of these alternative frameworks impose pre- and post-conditions, or other expectations.

For example, in several other MapReduce tools, you must preformat, filter, or import your data into the Hadoop Filesystem (HDFS) prior to running the application. That step of preparing the data must be performed outside of the programming abstraction. In contrast, Cascading provides means to prepare and manage your data as integral parts of the programming abstraction.

This case study begins with an introduction to the main concepts of Cascading, then finishes with an overview of how ShareThis (*http://www.sharethis.com/*) uses Cascading in its infrastructure.

Please see the Cascading User Guide on the project website for a more in-depth presentation of the Cascading processing model.

Fields, Tuples, and Pipes

The MapReduce model uses keys and values to link input data to the Map function, the Map function to the Reduce function, and the Reduce function to the output data.

But as we know, real-world Hadoop applications are usually more than one MapReduce job chained together. Consider the canonical word count example implemented in MapReduce. If you needed to sort the numeric counts in descending order, not an unlikely requirement, it would need to be done in a second MapReduce job.

So, in the abstract, keys and values not only bind Map to Reduce, but Reduce to the next Map, and then to the next Reduce, and so on (Figure 14-11). That is, key-value pairs are sourced from input files and stream through chains of Map and Reduce operations and finally rest in an output file. When you implement enough of these chained MapReduce applications, you start to see a well-defined set of key/value manipulations used over and over again to modify the key/value data stream.

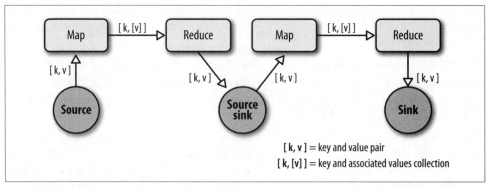

Figure 14-11. Counting and sorting in MapReduce

Cascading simplifies this by abstracting away keys and values and replacing them with tuples that have corresponding field names, similar in concept to tables and column names in a relational database. And during processing, streams of these Fields and Tuples are then manipulated as they pass through user-defined operations linked together by Pipes (Figure 14-12).

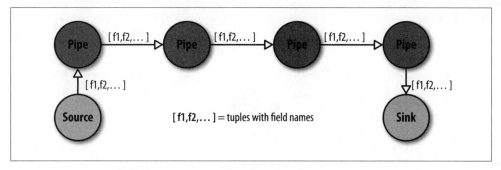

Figure 14-12. Pipes linked by Fields and Tuples

So, MapReduce keys and values are reduced to:

Fields

Fields are a collection of either `String` names (like "first_name"), numeric positions (like 2, or –1, for the third and last position, respectively), or a combination of both, very much like column names. So Fields are used to declare the names of values in a Tuple, and to select values by name from a Tuple. The later is like a SQL `select` call.

Tuple

A Tuple is simply an array of `java.lang.Comparable` objects. A Tuple is very much like a database row or record.

And the Map and Reduce operations are abstracted behind one or more Pipe instances (Figure 14-13):

`Each`

The `Each` pipe processes a single input Tuple at a time. It may apply either a `Func tion` or a `Filter` operation (described shortly) to the input tuple.

`GroupBy`

The `GroupBy` pipe groups tuples on grouping fields. It behaves just like the SQL `group by` statement. It can also merge multiple input tuple streams into a single stream, if they all share the same field names.

`CoGroup`

The `CoGroup` pipe both joins multiple tuple streams together by common field names, and it also groups the tuples by the common grouping fields. All standard join types (inner, outer, etc.) and custom joins can be used across two or more tuple streams.

`Every`

The `Every` pipe processes a single grouping of tuples at a time, where the group was grouped by a `GroupBy` or `CoGroup` pipe. The `Every` pipe may apply either an Aggregator or a Buffer operation to the grouping.

SubAssembly

The SubAssembly pipe allows for nesting of assemblies inside a single pipe, which can in turn be nested in more complex assemblies.

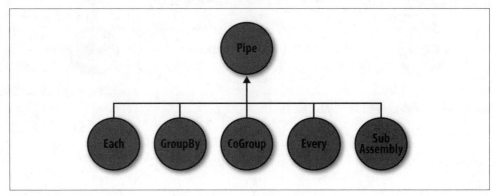

Figure 14-13. Pipe types

All these pipes are chained together by the developer into "pipe assemblies" in which each assembly can have many input Tuple streams (sources) and many output Tuple streams (sinks) (see Figure 14-14).

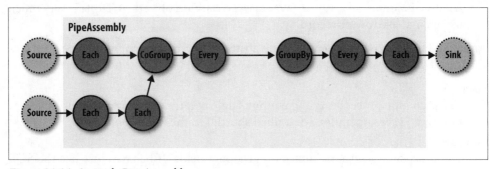

Figure 14-14. A simple PipeAssembly

On the surface, this might seem more complex than the traditional MapReduce model. And admittedly there are more concepts here than Map, Reduce, Key, and Value. But in practice, there are many more concepts that must all work in tandem to provide different behaviors.

For example, if a developer wanted to provide a "secondary sorting" of reducer values, she would need to implement Map, Reduce, a "composite" Key (two Keys nested in a parent Key), Value, Partitioner, an "output value grouping" Comparator, and an "output key" Comparator, all of which would be coupled to one another in varying ways, and very likely nonreusable in subsequent applications.

In Cascading, this would be one line of code: new GroupBy(<previous>, <grouping fields>, <secondary sorting fields>), where previous is the pipe that came before.

Operations

As mentioned earlier, Cascading departs from MapReduce by introducing alternative operations that either are applied to individual Tuples or groups of Tuples (Figure 14-15):

Function

> A Function operates on individual input Tuples and may return zero or more output Tuples for every one input. Functions are applied by the Each pipe.

Filter

> A Filter is a special kind of function that returns a boolean value indicating whether the current input Tuple should be removed from the Tuple stream. A Function could serve this purpose, but the Filter is optimized for this case, and many filters can be grouped by "logical" filters like And, Or, Xor, and Not, rapidly creating more complex filtering operations.

Aggregator

> An Aggregator performs some operation against a group of Tuples, where the grouped Tuples are grouped by a common set of field values. For example, all Tuples having the same "last-name" value. Common Aggregator implementations would be Sum, Count, Average, Max, and Min.

Buffer

> A Buffer is similar to the Aggregator, except it is optimized to act as a "sliding window" across all the Tuples in a unique grouping. This is useful when the developer needs to efficiently insert missing values in an ordered set of Tuples (like a missing date or duration), or create a running average. Usually Aggregator is the operation of choice when working with groups of Tuples, since many Aggregators can be chained together very efficiently, but sometimes a Buffer is the best tool for the job.

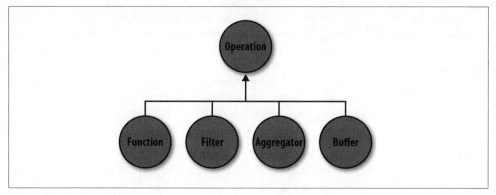

Figure 14-15. Operation types

Operations are bound to pipes when the pipe assembly is created (Figure 14-16).

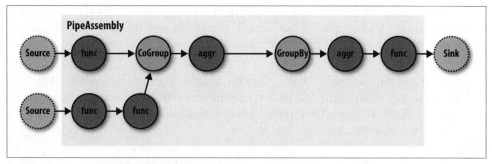

Figure 14-16. An assembly of operations

The Each and Every pipes provide a simple mechanism for selecting some or all values out of an input tuple before being passed to its child operation. And there is a simple mechanism for merging the operation results with the original input Tuple to create the output Tuple. Without going into great detail, this allows for each operation to only care about argument Tuple values and fields, not the whole set of fields in the current input Tuple. Subsequently, operations can be reusable across applications the same way Java methods can be reusable.

For example, in Java, a method declared as concatenate(String first, String second) is more abstract than concatenate(Person person). In the second case, the concatenate() function must "know" about the Person object; in the first case, it is agnostic to where the data came from. Cascading operations exhibit this same quality.

Taps, Schemes, and Flows

In many of the previous diagrams, there are references to "sources" and "sinks." In Cascading, all data is read from or written to Tap instances, but is converted to and from Tuple instances via Scheme objects:

Tap

> A Tap is responsible for the "how" and "where" parts of accessing data. For example, is the data on HDFS or the local filesystem? In Amazon S3 or over HTTP?

Scheme

> A Scheme is responsible for reading raw data and converting it to a Tuple and/or writing a Tuple out into raw data, where this "raw" data can be lines of text, Hadoop binary sequence files, or some proprietary format.

Note that Taps are not part of a pipe assembly, and so they are not a type of Pipe.

But they are connected with pipe assemblies when they are made cluster-executable. When a pipe assembly is connected with the necessary number of source and sink Tap instances, we get a Flow. A Flow is created when a pipe assembly is connected with its required number of source and sink taps, and the Taps either emit or capture the field names the pipe assembly expects. That is, if a Tap emits a Tuple with the field name "line" (by reading data from a file on HDFS), the head of the pipe assembly must be expecting a "line" value as well. Otherwise, the process that connects the pipe assembly with the Taps will immediately fail with an error.

So pipe assemblies are really data process definitions, and are not "executable" on their own. They must be connected to source and sink Tap instances before they can run on a cluster. This separation between Taps and pipe assemblies is part of what makes Cascading so powerful.

If you think of pipe assemblies like a Java class, then a Flow is like a Java Object instance (Figure 14-17). That is, the same pipe assembly can be "instantiated" many times into new Flows, in the same application, without fear of any interference between them. This allows pipe assemblies to be created and shared like standard Java libraries.

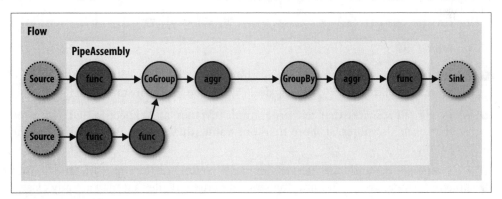

Figure 14-17. A Flow

Cascading in Practice

Now that we know what Cascading is and have a good idea how it works, what does an application written in Cascading look like? See Example 14-2.

Example 14-2. Word count and sort

```
Scheme sourceScheme =
  new TextLine(new Fields("line")); ❶
Tap source =
  new Hfs(sourceScheme, inputPath); ❷

Scheme sinkScheme = new TextLine(); ❸
Tap sink =
  new Hfs(sinkScheme, outputPath, SinkMode.REPLACE); ❹

Pipe assembly = new Pipe("wordcount"); ❺

String regexString = "(?<!\\pL)(?=\\pL)[^ ]*(?<=\\pL)(?!\\pL)";
Function regex = new RegexGenerator(new Fields("word"), regexString);
assembly =
  new Each(assembly, new Fields("line"), regex); ❻

assembly =
  new GroupBy(assembly, new Fields("word")); ❼

Aggregator count = new Count(new Fields("count"));
assembly = new Every(assembly, count); ❽

assembly =
  new GroupBy(assembly, new Fields("count"), new Fields("word")); ❾

FlowConnector flowConnector = new FlowConnector();
Flow flow =
  flowConnector.connect("word-count", source, sink, assembly); ❿

flow.complete();⓫
```

❶ We create a new Scheme that can read simple text files, and emits a new Tuple for each line in a field named "line," as declared by the Fields instance.

❷ We create a new Scheme that can write simple text files, and expects a Tuple with any number of fields/values. If more than one value, they will be tab-delimited in the output file.

❸ We create source and sink Tap instances that reference the input file and output
❹ directory, respectively. The sink Tap will overwrite any file that may already exist.

❺ We construct the head of our pipe assembly, and name it "wordcount." This name is used to bind the source and sink taps to the assembly. Multiple heads or tails would require unique names.

❻ We construct an Each pipe with a function that will parse the "line" field into a new Tuple for each word encountered.

❼ We construct a `GroupBy` pipe that will create a new `Tuple` grouping for each unique value in the field "word."

❽ We construct an `Every` pipe with an `Aggregator` that will count the number of `Tuples` in every unique word group. The result is stored in a field named "count."

❾ We construct a `GroupBy` pipe that will create a new `Tuple` grouping for each unique value in the field "count," and secondary sort each value in the field "word." The result will be a list of "count" and "word" values with "count" sorted in increasing order.

❿ We connect the pipe assembly to its sources and sinks into a `Flow`, and then execute
⓫ the `Flow` on the cluster.

In the example, we count the words encountered in the input document, and we sort the counts in their natural order (ascending). And if some words have the same "count" value, these words are sorted in their natural order (alphabetical).

One obvious problem with this example is that some words might have uppercase letters; for example, "the" and "The" when the word comes at the beginning of a sentence. So we might decide to insert a new operation to force all the words to lowercase, but we realize that all future applications that need to parse words from documents should have the same behavior, so we decide to create a reusable pipe `SubAssembly`, just like we would by creating a subroutine in a traditional application (see Example 14-3).

Example 14-3. Creating a SubAssembly

```
public class ParseWordsAssembly extends SubAssembly ❶
  {
  public ParseWordsAssembly(Pipe previous)
    {
    String regexString = "(?<!\\pL)(?=\\pL)[^ ]*(?<=\\pL)(?!\\pL)";
    Function regex = new RegexGenerator(new Fields("word"), regexString);
    previous = new Each(previous, new Fields("line"), regex);

    String exprString = "word.toLowerCase()";
    Function expression =
      new ExpressionFunction(new Fields("word"), exprString, String.class); ❷
    previous = new Each(previous, new Fields("word"), expression);

    setTails(previous); ❸
    }
  }
```

❶ We subclass the `SubAssembly` class, which is itself a kind of `Pipe`.

❷ We create a Java expression function that will call `toLowerCase()` on the `String` value in the field named "word." We must also pass in the Java type the expression expects "word" to be, in this case, `String`. (*http://www.janino.net/* is used under the covers.)

❸ We must tell the SubAssembly superclass where the tail ends of our pipe subassembly are.

First, we create a SubAssembly pipe to hold our "parse words" pipe assembly. Since this is a Java class, it can be reused in any other application, as long as there is an incoming field named "word" (Example 14-4). Note that there are ways to make this function even more generic, but they are covered in the Cascading User Guide.

Example 14-4. Extending word count and sort with a SubAssembly

```
Scheme sourceScheme = new TextLine(new Fields("line"));
Tap source = new Hfs(sourceScheme, inputPath);

Scheme sinkScheme = new TextLine(new Fields("word", "count"));
Tap sink = new Hfs(sinkScheme, outputPath, SinkMode.REPLACE);

Pipe assembly = new Pipe("wordcount");

assembly =
  new ParseWordsAssembly(assembly); ❶

assembly = new GroupBy(assembly, new Fields("word"));

Aggregator count = new Count(new Fields("count"));
assembly = new Every(assembly, count);

assembly = new GroupBy(assembly, new Fields("count"), new Fields("word"));

FlowConnector flowConnector = new FlowConnector();
Flow flow = flowConnector.connect("word-count", source, sink, assembly);

flow.complete();
```

❶ We replace the Each from the previous example with our ParseWordsAssembly pipe.

Finally, we just substitute in our new SubAssembly right where the previous Every and word parser function was used in the previous example. This nesting can continue as deep as necessary.

Flexibility

Take a step back and see what this new model has given us. Or better yet, what it has taken away.

You see, we no longer think in terms of MapReduce jobs, or Mapper and Reducer interface implementations, and how to bind or link subsequent MapReduce jobs to the ones that precede them. During runtime, the Cascading "planner" figures out the optimal way to partition the pipe assembly into MapReduce jobs, and manages the linkages between them (Figure 14-18).

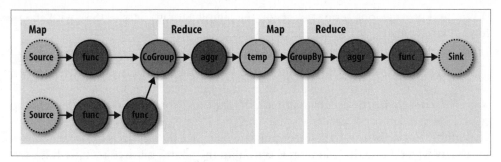

Figure 14-18. How a Flow translates to chained MapReduce jobs

Because of this, developers can build applications of arbitrary granularity. They can start with a small application that just filters a logfile, but then can iteratively build up more features into the application as needed.

Since Cascading is an API and not a syntax like strings of SQL, it is more flexible. First off, developers can create domain-specific languages (DSLs) using their favorite language, like Groovy, JRuby, Jython, Scala, and others (see the project site for examples). Second, developers can extend various parts of Cascading, like allowing custom Thrift or JSON objects to be read and written to and allowing them to be passed through the Tuple stream.

Hadoop and Cascading at ShareThis

ShareThis is a sharing network that makes it simple to share any online content. With the click of a button on a web page or browser plug-in, ShareThis allows users to seamlessly access their contacts and networks from anywhere online and share the content through email, IM, Facebook, Digg, mobile SMS, etc. without ever leaving the current page. Publishers can deploy the ShareThis button to tap the service's universal sharing capabilities to drive traffic, stimulate viral activity, and track the sharing of online content. ShareThis also simplifies social media services by reducing clutter on web pages and providing instant distribution of content across social networks, affiliate groups, and communities.

As ShareThis users share pages and information through the online widgets, a continuous stream of events enter the ShareThis network. These events are first filtered and processed, and then handed to various backend systems, including AsterData, Hypertable, and Katta.

The volume of these event can be huge, too large to process with traditional systems. This data can also be very "dirty" thanks to "injection attacks" from rogue systems, browser bugs, or faulty widgets. For this reason, ShareThis chose to deploy Hadoop as the preprocessing and orchestration frontend to their backend systems. They also chose to use Amazon Web Services to host their servers, on the Elastic Computing Cloud

(EC2), and provide long term storage, on the Simple Storage Service (S3), with an eye toward leveraging Elastic MapReduce (EMR).

In this overview, we will focus on the "log processing pipeline" (Figure 14-19). The log processing pipeline simply takes data stored in an S3 bucket, processes it (described shortly), and stores the results back into another bucket. Simple Queue Service (SQS) is used to coordinate the events that mark the start and completion of data processing runs. Downstream other processes pull data that load AsterData, pull URL lists from Hypertable to source a web crawl, or pull crawled page data to create Lucene indexes for use by Katta. Note that Hadoop is central to the ShareThis architecture. It is used to coordinate the processing and movement of data between architectural components.

Figure 14-19. The ShareThis log processing pipeline

With Hadoop as the frontend, all the event logs can be parsed, filtered, cleaned, and organized by a set of rules before ever being loaded into the AsterData cluster or used by any other component. AsterData is a clustered data warehouse that can support large datasets and allow for complex ad hoc queries using a standard SQL syntax. ShareThis chose to clean and prepare the incoming datasets on the Hadoop cluster and then to load that data into the AsterData cluster for ad hoc analysis and reporting. Though possible with AsterData, it made a lot of sense to use Hadoop as the first stage in the processing pipeline to offset load on the main data warehouse.

Cascading was chosen as the primary data processing API to simplify the development process, codify how data is coordinated between architectural components, and provide the developer-facing interface to those components. This represents a departure from more "traditional" Hadoop use cases, which essentially just query stored data. Instead, Cascading and Hadoop together provide better and simpler structure to the complete solution, end-to-end, and thus more value to the users.

For developers, Cascading made it easy to start with a simple unit test (by subclassing `cascading.ClusterTestCase`) that did simple text parsing and then to layer in more processing rules while keeping the application logically organized for maintenance. Cascading aided this organization in a couple of ways. First, standalone operations (Functions, Filters, etc.) could be written and tested independently. Second, the application was segmented into stages: one for parsing, one for rules, and a final stage for binning/collating the data, all via the `SubAssembly` base class described earlier.

The data coming from the ShareThis loggers looks a lot like Apache logs with date/timestamps, share URLs, referrer URLs, and a bit of metadata. To use the data for analysis downstream the URLs needed to be un-packed (parsing query-string data, domain names, etc.). So a top-level *SubAssembly* was created to encapsulate the parsing, and child SubAssemblies were nested inside to handle specific fields if they were sufficiently complex to parse.

The same was done for applying rules. As every `Tuple` passed through the rules `SubAssembly`, it was marked as "bad" if any of the rules were triggered. Along with the "bad" tag, a description of why the record was bad was added to the `Tuple` for later review.

Finally, a splitter SubAssembly was created to do two things. First, to allow for the tuple stream to split into two, one stream for "good" data and one for "bad" data. Second, the splitter binned the data into intervals, such as every hour. To do this, only two operations were necessary. The first to create the interval from the *timestamp* value already present in the stream, and the second to use the *interval* and *good/bad* metadata to create a directory path; for example, "05/good/" where "05" is 5am and "good" means the tuple passed all the rules. This path would then be used by the Cascading TemplateTap, a special Tap that can dynamically output tuple streams to different locations based on values in the `Tuple`. In this case, the TemplateTap used the "path" value to create the final output path.

The developers also created a fourth SubAssembly, this one to apply Cascading Assertions during unit testing. These assertions double-checked that rules and parsing SubAssemblies did their job.

In the unit test in Example 14-5, we see the splitter isn't being tested, but it is added in another integration test not shown.

Example 14-5. Unit testing a Flow

```
public void testLogParsing() throws IOException
  {
  Hfs source = new Hfs(new TextLine(new Fields("line")), sampleData);
  Hfs sink =
    new Hfs(new TextLine(), outputPath + "/parser", SinkMode.REPLACE);

  Pipe pipe = new Pipe("parser");

  // split "line" on tabs
  pipe = new Each(pipe, new Fields("line"), new RegexSplitter("\t"));
```

```
pipe = new LogParser(pipe);

pipe = new LogRules(pipe);

// testing only assertions
pipe = new ParserAssertions(pipe);

Flow flow = new FlowConnector().connect(source, sink, pipe);

flow.complete(); // run the test flow

// verify there are 98 tuples, 2 fields, and matches the regex pattern
// for TextLine schemes the tuples are { "offset", "line }
validateLength(flow, 98, 2, Pattern.compile("^[0-9]+(\\t[^\\t]*){19}$"));
}
```

For integration and deployment, many of the features built into Cascading allowed for easier integration with external systems and for greater process tolerance.

In production, all the SubAssemblies are joined and planned into a Flow, but instead of just source and sink Taps, trap Taps were planned in (Figure 14-20). Normally when an operation throws an exception from a remote Mapper or Reducer task, the Flow will fail and kill all its managed MapReduce jobs. When a Flow has traps, any exceptions are caught and the data causing the exception is saved to the Tap associated with the current trap. Then the next Tuple is processed without stopping the Flow. Sometimes you want your Flows to fail on errors, but in this case, the ShareThis developers knew they could go back and look at the "failed" data and update their unit tests while the production system kept running. Losing a few hours of processing time was worse than losing a couple of bad records.

Using Cascading's event listeners, Amazon SQS could be integrated. When a Flow finishes, a message is sent to notify other systems that there is data ready to be picked up from Amazon S3. On failure, a different message is sent, alerting other processes.

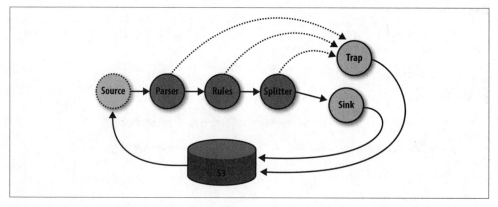

Figure 14-20. The ShareThis log processing Flow

The remaining downstream processes pick up where the log processing pipeline leaves off on different independent clusters. The log processing pipeline today runs once a day, so there is no need to keep a 100-node cluster sitting around for the 23 hours it has nothing to do. So it is decommissioned and recommissioned 24 hours later.

In the future, it would be trivial to increase this interval on smaller clusters to every 6 hours, or 1 hour, as the business demands. Independently, other clusters are booting and shutting down at different intervals based on the needs of the business unit responsible for that component. For example, the web crawler component (using Bixo, a Cascading-based web-crawler toolkit developed by EMI and ShareThis) may run continuously on a small cluster with a companion Hypertable cluster. This on-demand model works very well with Hadoop where each cluster can be tuned for the kind of workload it is expected to handle.

Summary

Hadoop is a very powerful platform for processing and coordinating the movement of data across various architectural components. Its only drawback is that the primary computing model is MapReduce.

Cascading aims to help developers build powerful applications quickly and simply, through a well-reasoned API, without needing to think in MapReduce, while leaving the heavy lifting of data distribution, replication, distributed process management, and liveness to Hadoop.

Read more about Cascading, join the online community, and download sample applications by visiting the project website at *http://www.cascading.org/*.

—Chris K Wensel

TeraByte Sort on Apache Hadoop

This article is reproduced from the http://sortbenchmark.org/YahooHadoop.pdf, which was written in May 2008. Jim Gray and his successors define a family of benchmarks to find the fastest sort programs every year. TeraByte Sort and other sort benchmarks are listed with winners over the years at http://sortbenchmark.org/. In April 2009, Arun Murthy and I won the minute sort (where the aim is to sort as much data as possible in under one minute) by sorting 500 GB in 59 seconds on 1,406 Hadoop nodes. We also sorted a terabyte in 62 seconds on the same cluster. The cluster we used in 2009 was similar to the hardware listed below, except that the network was much better with only 2-to-1 oversubscription between racks instead of 5-to-1 in the previous year. We also used LZO compression on the intermediate data between the nodes. We also sorted a petabyte (10^{15} bytes) in 975 minutes on 3,658 nodes, for an average rate of 1.03 TB/minute. See http://developer.yahoo.net/blogs/hadoop/2009/05/hadoop_sorts_a_petabyte_in_162 .html for more details about the 2009 results.

Apache Hadoop is an open source software framework that dramatically simplifies writing distributed data-intensive applications. It provides a distributed filesystem, which is modelled after the Google File System,[*] and a MapReduce[†] implementation that manages distributed computation. Since the primary primitive of MapReduce is a distributed sort, most of the custom code is glue to get the desired behavior.

I wrote three Hadoop applications to run the terabyte sort:

1. TeraGen is a MapReduce program to generate the data.
2. TeraSort samples the input data and uses MapReduce to sort the data into a total order.
3. TeraValidate is a MapReduce program that validates the output is sorted.

The total is around 1,000 lines of Java code, which will be checked in (*http://issues .apache.org/jira/brows/HADOOP-3402*) to the Hadoop example directory.

TeraGen generates output data that is byte-for-byte equivalent to the C version including the newlines and specific keys. It divides the desired number of rows by the desired number of tasks and assigns ranges of rows to each map. The map jumps the random number generator to the correct value for the first row and generates the following rows. For the final run, I configured TeraGen to use 1,800 tasks to generate a total of 10 billion rows in HDFS, with a block size of 512 MB.

TeraSort is a standard MapReduce sort, except for a custom partitioner that uses a sorted list of N–1 sampled keys that define the key range for each reduce. In particular, all keys such that $sample[i–1] <= key < sample[i]$ are sent to reduce i. This guarantees that the output of reduce i are all less than the output of reduce i+1. To speed up the partitioning, the partitioner builds a two-level trie that quickly indexes into the list of sample keys based on the first two bytes of the key. TeraSort generates the sample keys by sampling the input before the job is submitted and writing the list of keys into HDFS. I wrote an input and output format, which are used by all 3 applications, that read and write the text files in the right format. The output of the reduce has replication set to 1, instead of the default 3, because the contest does not require the output data be replicated on to multiple nodes. I configured the job with 1,800 maps and 1,800 reduces and io.sort.mb, io.sort.factor, fs.inmemory.size.mb, and task heap size sufficient that transient data was never spilled to disk other at the end of the map. The sampler used 100,000 keys to determine the reduce boundaries, although as can be seen in Figure 14-21, the distribution between reduces was hardly perfect and would benefit from more samples. You can see the distribution of running tasks over the job run in Figure 14-22.

---

[*] S. Ghemawat, H. Gobioff, and S.-T. Leung. "The Google File System." In *19th Symposium on Operating Systems Principles* (October 2003), Lake George, NY: ACM.

[†] J. Dean and S. Ghemawat. "MapReduce: Simplified Data Processing on Large Clusters." In *Sixth Symposium on Operating System Design and Implementation* (December 2004), San Francisco, CA.

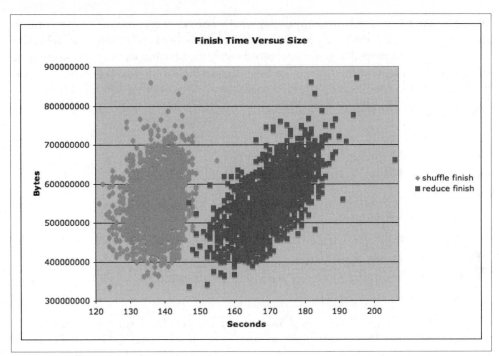

Figure 14-21. Plot of reduce output size versus finish time

Figure 14-22. Number of tasks in each phase across time

TeraValidate ensures that the output is globally sorted. It creates one map per file in the output directory, and each map ensures that each key is less than or equal to the previous one. The map also generates records with the first and last keys of the file, and the reduce ensures that the first key of file *i* is greater than the last key of file *i*–1. Any problems are reported as output of the reduce with the keys that are out of order.

The cluster I ran on was:

- 910 nodes
- 2 quad core Xeons at 2.0ghz per a node
- 4 SATA disks per a node
- 8 G RAM per a node
- 1 gigabit Ethernet on each node
- 40 nodes per a rack
- 8 gigabit Ethernet uplinks from each rack to the core
- Red Hat Enterprise Linux Server release 5.1 (kernel 2.6.18)
- Sun Java JDK 1.6.0_05-b13

The sort completed in *209 seconds (3.48 minutes)*. I ran Hadoop trunk (pre-0.18.0) with patches for HADOOP-3443 (*http://issues.apache.org/jira/browse/HADOOP-3443*) and HADOOP-3446 (*http://issues.apache.org/jira/browse/HADOOP-3446*), which were required to remove intermediate writes to disk. Although I had the 910 nodes mostly to myself, the network core was shared with another active 2,000-node cluster, so the times varied a lot depending on the other activity.

—Owen O'Malley, Yahoo!

Installing Apache Hadoop

It's easy to install Hadoop on a single machine to try it out. (For installation on a cluster, please refer to Chapter 9.) The quickest way is to download and run a binary release from an Apache Software Foundation Mirror.

In this appendix, we cover how to install Hadoop Core, HDFS, and MapReduce. Instructions for installing Pig, HBase, and ZooKeeper are included in the relevant chapter (Chapters 11, 12, and 13).

Prerequisites

Hadoop is written in Java, so you will need to have Java installed on your machine, version 6 or later. Sun's JDK is the one most widely used with Hadoop, although others have been reported to work.

Hadoop runs on Unix and on Windows. Linux is the only supported production platform, but other flavors of Unix (including Mac OS X) can be used to run Hadoop for development. Windows is only supported as a development platform, and additionally requires Cygwin to run. During the Cygwin installation process, you should include the *openssh* package if you plan to run Hadoop in pseudo-distributed mode (see following explanation).

Installation

Start by deciding which user you'd like to run Hadoop as. For trying out Hadoop or developing Hadoop programs, it is simplest to run Hadoop on a single machine using your own user account.

Download a stable release, which is packaged as a gzipped tar file, from the Apache Hadoop releases page (*http://hadoop.apache.org/core/releases.html*) and unpack it somewhere on your filesystem:

```
% tar xzf hadoop-x.y.z.tar.gz
```

Before you can run Hadoop, you need to tell it where Java is located on your system. If you have the `JAVA_HOME` environment variable set to point to a suitable Java installation, that will be used, and you don't have to configure anything further. Otherwise, you can set the Java installation that Hadoop uses by editing *conf/hadoop-env.sh*, and specifying the `JAVA_HOME` variable. For example, on my Mac I changed the line to read:

```
export JAVA_HOME=/System/Library/Frameworks/JavaVM.framework/Versions/1.6.0/Home
```

to point to version 1.6.0 of Java. On Ubuntu, the equivalent line is:

```
export JAVA_HOME=/usr/lib/jvm/java-6-sun
```

It's very convenient to create an environment variable that points to the Hadoop installation directory (`HADOOP_INSTALL`, say) and to put the Hadoop binary directory on your command-line path. For example:

```
% export HADOOP_INSTALL=/home/tom/hadoop-x.y.z
% export PATH=$PATH:$HADOOP_INSTALL/bin
```

Check that Hadoop runs by typing:

```
% hadoop version
Hadoop 0.20.0
Subversion https://svn.apache.org/repos/asf/hadoop/core/branches/branch-0.20 -r 763504
Compiled by ndaley on Thu Apr  9 05:18:40 UTC 2009
```

Configuration

Each component in Hadoop is configured using an XML file. Core properties go in *core-site.xml*, HDFS properties go in *hdfs-site.xml*, and MapReduce properties go in *mapred-site.xml*. These files are all located in the *conf* subdirectory.

 In earlier versions of Hadoop, there was a single site configuration file for the Core, HDFS, and MapReduce components, called *hadoop-site.xml*. From release 0.20.0 onward this file has been split into three: one for each component. The property names have not changed, just the configuration file they have to go in. You can see the default settings for all the properties that are governed by these configuration files by looking in the *docs* directory of your Hadoop installation for HTML files called *core-default.html*, *hdfs-default.html*, and *mapred-default.html*.

Hadoop can be run in one of three modes:

Standalone (or local) mode
> There are no daemons running and everything runs in a single JVM. Standalone mode is suitable for running MapReduce programs during development, since it is easy to test and debug them.

Pseudo-distributed mode
> The Hadoop daemons run on the local machine, thus simulating a cluster on a small scale.

Fully distributed mode
> The Hadoop daemons run on a cluster of machines. This setup is described in Chapter 9.

To run Hadoop in a particular mode, you need to do two things: set the appropriate properties, and start the Hadoop daemons. Table A-1 shows the minimal set of properties to configure each mode. In standalone mode, the local filesystem and the local MapReduce job runner are used, while in the distributed modes the HDFS and Map-Reduce daemons are started.

Table A-1. Key configuration properties for different modes

Component	Property	Standalone	Pseudo-distributed	Fully distributed
Core	fs.default.name	file:/// (default)	hdfs://localhost/	hdfs://*namenode*/
HDFS	dfs.replication	N/A	1	3 (default)
MapReduce	mapred.job.tracker	local (default)	localhost:8021	*jobtracker*:8021

You can read more about configuration in "Hadoop Configuration" on page 251.

Standalone Mode

In standalone mode, there is no further action to take, since the default properties are set for standalone mode, and there are no daemons to run.

Pseudo-Distributed Mode

The configuration files should be created with the following contents, and placed in the *conf* directory (although you can place configuration files in any directory as long as you start the daemons with the --config option).

```
<?xml version="1.0"?>
<!-- core-site.xml -->
<configuration>
  <property>
    <name>fs.default.name</name>
    <value>hdfs://localhost/</value>
  </property>
</configuration>

<?xml version="1.0"?>
<!-- hdfs-site.xml -->
<configuration>
  <property>
    <name>dfs.replication</name>
    <value>1</value>
  </property>
```

```
      </property>
    </configuration>

    <?xml version="1.0"?>
    <!-- mapred-site.xml -->
    <configuration>
      <property>
        <name>mapred.job.tracker</name>
        <value>localhost:8021</value>
      </property>
    </configuration>
```

Configuring SSH

In pseudo-distributed mode, we have to start daemons, and to do that, we need to have SSH installed. Hadoop doesn't actually distinguish between pseudo-distributed and fully distributed modes: it merely starts daemons on the set of hosts in the cluster (defined by the *slaves* file) by SSH-ing to each host and starting a daemon process. Pseudo-distributed mode is just a special case of fully distributed mode in which the (single) host is localhost, so we need to make sure that we can SSH to localhost and log in without having to enter a password.

First, make sure that SSH is installed and a server is running. On Ubuntu, for example, this is achieved with:

```
% sudo apt-get install ssh
```

 On Windows with Cygwin, you can set up an SSH server (after having installed the openssh package) by running ssh-host-config -y.

Then to enable password-less login, generate a new SSH key with an empty passphrase:

```
% ssh-keygen -t rsa -P '' -f ~/.ssh/id_rsa
% cat ~/.ssh/id_rsa.pub >> ~/.ssh/authorized_keys
```

Test this with:

```
% ssh localhost
```

You should be logged in without having to type a password.

Formatting the HDFS filesystem

Before it can be used, a brand-new HDFS installation needs to be formatted. The formatting process creates an empty filesystem by creating the storage directories and the initial versions of the namenode's persistent data structures. Datanodes are not involved in the initial formatting process, since the namenode manages all of the filesystem's metadata, and datanodes can join or leave the cluster dynamically. For the same reason, you don't need to say how large a filesystem to create, since this is determined

---

by the number of datanodes in the cluster, which can be increased as needed, long after the filesystem was formatted.

Formatting HDFS is quick to do. Just type the following:

```
% hadoop namenode -format
```

Starting and stopping the daemons

To start the HDFS and MapReduce daemons, type:

```
% start-dfs.sh
% start-mapred.sh
```

 If you have placed configuration files outside the default *conf* directory, start the daemons with the `--config` option, which takes an absolute path to the configuration directory:

```
% start-dfs.sh --config path-to-config-directory
% start-mapred.sh --config path-to-config-directory
```

Three daemons will be started on your local machine: a namenode, a secondary name-node, and a datanode. You can check whether the daemons started successfully by looking at the logfiles in the *logs* directory (in the Hadoop installation directory), or by looking at the web UIs, at *http://localhost:50030/* for the jobtracker, and at *http://localhost:50070/* for the namenode. You can also use Java's `jps` command to see whether they are running.

Stopping the daemons is done in the obvious way:

```
% stop-dfs.sh
% stop-mapred.sh
```

Fully Distributed Mode

Setting up a cluster of machines brings many additional considerations, so this mode is covered in Chapter 9.

Cloudera's Distribution for Hadoop

by Matt Massie and Todd Lipcon, Cloudera

Cloudera's Distribution for Hadoop is based on the most recent stable version of Apache Hadoop with numerous patches, backports, and updates. Cloudera shares this distribution in a number of different formats: compressed tar files, RPMs, Debian packages, and Amazon EC2 AMIs. Cloudera's Distribution for Hadoop is free, released under the Apache 2.0 license and available at *http://www.cloudera.com/hadoop/*.

Cloudera has an online configurator at *http://www.cloudera.com/configurator* to make setting up a Hadoop cluster easy (Figure B-1). The configurator has a simple wizard-like interface that asks targeted questions about your cluster. When you've finished, the configurator generates customized Hadoop packages and places them in a package repository for you. You can manage any number of clusters and return at a later time to update your active configurations.

To simplify package management, Cloudera shares RPMs from a `yum` repository and Debian packages from an `apt` repository. Cloudera's Distribution for Hadoop enables you to install and configure Hadoop on each machine in your cluster by running a single, simple command. Kickstart users benefit even more by being able to commission entire Hadoop clusters automatically without any manual intervention.

Prerequisites

Cloudera's Distribution for Hadoop requires Sun Java 6 or later to be installed. The Sun Java Debian and RPM packages require that you agree to the Sun license before use. For a Debian-based system, you will want to enable the `non-free` apt repository, as it contains the `sun-java6-*` packages. For a Red Hat–based system, download the Sun Java RPM package from *http://java.sun.com/javase/downloads/*.

Before you can use your favorite package manager (e.g., `yum`, `apt-get`, `aptitude`) to install Cloudera packages, you'll need to add the Cloudera repositories to your list of `yum` and/or `apt` sources.

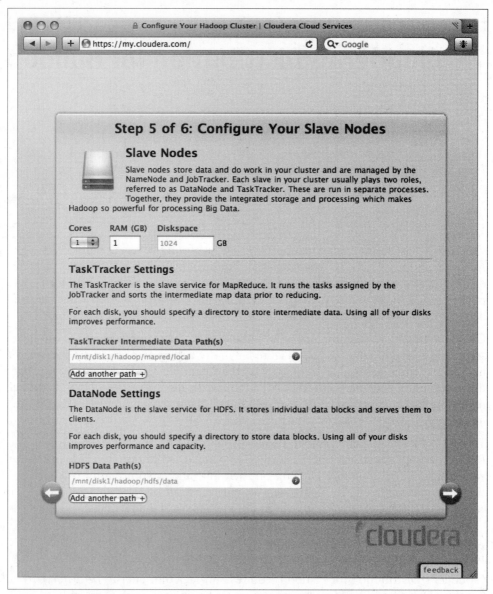

Figure B-1. Cloudera's on-line configurator makes it easy to set up a Hadoop cluster

Please refer to *http://www.cloudera.com/hadoop/* for up-to-date instructions on the simplest way to satisfy these prerequisites.

Standalone Mode

To install Hadoop standalone mode, run the following command on Red Hat–based systems:

```
% yum install hadoop
```

Or on Debian-based systems, run the command:

```
% apt-get install hadoop
```

The hadoop package include a man page. To read the man page, run the command:

```
% man hadoop
```

If you want to install the full Hadoop documentation on a machine, install the hadoop-docs package. On Red Hat–based systems, run the command:

```
% yum install hadoop-docs
```

To install the documentation on Debian-based systems, run the command:

```
% apt-get install hadoop-doc
```

Pseudo-Distributed Mode

To install Hadoop in pseudo-distributed mode, run the following command on Red Hat–based systems:

```
% yum install hadoop-conf-pseudo
```

Or on Debian-based systems, run the command:

```
% apt-get install hadoop-conf-pseudo
```

Once you've installed the Hadoop pseudo-distributed configuration package, you start the Hadoop services by running the same command on both Red Hat– and Debian-based systems:

```
% for x in namenode secondarynamenode datanode jobtracker tasktracker ;
    do /etc/init.d/hadoop-$x start ; done
```

There is no need to worry about creating a hadoop user or formatting HDFS, as that is handled automatically by the hadoop-conf-pseudo package. You can use Hadoop immediately after installing the package and starting the Hadoop services. The hadoop-conf-pseudo package will also ensure that your Hadoop services are started at system boot.

Fully Distributed Mode

For details about deploying a fully distributed Hadoop cluster, visit Cloudera's Distribution for Hadoop web page at *http://www.cloudera.com/hadoop/*.

When you run Cloudera's online configurator, it creates a personalized `apt` or `yum` repository to hold the configuration packages for every cluster you manage. For example, let's say you gave one of your clusters the name `mycluster`. To see a list of all the configuration packages for `mycluster`, run the following command on Red Hat–based systems:

```
% yum search hadoop-conf-mycluster
```

or on Debian-based systems, run the command:

```
% apt-cache search hadoop-conf-mycluster
```

These commands will return a list of configuration packages for the `mycluster` cluster. The number and types of configuration packages depends on how you answered the questions posed by the Cloudera configurator. Some of the packages will be generated for specific hosts in your cluster; others will be for groups or classes of machines in your cluster. For host-specific configurations, the fully qualified hostname will be added to the package name. For example, there may be a configuration for `myhost.mydomain` in the `mycluster` cluster. To install Hadoop on `myhost.mydomain` on Red Hat–based systems, run the command:

```
% yum install hadoop-conf-mycluster-myhost.mydomain
```

or on Debian-based systems, run the command:

```
% apt-get install hadoop-conf-mycluster-myhost.mydomain
```

The Hadoop configuration packages will ensure that your services are set up to run at system boot.

Hadoop-Related Packages

Cloudera's Distribution for Hadoop allows you to easily deploy tools built on top of Hadoop like Hive and Pig. Hive is a data warehouse infrastructure that allows you to query data in Hadoop with a query language based on SQL. For more information on Hive, see "Hadoop and Hive at Facebook" on page 414. Pig is a platform for analyzing large datasets using a high-level language; it is covered in Chapter 11.

To install Hive and Pig on Red Hat–based systems, run the command:

```
% yum install hadoop-hive hadoop-pig
```

To install Hive and Pig on Debian-based systems, run the command:

```
% apt-get install hadoop-hive hadoop-pig
```

More Hadoop-related packages will be added to Cloudera's Distribution for Hadoop over time.

Preparing the NCDC Weather Data

This section gives a runthrough of the steps taken to prepare the raw weather data files so they are in a form that is amenable for analysis using Hadoop. If you want to get a copy of the data to process using Hadoop, you can do so by following the instructions given at the website which accompanies this book at *http://hadoopbook.com/*. The rest of this section explains how the raw weather data files were processed.

The raw data is provided as a collection of *tar* files, compressed with *bzip2*. Each year of readings comes in a separate file. Here's a partial directory listing of the files:

```
1901.tar.bz2
1902.tar.bz2
1903.tar.bz2
...
2000.tar.bz2
```

Each *tar* file contains a file for each weather station's readings for the year, compressed with *gzip*. (The fact that the files in the archive are compressed makes the *bzip2* compression on the archive itself redundant.) For example:

```
% tar jxf 1901.tar.bz2
% ls -l 1901 | head
011990-99999-1950.gz
011990-99999-1950.gz
...
011990-99999-1950.gz
```

Since there are tens of thousands of weather stations, the whole dataset is made up of large number of relatively small files. It's generally easier and more efficient to process a smaller number of relatively large files in Hadoop (see "Small files and CombineFileInputFormat" on page 190), so in this case, I concatenated the decompressed files for a whole year into a single file, named by the year. I did this using a MapReduce program, to take advantage of its parallel processing capabilities. Let's take a closer look at the program.

The program has only a map function: no reduce function is needed since the map does all the file processing in parallel with no combine stage. The processing can be done with a Unix script so the Streaming interface to MapReduce is appropriate in this case; see Example C-1.

Example C-1. Bash script to process raw NCDC data files and store in HDFS

```bash
#!/usr/bin/env bash

# NLineInputFormat gives a single line: key is offset, value is S3 URI
read offset s3file

# Retrieve file from S3 to local disk
echo "reporter:status:Retrieving $s3file" >&2
$HADOOP_INSTALL/bin/hadoop fs -get $s3file .

# Un-bzip and un-tar the local file
target=`basename $s3file .tar.bz2`
mkdir -p $target
echo "reporter:status:Un-tarring $s3file to $target" >&2
tar jxf `basename $s3file` -C $target

# Un-gzip each station file and concat into one file
echo "reporter:status:Un-gzipping $target" >&2
for file in $target/*/*
do
  gunzip -c $file >> $target.all
  echo "reporter:status:Processed $file" >&2
done

# Put gzipped version into HDFS
echo "reporter:status:Gzipping $target and putting in HDFS" >&2
gzip -c $target.all | $HADOOP_INSTALL/bin/hadoop fs -put - gz/$target.gz
```

The input is a small text file (*ncdc_files.txt*) listing all the files to be processed (the files start out on S3, so the files are referenced using S3 URIs that Hadoop understands). Here is a sample:

```
s3n://hadoopbook/ncdc/raw/isd-1901.tar.bz2
s3n://hadoopbook/ncdc/raw/isd-1902.tar.bz2
...
s3n://hadoopbook/ncdc/raw/isd-2000.tar.bz2
```

By specifying the input format to be `NLineInputFormat`, each mapper receives one line of input, which contains the file it has to process. The processing is explained in the script, but, briefly, it unpacks the *bzip2* file, and then concatenates each station file into a single file for the whole year. Finally, the file is gzipped and copied into HDFS. Note the use of `hadoop fs -put -` to consume from standard input.

Status messages are echoed to standard error with a `reporter:status` prefix so that they get interpreted as a MapReduce status update. This tells Hadoop that the script is making progress, and is not hanging.

The script to run the Streaming job is as follows:

```
% hadoop jar $HADOOP_INSTALL/contrib/streaming/hadoop-*-streaming.jar \
  -D mapred.reduce.tasks=0 \
  -D mapred.map.tasks.speculative.execution=false \
  -D mapred.task.timeout=12000000 \
  -input ncdc_files.txt \
  -inputformat org.apache.hadoop.mapred.lib.NLineInputFormat \
  -output output \
  -mapper load_ncdc_map.sh \
  -file load_ncdc_map.sh
```

I set the number of reduce tasks to zero, since this is a map-only job. I also turned off speculative execution so duplicate tasks didn't write the same files (although the approach discussed in "Task side-effect files" on page 173 would have worked, too). The task timeout was set high so that Hadoop didn't kill tasks that are taking a long time (for example, when unarchiving files, or copying to HDFS, when no progress is reported).

Last, the files were archived on S3 by copying them from HDFS using *distcp*.

Index

We'd like to hear your suggestions for improving our indexes. Send email to *index@oreilly.com*.

HadoopPipes::runTask method, 38
HADOOP_CLASSPATH environment
    variable, 24
HADOOP_INSTALL environment variable,
    38
HADOOP_LOG_DIR setting, 256
HADOOP_MASTER setting, 257
hanging tasks, 160
.har file extension, 72
HAR files (Hadoop Archives), 72
    limitations of, 73
hardware
    commodity hardware, Hadoop on, 42
    specification for Hadoop clusters, 245
HarFileSystem, 47
HashComparator objects, 434
HashPartitioner class, 98, 181
    default, using to sort SequenceFile with
        IntWritable keys, 219
HBase, 343–368
    brief history of, 344
    clients, 350–354
        Java, 351
        using REST and thrift, 353
    data model, 344
        locking, 345
        regions, 345
    defined, 13
    example, 354–360
        loading data from HDFS into table, 355–
            358
        schemas for Stations and Observations
            tables, 354
        web queries, 358–360
    implementation
        clients, slaves, and coordinating master,
            346
        operation of HBase, 346
    installation, 348–350
        testing, 349
    listing command-line options, 348
    practical issues running HBase instance,
        365–368
        HBase and HDFS, 366
        metrics, 367
        schema design, 368
        UI, 367
        versions of Hadoop and HBase, 366
    RDBMS versus, 361

HBase characteristics, 363
    successful RDBMS service, 362–365
    use case, HBase at streamy.com, 363
shutting down an instance, 350
TableInputFormat and
    TableOutputFormat, 202
HBaseAdmin class, 351
HDFS (Hadoop Distributed Filesystem), 3, 41–
    73
    audit logging, 280
    backups, 292
    balancer for block distribution over
        datanodes, 284
    benchmarking with TestDFSIO, 267
    block size, property for, 265
    blocks, 43
    client reading file from, 63
    client writing files to, 66
    coherency model, 68
    command-line interface, 45
        basic filesystem operations, 45
    data integrity, 75
    datanode block scanner, 283
    defined, 12
    design of, 41
    dfsadmin tool, 280
    file permissions, 47
    formatting, 469
    fsck utility, 281
    HAR files (Hadoop Archives), 71
    HBase persistence to, 346
    HBase use of, problems with, 366
    HTTP and FTP interfaces, 50
    important daemon properties, 260
    include and exclude file precedence, 295
    installation, MapReduce installation and,
        250
    keeping clusters balanced, 71
    namenodes and datanodes, 44
    parallel copying with distcp, 70
    persistent data structures, 273–278
        datanode directory structure, 277
        filesystem image and edit log, 274
        namenode directory structure, 273
        secondary namenode directory
            structure, 276
    relationship between input splits and
        blocks, 197
    safe mode, 278

Utf8StorageConverter class, 330

V

validation, Pig Latin schemas and, 318
variable expansion, 118
versioned cells in HBase, 344
versions
    Hadoop and HBase, compatibility, 366
    Hadoop components, compatibility of, 296
very large files, 41
void return types in ZooKeeper, 382
volunteer computing, 8

W

Walters, Chad, 344
Watcher interface
    ConnectionWatcher class (example), 375
    CreateGroup (example), 373
    functions of, 390
    process( ) method, 374
Watcher.Event.KeeperState enum, 374
watches, 380
    creation operations and corresponding
        triggers, 383
    on read operations, 382
weather dataset, 15
    analyzing with Unix tools, 17
    NCDC format, 15
web page for this book, xviii
web queries in HBase, 358–360
    methods retrieving range of rows from
        HBase table, 359
    using Scanners, 359
web search engines
    Apache Lucene and Nutch, 9
    building from scratch, 9
web UI for MapReduce, 134–136, 139
    job page, 136
    jobtracker page, 134
    task details page, 141
    tasks page, 140
WebDAV, 50
webinterface.private.actions property, 141
WebMap, 11
webtable, 343
whoami command, 120
WholeFileInputFormat class, 192

using to package small files into
    SequenceFiles, 194
Windows, Hadoop on, 465
work units, 8
workflows, MapReduce, 149–151
    decomposing problem into MapReduce
        jobs, 149
    running dependent jobs, 151
Writable classes
    BytesWritable, 94
    collections, 95
    implementing custom, 96–101
    NullWritable, 95
    ObjectWritable and GenericWritable, 95
    Text, 91–94
    wrappers for Java primitives, 89
Writable interface, 87–89
WritableComparable interface, 88, 220
WritableSerialization class, 101
write operations in ZooKeeper, 382
WriteLock class, 400
writers, multiple, HDFS and, 42

X

XML, text input as XML documents, 199

Y

Yahoo!, Hadoop at, 10

Z

Zab protocol, 385
zettabytes, 1
znodes, 372, 379
    ACLs (access control lists), 383
    deleting, 378
    deletion of, watch event types and, 383
    ephemeral, 379
    ephemeral and persistent, 374
    paths, 379
    program creating znode to represent group,
        372–374
    sequence numbers, 380
    version number, 381
    watches on, 380
zoo.cfg file, 371
ZOOCFGDIR environment variable, 371
ZooDefs.Ids class, 384
ZooKeeper, 369–403

About the Author

Tom White has been an Apache Hadoop committer since February 2007, and is a member of the Apache Software Foundation. He works for Cloudera, a company that offers Hadoop support and training. Previously, he was an independent Hadoop consultant, working with companies to set up, use, and extend Hadoop. He has written numerous articles for oreilly.com, java.net, and IBM's developerWorks, and has spoken about Hadoop at several conferences. Tom has a B.A. from the University of Cambridge and an M.A. in philosophy of science from the University of Leeds, UK He lives in Powys, Wales, with his family.

Colophon

The animal on the cover of *Hadoop: The Definitive Guide* is an African elephant. They are the largest land animals on earth (slightly larger than their cousin, the Asian elephant) and can be identified by their ears, which have been said to look somewhat like the continent of Asia. Males stand 12 feet tall at the shoulder and weigh 12,000 pounds, but they can get as big as 15,000 pounds, whereas females stand 10 feet tall and weigh 8,000–11,000 pounds.

They have four molars; each weighs about 11 pounds and measures about 12 inches long. As the front pair wears down and drops out in pieces, the back pair shifts forward, and two new molars emerge in the back of the mouth. They replace their teeth six times throughout their lives, and between 40–60 years of age, they will lose all of their teeth and likely die of starvation (a common cause of death). Their tusks are teeth—actually it is the second set of incisors that becomes the tusks, which they use for digging for roots and stripping the bark off trees for food, fighting each other during mating season, and defending themselves against predators. Their tusks weigh between 50–100 pounds and are between 5–8 feet long.

African elephants live throughout sub-Saharan Africa. Most of the continent's elephants live on savannas and in dry woodlands. In some regions, they can be found in desert areas; in others, they are found in mountains.

Elephants are fond of water. They shower by sucking water into their trunks and spraying it all over themselves; afterward, they spray their skin with a protective coating of dust. An elephant's trunk is actually a long nose used for smelling, breathing, trumpeting, drinking, and grabbing things, especially food. The trunk alone contains about 100,000 different muscles. African elephants have two finger-like features on the end of their trunks that they can use to grab small items. They feed on roots, grass, fruit, and bark. An adult elephant can consume up to 300 pounds of food in a single day. These hungry animals do not sleep much—they roam great distances while foraging for the large quantities of food that they require to sustain their massive bodies.

Having a baby elephant is a serious commitment. Elephants have longer pregnancies than any other mammal: almost 22 months. At birth, elephants already weigh approximately 200 pounds and stand about 3 feet tall.

This species plays an important role in the forest and savanna ecosystems in which they live. Many plant species are dependent on passing through an elephant's digestive tract before they can germinate; it is estimated that at least a third of tree species in west African forests rely on elephants in this way. Elephants grazing on vegetation also affect the structure of habitats and influence bush fire patterns. For example, under natural conditions, elephants make gaps through the rainforest, enabling the sunlight to enter, which allows the growth of various plant species. This in turn facilitates a more abundant and more diverse fauna of smaller animals. As a result of the influence elephants have over many plants and animals, they are often referred to as a *keystone species* because they are vital to the long-term survival of the ecosystems in which they live.

The cover image is from the Dover Pictorial Archive. The cover font is Adobe ITC Garamond. The text font is Linotype Birka; the heading font is Adobe Myriad Condensed; and the code font is LucasFont's TheSansMonoCondensed.

Related Titles from O'Reilly

Unix Administration

Classic Shell Scripting

DNS and BIND, *5th Edition*

DNS & BIND Cookbook

Essential System Administration, *3rd Edition*

Essential System Administration Pocket Reference

Postfix: The Definitive Guide

qmail

sendmail, *4th Edition*

sendmail Cookbook

System Performance Tuning, *2nd Edition*

Unix Basics

bash Cookbook

GNU Emacs Pocket Reference

Learning GNU Emacs, *3rd Edition*

Learning the bash Shell, *3rd Edition*

Learning the Korn Shell, *2nd Edition*

Learning the Unix Operating System, *5th Edition*

Learning the vi Editor, *6th Edition*

sed & awk Pocket Reference, *2nd Edition*

sed & awk, *2nd Edition*

Unix in a Nutshell, *4th Edition*

Using csh & tcsh

Unix Tools

BSD Hacks

CVS Pocket Reference, *2nd Edition*

Effective awk Programming, *3rd Edition*

Essential CVS, *2nd Edition*

GDB Pocket Reference

lex & yacc, *2nd Edition*

Managing Projects with GNU make, *3rd Edition*

Practical PostgreSQL

The Complete FreeBSD, *4th Edition*

Unix Power Tools, *3rd edition*

Version Control with Subversion

Our books are available at most retail and online bookstores.

To order direct: 1-800-998-9938 • *order@oreilly.com* • *www.oreilly.com*

Online editions of most O'Reilly titles are available by subscription at *safari.oreilly.com*

The O'Reilly Advantage

Stay Current and Save Money